Communications
in Computer and Information Science   **1195**

Commenced Publication in 2007
Founding and Former Series Editors:
Phoebe Chen, Alfredo Cuzzocrea, Xiaoyong Du, Orhun Kara, Ting Liu,
Krishna M. Sivalingam, Dominik Ślęzak, Takashi Washio, Xiaokang Yang,
and Junsong Yuan

More information about this series at http://www.springer.com/series/7899

Miguel Botto-Tobar · Marcelo Zambrano Vizuete ·
Pablo Torres-Carrión · Sergio Montes León ·
Guillermo Pizarro Vásquez ·
Benjamin Durakovic (Eds.)

Applied Technologies

First International Conference, ICAT 2019
Quito, Ecuador, December 3–5, 2019
Proceedings, Part III

 Springer

Editors
Miguel Botto-Tobar ⓘ
Eindhoven University of Technology
Eindhoven, The Netherlands

Pablo Torres-Carrión ⓘ
Universidad Técnica Particular de Loja
Loja, Ecuador

Guillermo Pizarro Vásquez ⓘ
Universidad Politécnica Salesiana
Guayaquil, Ecuador

Marcelo Zambrano Vizuete ⓘ
Universidad Técnica del Norte
Ibarra, Ecuador

Sergio Montes León ⓘ
Universidad de las Fuerzas Armadas (ESPE)
Quito, Ecuador

Benjamin Durakovic ⓘ
International University of Sarajevo
Sarajevo, Bosnia and Herzegovina

ISSN 1865-0929   ISSN 1865-0937 (electronic)
Communications in Computer and Information Science
ISBN 978-3-030-42530-2   ISBN 978-3-030-42531-9 (eBook)
https://doi.org/10.1007/978-3-030-42531-9

This Springer imprint is published by the registered company Springer Nature Switzerland AG
The registered company address is: Gewerbestrasse 11, 6330 Cham, Switzerland

Preface

The First International Conference on Applied Technologies (ICAT 2019) was held on the main campus of the Universidad de las Fuerzas Armadas (ESPE), in Quito, Ecuador, during December 3–5, 2019, and was jointly organized by the Universidad de las Fuerzas Armadas (ESPE), the Universidad Técnica Particular de Loja, and the Universidad Técnica del Norte, in collaboration with GDEON. The ICAT series aims to bring together top researchers and practitioners working in different domains in the field of computer science to exchange their expertise and discuss the perspectives of development and collaboration. The content of this three-volume set is related to the following subjects: technology trends, computing, intelligent systems, machine vision, security, communication, electronics, e-learning, e-government, and e-participation.

ICAT 2019 received 328 English submissions written by 586 authors from 23 different countries. All these papers were peer-reviewed by the ICAT 2019 Program Committee consisting of 191 high-quality researchers. To assure a high quality and thoughtful review process, we assigned each paper to at least three reviewers. Based on these reviews, 124 full papers were accepted, resulting in an acceptance rate of 38%, which was within our goal of less than 40%.

We would like to express our sincere gratitude to the invited speakers for their inspirational talks, to the authors for submitting their work to this conference, and the reviewers for sharing their experience during the selection process.

December 2019

Miguel Botto-Tobar
Marcelo Zambrano Vizuete
Pablo Torres-Carrión
Sergio Montes León
Guillermo Pizarro Vásquez
Benjamin Durakovic

Organization

General Chair

Miguel Botto-Tobar   Eindhoven University of Technology, The Netherlands

Organizing Committee

Miguel Botto-Tobar	Eindhoven University of Technology, The Netherlands
Marcelo Zambrano Vizuete	Universidad Técnica del Norte, Ecuador
Pablo Torres-Carrión	Universidad Técnica Particular de Loja, Ecuador
Sergio Montes León	Universidad de las Fuerzas Armadas (ESPE), Ecuador, and Universidad Rey Juan Carlos, Spain
Guillermo Pizarro	Universidad Politécnica Salesiana, Ecuador
Benjamin Durakovic	International University of Sarajevo, Bosnia and Herzegovina
Jose Bucheli Andrade	Universidad de las Fuerzas Armadas (ESPE), Ecuador

Steering Committee

Miguel Botto Tobar	Eindhoven University of Technology, The Netherlands
Ángela Díaz Cadena	Universitat de Valencia, Spain

Publication Chair

Miguel Botto-Tobar   Eindhoven University of Technology, The Netherlands

Program Chairs

Technology Trends

Jean Michel Clairand	Universidad de Las Américas, Ecuador
Miguel Botto-Tobar	Eindhoven University of Technology, The Netherlands
Hernán Montes León	Universidad Rey Juan Carlos, Spain

Computing

Miguel Zúñiga Prieto	Universidad de Cuenca, Ecuador
Lohana Lema Moreira	Universidad de Especialidades Espíritu Santo (UEES), Ecuador

Intelligent Systems

Janeth Chicaiza	Universidad Técnica Particular de Loja, Ecuador
Pablo Torres-Carrión	Universidad Técnica Particular de Loja, Ecuador
Guillermo Pizarro Vásquez	Universidad Politécnica Salesiana, Ecuador

Machine Vision

Julian Galindo	LIG-IIHM, France
Erick Cuenca	Université de Montpellier, France
Jorge Luis Pérez Medina	Universidad de Las Américas, Ecuador

Security

Luis Urquiza-Aguiar	Escuela Politécnica Nacional, Ecuador
Joffre León-Acurio	Universidad Técnica de Babahoyo, Ecuador

Communication

Nathaly Verónica Orozco Garzón	Universidad de Las Américas, Ecuador
Óscar Zambrano Vizuete	Universidad Técnica del Norte, Ecuador
Pablo Palacios Jativa	Universidad de Chile, Chile
Henry Ramiro Carvajal Mora	Universidad de Las Américas, Ecuador

Electronics

Ana Zambrano Vizuete	Escuela Politécnica Nacional (EPN), Ecuador
David Rivas	Universidad de las Fuerzas Armadas (ESPE), Ecuador

e-Learning

Verónica Falconí Ausay	Universidad de Las Américas, Ecuador
Doris Macías Mendoza	Universitat Politécnica de Valencia, Spain

e-Business

Angela Díaz Cadena	Universitat de Valencia, Spain
Oscar León Granizo	Universidad de Guayaquil, Ecuador
Praxedes Montiel Díaz	CIDEPRO, Ecuador

e-Government and e-Participation

Vicente Merchán Rodríguez	Universidad de las Fuerzas Armadas (ESPE), Ecuador
Alex Santamaría Philco	Universidad Laica Eloy Alfaro de Manabí, Ecuador

Program Committee

A. Bonci	Marche Polytechnic University, Italy
Ahmed Lateef Khalaf	Al-Mamoun University College, Iraq
Aiko Yamashita	Oslo Metropolitan University, Norway
Alejandro Donaire	Queensland University of Technology, Australia
Alejandro Ramos Nolazco	Instituto Tecnólogico y de Estudios Superiores Monterrey, Mexico
Alex Cazañas	The University of Queensland, Australia

Alex Santamaria Philco	Universitat Politècnica de València, Spain
Alfonso Guijarro Rodriguez	University of Guayaquil, Ecuador
Allan Avendaño Sudario	Escuela Superior Politécnica del Litoral (ESPOL), Ecuador
Alexandra González Eras	Universidad Politécnica de Madrid, Spain
Ana Núñez Ávila	Universitat Politècnica de València, Spain
Ana Zambrano	Escuela Politécnica Nacional (EPN), Ecuador
Andres Carrera Rivera	The University of Melbourne, Australia
Andres Cueva Costales	The University of Melbourne, Australia
Andrés Robles Durazno	Edinburg Napier University, UK
Andrés Vargas Gonzalez	Syracuse University, USA
Angel Cuenca Ortega	Universitat Politècnica de València, Spain
Ángela Díaz Cadena	Universitat de València, Spain
Angelo Trotta	University of Bologna, Italy
Antonio Gómez Exposito	University of Sevilla, Spain
Aras Can Onal	Tobb University Economics and Technology, Turkey
Arian Bahrami	University of Tehran, Iran
Benoît Macq	Université Catholique de Louvain, Belgium
Bernhard Hitpass	Universidad Federico Santa María, Chile
Bin Lin	Università della Svizzera italiana (USI), Switzerland
Carlos Saavedra	Escuela Superior Politécnica del Litoral (ESPOL), Ecuador
Catriona Kennedy	The University of Manchester, UK
César Ayabaca Sarria	Escuela Politécnica Nacional (EPN), Ecuador
Cesar Azurdia Meza	University of Chile, Chile
Christian León Paliz	Université de Neuchâtel, Switzerland
Chrysovalantou Ziogou	Chemical Process and Energy Resources Institute, Greece
Cristian Zambrano Vega	Universidad de Málaga, Spain, and Universidad Técnica Estatal de Quevedo, Ecuador
Cristiano Premebida	Loughborough University, ISR-UC, UK
Daniel Magües Martinez	Universidad Autónoma de Madrid, Spain
Danilo Jaramillo Hurtado	Universidad Politécnica de Madrid, Spain
Darío Piccirilli	Universidad Nacional de La Plata, Argentina
Darsana Josyula	Bowie State University, USA
David Benavides Cuevas	Universidad de Sevilla, Spain
David Blanes	Universitat Politècnica de València, Spain
David Ojeda	Universidad Técnica del Norte, Ecuador
David Rivera Espín	The University of Melbourne, Australia
Denis Efimov	Inria, France
Diego Barragán Guerrero	Universidad Técnica Particular de Loja (UTPL), Ecuador
Diego Peluffo-Ordoñez	Yachay Tech, Ecuador
Dimitris Chrysostomou	Aalborg University, Denmark
Domingo Biel	Universitat Politècnica de Catalunya, Spain
Doris Macías Mendoza	Universitat Politècnica de València, Spain

Edison Espinoza	Universidad de las Fuerzas Armadas (ESPE), Ecuador
Edwin Quel	Universidad de las Américas, Ecuador
Edwin Rivas	Universidad Distrital de Colombia, Colombia
Ehsan Arabi	University of Michigan, USA
Emanuele Frontoni	Università Politecnica delle Marche, Italy
Emil Pricop	Petroleum-Gas University of Ploiesti, Romania
Erick Cuenca	Université Catholique de Louvain, Belgium
Fabian Calero	University of Waterloo, Canada
Fan Yang	Tsinghua University, China
Fariza Nasaruddin	University of Malaya, Malaysia
Felipe Ebert	Universidade Federal de Pernambuco (UFPE), Brazil
Felipe Grijalva	Escuela Politécnica Nacional (EPN), Ecuador
Fernanda Molina Miranda	Universidad Politécnica de Madrid, Spain
Fernando Almeida	University of Campinas, Brazil
Fernando Flores Pulgar	Université de Lyon, France
Firas Raheem	University of Technology, Iraq
Francisco Calvente	Universitat Rovira i Virgili, Spain
Francisco Obando	Universidad del Cauca, Colombia
Franklin Parrales	University of Guayaquil, Ecuador
Freddy Flores Bahamonde	Universidad Técnica Federico Santa María, Chile
Gabriel Barros Gavilanes	INP Toulouse, France
Gabriel López Fonseca	Sheffield Hallam University, UK
Gema Rodriguez-Perez	LibreSoft, Universidad Rey Juan Carlos, Spain
Ginger Saltos Bernal	Escuela Superior Politécnica del Litoral (ESPOL), Ecuador
Giovanni Pau	Kore University of Enna, Italy
Guilherme Avelino	Universidade Federal do Piauí (UFP), Brazil
Guilherme Pereira	Universidade Federal de Minas Gerais (UFMG), Brazil
Guillermo Pizarro Vásquez	Universidad Politécnica de Madrid, Spain
Gustavo Andrade Miranda	Universidad Politécnica de Madrid, Spain
Hernán Montes León	Universidad Rey Juan Carlos, Spain
Ibraheem Kasim	University of Baghdad, Iraq
Ilya Afanasyev	Innopolis University, Russia
Israel Pineda Arias	Chonbuk National University, South Korea
Jaime Meza	Universiteit van Fribourg, Switzerland
Janneth Chicaiza Espinosa	Universidad Técnica Particular de Loja (UTPL), Ecuador
Javier Gonzalez-Huerta	Blekinge Institute of Technology, Sweden
Javier Monroy	Universidad de Málaga, Spain
Javier Sebastian	University of Oviedo, Spain
Jawad K. Ali	University of Technology, Iraq
Jefferson Ribadeneira Ramírez	Escuela Superior Politécnica de Chimborazo, Ecuador
Jerwin Prabu	BRS, India
Jong Hyuk Park	Korea Institute of Science and Technology, South Korea

Jorge Charco Aguirre	Universitat Politècnica de València, Spain
Jorge Eterovic	Universidad Nacional de La Matanza, Argentina
Jorge Gómez Gómez	Universidad de Córdoba, Colombia
Juan Corrales	Institut Universitaire de France et SIGMA Clermont, France
Juan Romero Arguello	The University of Manchester, UK
Julián Andrés Galindo	Université Grenoble Alpes, France
Julian Galindo	Inria, France
Julio Albuja Sánchez	James Cook University, Australia
Kelly Garces	Universidad de Los Andes, Colombia
Kester Quist-Aphetsi	Center for Research, Information, Technology and Advanced Computing, Ghana
Korkut Bekiroglu	SUNY Polytechnic Institute, USA
Kunde Yang	Northwestern Polytechnic University, China
Lina Ochoa	CWI, The Netherlands
Lohana Lema Moreira	Universidad de Especialidades Espíritu Santo (UEES), Ecuador
Lorena Guachi Guachi	Yachay Tech, Ecuador
Lorena Montoya Freire	Aalto University, Finland
Lorenzo Cevallos Torres	Universidad de Guayaquil, Ecuador
Luis Galárraga	Inria, France
Luis Martinez	Universitat Rovira i Virgili, Spain
Luis Urquiza-Aguiar	Escuela Politécnica Nacional (EPN), Ecuador
Maikel Leyva Vazquez	Universidad de Guayaquil, Ecuador
Manuel Sucunuta	Universidad Técnica Particular de Loja (UTPL), Ecuador
Marcela Ruiz	Utrecht University, The Netherlands
Marcelo Zambrano Vizuete	Universidad Técnica del Norte, Ecuador
María José Escalante Guevara	University of Michigan, USA
María Reátegui Rojas	University of Quebec, Canada
Mariela Tapia-Leon	University of Guayaquil, Ecuador
Marija Seder	University of Zagreb, Croatia
Mario Gonzalez Rodríguez	Universidad de las Américas, Ecuador
Marisa Daniela Panizzi	Universidad Tecnológica Nacional Aire, Argentina
Marius Giergiel	KRiM AGH, Poland
Markus Schuckert	Hong Kong Polytechnic University, Hong Kong
Matus Pleva	Technical University of Kosice, Slovakia
Mauricio Verano Merino	Technische Universiteit Eindhoven, The Netherlands
Mayken Espinoza-Andaluz	Escuela Superior Politécnica del Litoral (ESPOL), Ecuador
Miguel Botto-Tobar	Eindhoven University of Technology, The Netherlands
Miguel Fornell	Escuela Superior Politécnica del Litoral (ESPOL), Ecuador
Miguel Gonzalez Cagigal	Universidad de Sevilla, Spain
Miguel Murillo	Universidad Autónoma de Baja California, Mexico

Miguel Zuñiga Prieto   Universidad de Cuenca, Ecuador
Milton Román-Cañizares   Universidad de las Américas, Ecuador
Mohamed Kamel   Military Technical College, Egypt
Mohammad Al-Mashhadani   Al-Maarif University College, Iraq
Mohammad Amin   Illinois Institute of Technology, USA
Monica Baquerizo   Universidad de Guayaquil, Ecuador
  Anastacio
Muneeb Ul Hassan   Swinburne University of Technology, Australia
Nam Yang   Eindhoven University of Technology, The Netherlands
Nathalie Mitton   Inria, France
Nathaly Orozco   Universidad de las Américas, Ecuador
Nayeth Solórzano Alcívar   Escuela Superior Politécnica del Litoral (ESPOL),
                                 Ecuador, and Griffith University, Australia
Noor Zaman   King Faisal University, Saudi Arabia
Omar S. Gómez   Escuela Superior Politécnica del Chimborazo
                                 (ESPOCH), Ecuador
Óscar León Granizo   Universidad de Guayaquil, Ecuador
Oswaldo Lopez Santos   Universidad de Ibagué, Colombia
Pablo Lupera   Escuela Politécnica Nacional, Ecuador
Pablo Ordoñez Ordoñez   Universidad Politécnica de Madrid, Spain
Pablo Palacios   Universidad de Chile, Chile
Pablo Torres-Carrión   Universidad Técnica Particular de Loja (UTPL),
                                 Ecuador
Patricia Ludeña González   Universidad Técnica Particular de Loja (UTPL),
                                 Ecuador
Paúl Mejía   Universidad de las Fuerzas Armadas (ESPE), Ecuador
Paulo Batista   CIDEHUS.UÉ, Portugal
Paulo Chiliguano   Queen Mary University of London, UK
Paulo Guerra Terán   Universidad de las Américas, Ecuador
Pedro Neto   University of Coimbra, Portugal
Praveen Damacharla   Purdue University Northwest, USA
Priscila Cedillo   Universidad de Cuenca, Ecuador
Radu-Emil Precup   Politehnica University of Timisoara, Romania
Ramin Yousefi   Islamic Azad University, Iran
René Guamán Quinche   Universidad de los Paises Vascos, Spain
Ricardo Martins   University of Coimbra, Portugal
Richard Ramirez   Universitat Politècnica de Catalunya, Spain
  Anormaliza
Richard Rivera   IMDEA Software Institute, Spain
Richard Stern   Carnegie Mellon University, USA
Rijo Jackson Tom   SRM University, India
Roberto Murphy   University of Colorado Denver, USA
Roberto Sabatini   RMIT University, Australia
Rodolfo Alfredo Bertone   Universidad Nacional de La Plata, Argentina
Rodrigo Barba   Universidad Técnica Particular de Loja (UTPL),
                                 Ecuador

Rodrigo Saraguro Bravo	Universitat Politècnica de València, Spain
Ronald Barriga Díaz	Universidad de Guayaquil, Ecuador
Ronnie Guerra	Pontificia Universidad Católica del Perú, Peru
Ruben Rumipamba-Zambrano	Universitat Politècnica de Catalanya, Spain
Saeed Rafee Nekoo	Universidad de Sevilla, Spain
Saleh Mobayen	University of Zanjan, Iran
Samiha Fadloun	Université de Montpellier, France
Sergio Montes León	Universidad de las Fuerzas Armadas (ESPE), Ecuador
Stefanos Gritzalis	University of the Aegean, Greece
Syed Manzoor Qasim	King Abdulaziz City for Science and Technology, Saudi Arabia
Tatiana Mayorga	Universidad de las Fuerzas Armadas (ESPE), Ecuador
Tenreiro Machado	Polytechnic of Porto, Portugal
Thomas Sjögren	Swedish Defence Research Agency (FOI), Sweden
Tiago Curi	Federal University of Santa Catarina, Brazil
Tony T. Luo	A*STAR, Singapore
Trung Duong	Queen's University Belfast, UK
Vanessa Jurado Vite	Universidad Politécnica Salesiana, Ecuador
Waldo Orellana	Universitat de València, Spain
Washington Velasquez Vargas	Universidad Politécnica de Madrid, Spain
Wayne Staats	Sandia National Labs, USA
Willian Zamora	Universidad Laica Eloy Alfaro de Manabí, Ecuador
Yessenia Cabrera Maldonado	University of Cuenca, Ecuador
Yerferson Torres Berru	Universidad de Salamanca, Spain, and Instituto Tecnológico Loja, Ecuador
Zhanyu Ma	Beijing University of Posts and Telecommunications, China

Organizing Institutions

Sponsoring Institutions

Collaborators

Contents – Part III

Electronics

e-Learning

e-Government and e-Participation

Security

Safety Methodology for IoT Devices Based on Vulnerabilities in Agricultural Environments

Jorge Gomez[1]([⊠])(iD), Miguel Angel Zuñiga[2], and Alexander Fernandez[1]

[1] Departamento de Ingenieria de Sistemas, Universidad de Córdoba,
Monteria, Colombia
jegjorge@gmail.com
[2] Departamento de Informatica, Universidad Tecnica de Babahoyo,
Babahoyo, Ecuador

Abstract. The development of this proposal seeks to show what has been the impact of IoT-related technologies, focusing on IoT implementations in agriculture. A concise taxonomy of the devices and networks in use, as well as their vulnerabilities, is analyzed. It develops a methodology that seeks the implementation of good practices, the implementation of security elements in the development of IoT use. The conclusions have been adequate and show that it is possible to implement the proposed methodology.

Keywords: Security · Internet of Things · Precision agriculture · Intelligent environments · Security methodology

1 Introduction

Bearing in mind important aspects related to security, the world of Internet-based systems of things, has not suffered major contributions until recently. This is due to the urgent need to safeguard the resources available in such systems in order to make more efficient the collection, processing and delivery of data obtained [1]. However, with the evolution of this technology today it is necessary to develop new forms that lead to understandable processes and easy deployment without forgetting any element of security.

This work is framed in the need to control the safety elements related to the monitoring of some environmental parameters involved with crop verification and control [2]. Looking with the use of IoT technologies, the future improvement of food production, allowing these processes to be much more efficient and at the same time have the robustness to support their operation through different types of data analysis platform. It is also intended to ensure that possible security problems generated by vulnerabilities of origin, are controlled and mitigated generating the confidence needed by different types of users.

Nowadays, new and more adapted security standards regarding the different IoT technologies are in full development. The need to generate, organize

© Springer Nature Switzerland AG 2020
M. Botto-Tobar et al. (Eds.): ICAT 2019, CCIS 1195, pp. 3–12, 2020.
https://doi.org/10.1007/978-3-030-42531-9_1

and implement these new methodologies becomes necessary due to the growing impact that these systems have on people's daily activities [3].

It is clear that in the beginning IoT devices were developed thinking about efficiency, saving resources and finding ways that the deployment of various sensors and controllers was massive and economical, was left aside in principle, aspects related to security. This being a latent issue, it could flatly allow the possibility of taking advantage of the security gaps generated by any vulnerability found in one of these device architectures and IoT networks. In this article, he focuses precisely on the development of a methodology that allows the implementation of security elements in the different phases of monitoring environmental parameters in crop growth.

In general terms, it is possible to synthesize the main vulnerabilities that affect devices in a broad sense, usually related to aspects such as deficient authorization, different types of insecure interfaces, problems related to privacy and a lack of adequate encryption.

This document is divided as follows, the first part shows an introduction, the second part emphasizes the different related works, then in the third presents a proposed security methodology and fourth part its conclusions.

2   Related Work

The Internet has proven to be an efficient means to increase the way people interconnect, achieving as never before a rapid and almost instantaneous propagation of information, becoming a collaboration mechanism not restricted by a physical location [4].

From the beginning Internet that was only used by computers, today this has given way to its use to diverse types of devices, some not necessarily with a high computing power, for simple tasks, such as embedded sensors, but capable of interconnecting to each other and to network nodes.

At present various devices from a mobile phone to a television, can communicate with each other and through the network, as well as many other devices of everyday life are gradually having this possibility. This movement that has been incorporated is what is called IoT [5].

The current need to be able to control a specific environment has led to the development of ways of using technology in order to achieve this purpose. Thanks to the arrival of the Internet, it has been possible to achieve in the first instance, communication between people, being the Internet a platform capable of interconnecting the planet, this has been its first use.

2.1   Basic Architecture of IoT

An architecture for IoT device and/or networks, based on four layers [6], will be analyzed below:

Perception Layer. In the first instance this layer performs the identification of objects, collects data through sensors and other related devices [7].

In the perception layer, technologies such as WSN, RFID and recently Near Field Communications (NFC) can be found. Some overlap between WSN and RFID technologies, as semi-passive and active RFID tags can also be considered as wireless nodes with lower computational and storage capacity.

Network Layer. In the case of this layer, it is the one that allows the transmission of data obtained through the perception layer, through the Internet, the mobile network or otherwise, any type of communication network that is trusted [8].

In this layer, in the case of wireless sensors, they manage to interact with physical objects and their environment, as well as, when this is the case, with their neighbouring nodes or their respective gateways, integrating the networks through which the data are sent to a remote infrastructure for subsequent storage, analysis and processing, to then make use of the information that has been collected [9].

Mid-Level Layer. This layer is responsible for ensuring the same type of service between the physical objects linked in the IoT network, is also responsible for the management of the service and is linked to the storage of data.

Application Layer. This part of application management is of utmost importance and its success depends on the development of adequate models to process information, as well as on a correct analysis of the results obtained. It is in this part where IoT technologies present their true use and become a determining element in a decision-making process [10]. Figure 1 shows the distribution of the architecture.

2.2 IoT in Agriculture

The use of these elements based on IoT technologies comes at a crucial time. When the demand for more and better quality food is met by a growing demand to meet the growing population. As well as that these are healthy and safe for use. All this will be increasingly difficult for traditional agriculture.

It is necessary to implement all these advances in order to meet the demand of the population. All this will be possible thanks to the IoT family of technologies, which provides all the necessary tools to build and maintain such infrastructures and services, which are specially designed to support the processes originated in the agricultural sector [11].

Sensors, whether wired or wireless, have been widely used in recent years or even decades. Being able to measure the environment in which production occurs, and more recently, the responses that crop plants have to the impact that climate change is beginning to exert, are crucial for concrete and accurate decision making, thus optimizing productivity and crop quality [12].

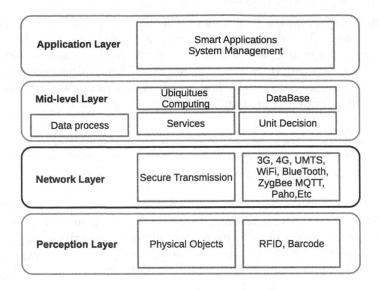

Fig. 1. Basic architecture of IoT [10].

As the use of IoT-related technologies becomes more common, new attack surfaces are born along with this growth, including at the same time new threats to the security of the operation of these. It is expected that at least 25% of the companies that register their attacks by 2020, 2021, will be involved in IoT technologies in this regard. All of this in spite of the precautions and predictions made by research, thus generating a safe growth in the number of attacks capable of doing harm and increasing over the years [13].

Next, a brief correlation of elements involved in the different layers of a basic IoT architecture is made. This allows a compression of the different vulnerabilities that could affect the different stages of this architecture. This is organized taxonomically as shown in Fig. 2.

As in other areas of systems using the Internet of Things (IoT) concept, in the deployment of IoT systems or networks in agriculture it is of utmost importance to identify possible attack surfaces. These must be known and understood, a specific risk assessment is necessary to identify efficiently the vulnerabilities that could be associated with these risks. With the implementation of these types of proposed methodologies, the development of controls seeks to eliminate these risks or, failing that, to achieve effective mitigation for them.

To describe the origin of the risks one can see a quick appreciation of the different vulnerabilities that have the possibility of being found in the elements that compose the deployed IoT systems. Among other risk factors can be analyzed elements such as little or no physical protection of the devices, causing damage or loss to equipment either through neglect or vandalism, is to understand that physical devices are exposed in areas of crops not permanently supervised.

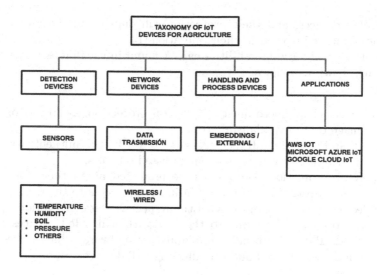

Fig. 2. Taxonomy of IoT devices for agriculture.

In addition, there may also be failures or lack of clarity in the identification or protection of processed data, which allows access by third parties or intruders with the risk of improper manipulation of elements such as actuators, climate and temperature controls, leading to damage or loss in the different stages of the cultivation process.

There is the possibility of finding networks with limited capacity, networks of devices framed in the IoT, are often vulnerable to various attacks due to the need to have little capacity to achieve its operation with few resources, an example of this are sensor networks, in some cases can be easily impacted with denial of service attack, leaving them inoperative and at the mercy of possible attackers.

Another element is the non-application of encryption processes, when this is ignored either in the stages of data acquisition or in the processes or sending, the packets can be exposed to readings and manipulation of third parties due to this vulnerability, this can be a catastrophic failure, when the data are processed and sent in clear or without any encryption either network or process.

Finally, it is necessary not to follow the security measures proposed in the administration sites or user interfaces with the known risks related to not following the standards and elements of good practices associated with their development.

2.3   Vulnerabilities According to Their Layer Within a IoT System

In this type of architecture the vulnerabilities of the IoT environments, must be appreciated from the approach of which affects the different surfaces of attacks, as well as the vulnerabilities associated with each part of a IoT system, as mentioned above the IoT ecosystems are composed of a wide variety of services and interconnected devices, and their protection will depend on the protection of each of the elements involved in their operation [14].

A sample of existing vulnerabilities can be found in the different elements of IoT systems, shown as follows.

For devices:

- Physical protection: There must be physical protection, avoid loss of equipment, damage due to vandalism, etc.
- Identification Protection: It is necessary to verify the authenticity of the devices and to protect the access control based on roles.
- Data privacy protection: Data must be protected at all times, as well as configuration, storage and firmware data. Direct access to the device should be avoided at all costs, avoided with the respective data encryption.
- Avoid back doors: This is due to the ease with which IoT devices can be compromised. These are usually implanted by malware, which is becoming more and more specialized and are affecting IoT devices.

For networks:

- Avoid low capacity: IoT networks can be very vulnerable to denial of service attacks because system resources are often not very powerful.
- Access to Port Scanning: It is important to know which ports are open, as there are now tools that can identify them very quickly.
- Danger of data injection: it is possible with the right tools to capture, transform and introduce packets with altered data to deploy future attacks.
- No network encryption processes: Little by little manufacturers are using TLS encryption for packet processing on IoT devices.

In terms of deployment:

- Intrusion: It is important to deploy detection tools such as IDS or IPS, detecting intrusions in time increases the security of the system.
- Incorporate isolation through isolators such as DMZ, firewall controls, in order to restrict traffic and create secure zones.
- Active detection, to avoid man-in-the-middle attacks, or false DNS replications, to avoid unauthorized access through false credentials.
- Breaking passwords through brute force or any other method.

3   Proposed Safety Methodology

The aim is to develop a methodology to increase security levels in working environments with devices and different types of IoT networks. Directed towards the processes linked to the development and growth of crops, through the monitoring of their environmental parameters, related to their production processes. Similarly, it is necessary to find mechanisms that can ensure these processes, in addition to identifying and mitigating possible safety failures. Figure 3 shows the proposed methodology.

The methodology focuses on the following phases:

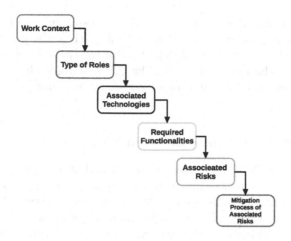

Fig. 3. Proposed methodology.

3.1 Work Context

This part defines the physical space and use of the IoT infrastructure, which will compose the working environment where the infrastructure will be deployed. In this case it will be clearly the area of crops.

3.2 Type of Roles

Here we will define and identify all the different types of roles that will be involved in the use of IoT technology deployed in this type of infrastructure. These can be a natural person or a business entity, taking into account that these must share common characteristics.

3.3 Associated Technologies

This phase seeks to identify any technology that is part or involved in the working environment of crop monitoring through an IoT infrastructure. Detailed knowledge of these technologies is needed to establish the possible onset of risks.

3.4 Required Functionalities

It is necessary here to identify all the functions that are involved with the use of IoT infrastructure in crops, in effect to identify the technologies proposed and analyzed above.

3.5 Associated Risks

An important part of the methodology is found here, this is because the risks associated with the vulnerabilities found in the IoT environment linked to crop monitoring can be identified. As well as the relationship that these risks have with the development of the different roles dealt with in the previous phases. It is important to identify the set of risks that affect the IoT environment to be analyzed, through the correlation with the different roles identified in the previous steps. It is essential to use tables to organize and interpret the correlation properly.

3.6   Mitigation Process of Associated Risks

This phase is used to implement the controls aimed at mitigating the risks managed in the previous phase, either to reduce them or to eliminate them in each of the technological elements used in the work environment. This should be enhanced by associating each mitigation with a given risk. It is necessary to identify the set of mitigations that will have for each risk, then it must be correlated with the role that can implement the suggested mitigation.

4   Expected Results of the Evaluation of the Proposed Methodology

The start-up and evaluation was carried out on a protected type of crop in which an IoT infrastructure was deployed to monitor environmental parameters and their impact on its growth.

According to the application of the proposed methodology, it was possible to identify which is the working environment, through the knowledge of the environment where the IoT infrastructure analyzed in this case is developed. Similarly, the different types of roles associated with the management of the protected crop were determined, where the IoT devices are deployed for the control of crop growth.

It was possible to classify with accuracy the different technologies involved in the operation of the software or physical devices, thus knowing the place it occupies within the infrastructure and determining its priority and possible performance capacity. Next, the risk present in the various functions was identified and its correlation with the roles involved and the use of the devices within the infrastructure.

After all this, the methodology shows the way to mitigate these risks by following the implementation of controls designed for this purpose under the guidelines provided by the standards and concepts of good practices on which the development of the proposed methodology is based.

5   Conclusion

An in-depth analysis was made of the elements that are involved in IoT systems used in agricultural infrastructure and how safety should be an important part of any design and evaluation. As more technological support is needed, the need to rely on it becomes greater and this is only possible if standards are raised so that safety can guarantee its proper and reliable use.

This document proposed a methodology that would allow through the knowledge of a taxonomy of devices/IoT networks and the identification of different vulnerabilities through the methodology exposed, since it is possible to determine the guidelines that are necessary to take into account when it comes to the identification of risk and mitigations for each of them through the application of controls.

References

1. Ashton, K.: That 'Internet of Things' thing. RFID J. (2009). http://www.rfidjournal.com/articles/view?4986
2. Gómez, J.E., Castaño, S., Mercado, T., Fernandez, A., Garcia, J.: Sistema de internet de las cosas (IoT) para el monitoreo de cultivos protegidos. Ingeniería e Innovación 5(1) (2017)
3. Evans, D.: Internet de las cosas: Cómo la próxima evolución lo cambia todo (2011)
4. Leiner, B.M., et al.: Una breve historia de Internet. Revista Novática. Números 130, 131 (1999)
5. Coetzee, L., Perez, N.B., Eksteen, J.: Internet of Things promise for the future? An introduction (2011)
6. Perez, N.B., Bustos, M.A., Berón, M., Rangel Henriques, P.: Análisis sistematico de la seguridad en internet of things. In: XX Workshop de Investigadores en Ciencias de la Computación, WICC 2018, Universidad Nacional del Nordeste (2018)
7. Zhang, Y.: Technology framework of the Internet of Things and its application. In: International Conference on Electrical and Control Engineering, pp. 4109–4112, September 2011
8. Yang, X., Li, Z., Geng, Z., Zhang, H.: A multi-layer security model for Internet of Things. In: Wang, Y., Zhang, X. (eds.) IOT 2012. CCIS, vol. 312, pp. 388–393. Springer, Heidelberg (2012). https://doi.org/10.1007/978-3-642-32427-7_54
9. Gubbi, J., Buyya, R., Marusic, S., Palaniswami, M.: Internet of Things (IoT): a vision, architectural elements, and future directions. Future Gener. Comput. Syst. 29(7), 1645–1660 (2013)
10. Khan, R., Khan, S.U., Zaheer, R., Khan, S.: Future internet: the Internet of Things architecture, possible applications and key challenges. In: 10th International Conference on Frontiers of Information Technology, pp. 257–260. IEEE, December 2012
11. Verdouw, C.N., Beulens, A.J.M., Van Der Vorst, J.G.A.J.: Virtualisation of floricultural supply chains: a review from an Internet of Things perspective. Comput. Electron. Agric. 99, 160–175 (2013)
12. Nishina, H.: Development of speaking plant approach technique for intelligent greenhouse. Agric. Agric. Sci. Procedia 3, 9–13 (2015)
13. Gartner: Leading the IoT. Gartner Insights on How to Lead in a Connected World (2017)
14. ENISA: Baseline Security Recommendations for IoT. ENISA, 20 November 2017. https://www.enisa.europa.eu/publications/baseline-security-recommendations-for-iot
15. Gilchrist, A.: IoT Security Issues. Walter de Gruyter GmbH & Co KG, Berlin (2017)

16. Hallman, R., Bryan, J., Palavicini, G., Divita, J., Romero-Mariona, J.: IoDDoS, el Internet de los ataques de denegación de servicio distribuidos (2017)
17. Enmanuel, D., et al.: Theoretical foundations of Web 2.0 for teaching in higher education. Revista de Ciencias Médicas Cienfuegos **15**, 190–196 (2017)
18. ISACA: Internet of Things: risk and value considerations. ISACA Academic J. (2015). http://www.isaca.org/knowledgecenter/research/researchdeliverables/pages/internet-ofthings-risk-and-value-considerations.aspx
19. Katsoulas, N., Bartzanas, T., Kittas, C.: Online professional irrigation scheduling system for greenhouse crops. Acta Hortic. **1154**, 221–228 (2017)
20. Kittas, C., Bartzanas, T., Jaffrin, A.: Temperature gradients in a partially shaded large greenhouse equipped with evaporative cooling pads. Biosyst. Eng. **85**(1), 87–94 (2003)
21. Larin, G., German, Y.: El internet de las cosas y sus riesgos para la privacidad, Bachelor's thesis, Universidad Piloto de Colombia (2017)
22. NISTIR: Interagency Report on Status of International Cybersecurity Standardization for the Internet of Things (IoT). NIST, February 2018. https://csrc.nist.gov/publications/detail/nistir/8200/draft
23. Popović, T., Latinović, N., Pešić, A., Zečević, Ž., Krstajić, B., y Djukanović, S.: Diseñar una plataforma habilitada para IoT para la agricultura de precisión y el monitoreo ecológico: un estudio de caso. Computadoras y Electrónica en la Agricultura **140**, 255–265 (2017)
24. Rozsa, V., et al.: An application domain-based taxonomy for IoT sensors. In: ISPE TE, pp. 249–258, October 2016
25. Sivakumar, B., GunaSekaran, P., SelvaPrabhu, T., Kumaran, P., Anandan, D.: The application of wireless sensor network in the irrigation area automatic system. Int. J. Comput. Technol. Appl. **3**(1), 67–70 (2012)
26. Tzounis, A., Katsoulas, N., Bartzanas, T., Kittas, C.: Internet of Things in agriculture, recent advances and future challenges. Biosyst. Eng. **164**, 31–48 (2017)
27. Welbourne, E., et al.: Construyendo el Internet de las cosas utilizando RFID: la experiencia del ecosistema RFID. IEEE informática en Internet **13**(3), 48–55 (2009)
28. Whitmore, A., Agarwal, A., Da Xu, X.: The Internet of Things-a survey of topics and trends. Inf. Syst. Front. **17**(2), 261–274 (2015)

Methodology for the Efficiency and Cybersecurity Improvement of the SCADA Communication Network in EmelNorte Substations

Erick Pozo[1]([✉]), Edison Eche[2]([✉]), Silvana Gamboa[1]([✉]), and Patricio Chico[1]([✉])

[1] Escuela Politécnica Nacional, 17-01-2759, Quito, Ecuador
{erick.pozo,silvana.gamboa,patricio.chico}@epn.edu.ec
[2] EmelNorte, Ibarra 100105, Ecuador
eeche@emelnorte.com

Abstract. This paper presents the development and pilot implementation of the methodological proposal for the improvement to the efficiency and cybersecurity of the SCADA communication network in EmelNorte substations. This is justified by the fact that the modern substations operation requires that the SCADA will become to an open system, which can be integrated with others systems related with administration and management of Energy Business. This situation, on the one hand, bring with it the need for a SCADA communication network that should be characterized by a high availability and efficiency, but on the other hand, as the SCADA becomes an open system, its cybersecurity could be compromised. In this regard, a design methodology for improving efficiency and cybersecurity of the SCADA communication network is developed by taking as references standards IEC-61850 and NERC-CIP-7. This methodology propose design guidelines for: (1) LAN architecture design in substations, (2) administration and management of SCADA communication network, and (3) cybersecurity of SCADA communication network. In order to validate the proposed guidelines, these were implemented in the communication network of substation "El Retorno", and then efficiency and cybersecurity were evaluated and contrasted to that of network before the implementation. The results show significant performance improvements, and with it the potential benefits of the methodology implementation are evidenced.

Keywords: Efficiency · Cybersecurity · SCADA · Communication network · Substation

1 Introduction

Nowadays, communication in the SCADA system at electric substations is becoming more relevant, justified in that modern substations requires a SCADA which must be an open system capable of providing multiple features and integrating with other systems related to energy management. But, enable these

© Springer Nature Switzerland AG 2020
M. Botto-Tobar et al. (Eds.): ICAT 2019, CCIS 1195, pp. 13–27, 2020.
https://doi.org/10.1007/978-3-030-42531-9_2

functions requires a proper administration and management of this communication network, as well as the implementation of mechanisms to ensure its cybersecurity, since as an open system the risk of suffering attacks of this type is increased [1]. This situation is not foreign to EmelNorte because its operations are supported by the SCADA system that integrates electrical substations and the control center. Currently, although the importance of communication system, one of the big problems which faces EmelNorte is that there are no guidelines for implementing an appropriate network architecture and structure in its electrical substations. This results in, among other things, difficulties for finding damages, or more complex problems such as the lack of redundancy in both the network equipment and communication links, since substation IEDs are concentrated to a single communication equipment. Therefore, the substation could go out of service if any failure in these equipment are presented. From an administrative point of view, the network is not enabled to face contingencies because the lack of a procedure and guidelines that establish how services should be performed within the network, it becomes disorganized and potentially vulnerable in relation to its cybersecurity. Then, It is necessary to establish guidelines for the administration, management and cybersecurity of the LAN networks of EmelNorte electrical substations. This requirement is not justified for a future modernization of the SCADA system only but also for a proper operation of the current SCADA system. According to this objective and taking into account that currently all substations have similar equipment and architectures, El Retorno substation is taken as a study case and in which the analysis of the communication network in regards to its physical architecture, as well as its administration and management is performed. Also, the existence of configurations related to the cybersecurity are checked. Subsequently, the methodology and design guidelines already mentioned were established. Then, they are applied and evaluated in El Retorno, the pilot substation, to analyze the feasibility of implementation in the remaining EmelNorte substations.

This paper is organized as follow. First, in Sect. 2, we present a Network Evaluation Criteria which are applicable to our issue. Then in Sect. 3, analysis for a pilot substation is described, while in Sect. 4 the development of proposed methodology is detailed. In Sect. 5, the implementation at the El Retorno Substation and its validation are presented. Finally, conclusions are drawn in Sect. 6.

2   Network Evaluation Criteria

There are several ways to evaluate a communications network, this evaluation will depend on the needs or the application which the network is oriented, in this case it is a LAN network for an electrical substation. Therefore, evaluations have been considered based on three aspects: (1) Analysis of the physical architecture, (2) Analysis of the administration and management of the network, and (3) Vulnerability analysis of the LAN network. After establishing the three evaluation aspects mentioned above we focus on specific criteria for these that result in a set of evaluation criteria, which are described in the following.

2.1 Analysis of the Physical Architecture [2]

For the analysis of the physical architecture of the network, evaluation criteria were structured based on the needs of an industrial network for electrical substations, then the standard IEC61850-7 were used as reference. These proposed criteria is described in the following.

Redundancy of Links. In a network, it is not enough to establish communications between the equipment only, at less two links must be maintained.

Redundancy of Switches. Generally, the relays among other equipment of the electrical substations have a dual-port network card then redundancy in the switches should be considered.

Redundancy of Router. Since it is intended to establish an internal network and an external network, it is necessary to place a router to connect them. However, this connection could be a weak point for the network, which is why it is important to consider a redundant configuration.

From the first three evaluation criteria, three subsequent criteria are considered and although they are general and can be applied in most networks, it is important to refer to them in this particular case of a LAN network in an electrical substation. These are the following:

Flexibility. This is the ability of the network devices to operate with devices from different brands. Moreover, it refers to the easiness to implement new technologies in the network.

Scalability. The network must have the capacity to be expanded it by the integration of the new equipment.

Availability. It is not allowable that the communications with a substation are interrupted for extended periods because the communication between substations and the control center must be permanent. It is recommended to consider the rule of the 5 nines.

2.2 Administration and Management Analysis [3]

Topology. From the administrative standpoint, there must be a defined architecture, which should have a redundant configuration to guarantee a proper operation of the network.

Physical Redundancy. It depends on the number of physical links through which data can be transported. Beside redundancy in network devices, redundancy at the border devices or routers and on the relays of the substation must be considered since these can be considered as critical points of the network.

Logical Redundancy [4]. The network must have redundant configurations. Then, protocols such as the RSTP (Rapid Spanning Tree Protocol) should be implemented. In addition, load balancing protocols such as PAgP (Port Aggregation Protocol) or LACP (Link Aggregate Control Protocol) should be considered.

Addressing. All equipment that is part of the LAN network must be addressed. Every device must have a unique address, the mask and the gateway, and as part of the procedure, all of this information must be documented.

Routing Configurations. Routing must be static and specified.

Basic Administrative Configurations. In most networking devices, it is possible to carry out basic configurations such as time of access to the equipment or number of attempts to register credentials, among others. It is recommended to modify them since it is not a good practice to maintain them in their default configurations.

Credentials [5]. A credential should never be maintained in its default configuration, besides the credentials must meet a minimum of characters between uppercase and lowercase letters. In addition, in all computers must be configured two types of users, one with administrative privileges and another with only visualization privileges.

Network Synchronization Protocol. All equipment must be associated with a synchronization server. The synchronization equipment is recommended to be in the substation.

Network Security Configurations [6]. The network must have a firewall that can be either a physical device or logical in a layer 3 device. In addition, the access to authorized personnel and relevant documentation must be restricted.

Memory and CPU Usage Status of Equipment. Memory as well as CPU usage of equipment must not exceed 85% of their resources.

Quality of Service Configurations. Although only process information should be exchanged through the substation network, it is recommended that quality of service should be enabled for the links used by the substation.

Security Policies [7]. As a structural part of network administration and management, procedures for assigning credentials to users as well as for information management must be established.

Administration and Management Procedures. Documentation that establishes a procedure for the administration and management of the network should be developed.

2.3 Vulnerability Analysis

Although vulnerability analysis could be performed through tests of network access, a network analysis accomplished by the Nessus software to be found as a more convenient. This software allows to establish the enabled ports, the vulnerabilities and how the vulnerabilities could be exploited. Then, it presents its results according to states summarized in Fig. 1 [8]. For the analysis of the physical architecture of the network, evaluation criteria were initially generated which were structured based on the needs of the industrial network and also taking as reference the IEC61850-7 standard.

Assigned Color	Status	Description
	Informative	Information to consider
	Low	The system is safe
	Average	Certain improvements must be made
	High	Considerable corrections must be made
	Critical	High-risk corrections are needed as the system is considerably in danger

Fig. 1. Nessus evaluation chart

3   Network Analysis in "El Retorno" Substation

3.1 Physical Architecture

El Retorno substation presents the physical architecture depicted in Fig. 2, in which it is observed that all equipment are concentrated in a single switch that is connected to the corporate WAN network. Also, there are 3 switches and a router that communicate the data concentrator that communicates with the relays and meters of the electrical substation. Besides, it can be seen that the architecture does not show redundancy in its communication links.

3.2 Analysis of the Physical Architecture

The result of the analysis are detailed in Table 1. In Fig. 3, the results of the vulnerability analysis can be observed, in which it can see that its architecture is deficient according to the established evaluation parameters.

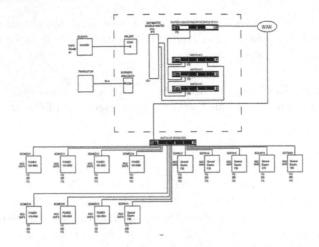

Fig. 2. Physical architecture of the LAN network

Table 1. Results of the physical architecture analysis

No.	Description	Status			
		Excellent	Good	Poor	Non-existent
1	Redundancy of links			●	
2	Switch redundancy				●
3	Router redundancy				●
4	Flexibility			●	
5	Scalability			●	
6	Availability			●	
7	Reliability			●	

Fig. 3. Global results of the physical architecture analysis

3.3 Analysis of the Administration and Management

The parameters of the evaluation and their status are those mentioned in the Table 2. In Fig. 4, the analysis results are shown, in which it is noted 43% is deficient and 43% present a lack of administration and management parameters in the network.

Table 2. Results of the LAN network administration and management analysis

No.	Description	Status			
		Excellent	Good	Poor	Non-existent
1	Topology			•	
2	Physical redundancy			•	
3	Logical redundancy				•
4	Addressing			•	
5	Routing settings		•		
6	Basic administrative configurations			•	
7	Credentials			•	
8	Network synchronization protocols				•
9	Network security settings			•	
10	Status of device memory and CPU	•			
11	Quality of service				•
12	Security policies				•
13	Administration and management procedures				•

Fig. 4. Results of administration and management analysis

3.4 Vulnerability Analysis

In Fig. 5, the results obtained by the software Nessus are detailed. According to the results of the vulnerability analysis that was executed in all the equipment in the substation, it was possible to determine that the communications system does not have an acceptable level of security since it presents high and critical states.

STATUS	PERCENTAGE
Informative	56%
Low	5%
Medium	27%
High	5%
Critical	7%

Fig. 5. Results of vulnerability analysis

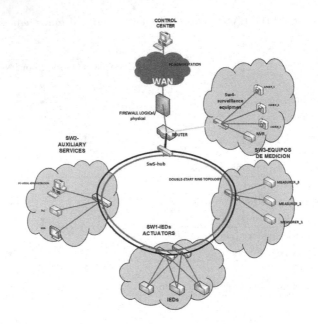

Fig. 6. Double ring architecture

3.5 Conclusions of the Network Analysis

From the results of network analysis, it is concluded that the network needs to be intervened. Therefore, it is necessary to generate a methodology that improve the operation of it by means of a solid infrastructure. Besides that, an administration and management guideline according to the needs of the network and the cybersecurity in order to keep the system available and protected. Such guidelines were established by this work and will be detailed in the following numbers.

4   Development of Proposed Guidelines

It is important to highlight that the guidelines that will be presented in this section to have been proposed focusing on reality of the EmelNorte substations needs.

4.1 Physical Architecture

It is necessary to implement an architecture that meets the requirements of redundancy as well as scalability. In this regard, although the ring architecture could satisfy these requirements, a communication network in a substation could be improved even more through a double ring architecture that is shown in Fig. 6 [2]. In this architecture, the switches concentrate devices that carry out similar functions, excepting switch sw5 that connects the router with the other switches. In sw1 are connected the substation relays with a redundant configuration. Ancillary equipment that allow a proper functioning of the substation facilities are concentrated to sw2, while in sw3 the measurement devices are connected. In addition, sw4 is proposed for integrating security cameras; however, sw4 can be omitted if there is a post-firewall equipment in which the cameras could be installed. Since the importance of the relays in the operation of the substation, an important aspect to consider is to install a dual-port network card in every of them for increasing the redundancy level at the substations, because this should enable to connect the relays to two redundant switches as sw1-IEDs. It is also important to highlight that a most convenient alternative is to implement a communication network dedicated to the SCADA and its industrial equipment. However, in the case of EmelNorte, there is not independent infrastructure, therefore the information of both the substations and the business areas share a unique infrastructure.

4.2   Network Administration and Management

After establishing the architecture, parameters and guidelines for a proper operation of this architecture must be determined.

Network Address Translation Process (NAT). It is important to differentiate the substation network from the other communications networks that may exist. In this regard, the concept of external network and internal network is proposed. Where the external network is that has access to the internet or to equipment that do not belong to SCADA system. While the internal network is that is integrated by equipment related to substation operation only. The NAT must accompany the proposed implementation.

Fully Specified Static Routing. Static routing is recommended since generally the equipment through which information circulates is known. Although the specification of static routing demands time and work, it has benefits such as decreasing broadcast messages. Also, since the route is established no intruder equipment can get the information packets avoiding "man in the middle" attacks.

Remote Administration. Protocols that allow to remote management of the substation equipment should be enabled. Therefore, Telnet and SSH that use ports 23 and 22 respectively could be considered. Telnet is a protocol that does not use any encryption algorithm during communication. Instead, SSH uses an encryption method, which allows a more secure communication. Then, the use of the SSH protocol is recommended. However, for the equipment that lacks it, Telnet could be used. But security must be improved at the higher level devices such as routers.

Redundancy in the Router Links. The router will be the device responsible for communicating the internal network to the external network. In this regard, it is proposed to implement two routers in a redundant configuration. In addition, redundancy protocols such as Hot Standby Router Protocol (HSRP) or Virtual Router Redundancy Protocol (VRRP) must be configured. The first of these protocols belongs to CISCO and the second is free, however both has the same features.

Redundancy in the Switch. For implementing the architecture proposed in Fig. 1, redundancy protocols such as Rapid Spanning Tree Protocol (RSTP) must be configured. This protocol has the ability to determine the most appropriate link to send the information when a device has two connections to another device. If this protocol is not enabled, a loop of information could be generated that may bring to device to saturate the memory buffers, which subsequently disinhibit the network card.

Load Balance and Link Aggregation Protocols. This type of protocols allows to communicate equipment through a double physical link by performing a load balance and a redundant communication. As result, the transmission speed is increased allowing a more efficient communication. Two protocols of this type are PAgP (port aggregation protocol) for CISCO equipment and LACP (link aggregation control protocol) for equipment of another brand.

Limit the Connection of External Devices through the Management of Physical Ports [5]. Only equipment authorized by the network administrator can be connected. With this objective, several configurations can be implemented in the equipment according to their capabilities. However the basic restrictions should be: (1) Shutdown: blocking the connected port, (2) Protect: restriction the sending of frames without blocking the port, and (3) Restrict: restriction the sending of frames without blocking the port and sending an alarm through the SNMP protocol.

Assignment of Addresses to the Devices. An IPV4 or IPV6 network must be defined, and its addressing configuration should be include the parameters detailed below, which are described by using an IPV4/class C network:

- Network address: 10.10.10.xx
- Network prefix: / 24
- Network mask: 255.255.xx.xx
- Address that begins the range: 10.10.10.xx
- Address that ends the range: 10.10.10.xx
- Gateway address

Synchronization of Networking Equipment [3]. It is important that the devices are synchronized. Then, the use of devices that manages the synchronization of all equipment in the substation network is recommended. In addition, a synchronization protocol in each of the devices on the network should be enabled. For this purpose, there are currently protocols such as SNTP (simple network time protocol) and PTP (precision time protocol).

Backup of Networking Equipment Configurations [2]. It is important to keep a backup of the configurations made in the networking equipment, since the availability of these backups allows fast emergency actions when any device goes out of operation and needs to be replaced. For this, the following parameters must be considered: (1) The equipment must allow to obtain backup of the configurations, (2) The settings must be stored digitally, (3) Verify the method by which the backup of the equipment must be obtained and how the configuration can be entered to the equipment.

4.3   Network Security

This section will emphasize about cybersecurity and provide guidelines for a "good use" of the data generated in the substation network, in addition to proper management of the credentials that were assigned. For this, the following parameters have been considered:

Access Control [5]. Access to the internal network must be restricted. With this objective, security settings such as Access Control Lists (ACLs) are available, in which could be determined the method by which access will be restricted. The most usual method is to restrict the access according to the MAC address or IP address. In both cases, the restrictions for every equipment must be specified. The restrictions can also be configured by ports; this will depend on the capabilities of the equipment in that will be configured the ACL.

Password Management in Networking Equipment. It is important that access credentials to the devices are generated considering the following requirements: (1) Determine the personnel, for which the credential is addressed. This refers to whether the person will have full access or a partial access that could be visualization only. It is advisable to generate both types of credentials, (2) Password will be structured by upper and lower case letters, numbers and characters.

Encryption Protocols. Encryption protocols allow to increase the security during transfer of information is performed by means of the use of cryptographic characters. Then, the Transport Layer Security Protocol (TLS) is recommended to be enabled in each of the networking equipment since many applications can use this encryption protocol such is the case of HTTPS.

Update of Patches. Regarding security, it is important that the equipment software be updated with the latest versions provided by the manufacturer, since new ways of violating the systems could appear or programming failures simply. In this regard, the NERC CIP-007-6 standard offers some recommendations for updates: (1) Determine the source of the patch, it must be officially issued by the manufacturer, (2) Document and keep a record of the updates, (3) After any update, verify the proper operation of the equipment and the whole network, (4) Implement a plan to mitigate the patch in the event that it affects the proper functioning of the system, and (5) Verify the patch first on a device isolated from the system.

Administration of Ports and Services. It is important to limit the use of ports in the substation network since in a SCADA system network referring to a substation, it is not necessary that ports that handle audio or video are enabled because these services "bull" type consume bandwidth. This type of services is not recommended to be enabled.

Security in the Facility. Although the topic of this project is not the safety of the facilities, it is important to consider it as part of the security that encompasses the communication system.

5   Application and Evaluation of the Methodology in El Retorno Susbstation

After developing the guidelines for the physical architecture, administration, management and cybersecurity, these were applied to the communication network of substation EL RETORNO to evaluate them.

5.1   Implementation Limitations

Prior to the implementation of the methodology in El Retorno substation, the particular limitations of this substation for the proposed implementation are established. These limitations will be mentioned below.

- The main ring of the current physical architecture is not entirely fiber optic
- VLAN configurations were not implemented
- Router redundancy was not implemented because an additional router is not availability

5.2   Proposed Physical Architecture

In Fig. 7 is depicted the proposed architecture for El Retorno substation, in which the equipment has been grouped according its functionality. This architecture with ring topology is currently implemented because a double ring topology could not be implemented due to the limitations mentioned above. However, the current architecture complies with the redundancy in its links that guarantee a good network availability (Fig. 8).

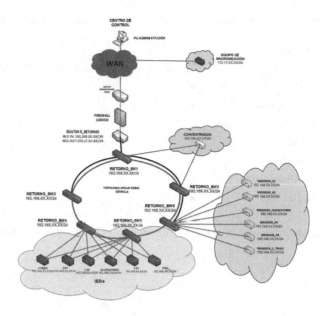

Fig. 7. Physical architecture applied to the El Retorno substation

■ Excelent ■ Good ■ Deficient ■ Non-existent

Fig. 8. Global results of the architecture analysis

5.3   Analysis Results for the Physical Architecture

The current architecture of the El Retorno substation network, which has the following characteristics:

– The current architecture has redundant links.
– The relays are connected to switches with redundant configuration.
– The architecture is scalable since more equipment can be integrated.
– The network is 100% available. However, it is recommended to perform an annual record of the time that the network goes out of service.

In Table 3 the results after the application of the mentioned guidelines are presented.

5.4   Analysis Results of Network Administration and Management

After making the proposed configurations in the networking equipment, the results shown in Table 4 and Fig. 9 were reached.

Table 3. Results of the evaluation of the physical architecture of El Retorno

No.	Description	Status			
		Excellent	Good	Poor	Non-existent
1	Redundancy of links	●			
2	Switch redundancy	●			
3	Router redundancy			●	
4	Flexibility	●			
5	Scalability	●			
6	Availability	●			
7	Reliability	●			

Table 4. Evaluation results of the LAN network management and administration

No.	Description	Status			
		Excellent	Good	Poor	Non-existent
1	Topology	●			
2	Physical redundancy	●			
3	Logical redundancy	●			
4	Addressing	●			
5	Routing settings	●			
6	Basic administrative configurations	●			
7	Credentials	●			
8	Network synchronization protocols	●			
9	Network security settings	●			
10	Status of device memory and CPU	●			
11	Quality of service		●		
12	Security policies	●			
13	Administration and management procedures	●			

■ excelent ■ good ■ deficient ■ Non-existent

Fig. 9. Results of the administration and management analysis of the LAN network

5.5   Global Results of Vulnerability Analysis

In order to perform the vulnerability analysis, the Nessus software was used. In Fig. 10 the results obtained are presented. In which is observed that there is no longer a critical state in the network and also the percentages in the high

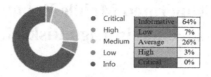

Fig. 10. Results from vulnerability analysis using NESSUS software

and medium states were reduced. Although it is ideal that the highest state be eliminated, this percentage is given by the limitations of the equipment to configure SSH.

6 Conclusions

Development of the methodology for improving the efficiency and cybersecurity of the communication network at EmelNorte substations has been proposed. In order to evaluate this methodology, it were used as a guideline for restructuring the communication network at El Retorno Substation. After the application of the methodology, the physical architecture, administration, management and cybersecurity of the network in the substation shown an improvement in their performance because, among other things, a separation between the substation network and the corporate network was achieved. Also remote and local access of substation equipment was restricted. Therefore, the proposed methodology is shown as feasible and achieves the aims for that this were proposed. Also, it is important to highlight that this methodology will allow a standardization of all communication networks of electrical substations of EmelNorte.

References

1. Rodríguez, A.: Sistemas SCADA, 3rd edn. Alfaomega Grupo Editor, S.A. de CV., México (2013)
2. International Electrotechnical Commission: IEC61850-7-1: Communication Networks and Systems in Substation - Part 7–1: Basic communication structure for substation and feeder equipment-Principles and Models, 1st edn. (2003)
3. Matousek, P.: Description of analysis of IEC 104 Protocol. Technical report. Faculty of Information Technology. FIT-TR-2017-12 (2017)
4. Pérez, E.: Los Sistemas SCADA en la Automatización Industrial. Tecnología en Marcha **28**(4), 3–14 (2015)
5. NERC-CIP: Standard CIP-007-6 (Cyber Security-System Security Management) V. 5 (2014)
6. Centre for the Protection of National Infrastructure: Firewall Deployment for SCADA and Process Control Networks (2005)
7. Chebyshev, V., Sinitsyn, F., Parinov, D., Liskin, A., Kupreev, L.: Desarrollo de las amenazas informáticas en el segundo trimestre de (2018). https://securelist.lat/it-threat-evolution-q2-2018-statistics/87391/. Accessed 6 Aug 2018
8. Tenable-Nessus. https://www.tenable.com/products/nessus/nessus-professional. Accessed 18 Nov 2018

Wireless Teleoperated Mobile Robot Prototype for Inspection in High Risk Places

Gallegos Alejandro, Ibarra Alexander[✉], Orozco Luis, and Tipán Edgar

Universidad de las Fuerzas Armadas - ESPE, Sangolquí, Av. General Rumiñahui s/n y Ambato, Sangolquí, Ecuador
oaibarra@espe.edu.ec

Abstract. This article presents the design and implementation of a wireless tele-operated mobile robot prototype, intended for the inspection of high risk locations where they could be developing criminal activities with the objective of safeguard the integrity and security of law enforcement officers. Robot design combines special geometry with posibility of high materials deformity and displacement, in order to withstand a free fall of up to 2 m, has an autonomy of up to 50 min, is manipulated by remote control with the possibility of real-time audio and video transmission at a distance of 250 m with sight line and 90 m when there are obstacles; this document is organized as follows: Sect. 1 presents a brief description of mobile robotics and commercial applications, Sect. 2 describes the methodology used for the design of the prototype, Sect. 3 presents the implementation of the prototype, Sect. 4 presents the results achieved and finally, in Sect. 5 the main conclusions of this document are presented.

Keywords: Teleoperated mobile robot · High risk · Law enforcement officers

1 Introduction

Due to the increase in organized crime, to its preparation and armament, it is important to provide police and law enforcement officers with new support technologies that help to safeguard their life and safety during the execution of anti-criminal operations. Thus, the need arises for police officers to monitor criminal activities from a safe point, before their intervention in the place where a possible crime is carried out, by means of a teleoperated robotic device.

To provide a solution to this problem, this paper proposes: (1) Develop a mobile robot prototype with mechanical robustness, autonomy, teleoperation with audio and video in real time, for political support in anti-criminal operations, in places of high risk. (2) Monitor anti-delinquency activities from a safe point, before the intervention in the place where a possible crime is carried out, by means of a tele-operated robotic device that enters the place of risk, through its locomotion or launch system by police personnel.

The contribution and importance of this work lies in the proposal of new alternatives in the methodology of technology integration and a robust structural and locomotion

M. Botto-Tobar et al. (Eds.): ICAT 2019, CCIS 1195, pp. 28–39, 2020.
https://doi.org/10.1007/978-3-030-42531-9_3

design, suitable for the development of a teleoperated mobile robot, which is useful for the monitoring of anti-criminal activities, before the intervention of police officers in places of high risk.

1.1 Movile Robots

The robots have been created with the purpose of replacing the human in repetitive, tedious, unpleasant, dangerous tasks, as well as to optimize human work in terms of accuracy, speed, efficiency and safety, among others. In particular, mobile robots are machines that can move in terrestrial, aquatic, aerial and space environments, using some form of locomotion, energy source and control system. Mobile robotics has in security one of its most important applications, its objective being the inspection and recognition of the place, to help people to know the situation of the site before moving forward or positioning themselves in it [1].

The design of a mobile robot implies proposing solutions for the mechanical system, actuation system, sensors, control system, energy source, autonomy; Additionally, several aspects such as robustness of vibrations and other effects of its movement must be considered: misalignment, friction, wear and finally its navigation and interaction with the environment. The robot control can be local or remote, teleoperation allows a human operator to control the robot remotely (remote station), giving a perspective of the place without the operator being physically immersed in there.

Teleoperated mobile robotics, with its constant development, is opening the field in different areas of industry and daily life, among which security applications stand out, both at the research level and at the commercial level. For example, in [2]., a platform is developed for the monitoring and teleoperation of several robot models, used for security roles, reconnaissance missions and detection of explosive devices improvised, the authors apply the concept that small low-cost systems capable of visual surveillance, are proving to be increasingly effective, in environments in which robots are even considered expendable, so it is intended that designed robots are Low-cost, fast-response, applicable in land-based urban search and rescue, that meet the growing expectations of being able to negotiate each and every one of the variations of the land, this work presents a comparative chart of three elaborate designs each with different operating characteristics and applications. Other related work is in [3], where the design of a teleoperated robotic platform for the inspection of industrial plants is proposed, to visualize the values of different analogue meters and through artificial vision allow the operator to verify the measured values and with the use of an actuator embedded in the mobile robot, Even regulating valves in order to adjust them and reach certain operating values, this work aims to prevent the entry of operators to dangerous areas in which their integrity and health can be jeopardized.

On a commercial level, within the field of security, there are different examples of mobile robots developed for work in hostile environments such as, the Throwbot XT robot, developed by the ReconRobotics company [4], this teleoperated robot has an audio and video system to locate armed suspects and listen to conversations, it is designed to be launched up to 36 m in narrow spaces, waterproof, capable of absorbing impacts from falls or shocks, it has a compact and portable size, thus becoming a reference in mobile robots oriented towards this type of operations, is used by the United States Army for exploration and rescue tasks in high risk situations.

2 Design Methodology

2.1 Selection of Alternatives

For the selection of design alternatives of the teleoperated robot, the Quality Development Function (QFD) methodology was used [5], through which 13 design requirements were identified, which had to be satisfied by the characteristics or technical specifications of the product, which are summarized in Table 1.

Table 1. Requirements and specifications for the QFD matrix.

Concept	No	Requirement	Power Interface	Motors with alternating power	Type of materials	Energy damping system	Reception Transmission System	Controlability	Energy consumption	Minimum operable distance	Locomotion System	Real-time percepion system
Function	1	Teleoperated	X	X			X	X	X			X
	2	Real Time Vision and Video					X			X		X
	3	Medium Autonomy					X		X		X	
	4	Wirelessly Commanded					X			X		X
Manufacture	5	Move on uneven terrain	X	X							X	
	6	Resistant to dynamic forces		X	X						X	
	7	Compact	X	X					X	X	X	
	8	Power attenuator system		X	X						X	
Control	9	Easy to operate	X				X	X		X		X
	10	Remote control	X				X	X		X		
	11	Rotation System	X	X								
	12	Adjustable speed	X						X			
Cost	13	Low cost			X					X	X	X

Next, Table 2 describes the seven modules with the alternatives analyzed to be developed in the design stage, complying with the main product characteristics defined in the QFD matrix presented above.

Table 2. Selected alternatives for design

Module	Focus	Alternative selected for development
Module 1	Locomotion system	Wheel locomotion system
Module 2	Mechanical structure	Frame and chassis made of aluminum with high deformity and displacement material
Module 3	Drives	Mobility: Motor with gearbox Positioning: Servo motor
Module 4	Power	H bridge with IC
Module 5	Teleoperation	FPV System Vision Remote control operation by RF module
Module 6	Control	Arduino card with On/Off control type
Module 7	Energy	Power supply per battery

2.2 Detail of the Module Design

Module 1, Locomotion system: It is considered that the place on which the robot is going to develop is flat; to which a four-wheel-based configuration is proposed for adequate stability (Fig. 1); and for its construction, aspects related to the suspension, traction and maneuverability system were considered with the following characteristics: (a) The left front wheel will have the same speed and direction of rotation as the left rear wheel. The right front wheel will have the same speed and direction of rotation as the right rear wheel. (b) The change of direction of the robot will be done by speed difference or rotation between the left and right wheels.

Fig. 1. Mechanical structure and possible contacts between the surface and the wheels

Module 2, Mechanical structure: It was divided into two parts, material of the frame and anti-shock system, determining that the wheels are responsible for receiving the impact, so its dimensions must protrude from the structure of the robot's base, considering that in any orientation that the robot can fall down, the wheels should always make contact with the surface, thus protecting the structure of the base (Fig. 2). With respect to the material to withstand the blows, after an analysis based on QFD matrices, it was decided to use silicone rubber with catalyst.

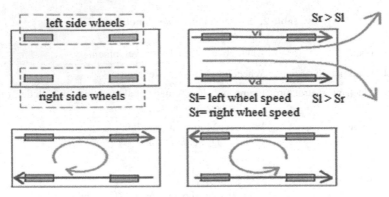

Fig. 2. Maneuverability of the mobile robot

In the same way, the wheels will serve as a suspension system as they will help in the damping of impacts. The complement of the suspension system in mobile robots can be simplified with the geometric design of the wheels, so that their flexibility, grant and maintain continuous contact of the wheels with the ground. For this, an impact simulation was designed and performed at 10 m/s, of three different wheel models (Fig. 3); concluding that the best alternative is model being semi-hollow and having connections to other parts of the material, it grants a network of efforts transmission links from the first point to the other ties, resulting in a lower effort of Von Mises.

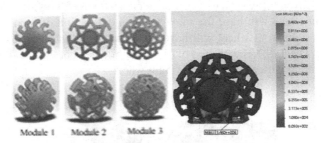

Fig. 3. Wheel models and impact simulation

The construction of these wheels was carried out using a mold manufactured in a 3D printer. The connection between the engine and the wheel was made through a ring made of ABS with a minimum of 80% padding considering that the wheel is very flexible and it is intended that the ring has better grip inside the wheel (Fig. 4).

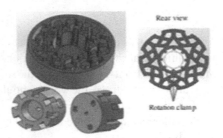

Fig. 4. Wheel mold, hoop and clamping system

Additionally, the hoop has 3 holes, so silicone rubber will enter the curing process, offering greater transmission of rotational movement and avoiding lateral decoupling (Fig. 5).

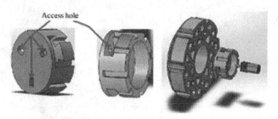

Fig. 5. Coupling, motor, hoop and wheel

Understanding that the size and weight of the robot, are defined by the dimensions of the electronic components, to finalize the design process, the structural characteristics of the robot will be established, which are shown in Table 3.

Table 3. Robot structural specifications

Design	Specification	Unit
Wheels	7–12	cm
Height	7–12	cm
Width	11–17	cm
Long	17–22 framework	cm
	20–30 wheel to wheel	cm
Weight	0.9–1.8	Kg
Minimum autonomy	30	minutes
Maximum resistance to falls	2	m
Minimum reach	250 outdoors 50 indoor	m

The chassis was manufactured with sheets aluminum 1060, 1 mm thick due to its characteristics, it will be designed based on criteria applied in the automotive industry, selecting a mono-hull design since it facilitates the coupling of both mechanical components and electronic, so the coupling is intended to be sufficiently rigid to keep the elements stable. The base plate of the chassis will be constructed of aluminum and the support elements in ABS to give greater support.

To validate the chassis design, a CAE software was used as a simulation tool to assess the strength of the structure (Fig. 6).

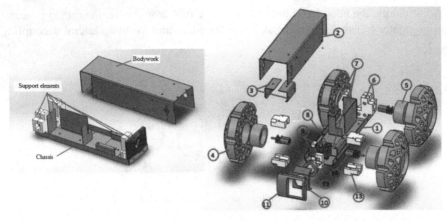

Fig. 6. Elements of the mobile robot

The elements of the mobile robot are described below in the Table 4.

Table 4. Elements of the mobile robot

Number	Elements	1Number	Elements
1	Motherboard	8	Servo Motor
2	Bodywork	9	Servo motor couplings
3	Body support plates	10	Camera turn coupling
4	Rolling	11	Front support
5	Hoop	12	Camera coupling
6	Rear engine support	13	Fastening for front engine
7	PCB board coupling	14	Gearmotor

The most critical fall was simulated where a wheel must withstand the impact of a free fall of 2 m in height and on rigid ground, which presented a greater effort of Von Mises: 56.93 MPa located in the chassis, after the union of the support of the engine and considering that the elasticity limit of the aluminum used is 90 MPa, the design meets the requirements.

The greatest deformation in the rolling of the wheel is measured, since it absorbs most of the impact, having a resulting displacement of 8.6 mm and the resulting displacement in the area of greatest effort, between the joint of the bodyriver and engine clamping, the highest value being 0.266 mm. Subsequently, the fatigue simulation is performed, resulting in a life cycle of 306 falls.

Module 3, Drives: The torque is calculated to select a motor that exceeds the inertia and the strength of the robot's weight. Carrying out a free-body diagram for a slope of 60° with respect to the ground and considering a safety factor of 1.3, a gearmotor with torque of 3.6 kg/cm, of 6 VDC is chosen and, considering the radius of the wheel produces a speed of 0.806 m/s.

For the actuator that controls the rotation of the camera, it is considered a 180° rotation servomotor that will facilitate the positioning of the camera regardless of the position in which it falls, its calculated the necessary torque that the motor must have to rotate the support structure and the camera, two H301 micro servos with 0.4 kg/cm torque were selected that will be implemented for up and down rotation in order to have a sufficiently wide viewing angle.

Module 4, Power: For the control of DC motors, an H Bridge L293D will be used that supplies currents of up to 600 mA, which conforms to the motor characteristics.

Module 5, Teleoperation: It is divided into two parts, a band for the transmission of control signals and another for the transmission of video, thus avoiding interference and delays in communication by sharing a single channel. For the video transmission, an FPV system commonly used in drones and mobile devices at high frequencies (1 GHz– 5.9 GHz) and with a wide bandwidth was selected. It consists of four elements: camera, transmitter, receiver and screen (Fig. 7).

For the transmitter, a Mini Audio/Video transmitter Eachine TX526 has been selected, as a receiver to the Mini Audio/Video receiver Eachine ER32, choosing a common channel and transmission frequency to guarantee 5645 MHz communication, which is supported by both dispositives. A camera with a small microphone included compatible with the transmitter and a screen with a resolution of 800×480 pixels 5-in. TFT-LCD are selected.

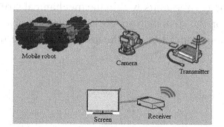

Fig. 7. FPV system

Module 6, Control: A low amount of data transmission is established and a high transmission frequency is not required, the main selection parameter is the 250 m range with line of sight; The NRF24L01 transceiver is selected for its low cost, consumption and long range. 2 transceiver are used in the simplex communication system, one in the robot as a receiver and another in the command as a transmitter.

According to the number of inputs, outputs and communication of the transceiver, it was decided to use an Arduino mini board, one for each station; for the control of the gearmotors, the use of a 2-axis analog joystick with a push button in the control system is proposed, with 4 speeds being proposed according to the joystick controllability, as indicated in Table 5.

Table 5. Speed controllability vs voltage range

Voltage Range (V)	Speed (m/s)	Voltage Range (V)	Speed (m/s)
2.51–3.125	0.1	2.49–1.875	−0.1
3.126–3.75	0.3	1.874–1.25	−0.3
3.751–4.375	0.7	1.24–0.62	−0.7
4.376–5.0	1	0.61–0	−1

Module 7, Energy: It is responsible for the energy supply to electronic devices both at the operator's control and at the remote control station (mobile robot). For the dimensioning of the battery, the electrical consumption of the elements of each station will be taken into account, being for the operator control of 15.45 W with a current of 1.55 A and for the robot 18.88 W with a current of 3.22 A. An 11.1 VDC AR Drone battery with 22 WH power and maximum 40 A supply is selected, additionally voltage regulators are placed for the elements to be fed. For the operator control station, a rechargeable lithium battery DC 12680 with a capacity of 6800 mAH and 12 VDC was selected.

2.3 Electronic Design

Once all the elements have been selected, the electronic circuits are designed using dedicated software, for the robot it was decided to prepare three printed plates in order to distribute the electronic components within the mechanical structure of the same, the first board is intended for the distribution of the power supply for each element, the second destined to the robot controller and the third is the power to control the system's motors (Fig. 8).

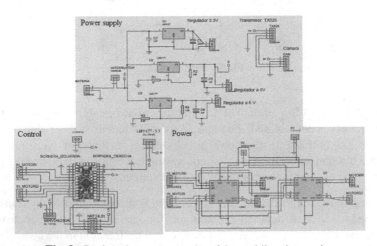

Fig. 8. Design electronic circuits of the mobile robot station

Two plates will be used for the control station, one for data transmission and another for audio/video reception and audio amplification. Subsequently, the PCB boards were designed and manufactured, for the assembly and welding of the components (Fig. 9).

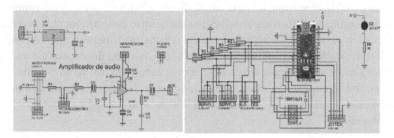

Fig. 9. Design of electronic circuits for the control station

3 Implementation

The machining of the mechanical parts is carried out prior to the manufacture of the robot's metal structure, together with the 3D printing of the most complex components. The process of assembling all the systems continues, includes the production of the wheels based on silicone rubber using the mold made in 3D printing (Figs. 10 and 11).

Fig. 10. Aluminum parts and 3D parts printing and manufacturing of bearings

Fig. 11. Final robot assembly and command station

4   Results

Once the implementation stage is completed, performance tests are performed to validate all established design criteria. Mechanical tests of inclination angle, traction on different surfaces and free fall, electronic tests, control, distance, audio and video transmission are executed; presenting the following results: free fall of up to 2 m without physical damage, highest elevation or tier that the robot can climb is 5 cm, maximum inclination angle was 50° in concrete, satisfactory mobility on wooden land, floating floor, ceramic and carpet, unsatisfactory mobility in grass (Fig. 12), energy autonomy of up to 50 min, correct connectivity and manipulation of the robot by remote control, correct transmission of audio and video in real time at a distance of 250 m with line of sight and 90 m when there are obstacles.

Fig. 12. Functionality test

5   Conclusions

A low-cost mobile robot was designed and implemented, operated wirelessly by a remote control, with an energy autonomy of up to 50 min, for police officers to use in the monitoring of criminal actions, before their intervention in places high-risk.

The robot can enter the place of risk, by its rolling locomotion system or by manual launch from heights of up to 2 m of free fall. The use of silicone rubber for the robot wheels of this project was very important due to its mechanical characteristics; Being a material of great deformation and displacement, 3 design parameters could be satisfied: suspension system, traction and shock systems.

The weight of the robot is a critical factor, since if the weight increases, it would generate a greater impact force, the robot currently weighs 1.8 kg. To do this, the wheels could be changed to a more rigid elastomer and that the width of the connections be smaller.

For monitoring high-risk locations, the prototype transmits audio and video in real time at a distance of 250 m with line of sight and 90 m when there are obstacles; Its real-time teleoperation design parameters were resolved through transmission criteria such as: data speed, information processing capacity to reduce system limitations and obtain the best performance between human-robot coordination, since the critical point It is the perception of signal delays.

Future works have been considered for the analysis of elastomers, reduction of the size and weight of the prototype to improve the ante-impact system, the exploration of other locomotion options, the Investigation of new alternatives of teleoperation and navigation of the robot using computer vision techniques, cloud computing and cloud robotic.

References

1. Arranz, J.B.Á.: Aplicaciones de robots móviles, Universidad de Alcalá (2006)
2. Fielding, M., Mullins, J., Horan, B., Nahavandi, S.: OzBotTM - Haptic Augmentation of a tele-operated robotic platform for search and rescue operations. In: International Workshop on Safety, Security and Rescue Robotics Rome, Italy (2007)
3. Hilario, J., et al.: Late Breaking Report - Development of a mobile robot for industrial plants inspections us-ing computer vision. In: 2019 IEEE International Symposium on Safety, Security, and Rescue Robotics (SSRR), Alemania, pp. 108–109 (2019)
4. Reconrobotics. https://www.policemag.com/367996/throwbot-xt. Accessed 07 Oct 2019
5. Ulrich, K.T.: Diseño, y desarrollo de productos: enfoque multidisciplinario, 5th edn. McGraw Hill, New York (2004)
6. Ollero, A.: Robótica manipuladores y robots móviles. Marcobo, Barcelona (2001)
7. Romeva, C.R.: Diseño concurrente. UPC, Barcelona (2002)
8. Braunl, T.: Embedded Robotics Mobile Robot Design and Applicationas with Embedded Systems. Springer, Berlin (2006)
9. EPRI. Plant Support Engineering: Elastomer Handbook for Nuclear Power Plants. California: Electric Power Reseach Institute (2006)
10. González Pino, M.A.: El Tmr-1. Un Robot Móvil Teleoperado. Santander: Revista Colombiana de Tecnologías de Avanzada (2009)
11. Hernandez, S., Menga, E.: Computational modelling of elastomeric materials to fit experimental data. Coruña: School of Civil Engineering, Universidad of Coruña (2015)
12. Siegwart, R.: Introduction to Autonomous Mobile Robots, London (2004)
13. Stachniss, C.: Robotic Mapping and Exploration. Springer, Berlin (2009)
14. Wood, L.: Robotic Mobile Manipulation Experiments at the U.S. Army Maneuver Support Center, Missouri (2001)

Communication

Comparative Analysis of Cooperative Routing Protocols in Cognitive Radio Networks

Pablo Palacios Játiva[1]($\boxtimes$), Carlos Saavedra[2], José Julio Freire[3],
Milton Román Cañizares[3], and David Zabala-Blanco[4]

[1] Department of Electrical Engineering, University of Chile, Santiago, Chile
`pablo.palacios@ug.uchile.cl`
[2] Faculty of Electrical and Computation Engineering,
ESPOL Polytechnic University, Guayaquil, Ecuador
`casaaved@espol.edu.oc`
[3] Departamento de Redes y Telecomunicaciones,
Universidad De Las Américas, Quito, Ecuador
`{jose.freire,milton.roman}@udla.edu.ec`
[4] Department of Computing and Industries,
Universidad Católica del Maule, Talca, Chile
`davidzabalablanco@hotmail.com`

Abstract. In this work, we investigate and compare cooperative routing protocols for channel selection purposes. In specific, the following efficient protocols: Channel Selection Scheme for Cooperative Routing Protocols (CSCR) and Cooperative Multi-channel MAC Protocol (MC-MAC) applied to Cognitive Radio Networks (CRNs). Cooperative protocol schemes allow Secondary Users (SUs) to detect the presence of Primary Users (PUs). SUs employ their spectrum sensing phase in a multi-channel architecture and, then, transmit this detection to the neighboring SUs cooperatively. The studied protocols are analyzed and evaluated through a CRN simulator, which consists of all stages of the cognitive cycle, namely spectrum sensing, decision, sharing, and mobility. The evaluation is carried out in terms of probability of detection of the PU, packet delivery ratio in terms of SUs, and end-to-end delay as a function of SUs.

Keywords: Channel Selection Scheme for Cooperative Routing Protocols · Cognitive Radio Network · Cooperative routing protocols · Multi-channel MAC protocol · Multi-channel scheme

1 Introduction

The exponential increase in wireless communications has led to an overwhelming growth of the radio-electric spectrum use and since it is a limited resource, new mechanisms must be studied to make its use more efficient. Cognitive Radio (CR), appeared some years ago as a growing solution for the under-utilization

© Springer Nature Switzerland AG 2020
M. Botto-Tobar et al. (Eds.): ICAT 2019, CCIS 1195, pp. 43–56, 2020.
https://doi.org/10.1007/978-3-030-42531-9_4

and saturation problem of the radio spectrum use. In Cognitive Radio Networks (CRNs), the primary users (PUs) have the permission to use the spectrum as a priority (Licensed Users) [1]. However, secondary users (SUs) also called CR users, can use the spectrum as well, but under the premise of not interrupt the PUs transmissions. The CRN operating scheme is based on a cycle of four stages: Detection, Decision, Sharing and Mobility. It should be noted that the largest number of studies are focused on the detection and decision stages, as these are the most critical stages in the entire cognitive cycle [2,3].

With the motivation to improve the CRNs performance, Multiple routing protocols have been designed to build efficient links with optimal routes between SUs, with its own criteria and methods. Thus, the design of a routing protocol also called the MAC layer protocol for CRNs is not trivial [11]. There are several problems of the MAC layer for this type of network that can be improved when designing the protocol, among them the design of the control channel, the spectrum detection policy, the cooperative detection of the spectrum and the multi-channel problem.

The main paradigm of CR states that the activities of the SUs should not interfere with the PUs [1]. In conventional multi-channel networks, the MAC protocol implements mechanisms to prevent data sent between neighboring nodes suffer collisions. While, in the CRNs, the protocol should focus on avoiding the interference between SUs and PUs [12]. Thus, in this study, we evaluated some cooperative communication techniques in the routing process, which according to the literature, are more effective than non-cooperative techniques [13]. It is important to mention that to obtain the best results from these protocols, the PU detection (sensing spectrum), must be reliable before the transmission begins.

The main contribution of this research is the implementation, analysis, and comparison of two cooperative routing protocols for CRNs, called MC-MAC and CSCR, in an environment based on LTE and WiFi primary network, and a secondary decentralized CRN. In order to meet the CR paradigm requirements, the model system is simulated in *Network Simulator 3* (NS-3), that has been set-up taking into account the CR constraints. In addition, it has each of the stages of the cognitive cycle, which will verify the efficiency of these protocols in the system based on Packet Delivery Radio (PDR), End-to-end Delay and Probability of PU detection (P_d).

The paper organization is presented as follows: In section two, related research on specific cooperative routing protocols for CR are presented. The mathematical system model for the spectrum sensing phase is analyzed in Section three. Then, in Section four, the proposed cooperative routing protocols applied to the CR system are analyzed. After that, in Section five, parameters used in the simulation are shown to evaluate the routing algorithms performance, in addition to their results. The conclusions are given in Section six.

2   Related Works

In the current literature, there are multiple MAC protocols, for traditional mobile networks and CRNs (CR-MAC). The main difference between conventional protocols and CR-MAC protocols are the interaction between physical and MAC layers, in addition to the dependence of hardware architecture.

In [4], a comparative study of decentralized protocols for CRNs was proposed. In this approach, the concept of decentralization implies not having a central device that controls the functions of the PUs and SUs. Moreover, cooperative protocols are chosen as a subject of study because they allow to generate a more flexible and scalable scheme, cooperating among adjacent users. The importance of this research, in addition to the theoretical precedent of the protocols, is to verify the direct relationship between the physical and MAC layers, concluding that the spectral detection has a direct impact on the information that reaches the MAC layer for the decision to access a channel. A multi-channel MAC protocol for CRNs is proposed in [5], compatible with the dynamics use of a licensed channel by the SUs, which allows an adequate performance of the SUs in a multi-channel data transmission simultaneously and without interfering with each other.

Another channel selection scheme for cooperative routing protocols in CRNs, called CSCR, is proposed in [6]. According to the results shown by the authors, the mechanism proposed allows increasing the efficiency of the spectrum use by integrating the selection of channels in the initial phase of route discovery. Congested, they are chosen to form the cooperative coalition. For its efficiency, it is the other protocol chosen to analyze it in our work.

3   Proposed System Model

In this section, the basic system model used and the assumptions made, for the subsequent planning and implementation of the cooperative routing protocols in the system MAC layer are presented.

3.1   System Model Scheme

The system model scheme considers a primary network, composed of LTE and WiFi technologies that coexist in the same environment, considering only the downlink stage. The devices considered in the model are a evolved NodeB (eNB) for LTE technology, which will serve PU_l LTE. A Access Point (AP) for WiFi technology, which will serve PU_w WiFi users. For the model simplicity, both LTE and WiFi users are considered as PUs, being a total of M PUs. In addition, we will refer to the Primary Transmitters (eNB and AP), as T_p.

A secondary network is also considered in the model, focused on the downlink taking the CR interweave paradigm, which we will call CRN, which consists of N SUs. These are sensing the primary channels and only transmits in those frequency bands not used by the primary network (idle bands of transmission of the eNB and AP).

For all wireless channels between the PUs and the Primary Transmitter and all the SUs and the Primary Transmitter, a slow fade Rayleigh channel is assumed. We assume that the estimation of channels has already been done before the data transmission among nodes throughout the CRN. In addition, it is assumed that SUs transmit control packets through a common control channel (CCC).

To analyze the proposed protocols, we will consider two types of channels, a dedicated CCC and data channels (DC). The SUs will use CCC to do the channel negotiation and inform the presence of the PUs in the channel to the SUs. We assume that this channel works in the ISM spectrum (for example, a wireless local area network channel) as a dedicated channel. Finally, we assume that the SUs can sense and detect the PUs activity around them. Therefore, the primary network adopts a transmission policy, which indicates that SUs can transmit data only in two cases: when the PUs around them are not active at the time of detection, or when the SUs use their cooperative links between them, so that their transmissions can not interfere with the PUs. The network topology, with all the parameters described in this section, is shown in Fig. 1.

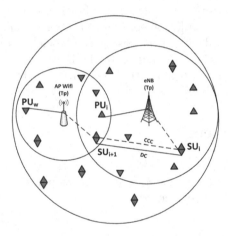

Fig. 1. Proposed CRN topology.

The protocols considered for the evaluation in this work, will be implemented using as a baseline, the detailed investigation in [3], in which the spectrum sensing by the SUs, is done through a Singular Value Decomposition (SVD) detection method, described briefly below.

3.2 Spectrum Sensing via SVD Detection Method

The detection problem can be formulated according to a hypothesis test. [3]. The binary hypothesis test is formulated as follow

$$x(t) = \begin{cases} n(t) & H_0 \\ h(t) * s(t) + n(t) & H_1 \end{cases},$$ (1)

where $x(t)$ is the signal that the SU receives, $s(t)$ is the signal that the PU transmits, $n(t)$ is the AWGN with known mean and variance and $h(t)$ is the channel gain.

For the application of the SVD method, samples must be taken by the SU, for the subsequent elaboration of a covariance matrix, given by the following expression [3]

$$R(N) = \frac{1}{N} \sum_{n=L}^{L-1+N} \hat{x}(n)x^{\dagger}(n), \qquad (2)$$

The details about the SVD method to obtain the singular values and the decision threshold on the use of a channel by some PU, are explained and analyzed in depth in [3].

4   Proposed Cooperative Routing Protocols

According to the previous review, of cooperative routing protocols focused on CR, the Channel Selection Scheme for Cooperative Routing protocol (CSCR) and the Cooperative Multichannel MAC Protocol (MC-MAC) protocol were chosen for analysis and implementation. This is due to its simplicity, multi-channel capacity and characteristics adaptable to the proposed system.

4.1   Channel Selection Scheme for Cooperative Routing Protocol

The main goal of this scheme is to dynamically choose the most optimal channel to use in each hop along the route, for a SUs cooperative coalition. Also, avoid choosing channels with high PU activity. The decentralized approach of this method allows each coalition of SUs to choose the channel to which they will send the data independently, considering that a CRN can have a variable data flow, with this being able to interfere in less proportion with PU activities.

When assuming a multi-channel environment, the channel change delay is also critical, since there may be cases in which a group of SUs have no option but to make a channel change, if this is occupied by a PU. Therefore, it is essential to minimize this delay. In Fig. 2 we can see the advantage of this mechanism when choosing the optimal channel to for transmission. We will consider for the example, and without losing the generality, a cooperative coalition composed of three SUs that are required to choose a channel (assuming that channel 1 is the default) for sending data. In this case, sending on channel 1 is a bad option due to the high number of nearby PUs and the channel activity (Fig. 2a). In addition, sending on channel 9 (Fig. 2c) is also a bad option, due to the time it will take to change from channel 1 to channel 9, since it is farther from the predetermined channel. Therefore, the best option is the channel 3 (Fig. 2b) because it achieves the trade-off between avoiding PUs with a lot of activity and minimizing channel switching time. The protocol model is described below.

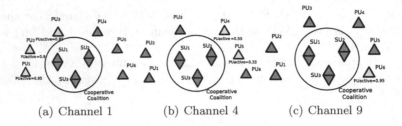

(a) Channel 1   (b) Channel 4   (c) Channel 9

Fig. 2. Case of the effect produced when selecting the best channel for transmission, where PU_{active} is the probability that a PU is using a certain channel.

Routing Metric: In the first stage, the coalition formation method is taken based on [2]. The channel selection algorithm is added to the formation phase of the coalitions, to ensure choosing the optimal channel for transmission. This allows to eliminate the overhead of choosing a channel when transmitting data and also decreases the possibility that the data will be lost due to the interruption that the other active flows may cause. Therefore, each network coalition independently and periodically chooses the best channel for transmission. This decision allows the algorithm to adapt to the CRN.

Then, we determine the routing metric in which the SU i, which wishes to transmit data, can achieve in a selected cooperative coalition, while transmitting the data to SU j by

$$R_{i,j} = \frac{C_{i,j}}{(I_f + \alpha(I_n - I_f))P_{PU}T_s}, \tag{3}$$

where $C_{i,j}$ is the maximum effective capacity between the SU i and the SU j, which depends on the bandwidth that is available and the maximum power that can be obtained by the nodes, I_n is the number of SUs active and close to all members of the coalition, I_f is the flows amount that can cause interference in the coalition, α is a variable that can modify the behavior of the cooperative coalition, P_{PU} is the probability that leastwise one of the nearby PUs is active, in the validated channel, in a set period of time and T_s is a cost related to the delay resulting from changing all coalition members from one selected channel to another. T_s is given by

$$T_s = \max_{m \in G} d_{ch,m}c, \tag{4}$$

where, G is the set of SUs of the coalition, $d_{ch,m}$ represents the distance between the current channel of the node m with the target channel, and c is a constant that represent the switching cost between two consecutive channels. Because all members of the coalition can change their channels at the same time, the total cost of change can be derived as the delay of the SU using the channel farthest from the target channel.

Information Exchange Process: In order to make an optimal channel selection, the SUs must know a set of information that is periodically updated

- The direct neighbors of the SUs and their available channels.
- All the PUs that are detected by the direct neighbors with their use probabilities and activity channels.

This information is communicated among the SUs through periodic packages (beacons). Besides, each node consider some parameters when choosing a channel to transmit including the free channels ID, the actual channels occupied by other flows, and the channel used to transmit.

The flow diagram of the CSCR algorithm is shown in the Fig. 3. The protocol approach, which seeks the most optimal channel for transmission, is developed in the creation phase of the coalition. At this stage, all CRN channels are validated in terms of their viability. If the channel is not optimal, it is added to the table of non-viable channels and the verification of the next channel is continued. However, if the channel is optimal, the protocol considers different cooperative groups based on [2]. For each coalition, the route metric is calculated according to the Eq. 3 and remains with the SU, if it exceeds the best metric that the SU node has. In the end, the most optimal value of the routing metric should be considered.

4.2 Cooperative Multi-channel MAC Protocol for Cognitive Radio Networks

This protocol proposed in [5], consists of three phases, described below

Sensing Phase: All SUs collaborate in the detection of channel use by PUs and then send this information to neighboring SUs, based on [2,3]. The SU during this phase, randomly detect a particular channel, adding the status of that channel to its channel table. The SUs through a CCC can exchange the detection result to the neighboring SUs. In addition, SUs use their channel table to determine the optimal channel for transmission.

Contention Phase: At the beginning, an SU needs to send data through a licensed channel. After booking the channel, adopting the CSMA/CA mechanisms validated by IEEE 802.11, the SU agrees to use the channel. Then, it performs a channel negotiation. Check your channel status table (CST) to check if the given channel is free to use any PU. If this premise is fulfilled, the SU begins the contention stage by the channel use. A back-off value t_b of the SU is chosen to define a backspace timer, with a value $t_b \in [(cw + 1)/2, cw]$, where cw is the CSMA/CA contention window.

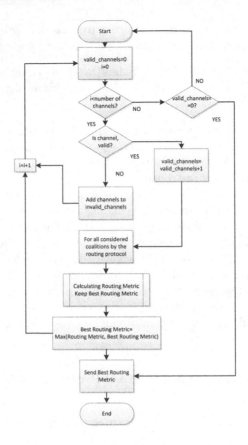

Fig. 3. Flow diagram of the CSCR algorithm.

Transmission Phase: As soon as SU wins the containment stage, it enters the transmission phase. Based on the transmission stage of the IEEE 802.11 protocol, it sends a Ready to send (RTS) frame to the SU at the other end of the transmission. This SU should respond with a Clear to Send (CTS) frame if it is willing to receive data. When the sender receives the CTS frame, it checks in its channel table. If the channel is not occupied by a PU, then the data is transmitted immediately. When the receiver receives the data, it transmits an acknowledgment (ACK) frame. It is important to consider that this protocol requires that all SUs detect the channel before starting the transmission. In the event that a PU transmits an RTS frame that indicates that it wants to use a channel. In the event that a PU broadcasts an RTS frame requesting to use the channel, the SU that listens to it immediately transmits an emergency request channel (RQS) frame to its SU neighbors. The RQS frame contains the SU ID and the channel requested by the PU. Coalition members receive the RQS and update their channel tables.

This cooperative protocol has two important benefits. First, an SU that needs to transmit can know that the channel is busy, although it does not directly see the occupation. This cooperative action by the SUs prevents a transmission from being made when the broadcast message is received. Moreover, when an SU maintains communication and is in active liaison with another SU and one of the parties listens to the RQS frame, the channel must be left quickly and the transmission is made through another channel that is unoccupied. In the event that there is no free channel, the SUs must wait for the contention stage. The flow diagram of the MC-MAC protocol is shown in Fig. 4.

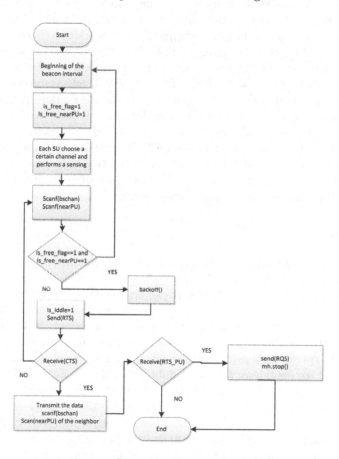

Fig. 4. Flow diagram of the MC-MAC algorithm.

5   System Performance Evaluation

In this section, the performance of the implemented protocols, CSCR and MC-MAC, is evaluated in the CRN. First, the assignment of the simulation parameters and performance metrics to be analyzed is explained. Then, the results are presented with their respective analysis.

5.1   Simulation Parameters

We implemented the cooperative routing protocols and simulated it in a secondary CRN, which coexists with a primary network, based on LTE and WiFi technologies, creating a module developed in Network Simulator 3 (NS-3.23) [8]. This module contains the cognitive cycle, which are spectrum detection and decision using the SVD detection method [3] and Coalition Game Theory [2], and spectrum Sharing and mobility based on the power parameter RSSI [9].

For the type of channel applied to the SUs and PUs, we will assume the slow fading of the Rayleigh channel. The path loss exponent α is set to 2.7, because this value generally represents the propagation in an urban area [10]. The propagation and mobility models applied in our work have been chosen from the models that the NS-3 simulator provides based on its modules [8].

The basic parameters applied in our work are presented in Table 1. For both protocols, the MAC layer used is taken from the IEEE 802.11 protocol. The SU transmitter/receiver of each connection link are chosen randomly. The SU and PU move randomly with a speed provided by the simulator and in a defined coverage area. The standard size of the transmitted data packets is 1000 bytes, which are transmitted based on the ON-OFF distribution. We also assume that the number of channels available for the SU and PU transmissions is ten. Finally, the duration of the beacon is 100 ms and the total simulation time is 1200 s, distributed according to the Monte-Carlo scheme.

5.2   Results

The results of the routing protocols algorithms implementation in the simulator are presented in Figs. 5, 6 and 7. In Fig. 5, the Pd of a PU by some SU is presented for different number of SUs. It can be seen that the behavior is similar for the two schemes analyzed, making the system more efficient as the number of SUs increases, due to the fact that the existence of more SUs, the decision of presence or not of a PU improves by factors such as the increase of coalitions, the continuous spectrum sensing and the fast update of the channel status tables of each SU and its neighbors for the collaboration that exists between them.

In Fig. 6, the average End-to-end delay of the system is shown. It is possible to observe several important points. By increasing the number of SUs in the network, it is possible to obtain new and better routes, however, this results in increasing the end-to-end delay of all transmitted packets based on the MC-MAC protocol. Increasing the number of transmissions between SUs causes congestion in the MAC layer, increasing queues and total end-to-end delay. However, for CSCR, when the SUs increase, the end-to-end delay decreases, based on the CSCR protocol making the decision to choose the most optimal channel to transmit. According to the operation of CSCR, this channel has the least PU activity and less interference with existing flows, so only new data flows are introduced without interfering with PU or SU flows.

Table 1. System parameters

Parameters	Nominal values	Range values
AP Range of Coverage	100 m	0–300 m
Available Channels	10	1–15
Channel model PU	Slow Rayleigh fading [8]	idem
Channel model SU	Slow Rayleigh fading [8]	idem
CR SU	30	0–30
Data Packet	1000 bytes	0–10000 bytes
Deployment Area Side Length	500 m	0–1000 m
eNB Range of Coverage	350 m	0–1000 m
LTE Bandwidth	20 MHz [3]	5–100 MHz
LTE Frequency	729 MHz [3]	No range
Mobility model	Random Waypoint [8]	No range
Noise	AWGN, $\sigma=1$	No range
Path loss exponent (*alpha*)	2.7 [10]	No range
Propagation model	Range Propagation Loss [8]	No range
PU	8	0–30
PU Activity	50%	0–100%
Samples	16000	0–30000
SU, PU distribution	Uniform Random Distribution [8]	idem
Time of Simulation	1200 s	0–12000 s
Traffic	TCP	No range
WiFi Bandwidth	20 MHz [3]	0–100 MHz
WiFi Frequency	2400 MHz* [3]	No range

*Note: According to the research in [8], NS-3 has not implemented any module for the band of 5.9 Mhz, for this reason, it was decided to evaluate the system in 2.4 Ghz.

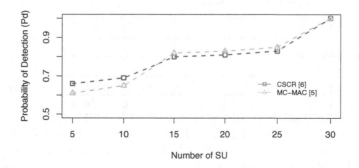

Fig. 5. Probability of detection in terms of the number of SUs.

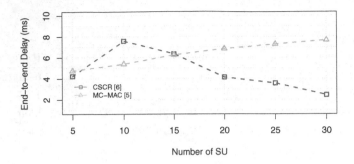

Fig. 6. End-to-end delay as a function of the number of SUs.

In Fig. 7 the *PDR* system parameter is presented. It is easy to observe that the behavior of both protocols is similar, where the improvement of PDR occurs because the protocols can avoid discarding and losing data that SUs transmit, since cooperation between them provides a reporting mechanism in the coalition. Therefore, an SU when receiving from a neighbor some information frame of the PU presence, stops the transmission and postpones the data sending through the channel that has been occupied.

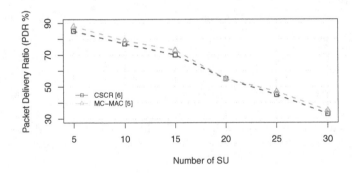

Fig. 7. Packet delivery ratio vs number of SU

6   Conclusions

In this paper, two cooperative routing protocols applied to CRN are studied, analyzed and compared. The CSCR and MC-MAC protocols were evaluated in a secondary CRN based on the interweave paradigm. In addition, there is a primary network based on WiFi and LTE technologies that coexist with the CRN. The protocols analyzed are based on cooperative communications techniques between SUs of the same coalition, forming optimal routes, channel status tables and PU activity of each SUs and their neighbors. This allows less interference of the SUs with the PUs. It is verified through simulations that these protocols improve the efficiency of the system in terms of Pd, End-to-end Delay and PDR, varying the number of SUs. Specifically, it was observed that the CSCR protocol outperform the MC-MAC in terms of End-to-end Delay, given its ability to choose the channel with less PU activity, to perform communication between SUs.

Acknowledgment. This work was funded by CONICYT PFCHA/Beca de Doctorado Nacional/2019 21190489 and SENESCYT "Convocatoria abierta 2014-primera fase, Acta CIBAE-023-2014", and UDLA Telecommunications Engineering Degree.

References

1. Haykin, S.: Cognitive radio: brain-empowered wireless communications. IEEE J. Sel. Areas Commun. **23**(2), 201–220 (2005)
2. Palacios, P., Saavedra, C.: Coalition game theory in cognitive mobile radio networks. In: Botto-Tobar, M., Pizarro, G., Zúñiga-Prieto, M., D'Armas, M., Zúñiga Sánchez, M. (eds.) CITT 2018. CCIS, vol. 895, pp. 3–15. Springer, Cham (2019). https://doi.org/10.1007/978-3-030-05532-5_1
3. Palacios, P., Castro, A., Azurdia-Meza, C., Estevez, C.: SVD detection analysis in cognitive mobile radio networks. In: 2017 Ninth International Conference on Ubiquitous and Future Networks (ICUFN), pp. 222–224, July 2017
4. Fihri, W.F., Salahdine, F., El Ghazi, H., Kaabouch, N.: A survey on decentralized random access MAC protocols for cognitive radio networks. In: 2016 International Conference on Advanced Communication Systems and Information Security (ACOSIS), pp. 1–7, October 2016
5. Sofwan, A., AlQahtani, S.A.: Cooperative multichannel MAC protocol for cognitive radio ad hoc. In: 2015 IEEE Global Communications Conference (GLOBECOM), pp. 1–6, December 2015
6. Guirguis, A., ElNainay, M.: Channel selection scheme for cooperative routing protocols in cognitive radio networks. In: 2017 International Conference on Computing, Networking and Communications (ICNC), pp. 735–739, January 2017
7. Zeng, Y., Liang, Y.C.: Maximum-minimum eigenvalue detection for cognitive radio. In: 2007 IEEE 18th International Symposium on Personal, Indoor and Mobile Radio Communications, pp. 1–5, September 2007
8. NS-3 Model Library, Release NS-3.23. https://www.nsnam.org/docs/release/3.23/models/ns-3-model-library.pdf
9. Gerasimenko, M., Himayat, N., Yeh, S.P., Talwar, S., Andreev, S., Koucheryavy, Y.: Characterizing performance of load-aware network selection in multi-radio (WiFi/LTE) heterogeneous networks. In: 2013 IEEE Globecom Workshops (GC Wkshps), pp. 397–402, December 2013
10. Lv, L., Chen, J., Ni, Q., Ding, Z.: Design of cooperative non-orthogonal multicast cognitive multiple access for 5G systems: user scheduling and performance analysis. IEEE Trans. Commun. **65**(6), 2641–2656 (2017)
11. Kulkarni, S., Markande, S.: Comparative study of routing protocols in cognitive radio networks. In: 2015 International Conference on Pervasive Computing (ICPC), pp. 1–5, January 2015

12. Ping, S., Aijaz, A., Holland, O., Aghvami, A.H.: Energy and interference aware cooperative routing in cognitive radio ad-hoc networks. In: 2014 IEEE Wireless Communications and Networking Conference (WCNC), pp. 87–92, April 2014
13. Youssef, M., Ibrahim, M., Abdelatif, M., Chen, L., Vasilakos, A.V.: Routing metrics of cognitive radio networks: a survey. IEEE Commun. Surv. Tutor. **16**(1), 92–109 (2014)

On the Asymptotic BER of MMSE Detector in Massive MIMO Systems

Carlos Daniel Altamirano[1,3](✉) ⓘ, Juan Minango[2] ⓘ, Celso de Almeida[3] ⓘ, and Nathaly Orozco[4] ⓘ

[1] Departamento de Eléctrica, Electrónica y Telecomunicaciones,
Universidad de las Fuerzas Armadas - ESPE, Sangolquí, Ecuador
cdaltamirano@espe.edu.ec
[2] Instituto de Fomento de Talento Humano (IFTH),
Secretaria Nacional de Educación Superior, Ciencia,
Tecnología e Innovación (SENESCYT), Quito, Ecuador
jcarlosminango@gmail.com
[3] Faculdade de Engenharía Eléctrica e Computação,
Universidade Estadual de Campinas, Campinas, Brazil
celso@fee.unicamp.br
[4] Facultad de Ingeniería y Ciencias Aplicadas,
Universidad de Las Américas, Quito, Ecuador
nathaly.orozco@udla.edu.ec

Abstract. The minimum-mean-square-error (MMSE) detector is widely used in multiple-input multiple-output (MIMO) systems, since it is considered as the best linear detector. However, obtaining a tight bit error rate (BER) expression is not a straightforward task. In massive MIMO (M-MIMO) systems, due to the asymptotically orthogonal channel matrix property, the BER evaluation is less complex by using the random matrix theory. In this article, two closed-form BER expressions are derived for the MMSE detector in M-MIMO systems. The first one is an asymptotic result by using the Marchenko-Pastur distribution, and the second one is an accurate result by using an approximation of the ZF detector performance.

Keywords: BER · Massive MIMO · MMSE detector

1 Introduction

The technological transition to 5G systems is expected to offer a thousand-fold higher throughput [1]. Massive multiple-input multiple-output (M-MIMO) has emerged as one of the most promising technologies towards this direction. This is due to the large number of antennas at the base station (BS) serving a reduced number of user terminals (UTs) equipped with one antenna each, that can offers more degrees of freedom for the BS to multiply the throughput by using linear detection [3].

© Springer Nature Switzerland AG 2020
M. Botto-Tobar et al. (Eds.): ICAT 2019, CCIS 1195, pp. 57–68, 2020.
https://doi.org/10.1007/978-3-030-42531-9_5

The performance of M-MIMO systems as other communication systems is evaluated in terms of the ergodic capacity and in terms of the bit error rate (BER). In the literature, most of performance evaluations of M-MIMO systems are presented in terms of the ergodic capacity [14]. However, the BER evaluation is important, in order to analyze the modulation effects [2,10].

The performance of MIMO and M-MIMO systems depends on the linear detection. Among the linear detectors, the minimum-mean-square-error (MMSE) detector presents the best performance at the cost of more complexity [5,9]. However, the closed-form expressions for the mean symbol error rate (SER) and mean BER of the MMSE detector, are tricky to be obtained, as shown in [8,13], because the SER and BER are a function of the signal-to-noise-plus-interference ratio (SNIR), whose exact closed-form distribution is a complex expression.

In M-MIMO systems, there are some results based on the random matrix theory, such as the Marchenko-Pastur distribution [12], which could be useful to derive the BER performance of the MMSE detector by obtaining a simpler expression for the SNIR distribution. However, in the literature, Marchenko-Pastur distribution has been mostly used to evaluate the performance based on the ergodic capacity [6] or to propose detection algorithms with reduced complexity [7].

By the above, in the literature, there is a lack of studies of the BER performance evaluation in M-MIMO systems using the MMSE detector. Thus, in this paper, closed-form expressions of the mean BER are evaluated by approximating the SNIR of the MMSE detector by the Marchenko-Pastur distribution and by the distribution based on the zero-forcing (ZF) detector for M-MIMO. The Marchenko-Pastur approximation provides an asymptotic mean BER and the ZF approximation provides an accurate mean BER for any E_b/N_0 with lesser complexity. Besides, for comparison purposes, the approximated closed-form expressions of the mean BER are evaluated in MIMO systems.

The results show that for MIMO, the Marchenko-Pastur approximation, also provides an asymptotic mean BER and the ZF approximation provides an upper bound of the mean BER. This last result shows the well known result where the performance of the ZF detector is an upper bound of the MMSE detector due to the anti-noise property of the MMSE detector [5]. However, for M-MIMO this property is negligible as shown in the results.

The remainder of this paper is organized as follows. Section 2 reviews the system model. Section 3 derives the SNIR distribution of the MMSE detector. The mean BER performance is obtained in Sect. 4. Numerical results are presented in Sect. 5. Finally, the conclusions are highlighted in Sect. 6.

Notation: $(\cdot)^H$, $(\cdot)^{-1}$, $\mathbf{I}_N$, $\mathrm{E}\{\cdot\}$ and $\mathrm{Var}\{\cdot\}$ denote the conjugate transpose, matrix inversion, $N \times N$ identity matrix, expectation operator and variance operator, respectively. Finally, erfc (x) is the complementary error function, $\lfloor x \rfloor$ is the floor function, $(x)^*$ is the conjugate operation and $\binom{n}{x}$ is the binomial expansion.

2 System Model

Consider the uplink of a unicellular M-MIMO system employing N antennas at BS to serve simultaneously K single-antenna UTs, where $N \gg K$. Thus, at each symbol time interval, the received signal vector $\mathbf{y}$ of dimension $N \times 1$ at the BS is given by:

$$\mathbf{y} = \mathbf{Hx} + \mathbf{w}$$
$$= \sum_{j=1}^{K} \mathbf{h}_j x_j + \mathbf{w}, \tag{1}$$

where $\mathbf{x} = [x_1 \ x_2 \ \cdots \ x_K]^T$ is the $K \times 1$ transmitted symbols vector from the K users that employ a multilevel quadrature amplitude modulation (M-QAM), $\mathbf{H} = [\mathbf{h}_1 \ \mathbf{h}_2 \ \cdots \ \mathbf{h}_K]$ is the $N \times K$ slow flat Rayleigh fading channel matrix, whose entries are independent and identically distributed (i.i.d.) complex Gaussian random variables, i.e. $h_{i,j} \sim \mathcal{CN}(0, \overline{\alpha^2})$, where $\overline{\alpha^2}$ is the Rayleigh fading second moment and finally $\mathbf{w}$ represents the additive complex white Gaussian noise (AWGN) vector, whose entries are i.i.d. complex random variables with distribution $\mathcal{CN}(0, \sigma^2)$, where $\sigma^2 = N_0/T_s$ is the noise variance.

3 SNIR Distribution of the MMSE Detector

The symbols vector at the MMSE detector output is given by:

$$\hat{\mathbf{x}} = \mathbf{Ay}, \tag{2}$$

where $\mathbf{A} = \mathbf{R}_{\mathbf{xy}} \mathbf{R}_{\mathbf{yy}}^{-1}$ is the MMSE compensation matrix of dimension $(K \times N)$, with covariances matrices $\mathbf{R}_{\mathbf{xy}} = \mathrm{E}\{\mathbf{xy}^H\}$ and $\mathbf{R}_{\mathbf{yy}} = \mathrm{E}\{\mathbf{yy}^H\}$.

The kth UT detected symbol at BS can be rewritten as:

$$\hat{x}_k = \mathbf{a}_k \mathbf{h}_k x_k + \sum_{\substack{i=1 \\ i \neq k}}^{K} \mathbf{a}_k \mathbf{h}_i x_i + \mathbf{a}_k^H \mathbf{w}, \tag{3}$$

where $\mathbf{a}_k = \mathbf{h}_k^H \left(\mathbf{R}_{\mathbf{yy}}^{(k)} \right)^{-1}$ is the kth row of $\mathbf{A}$, $\mathbf{R}_{\mathbf{yy}}^{(k)} = \mathrm{E}\{\underline{\mathbf{y}}_k \underline{\mathbf{y}}_k^H\}$ is the covariance matrix of $\underline{\mathbf{y}}_k$, where $\underline{\mathbf{y}}_k$ defined as the received signal vector $\mathbf{y}$ excluding the kth user entry. The covariance matrix $\mathbf{R}_{\mathbf{yy}}^{(k)}$ can be rewritten as [5]:

$$\mathbf{R}_{\mathbf{yy}}^{(k)} = \overline{|x|^2} \underline{\mathbf{H}}_k \underline{\mathbf{H}}_k^H + \sigma^2 \mathbf{I}_N, \tag{4}$$

where $\underline{\mathbf{H}}_k$ is defined as the channel matrix $\mathbf{H}$ without the kth column vector and $\underline{\mathbf{H}}_k \underline{\mathbf{H}}_k^H = \mathbf{U}^H \mathbf{D} \mathbf{U}$ is the eigen-factorization of $\underline{\mathbf{H}}_k \underline{\mathbf{H}}_k^H$ where $\mathbf{U}$ is an orthonormal matrix that contains the eigenvectors and $\mathbf{D} = \mathrm{diag}[\lambda_1 \ \lambda_2 \ \cdots \ \lambda_{K-1} \ \overbrace{0 \ \cdots \ 0}^{N-K+1}]$

is a diagonal matrix that contains the eigenvalues. Notice that there are $K - 1$ random eigenvalues and $N - K + 1$ zero eigenvalues.

In (3), the first term is the kth user desired signal ($\mathcal{S}_k$), the second term is the multiple access interference ($\mathcal{MAI}$), and the last term is the noise ($\mathcal{W}$). The SNIR conditioned on the kth user channel vector is given by:

$$\gamma_{s|\mathbf{h}_k} = \frac{|\mathcal{S}_k|^2}{\mathrm{Var}\{\mathcal{MAI} \mid \mathbf{h}_k\} + \mathrm{Var}\{\mathcal{W} \mid \mathbf{h}_k\}}. \tag{5}$$

The kth user signal power is given by:

$$\begin{aligned}
|\mathcal{S}_k|^2 &= \mathbf{a}_k \mathbf{h}_k x_k x_k^* \mathbf{h}_k^H \mathbf{a}_k^H \\
&= |x_k|^2 \mathbf{h}_k^H \left(\mathbf{R}_{\mathbf{yy}}^{(k)}\right)^{-1} \mathbf{h}_k \mathbf{h}_k^H \left(\mathbf{R}_{\mathbf{yy}}^{(k)}\right)^{-1} \mathbf{h}_k.
\end{aligned} \tag{6}$$

The sum of the $\mathcal{MAI}$ and noise variances is:

$$\begin{aligned}
\mathrm{Var}\{\mathcal{MAI} \mid \mathbf{h}_k\} + \mathrm{Var}\{\mathcal{W} \mid \mathbf{h}_k\} &= \mathrm{E}\left\{ \left(\sum_{\substack{i=1 \\ i \neq k}}^{K} \mathbf{a}_k \mathbf{h}_i x_i + \mathbf{a}_k^H \mathbf{w} \right) \left(\sum_{\substack{i=1 \\ i \neq k}}^{K} \mathbf{a}_k \mathbf{h}_i x_i + \mathbf{a}_k^H \mathbf{w} \right)^H \right\} \\
&= \mathrm{E}\left\{ \mathbf{a}_k \left(\underline{\mathbf{H}}_k \underline{\mathbf{x}}_k + \mathbf{w} \right) \left(\underline{\mathbf{H}}_k \underline{\mathbf{x}}_k + \mathbf{w} \right)^H \mathbf{a}_k^H \right\} \\
&= \mathbf{h}_k^H \left(\mathbf{R}_{\mathbf{yy}}^{(k)} \right)^{-1} \mathbf{h}_k,
\end{aligned} \tag{7}$$

where we have used that $\mathbf{R}_{\mathbf{yy}}^{(k)} = \mathrm{E}\left\{ \left(\underline{\mathbf{H}}_k \, \underline{\mathbf{x}}_k + \mathbf{w} \right) \left(\underline{\mathbf{H}}_k \, \underline{\mathbf{x}}_k + \mathbf{w} \right)^H \right\}$ and that $\sum_{\substack{i=1 \\ i \neq k}}^{K} \mathbf{h}_i x_i = \underline{\mathbf{H}}_k \underline{\mathbf{x}}_k$.

By replacing (6) and (7) in (5), the SNIR can be rewritten as:

$$\gamma_{s|\mathbf{h}_k} = |x_k|^2 \mathbf{h}_k^H \left(\mathbf{R}_{\mathbf{yy}}^{(k)} \right)^{-1} \hat{\mathbf{h}}_k. \tag{8}$$

By using the eigen-factorization of $\mathbf{R}_{\mathbf{yy}}^{(k)}$ in (8), the SNIR is given by:

$$\begin{aligned}
\gamma_{s|\mathbf{h}_k, \lambda_i} &= |x_k|^2 \hat{\mathbf{h}}_k^H \left(\overline{|x|^2} \mathbf{U}^H \mathbf{D} \mathbf{U} + \sigma^2 \mathbf{I}_N \right)^{-1} \hat{\mathbf{h}}_k \\
&= |x_k|^2 \hat{\mathbf{h}}_k^H \mathbf{U}^H \left(\overline{|x|^2} \mathbf{D} + \sigma^2 \mathbf{I}_N \right)^{-1} \mathbf{U} \hat{\mathbf{h}}_k \\
&= |x_k|^2 \hat{\mathbf{h}}_k^H \left(\overline{|x|^2} \mathbf{D} + \sigma^2 \mathbf{I}_N \right)^{-1} \hat{\mathbf{h}}_k \\
&= |x_k|^2 \sum_{i=1}^{N} \frac{|h_{i,k}|^2}{\overline{|x|^2} \lambda_i + \sigma^2},
\end{aligned} \tag{9}$$

where λ_i is the ith eigenvalue of $\underline{\mathbf{H}}_k \underline{\mathbf{H}}_k^H$. Considering that $N - K + 1$ eigenvalues are equal to zero, the SNIR given by (9) can be rewritten as:

$$\gamma_{s|\mathbf{h}_k, \lambda_i} = \frac{|x_k|^2}{\overline{|x|^2}} \left(\sum_{i=1}^{K-1} \frac{|h_{i,k}|^2}{\lambda_i + \rho} + \frac{1}{\rho} \sum_{i=K}^{N} |h_{i,k}|^2 \right), \tag{10}$$

where we have used that $\rho = \frac{N_0}{E_s} = \frac{\sigma^2}{x^2}$ and $E_s = \overline{x^2}T_s$. In terms of the energy per bit $\rho = \frac{1}{\log_2 M \ E_b/N_0}$, where M is the modulation order.

Notice that the SNIR is conditioned on the kth UT channel vector and on the eigenvalues. In order to uncondition the SNIR in relation to the eigenvalues, the SNIR must be averaged over the eigenvalues distribution. In [12], the authors have derived the eigenvalues distribution resulting in a tricky expression. Therefore, to obtain the unconditioned SNIR is a quite complex task [13]. However, for M-MIMO, the distribution of the eigenvalues can be well approximated by the Marchenko-Pastur distribution, whose probability density function (PDF) is given by [12]:

$$f_\Lambda(\lambda) = \begin{cases} \frac{\sqrt{(\lambda-a)(b-\lambda)}}{2\pi\lambda}, & a \leq \lambda \leq b \\ 0, & \text{otherwise} \end{cases} \tag{11}$$

where $a = (1 - \sqrt{\beta})^2$, $b = (1 + \sqrt{\beta})^2$ and $\beta = \frac{K-1}{N}$. By using (11), the unconditioned SNIR on the eigenvalues is given by:

$$\begin{aligned}
\gamma_{s|\mathbf{h}_k} &= \int_a^b \gamma_{s|\mathbf{h}_k,\lambda_i} f_\Lambda(\lambda_i)d\lambda_i \\
&= \frac{|x_k|^2}{|x|^2} \left(\Omega \sum_{i=1}^{K-1} |h_{i,k}|^2 + \frac{1}{\rho} \sum_{i=K}^{N} |h_{i,k}|^2 \right),
\end{aligned} \tag{12}$$

where Ω is given by:

$$\begin{aligned}
\Omega &= \int_a^b \frac{1}{\lambda_i + \rho} f_\Lambda(\lambda_i)d\lambda_i \\
&= \frac{1}{2\rho} \left[\sqrt{(a+\rho)(b+\rho)} - (\rho + \sqrt{ab}) \right].
\end{aligned} \tag{13}$$

The SNIR given by (12) corresponds to the sum of two chi-square distributions with different variances. The sum of chi-square distributions with different variances is known as generalized chi-square distribution [13]. In particular, for our work, the generalized chi-square distributions can be rewritten as:

$$f_{\Gamma_s}(\gamma_s) = \prod_{m=1}^{2} \frac{1}{\varsigma_m^{2r_m}} \sum_{k=1}^{2} \sum_{l=1}^{r_k} \frac{\psi_{k,l,\mathbf{r}}}{(r_k-l)!} (-\gamma_s)^{r_k-l} e^{-\frac{\gamma_s}{\varsigma_k^2}}, \tag{14}$$

where $\mathbf{r} = [r_1 \ r_2]$ is a vector containing the two degrees of freedom of each chi-square random variables. The first chi-square random variable has $r_1 = K - 1$ degrees of freedom with variance $\varsigma_1^2 = \Omega$ and the second chi-square random variable has $r_2 = N - K + 1$ degrees of freedom with variance $\varsigma_2^2 = 1/\rho$. Finally, $\psi_{1,l,\mathbf{r}}$ and $\psi_{2,l,\mathbf{r}}$ are given by:

$$\psi_{1,l,\mathbf{r}} = (-1)^{r_1-1} \binom{l+r_2-2}{l-1} \left(\frac{1}{\varsigma_2^2} - \frac{1}{\varsigma_1^2} \right)^{-(r_2+l-1)} \tag{15}$$

$$\psi_{2,l,\mathbf{r}} = (-1)^{r_2-1} \binom{l+r_1-2}{l-1} \left(\frac{1}{\varsigma_1^2} - \frac{1}{\varsigma_2^2} \right)^{-(r_1+l-1)}. \tag{16}$$

62   C. D. Altamirano et al.

A SNIR approximation can be made for M-MIMO by considering that the first summation in (12) is negligible, because $K \ll N$. Thus, the SNIR distribution can be approximated by a chi-square distribution which is the SNIR PDF of the ZF detector, given by [5]:

$$f_{\Gamma_s,\text{ZF}}(\gamma_s) = \frac{\rho^{N-K+1}}{(N-K)!}\gamma_s^{N-K}e^{-\rho\gamma_s}. \tag{17}$$

The PDF of the SNIR given by the Marchenko-Pastur approximation shown in (14) has two summations with binomial expansions and one product, while the PDF of the SNIR using the ZF approximation given by (17) has not summation nor product operators. As a consequence, the Marchenko-Pastur PDF is computationally more complex than the ZF approximation.

4 BER Performance

Using any SNIR distribution, it is possible to derive the mean BER by [11]:

$$\overline{P_b} = \int_0^\infty P\left(b|\gamma_s\right) f_{\Gamma_s}\left(\gamma_s\right) d\gamma_s, \tag{18}$$

where $P\left(b|\gamma_s\right)$ is the bit error probability conditioned on the SNIR random variable and $f_{\Gamma_s}\left(\gamma_s\right)$ is the PDF of the SNIR.

By using the exact BER for M-QAM modulation given by [4], the mean BER using Gray mapping is:

$$\overline{P_b} = \frac{2}{\log_2\sqrt{M}} \sum_{\kappa=1}^{\log_2\sqrt{M}} \frac{1}{\sqrt{M}} \sum_{i=0}^{(1-2^{-\kappa})\sqrt{M}-1} \left\{ (-1)^{\left\lfloor \frac{i\cdot2^{\kappa-1}}{\sqrt{M}} \right\rfloor} \right.$$
$$\left. \left(2^{\kappa-1} - \left\lfloor \frac{i\cdot2^{\kappa-1}}{\sqrt{M}} + \frac{1}{2} \right\rfloor \right) \mathcal{I}(\nu_i) \right\}, \tag{19}$$

where $\mathcal{I}(\nu_i)$ is an integral defined by:

$$\mathcal{I}(\nu_i) = \frac{1}{2} \int_0^\infty \text{erfc}\left(\sqrt{\frac{\gamma_s}{\nu_i}} \right) f_{\Gamma_s}\left(\gamma_s\right) d\gamma_s \tag{20}$$

which depends on the SNIR distribution and on $\nu_i = \frac{2(M-1)}{3(2i+1)^2}$.

The solution of (20) using the SNIR distribution obtained by the Marchenko-Pastur PDF given by (14), is equal to:

$$\mathcal{I}[l,\nu_i] = \prod_{m=1}^{2} \frac{1}{\varsigma_m^{2r_m}} \sum_{k=1}^{2} \sum_{l=1}^{r_k} \psi_{k,l,\mathbf{r}}(-1)^{r_k-l}\varsigma_k^{2(r_k-l+1)}$$
$$p_k^{r_k-l+1} \sum_{j=0}^{r_k-1} \binom{r_k-l+j}{j} (1-p_k)^j, \tag{21}$$

where $p_k = \frac{1}{2}\left(1 - \sqrt{\frac{\varsigma_k^2}{\nu_i + \varsigma_k^2}}\right)$.

On the other hand, the solution of (20) using the ZF SNIR distribution in (17), is given by:

$$\mathcal{I}(\nu_i) = p^{N-K+1} \sum_{j=0}^{N-K} \binom{N-K+j}{j} (1-p)^j \tag{22}$$

where $p = \frac{1}{2}\left(1 - \sqrt{\frac{1/\rho}{\nu_i + 1/\rho}}\right)$.

5 Numerical Results

In this section we present the numerical results. The PDFs of the derived SNIRs expressions are plotted in different scenarios. Besides, the mean BER expressions are plotted and compared with Monte Carlo simulations to verify the validity of the derived expressions.

Figure 1 shows the SNIR PDF, for $E_s/N_0 = 0$ dB, $N = 128$ and $K = 16$. The Marchenko-Pastur PDF given by (14) is plotted together with the ZF PDF given by (17) and the Monte-Carlo simulation. All three PDFs present the same shape for $N \gg K$, which is a M-MIMO scenario. However, the ZF PDF approximation is accurate than the Marchenko-Pastur PDF approximation, when compared to the simulated PDF.

Figure 2 shows the SNIR PDF of the SNIR, for $E_s/N_0 = 0$ dB, $N = 8$ and $K = 4$. Notice that in this case, N is not much bigger than K, which represents a MIMO scenario. Figure 2 shows the Marchenko-Pastur PDF approximation, the ZF PDF and the simulation of the PDF are plotted. Observe that in this case the SNIR PDF approximations have different shapes compared to the simulation. This is evident because our approximations were made by considering a M-MIMO scenario.

The asymptotic complexity in big-O notation of the PDF approximated by Marchenko-Pastur is $O(n^{N-K+1})$ and of the ZF PDF is $O(n^{N-K})$. Observe that both PDFs have the same complexity. However, considering the computational time, the complexity of the Marchenko-Pastur PDF approximation is higher than the ZF PDF, because for the Marchenko-Pastur PDF approximation binomial expansions, summations and products are necessary to do, where as for the ZF PDF not. Table 1 presents the computational time given in seconds in order to obtain each curve shown in Figs. 1 and 2.

Figure 3 presents the mean BER as a function of E_b/N_0 for M-MIMO systems with $N = 128$, $K = 16$, and M-QAM modulation for $M = 4$, 16, and 64. The mean BER is simulated and compared to the mean BER, given by (19), for the Marchenko-Pastur PDF approximation and the ZF PDF. The simulation is presented in just the low E_b/N_0 region, i.e. for $\overline{P_b} < 10^{-6}$. Observe that the mean BER using the ZF PDF SNIR is tight as to the simulated BER. The Marchenko-Pastur PDF approximation is a BER asymptote, which becomes

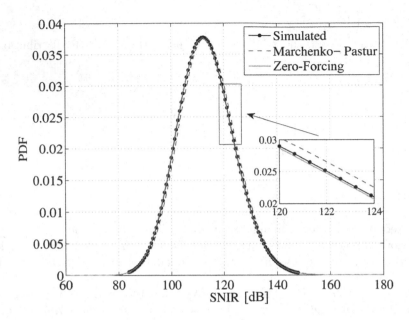

Fig. 1. Probability density function of the SNIR for the MMSE detector in M-MIMO systems for $E_s/N_0 = 0$ dB, $N = 128$ and $K = 16$.

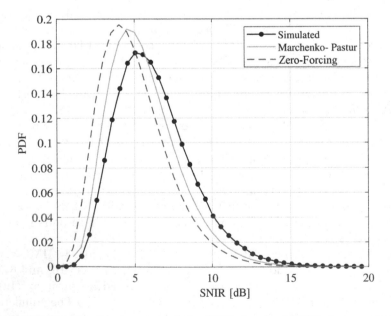

Fig. 2. Probability density function of the SNIR for the MMSE detector in MIMO systems for $E_s/N_0 = 0$ dB, $N = 8$ and $K = 4$.

Table 1. PDF computational time

PDF	MIMO	M-MIMO
Zero-Forcing	3.1×10^{-4} [s]	3.9×10^{-3} [s]
Marchenko-Pastur	8.3×10^{-2} [s]	5.1 [s]
Simulation	83 [s]	1973.8 [s]

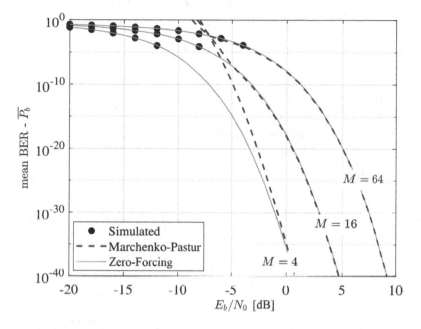

Fig. 3. Mean BER as a function of E_b/N_0 for the MMSE detector in a M-MIMO systems with $N = 128$, $K = 16$, and M-QAM modulation.

more accurate in the high E_b/N_0 region. Notice that as M increases the BER asymptote becomes more tight.

Figure 4 presents the mean BER as a function of E_b/N_0 for MIMO systems with $N = 8$, $K = 4$, and M-QAM modulation, for $M = 4$, 16, and 64. The simulated mean BER is compared to the mean BER given by the Marchenko-Pastur PDF approximation and the ZF PDF. Although the approximations were derived for M-MIMO, Fig. 4 shows that the ZF BER behaves as an upper bound and the Marchenko-Pastur BER in an asymptote in the high E_b/N_0. Notice that Marchenko-Pastur approximation becomes tighter in the asymptotic region.

Figure 5 shows the mean BER as a function of N for $K = 8$ and 16, $M = 64$ and $E_b/N_0 = 0$. As N increases, the system performance is improved, and both becomes tight. On the other hand, as K increases, the system performance get worse. However, as expected, the performance reduction is relieved by increasing the number of antennas.

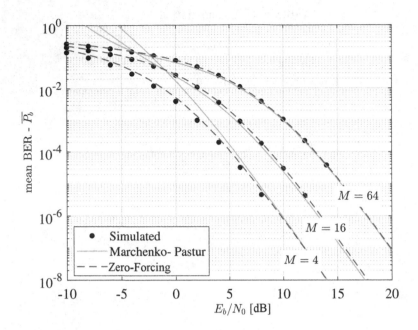

Fig. 4. Mean BER as a function of E_b/N_0 for the MMSE detector in MIMO systems with $N = 8$, $K = 4$, and M-QAM modulation.

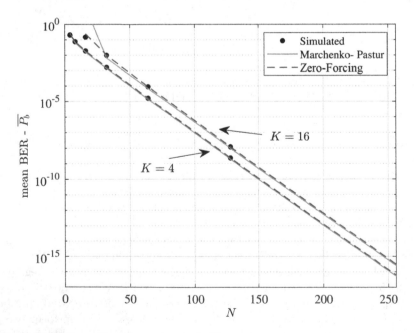

Fig. 5. Mean BER as a function of N for MIMO and M-MIMO systems with $K = 4$, 16, $M = 64$ and $E_b/N_0 = 0$ [dB].

6 Conclusion

In this paper, two closed-form expressions of the mean BER for the MMSE detector in M-MIMO systems have been derived. The Marchenko-Pastur PDF approximation is a precise mean BER asymptote. For M-MIMO, a less complex and more accurate result is given by the ZF PDF, as shown in the numerical results. The ZF PDF is less complex, because the PDF SNIR is a much simpler expression without summations or binomial expansions. The results also show that the derived mean BER expressions can be used for MIMO systems. For this case in particular, the ZF BER is an upper bound and the Marchenko-Pastur PDF is an asymptotic bound.

References

1. Al-Falahy, N., Alani, O.Y.: Technologies for 5G networks: challenges and opportunities. IT Prof. **19**(1), 12–20 (2017). https://doi.org/10.1109/MITP.2017.9
2. Beiranvand, J., Meghdadi, H.: Analytical performance evaluation of MRC receivers in massive MIMO systems. IEEE Access **6**, 53226–53234 (2018). https://doi.org/10.1109/access.2018.2866795
3. Björnson, E., Larsson, E.G., Marzetta, T.L.: Massive MIMO: ten myths and one critical question. IEEE Commun. Mag. **54**(2), 114–123 (2016). https://doi.org/10.1109/mcom.2016.7402270
4. Cho, K., Yoon, D.: On the general BER expression of one- and two dimensional amplitude modulations. IEEE Trans. Commun. **50**(7), 1074–1080 (2002). https://doi.org/10.1109/TCOMM.2002.800818
5. Jiang, Y., Varanasi, M.K., Li, J.: Performance analysis of ZF and MMSE equalizers for MIMO systems: an in-depth study of the high SNR regime. IEEE Trans. Inf. Theory **57**(4), 2008–2026 (2011). https://doi.org/10.1109/tit.2011.2112070
6. Marzetta, T.L., Larsson, E.G., Yang, H., Ngo, H.Q.: Fundamentals of Massive MIMO. Cambridge University Press, Cambridge (2016). https://doi.org/10.1017/CBO9781316799895
7. Minango, J., de Almeida, C., Altamirano, C.D.: Low-complexity MMSE detector for massive MIMO systems based on damped Jacobi method. In: 2017 IEEE 28th Annual International Symposium on Personal, Indoor, and Mobile Radio Communications (PIMRC). IEEE, October 2017. https://doi.org/10.1109/pimrc.2017.8292627
8. Mora, H.C., Garzón, N.O., de Almeida, C.: Performance analysis of MC-CDMA cellular systems employing MMSE multiuser detector in presence of own-cell and co-cell interference. AEU - Int. J. Electron. Commun. **80**, 19–28 (2017). https://doi.org/10.1016/j.aeue.2017.06.020
9. Ngo, H.Q., Larsson, E.G., Marzetta, T.L.: Energy and spectral efficiency of very large multiuser MIMO systems. IEEE Trans. Commun. **61**(4), 1436–1449 (2013). https://doi.org/10.1109/TCOMM.2013.020413.110848
10. Ngo, H.Q., Matthaiou, M., Duong, T.Q., Larsson, E.G.: Uplink performance analysis of multicell MU-SIMO systems with ZF receivers. IEEE Trans. Veh. Technol. **62**(9), 4471–4483 (2013). https://doi.org/10.1109/tvt.2013.2265720
11. Simon, M.K., Alouini, M.S.: Digital Communication over Fading Channels, 2nd edn. Wiley, Newark (2005)

12. Tulino, A.M., Verdú, S.: Random matrix theory and wireless communications. Commun. Inf. Theory **1**(1), 1–182 (2004). https://doi.org/10.1516/0100000001
13. Zhai, K., Ma, Z., Lei, X.: Closed-formed distribution for the SINR of MMSE-detected MIMO systems and performance analysis. AEU - Int. J. Electron. Commun. **97**, 16–24 (2018). https://doi.org/10.1016/j.aeue.2018.09.038
14. Zheng, K., Zhao, L., Mei, J., Shao, B., Xiang, W., Hanzo, L.: Survey of large-scale MIMO systems. Commun. Surv. Tutor. **17**(3), 1738–1760 (2015). https://doi.org/10.1109/COMST.2015.2425294

MPTCP Multipath Protocol Evaluation in Packet Networks

Jecenia Luzuriaga-Jiménez[✉], Rommel Torres-Tandazo,
Patricia Ludeña-González, and Katty Rohoden-Jaramillo

Universidad Técnica Particular de Loja, Loja, Ecuador
{jpluzuriaga3,rovitor,pjludena,karohoden}@utpl.edu.ec

Abstract. In data networks, multipath algorithms use more than one path to transport information from one source to a destination node. Even though, there are many algorithms about multipath solutions, performance evaluation in simulators and testbeds still need to be widely analyzed. The present work analyzes the MPTCP protocol performance through its implementation in NS-3 network simulator. Besides, MPTCP is compared with the TCP protocol in order to evaluate the impact of the number of nodes in the performance of each protocol. The performance metrics considered in this work are window size, jitter, and throughput. The simulation results show that MPTCP improves the throughput compared with the TCP protocol. In addition, MPTCP windows size has a better behavior and the full delivery information is achieved in less time.

Keywords: Multipath · Window size · Packet network · Routing multipath algorithm · MPTCP

1 Introduction

Nowadays, the networking technology advances leads to the implementation of multipath protocols, which allows the use of several network routes in a single connection. This improves performance through the efficient use of resources. The implementation of these types of protocols will be carried out in data centers with a high analysis level, in mobile devices with multiple interfaces such as WiFi, in cell phones with 4G-5G technologies, and in cloud computing.

The present work studies the multipath protocol MPTCP (Multipath Transport Control Protocol), a TCP extension that has been standardized by IETF (Internet Engineering Task Force). The aforementioned protocol supports multiple simultaneous connections in the transport layer with the purpose of hosts to send data through several paths or interfaces, providing greater performance and reliability to the user.

In recent years, multipath networks have been widely studied due to its connection with the requirements of IoT (Internet of Things), data centers, and

Supported by the Grupo de Investigación de Redes seguras y sustentables, UTPL.

cloud computing. MPTCP has been selected because of its compatibility with TCP, and since it is the existing standard multipath solution that attempts to increase the network throughput and to reduce the delivery time per TCP flow. The multipath network relevance and the standardization of MPTCP allow having a knowledge base of the multipath strategies, thus in future studies, new versions or improves for multipath behavior can be proposed.

Research studies have focused their attention on the analysis of MPTCP protocol [4,5,8,10,17]. For instance, in [10], the performance of MPTCP is studied by considering slow start and congestion avoidance phases. In [4], TCP, SCTP, and MPTCP protocols are compared in a wireless sensor network environment. In the proposed work, TCP and MPTCP protocols are analyzed to determine which one has better performance in IoT scenarios. MPTCP protocol simulations were carried out under three different scenarios, each one with a different number of nodes. In addition, three metrics were evaluated, performance, window size, and average delay are evaluated.

This document is structured in five sections. In the first section an introduction to the work is presented. In section two, we study how to implement the MPTCP protocol in the network simulator NS-3. The methods and materials are detailed in the third section. In the fourth section, the analysis of the results is presented. Finally, the conclusions are detailed in the fifth section.

2   MPTCP Fundamentals

According to [8], MPTCP is a propagation of a TCP connection across multiple routes. MPTCP distributes the traffic-load by creating separate subflows through potentially disjoint roads. On the other hand, [17] defines MPTCP as a protocol that manages different bandwidths on the network topology thanks to the congestion control mechanism. This mechanism is responsible for controlling traffic on a congested route by transferring it to a less congested link, thus balancing the load. MPTCP allows the use of several IP addresses/interfaces simultaneously through a TCP modification that presents a regular and unique TCP interface to applications while distributes data through several subflows [3].

2.1   Characteristics

The main characteristics of MPTCP protocol are explained below.

- *Performance:* The use of two or more network interfaces in a simultaneous way increases the bandwidth in a TCP connection. This happens in favorable conditions, e.g. added paths should have neither high delay nor packet loss [13].
- *Connection Robustness:* The addition of paths allows introducing redundancy in packets. By using this mechanism, MPTCP reduces the loss, guarantees a stable connection and is less propense to failures. MPTCP distributes the load between the existing flows, flow with less congestion, fewer losses, etc., receives a high amount of traffic [7].

To tackle NAT (Network Address Translation) in the path, the addresses are represented by an address ID. In the case the address of an IP source packet is modified by NAT, MPTCP allows the creation of subflows when end connections are behind of NAT, using the MPTCP ADD_ADDR message.

2.2 MPTCP Architecture

In this section, the architecture of MPTCP is described, which is based on [14]. The Fig. 1 shows the MPTCP protocol stack, located in the transport layer, between the application layer and the network layer. MPTCP is designed to achieve the following goals:

– Be able to use network multipaths for only one TCP connection.
– Be able to use the available network paths without traffic losses as TCP does.
– Be useful as TCP for existing applications.
– The activation of MPTCP must not avoid connectivity in network paths where TCP is working.

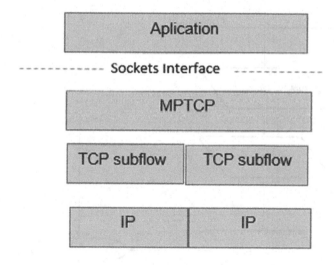

Fig. 1. MPTCP architecture

2.3 MPTCP Operation

MPTCP protocol works as a TCP extension in hosts that are able to use multipath. MPTCP maintain connections in four steps as can be seen in Fig. 2.

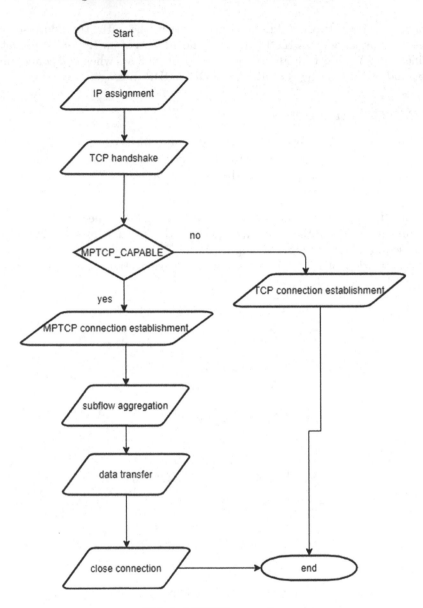

Fig. 2. MPTCP operation

Connection Establishment

MPTCP and TCP connections are similar between, in the Fig. 3, host A sends a SYN packet to host B, MPTCP includes the MP_CAPABLE option. The host that requires to establish a connection sends the MP_CAPABLE option. If the destiny node is able to receive a MPTCP connection, it will answer with

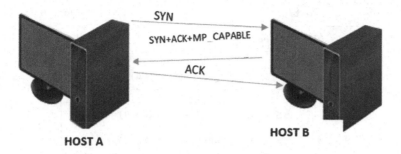

Fig. 3. MPTCP connection establishment

SYN/ACK including the MP_CAPABLE response, otherwise it will respond with SYNACK, which establishes a standard TCP connection only.

Subflows Aggregation

According to [1], the MP_JOIN option is used for the aggregation of subflows. In Fig. 4, host A starts a new subflow between the IP addresses. The token is used to generate the key that serves to identify the connection that is adding the subflow. The field HMAC is used for authentication, it is generated from the nodes and is interchanged with the keys in the established connection. Address indicators are also sent to refer the flow source, preventing changes when NAT is used.

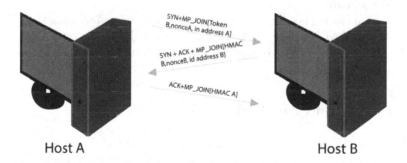

Fig. 4. Subflows aggregation

Data Transmission

To ensure that the data is transmitted correctly, MPTCP adds a 64-bit sequence numbers, used to enumerate the MPTCP flow data. So, the information is sent by different subflows in case of retransmission, this is possible thanks to Multipath_Capable and Multipath_Join fields. In Fig. 5, the establishment of the MPTCP transmission is presented.

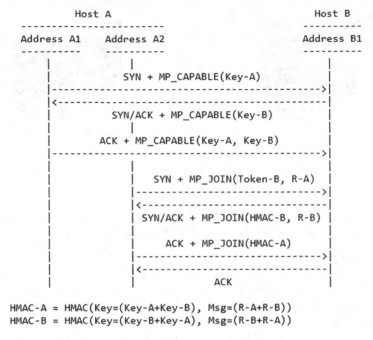

HMAC-A = HMAC(Key=(Key-A+Key-B), Msg=(R-A+R-B))
HMAC-B = HMAC(Key=(Key-B+Key-A), Msg=(R-B+R-A))

Fig. 5. MPTCP transmission

Close Connection

The connection closing is similar to TCP except that instead of using the FIN flag from TCP, the DATA_FIN flag of MPTCP is used. However, once this process is finished, it is necessary to terminate the individual TCP connections of each subflow.

3　Materials and Methods

In this section, the scenarios according to IoT network topologies are defined. In addition, the metrics to analyze the protocols performance are presented.

3.1　Scenarios

In this section, the scenarios used to test the proposed model are specified. Furthermore, the simulation parameters are shown in Table 1.

The topologies shown in Figs. 6, 7, and 8 consist of 12, 20, and 30 nodes, respectively. It is important to notice that nodes are connected with the aim of achieving the creation of several paths for the information interchange.

Table 1. Simulation parameters

Parameters	Values
Number of nodes	12, 20, 30
Simulation time	10 s
Total traffic	2 Gbps
Data rate	2 Mbps
Packet size	1024 bytes
Transport layer protocols	MPTCP, TCP
Segment size	1024 bytes

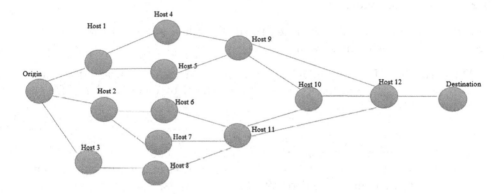

Fig. 6. Topology with 12 nodes

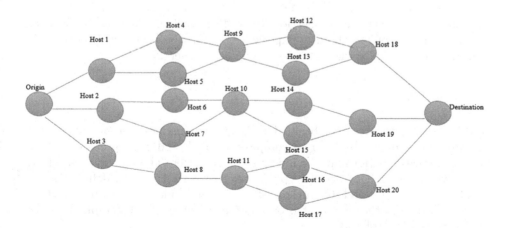

Fig. 7. Topology with 20 nodes

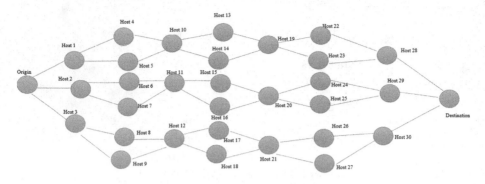

Fig. 8. Topology with 30 nodes

3.2   Evaluation Metrics

In order to analyze the performance of MPTCP when compared with the TCP protocol, the following metrics are used.

1. **Performance:** It is the amount of data received correctly at a certain time. To calculate the performance R, divide the total bytes received Tbr for the simulation time Ts.

$$R = \frac{Tbr}{Ts} \tag{1}$$

2. **Window size:** It determines the number of segments that the source can send without waiting for ACK from the receiver, ensuring that the capacity of the network is not exceeded [12]. In other words, it is the ability of the destination node to accept and process a certain amount of data in a given time, minimizing the loss or retransmission of data.
3. **Jitter:** It is the variation in the latency given in milliseconds (ms) between received packets over a data network. The packet delay variance can be a consequence of network congestion, buffer load, and large queues. Since jitter can be deleterious to the user experience, it must be kept low. Besides, it is used to determinate the end to end congestion level [2].

4   Results

In this section, the results obtained through the simulated scenarios in ns-3 software are analixed. In order to compare MPTCP and TCP protocols, three metrics are used: performance, window size, and jitter. These metrics obtained from several research works. The performance metric has been defined in [9], [11], and [15]. In [11] and [6], authors showed that window size is an important metric to evaluate the transport protocol. On the other hand, the jitter metric has been used by [16] and [2].

4.1   Performance at Destination Node

We analyzed the performance of MPTCP and TCP through the results obtained from the three topologies and from previously defined parameters.

Figures 9, 10, and 11 showed that MPTCP has a better performance than TCP in all scenarios. In addition, MPTCP receives more quantity of bytes during the simulation time. Thus, MPTCP achieves to deliver the traffic in less time than TCP. Consequently, MPTCP delivers all the information in less time than TCP. MPTCP sends an amount of initial information that increases until it finishes sending all the information approximately one second before TCP. Therefore, it is concluded that MPTCP is more efficient than TCP with respect to the effective sending of information.

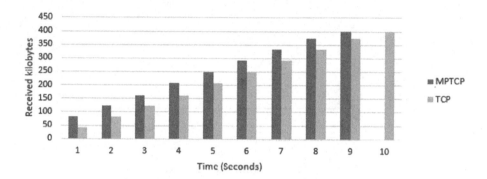

Fig. 9. Performance with 12 nodes.

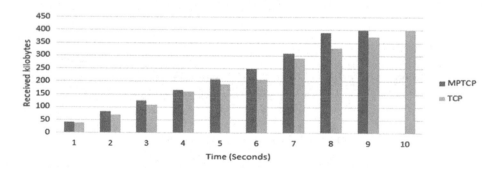

Fig. 10. Performance with 20 nodes.

4.2   Window Size at Source Node

Figures 12, 13 and 14 show that MPTCP provides a cumulative window size greater than TCP, impacting directly the time of information reception. With MPTCP, the same amount of information is sent as TCP but in less time due to the simultaneous sending of information through TCP subflows.

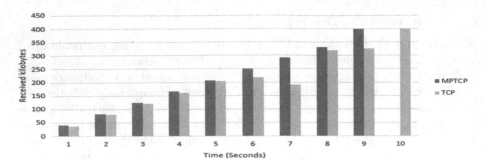

Fig. 11. Performance with 30 nodes.

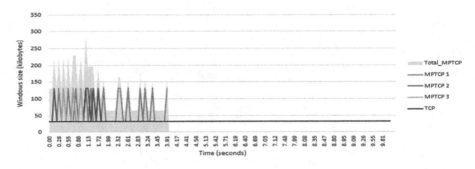

Fig. 12. Windows size 12 nodes

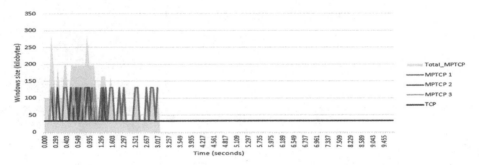

Fig. 13. Windows size 20 nodes

4.3   Jitter

Figure 15 demonstrates that MPTCP has better average jitter values than TCP in all scenarios, as long as the values are closer to 0 the stability of the network is better.

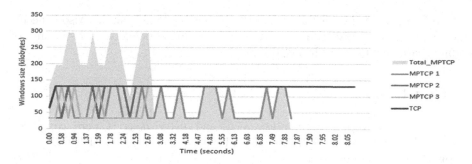

Fig. 14. Windows size 30 nodes

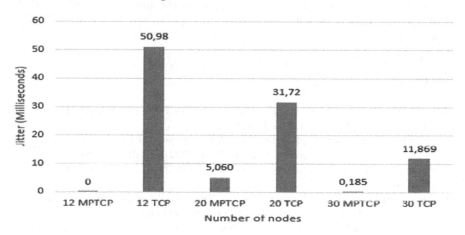

Fig. 15. Jitter

5   Discussion

The IoT paradigm requires that users have greater bandwidth and less latency, for these important reasons is necessary to analyze and identify the methodologies and techniques that improve these requirements. The use of multipath algorithms and protocols focuses on the efficient use of resources available in a data network. It has been analyzed in this investigation that the results obtained from the study of the MPTCP multipath protocol in relation to performance, window size and delivery time metrics have a considerable improvement with respect to TCP and that effectively address the IoT requirements. In the same way, IoT must support the growing demand for multimedia traffic in which the variation of the delay or jitter is one of the indicators that can change and improve the user experience, in this investigation the results show that the use of multiple roads improves the jitter in relation to standard connections.

The data contributes a clearer understanding of the behavior of multipath strategies and their relationship with IoT requirements. Future studies should take into account the processing time in each node when the setup process connection is established especially when the packet payload is small. Also is necessary to determine more realistic scenarios including topologies with the mix of a single path and multipath nodes.

6   Conclusions

In this work, performance, window size, and jitter metrics were compared between TCP and MPTCP protocols. The results show that MPTCP protocol provides better performance compared to TCP, because the total delivery of information is done in less time since MPTCP uses subflows in parallel. This work can provide the basis for future research on the implementation of multipath in VANET networks, especially in the IoT paradigm in the area of smart transportation.

References

1. Álvarez Méndez, S.: Análisis del protocolo MPTCP en plataformas Linux. B.S. thesis, Universidad Carlos III de Madrid (2015)
2. Andreadis, A., Rizzuto, S., Zambon, R.: A cross-layer jitter-based tcp for wireless networks. EURASIP J. Wirel. Commun. Netw. **2016**(1), 191 (2016)
3. Autores, V.: Multipath TCP-linux kernel implementation (2013). https://www. multipath-tcp.org/
4. Becke, M., Adhari, H., Rathgeb, E., Fa, F., Yang, X., Zhou, X.: Comparison of multipath TCP and CMT-SCTP based on intercontinental measurements. In: GLOBECOM - IEEE Global Telecommunications Conference, pp. 1360–1366, December 2013. https://doi.org/10.1109/GLOCOM.2013.6831263
5. Binet, D., et al.: Multipath TCP (MPTCP): motivations, status, and opportunities for the future internet. In: Handbook of Research on Redesigning the Future of Internet Architectures, pp. 190–213. IGI Global (2015)
6. Cui, Y., Wang, L., Wang, X., Wang, H., Wang, Y.: FMTCP: un protocolo de control de transmisión de múltiples rutas basado en código fuente. Transacciones IEEE / ACM en redes (ToN) **23**(2), 465–478 (2015)
7. Del Toro Domínguez, A.M.: Validación y corrección del protocolo de transporte MPTCP (Multipath TCP) para Ns3. B.S. thesis, Universidad de Sevilla (2018)
8. Ford, A., Raiciu, C., Handley, M., Barre, S., Iyengar, J.: Rfc 6182, architectural guidelines for multipath TCP development (2011)
9. Korowajczuk, L.: LTE, WiMAX and WLAN Network Design Optimization and Performance Analysis. John Wiley, Hoboken (2011)
10. Lee, J., Im, Y., Lee, J.: Modeling MPTCP performance. IEEE Commun. Lett. **23**(4), 616–619 (2019). https://doi.org/10.1109/LCOMM.2019.2898664
11. Raiciu, C., Barre, S., Pluntke, C., Greenhalgh, A., Wischik, D., Handley, M.: Improving datacenter performance and robustness with multipath TCP. ACM SIGCOMM Comput. Commun. Rev. **41**, 266–277 (2011)
12. Rattalino, D., Crespo, A.: Simulación de algoritmos de control de congestión en TCP bajo user mode linux. In: Revista Tecnología y Ciencia, November 2015. https://doi.org/10.13140/2.1.3970.3843

13. Moyano, R.F.: Diseño e implementación de escenarios virtuales de red para evaluar el funcionamiento de MPTCP. B.S. thesis, Universidad Politécnica de Madrid (2013). http://www.dit.upm.es/~posgrado/doc/TFM/TFMs2012-2013/ TFM_Ricardo_Flores_2013.pdf
14. Scharf, M., Ford, A.: Multipath TCP (MPTCP) application interface considerations. Technical report, RFC 6897, March (2013)
15. Singh, A., Goerg, C., Timm-Giel, A., Scharf, M., Banniza, T.R.: Performance comparison of scheduling algorithms for multipath transfer. In: 2012 IEEE Global Communications Conference (GLOBECOM), pp. 2653–2658. IEEE (2012)
16. Suarez, J., Salcedo, M., Carmona, C., Ramirez, J., Serna, G.: Effects of IPv6-IPv4 tunnel in jitter of voice over IPv6, measured in laboratory and over the national research and education network of colombia "renata". IEEE Latin Am. Trans. **14**(3), 1380–1386 (2016)
17. Van Der Pol, R., et al.: Multipathing with MPTCP and openflow. In: 2012 SC Companion: High Performance Computing, Networking Storage and Analysis, pp. 1617–1624. IEEE (2012)

Propagation Features of Visible Light Communication in Underground Mining Environments

Pablo Palacios Játiva[1(✉)], Cesar A. Azurdia-Meza[1], Milton Román Cañizares[2], David Zabala-Blanco[3], and Carlos Saavedra[4]

[1] Department of Electrical Engineering, University of Chile, Santiago, Chile
`pablo.palacios@ug.uchile.cl, cazurdia@ing.uchile.cl`
[2] Departamento de Redes y Telecomunicaciones,
Universidad De Las Américas, Quito, Ecuador
`milton.roman@udla.edu.ec`
[3] Department of Computing and Industries,
Universidad Católica del Maule, Talca, Chile
`davidzabalablanco@hotmail.com`
[4] Faculty of Electrical and Computation Engineering,
ESPOL Polytechnic University, Guayaquil, Ecuador
`casaaved@espol.edu.ec`

Abstract. Due to the problems that radio-frequency technology presents in hostile environments, especially in mining environments, other forms of more robust as well as efficient communication have been explored in recent years. Among these, Visible Light Communication (VLC) can be highlighted. In this work, the analysis of a VLC system applied to underground mining (UM) environments is presented. This scheme supports communication and lighting at the same time. This VLC study is done based on the mathematical models of optical transmitters, optical receivers, channel model, and propagation model. In addition, two UM scenarios are exposed, which are tested by numerical simulations. In particular, characteristics of the VLC channel such as gain, impulse response, and reception power are obtained, together with the fulfillment of the necessary lighting parameters in the mining scenarios. As a consequence, we observe that VLC systems comply with the lighting standards in UM environments and have favorable characteristics for reliable communication within these noisy environments.

Keywords: Illuminance · Underground mining communications · Visible Light Communications

1 Introduction

The underground mining (UM) industry is providing a significant boost to global economy. However, there are problems related to the mining environment, such as the presence of poisonous substances, toxic gases and corrosive water along

© Springer Nature Switzerland AG 2020
M. Botto-Tobar et al. (Eds.): ICAT 2019, CCIS 1195, pp. 82–93, 2020.
https://doi.org/10.1007/978-3-030-42531-9_7

with dust [3]. A reliable communication, tracking and monitoring system is required to guarantee safety in order to maximize the productivity in mines. Thus, designing a communication system in UM is considered as a challenging task. The information in UM includes detecting smoke, hazardous gases, monitoring miners location when disaster occurs. These details, added to the hostile environment of a mining company, make the design of UM communications systems an engineering challenge, which, if properly implemented, would guarantee work safety and optimize the productivity of the mines.

The main communication modes in UM are wireless, wired or the combination of both types of communication [1,5,14]. The common types of wired data transmission medium includes coaxial, fiber-optic and twisted pair. However, wired communication is susceptible to be damaged and cannot be a reliable mode of communication in UM. Furthermore, the wireless communication also cannot be used in the UM due to signal attenuation. Thus, the concept of Visible Light Communication (VLC) has been introduced for UM communication. The VLC compared to Bluetooth, ultra-wide band performs better in the scenario of short range communications [16].

There are several benefits of using VLC technology compared to other techniques, like unlicensed spectrum, reasonable prices, faster data transfer rate, and resistant to electromagnetic interference [9]. In UM, VLC can be used as a reliable mode of communication. The main components of an UM VLC system are: light-emitting diodes (LEDs), which are cold light sources used to form LED lamps that could be installed on the top surface of UM and photo-diodes (PDs) that could be installed on the worker's helmet, to create a VLC link between workers and mining infrastructure, or between workers, depending on the required application. The channel modeling is also an important stage for efficient, reliable, and robust VLC system design. There is an increasing research associated with characterization of indoor VLC channels that can more accurately model a VLC link [8], in addition to considering all the factors that can influence the link behavior. However, for underground mines only a few studies have concentrated on describing VLC channels [13].

Compared to typical VLC indoor systems, VLC environments for UM are more complex to model. A typical UM scenario consists of small tunnels with irregular walls, so the VLC channel can be modeled considering the line-of-sight (LoS) and No-line-of-sight (NLoS) components, provided by the direct signal emitted by the LED (optical transmitter) to the PD (optical receiver) and the signals reflected on the walls that also reach the receiver, respectively [12,13]. Further, due to the light characteristics, as well as the LEDs and PDs, intensity modulation (IM) techniques in the transmitter and direct detection (DD) in the receiver must be implemented in these systems.

In this study, a detailed underground VLC system model, in which, we consider LoS and NLoS components with their channel direct current (DC) gains, analyzing its propagation characteristics in terms of channel gain, channel impulse response and received power, important parameters to know the behavior of VLC in UM environments. Furthermore, a brief analysis of the lighting in the proposed mining scenarios is considered.

The remainder of this paper is organized as follows: In Sect. 2 we present some works related to the field of VLC in UM. In Sect. 3 the detail of the UM VLC system is analyzed. The performance analysis of the VLC system, depending on its propagation features, with their respective numerical results are presented in Sect. 4. Finally, in Sect. 5, the general conclusions of this research are presented.

2   Related Works

In specialized literature, only few authors have focused on the study of VLC channels model in UM. Several proposals for the characterization of the UM VLC channels are presented in [12,13]. In these works, a general VLC channel model for UM environments is presented, which involves the application of two communication scenarios. Regarding the mathematical model of the VLC channel, the LoS and NLoS components are considered, applied in two UM environments, in which the dimensions of the scenarios are varied, as well as the number of optical transmitters and the route that the helmets that the optical receivers take. The analysis carried out in these works is based on the determination of the channel path loss, the large-scale fading and scattering. The lighting parameter of mining environments is also briefly reviewed. The results determine an empirical path loss model of the VLC channel. For their contributions, these works are considered the starting point for our research. However, these still present opportunities for improvement. Among the details that must be addressed are the analysis of the of the propagation factors, power levels that can be achieved, and channel gains, among others.

An interesting research of VLC in hostile environments is applied in [15], where a energy coupling model of a VLC system applied to a coal mine is presented, specifically a theoretical study of the effects of coal dust particles on VLC. As a result, an optimal position of the optical transmitter is found, to maximize the coupled energy. It should be noted that when addressing a specific problem of mining VLC environments, when only addressing the problem from the optical transmitter, it leaves open the possibilities for other solutions in optical reception.

An application of a Li-Fi communication system for UM is presented in [11], which allows the sending of emergency messages in the mine. Finally, several works applied to localization in mining environments based on VLC systems are presented in [6,7]. As we can see, many of the works focus on applications in which VLC technology can be used in UM environments, however, is necessary to approach studies from the field of channel behavior and propagation models in these systems, to verify that all the applications that can be proposed on these environments, work efficiently.

3   Proposed VLC System Model

In general, UM can be divided into two sections, one where mining workers can walk and carry the extracted materials, called *mining roadway* [12] and another where mineral extraction work is carried out, called *mine working face* [12]. This model of mining system is presented in Fig. 1, which we describe below.

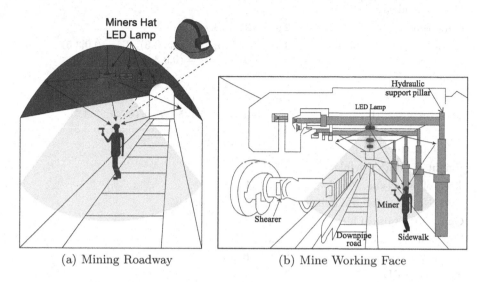

(a) Mining Roadway   (b) Mine Working Face

Fig. 1. Mining environment model for VLC based on [13].

- **Mining Roadway**: This part of the UM environment is generally a tunnel or a narrow chamber, where workers are mobilized and materials extracted from the mine are transported. In addition, it is characterized by being very narrow, with a short visibility distance and irregularities in the shapes of the walls and roof. In our work, we will use a horseshoe-shaped environment to represent this mine section, where the LEDs will be located in a row on the roof, equidistant from each other, to provide communication and lighting simultaneously, as we can see in Fig. 1(a).
- **Mine Working Face**: In this mine section, material extraction works are carried out using specialized equipment. In the extraction process, electromagnetic radiation, water vapor and flammable gas are produced. For our work, we will assume that this environment is rectangular, where the LEDs are located in rectangular form, equidistant from the center of the work section, to provide lighting and communication, as we can see in Fig. 1(b).

Both sections are equipped with LED lamps, and to optimize the effect of communication, the light intensity in the spaces should be distributed as uniformly as possible. Therefore, multiple LED lamps must be installed on the roof of each mining section, whose dimensions, LED lamps locations, and key parameters of the proposed underground mining VLC system are detailed in the Table 1. In addition, this communication model considers LoS and NLoS propagation components, which favors us to propose a complete channel mode.

Table 1. System UM VLC parameters

System Model Parameters	Values
Mining roadway	
Dimensions	$2\,m \times 10\,m \times 3.7\,m$
Coordinates of the $T_x s$	$T_1 = (0,4,3.5)$, $T_2 = (0,2,3.5)$, $T_3 = (0,0,3.5)$, $T_4 = (0,0,3.5)$, $T_5 = (0,0,3.5)$
Mine working face	
Dimensions	$2\,m \times 10\,m \times 4.7\,m$
Coordinates of the $T_x s$	$T_1 = (-0.5,-1.25,3.5)$, $T_2 = (0.5,1.25,3.5)$, $T_3 = (0.5,-1.25,3.5)$, $T_4 = (-0.5,1.25,3.5)$
Other parameters	
Height of miner's helmet	$1.7\,m$
Area of detection	$1\,cm^2$ [4]
AWGN power spectral density	2.5×10^{-23} A/Hz [4]
Gain of the optical filter	1 [4]
Modulation bandwidth	$10\,MHz$ [4]
Modulation	OOK [4]
Number of PDs	1 [4]
Number of R_x	1
Refractive index	1.5 [4]
Responsivity	0.53 A/W [4]
Rx FOV	60° [4]
Tx semi-angle	60° [4]
Transmission power	$10\,W$ [4]

3.1 Optical Transmitter

Given the uniform distribution of LED lamps in mining scenarios, multiple of them must be installed. Thus, we generalize the concept that each LED array will be considered as a optical transmitter T_x. Assuming that each LED lamp of the T_x has the same generalized Lambertian radiation pattern, and since this model is widely used for the light emission distribution of the LEDs, the angular distribution $S(\phi)$ of the intensity radiation pattern is defined, given as [12]

$$S(\phi) = \begin{cases} \frac{m+1}{2\pi} \cos^m(\phi) & \text{if } \phi \in [-\frac{\pi}{2}, \frac{\pi}{2}] \\ 0 & otherwise \end{cases}, \tag{1}$$

where ϕ is the incidence angle and m is the Lambertian mode number that is related to the half angle $\phi_{1/2}$ of the half power emitted by the T_x; m is defined as follows [12]

$$m = \frac{-ln(2)}{ln(cos(\phi_{1/2}))}. \tag{2}$$

The maximum intensity will be given when it $\phi_{1/2} = 0$. In addition, when m is increased, the T_x beam may be more directional.

3.2 VLC UM Channel Model

Given the characteristics involved in a UM environment, the location of the T_x on the roof of the mining scenarios, we will call the optical receivers as R_x, which will be located at the top of the mining workers' helmets. Due to the mobility that workers have in mining environments, the optical link will be different according to the location at some time of the R_x. For the details mentioned above, several gain components for the optical channel should be considered. In our work, the LoS path is adopted as the first and principal gain component, since it is the largest source of energy obtained from the T_x. Therefore, short-distance LoS links are often modeled as linear attenuation and delay. In this sense, the impulse response of the LoS component applied to underground mining environments is given as [4]

$$h_0(t) = \frac{A_p(m+1)}{2\pi d_0^2} \cos^m(\phi_0) T_s(\theta_0) g(\theta_0) \cos(\theta_0), \qquad (3)$$

where A_p is the physical area of the R_x, d_0 is the distance between T_x and R_x, ϕ_0 is the LoS transmission angle, θ_0 is the reception angle, $T_s(\theta_0)$ is the optical filter gain, and $g(\theta_0)$ is the optical concentrator gain, whose expression we will present later. Also, it is assumed that $\phi_0 < 90°$ and $\theta_0 < \Theta$, where Θ is the R_x Field-of-View (FoV).

Not only does the LoS path contribute energy in mining scenarios, as these hostile environments, multiple factors affect the energy received in the R_x, such as non-uniform walls, dust particles or extracted materials, reflectivity of the ceiling, walls or others objects, dimensions of the environment, position and orientation of the T_x and R_x, among others, which creates non-directed LOS (NLoS) and diffuse links. However, several researches show that the strongest NLOS component is much lower in terms of energy compared to the LOS component, specifically in indoor VLC environments [2], so it will not be considered in this work.

3.3 Optical Propagation Model

Considering the physical characteristics of the UM environments we are studying, there must be multiple T_x and R_x, we will denote N_{T_x} as the total number of T_x, whose indexes for any T_x is $a = 1, 2..., N_{T_x}$. Therefore, the equivalent base-band model that we will use in our work to describe an UM IM/DD VLC link is as follows

$$y_p(t) = \tau P_{op} x_{op}(t) \otimes h_{op}(t) + \sum_{a=1, a \neq op}^{N_{T_x}} \tau P_a x_a(t) \otimes h_a(t) + n(t), \qquad (4)$$

where $y_p(t)$ is the electrical signal received by the pth PD, τ is the electric-optical conversion efficiency, furthermore, since there are multiple T_x and R_x, we will assume for this model that only one T_x should be selected as the optimum, where op is the index of this T_x. Hence, $x_{op}(t)$ and $x_a(t)$ are the electrical signals transmitted from $T_{x_{op}}$ and T_{x_a} respectively, $h_{op}(t)$ is the channel impulse response between the Tx_{op} and the R_x, $h_a(t)$ is the channel impulse response between the T_{x_a} and the R_x, P_{op} and P_a are the average output optical power from $T_{x_{op}}$ and T_{x_a} respectively. We will consider $n(t)$, modeled as additive white Gaussian noise (AWGN).

3.4   Optical Receiver

Generally, VLC systems use PDs in R_x, which are composed of a non-imaging concentrator (lens) and a physical area A_p. PDs collect the incident power produced by the light intensity of T_x. The optical gain of a PD, $g(\theta_0)$, based on a non-imaging concentrator is given as follows

$$g(\theta_0) = \begin{cases} \frac{\eta^2}{sin^2(\theta_0)}, & \text{if } 0 \leq \theta_0 \leq \Theta \\ 0, & \text{if } \theta_0 \geq \Theta \end{cases} , \tag{5}$$

where η is the refractive index of concentrator. Together with the PD lens, an optical transmission gain band-pass filter $T_s(\theta_0)$ is also added.

Among the goals of this research is the study of the VLC channel model features used, the propagation model used and the environment illuminance. This research will be presented in terms of illuminance distribution, received power and the channel impulse response in the next section.

4   UM VLC System: Performance Analysis, Results and Discusion

In simulations developed using the Matlab program, all the parameters applied to the VLC UM model are described in the Table 1. In addition, Monte-Carlo method with 21 iterations, for more robust and statistically significant results was applied. The parameters we will analyze were obtained by varying the R_x position in all possible locations in the VLC UM scenarios and estimating the respective values.

4.1   Environment Illuminance

Since one of the basic benefits of VLC is to provide lighting and communication at the same time in UM environments, the analysis of the illuminance that the scenarios presented must have is considered. To comply with this, the simulations are validated with the standard lighting in [10], which indicates that for the UM environments to have a correct illumination, it must exceed 107.65 lux. The simulation results are shown in Fig. 2. For the illuminance in the mining roadway scenario shown in Fig. 2(a), it is possible to note that illuminance is in the range of [700–1400] lux, it is also observed that the illuminance peaks occur precisely in the location of the T_x, which are in a row in this scenario, taking into consideration that the T_xs are located at 3.7 m and the height of the R_x is 1.7 m, to emulate the average height of a mining worker.

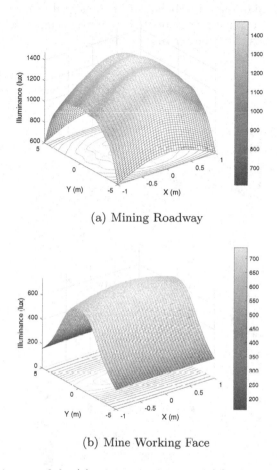

(a) Mining Roadway

(b) Mine Working Face

Fig. 2. Illuminance of the (a) mining roadway and (b) mining working face.

Secondly, in Fig. 2(b), illuminance for the mine working face scenario is illustrated. The location of the T_xs changes to have a rectangular order, in addition to the height of the stage being increased to 4.7 m. Due to these variations, since the T_xs are further from the mining helmets, it is observed that the illuminance is in the range between [200–700] lux, less than the previous scenario. However, in both scenarios it is possible to note that the illuminance standard for UM scenarios is met.

4.2   Channel Impulse Response

In Fig. 3, The Channel Impulse Response, calculated and illustrated for both mining roadway and the mine working face environments, is presented. This parameter is basic to observe the behavior of the signal propagation of the UM scenarios. In order to physically model the environments, Sect. 3 presents the shape of the scenarios, for a better understanding.

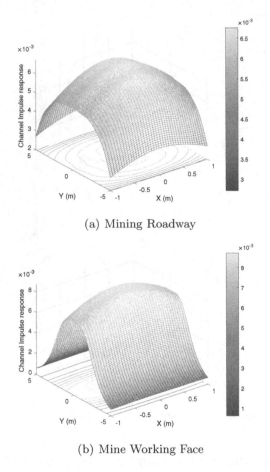

(a) Mining Roadway

(b) Mine Working Face

Fig. 3. Channel impulse response of the (a) mining roadway and (b) mining working face.

In Fig. 3(a), the Channel Impulse Response of the mining roadway is shown, caused by the LoS signal as a delta function, whose maximum and minimum values are given by 6.5×10^{-3} and 3×10^{-3} respectively. In Fig. 3(b), the Channel Impulse Response of the mine working face is shown, whose maximum and minimum values are given by 1×10^{-3} and 3×8^{-3} respectively. It is possible to identify that, in both scenarios, the Channel Impulse Response values are quite similar, in the order of 10^{-3}, this is because both environments have the same width that is 2 m, so that optical paths are not long, which indicates that the propagation of the signal in small and hostile areas has a favorable performance.

4.3   Received Power Distribution

In Fig. 4. The power distribution in reception for the mining roadway and mine working face scenarios is observed. The minimum power received in the mining roadway environment is −160 dBm. The maximum power received in the same environment is −110 dBm. For the mine working face environment the minimum power received is −140 dBm and the maximum power received is −90 dBm.

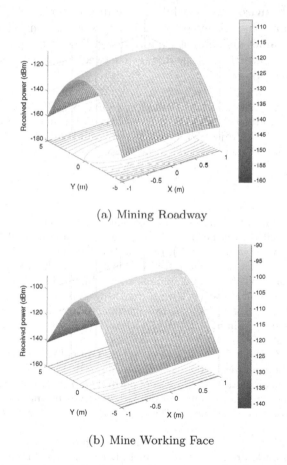

(a) Mining Roadway

(b) Mine Working Face

Fig. 4. Power distribution of the (a) mining roadway and (b) mining working face.

The results for the two scenarios show that despite the fact that there is greater distance between the T_xs and the R_xs in the mine working face environment, the rectangular location of the T_xs produces that the power that the R_xs receive is greater compared to the environment mining roadway. In addition, it can be seen that as the distance between T_xs and R_xs decreases, the received power also drops.

5   Conclusions

In this paper, the behavior of the VLC channel in mining environments is analyzed and the propagation features of the optical signal in two UM scenarios are also studied. The models proposed in this work are analyzed in terms of illuminance, channel impulse response and power distribution in reception, through simulations. The results show that the illuminance in both scenarios meets the standard for UM environments, while the results in terms of channel impulse response show that the LoS component provides the strongest signal in both scenarios, whose values are similar. Finally, depending on the power distribution in reception, it is shown that as the distance between optical elements decreases, so does the received power.

Acknowledgment. This work was funded by CONICYT PFCHA/Beca de Doctorado Nacional/2019 21190489, SENESCYT "Convocatoria abierta 2014-primera fase, Acta CIBAE-023-2014", Project STIC-AMSUD 19-STIC-08, and UDLA Telecommunications Engineering Degree.

References

1. Changsen, Z., Yan, M.: Study on mine communication network based on ethernet and WSN. In: 2015 International Conference on Computational Intelligence and Communication Networks (CICN), pp. 183–187, December 2015
2. Chen, C., Basnayaka, D., Haas, H.: Non-line-of-sight channel impulse response characterisation in visible light communications. In: 2016 IEEE International Conference on Communications (ICC), pp. 1–6, May 2016
3. Dong, L., Tong, X., Li, X.: Some developments and new insights of environmental problems and deep mining strategy for cleaner production in mines. J. Cleaner Prod. **210**, 1562–1578 (2018)
4. Ghassemlooy, Z., Popoola, W., Rajbhandari, S.: Optical Wireless Communications: System and Channel Modelling with Matlab®. CRC Press, Boca Raton (2019)
5. Indra, S., Barik, S., Pati, U.C.: Design of portable indicator for underground mines using 433 MHz wireless communication. In: 2018 2nd International Conference on Electronics, Materials Engineering Nano-Technology (IEMENTech), pp. 1–5, May 2018
6. Iturralde, D., Seguel, F., Soto, I., Azurdia, C., Khan, S.: A new VLC system for localization in underground mining tunnels. IEEE Lat. Am. Trans. **15**(4), 581–587 (2017)
7. Krommenacker, N., Vásquez, C., Alfaro, M.D., Soto, I.: A self-adaptive cell-id positioning system based on visible light communications in underground mines. In: 2016 IEEE International Conference on Automatica (ICA-ACCA), pp. 1–7, October 2016

8. Palacios, P., Azurdia-Meza, C., Roman, M., Zabala-Blanco, D., Soto, I.: Ber performance of OFDM-based visible light communication systems. In 2019 CHILEAN Conference on Electrical, Electronics Engineering, Information and Communication Technologies (CHILECON), October 2019

9. Seguel, F., Soto, I., Adasme, P., Krommenacker, N., Charpentier, P.: Potential and challenges of VLC based IPS in underground mines. In: 2017 First South American Colloquium on Visible Light Communications (SACVLC), pp. 1–6, November 2017

10. Statham, C.D.J.: Underground lighting in coal mines. Proc. IEE - Part A: Power Eng. **103**(10), 396–409 (1956)

11. Vivek Priyan, R., Dinesh, S., Ilanthendral, J., Ramya, B.: Communication system for underground mines using Li-Fi 5G technology, vol. III, pp. 80–85 (2014)

12. Wang, J., Al-Kinani, A., Zhang, W., Wang, C.: A new VLC channel model for underground mining environments. In: 2017 13th International Wireless Communications and Mobile Computing Conference (IWCMC), pp. 2134–2139, June 2017

13. Wang, J., Al-Kinani, A., Zhang, W., Wang, C., Zhou, L.: A general channel model for visible light communications in underground mines. China Commun. **15**(9), 95–105 (2018)

14. Wen, R., Tong, M., Tang, S.: Application of bluetooth communication in mine environment detection vehicle. In: 2017 7th IEEE International Conference on Electronics Information and Emergency Communication (ICEIEC), pp. 236–239, July 2017

15. Zhai, Y., Zhang, S.: Visible light communication channel models and simulation of coal workface energy coupling. Math. Prob. Eng. **2015**, 1–10 (2015)

16. Zhang, Y., Zhang, Y., Li, C.: Research of short distance wireless communication technology in the mine underground. In: 2014 Fourth International Conference on Instrumentation and Measurement, Computer, Communication and Control, pp. 955–959, September 2014

Design of a Non-deterministic Model for a Propagation of VHF Radio Signal in the Ecuadorian Jungle

Federico Rodas[1]([✉]), Manolo Paredes[2]([✉]), Elena Gimenez[3]([✉]), Diego Garzón[2]([✉]), and Emilia Ayala[2]([✉])

[1] Dep. Análisis Matemático, Universidad de Málaga, Campus Teatinos, Málaga, Spain
federicorodas@uma.es
[2] Universidad de las Fuerzas Armadas- ESPE, Av. El Progreso, Sangolquí, Ecuador
{dmparedes,dfgarznf,epayala3}@espe.edu.ec
[3] Universidad Internacional de la Rioja, Av. de la Paz, 137, Logroño, La Rioja, Spain
elena.gimenez@unir.net

Abstract. This paper develops a propagation model of electromagnetic signals emitted at frequencies of 20 and 40 MHz for the Ecuadorian jungle. The expected results of this research will be applied to produce a complete coverage map for wireless communications technologies, which will optimize the radio spectrum in operation carried out by the Armed Forces in Ecuadorian border jungle. The final expression found is an adjustment function that relates the Receiving Power (P_{RX}) to factors that determine the geometry of the Fresnell Zone (Conectivity). The resulting model of the research improves the discrepancy between the simulated power (P_{RL}) in commercial software and a sample of measured wireless transmissions *in situ*. The analysis was based on the results and methodology presented by Longley-Rice. It was determined the non-normality of the discrepancy between the losses (L_{IR}) calculated by Longley Rice Model (LMR) and the data obtained in the field. To solve this point, correction coefficients were added on the expression of LMR. Subsequently, the mathematical expression was linearized to implement multivariate linear adjustment techniques. Alternative formulations to the Linear Regression model were sought and their goodness of fit was compared; all these techniques are introduced theatrically. To conclude, the study includes a Kolmogorov Test to grant normality and goodness of fit. Mathematical modelling software such as Matlab, R and SPSS were used for the formulation and numerical analysis. Finally, we found a model that have a R^2 of 99.995%.

Keywords: Mathematical model · Longley Rice · Propagation model

1 Introduction

Ecuador is a megadiverse country that has different geographical and urban scenarios, due to its four regions with respective weather conditions [1]. Beginning with a fairly biodiverse Amazon jungle in the East, an Andes mountain range in the center, a

© Springer Nature Switzerland AG 2020
M. Botto-Tobar et al. (Eds.): ICAT 2019, CCIS 1195, pp. 94–103, 2020.
https://doi.org/10.1007/978-3-030-42531-9_8

coast between the Pacific Ocean and the aforementioned mountain range and finally the Galapagos Islands. All these conditions difficult to have a model that generalized the 4 regions [2].

Currently, the Armed Force of Ecuador has a wide wireless telecommunications equipment, in order to work as efficiently as possible. There are basic systems such as mobile telephony, wireless data networks, digital television or radio, which helps the army to communicate through data, voice or video at long distances. Unfortunately, the communication between these devices is not strong enough to work on borders. Taking into account that 80% of these places are covered by jungle and that military operations must be carried out permanently to control drug traffic and guerillas operations, it is necessary to have a robust model that allows the communication in the best way for the conditions [3].

The Longley-Rice propagation model (MLR), is an analysis for propagation calculation for point to point and point-zone links, applied in rural or extremely complex scenarios [4]. Based on this model the objective of this work is to determine a propagation regression model of electromagnetic signal that allows to predict an error less or equal to the Longley-Rice model in the reception power (P_{RX}) under the conditions of the Ecuadorian jungle.

2 Methodology

The methodology for the sampling and the experimental process, was based on the work done by Kasampalis, Lazaridis, Bizopoulos, Zettas & Cosmas in 2014 [5]. The main variable of the study was the Receiving power in dB (P_{RX}), which was determined through the measurement of VHF signal transmissions in the Ecuadorian jungle, at distances less than 20 [Km], with frequencies within the band of 20 to 40 [MHz], and low, medium and high Transmission Power (P_{TX}) corresponding to 1 W, 5 W and 20 W respectively. The data collection has a size of 1000 for each of the mentioned factors.

Filtered data of the powers obtained using technical parameters such as thermal noise levels, that means that the data below −120[dB] was eliminated. The statistical analysis was carried out with the new debug database. The obtained data were compared with those predicted by the MLR and determined the normality of the resulting residue vector. This indicates if the error is random and the randomness corresponds to a characteristic of the sample and not to external factors such as the meteorological conditions of the sampling place or the dissipation of the signal due to the vegetation area. If there is no normality in the residue vector, the error could be searched for an adjustment function that allows discriminating the influence of each of the mentioned factors.

Given the nature of our study, the use of adjustment processes is proposed for the determination of the non-deterministic model, using statistical and mathematical software such as Matlab, SPSS and R. The models were determined through of a regression analysis and an adjustment of Least Squares Regression (LSR), Least absolute residuals (LAR) and Least Trimmed Squares (LTS), moreover the comparison between the different models obtained from each adjustment. Furthermore, to the regression analysis, the behavior of the random error was observed between the MLR and the experimental data collected in the field for the interpretation.

3 Results

3.1 Propagation Modeling P_{RX}[DB]

The objective is to find an adjustment function to L. Based on the Longley-Rice model, different linear regressions has been performed, obtaining the results delivered by SPSS and R and shown in Table 1.

Table 1. Possible linear regressions made on SPSS and R.

#Model	Type	Coefficients	Std.Error	R^2
1st	Constant	71.806	4.997	0.798
1st	Log(d)	−48.215	1.545	−
2nd	Constant	136.378	11.181	0.8253
2nd	Log(f)	−50.903	1.491	−
2nd	Log(d)	−38.646	6.093	−
3rd	Constant	187.903	19.502	0.842
3rd	H	−0.147	−0.089	−
3rd	Log(f)	−52.443	−34.050	−
3rd	Log(d)	−43.908	−7.083	−

Given the significance of the variables, based on the comparison of the tolerance with the Variance Inflation Factor (VIF), the use of the variable that represents the height was discarded in the first and second model. This have some physical logic, because the variation of the height in the sample was very small and never exceeds tens units. However, into account the sum of the adjustment distances, the third model with the biggest R^2 of 0.842 was chosen, which in summary is the one shown below.

$$L = 187.90 - 0.147 * h - 52.443 * \log(d) - 43.908 * \log(f)$$

This model was compared with the Longley Rice model obtaining a 9% error which is less than 11% of the MLR, however, to improve the error, and adjustment was made.

3.2 Error in the Longley Rice Propagation Model and Reception Power (P_{LR})

In order to make an adjustment, is important to demonstrate that a dependent variable is not random, a form to verify this is by observing that it does not meet normally, and this can be done using the distribution function (CDF), which must fail in the adjustment with the graph of a CDF for an $\mathcal{N}(\mu = 0, \sigma^2)$. As seen in Fig. 1, the adjustment to a normal CDF is poor, also using the Kolgomorov test in Matlab and R, the statistic near zero confirms the non-normality of the waste vector. In this way we assume that there is no randomness in the e_{LR} data and the function can be adjusted.

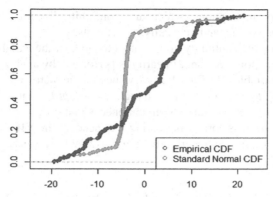

Fig. 1. Normality graphic test of the residual vector for the non-deterministic developed model.

The adjustment was done with error for that, first the error (e) of the Longley Rice model was define as the difference between the value of the receiver power (P_{RX}) and the power forecast delivered by the Longley Rice model (P_{LR}), such that:

$$e_{LR} = \log(P_{RX}) - \log(P_{LR})$$

By equating the error equation, and the equation of the model obtained above, a logarithmic type adjustment equation can be generated because the MLR was linearized by taking logarithms on both sides of the error equation, so we could say that the adjustment model can be expressed as follows:

$$\log(P_{Rx}) = \log(P_{LR}) \pm e_{LR}$$

where the P_{LR} is the power forecast delivered by the MLR and e_{LR} represents the random error. It was expected that since the P_{LR} is a function of h, f and d, therefore the fit model will be defined as:

$$\log(P_{Rx}) = A * \log(P_{LR}(h, f, d)) - B * \log(f) - C * \log(d) - D * h + E$$

The linear regression analysis was done by using SPSS and R, which delivered the coefficients for a linear regression adjustment with R^2 of 0.8979 and an error of 5,84% as follows:

$$\log(P_{Rx}) = 0.7 * \log(P_{LR}(h, f, d)) - 24.89 * \log(f) - 17 * \log(d) - 0.023 * h + 66.95$$

3.3 Adjustment of the Longley Rice Model Error by Least Squares Using Least Absolute Residuals (LAR)

The linear model of least squares allows the minimization of the sum of the squares of the residuals. In the case of a linear model there is no difference between the regression model and the least squares model, so the mathematical management is the same which means guaranteeing the six assumptions, which are: continuity, linearity, multicollinearity, homoscedasticity, parsimony and normality of residuals.

First to determine the continuity, it is enough to say that the variables take decimal data to guarantee this point. Second, linearity is performed by analyzing the degree of correlation of the variables. In Fig. 2, high values of the statistic r are observed for $log(P_{Rx}) - log(P_{LR})$, $log(P_{LR}) - log(d)$ and $log(P_{Rx}) - log(d)$, so it is defined that there is a linear relationship between the aforementioned variables except for height (h), so the generation of a linear is correct but taking into account the VIF index greater than the tolerance to avoid multicollinearity, the height variable is separated, resulting in a canonical model of form:

Table 2. Linear models with and without data filtering using LAR.

#Model	Type	Coefficients	R^2
Without filtering	Constant	16.91	0.9651
	Log(d)	−6.982	
	Log(f)	−4.942	
	P_{RL}	1	
With filtering	Constant	8.762	0.9746
	Log(d)	−4.218	
	Log(f)	−2.955	
	P_{RL}	1	

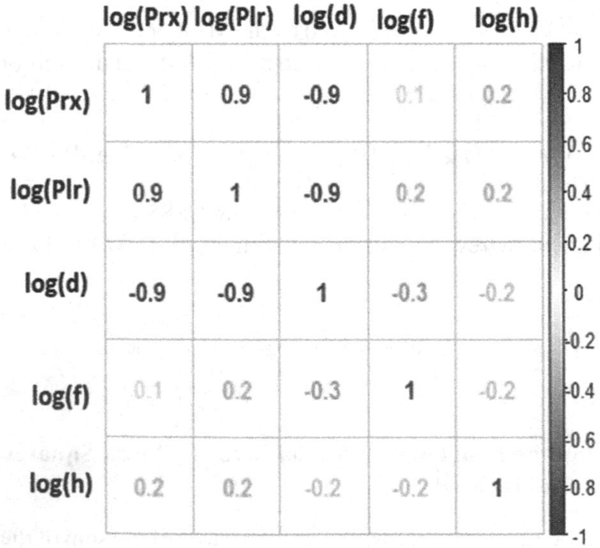

	log(Prx)	log(Plr)	log(d)	log(f)	log(h)
log(Prx)	1	0.9	-0.9	0.1	0.2
log(Plr)	0.9	1	-0.9	0.2	0.2
log(d)	-0.9	-0.9	1	-0.3	-0.2
log(f)	0.1	0.2	-0.3	1	-0.2
log(h)	0.2	0.2	-0.2	-0.2	1

Fig. 2. Collinearity matrix of the proposed propagation model.

$$e_{Lr}[dB] = A * \log(f) + B * \log(d) + C$$
$$\log(P_{RX})[dB] = A * \log(P_{LR}) + B * \log(d[m]) + C * \log(f[Mhz]) + D$$

For the calculation of the homoscedasticity of the model, an ANOVA analysis was carried out, where it can be concluded that the statistic being close to zero, shows that the sample of the model has homoscedasticity, however to improve the homoscedasticity of the model, it is important to filter the data to avoid anomalous data. The criterion that was used for the elimination of anomalous data was a technical criterion, since the reception powers below 120 dB, are considered noise. The result of the filtering is justified by observing the increase of the R^2 factor from 0.96 to 0.9747 (Table 2), which implies an improvement in the representativeness of the model with the respect to the variance of the sample, also obtaining an error of 4.9%. The model obtained was:

$$\log(P_{Rx}) = \log(P_{LR}(h, f, d)) - 2.955 * \log(f) - 4.218 * \log(d) + 8.762$$

3.4 Analysis of the Error and the Residual Vector of the Model Generated by LAR

To finalize the evaluation of the model, it is important to determine if the resulting residual vector meets the normal condition. Then a Kolmogorov test is performed with the residue vector. Comparing the significance of model (P value) with the Longley Rice model, while larger at 0.05 s better, this shows that ostensibly the error generated by the non-deterministic model improves the behavior compared to the MLR, however,

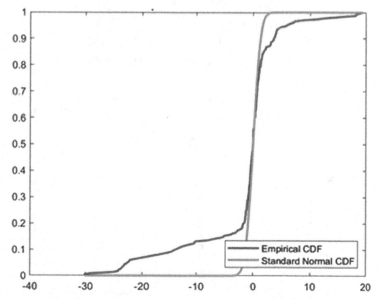

Fig. 3. Normality graphic test of the residuals vector for the non-deterministic model generated by LAR.

it continues to reject the null hypothesis of the Kolmogorov test, which implies non-normality. The summary of the tests carried out on both residuals vectors is observed in the Table 3. The improvement of the model is seen Fig. 3, where we see that the curve of residuals vectors is adjusted in better way to a normal CFD function than the first model.

3.5   Adjustment of the Longley Rice Model Error by Least Trimmed Squares (LTS)

To improve the previous model obtained, the LTS method was tested, using the *ltsreg ()* function, which is responsible for the elimination of the data considered as outliers. The resulting model was as follows:

$$\log(P_{Rx}) = 1.13 * \log(P_{LR}(h, f, d)) - 0.475 * \log(f) - 0.122 * \log(d) + 1.135$$

This model showed a better adjustment because it increased the representativeness of the data ($R^2 = 0.9995$), compared to the model previously developed. This shows that performing a debug of the outliers greatly improves the adjustment of the model.

3.6   Analysis of the Error and the Residual Vector of the Model Generated by LTS

To evaluate the improvement in the model, is important to determine if the resulting residuals vector meets the normal condition. For this, the Kolmogorov test with the

Table 3. Kolmogorov test comparison for the MLR and the developed models.

#Model	K-Statistical	P value	Error
Longley Rice	$1.82 * 10^{-6}$	0.175	11.85
LAR	$1.16 * 10^{-15}$	0.858	4.90
LTS	$2.68 * 10^{-6}$	0.169	4.75

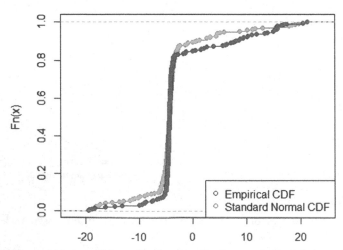

Fig. 4. Normality graphic test of the residuals vector for the non-deterministic model generated by LTS.

residuals vector and the graphic comparison is performed. Table 3 shows that the error generated by the model using LTS improves the behavior; compared to the other two models, however, it does not reach the normality. Moreover, Fig. 4 shows graphically that this model has a best curve fit than the other models.

4 Discussion

The strong LTS method provided greater representation and accuracy than the MLR and LAR, which statistically demonstrates the best model is to obtain the method by the LTS. This is due to the filtering performed by the method of outliers. This filtering consists in the iteration several times of the distances between the data errors, filtering those that are furthest from the set of similar errors [6].

Translating this filtering into technical terms, it can be seen in Table 4, that outliers do not correspond to data lees than −120 dB, so it is not possible to justify the thermal noise. These variations may be due to the wide range of climatic variations, that exist in the Amazon rainforest in short periods of time. This is corroborated by Al Hadidi and his collaborators [7] in 2016, who mention that radio signals have a direct dependence on the climatic conditions that exist in the medium through which it is being transmitted. Moreover, Armanjama [8] similarly in 2016, mentioned that the conditions that would most affect the emergence of outliers are atmospheric temperature, pressure and humidity.

Therefore, in future investigations it is recommended to take into account weather conditions to verify that the outliers are produced by climatic conditions and not by any other interference.

Table 4. Outliers data of the LTS model.

P_{RX}	d	f	P_{TX}
−92,36	1810	20	1
−90,12	1810	20	1
−95,7	1810	20	1
−96,36	1810	20	1
−95,07	1810	20	1
−89,2	1810	20	20
−60,1	2060	20	20
−68	2060	20	5
−78	2060	20	1

(continued)

Table 4. (*continued*)

P_{RX}	d	f	P_{TX}
−76	2060	20	1
−72	2060	20	1
−71	2060	20	1
−79	2060	20	1
−112,92	11650	30	5
−110,91	11650	30	5
−112,36	11650	30	5
−111,3	11650	30	5
−144	11650	30	5
−147,1	11650	30	1
−147,91	11650	30	1
−148,17	11650	30	1
148,05	11650	30	1

5 Conclusions

The adjustment model for the calculation of the P_{RX} power that best marches the conditions of the Ecuadorian rainforest is that obtained by the LTS method, which represents 99.995% of the total variance of the sample, and generates an error of less than 5%, reducing more than half of the error generated by the Longley Rice model. Furthermore, since the residue vector of the Longley Rice model does not meet the normality characteristics, is exposed that after the adjustments there is still a dependence of the model to the variables already taken into account in the process. Finally, it was shown that the addition of the multiplier coefficient of the P_{LR} power of the linear regression could be understood as a correction of the MLR.

References

1. Cruz, C.: Mapa bioclimático y ecológico del Ecuador, 1st edn. Central Bank of Ecuador, Quito (1983)
2. Villavicencio, M.: Geografía de la República del Ecuador, 3rd edn. Scholar select, New York (2015)
3. Luzuriaga, G., Semanate, A.: Análisis de las capacidades del sistema de comunicaciones troncalizado del ejército y su viabilidad futura, 1st edn. Force Army University, Quito (2018)
4. Kasampalis, S., Lazaridis, P., Zharis, Z., Cosmas, J.: Comparison of Longley-Rice ITM and ITWOM propagation moldes for DTV and F broadcasting. In: International Symposium on Wireless Personal Multimedia Communications, vol. 16, no. 1, pp. 1546–1553 (2013)

5. Kasampalis, S., Lazaridis, P., Zharis, Z., Cosmas, J.: Comparison of Longley-Rice, ITU-R P.1546 and Hata-Davidson propagation models for DVB-T coverage prediction. In: IEEE International Symposium on Broadband Multimedia Systems and Broadcasting, vol. 14, no. 1, pp. 1–4 (2014)
6. Roozbeth, M., Arashi, M.: Least-trimmed squares: asymptotic normality of robust estimator in semiparametric regression models. J. Stat. Comput. Simul. 1(6), 1130–1147 (2016)
7. Al Haddi, M., Al-zzeh, J., Odarchenko, R., Gnatyuk, S., Abakumova, A.: Adpative regulation of radiated power radio transmitting devices in modern cellular network depending on climatic conditions. Contemp. Eng. Sci. 9(10), 473–485 (2016)
8. Armajama, J.: Impact of weather components on (UHF) radio signal. Int. J. Eng. Res. Gen. Sci. 4(3), 481–494 (2016)

Performance Analysis of Radio Frequency Identification Technology in Race Timing Systems

Daniel Iturralde$^{(\boxtimes)}$ (iD), Pedro Peralta (iD), Andrés Cabrera (iD),
and Gabriel Delgado (iD)

Universidad del Azuay, Cuenca, Ecuador
{diturralde,santiago193,apcabrera,gabrieldelgadoes}@uazuay.edu.ec

Abstract. The following work implements a race timing system for running events using Radio Frequency Identification technology (RFID). We determined the best position to place the tags on athletes and antennas in the finish line. For this, several tests were made placing the antennas and tags in different configurations and heights. The results show that the hip tagging on athletes with antennas placed on the ground is the suitable configuration.

Keywords: RFID · Race timing systems · Performance

1 Introduction

There are several factors that can create difficulties in a running event organization, namely the assignment of personnel to register the participants and to carry out the monitoring and verification of athletes, both at the starting line and at the finish line. In addition, the personnel assigned to control and monitor the race usually makes mistakes when registering partial time records, which is detrimental in the final outcome of the race. These processes should be executed with greater precision and efficiency by an automated system in order to provide better and accurate results [1].

Manual timing systems introduce errors that create issues for participants and organizers, so it is necessary to improve the acquisition method through a system that eliminates human error. This work aims to implement a useful tool to improve the time acquisition of participants in athletic races and reduce the measurement error introduced by the human factor. By using radio frequency identification (RFID) systems, it is possible to reduce delays in data acquisition processes and provide quick access to a large amount of information, in addition to be suitable to be used outdoors.

The paper is organized as follows. Section 2 is dedicated to the analysis of the state of the art, Sect. 3 shows the methods to tag runners, Sect. 4 establishes the hardware design, Sect. 5 shows the tests and results. Finally, Sect. 6 is dedicated to conclusions based on the results obtained.

© Springer Nature Switzerland AG 2020
M. Botto-Tobar et al. (Eds.): ICAT 2019, CCIS 1195, pp. 104–112, 2020.
https://doi.org/10.1007/978-3-030-42531-9_9

2   State of the Art

The work in [5] aims to implement a bicycle theft management system, certification and competition, to assist the bicycle production industry with an after-sales service. Authors describe the problem of effective management in the certification, sales and control of bicycle theft. In addition, it is mentioned that industries have tried to solve these problems using RFID tags placed under bicycle seats with an antenna and a special reader. However, authors point out that privacy is one of the main problems because customers don't want their belongings to be tracked all the time.

In [7], the optimization of a standard UHF (Ultra High Frequency) RFID system for the identification of athletes in mass races was proposed, implemented and verified. This work based its execution studying the main causes of failures in previous systems. The improvements proposed and implemented were focused on the development of more efficient and directive antennas for both the reader and the transponder, and the optimization of their location and orientation. The propagation model used was able to describe the existing fading phenomena and predict the signal levels received anywhere in a 5 m wide finishing corridor. The optimized RFID system was tested in a standard outdoor operation, and results showed an identification reliability of 100%.

In [8], authors describe that running events in local communities count with low budgets and limited personnel assigned for managing. This causes that the investment in ultra-high frequency identification systems and existing timing systems becomes too expensive to be considered in the use of such events. To solve these problems, authors propose a cost-effective interactive platform based on low frequency RFID devices, which helps to manage racing events, store runner specifications, manage data through a centralized database, and show the participant information such as time and total laps in real time. Finally, authors specify that the proposed system was used in a race running event at the Assumption University between January 23-February 28, 2017.

The project's main objective in [6] is to implement RFID tags and high frequency RFID readers as detectors, which connect directly to the event organizer's computer without using an interface circuit. This system has been developed using Microsoft Visual Basic, which offers the possibility of creating a graphical user interface (GUI) to show the results. The database for this system is developed in Microsoft Access (MA).

At [4], a low-cost, high-performance UHF RFID system that uses Arduino based on IoT (Internet of Things) applications for a marathon competition is presented. An antenna for readers, tag antennas, a reading and writing program for labels and the application screen in Android operating system were designed and built. In addition, the system was manufactured at a very low cost. The measurement results of the reader antenna have a gain of 7.24 dBi with a directional radiation pattern; the tag antenna has a gain of 2.05 dBi with an omnidirectional radiation pattern and the system presents good test results. The results of the coverage range are enough for 8 race lanes and the program can correctly classify runners. The system can store race data in a cloud storage system.

3   RFID Applied in Race Timing Systems

The system proposed in this work uses a configuration of two panel type antennas and a reader. This configuration works well with a group of 50 to 200 athletes. Since there are only two antennas for reading, this configuration must have a reading area of 1.83 m to guarantee tags reads. It is necessary to adapt the structure to be able to position the antennas so that they have a clear view with respect to the tag to increase the reading success [3].

As for the most efficient way to obtain information from athletes, there are four ways to attach tags on them, these are [2]:

- Bib tagging: in this type of tagging the runner uses a tag in the chest area, as can be seen in Fig. 1. In this case the tag can be aligned horizontally or vertically, depending on the polarization of the antenna. This type of tagging reduces the risk that the runner movements cause errors in the reading. However, the reading range may be limited due to the interference that can be caused by the human body. It is possible to reduce this problem by creating a separation between the tag and the body of the runner by using a foam spacer. As for the configuration of the antenna, if a panel type antenna is used, it is recommended to use two on the sides of the track focused towards the center of the control point and at chest height. It is also recommended to use circularly polarized antennas to avoid reading problems regarding the position of the tag in the participant. An alternative arrangement for panel type antennas may be to use four antennas, two at the top of the control point, and two at the sides at chest height. If carpet type antennas linearly polarized are to be used, it is recommended that the tag be placed vertically. It is necessary to test the tags angles with respect to the antenna in any configuration to achieve efficient reading levels.

Fig. 1. Bib tagging.

– Double bib tagging: This type of tagging consists of two tags in the chest area, each aligned differently or in the same way, as seen in Fig. 2. The main advantage of using this method is that the chances of obtaining a reading are increased. However, there are two main problems related to this method: the first has to do with the increase in the cost of the system due to the use of two tags, and the second has to do with the reduction of the reading range due to the interference that can cause the human body, as in the previous case. It is possible to reduce the latter by creating a separation between the tag and the runner's body by using a foam spacer. The same antenna configuration of the bib tagging method can be used.

Fig. 2. Double bib tagging.

– Shoe tagging: shoe tagging consists of placing a tag on one of the runner's shoes as shown in Fig. 3. This method is used in races with a small number of participants and the tag is secured in the shoe laces of the runner. This method is used to increase the probability of reading, because there is less interference due to its location in a relatively small part of the body. A disadvantage presented by this method is that the orientation of the tag cannot be determined due to the movement generated by the runner, thus the polarity of the antenna has to be circular. Due to this inconvenience, this method is not recommended for races with a large number of participants. In this type of tagging method at least two panel antennas circularly polarized are used at the sides of the control point, and the antennas must be located at a height of 0.3 m from the ground.

– Hip tagging: this type of tagging is used for small races. In this method two tags are placed on the hips of the runners, one on the left side and one on the right, as can be seen in Fig. 4. This method allows to increase the probability of obtaining a reading in one or both of the tags. However, the cost is increased, and the density of the area of the human body in which is attached can generate attenuation, and therefore the reading range is reduced. As for the configuration of the antennas, it is possible to use a linear or circular

Fig. 3. Shoe tagging.

polarization, with two panel type antennas that are at the height of the hip at the sides of the control point. The antennas should point as far as possible to the location of the tags to obtain the best results.

Fig. 4. Hip tagging.

4   Hardware Design

To determine the ideal position for the antennas a series of tests were carried out with the antennas and tags at different heights (10 cm, 75 cm, 1 m, 1.25 m, and 1.50 m from the ground). In the first case the antennas were set at ground level, and a power measurement was performed at the tags at each height. In the second case the antennas were placed on the sides at 1.25 m from the ground, and the power measurement procedure with the tags was the same as in the previous case. In the third case the antennas were placed 2.5 m from the ground and the measurement was the same as in the previous two cases. Figure 5 shows the antenna and tag configuration for each case.

Fig. 5. Experimental design.

5   Results

With the information obtained through the graphs mentioned above, a better understanding of the behavior of the power surfaces in each of the cases presented can be achieved. However, to perform a better analysis it is necessary to develop the power profile of each surface. Table 1 presents each of the profiles for all antenna and tag configurations.

The first thing that can be observed is that most of the profiles have a power level above the 70 Received Signal Strength Indicator (RSSI) scale. This indicates that it is possible to use any of the antenna and tag configurations for the 3 m wide by 2.5 m height portal. However, certain configurations do not guarantee that in every case a tag reading occurs when it passes through the antenna reading fields.

Due to this, it was decided to verify which of the different profiles presented had the largest coverage area with a power level that guarantees the reading of the tag on the finish line area. After analyzing the graphs, it can be observed that the configuration of antennas at ground level and tags at 75 cm covers the largest possible area and guarantees that a reading of the tags takes place within the target area. This is because the RSSI power level is in a range greater than or equal to 90 RSSI.

To determine the accuracy of each antenna and tag configuration, 100 measurements were made at different speeds. Table 2 shows the results obtained, and the configuration with greater precision again the one with tags at 75 cm and antennas at ground level.

Table 1. RSSI power profiles for different tag and antenna settings

	Tags at 10cm	Tags at 75cm	Tags at 1m	Tags at 1,25m	Tags at 1,5m
Antennas at floor level					
Antennas at 1,25 m from floor					
Antennas at 2,5 m from floor					

■ 60-65   ■ 65-70   ■ 70-75   ■ 75-80   ■ 80-85
■ 85-90   ■ 90-95   ■ 95-100   ■ 100-105   ■ 105-110

Table 2. Percentage of precision of each configuration

	Tags at 10cm	Tags at 75cm	Tags at 1m	Tags at 1,25m	Tags at 1,5m
Antennas at floor level					
Antennas at 1,25 m from floor					
Antennas at 2,5 m from floor					

6   Conclusions

After having carried out a series of tests on the proposed timing system, it was observed that it improved the acquisition times of the participants because the software together with the hardware developed allowed storing the information of a runner in a database at the moment that it passes through the reading field located at the starting and finish line. Because the system is responsible for reading all the runners information, it can be established that the runners will not be affected in their times by human errors.

It is important to emphasize that the system, in addition to improving the acquisition times of the participants, allowed to establish that the best tag method for a system with two panel type antenna configuration is the hip tagging. This is due to the analysis performed in each of the power profiles obtained in Table 1 and the precision of the system of Table 2, which shows that this configuration has the largest coverage area, and therefore, the least loss of data in the reading process.

Acknowledgements. This research was funded by Project UDA 2019-0083, UDA 2019-0084 and UDA 2019-0230.

References

1. atlasRFIDstore.com: A guide to building your own timing system (2015)
2. atlasRFIDstore.com: How to properly tag racers (2015)
3. atlasRFIDstore.com: Selecting the right equipment (2015)
4. Chokchai, C.: Low cost and high performance UHF RFID system using Arduino based on IoT applications for marathon competition. In: 2018 21st International Symposium on Wireless Personal Multimedia Communications (WPMC), pp. 15–20, November 2018. https://doi.org/10.1109/WPMC.2018.8713018
5. Lin, K.-Y., Hsu, M.-W., Liou, S.-R.: Bicycle management systems in anti-theft, certification, and race by using RFID. In: Proceedings of 2011 Cross Strait Quad-Regional Radio Science and Wireless Technology Conference, vol. 2, pp. 1054–1057, July 2011. https://doi.org/10.1109/CSQRWC.2011.6037138
6. Misran, M.H., et al.: Smart le tour checkpoint using RFID. In: 2014 International Symposium on Technology Management and Emerging Technologies, pp. 246–251, May 2014. https://doi.org/10.1109/ISTMET.2014.6936514
7. Polivka, M., Svanda, M., Hudec, P.: The optimization of the RFID system for the identification of sportsmen in mass races. In: 2007 European Microwave Conference, pp. 732–735, October 2007. https://doi.org/10.1109/EUMC.2007.4405296
8. Satitsuksanoh, P., Jiamthapthaksin, R., Kim, S.W., Setthawong, P.: A cost-effective interactive platform for the management of a small scale lap-based jogging competition using low-frequency RFID technology. In: 2017 3rd International Conference on Science in Information Technology (ICSITech), pp. 360–365, October 2017. https://doi.org/10.1109/ICSITech.2017.8257139

Low Power Wide Area Network: Technical Review for Wireless sensor Networks and Its Utilization in Smart Cities Deployment Through Internet of Things (IoT) System

Diego F. Paredes-Páliz$^{(\boxtimes)}$ (ID), Edgar Maya-Olalla (ID), José C. Nogales-Romero (ID), and Cristian A. Padilla-Calderón (ID)

Universidad Técnica del Norte, Ibarra 100105, Ecuador
{dfparedes,eamaya,jcnogalesr,capadillac}@utn.edu.ec

Abstract. World communications are changing very fast due mainly for technology advances where new and all type of devices have been connected to present and future networks that requires low information amount transmission while increasing the time and periods when data is transmitted. The scenario is ideal for Low Power Wide Area Network (LPWAN) technologies that allows efficient communications, reliable and with low power consumption. This work proposes a technical review using simulation software to determine which LPWAN technology offers a realistic implementation solution for wireless sensor networks (WSN) to build smart cities that connects a diversity of mobile and fixed devices with an Internet of Things (IoT) architecture and reliable data transmission, protocol operation, data transfer rate configuration and frequency assignment. All these duties are results of network simulations modifying user interface parameters and simulation conditions, giving an accurate diagram network when it is possibly to configure protocol, network topology, data flow, frequency band, receiver sensibility, power transmission and others.

Keywords: LPWAN · IoT · Smart cities · LoRA · NB-IoT · Wireless Sensor Networks

1 Introduction

Low Power Wide Area Network (also known as LPWAN, LPWA, or LPN) is a wireless transport data protocol, today is the principal and most used protocol to develop mainly Internet of things networks. Internet of things (IoT) is defined as a system that interconnects devices no matter their nature or purpose, these devices can be mechanical or digital and generates a signal, also allows to interrelate persons, objects and animals with a unique identifier (UID) to transfer information over a network without H2H or human-to-computer interaction [1].

© Springer Nature Switzerland AG 2020
M. Botto-Tobar et al. (Eds.): ICAT 2019, CCIS 1195, pp. 113–126, 2020.
https://doi.org/10.1007/978-3-030-42531-9_10

IoT Networks require low power consumption devices, a long range coverage and variable data rate transfer. Previous research works present results analyzing transmission data amount, devices number, network topology, data flow control, data storage, device power consumption and so on. Main conclusion aims to increase autonomous operation with a proper battery duration on devices. All this launch LPWAN as major IoT technology around the world.

All these networks are designed to work over next generation wireless networks and 5G networks, then frequency bands assignation should share spectral occupancy with existing mobile networks and technologies. This work proposes 2G frequency bands re utilization, thus the hypothesis is to try a Wireless Sensor Network deployment over LPWAN, to accomplish a simulation scenario, two technologies are tested: one LoRaWAN with out a standard supported and a defined standard, Narrowband IoT (NB-IoT).

Previous works mention that coverage range for bidirectional connections between the end device (node in LoRaWAN and mote in NB-IoT) for urban and rural areas are known. LoRaWAN in urban areas allows a maximum coverage range of 5 Km and for rural areas reach a coverage range of 20 Km. Same situation occurs in NB-IoT networks, where the maximum coverage range is 1 Km for urban areas and 10 Km in rural areas [2].

The LoRaWA (Long Range Wide Area) network is a non standardized protocol that use the LoRa modulation technology to communicate and manage LoRa devices with an architecture where gateways and nodes connects each other. The LoRaWA (Long Range Wide Area) network is a non standardized protocol that use the LoRa modulation technology to communicate and manage LoRa devices with an architecture where gateways and nodes connects each other. To consider as a important point the difference between LoRa and LoRaWAN, these are not the same, LoRaWAN is network protocol while LoRa is the type of radio-frequency modulation patented by Semtech with several characteristics and advantages, where main are: interference tolerance, high sensitivity, on chirp modulation based, low power consumption, long range coverage, P2P connection [3].

Authentication and encryption issues in LoRaWAN technology are solved in previous research works, employing 128-byte AES authentication and defines two main security keys: NwkSKey and AppSKey where each key has a length of 128 bits. The NwkSKey session key is used to provide data integrity between the end user and the network server (i.e. it is used for network layer security and checking the message validity). The AppSKey is used to provide data confidentiality between the end node and network server or end user application (i.e. it is used to encrypt and decrypt application payload). The application payload is encrypted using AES-128 algorithm [4].

Narrowband IoT (NB-IoT) technology is a standardized type of LPWA network, with very similar characteristics between the other types of LPWAN such as LoRaWAN and SigFox in coverage range terms, energy consumption and frequency band configuration. It is ideal for devices that generate not very high data traffic and have a long life cycle. It uses the existing mobile network to connect all these devices. The advantages are: improvement of indoor coverage, low cost, reliable, simple network deployment, adequate number of connections by cell.

On the other hand, NB-IoT technology has its authentication and encryption given by the parameters of IEEE 802.15.4 and 3GPP [5].

This work analyzes both technologies in order to compare their behaviour and performance in simulation environments to determine devices parametrization to be used in LPWA networks. Network topology scheme is star, because all the devices or nodes will be connected directly to a central point acting as a gateway (node) and also the nodes could be connected between them. More details and explanation is further presented.

2 Methodology

LPWA network deployment at moment proposes new applications for devices connectivity, for this reason is necessary define a wireless network operation scenario employing some licensed or unlicensed simulation software as a previous step to design network solutions. Some developers that are working on LPWAN are working with NS3 software, that allows to access to python and C archives of source. One found issue refer to graphic interface user is nos available, simulations results are saved over virtual machine files and exportation of these is complex. Due this limitations this work discard NS3 as an accurate simulation software in this research.

After that, was time to evaluate GNS3 software, the main difference with previous one is the possibility to work over a graphic interface where devices can be displayed. However simulation software results obsolete in terms of older libraries and the absence of new technologies for LPWAN networks, therefore this software was discarded too.

Simple Soft® has developed a demo software called SimpleioTSimulator that allows analyze LoRa network whit defined network configuration where all parameters are defined as default, thus results can not be exported or processed to obtain network behaviour or establish a new design. This determine over other reasons to exclude any possibility to continue with a trial software, where data results analysis and user network configuration is essential for this work.

After a practice analysis of many other simulation software there are two unlicensed software with a graphic interface, allows network and device configuration also export results to evaluate network design performance for LPWAN. Both simulation software are installed on two computers, Omnet++ for the LoRa networks in a physical machine and Cooja from Contiki for NB-IoT networks that works with a virtual machine respectively.

Around the world there are several tends around Internet of Things (IoT) applications for this technology. As happen in wireless design networks a software simulation gives the opportunity to RF engineers define network operation parameters and adjust to user design and simulation environment, where results approximate as much as can to real network performance.

OMNeT++ Networks simulator (OMNeT++: Version: 5.2.1, Build id: 171211-da8f6bc, 2017-INet Framework 3.6.3) [6] in one of its most recent and stable versions (5.2.1), this tool help us with the task mentioned above and works together with a specific Framework for this type of applications, specifically INET Framework 3.6.3, to simulate devices with a specific LoRa configuration, using an external framework created called FLoRa, that is "FLoRa (Framework for LoRa) is a simulation framework for carrying out end-to-end simulations for LoRa networks. It is based on the OMNeT++ network simulator and uses components from the INET framework as well." [7], aiming at analyzing characteristic requirements of the Internet of Things, going from secure bidirectional data connections between a main entity and a node, for the study, observation and parameterization of all the phenomena and main characteristics that are presented over a wireless link.

A network can work with LoRa protocol, understanding that devices need connection with a equipment in a central point, configuring star topology for network simulation. This scenario can be recognized as node where all devices connects to a gateway that collects data from user devices or several nodes where all these can communicate each other, to finally carry all information to a main server.

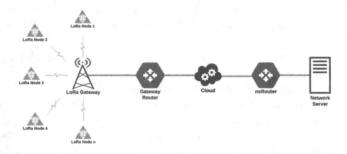

Fig. 1. Network topology used during the investigation in both softwares

As is shown in Fig. 1, each LoRa node has a direct link with the LoRa gateway, which collects data generated for each node, and then sends information to main gateway and proceed to route it, either directly to a local server to process the information or use internet protocol to access from an ISP for data processing in local or remote way. Each one of the LoRa nodes has similar characteristics, which allows an effective communication with the main node (LoRa Gateway), where assigned frequency band from 900 MHz to 1800 MHz, specifically 915 MHz, that means 2G mobile band is used for this type of communications, thanks to the use of this portion of the frequency spectrum we can say that LoRa is a long-range wireless platform, efficient and low power consumption that demands few resources, and that over the past few years has become in de facto standard for Internet of Things (IoT) around the world, that configure intelligent IoT applications development to solve some of the greatest challenges in so many areas of interest as it could be: energy efficiency, natural resources reduction, pollution control, sensor control administration, infrastructure efficiency, disaster prevention and more [8].

NB-IoT case, network specifications are similar to LoRa networks, so this work is centered to determinate which one support a more realistic network design to develop a LPWAN that can be used as technology for Internet of Things and identify on configuration differences between NB-IoT and LoRa. One more detail, NB-IoT software simulation uses Cooja for Contiki for Ubuntu 12.04 for 32 bits (Table 1).

Table 1. Details of the virtual machine used for Cooja.

Host	User (Instant Contiki)
Operating system	Ubuntu 12.04.2 LTS (32-bits)
Operating system version	#77-Ubuntu SMP Wed Jul 24 20:40:32 UTC 2013
OS manufacturer	Linux Corporation
Configuration	Instant Contiki
OS compilation	GNU C Compiler version 4.6.3
Type of system	x32
Processor(s)	Authentic AMD 2700 MHz
KERNEL version	Linux 3.2.0-51-generic-pae(i686)
Total RAM	4.127 MB

A virtual machine was used: Oracle® VM Virtual Box 6.0 GUI, 6.0.8 r130520 Version, to execute the Ubuntu Operating System (Ubuntu 12.04/32bits) to run Contiki Software. Contiki software (Cooja: The Contiki Network Simulator, Java version: 1.7.0_25(Oracle Corporation) System "os.arch" : i386, System "sun.arch.data.model":32) [9] uses a configuration based in motes (hardware interface) that emulates any device with a connectivity requirement to LPWAN or data server. Graphic interface calls some of motes to make the performance analysis of network design. The motes, also called sensor node, are sensors where are established the wireless node in order to communicate the gateway between them.

The mote employed for NB-IoT network technology analysis is Tmote Sky. This mote is a low power wireless sensor module that has many things to offer like high data rate sensor network applications requiring ultra-low power. Some other features to look out for are high reliability and ease of deployment summing that It is widely proven platform for wireless sensor systems installation.

The key features of the Tmote Sky are as follows: 1. Inter-operability with many different IEEE 802.15.4 devices 2. Integrated on-board antenna, with 50 m range for indoors and 125 m range at outdoors. 3. Optional Integrated humidity, temperature and light sensors 4. Ultra low current consumption. 5. Fast wake up from sleep 6. Programming data fed via USB and data collected via USB too.

7. SMA antenna connector and 16 pin expansion support. 8. TinyOS support, also the implementation of communication and mesh networking. 9. The FCC modular certification provided conforms to all US and Canada regulations. 10. User and reset button 11. CC2420 RF Chip, TI MSP430F1611 Microcontroller 12. IEEE 802.15.4 WSN mote fully compatible with TelosB platform" [10].

Another considerably difference between LoRa and NB-IoT is that Tmote Sky operates at 2.4 GHz frequency only, this is an universal band worldwide assigned, also energy consumption is a characteristic that is not available to configure because Tmote already exists in market and has a very low power consumption.

Network topology was the same used in the LoRa analysis but in this case with specifications given by the manufactures of the Tmote Sky and the gateway equipment. The objective of this research is to obtain results of how much the bit rate, and energy consumption change in both cases, considering several network design environments.

It is necessary consider data collection from all simulations to obtain desired results and its post processing due that any simulation has their aforementioned configuration. Data results is centered in terms of bit rate, energy consumption, reliability, range, losses, operating frequency and so on.

3   Results

3.1   Pre-simulation Parameters

To start the simulations, it is necessary to parameterize the network elements, as well as the medium in which each of the technologies (LoRa and NB-IoT) will be analyzed taking as reference network topology cited on methodology section. Since the operating frequencies are different, each of the network elements will have different characteristics in terms of transmission and reception, as well as the medium in which the simulation will be carried out, based on LoRa Medium for LoRa WAN and UDGM medium simulations for NB-IoT simulations (Table 2).

The UDGM (Unit Disk Graph Medium) Medium is a parameterization already established by the Cooja program, where the transmission, reception, signal, noise and interferences, are given in function of the losses due to the distance between the motes (Table 3).

Thus, the nodes and motes are parameterized following the guidelines of the medium and the established operating frequencies. NB-IoT technology uses Sky motes, according to Release 13 of 3GPP [5] which force the use of wireless network standard IEEE 802.15.4. In this part of the investigation, it was made tests with different motes Sky type in the Cooja software until achieving stability and better results with the mote Tmote Sky, for which it is necessary the access to the data sheet of the mote MTM-CM5000-MSP [10] to approach in a better way the parameterizations of the same ones (Table 4).

For LoRa WAN node parameters, it is important to take into account that parameters mentioned above are based on devices that are currently on the

Table 2. Details of LoRaWAN and NB-IoT Gateway

Gateway parameters		
Parameter	LoRa WAN	NB-IoT
Antenna type	Isotropic antenna	Microstrip antenna
Carrier frequency	915 MHz	2450 MHz
Bandwidth	0.915 MHz	0.180 MHz
Bitrate	91.5 kbps	200 kbps
Receiver sensitivity	−100 dBm	−141 dBm
Minimum interference power	−120 dBm	−76 dBm
Minimum SNIR	−8 dB	−7 dB (13 dB of re−Tx)
Transmission power	2.24 mW	199.53 mW
Preamble duration	0.001 s	0.0056 s
Antenna gain	2 dB	5 dBi

Table 3. Medium LoRa and NB-IoT

LoRa and NB-IoT medium		
Parameter	LoRa WAN	NB-IoT
Propagation type	Constant speed propagation	UDGM: distance loss
Model type	LoRa analog model	UDGM: distance loss
Path loss type	Normal shadowing (d = 40 m; gamma = 2,08; sigma = 3,57)	UDGM: distance loss
Background noise power	−96.616 dBm	UDGM: distance loss

Table 4. Parameters of the sensors in NB-IoT and LoRa WAN.

Mote and node parameters		
Parameters	LoRa WAN	NB-IoT
Antenna type	Isotropic antenna	Dipole/PCB antenna
Carrier frequency	915 MHz	2450 MHz
Bandwidth	0.915 MHz	0.180 MHz
Bitrate	91.5 kbps	200 kbps
Receiver sensitivity	−137 dBm	−95 dBm
Minimum interference	−120 dBm	−25 dBm
Minimum SNIR	−8 dB	−7 dB
Transmission power	25.11 mW	45.24 mW
Preamble duration	0.001 s	0.056 s
Antenna gain	2 dB	5 dBi

market, so it can be said that it is possible to take reference values from different brands or systems with very similar characteristics, to perform a simulation with a good approximation of wireless link communication.

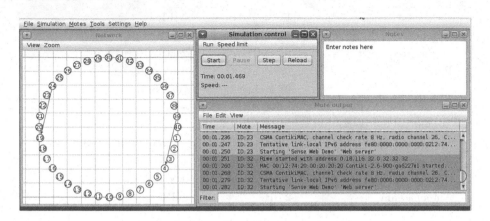

Fig. 2. Network topology used by NB-IoT Technology in Cooja, the Contiki Simulator

Simulations requires nodes and motes distribution, given as result a network topology, devices are distributed in an elliptical way as is shown in Figs. 2 and 3, where the number of nodes and motes changes, at beginning doubling their number to observe the behavior where network throughput increases with same proportion when devices number rises, starting with 10 devices in both cases.

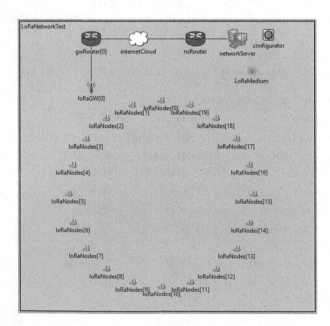

Fig. 3. Network topology used by LoRaWAN technology in Omnet++ simulator

It is important to analyze that when making an IoT simulation it is necessary to take into account the application to which the study is going to be submitted, that is why it is necessary to have a previous knowledge of the environment in which we will work, and because LPWAN applications are intended to facilitate communication between potentially nearby nodes and assigned specific jobs, they become best options for tasks that demand a low data flow, so once the information is collected through LoRa nodes, the data must be post processed, however, when an analysis is made of those data and the context in which they have been obtained, they become information.

3.2 Simulation Results

Tmote Sky uses IEEE 802.15.4 wireless network protocol, under this condition, simulation automatically assigns IP addresses using IPv6. The positions of the nodes and motes are given in geographical coordinates, center of ellipse is located in center of this and from here can be measured major radio and minor radio, where nodes or motes assignment follow clockwise direction (Figs. 2 and 3) with a appropriate distance between them for a better analysis of wide area network.

Each mote work in cycles, it has a storage buffer to save reading information for a while, after that it is sent to eNodeB gateway and network server. This cycle is given by a read period, a storage period, and the last writing period. For other side Tmote Sky has a micro-controller where storage of information is made.

As can be seen in Tables 5 and 6, devices energy consumption is extremely low, the currents consumed for each cycle is very low and the total energy consumption per cycle does not even exceed 0.7% of total battery consumption, so devices useful life estimates about 10 years [11].

Table 5. LoRa WAN simulations results

LoRaWAN results	
Amount of data	4 octets prelude, 1 octet info, 7 bit frame length, 1 bit reserved
Number of nodes	20
Total devices	25
Modulation	DSSS (Direct Sequence Spread Spectrum)
Distribution scheme	Elliptical
Power consumption	9.6 mA in RX mode - 16.4 mA in TX mode
Frequency band	902–928 MHz
Channels	64
UpLink channel	125/500 kHz
DownLink channel	500 kHz
BitRate	980 bps–211.9 kbps

Results analysis present graphs of bit rate as a function of the distance between nodes, for LoRaWAN technology (Fig. 4):

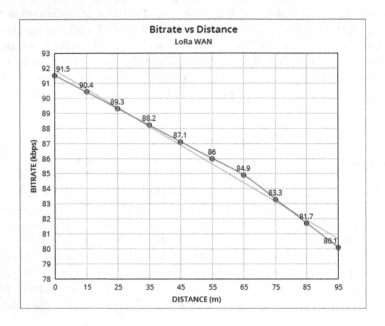

Fig. 4. Bitrate (kbps) vs. distance (m)

Table 6. NB-IoT simulations results

NB-IoT results			
Parameters	10 Motes	20 Motes	40 Motes
Data quantity	Packet data (64 bytes)	Cross level packet data (62 Bytes)	Cross level packet data (62 Bytes)
Devices number	14 total devices	24 total devices	44 total devices
Topology network	Ellipse motes	Ellipse motes	Ellipse motes
Data flow control	Multipoint real time	Multipoint real time	Multipoint real time
Data storage	64 Bytes per cycle	62 Bytes per cylce	62 Bytes per cylce
Energy consumption	0.14% Tx 0.01% Rx	0.24% Tx 0.04% Rx	0.57% Tx 0.09% Rx

NB-IoT technology results are presented below:

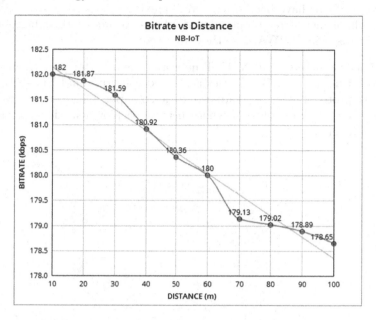

Fig. 5. Bitrate (kbps) vs. distance(m)

From the perspective of nodes communication and LoRa Gateway, it is necessary to consider all the parameters that can be settled in wireless medium, where the distance from a node to Gateway takes an important role, because if longer is length to be covered, more obstacles could be appear, then communication became less reliable and the bit rate decreases. This pushes LoRa devices usage as a alternative medium range applications with a low data flow because they have high interference tolerance characteristics provided by the frequency band used on this technology (Fig. 5).

As is showed in the graph above bit rate decreases if distance increases, in any wireless network there are some variables that responds to a specific propagation model, free space losses explains results obtained in this work, moreover simulation software user must be clear that over RF link appear obstacles that also affect power signal. In any case, LoRa devices work with 2G frequency bands and have excellent reception sensitivity characteristics (from -145 to -168 dB) it can be said that a reliable connection can be established regardless of the number of obstacles for a medium distance (<1 km), taking into account that it will always be a communication with low resources in terms of data flow.

In both cases data transmission rate decreases with distance, however bit rate reduction is quite small, where there is not data information losses. The graphs made for both technologies show the inverse proportional relationship that exists between distance and bit rate, thus for a bigger distance between nodes a lower bit rate is measured, and at the same time energy consumption will be greater.

There are several parameters where it is possible define an importance impact, some of this have been discussed in previous research works. Said that, different technologies were compared and related to predict their behaviour in sensor networks using LPWAN, so they are cited:

– **QoS**: Quality of service in NB-IoT networks has a better performance than LoRaWAN networks, NB-IoT uses a licensed spectrum and LTE-based synchronous protocol, this is traduced in a cost per megahertz, meanwhile LoRaWAN is a good solution where network deployment does not require such characteristic.

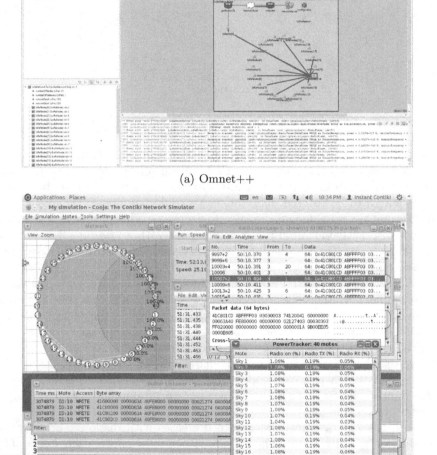

(a) Omnet++

(b) Cooja

Fig. 6. Simulation in Omnet++ for LoRa Network (a) and Cooja, the Contiki Simulator for NB-IoT network (b)

- **Latency Performance**: NB-IoT performs low latency networks. In other hand LoRa class C provides low bidirectional latency with energy consumption increasing.
- **Scalability & Payload length**: Both technologies work well with a large number of connected devices. There were registered a huge quantity of end devices working with NB-IoT reaching up to 100 K per cell compared to 50 K per cell for LoRa [2].

Finally, the following figures show the final simulation environments for each technology (Fig. 6).

4 Discussion and Conclusions

Network simulations need a significant processing capacity mainly for devices quantity as occur in large scale network design, in many cases is required a server that supports more than one simulation software and creation of user profiles for custom configurations. This work affords technical information and procedures to continue with a more realistic design for a useful application of LoRa and NB-IoT.

Smart City involves a wide and varied meaning, most part of times uses Internet of Things to connect a huge devices number as sensors, computers, BAN (Body Area Network), mobile phones and so on. This research study define main characteristics to deploy LPWAN with LoRa and NB-IoT employment, logically technical features are a very important variable to consider, because here is presented bitrate variation respect to distance from gateway and number of devices as well as energy consumption in a different transmission media and protocol and above all operation frequency band influence.

Today discussions promote vulnerable human bean careful and there is a special interest on medial care of children and persons with catastrophic diseases. A big challenge is launched to engineers, medics, software developers and other science actors, when available technology as LoRa and NB-IoT can configure a practical resource to attend this society segment.

It is opened the possibility that in the future this work serves as reference to research on 1. Patients health smart monitoring, 2. Enhanced drugs management, 3. Smart continuous glucose monitoring (CGM), 4. Digestible sensors, 5. Remote medical assistance, 6. Healthcare charting, where technology support medicine areas, thus providing a different perspective when it comes to more automated medical processes [12].

References

1. Rouse, M.: What is internet of things (IoT)? - Definition from WhatIs.com, IoT Agenda. https://internetofthingsagenda.techtarget.com/definition/Internet-of-Things-IoT. Accessed 12 Sept 2019
2. Mekki, K., Bajic, E., Chaxel, F., Meyer, F.: A comparative study of LPWAN technologies for large-scale IoT deployment. ICT Exp. **5**(1), 1–7 (2019)

3. Sabas: Haciendo IoT con LoRa: Capítulo 1.- ¿Qué es LoRa y LoRaWAN?, Medium, 20 November 2017. https://medium.com/beelan/haciendo-iot-con-lora-cap%C3%ADtulo-1-qu%C3%A9-es-lora-y-lorawan-8c08d44208e8. Accessed 12 Sept 2019

4. Al-Kashoash, H.A.A., Kemp, A.H.: Comparison of 6LoWPAN and LPWAN for the Internet of Things. Aust. J. Electr. Electron. Eng. **13**(4), 268–274 (2016)

5. 3GPP: Release 13 analytical view version 9th September 2015. MCC Work Plan Manager (Alain Sultan), 14 September 2015

6. OpenSim: OMNeT++ documentation. https://omnetpp.org/documentation/. Accessed 28 Sept 2019

7. Mariusz Slabicki, G.P.: Home—FLoRa - A framework for LoRa simulations. https://flora.aalto.fi/. Accessed 20 Oct 2019

8. Semtech: What is LoRa?—Semtech LoRa Technology—Semtech. https://www.semtech.com/lora/what-is-lora. Accessed 28 Sept 2019

9. Contiki-NG. https://www.contiki-ng.org/. Accessed 18 Oct 2019

10. Moore, S.: Tmote sky, Wireless Sensor Networks. http://wirelesssensornetworks.weebly.com/1/post/2013/08/tmote-sky.html. Accessed 15 Oct 2019

11. Accent Advanced Systems: NB-IoT, la nueva revolución del mundo conectado, Accent Systems

12. Bui, N., Zorzi, M.: Health care applications: a solution based on the internet of things. In: Proceedings of the 4th International Symposium on Applied Sciences in Biomedical and Communication Technologies - ISABEL 2011, Barcelona, Spain, pp. 1–5 (2011)

Electronics

Acquisition Protocol and Comparison of Myoelectric Signals of the Muscles Innervated by the Ulnar, Radial and Medial Nerves for a Hand Orthoses

Leonardo A. Bermeo Varon[1]([⊠]) [iD], John Jairo Villarejo Mayor[2] [iD], Edgar F. Arcos[1] [iD], Diana M. Quiguanas[1] [iD], Andrea A. Bravo[1], and Vanessa Perez Plaza[1]

[1] Universidad Santiago de Cali, Street 5 No. 62-00, Cali, Colombia
leonardo.bermeo00@usc.edu.co
[2] Department of Physical Education, Universidade Federal de Parana, Street Coração de Maria 92, Curitiba, PR, Brazil

Abstract. This paper proposes a protocol for obtaining surface myoelectric signals in muscles of the upper limb for characterization of hand movement patterns. To characterize the movement patterns, the magnitude of the signal from each muscle is compared, for eight movements: (i) flexion, (ii) extension, (iii) ulnar and (iv) radial deviation of the hand, (v) metacarpophalangeal flexion, (vi) metacarpophalangeal extension, (vii) opposition and (viii) adduction thumb. Specific points were considered to acquire the signals from muscles innervated by the radial, medial and ulnar nerve, following the recommendations of the SENIAM project, in six intact people, using a myoelectric signal acquisition system. Seven protocols with recommendations for the location of sensors in the muscles were obtained, intended to establish combinations to reduce the number of sensors for future designs of assistive technologies, such as active orthoses. The suitable characteristic patterns for the hand movements studied allows the identification of a reduced set of sensors, considering the same eight movements. In this way, the functionality and rehabilitation processes of hand injuries are improved, facilitating the execution of activities of daily living.

Keywords: Radial nerve · Ulnar nerve · Medial nerve · Active orthoses · Myoelectric signals

1 Introduction

An orthosis is an external device adapted to the human body, intended to maintain, correct and improve the function of the musculoskeletal system, in order to replace a function when this system has suffered an injury, causing a deficit in its functionality [1]. An orthosis helps people in a disability condition to potentiate the reduced mobility on daily activities, by performing controlled movements in a more natural way, reducing those limitations and providing a better quality of life.

© Springer Nature Switzerland AG 2020
M. Botto-Tobar et al. (Eds.): ICAT 2019, CCIS 1195, pp. 129–140, 2020.
https://doi.org/10.1007/978-3-030-42531-9_11

Over the past years, orthoses have demonstrated to be a suitable tool when incorporated in therapeutic treatments for rehabilitation of spinal injuries that directly affect the hand [2–6]. The success of those treatments is closely linked to rigorous diagnoses to identify the condition of each person, with their particular reality and pathology, in order to indicate specific and personalized solutions.

Functional-oriented active orthoses are devices that can be controlled by myoelectric signals [7, 8] to perform movements according to decoded patterns into the signal. This signal is based upon action potentials at the muscle fiber membrane resulting from muscle activation, due to contractions or distentions of muscle fibers, leading to exchange of ions through muscle membranes [9]. The study of myoelectric signals is important to understand the patterns of muscle activation from people with altered movements [10], to assess the possibilities to control specific motor tasks with support of the orthoses. However, these patterns can be altered due to the injuries, requiring following protocols to assess the abilities for each user.

This study describes the suitable location of superficial electrodes in the muscles innervated by the radial, ulnar and medial nerve, for a set of movements of a hand orthosis. Also, this study compares the magnitude of the myoelectric signal of different movements, in order to select the number of electrodes and their location and to provide recommendations for the sensor placement procedures.

2   Methodology

A protocol for the acquisition of myoelectric signals was proposed to determine the points of greater innervation detected by the superficial electrodes in the muscles involved in the movements of the hand.

2.1   Subjects

This study was conducted on six intact volunteers, including four women and two men, aged 19 to 41 years. Inclusion criteria: have no disability in the upper limbs, no history of neurological or neuromuscular disorders. The study was approved by the ethical committee of the Universidad Santiago de Cali, Colombia.

2.2   Sensors Locations

The locations of the sensors for the acquisition of myoelectric signals were assessed through the identification of muscles according to the literature and the Human Anatomy Atlas [11]. All the muscles related to the above movements were collected to the study: (i) flexion, (ii) extension, (iii) ulnar and (iv) radial deviation of the hand, (v) metacarpophalangeal flexion, (vi) metacarpophalangeal extension, (vii) opposition and (viii) adduction thumb. Moreover, the origin, innervation, insertion and the action performed by those muscles were studied.

Once the identification of muscles was carried out, an evaluation of the most appropriate location for obtaining myoelectric signals was performed, following the muscular anatomical theory of the upper limb, considering the greatest dimension. This is the most dominant middle portion of the muscle belly for better selectivity.

The movements were organized into two groups: (i) extension, flexion, ulnar and radial deviation of the hand and (ii) metacarpophalangeal flexion and extension, and opposition and adduction of the thumb.

For the test, each movement was performed six times, with intervals of 10 s, within one minute, obtaining a set of 6 repetitions. It was repeated for each movement of both groups, for each sensor location, in order to identify the maximum amplitude of the signal. Finally, volunteers performed five repetitions of the overall test. In total, each movement was composed of 30 repetitions for each movement for each sensor location.

2.3 Acquisition System

Myoelectrical signals were acquired in a non-invasive way using a MyoWare™ Muscle Sensor, with polarity reversal protection [12]. Covidien H124SG disposable surface electrodes, with 23.9 mm of diameter, weight of 0.6 g, and non-irritating gel and latex-free foam surface were used. The measurements of myoelectric signals were obtained from the processed output signal (SIG) of the sensor which provides a rectified and integrated signal. The signal was digitalized using an Arduino microcontrolled board with a sample time of 4 ms (sampling of 250 Hz). The power supply of the system was of +5.0 V.

2.4 Data Analysis

For the data analysis, signals were split into windows of four seconds within each trial of the movements, considering four seconds as enough time to cover the entire signal, obtaining 30 sets of data from each experiment for evaluation.

Once the signals were obtained, 95% confidence interval (CI) (Eq. 1) was calculated in the eight sensors locations, where $\bar{X}$ is the mean of the signals for each specific movement, σ is the standard deviation and n is the number of samples. In addition, a comparison of the statistical values of different groups was performed through box and whisker analysis, by comparing the current movement with the maximum amplitude among the three remaining movements of the group. Thus, patterns for each movement and a reduced number of sensors were identified for a specific disability.

$$IC(95\%) = [\bar{X} \pm 1.96(\sigma/\sqrt{n})] \tag{1}$$

3 Results and Discussions

3.1 Muscles Involved in the Movements

Figures 1, 2, 3, 4, 5, 6, 7 describe the muscles involved in each movement performed: Fig. 1, Flexion of the Hand; Fig. 2, Extension of the Hand; Fig. 3, Radial Deviation of the Hand; Fig. 4, Ulnar Deviation of the hand; Fig. 5, Metacarpophalangeal flexion; Fig. 6, Metacarpophalangeal Extension; and Fig. 7, Opposition and Adduction of the Thumb.

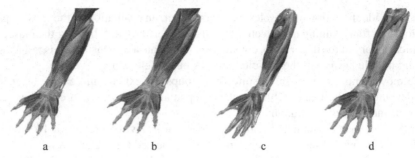

Fig. 1. Flexion of the hand. (a) Flexor carpi radialis, (b) Palmaris longus, (c) Flexor carpi ulnaris, (d) Flexor digitorum superficialis.

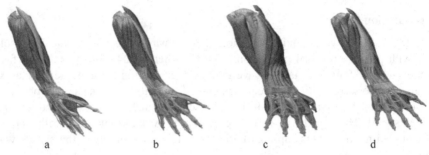

Fig. 2. Extension of the hand. (a) Extensor carpi radialis longus, (b) Extensor carpi radialis brevis, (c) Extensor carpi ulnaris, (d) Extensor digitorum comunis.

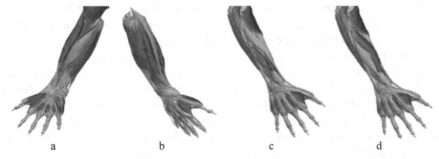

Fig. 3. Radial Deviation of the hand. (a) Flexor carpi radialis longus, (b) Extensor carpi radialis longus, (c) Abductor pollicis longus, (d) Extensor pollicis brevis.

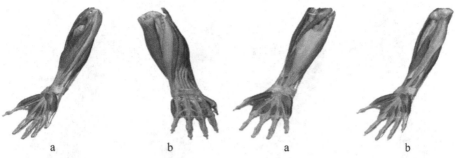

Fig. 4. Ulnar Deviation of the hand. (a) Flexor carpi ulnaris, (b) Extensor carpi ulnaris.

Fig. 5. Metacarpophalangeal flexion. (a) Flexor digitorum superficialis, (b) Flexor digitorum profundus.

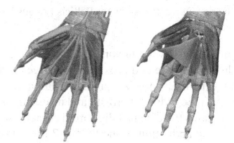

Fig. 6. Metacarpophalangeal extension. Extensor digitorum comunis.

Fig. 7. Opposition and adduction of the thumb. (a) Opponens pollicis, (b) Abductor pollicis brevis.

3.2 Sensor Locations

Based on the muscular anatomical theory of the upper limb, and considering the greater dimension, Figs. 8 and 9 present the most appropriate sensor locations in the muscle for each case, being this the most dominant middle portion of the muscle belly for better selectivity.

Figure 8a shows the flexor carpi radialis whose functions are the flexion and extension of the hand. It originates on the humeral epicondyle and inserts in the base of the second metacarpal and the base of the third metacarpal. Figure 8b shows the extensor carpi radialis brevis whose functions are the extension and radial deviation of the wrist. It originates on the lateral epicondyle of the humerus, by the common tendon and inserts in the dorsal base of the third metacarpal bone. Figure 8c shows extensor carpi ulnaris whose functions are the extension and adduction of the wrist. It originates on the lateral epicondyle of the humerus, by the common tendon and dorsal surface of the humerus and inserts in the tuber of the ulnar side of the base of the fifth metacarpal. Figure 8d presents the abductor pollicis longus whose functions are the radial deviation wrist and pollicis. It originates on the lateral dorsal surfaces of the radius and ulnar, as well as the interosseous membrane and inserts in the lateral radial side of the base of the first metacarpal bone.

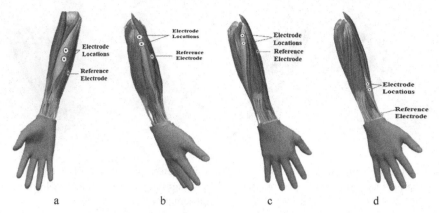

Fig. 8. (a) Flexor Carpi Radialis Muscle, (b) Extensor Carpi Radialis Brevis Muscle, (c) Extensor Carpi Ulnaris Muscle, (d) Abductor Pollicis Longus Muscle.

Figure 9a shows the flexor digitorum superficialis whose functions are flexing the wrist, flex the middle and proximal phalanges of the fingers 2 to 5. It originates on the head of the humerus: medial epicondyle, ulnar head: coronoid apophysis and head of the radius: under the radial tuberosity and inserts in the middle phalanx of the fingers 2 to 5. Figure 9b shows the extensor digitorum comunis whose functions are the wrist extension, extension and abduction of the fingers 2 to 5. It originates on the lateral epicondyle of the humerus, by the common tendon and inserts in the dorsal digital finger expansions 2 to 4. Figure 9c shows the opponens pollicis whose function is the opposition of the thumb. It originates on the flexor retinaculum, scaphoid and trapezius, and inserts in the lateral edge of the metacarpal bone of the first finger.

Figure 9d shows adductor pollicis brevis whose function are the abduct the carpometacarpal and metacarpophalangeal joints of the thumb in a ventral direction perpendicular to the plane of the palm, assists in opposition and may assist in flexion of the

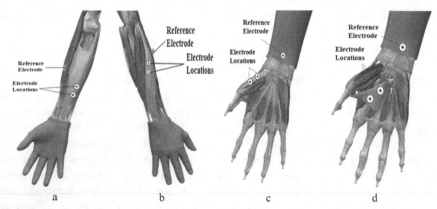

Fig. 9. (a) Flexor Digitorum Superficialis Muscle, (b) Extensor Digitorum Comunis Muscle, (c) Opponens Pollicis Muscle, (d) Adductor Pollicis Brevis Muscle [13].

metacarpophalangeal joint. This muscle originates on the flexor retinaculum, tubercle of trapezium bone and tubercle of scaphoid bone and inserts in the base of proximal phalanx of thumb, radial side, and extensor expansion [13].

The recommendations sensor placement procedure is sitting or supine position with the back of the hand stabilized on a table. The electrode size is 23.9 mm maximum, electrode distance is 5 mm for dynamic contractions and 7.5 mm for isometric contractions and the fixtion on the skin can be carried out tapes, rings (double sided) or elastic band. Tables 1, 2, 3, 4, 5, 6, 7, 8 presents the electrode placement for each muscle indicating the location, orientation, fixation on the skin, reference electrode and clinical test.

It is worth to mention that only one of these recommendations is registered by SENIAM (Surface ElectroMyoGraphy for the Non-Invasive Assessment of Muscles) [13], referring to the adductor pollicis brevis muscle of the thumb. The remaining recommendations for muscles not registered by SENIAM are part of the contribution of this paper.

Table 1. Flexor carpi radialis muscle

Location	Slightly medial of the upper third of the forearm
Orientation	Ventral, slightly medial
Reference electrode	On the inner edge of the forearm
Clinical test	Bend wrist slightly, bringing the front of the hand toward the front of the forearm

Table 2. Extensor carpi radialis brevis muscle

Location	Lateral upper third of the forearm, close to the common tendon of the fingers
Orientation	Dorsal
Reference electrode	On the inner edge of the forearm
Clinical test	Extend the wrist so that the back of the hand is directed towards the back of the forearm

Table 3. Extensor carpi ulnaris muscle

Location	Upper dorsal third of the forearm, near the common extensor tendon of the fingers
Orientation	Dorsal
Reference electrode	On the outer side of the forearm
Clinical test	Turn hand horizontally in the direction of the ulna bone, bringing the inner edges of the hand and forearm closer together

Table 4. Abductor pollicis longus muscle

Location	Lateral lower third of the forearm, radial side
Orientation	Dorsal
Reference electrode	On or around the wrist
Clinical test	Turn your hand horizontally in the direction of the radius bone, bringing the outer edges of the hand and the forearm closer together

Table 5. Flexor digitorum superficialis muscle

Location	Lower third medial of the forearm, ventral side
Orientation	Ventral medial
Reference electrode	On the outer edge of the forearm
Clinical test	Abduct the thumb ventrally towards the palm while applying pressure against the proximal phalanx in the direction of adduction towards the palm

Table 6. Extensor digitorum comunis muscle

Location	Third dorsal middle of the forearm
Orientation	Dorsal
Reference electrode	On the front side of the forearm
Clinical test	Abduct the pollici ventrally towards the palm while applying pressure against the proximal phalanx in the direction of adduction towards the palm

Table 7. Opponens pollicis muscle

Location	Slightly lateral in the bone of the first metacarpal
Orientation	On first metacarpal.
Reference electrode	On/around the wrist
Clinical test	Abduct the thumb ventrally towards the palm while applying pressure against the proximal phalanx in the direction of adduction towards the palm

Table 8. Adductor pollicis brevis muscle [13]

Location	Slightly medial of the distal 1/4 of the 1st ossa metacarpalia
Orientation	Parallel to the 1st ossa metacarpalia
Reference electrode	On/around the wrist
Clinical test	Abduct the thumb ventral ward from the palm while applying pressure against the proximal phalanx in the direction of adduction toward the palm

3.3 Data Analysis and Discussions

Table 9 present a summary of the potential mean and a 95% confidence interval for 30 repetitions of each movement. A closeness is observed in the myoelectric potentials of the main muscles of each movement. Despite this similarity, the myoelectric signal is identifiable in the instant to occur a specific movement, because the values in maximum mean do not overlap in any case. This is important to determine a reduced number of sensors to perform more movements, identifying which movement is being done by the classification of different myoelectric signals at the instant of performing a specific movement.

Table 9. Myoelectric signals potentials

Movimiento	Maximum mean (V)	Confidence interval (V)
Flexion of the hand (FH)	1.072	0.905–1.239
Extension of the hand (EH)	1.794	1.682–1.897
Radial Deviation of the hand (RDH)	2.294	2.196–2.391
Ulnar Deviation of the hand (UDH)	1.282	1.252–1.312
Metacarpophalangeal Flexion (MF)	0.821	0.775–0.868
Metacarpophalangeal Extension (ME)	0.688	0.622–0.755
Opposition of the thumb (OT)	3.261	2.937–3.584
Adduction of the thumb (AT)	2.765	2.365–3.088

Figures 10 and 11 presents the mean of the flexion of the hand and metacarpophalangeal flexion, respectively. It is possible to observe that all the signals have different amplitudes, which is an important aspect for the signal processing and the control of the

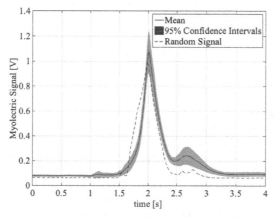

Fig. 10. Flexion of the hand.

orthosis. Additionally, the confidence interval for each movement and a random signal of the process is presented to verify that 95% of the signals are into the confidence interval.

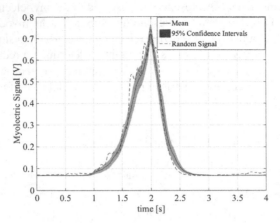

Fig. 11. Metacarpophalangeal Flexion.

Figure 12 shows the comparison of the signal strength of the flexor carpi radialis muscle executing the flexion of the hand (FH), corresponding to a characteristic movement for this muscle, extension of the hand (EH), radial deviation of the hand (RDH) and ulnar deviation of the hand (UDH). Moreover, Fig. 13 shows the intensity of the signals of the flexor digitorum superficialis muscle executing metacarpophalangeal flexion (MF), corresponding to a characteristic movement for this muscle, metacarpophalangeal extension (ME), opposition of the thumb (OT) and adduction of the thumb (AT). In these figures, it is observed that the greatest potential obtained in each of the experiments corresponds to the main movement associated with the muscle, while the three (3) remaining movements have lower potential. These results are important because it allows identifying

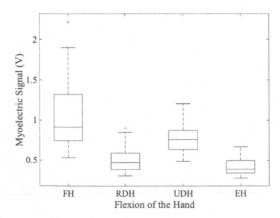

Fig. 12. Flexor carpi radialis muscle.

which movement is being carried out and define a minimum number of sensors for the execution of the eight (8) movements with a processing stage.

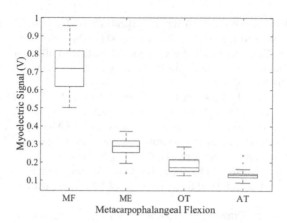

Fig. 13. Flexor digitorum superficialis muscle.

4 Conclusions

This work outlines a protocol to analyze characteristic patterns obtained from the magnitude of myoelectric signals, and the trend for a set of movements, generating commands for a system able to classify movements of an active hand orthosis. It could be verified that the amplitude of the signals obtained was consistent when compared to the main muscle for each movement, showing significant differences with the signals of the other ones. The comparison of magnitude of the signal from the different movements allows the possibility of combine and select an adequate number of sensors to perform until eight (8) movements. The proposed protocol can be applied for the control of an orthosis by using a machine learning system. This outcome can be relevant for the designing and manufacturing of an orthosis in order to improve their functionality, providing a more accurate classification of the movements for people in disability conditions.

This study will allow future development of an orthosis in a personalized way for persons in disability conditions related to the radial, ulnar and medial nerves, which will establish an optimal performance in the design and construction of active orthoses for the hand.

Acknowledgments. The authors are thankful for the support provided by CNPq, CAPES (Brazil) and DGI of Universidad Santiago de Cali, Colombia, project No. 819- 621119-487.

Disclosure Statement. No potential conflict of interest was reported by the authors.

References

1. Viladot, R., Riambau, O.C., Paloma, S.C.: Ortesis y prótesis del aparato locomotor. Elsevier, Espana (1998)
2. Watanabe, H., Ogata, K., Okabe, T., Amano, T.: Hand orthosis for various finger impairments–the K U finger splint. Prosthet. Orthot. Int. **2**, 95–100 (1978)
3. Ryser, F., Butzer, T., Held, J.P., Lambercy, O., Gassert, R.: Fully embedded myoelectric control for a wearable robotic hand orthosis. In: IEEE International Conference Rehabilation Robotics 2017, pp. 615–621 (2017)
4. Makaran, J.E., Dittmer, D.K., Buchal, R.O., MacArthur, D.E.: The SMART Wrist-Hand Orthosis (WHO) for Quadriplegic Patients. JPO J. Prosthetics Orthot. **5**(3), 73 (1993)
5. Meeker, C., Park, S., Bishop, L., Stein, J., Ciocarlie, M.: EMG Pattern Classification to Control a Hand Orthosis for Functional Grasp Assistance after Stroke. In: IEEE International Conference Rehabilation Robotics, pp. 1203–1210 (2017)
6. Zhao, H., Jalving, J., Huang, R., Knepper, R., Ruina, A., Shepherd, R.: A helping hand: soft orthosis with integrated optical strain sensors and EMG control. IEEE Robot. Autom. Mag. **23**, 55–64 (2016)
7. Ganesan, Y., Gobee, S., Durairajah, V.: Development of an upper limb exoskeleton for rehabilitation with feedback from EMG and IMU sensor. Procedia - Procedia Comput. Sci. **76**, 53–59 (2015)
8. Hussain, S., Xie, S.Q., Jamwal, P.K.: Control of a robotic orthosis for gait rehabilitation. Rob. Auton. Syst. **61**, 911–919 (2013)
9. Konrad, P.: The ABC of EMG. A Practical Introduction to Kinesiological Electromyography (2005)
10. Hamonet, C., Boulongne, D., Simon, S., Bedhet, P.: A myoelectric-controlled orthosis: Recent development. Hand. **7**, 63–66 (1975)
11. Argosy Publishing Inc.: Human Anatomy Atlas. www.visiblebody.com. Accessed 29 June 2019
12. Advancer Technologies: MyoWare. www.AdvancerTechnologies.com. Accessed 23 Oct 2019
13. Seniam: Surface ElectroMyoGraphy for the Non-Invasive Assessment of Muscles, www.seniam.org. Accessed 03 Nov 2019

Estimation of Electrical Conductivity from Radiofrequency Hyperthermia Therapy for Cancer Treatment by Levenberg Marquardt Method

Jorge Iván López Perez⬤, Rafael Daniel Serna Maldonado⬤,
Leonardo A. Bermeo Varon$^{(\boxtimes)}$ ⬤, and Javier Ferney Castillo García⬤

Universidad Santiago de Cali, Street 5 No. 62-00, Cali, Valle del Cauca, Colombia
leonardo.bermeo00@usc.edu.co

Abstract. Introduction: The radiofrequency hyperthermia is a technique that by induction of the electromagnetic waves produces the heating in the biological tissues. The increase in body temperature in a range of 40 °C to 46 °C causing heat-induced necrosis, protein inactivity, and inhibition of DNA recovery mechanisms in the cancer cell. The application of this therapy depends on parameters like the frequency and power and physical properties of the tissue, which vary from person to person. One of the important properties is the electrical conductivity of the tissue, which varies depending on the tissue and frequency. In this paper, the electrical conductivity estimation is performed in hyperthermia therapy with different frequencies. **Methodology:** The estimation process of electrical conductivity is carried out through the Levenberg Marquardt method. The process is performed on simulated experimental data and mathematical model of the system with different frequencies. The geometry used is a copper coil that induces radiofrequency to a domain located in the center of the coil. **Results:** The estimation of electrical conductivity is obtained to different frequencies from radiofrequency hyperthermia therapy for cancer treatment by the Levenberg Marquardt method. Also, these results allow that by identifying the electrical conductivity of each patient. **Conclusions:** The estimation of physical properties in the application of cancer treatment is important, in this case with radiofrequency hyperthermia therapy, because it is possible to plan appropriate treatment, due to a better knowledge of the system.

Keywords: Hyperthermia · Radiofrequency therapy · Parameter estimation · Electrical conductivity

1 Introduction

According to WHO statistical data, cancer is considered the second leading cause of death in the world. 8.8 million deaths occurred in 2015 and it is estimated that around 20.2 million will occur in 2030 per year [1]. Almost 70% of these deaths were registered in middle and low-income countries, which reveals that less than 30% of these countries

© Springer Nature Switzerland AG 2020
M. Botto-Tobar et al. (Eds.): ICAT 2019, CCIS 1195, pp. 141–152, 2020.
https://doi.org/10.1007/978-3-030-42531-9_12

offer treatment to cancer patients. Although there are therapies, medications, and treatments to deal with the disease, death rates continue to rise due to high costs and poor accessibility [2].

There are different alternatives for cancer treatment, such as chemotherapy, radiotherapy, and surgery. Where the type of treatment chosen is determined by conditions presented by each patient, such as the stage of cancer and its location. Commonly, these treatments, at the time of execution and compromise healthy tissues causes discomfort to the patient [3, 4]. For this reason, other alternatives are being developed, such as hyperthermia, which is implemented individually or as adjuvant therapy in traditional therapies to reduce their side effects [5].

Hyperthermia is an increase in body temperature in a range of 40 °C to 46 °C causing heat-induced necrosis, protein inactivity, and inhibition of DNA recovery mechanisms in the cancer cell [6]. Hyperthermia therapy is performed locally, regionally or completely body. This therapy causes a temperature increase, invasively with the use of electrodes or needles, and non-invasively through the induction of electromagnetic waves in the infrared, microwave and radiofrequency waves [7–17]. Radiofrequency (RF) hyperthermia therapy has been used demonstrating its efficiency in the frequency range of 0.1 MHz to 27 MHz [9]. The frequency range the most common are: 0.1–10 MHz, 13.56 MHz and 27.24 MHz [12].

The heat generation by RF hyperthermia therapy it is induced by two mechanisms: (i) the Joule effect, which is given by the opposition of the tissues to the passage of the electric current generating heating and (ii) the absorption of electromagnetic radiation which excites the water molecules causing a rapid rotation producing a mechanical friction effect generating heat [18]. Heat generation in the application of this therapy depends on the physical properties of the biological tissues that differ in each patient, which suggests a specific treatment.

In that sense, there is a need to identify the parameters of biological tissues. For example, the electrical conductivity of tissues is a property that depends on the number of ions present in the medium and the frequency ranges in which they are exposed, an adequate knowledge of this parameter will allow a more specific therapy in patients.

Engineering has developed tools capable of helping to understand the behavior of tissues and their properties. The development of mathematical models and optimization algorithms has been important to know more about a problem, using the information available to estimate the variables present in the system to identify a more appropriate behavior for each type of tissue and patient [19].

There are several methods for estimating parameters such as Levenberg Marquardt (LM) [20–23], which is widely used to estimate parameters in different problems, being one of the most effective for this purpose. Other methods such as Gauss-Newton method [24], Conjugated Gradient method and Monte Carlo with Markov Chains [25] have also had good results in parameter estimation. These methods correlate the mathematical model that describes the physics of the problem and the experimental measures in order to know more about a system.

LM method is a technique with a high level of effectiveness in the estimation of biological parameters [26], like electrical conductivity, of great interest to understand the behavior of tissues in the presence of an electromagnetic field and its application in different fields of medicine [27].

In this paper, the estimation of the electrical conductivity in biological tissues is carried out through the LM method. The study includes the mathematical model of a hyperthermia system with RF wave induction and simulated experimental measurements. The electrical conductivity is estimated for three different frequencies on a biological tissue with standard properties.

2 Methodology

Figure 1 shows the sequence to implementation for the estimation of electrical conductivity in RF hyperthermia therapy for cancer treatment.

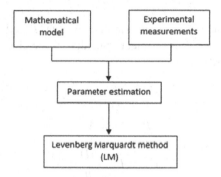

Fig. 1. Sequence to estimation of the electrical conductivity

2.1 Mathematical Model

The forward model was implemented in Comsol Multiphysics® 5.3 software [28], the mathematical models are described in Eqs. 1–9, which solves the electromagnetic and thermal system, which involves RF hyperthermia therapy for cancer treatment.

Figure 2 is showed the domain system to simulate the RF hyperthermia therapy. RF induction is carried out using a copper coil of three turns with internal cooling on a Phantom located in the center of the coil. The material has the physical properties of the typical human muscle. The geometry of the model was a rectangular two-dimensional axisymmetric domain with dimensions $r = 100$ mm and $z = 100$ mm, and the Phantom was a rectangular domain with dimensions $r = 40$ mm and $z = 80$ mm, the coil is located 20 mm from the boundary of the Phantom. The water parameters for cooling, air, and copper are used by default of Comsol Multiphysics® 5.3 and muscle properties were taken from the ITIS Foundation [29].

The physical models of a hyperthermia system with electromagnetic wave induction is calculated by the Maxwell equations [30] coupled to the heat transfer equation [31]. Equations (1–4) the electromagnetic fields were defined, where H is the induction of the

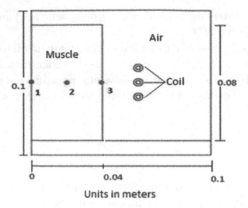

Fig. 2. Domain system

magnetic field, J is the induction of electric field current, B is the magnetic field, A is the magnetic potential vector, E is the electric field, σ is the electrical conductivity and D is the electric flux density.

$$\nabla \times H = J \tag{1}$$

$$B = \nabla \times A \tag{2}$$

$$J = \sigma E + \frac{\partial D}{\partial t} \tag{3}$$

$$E = -\frac{\partial A}{\partial t} \tag{4}$$

Equation (5) defines heat transfer and Eqs. (6–8) determines the heat source which couples the electromagnetic model to the thermal model [6], where ρ is the density, c_p is the heat capacity, μ is the speed, T is the temperature, k is the thermal conductivity, Q_e is the heat source, composed of Q_{rh} are the electrical losses and Q_{ml} are the magnetic losses. Re specific the real part of the magnitude.

$$\rho c_p \frac{\partial T}{\partial t} + \rho c_p \mu \cdot \nabla T = \nabla \cdot (k\nabla T) + Q_e \tag{5}$$

$$Q_e = Q_{rh} + Q_{ml} \tag{6}$$

$$Q_{rh} = \frac{1}{2}\mathrm{Re}(J \cdot E') \tag{7}$$

$$Q_{ml} = \frac{1}{2}\mathrm{Re}(i\omega B \cdot H') \tag{8}$$

Due to the excessive heating of the coils, cooling pad is necessary. Equation (9) defines heat source Q_o, where M_t is the mass flow rate, c_{pw} is the heat capacity of water,

T_{in} is the inlet temperature of the cooling water, r and A_c is the internal radius and cross section of the coil, respectively.

$$Q_0 = M_t c_{pw} \frac{T_{in} - T}{2\pi r A_c} \tag{9}$$

The initial conditions of the system was the initial temperature $T_i = 24\,°C$, cooling pad temperature $T_{in} = 20\,°C$, convection coefficient in the middle $h = 10\,W/m^2.K$, $\mu = 0$ and prescribed temperature in the Phantom of $20\,°C$ in $r = 0.04$; $-0.04 < z < 0.04$. Table 1 shows the electrical properties of phantom that depending of the frequency, and Table 2 shows the physical properties of the domain [28, 29].

Table 1. Electric properties of the Phantom (muscle properties) [29]

Nominal frequency (MHz)	0.1	1	10
Power (W)	1,000	600	300
Electrical conductivity (S/m)	0.362	0.503	0.617
Permittivity	8,090	1,840	171

Table 2. Physical properties of the domain [28, 29]

	k (W/(mK))	c_p (J/(kg.K)	ρ (kg/m^3)	σ (S/m)	εr	μ_r
Cooper	400	385	8,960	5.998×10^7	1	1
Air	0.024	0.240	1.086	0	1	1
Water	0.580	4,230	997	5.500×10^{-6}	1	80
Phantom	0.49	3,421	1,090	see Table 1		159

2.2 Levenberg Marquardt (LM) Method

The Levenberg Marquardt method is widely used to solve problems of iterative linear and nonlinear least squares for parameter estimation, the method combines the Gauss-Newton and gradient descent methods, where the dumpling factor (u) approaches at zero its convergence is fast and when the factor approaches infinity, its convergence is slow. The LM method allows a smooth transition between these two methods [21].

The implementation of the LM algorithm for the estimation of the electrical conductivity is described in Fig. 3, where Y are the simulated experimental temperature obtained by numerical solution with a Gaussian additive error of mean zero and standard deviation of 10%, T is the numerical temperature transient, P is the parameter, u is the dumpling factor, J is the sensitivity matrix, W is the measurements error covariance matrix, Ω is the diagonal matrix of $J^T WJ$ and S likelihood objective function.

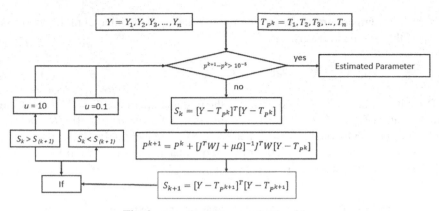

Fig. 3. Levenberg Marquardt Algorithm

A sensitivity study was performed by finding that all parameters are linearly dependent which indicates that only one parameter can be estimated.

The numerical simulation was realized on a computer with an A10 processor and 16 GB of RAM and the optimization algorithm was performed 39 times to calculate the mean, standard deviation and a 95% confidence interval.

3   Results and Discussions

Figures 4, 5 and 6 shows the temperature distributions at three (3) cut-off points to analyze the variation in temperature at each of the frequencies evaluated, cut point 1 corresponds to the core of the domain localized at the coordinates (0.00; 0.00), cut point 2 it is located between the center and the boundary of the Phantom (0.02; 0.00) and the cut point 3 is located on the boundary of the Phantom (0.04; 0.00). The frequency transient study was performed in Comsol Multiphysics® 5.3 at time $t = 300$ s with 688 elements.

Figure 4 shows the behavior at the three cut-off points at a frequency of 0.1 MHz and a power of 1,000 W. It is observed that the center of the Phantom (cut point 2) is the one with the highest temperature increase 0.7 °C, approximately. This increase allows a mild hyperthermia treatment.

Figure 5 presents the temperature transient at the three cut-off points at a frequency of 1.0 MHz and a power of 600 W. The temperature increases 22 °C in 300 s at the cut point 2. In this frequency, a higher temperature increase is reached that would allow hyperthermia treatment to be performed at 230 s. The temperature increase in the center of the domain is around 1.7 °C, that indicates that this area will not be affected.

Figure 6 shows temperature transient at the same cut-off points at a frequency of 10.0 MHz and a power of 300 W. Note, that the temperature increase is even greater. This frequency reaches a higher temperature increase that allows making an ablation treatment. Also, is observed a higher temperature increase in the center domain the 5.7 °C.

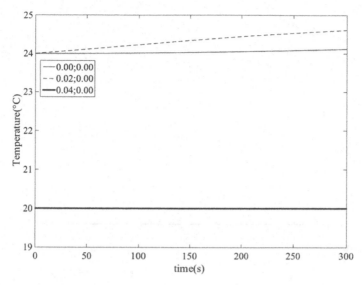

Fig. 4. Temperature transient at a frequency of 0.1 MHz and power of 1,000 W

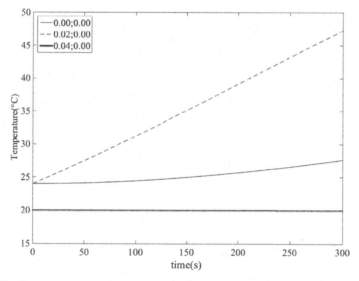

Fig. 5. Temperature behavior at a frequency of 1 MHz and power of 600 W

From these results, it is observed that the temperature increase is proportional to the increase in frequency. The choice of frequency and power will depend on what type of cancer is being treated in terms of stage and depth.

Figures 7, 8 and 9 presents the numerical solution and simulated experimental of the system to $f = 0.1$ MHz at 1,000 W, $f = 1.0$ MHz at 600 W and $f = 10.0$ MHz at 300 W, respectively. The simulated experimental temperature is performed with 6,085 elements,

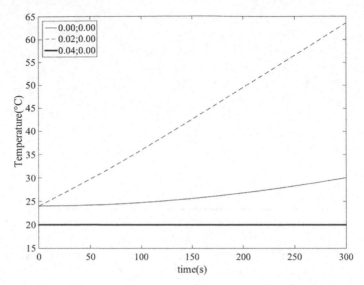

Fig. 6. Temperature transient at a frequency of 10 MHz and power of 300 W

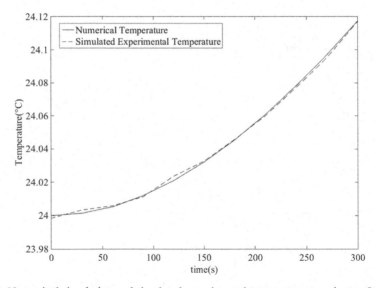

Fig. 7. Numerical simulation and simulated experimental temperature transient to 0.1 MHz.

in a unique cut point (0.02; 0.00) in 300 s with a Gaussian additive error with mean zero and a standard deviation of 1% establishing a difference with numerical simulation.

Table 3 shows a statistical analysis of the three frequencies. It is observed the mean of electrical conductivity, the standard deviation, and the 95% confidence interval. Note, that the estimation values are very close to the exact values. The standard deviation for the 39 estimation values is very small indicating that the algorithm had an excellent

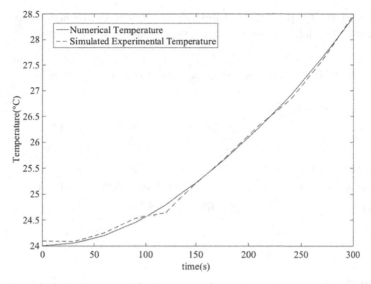

Fig. 8. Numerical simulation and simulated experimental temperature transient to 1 MHz.

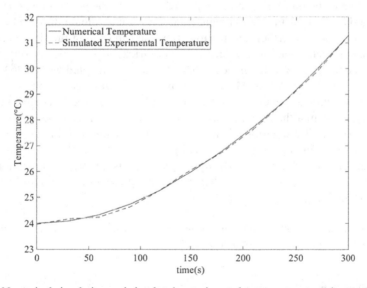

Fig. 9. Numerical simulation and simulated experimental temperature transient to 10 MHz.

convergence and repeatability. The confidence interval is very close to the exact values suggesting a possible implementation in hyperthermia therapies, take to account the differences of the physical properties for each patient.

The results obtained in the estimation of the electrical conductivity that the implementation of the LM algorithm is more effective in the frequencies of 1.0 MHz and 10.0 MHz, due to the high-temperature variation.

With this study, it is possible to determine the appropriate frequency depending on the treatment and establish a specific parameter depending on the patient.

Table 3. Results of the estimation of the electrical conductivity (σ)

Nominal frequency (MHz)	0.1	1	10
Exact σ (S/m)	0.3620	0.5030	0.6170
Mean (S/m)	0.3642	0.4988	0.6133
Standard Deviation (S/m)	0.0034	0.0126	0.0011
Confidence Interval (S/m)	0.3631–0.3653	0.4948–0.5028	0.6130–0.6136
Run-time (min)	19.1000	15.3000	8.1300

4 Conclusions

In this paper, an estimation of the electrical conductivity of the phantom was performed in the forward problem with a two-dimensional rectangular domain through Levenberg Marquardt in the RF hyperthermia therapy. The result indicating that it is possible to estimate the parameter obtaining values of the electrical conductivity to very close to the exact value to different frequencies, where the values estimated were 0.364, 0.4988 and 0.6133 to 0.1, 1.0, and 10.0 MHz, respectively. The numerical results show that it is expected to develop a cancer treatment with simulated and experimental temperature in the RF hyperthermia therapy considering the differences in physical properties for each person. The implementation of the algorithm demonstrates that it has a high level for the estimation of biological parameters of great complexity and of great importance for the optimization in this case of RF hyperthermia. It is important to mention that it is pertinent to consider estimates of other parameters present in the tissues to ensure a more effective therapy.

Acknowledgments. The authors are thankful for the support provided by DGI of Universidad Santiago de Cali, Colombia, project No. 819-621118-120.

Disclosure Statement. No potential conflict of interest was reported by the authors.

References

1. WHO: Cancer. www.who.int. Accessed 1 Oct 2019
2. Rangel-Sosa, M.M., Aguilar-Córdova, E., Rojas-Martínez, A.: Immunotherapy and gene therapy as novel treatments for cancer. Colomb. medica **48**, 138–147 (2017)
3. Oun, R., Moussa, Y.E., Wheate, N.J.: The side effects of platinum-based chemotherapy drugs: a review for chemists. Dalton Trans. **47**, 6645–6653 (2018)

4. Palesh, O., Scheiber, C., Kesler, S., Mustian, K., Koopman, C., Schapira, L.: Management of side effects during and post-treatment in breast cancer survivors. Breast J. **24**, 167–175 (2018)
5. Curto, S.: Antenna development for radio frequency hyperthermia applications. Doctoral thesis. Dublin Institute of Technology. Technological University Dublin (2010)
6. Mallory, M., Gogineni, E., Jones, G.C., Greer, L., Simone, C.B.: Therapeutic hyperthermia: the old, the new, and the upcoming. Crit. Rev. Oncol. Hematol. **97**, 56–64 (2016)
7. Gas, P.: Study on interstitial microwave hyperthermia with multi-slot coaxial antenna. Génie biomédicale. **59**, 215–224 (2014)
8. Vrba, D., Vrba, J., Rodrigues, D.B., Stauffer, P.: Numerical investigation of novel microwave applicators based on zero-order mode resonance for hyperthermia treatment of cancer. J. Franklin Inst. **354**, 8734–8746 (2017)
9. Guirado, N., Mart, J.C.: Hipertermia oncológica profunda conformada provocada por campos electromagnéticos no ionizantes Conformed deep oncologic hyperthermia caused by electromagnetic. Rev. Fis. Med. **19**, 11–44 (2018)
10. Kurgan, E., Gas, P.: Estimation of Temperature Distribution Inside Tissues in External RF Hyperthermia. Prz. Elektrotechniczny **86**, 100–102 (2010)
11. Gas, P.: Essential Facts on the History of Hyperthermia and their Connections with Electromedicine. Prz. Elektrotechniczny **87**, 37–40 (2011)
12. Bermeo Varon, L.A., Orlande, H.R.B., Elicabe, G.: Estimation of state variables in the hyperthermia therapy of cancer with heating imposed by radiofrequency electromagnetic waves. Int. J. Therm. Sci. **98**, 228–236 (2015)
13. Eibner, S., et al.: Near Infrared Light Heating of Soft Tissue Phantoms Containing Nanoparticles. Eng. térmica. **13**, 13–18 (2014)
14. Lamien, B., Bermeo Varon, L.A., Orlande, H.R.B., Eliçabe, G.E.: State Estimation in Bioheat Transfer: a Comparison of Particle Filter Algorithms. Int. J. Numer. Methods Heat Fluid Flow. **27**, 1–53 (2017)
15. Majchrzak, E., Paruch, M.: Numerical modelling of temperature field in the tissue with a tumor subject to the action of two external electrode. Sci. Res. Inst. Math. Comput. Sci. **1**, 1–8 (2009)
16. Miaskowski, A., Sawicki, B., Krawczyk, A., Yamada, S.: The application of magnetic fluid hyperthermia to breast cancer treatment. Prz. Elektrotechniczny, 99–101 (2010)
17. Gas, P., Miaskowski, A.: Specifying the ferrofluid parameters important from the viewpoint of Magnetic Fluid Hyperthermia. Sel. Probl. Electr. Eng. Electron., 1–6 (2015)
18. Sun, J., Wang, W., Yue, Q.: Review on microwave-matter interaction fundamentals and efficient microwave-associated heating strategies. Mater. **9**, 231 (2016)
19. Beck, J.V.: Sequential methods in parameter estimation. Michigan State University, East Lansing (1999)
20. Borzou, P., Ghaisari, J., Izadi, I., Gheisari, Y.: An iterative LMA method for parameter estimation in dynamic modeling of TGFβ pathway using ODE, pp. 1140–1144 (2019)
21. Madsen, K., Nielsen, H.., Tingleff, O.: Method for Non-Linear Least Squares Problems, pp. 24–29. Informatics and Mathematical Modelling Technical University of Denmark (2004)
22. Ghosh, S., Chattopadhyay, B.P., Roy, R.M., Mukherjee, J., Mahadevappa, M.: Estimation of echocardiogram parameters with the aid of impedance cardiography and artificial neural networks. Artif. Intell. Med. **96**, 45–58 (2019)
23. Huang, C.-H., Huang, C.-Y.: An inverse problem in estimating simultaneously the effective thermal conductivity and volumetric heat capacity of biological tissue. Appl. Math. Model. **31**, 1785–1797 (2007)
24. Gill, P.E., Murray, W.: Algorithms for the solution of the nonlinear least-squares problem. SIAM J. Numer. Anal. **15**, 977–992 (1978)

25. Andrieu, C., De Freitas, N., Doucet, A., Jordan, M.I.: An introduction to MCMC for machine learning. Mach. Learn. **50**, 5–43 (2003)
26. Tan, C., Xu, Y., Dong, F.: Determining the boundary of inclusions with known conductivities using a Levenberg-Marquardt algorithm by electrical resistance tomography. Meas. Sci. Technol. **22**, 104005 (2011)
27. Xu, Y., Dong, F., Tan, C.: Electrical resistance tomography for locating inclusions using analytical boundary element integrals and their partial derivatives. Eng. Anal. Bound. Elem. **34**, 876–883 (2010)
28. Comsol Multiphysics: Comsol Multiphysics Modelling Software. www.comsol.com. Accessed 8 Oct 2019
29. Hasgall, P.A., Neufeld, E., Gosselin, C., Klingenb, M.A., Kuster, N.: IT'IS Database for thermal and electromagnetic parameters of biological tissues (2015). www.itis.ethz.ch/database
30. Maxwell, J.C.: A dynamical theory of the electromagnetic field. Philos. Trans. R. Soc. London. **155**, 459–512 (1865)
31. Ozisik, N.: Heat Conduction. Wiley, New York (1993)

Retrofit to IEC 61850 of a Line-Bay in Transmission Substation. Case Study: INGA1/SE Pomasqui

Ana Mosquera[1]([⊠]), Rommel Proaño[2]([⊠]), Carlos Vallejo[2]([⊠]),
Silvana Gamboa[1]([⊠]), and Ana Rodas[1]([⊠])

[1] Escuela Politécnica Nacional, 17012759, Quito, Ecuador
{ana.mosquera,silvana.gamboa,ana.rodas}@epn.edu.ec
[2] CELEC EP, TRANSELECTRIC, Quito 170133, Ecuador
rommel.proano@celec.gob.ec, vallejo.caredu@gmail.com

Abstract. Ecuador's Transmission System (SNT) is integrated by 60 substations, 44 of them have a Substation Automation System (SAS) and 5 of these SAS are obsolete. When a failure of any protection/control device occurs in an obsolete SAS, the lack of spare parts drives the substation to a critical state that could compromise the service availability since a proper substation operation cannot be accomplished. In this regard, TRANSELECTRIC set up the plan to update around 20 substations which are within its field of action. To this end, retrofit engineering of a transmission line-bay under the IEC 61850 guidelines is developed and includes the standardization of signals, the reengineering of SAS components, and the standardization of the substation operator interfaces. This engineering is then applied to INGA 1 Bay (Pomasqui Substation) and its evaluation is accomplished in laboratory by the emulation of such bay with the designed automation system. To validate the proposed retrofit, the architecture and dataflow of Pomasqui Substation are emulated as well, to evaluate the automation system performance under practical operational scenarios. After the experiments, the results show the feasibility of the proposed retrofit.

Keywords: Retrofit · IEC 61850 · Substation · Line-bay · Transmission system

1 Introduction

Ecuador's National Transmission System (SNT) is integrated by 60 substation, 44 of them have a Substation Automation System (SAS) and 5 of these SAS are obsolete (Machala, San Idelfonso, Tena, Pomasqui, Orellana). The obsolescence of these systems make the real-time supervisory control and with it the operation of substation difficult. Such situation could worsen if any SAS failure would occur because spare parts or technical support are not available currently for these obsolete systems. This condition would cause a loss of supervision and control,

© Springer Nature Switzerland AG 2020
M. Botto-Tobar et al. (Eds.): ICAT 2019, CCIS 1195, pp. 153–165, 2020.
https://doi.org/10.1007/978-3-030-42531-9_13

thus, energy supply in areas in which these substations provide their service could be affected [1]. In this regard, TRANSELECTRIC as responsible for the operation and maintenance of substations that make up the SNT, has taken over responsibility for presenting the retrofit plan of the automation systems installed in these substations.

Retrofit is the migration from obsolete or discontinued equipment to new technology equipment. An important aspect in a retrofit is that changes to infrastructure must be minimal, and only some adaptations should be required to put in operation the new equipment [2]. A retrofit is justified in some conditions that in the present work are: (1) obsolescence of equipment, (2) lack of spare parts in the market for these obsolete equipment and (3) ensure continuity of the energy supply.

With this background, this work begins in order to accomplish the following objectives: (1) to generate retrofit to IEC 61850 specifications for line bays of transmission substations, (2) to standardize control and protection signals and (3) to validate the proposed specifications by emulating its implementation on INGA 1 Bay.

This paper is organized as follows. First, in Section 2, a review about IEC 61850 topics applicable to our issue are presented. Then in Sect. 3, requirements for the proposed retrofit are raised, while in Sect. 4 the proposed retrofit development is detailed. In Sect. 5, implementation at TRANSELECTRIC Laboratory and its validation are presented. Finally, conclusions are drawn in Sect. 6.

2   IEC 61850 Standard

IEC 61850 is a standard that provides guidelines for, among other aspects, design and implementation of SAS architecture, communication between intelligent electronic devices (IEDs) in a substation and the requirements of the systems associated with SAS [3]. Their main objectives are: (1) interoperability, (2) free communication and (3) long-term stability. Between them, and without underestimating the other objectives, interoperability is an important objective, since this will enable the use of equipment from different manufacturers as long as they are certified with the IEC 61850 standard [3]. Although this standard includes several aspects, only those that contemplate the interaction between the automation levels and the data model are addressed in this document because they are in the scope of this work. These are described below.

2.1   Interaction Between Automation Levels

As in any process automation system, substation automation requires a hierarchical organization of automation devices in automation levels, which in the case of a SAS are: Process Level or Level 0 (N0), Bay Level or Level 1 (N1) and Station Level or Level 2 (N2). Where level N0 is integrated by yard equipment (i. e. switches, voltage or current transformers), N1 comprises bay protection and

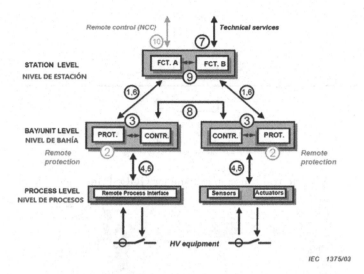

Fig. 1. SAS logical interfaces [3]

control equipment, and N2 includes the platform for the entire substation supervisory control. In this aspect, IEC 61850 states that the interaction between SAS components within a substation takes place through logical interfaces, which are a representation of the communication connections for data exchange between such devices. This information exchange can occur between devices of the same level and between devices of different levels. The logical interfaces proposed by this standard are summarized in Fig. 1.

For this retrofit the interfaces used for the design are:

- (1): protection data exchange between bay and station level,
- (3): data exchange within bay level, and
- (6): control data exchange between bay and station level.

Interface 3 is where GOOSE messages are transmitted. GOOSE is a multicast message of great interest since it belongs to the Generic Substation Event (GSE) model. It is characterized for a rapid distribution of information, but at the same time for a reliable communication [4] due to its periodic re-transmission scheme that is shown in Fig. 2 [5]. This scheme establishes that a message with selected information must be sent periodically with a long transmission period when there is no change in the states [5]. But if a change occurs, the initial transmissions will be done with short transmission periods that progressively increase until reaching its regular period. For this reason, GOOSE are used for a fast exchange of data related to relays operation or data that allow calculation of interlocking conditions [6]. Instead, for interfaces 1 and 6, MMS (Manufacturing Message Specification) messages are defined as one of the mechanisms for transmitting information in them. In this case, MMS messages are proposed to map data from level 1 equipment to level 2 equipment, and to send commands from level 2 to

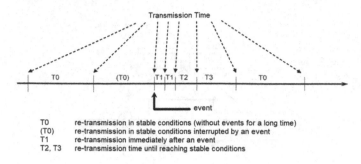

T0	re-transmission in stable conditions (without events for a long time)
(T0)	re-transmission in stable conditions interrupted by an event
T1	re-transmission immediately after an event
T2, T3	re-transmission time until reaching stable conditions

Fig. 2. Re-transmission scheme for GOOSE messages [5]

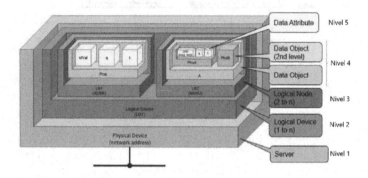

Fig. 3. Data model - hierarchical organization [7]

devices in lower levels [5]. Information is group in a data set depending on their transmission priority and on the kind of messages to be transmitted, GOOSE or MMS.

2.2 Data Model

IEC 61850 states that physical devices could be represented through a set of relevant data for the execution of SAS tasks. This data-set is defined as a logical device since is a virtual representation of a physical device. Also, the standard proposes a hierarchical organization of the substation information (see Fig. 3) in which lower level data-sets can be contained by a higher level data-set [7]. This structure in addition to provide a way of organizing data, models the power system as the integration of smaller models which are the data-sets that represent its components, bringing this virtual representation closer to the physical structure of the power system.

3 Retrofit Requirements

TRANSELECTRIC not only seeks a change in the technology of its equipment with the retrofit to IEC 61850 but also aims to incorporate other aspects such as current trends for substation control and protection that will allow to improve the operation of its line bays. In this regard, the requirements for retrofit were established based on the guidelines of the applicable regulations and also from specifications established by the Operation and Maintenance Area [1]. Such requirements are described in the following numbers.

3.1 Requirements in Accordance with IEC 61850

Communication Protocols. As part of the retrofit, all messages currently transmitted between level 1 equipment by wiring must be replaced by GOOSE messages while in the case of messages between level 1 devices and level 2 devices must be transmitted through MMS messages.

Signal Grouping. Bay signals must be grouped and organized according to the logical nodes established by the standard. In case there is no logical node for a specific device or element, a name according to the characteristics or functions of the device and its signals will be used.

3.2 Operation and Maintenance Requirements

Criteria for Line Protections. A redundant protection system must be implemented. With this objective, there must be two similar protection devices in the bay, if one of them fails the other device must be able to fulfil all the protection functions.

Criteria for Control of Line Bays. Maintenance maneuvers of level 0 equipment will be carried out only from board at this level, control commands cannot be sent from level 1 or level 2 in this type of operations.

Interlock Logics for Level 1 Equipment. Hard-wired interlocks will be migrated to software interlocks, as long as this does not compromise security during the operation of the bay or the substation.

Standard Operator Interface for Substations. An operator interface or HMI must be designed according to the needs and requirements of TRANSE-LECTRIC. This designed HMI will be implemented in all substations in which the retrofit will be applied.

4 Re-engineering and Development of Specifications

4.1 Re-engineering for INGA 1 Bay

Re-engineering is intended to establish: (1) the operating philosophy of the line bay after retrofit to IEC 61850, (2) the functioning of the operation circuits of level 0 equipment, and (3) equipment and other components for control, protection or measurement that will be installed in the control panel of the bay. The re-engineering also establishes the equipment or elements that will be installed, maintained or removed in INGA 1 bay since the previous engineering of this bay was taken as a reference for the re-engineering, also, the retrofit validation was developed taking as a reference such bay.

This work includes the retrofit of the bay from level 1 to level 2. For level 1, MiCOM C264 (bay control unit) and MiCOM P543 (line protection relay) devices were used. These equipment were selected because they are IEC 6185 certified and TRANSELECTRIC has them in its laboratory. In addition, the protection relay is similar to the one currently installed in INGA 1 bay. This will make it easier for the retrofit future implementation within Pomasqui substation. EcoSUI Server and EcoSUI HMI were developed under IEC 61850 standard, for that reason they have been used to implement the operator interface at level 2.

In order to maintain all functions currently implemented, during the development of the re-engineering, control and protection functions currently carried out were analysed, as well as what information and how it is exchanged within the bay, besides the equipment involved in such exchange. Then, necessary modifications were established and the most important ones that took place are:

- Replacement of hard-wired digital signals by GOOSE messages for communication between level 1 equipment.
- 52 (circuit breaker)closing sequence modification so that line protection equipment operates alone after function 25 has started.
- Configuration of two similar and redundant line protections.
- Association of functions 21, 67 and 87 to a single output contact of the line protection relay.
- Removal of local operation permits for level 0 equipment by level 1 equipment.
- Removal of power meter since the bay control unit (BCU) will perform this function.
- Removal of function 32 at Pomasqui substation since this function will be carried out by Pimampiro substation.

4.2   Standardization of Control and Protection Signals

Generally, control and protection signals are the same or very similar in all bays, except in some cases where there are more or less signals due to restrictions or intrinsic characteristics of level 0 or level 1 equipment. Therefore, a generic list of control and protection signals in a line-bay is defined. In addition, the signal names were standardized for level 1 to facilitate their recognition by the operator and by the maintenance staff. In this regard, due to the lack of official guidelines to assign a name to signals within a substation, a structure for naming them according to their type is proposed. The structure presented in Table 1 establishes that the signal names will have 4 terms whose combination will identify the type of signal, as well as the related equipment. This structure is complemented by the representation established for keywords of which a summary is shown

Table 1. Structure to name a signal according to its type [1]

Signal type	1st term	2nd term	3th term	4th term
Fault (F)	F	Fault type	N0 or N1 Device	Description
Command (CMD)	CMD	Device	Command type	-
Permissive (P)	P	Type	N0 Device	Description
Alarm (ALRM)	N0 Device	Type	ALRM	-
Position (POS)	N0 Device	POS	-	-
Local/Remote (L/R)	N0 Device	L/R	-	-
Starting (ARR)	Function	ARR	Description	Device
Trip (DISP)	Function	DISP	Description	Device
Analog IN	Signal type	Fase	-	-

Table 2. Keywords for signal names [1]

Keyword	Representation
Open	A
Opened	ABT
Active	ACT
Alarm	ALRM

a. Falla MCB motor 52-272
b. Falla circuito de disparo 1 52-272

Fig. 4. Structure example to name "fault" signals

in Table 2. An example of how to name a signal using the proposed structure is shown in Fig. 4.

4.3 Standardized Operator Interface

An HMI template is established and the aspects that were taken into account during its design were: (1) Establishing areas for different system views within the HMI screen, (2) Defining the information to be presented in each view of the system, (3) Defining colors for spaces and elements in the HMI.

The defined template shown in Fig. 5 exhibits areas 1 and 2 correspond to the electrical or system views, which will change depending on the required information, while areas 3 and 4 are permanent since they are the menu bar and substation alarms respectively. Data presented in area 3, corresponding to

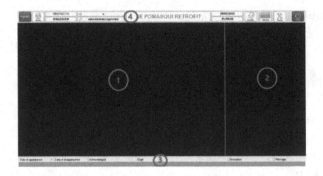

Fig. 5. Established template for operator interface

the bay view, were carefully selected since maneuvers of level 0 equipment will be performed, among other operations. Then, although it is necessary for the operator to have enough information to perform tasks, this does not mean overloading such area with too much data. Therefore, it was established that data enumerated below to be deployed in the bay view. A view of this area is shown in Fig. 6.

- Bay single line diagram.
- Measurements of CTs, PTs and power measurements.
- Status of synchronism elements.
- Operating permits for level 0 equipment.
- Bay alarms.
- Status and reset command of relay 86L.
- Status and enable/disable command of reclose (79).

5   Validation Tests

5.1   Test Platform

A test platform was implemented in TRANSELECTRIC's engineering laboratory to validate the retrofit. This platform aims to emulate the architecture and data flow of Pomasqui substation. For this reason, control levels of this substation with their respective equipment were implemented in the platform according to architecture depicted in Fig. 7 and the information flow shown in Fig. 8. Also, simulators of level 0 equipment were installed.

5.2   Functional Tests

It should be noted that this stage was performed in accordance with protocols and commissioning procedures established by TRANSELECTRIC.

Fig. 6. Bay view (INGA 1)

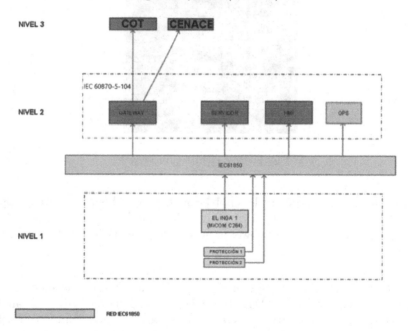

Fig. 7. Control architecture for the test platform

Verification of Failure Effect and Recovery of Auxiliary Power in IEDs.
An IED in bay is selected and its power supply is removed. Then, it is verified
that this event is notified in the bay communication architecture view in the

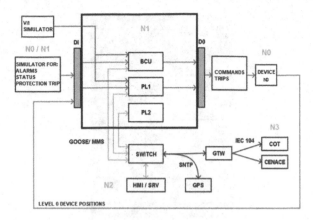

Fig. 8. Information flow for the test platform

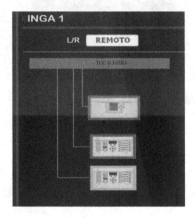

Fig. 9. Bay architecture view

HMI and any other equipment has not been affected. This procedure is applied to each IED in bay. The test for PL2 relay is shown in Fig. 9, in which is observed that although PL2 has lost its power supply neither the BCU nor PL1 have been affected.

Verification of HMI Views Deployment Time. This experiment aims to verify the deployment time of HMI views when a change from one view to another occurs. To carry it out several tests, some views are selected from and to where the tests will be performed. In order to verify that this time is adequate, the following evaluation reference is taken into account: (1) Not noticeable: 0–2 s, (2) Acceptable: 2–5 s, and (3) Unacceptable: >5 s.

Verification of System Response to Control Commands from Different Control Levels. The objective of the test is to verify execution times of

Fig. 10. Level 1 event log

PROYECTO	a	SE POMA
HMI 1	administrator;operator	

Origin	Description	Message
POMASQUI / 230 kV / INGA 1_BCU / 89-271	PERMISIVO 89-271 CERRAR	ON
POMASQUI / 230 kV / INGA 1_BCU / 89-273	PERMISIVO 89-273 CERRAR	OFF
POMASQUI / 230 kV / INGA 1_BCU / 79	CMD 79_PL1 GOOSSE	OFF
POMASQUI / 230 kV / INGA 1_BCU / 89-271	PERMISIVO 89-271 ABRIR	OFF
POMASQUI / 230 kV / INGA_1_PL1 / ESTADOS	CONTACTO DE VIDA BCU	NORMAL
POMASQUI / 230 kV / INGA 1_BCU / 52-272	ORDEN CIERRE DESDE BCU	OFF
POMASQUI / 230 kV / INGA 1_BCU / 79	On/Off order SPS	OFF
POMASQUI / 230 kV / INGA 1_BCU / BCU LOCAL/REMOTO	BCU LOCAL/REMOTO	LOCAL

Fig. 11. Level 2 event log

commands sent to level 0 equipment from level 1 and level 2 equipment. The referents for the evaluation were: (1) Not noticeable: execution time <1 s, (2) Acceptable: execution time between 1 and 3 s, and (3) Unacceptable: execution time >3 s.

Verification of Digital Signals Acquisition at Different Control Levels. In this test, mapping of signals to level 1 and 2 is checked. In line with this objective, it is verified that each signal is shown in the level 1 equipment (see Fig. 10) and in level 2 equipment (Fig. 11). This test was the most extensive, since 321 signals were validated.

Verification of Analog Signal Mapping to BCU and HMI. All signals from current or voltage transformers must be mapped to BCU and HMI. To carry out this verification, signals were emulated by means of current injectors for testing relays.

Validation of Function 25. This test aims to verify that the bay switch closes only when synchronism conditions are met. A current injector and its test software were used for creating two kind of conditions. First, conducive conditions to close the switch were emulated and the close command was actuated in

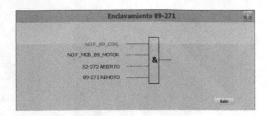

Fig. 12. Interlock tests for 89-271 using the HMI

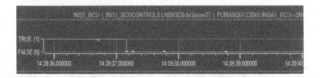

Fig. 13. Display of the first re transmission periods of a GOOSE message

Fig. 14. Display of the GOOSE transmission scheme

the HMI. Second, the close command was tested when synchronism conditions were not met. Proper operation of this function was verified in both cases.

Interlock Tests for Level 0 Equipment Operation. Compliance with interlock logic for operating level 0 equipment is evaluated by this test. In this regard, a first experiment places all the required conditions that actuate the permissive and verifies its activation. Then, all conditions are removed and restored one by one and using the HMI to graphically display of their status (see Fig. 12), it is verified that in the absence of at least one condition the permit will not be enabled [1].

GOOSE Message Test. In this test, the transmission time of a GOOSE message was approximately measured. The measured time was around 4.6 ms, which is less than 10 ms, thus, meeting operating requirements established for performance class P1. Additionally, GOOSE re-transmission scheme was verified as shown in Figs. 13 and in 14.

It is important to highlight that all the tests described previously were satisfactorily completed, validating the design of the proposed retrofit.

6   Conclusions

Development of guidelines for retrofit to IEC 61850 of a line-bay in transmission substations and their corresponding validation have been presented. These guidelines contemplate the re-engineering for a line-bay in order to define the operating philosophy, the functioning of the operation circuits of level 0 equipment, and equipment that will be installed in the control panel of the bay. So too the standardization of control and protection signals as well as the standardization of the operator interface for substations. Since interoperability is an important objective of IEC 61850, the guidelines will be applicable to any line-bay regardless of the equipment and by simple adaptations only. It is also important to note that although this retrofit is carried out based on a particular standard, it was not limited to a change of technology. Instead a comprehensive update process was established, since current control and protection criteria handled by operation and maintenance department was considered. This shows the flexibility of the standard to adapt to different practical cases that could arise. Among future works, the validation of the retrofit in line-bays with control and protection equipment from different manufacturers than the used in this work is proposed.

References

1. Mosquera, A.: Actualización de una bahía de línea tipo para subestaciones del Sistema Nacional Interconectado utilizando la norma IEC 61850 y estandarización de señales de control y protección. Escuela Politécnica Nacional, Quito (2019)
2. Electric System Mexico 2018: Modernización o Retrofit. http://electric-system.mx/servicios/modernizacion-o-retrofit/. Accessed 24 Feb 2019
3. International Electrotechnical Commission. IEC61850-1: Introduction and overview. Ginebra (2004)
4. International Electrotechnical Commission. IEC61850-7-2: Basic communication structure for substation and feeder equipment - ACSI. Ginebra (2004)
5. International Electrotechnical Commission. IEC61850-8-1: Speecific Communication Service Mapping (SCSM) - Mappings to MMS. Ginebra (2004)
6. International Electrotechnical Commission. IEC61850-7-1: Basic communication structure for substation and feeder equipment - Principles and models. Ginebra (2004)
7. International Electrotechnical Commission. IEC 61850–5: Communication requirements for functions and device models. Ginebra (2004)

Robohip: Robotic Platform for Hippotherapy in Children with Disabilities

Luis Carlos Murillo Penagos(iD), Aura María Millán Castro(iD),
and Javier Ferney Castillo Garcia(✉)(iD)

Universidad Santiago de Cali, Calle 5 No. 62-00 Barrio Pampalinda, Cali, Colombia
javier.castillo00@usc.edu.co

Abstract. The problems inherent to the intervention of animals in therapies are associated with risks that imply this interaction and the low capacity to carry out a quantitative assessment. This document aims to offer patients with motor, sensory and cognitive disabilities a different and safe treatment option. The approach to this problem uses a robotic platform divided into three systems, integrating elements for motor, cognitive and sensory rehabilitation: The first emulating the head and neck of the animal; the second emulating movements of rotation and translation of the horse's back in the three axes (base); the third to calculate the force vector relating the distribution of the child's weight, performing emulation of temperature ranging from 38 °C to 42 °C depending on the speed of work (seat), recording articular angles of the cervical region, thoracic cage, lumbar and hip; The patient is evaluated posturally, in-corporating a set of lights that make it easier to observe to which side the resulting force vector is directed, allowing him to modify his posture and improve his proprioception. The system comprises interaction of commands for the user so that he can develop new psychomotor skills and abilities. The data obtained can serve as indicators for the differential evaluation of each patient, as well as the possibility of monitoring variables such as Temperature, joint angles, and weight.

Keywords: Hippotherapy · Parallel robot · Robotic platform · Rehabilitation robotics

1 Introducción

The hippotherapy is a therapy that counts on the help of a horse, in this treatment a physiotherapist, a specialized horse, and a horse trainer are those who manage to integrate the movement of the horse in an alternative therapy [1]; it also provides a dynamic base of support, which turns it into an excellent therapeutic tool to improve the balance, the control and the strength of the trunk of the patients. Likewise, hippo-therapy acquires its distinctive effect through neuronal facilitation, vestibular stimulation, proprioceptive stimulation and psychosomatic influence [2].

Hippotherapy can treat different medical pathologies such as: autism spectrum disorder, substance abuse, multiple sclerosis, muscular dystrophy, amputation, developmental disorders, spinal cord injury, brain injury, cerebral palsy, convulsive disorders,

© Springer Nature Switzerland AG 2020
M. Botto-Tobar et al. (Eds.): ICAT 2019, CCIS 1195, pp. 166–178, 2020.
https://doi.org/10.1007/978-3-030-42531-9_14

visual, hearing impairment, learning disorders, emotional problems, anxiety disorders, behavioral problems, among others [3, 4]. Hippotherapy can be used in a wide range of pathologies but because animals are used in its application, this implies risks for both the patient and the therapist. At the same time, it is difficult to measure any variable on it, besides being able to replicate and quantify the movements that the animal generates and radiates towards the patient.

This research aims to present a proposal for a robotic platform for hippotherapy in children with disabilities, showing the elements that compose it and the functionalities that can be applied with this platform and the impacted areas of hippotherapy.

For the development of this document a contextual framework is developed wherein Sect. 1 the introduction is presented and the three-dimensional movements produced in a team are described, the three-dimensional movements in hippotherapy are described, parallel robots vs robots series, horse heat, areas of impact of hippotherapy, rehabilitation robotics and research related to this document, which are explained below.

1.1 Three-Dimensional Movements in Hippotherapy

The horse that fulfills the function of the physical therapist moves tridimensionally, therefore, it moves of horizontal, vertical and circular way. These movements generate stimuli in the patient's body focusing on the hip, which in turn affects the spine, pelvis, and medulla. To be able to carry out this therapy the horse must be meek, docile, agile, receptive and have crossed trot which leads to difficulties when it comes to having available cash with these characteristics. The structure made and expressed in this article allows at a much lower cost to have all these advantages with the movements made by the horse that are effective to help in the recovery of the patient. Before making any movement therapy the patient must balance in the horse to activate their reflexes of protection in the first movement giving benefits in both hypotonia and increased tone.

First movement: Abduction-adduction. As a first instance this movement is observed in the frontal plane (divides the body into anterior and posterior). The horse begins its march lifting its lumbar muscles vertically generating that the patient also rises vertically away from the back of this about 4 cm, this elevation affects the pelvis that performs lateral movements of 8 to 9 cm, when moving to the sides the patient with his spine seeks to stabilize. In other words, in the hip is made opening and closing movement which is called abduction and adduction. It has an equal gait that we perform daily under normal conditions [5].

Second movement: extension-flexion. As a first instance this movement is observed in the sagittal plane (divides the body into left and right). The previous movement is for the vertical part, extension-flexion elaborates on a horizontal march. The horse moves the front limbs and pushes the hind limbs both at the same time transmitting its point of gravity from the back to the center of gravity of the rider. The pelvis ex-tends and picks up rhythmically concerning the forward and backward displacement mentioned above resulting in the extension-flexion over this area of the body. As a great advantage, it reduces the postural tone so that the person takes a more relaxed and comfortable natural posture [5].

Third movement: inter-external rotation. As a first instance this movement is observed in the transverse plane (divides the body into upper and lower). The horse advances the anterior ones and gathers the posterior ones, generating that the ventral muscles give the accordion movement that is nothing more than the contraction-extension. The patient's pelvis responds with a rotation of 20°. The circular movement that results from the rotation gives internal and external extensions in the pelvis and the heads of the femurs in the acetabulum.

As great benefits, it achieves the correction of the posture unleashing reference and error signals that are used to maintain posture and balance. Many of the patients do not have these two signals that consist of identifying when it is time to march and when not to do so, thus giving feedback to the patient who may never have walked showing the information that was not present in him to do so [5].

1.2   Horse Heat

The heat of the horse is a primordial aspect in the hippotherapy and of the characteristics of the most difficult rehabilitation to simulate in the robotic platforms of this nature, where according to the step of the horse the heat is transferred to the rider, improving considerably all the stimuli of the pelvic belt and the spinal cord of the person, used to distend and to relax the musculature, to stimulate the tactile sense perception and to improve the blood flow that stimulates the circulatory system, which benefits in general the physiological function of the internal organs

1.3   Impact Areas of Hippotherapy

Bearing in mind that hippotherapy can be recommended for different medical pathologies, the areas and characteristics that are impacted by the use of this therapy are listed below.

Psychological/Cognitive: In people who do not present a cognitive deterioration associated with a disease, the objective of cognitive stimulation (cognitive training) is to achieve the stimulation, improvement and optimal functioning of the cognitive abilities important for people's daily life. Achieving improved well-being and personal autonomy, self-esteem, and self-efficacy, as well as the acquisition of skills necessary to deal satisfactorily with situations of stress and emotional imbalance, however, when the person presents cognitive impairment, the main objective of cognitive stimulation (cognitive rehabilitation) will be the recovery and restoration of altered functions. In this way, the slowdown of deterioration is attempted, achieving greater functional autonomy for a longer period. The metrics used are the Australian Scale for Asperger's Syndrome ASAS [6] and the Childhood Asperger Syndrome Test-CAST [7].

Communication and Language: Improves/increases gestural and oral communication, increases vocabulary, helps in the process of building sentences correctly and improves the articulation of words [8].

Psychomotor: Development of horizontal and vertical position, construction of body symmetry, promotes gross and fine psychomotor coordination, helps in the development of laterality. Psychomotor Development Assessment Scale [8].

Acquisition of New Learning and Riding Technique: Get on and off the horse as automatically as possible, learn to lead the horse to step, trot and gallop.

Socialization: To relate to people who do not belong to their family or school environment, to create friendly relationships with peers, to develop respect and love for animals, to increase the number of experiences.

Medical: Stimulation of peristalsis, stimulation of the circulatory system and stimulation of the respiratory system.

Motor: Regulation of muscular tone, inhibition of tonic reflexes and associated movements, recording and automation of the locomotion pattern, stabilization of the trunk and head, increase in elasticity, agility, muscular strength and development of the proprioceptive system. Gross motor function measure - GMFM [9]. Sitting assessment scale SAS [10].

1.4 Rehabilitation Robotics

The term rehabilitation engineering can be defined as the application of technological solutions to the different problems that people with special needs could face in everyday life. Robotic rehabilitation is a subfield of rehabilitation engineering and is part of the new technologies being implemented in occupational therapy and physiotherapy [11].

In Colombia, because of motor and cognitive disabilities, children are excluded from the educational system and adults have almost no employment opportunities, resulting in high social and economic costs [12]. Therefore, there is a valuable opportunity to implement technologies based on rehabilitation robotics that promote the inclusion and growth of the potentialities of the disabled population, as well as promoting the cognitive and physical rehabilitation of children in special conditions, in which a therapy protocol could be proposed with a system to measure and evaluate certain parameters that can be taken into account when evaluating a patient.

In relation to this work and after carrying out a bibliographic review, documents were found that can contribute to the development of this research, bearing in mind that although this type of rehabilitation has years of approach using a horse in itself, there are some applications in this field that seek to study the interaction with therapies assisted by robotic platforms in children, in order to observe the acceptance on the part of the patient and therapist as described below:

Caren System: This platform is used for motor control and motor learning, it impacts the medical and motor areas. Tests were performed in 11 children, patients had no disability condition and the results obtained suggest that the use of assisted systems can positively affect therapy [13].

Joba: This platform analyzes the therapeutic effects and contraindications of the use of a professional hippotherapy simulator in children with cerebral palsy, and evaluates motor development, control of sitting posture and hip abduction. The impacted areas were the medical and motor areas. The metrics used for patient assessment were GMFCS and SAS. The number of participants in this study was 38 children (4–18 years) [14].

Fortis-102: This robotic system is used for hippotherapy, the impacted area is the motor area, the validation metric was acceleration. The results obtained show that the accelerations between the robot and the real horse are very similar [15].

Gough-Stewart Platform: It is a robotic system of 6° of freedom for hippotherapy, the impacted areas were the learning of riding and motor techniques. The simulator developed performs the three basic maneuvers: walking, jogging, and galloping. The rider can control the behavior of the simulator through sensors and an interactive interface. The control aids used by the interface are the tension of the reins, the pressure of the calf and the angle of the stirrup [16].

IM-hirob: It is a robotic system of 6° of freedom for hippotherapy, its impact area is the motor. It achieves movements similar to those of a horse in its three axes. It allows assisting the patient until getting on the horse [17].

Robot-HBRT: It is a platform used in patients with progressive neuromuscular scoliosis before and after therapy, it impacts the medical and motor area. The patient assessment metric used is the Gross Motor Function Measure and muscle testing manual. This study involved 12 11-year-old children, the first study to provide evidence of the therapeutic efficacy of a new form of robot-HBRT on motor function and associated improvements in structural and motor control [18].

This type of research seeks to deepen aspects that generate options and from this offer, significant improvements in patients, compared to traditional therapy with the horse, along with greater comfort for both users and the physiotherapist.

2 Materials and Methods

2.1 Materials

MPU6050 Sensors. Patient posture monitoring is carried out with inertial sensors MPU6050-GY521, this is a six degrees of freedom (6DOF) inertial measurement unit (IMU), combining a 3-axis accelerometer and a 3-axis gyroscope [19]. The communication can be done both by SPI and by the I2C bus, so it is easy to obtain the measured data, the latter being the form of communication implemented because it used an I2C multiplexer. This sensor plays an important role since, apart from monitoring the patient's posture, it allows recording the orientation of the chair.

Load Cells. Made up of strain gauges, which at the minimum stress change of the resistance subjected to tensions together with an HX 711 module is responsible for converting the analog signal into a digital signal proportional to the deformation of the cell.

Temperature Sensors. In this project 2 different temperature sensors were used which are responsible for obtaining the temperature in the modes that emulate a horse at rest, walking and jogging, with temperatures from 38 to 42 °C respectively. One of the sensors together with a Solid State Relay 24–380vac 40a Ssr-40da, are the ones in charge, using a PI system (proportional, integral), of controlling the heat generation system that is carried by a nichrome thread lined with silicone capable of withstanding temperatures of up to 55 °C.

Power Supply. Two S-400 power supplies of 24 volts 16.6 amps each were used for the proposal.

High Torque Servomotor. For the development of the proposed robotic platform are used 8 servomotors of high torque ASMB04B, Working voltage: DC 11–24 V, torque Max: 380 kg.cm, Angle of rotation: 300° MAX (±150° or 0°–300° MAX [20].

Arduino One and Mega 2560. These devices were used to process the mathematical equations and to create the three-dimensional movements on the Stewart platform, the movement of the head and neck, the processing of the temperature control, the taking of data from the MPU6050 sensors, the control of the RGB LED ring, the control of the load cells and the orders of the resistive force sensors (fsr402).

2.2 Methods

Stewart Platform. For the development of the proposal, the solution to the mathematical problem of a Stewart Gough platform was used, the real data of the structure are calculated and implemented in the algorithm in charge of the mobility of the servos [21]. Figure 1 presents the coordinates of a Stewart platform.

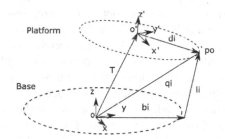

Fig. 1. Stewart platform and its coordinates.

However, using the mathematics presented [21], 40 possible solutions were found, although in practice many of these solutions would not be useful, it was chosen to select rotary servos, instead of linear servos to reduce the complexity of implementation.

Three-Dimensional Movements of the Stewart Structure. Seen in the section on three-dimensional movements of the horse, it was proposed as a solution the incorporation of the 3 movements of the different planes in one, where the therapist is the one who decides how many degrees in the x-axis, y, and z or how much distance in x, y, z needs the patient in the current state of his preliminary examination along with the 3 levels of intensity (walking, trotting, and galloping).

In Hippotherapy the horse must meet certain requirements such as their gait, size, height, temperature, and age, while with the Stewart platform solution we solve these prerequisites having a standard model based on mathematical solutions and programming. The terrain greatly influences the therapy because it has to be flat, different from the structure that does not need an environment outside the facilities of a clinic.

The software made for the structure is designed in an Arduino microcontroller, which offers a menu to the therapist with which he has to enter the respective values in position of x, y, z and rotational angles on the x, y and z axes for the current stage of the patient together with the appropriate intensity level for it. At any time of therapy (usually 20 to 30 min), the therapist is free to change the parameters to improve the outcome that is reflected in the patient and seek better results.

Temperature. The temperature in hippotherapy allows relaxing and distending the muscles and for this purpose was implemented on the seat of the structure with silicone lined nichrome thread, controlled by a solid-state relay and a microcontroller in which was developed a proportional control, integral (PI) based on an internal control model (IMC), which allows to obtain the model of plant data (with respect to an input step).

Once the model is obtained and the controller is designed for the object system, it is possible to apply different controller tuning methods such as the Ziegler Nichols method, the Cohen Coon method, or the internal control model (IMC) among others, which are used to meet the system requirements.

To tune a controller means to adjust the gains of each of the control actions to obtain an acceptable response of the process variable [22]. The tuning methods for proportional, integral and derivative controllers determine the adjustment of system requirements such as gain, derivative time and integral time. In the tuning of controllers, first the dynamics of the process must be identified, then the method of tuning controllers is selected and from this response the parameters of the controller to be implemented are determined.

Since there is the mathematical inverse of the operator describing the plant, this inverse is used as a controller and the closed-loop system is stable with this controller [23]. The IMC has been used as a control strategy that provides excellent results, thanks to its robustness against disturbances caused by disturbances.

The control by the internal model depends directly on the structure of the system and its mathematical model, this method consists of designing the controller according to the system requirements. To apply this tuning method, the plant must be tested to see how it responds. From this response the design parameters are chosen, with these parameters the controller is designed and finally, this controller is applied to the plant to see its response. The case study will focus on first-order models plus downtime.

Postural Monitoring. For the inertial sensors tests, a harness was used, adjusted to the child's body, placing the sensors as shown in Fig. 2, and locating them: (1) in the head, (1) in cervical vertebrae, (1) in lumbar vertebrae and (2) in the hip. These allowed the lateral movement of the entire trunk segment to be examined.

Weight Distribution and Cognitive Stimulation. For the development of the proposal, 5 ELN0418 load cells with their respective HX711 modules were used. Figure 3 shows three load cells that allow determining the location of the patient in the seat using

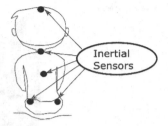

Fig. 2. Location of MPU6050 sensors

the resulting calculation between one load cell and the other. The location of the patient in the seat of the platform is shown by a ring of 24 programmable RGB LEDs, this ring is fed at 5 volts and commanded by a PWM signal from the micro, which depending on the location of the patient will illuminate a color in the direction in which it is, informing the patient to correct the location of his body in the structure.

Fig. 3. Load cells for weight distribution.

The two remaining load cells were used to instruct the servos of the head and neck determining braking and direction of the structure, commanded by a microcontroller ATMEGA16u2 being this the one in charge of sending the PWM signal to each servo of the head and neck. To increase the speed of the structure, the FSR402 sensors were used to simulate the stirrups of the horse.

Stimuli. The ring of LEDs used to determine the patient's location was also programmed to be used in visual stimuli, which work with a serial communication protocol of a line which means that each color corresponds to a signal. Auditory stimuli are achieved with an mp3 module and the signal is amplified and reproduced by a 3w speaker.

3   Results and Discussion

Figure 4 presents the design and implementation of the robotic platform for hippotherapy.

The movements performed by the platform emulate the therapeutic movements for hippotherapy, since there are no equations that model these movements, we proceeded to establish the precision with which the platform performed the angular and translation movements in the X, Y, and Z axes.

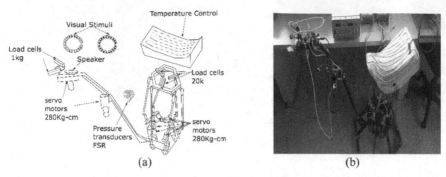

(a)   (b)

Fig. 4. Robotic platform for hippotherapy. (a) Schematic design, (b) Platform implementation.

Table 1 presents error percentages concerning the 3 axes of the Stewart platform, these error percentages are less than 5%, this compared to the little repeatability that can be achieved with a horse is a satisfactory result. These results were obtained using distance sensors placed on the platform and performing the different positions shown in Table 1.

Table 1. Percentage of error (z-axis).

Z-Axis	Distances (cm)								
	0	2	4	6	8	−2	−4	−6	−8
X (% error)	4,1	2,3	1,6	4,0	2,2	2,0	3,3	2,0	4,1
Y (% error)	2,3	0,7	2,3	2,0	2,9	1,9	2,5	1,8	2,3
Z (% error)	5,2	1,7	4,5	4,7	1,4	3,7	0,6	1,5	5,2

Table 2 presents the error percentages obtained for minimum and maximum rotational movements for the three axes, the angle reading was obtained by acquiring an inertial sensor MPU6050 which is integrated with the platform.

Table 2. Percentage of error concerning the min and max angles

Axis	Angles (degree)	
	Min (% error)	Max (%error)
X (% error)	−5° (9,4)	7° (8,7)
Y (% error)	−10° (5,3)	10° (7,6)
Z (% error)	−20° (11,2)	20° (9,8)

The importance of the heat of the horse in the hippotherapy is fundamental for the patients since this one helps to relax and to relax the muscles, and as solution a thermal blanket was implemented capable of generating 38 °C in state of rest and up to 42 °C in trot, emulating the corporal heat of the horse.

3.1 Heat Generation System

The temperature control was implemented in an Arduino microcontroller based on PID control (Proportional, Integral, and Derivative Controller). This is a feedback controller, which calculates the deviation or error between a mean value and the desired value. The actuator is a solid-state relay, which switches a load through an activation signal PWM (Pulse Width Modulation) generated from the Arduino. The temperature sensor used was a DS18B20.

Table 3 presents the time and temperature measurement values for the open-loop heat generator system, the heat generator system is excited by a voltage of 4.3 V (DC) from the Arduino PWM and reaches the actuator (solid-state relay) and heats the electrical resistance of 110 V (AC). These data allow us to calculate the equation of the first-order transfer function that best matches the data taken.

Table 3. Temperature opening point ratio

Temperature (°C)	Time (Seconds)
29.3	122
33.6	205
37,9	298
42,2	396

The process of tuning controllers can be empirical or using more elaborate techniques such as ZyN, CyC, and the IMC, the performance indices of the PI controller implemented using the different performance techniques are presented in Table 4.

Table 4. Performance index system variation with PI controller.

Methods	UAE	ISE	Mp	Ts/seg
Empirical	222.1535	135.4448	1.2	484
ZyN	311.4675	135.4925	1.3	520
CyC	242.5618	122.3332	1.35	601
IMC	38.6743	39.9203	1.0	360

The method of tuning by internal model or IMC is the one that presents the best results since it presents a smaller time of establishment, the smaller surpass, the smaller dynamic error and the smaller absolute error.

On the other hand, the seat of the platform makes it possible to evaluate and train the position of the child, since it records the values of the force vector expressed by the angular value and magnitude of the vector resulting from the tensions present in the three load cells, located at the base of the seat and whose output is sent and represented by an arrangement of LEDs in a circular shape.

The head and neck of the platform can be controlled to emulate the movements of the horse, the control of the turn of the head is achieved by the variation of the two load cells connected to the reins, to make greater tension on one side than on the other, the platform turns the head. When the stirrups are pressed (fsr 402 sensors), the system increases speed and when equal tension is applied to both sides of the reins, the system reduces speed.

The proposed system has 3 functionalities, which are:

– Motor.
– Cognitive (posture and stimulation).
– Motor + Cognitive.

The motor function works exclusively on the base of the platform, making soft movements to stimulate the lower back and hip; in the cognitive function, it is oriented to the use of the head and neck making the patient with his own hands interact with them through auditory and visual stimuli. The motor and cognitive function groups all the capacities offered by the platform, leading the patient to interact directly with the platform being the same who makes the structure always move in safe conditions.

As stated in the section on robotic platforms used for hippotherapy in which similar platforms are mentioned, also, the impact areas which can be compared with Table 5, which presents a relationship of the areas impacted by the platform and the pathologies that can be studied with the development of this project.

Table 5. Platform functionalities and pathologies associated with the intervention areas impacted by hippotherapy.

Functionalities	Similar platforms	Impacted areas						
		Ps/Cg	C& L	PsM	A&T	S	Me	Mt
Motor	Caren system			x			x	x
	Fortis-102 IM-hirob			x			x	x
Cognitive postural	Joba			x			x	x
Cognitiva-stimuli	Gough-Stewart platform				x			
					x			
Motor-cognitive	Robot-HBRT			x	x		x	x
	Gough-Stewart platform			x	x		x	x
				x	x		x	x
All functions	Proposed system	x	x	x			x	x

Ps/Cg-Psychological/cognitive,   **C&L**-Communication   and   language,   **PSM**-Psychomotor, **A&T**-Acquisition of new learning and riding technique, **S**-Socialization, **Me**-Medical, and **Mt**-Motor.

4 Conclusions

The platform proposed in comparison with the robotic platforms used for hippotherapy achieves multiple impact areas which shows the versatility of the system which will allow cognitive and motor assessment in children with special needs. With the development of the platform, a general error rate of less than 10% was found in the rotation and translation movements. This is significant but if we take into account that when validating hippotherapy, the movements generated by the platform prevail over its accuracy.

The designed platform has functionalities oriented to:

- Motor rehabilitation - emulation of equine movements.
- Cognitive - Teaching basic aspects of control of an equine.
- Cognitive-motor - Related to proprioception by properly sitting on the platform and preserving its postural location

References

1. Berneche García, M.: Terapias asistidas por caballos (TAC): El arte de la rehabilitación al paso y el rol del psicólogo: La Equinoterapia. Pre-proyecto de investigación. Universidad de la República (Uruguay). Facultad de Psicología (2015)
2. McGibbon, N.H., Benda, W., Duncan, B.R., Silkwood-Sherer, D.: Immediate and long-term effects of hippotherapy on the symmetry of adductor muscle activity and functional ability in children with spastic cerebral palsy. Arch. Phys. Med. Rehabil. **90**(6), 966–974 (2009)
3. Snider, L., Korner-Bitensky, N., Kammann, C., Warner, S., Saleh, M.: Horseback riding as therapy for children with cerebral palsy: is there evidence of its effectiveness? Phys. Occup. Ther. Pediatr. **27**(2), 5–23 (2007). (17442652)
4. Zadnikar, M., Katrin, A.: Effects of hippotherapy and therapeutic horseback riding on postural control or balance in children with cerebral palsy: a meta-analysis. Dev. Med. Child Neurol. **53**(8), 684–691 (2011)
5. Luz Stella Espinosa A: Generalidades de hipoterapia (2007). https://uscfisioavanzados.files. wordpress.com/2013/08/generalidades-de-hipoterapia
6. Attwood: The Complete Guide to Asperger's syndrome (2008). http://www.autismforthvalley. co.uk/files/5314/4595/7798/Attwood-Tony-The-Complete-Guide-to-Aspergers-Syndrome. pdf
7. Scott, F.J., Baron-Cohen, S., Bolton, P., Brayne, C.: The CAST (Childhood Asperger Syndrome Test): Preliminary Development of a UK Screen for Mainstream Primary-School-Age Children (2002)
8. Madrona, P.G., Contreras, O.R., Gómez, I.M.: Habilidades motrices en la infancia y su desarrollo desde una educación física animada. Revista Iberoamericana de Educación **47** (2008). https://rieoei.org/historico/documentos/rie47a04.htm
9. Rosenbaum, P.L., et al.: Prognosis for gross motor function in cerebral palsy: creation of motor development curves. JAMA **288**(11), 1357–1363 (2002)
10. Angsupaisal, M.: Effects of forward tilted seating and foot-support on postural adjustments in children with spastic cerebral palsy: an EMG-study. Eur. J. Paediatr. Neurol. (2019) https:// doi.org/10.1016/j.ejpn.2019.07.001
11. Acevedo, J., Caicedo, E., Castillo-Garcia, J.: Aplicación de tecnologías de rehabilitación robótica en niños con lesión del miembro superior (2017). ISSN: 0121-0807. http://www. scielo.org.co/scielo.php?pid=S0121-08072017000100103&script=sci_abstract&tlng=es

12. DANE: Proyecciones de población (2005). https://www.dane.gov.co/index.php/estadisticas-por-tema/demografia-y-poblacion/proyecciones-de-poblacion
13. Barton, G.J., Moine, C., Hawken, M.B.: Hippotherapy without a horse: the effects of passive movement on core control. Gait Posture **42**, S29 (2015)
14. Herrero, P., et al.: Study of the therapeutic effects of an advanced hippotherapy simulator in children with cerebral palsy: a randomized controlled trial. BMC Musculoskelet. Disord. **11**(1), 71 (2010)
15. Kim, M.J., Kim, T., Oh, S., Yoon, B.: Equine exercise in younger and older adults: simulated versus real horseback riding. Percept. Mot. Skills **125**(1), 93–108 (2018). https://doi.org/10.1177/0031512517736463
16. Eskola, R., Handroos, H.: Novel horseback riding simulator based on 6-DOF motion measurement, a motion base, and interactive control of gaits (2013). https://doi.org/10.1080/01691864.2013.824134
17. Mayr, A., Kofler, M., Saltuari, L.: IM-hirob: robotic hippotherapy or improvement of impaired trunk function-preliminary results. Neurorehabilitation Neural Repair (2012)
18. Kwon, J., Chang, H., Yi, S., Lee, Y., Shin, H., Kim, Y.: Effect of hippotherapy on gross motor function in children with cerebral palsy: a randomized controlled trial. J. Altern. Complement. Med. **21**(1), 15 (2015)
19. InvenSense: TDK | Atrayendo el Mañana (2019). https://www.invensense.com/
20. Moog: High torque direct drive rotary, advanced direct drive technology in a compact, customized package for high-power applications (2006). Moog.com/industrila/globallocato
21. Barona, R., Prado, G.: Plataforma robótica para emular los movimientos de un equino en tratamientos de hipoterapia, graduate thesis. Universidad Santiago de Cali (2018)
22. Alfaro, V.: Ecuaciones Para Controladores Pid Universales (2011). https://doi.org/10.15517/ring.v12i1-2.6429
23. Puerto Jorge, A., Rincon Liz, K., Edwar, J.: Control robusto por modelo interno aplicado como laboratorio virtual a un péndulo motorizado (2011)

Estimation of Non-physiological Parameter for Electric Power Generation Using a Conventional Bicycle

Daniel Salazar Muñoz⊙, Aura María Millán Castro⊙,
and Javier Ferney Castillo García⁽✉⁾ ⊙

Grupo de Investigación en Electrónica Industrial y Ambiental – GIEIAM,
Universidad Santiago de Cali, Cali, Colombia
javier.castillo00@usc.edu.co

Abstract. The need to find new alternative energy sources brings with it the use of unconventional power generation sources such as bicycles and the question arises as to how safe these sources are from the user's perspective. The present work consists in the estimation of a parameter of easy evaluation, for the safe use of a conventional bicycle in the generation of electrical energy. The generation of energy is achieved by coupling a bicycle to an electric alternator and this to an inverter. The load used was a 100 W lamp. The measurement of non-physiological parameters such as vibration, ambient temperature and pedaling speed as well as certain physiological parameters such as heart rate (HR) and body temperature, were used to determine both physiological and electrical signals when the user is overexerting. A protocol oriented to two routines was defined to evaluate the use of the bicycle in conditions of maximum effort and conditions of safe operation. Eight people between the ages of 22 and 32, body weights from 56 kg to 80 kg and heights from 1.59 m to 1.84 m participated. Voltage and current readings were taken to estimate the power and energy generated by the participants. In the process of user-bike interaction it was found that when the participant overexerted, he/she resorted to compensatory postural movements to maintain the pedaling speed. These compensatory movements made it possible to observe a relationship between the first derivative of vibration and HR.

Keywords: Bicycle · Non-conventional energy · Physiological signals · Non-physiological signals

1 Introduction

The pollution produced by thermal activity derived from the generation of electrical energy has caused the need to look for unconventional and environment-friendly energy sources [1]. A recent initiative is to implement bicycles coupled to an electrical generator [2] in domestic environments, which enables users to obtain electrical energy in exchange for physical activity, which alone has benefits such as improving heart failure problems, obesity and diabetes [3–5]. However, it is important to recognize that people cannot be compared with the performance of machines, and their health must be considered

© Springer Nature Switzerland AG 2020
M. Botto-Tobar et al. (Eds.): ICAT 2019, CCIS 1195, pp. 179–191, 2020.
https://doi.org/10.1007/978-3-030-42531-9_15

paramount. Therefore, the need arises to validate whether their use is safe or not, through the analysis of physiological and non-physiological parameters [6]. This procedure may require expensive equipment and specialized use, which are not appropriate to implement in this type of environment, leading to the need to seek simpler ways for the detection of health risks to avoid them.

Some authors had proposed the use of bicycles coupled to electric generators as a potential element to save energy in environments such as gyms, allowing to produce in an isolated way or with connection to the electric network [7], also experiments have been carried out that suggest that harnessing human energy is a method with a promising contribution, carrying out experiments with different types of generators, with a production capacity between 60 w and 200 w [8], however there is no clarity or suggestions on the risks to which users can be exposed when carrying out this type of activities.

The use of electric bicycles is a method that allows reducing vehicle congestion and pollution. However, they present the need to recharge the system and an added weight, as a solution was proposed the implementation of a hybrid electric bicycle with self-sufficient shits control based on the consumption of oxygen-gene, heart rate and the state of fatigue of the user, providing energy when the pedaling is inefficient and recovering it in the opposite case, thereby maintaining the charge of the battery for a longer time [9].

The following article goal is the estimation of a non-physiological parameter for the safe use of a conventional bicycle in the generation of electrical energy, based on the comparison analysis between physiological and non-physiological parameters of the individual, looking for a relationship between the parameters: heart rate and vibration, in order to offer a simple and easy to evaluate method to avoid risk conditions and use of complex equipment in domestic environments.

2 Materials and Methods

2.1 Materials

A system was designed to estimate safe conditions of use for users by measuring physical and electrical performance. The system was divided into three parts:

A Stage for the Acquisition of Physiological and Non-physiological Parameters: Designing a module to measure heart rate, body temperature, environment and vibration in a non-invasive manner. Transmitting information using radio frequency signals, and feeding the module with Ni-Cd batteries, working in an isolated way.

Power Stage: The bicycle was adapted on a fixed base, with the rear wheel attached to a three-phase electromagnet alternator with 14.3 V DC output and 500 W power, connected to a regulator to avoid voltage changes; storing the energy in a 12 V 7.5 ampere-hour (Ah) lead-acid bathtub, which was later raised to 110 V AC by means of a 1 kW inverter, and finally supplying a 100 W incandescent bulb.

Measurement Stage of System Parameters: It was designed to measure the rotation speed in Rpm of the alternator by means of an encoder with hall effect sensor [10], RMS current and RMS output voltage with isolation of the power system, by means of a circuit to condition the signal to the microcontroller; A panel of bars was constructed that indicates the velocity of the generator that the user must maintain, composed by 9 LEDs, 4 red LEDs to indicate a speed below the necessary one, 1 blue led to indicate an optimal speed and 4 green LEDs for speeds greater than the necessary ones, taking charge of receiving the information coming from the module for measurement of physiological and non-physiological parameters by means of a radiofrequency receiver, and transmitting all the information of the system to a file of Microsoft Excel, allowing to monitor the communication.

The design was implemented with an all-terrain bicycle size M or 18 inches with adjustable seat height, sprocket of 3 front and 6 rear gears, for tests was used a configuration of fixed sprockets in a ratio of 2 to 4. Figure 1 shows a general scheme of the system where the LED panel is illustrated and the device for acquiring signals from the user. Figure 2 shows the implemented system.

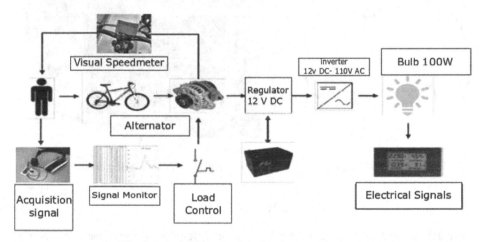

Fig. 1. Block diagram of the implemented system.

2.2 Methods

Heart Rate: A Myoware sensor was used for electromyographic signal acquisition (EMG) because of its high noise rejection capacity [11], positioning 3 electrodes as shown in Fig. 3A, the signal obtained can be seen in Fig. 3B, here are the peaks represent the time when there is a cardiovascular contraction, the operation was validated by comparing the signal with that delivered by circuits for obtaining photopletimographic and electrocardiographic signal (ECG) [12–15] in rest conditions and during physical activity and physical activity, obtaining a signal with optimal quality and adequate characteristics for the measurement of heart rate during physical activity, we used the so-rhythm energy signal threshold [16], to obtain pulses per minute - PPM, Eq. 1, shows the procedure used for the detection of the parameter.

Fig. 2. Implemented system.

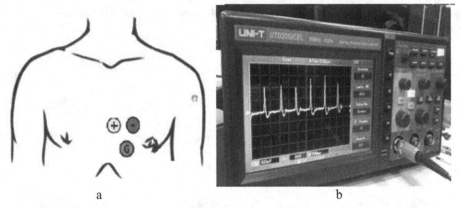

a   b

Fig. 3. Heart rate measurement. (a) Position of electrodes and (b) signal obtained.

$$HR = 60/RRa \tag{1}$$

where HR is the heart rate and RRa is the time difference between each contraction detected.

Body Temperature and Environment: Monitoring the thermoregulation of the participants and the temperature of the environment, using the difference between temperatures it was detected that the user wears the measurement system disabling the generation in the opposite case.

Generator Speed (rpm): It was used as a control parameter to estimate optimal conditions for a generation. [17], this allows to determine the optimal conditions for the generation and the physical performance during the activity, counting the peaks produced by the encoder during intervals of 1 s, multiplying the result by 60, obtaining rpm of the engine; Eqs. 2 and 3, describe the procedure used in the obtaining algorithms.

$$c(n) = \sum_{t(n)}^{t(n+1)} P(t) \tag{2}$$

$$Rpm = \left(\frac{c(n) - c(n-1)}{t2 - t1} \right) \times 60 = \left(\frac{\Delta y}{\Delta t} \right) \times 60 \qquad (3)$$

Where,
c(n) is the count of peaks during a second, t is time, and P are signal peaks.

Vibration: The count of the pulses activated by the intensity of the movement from the beginning to the end of the activity was carried out, producing a signal with positive ascending slope, which allowed to reflect the index of movement of the user, and to precise the moments of where there were more frequent changes of position, the Eq. 4 contains the procedure implemented for the obtaining of the parameter inside the algorithms.

$$Vb = \sum_{t(0)}^{\infty} P(t) \qquad (4)$$

Where,
Vb is vibration and p are the pulses produced in its time.

Electrical Parameters and Energy: A signal adequacy circuit was used to measure a maximum voltage signal of 180 V AC RMS, a hall effect sensor ACS712-20 to measure the current, obtaining in both cases a sinusoidal signal that had to go through a signal processing using calibration algorithms, with the product of the values obtained in time the apparent power was obtained as shown in Eq. 5 in Watts values [18].

$$S = V_{RMS} * I_{RMS} \qquad (5)$$

From the power, the transfer of energy in the system was calculated in watts per hour (Wh) using Eqs. 6 and 7, the conversion of equivalence to calories (Cal) was carried out using Eq. 7.

$$Wh = x \, W \frac{t(s)}{3600} \qquad (6)$$

$$1Wh = 0.860 \, Kcal \qquad (7)$$

where x corresponds to the average of Wh consumed during a time interval(t(s)) [19].

Electrical Safety: The measurements made to the test subjects were made taking into account the guidelines of the Colombian Technical Standard for "Electro-medical equipment" NTC-IEC60601-1, [20–22] of "Effects of current on humans and domestic animals" NTC 4120 [23] and the "Technical Regulation of Electrical Installations" RETIE [24]; the feeding of the measuring equipment was done by means of Ni-Cd batteries, isolating all exposed contacts from skin and sweat, with a power supply of 5 V Dc.

Calorie Consumption in the Human Body: The energy used for the functioning of the human body is obtained from the food ingested, the average diet of a normal person is approximately 2000 kilocalories per day (Kcal/d), which is distributed mainly for the function of the heart, respiratory and digestive system; The execution of physical exercise is estimated to have an approximate consumption of 27% of the total caloric consumption with amounts close to 600 kcal [25], however the high-performance athletes can reach higher energy consumption, the participants of events such as the Tour de France have an average consumption of 7000 kcal/d, which implies a diet of at least 17000 kcal/d [26].

An Estimate of a Person's Maximum Heart Rate During Exercise: The basic rule of clinical use stipulated by the American Heart Association dictates that the estimation of an individual's maximum heart rate is calculated by Eq. 8, reaching levels between 50–69% of the total during moderate exercise routines and values between 70 and 90% during hard exercise routines [27].

$$\text{Maximum heart rate} = 220 - \text{age of the individual} \qquad (8)$$

Overexertion and Risk Conditions: The development of physical activities where there is overexertion can have harmful consequences on human health, such as: supraventricular arrhythmias, exercise arrhythmias or arrhythmias that alter heart function, unstable angina, congestive heart insufficiency, severe valvular stenosis, complete atrioventricular block without pacemaker, frequent ventricular extrasystoles, arterial hypertension with figures >200/115 mm Hg, moderate valvular stenosis, moderate cardiomyopathy, fixed frequency pacemaker carrier, chronic infection, rheumatic or neuromuscular or bone disease aggravated by exercise, complicated gestation, untrained sedentary person, and over 40 years of age [28].

Test Subjects: He subjects of this investigation were 7 men and 1 woman. The participants were surveyed with a form where they voluntarily gave personal information and signed an informed consent form, the trial protocol was endorsed by the ethics committee of the University Santiago de Cali, the age of the subjects was in a range of 22–32 years, their weights in 56–80 kg, and heights between 1.59–1.84 m. The participants were surveyed with a form where they voluntarily gave personal information and signed an informed consent form, the trial protocol was endorsed by the ethics committee of the University Santiago de Cali, the age of the subjects was in a range of 22–32 years, their weights in 56–80 kg, and heights between 1.59–1.84 m.

Protocol for Carrying Out Tests: Test subjects must meet the following requirements:

- Be of legal age.
- You must not have smoked or eaten three hours before the test.
- Respond to a form with personal information informing if they suffer from any type of pathology or habits that may determine if it is convenient to perform the test.
- Fill out an informed consent form.

The patient should be given a clear and detailed explanation of the evaluation protocol, its risks and possible complications [29].

After the requirements have been met, the test will be performed at three intervals: rest interval (basal state), physical activity interval, and recovery interval, proceeding with the following steps:

- The measuring devices are placed on the user, calibrating and reading the variables.
- The user gets on the bicycle and remains at rest for 5 min.
- The subject begins pedaling without a load of the system, which holds for 1 min to adapt and achieve the optimum speed to generate.
- The participant is told that a change of effort will occur and tries to maintain the rhythm, the load is connected, and the user maintains the pedaling for a maximum time of 15 min and stops when entering fatigue (we understand fatigue from the point of view of not being able to maintain the rhythm of pedaling), by detection of the system or if the people who supervise the activity consider it is not convenient to continue, in which case, the load is disconnected from the system.
- At the end of the process of pedaling with load, the user is instructed to hold the bicycle for 5 min.
- The patient is no longer monitored when his vital signs return to the same basals. Figure 4 shows the timing diagram of the test performed on the subjects.

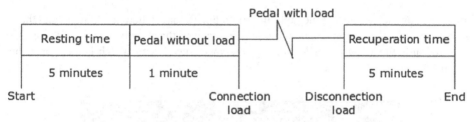

Fig. 4. Experimental protocol.

Experimental Analysis: The data obtained during the procedure were treated under the principle of ethics in research, contemplated in resolution 8430 of 1993, law 842 of 2013; under the principle of disciplinary engineering law, the statutory law of 1581 of 2012 and resolution 1377 on data protection, enshrined in the political constitution of Colombia.

Speed was used as control. The objective of the subjects during the pedaling stage is to maintain an adequate speed range, keeping the blue LED on the panel, making the system can generate electricity.

Two routines were performed, the first with the participation of 5 people in maximum effort condition, monitoring their heart rate, seeking to find a relationship with the vibration; the second routine with the participation of 3 people, who were disconnected from the load of the system as a result of the estimation of the instant of fatigue by analyzing the behavior of heart rate and vibration in both cases.

The exclusion criteria [29] for carrying out the tests were as follows:

- People with dehydration problems.
- People with osteogenesis imperfecta (crystal bones).
- People with AIDS.
- People with cancer.

- People with type I and II diabetes.
- People with kidney problems.
- People with scoliosis.
- People who are pregnant.
- People with morbid obesity.
- People with cardiac or respiratory conditions.
- Persons were unable to follow commands.
- People with balance problems.
- People over 60 years of age.

These parameters were selected as exclusion, because people who comply with these parameters may have some type of health risk during the development of the activity.

3   Results and Discussion

Figure 5 shows a user during the pedaling routine with load, where it is evident that there are no elements that inconvenience the performance of the activity, the user focuses his view towards the LED panel to identify the speed level with which it maintains the pedaling.

Fig. 5. User using the designed system, during the loaded pedaling stage

During pedaling it was identified that speeds below 1300 Rpm there was no generation, in the range of 1300–1400 Rpm presented a resistance in the movement of the generator that required additional effort on the part of the user, beyond this threshold the resistance decreased while maintaining the speed, providing optimal conditions of generation, it was determined that speeds above 1800 Rpm had no contribution to the generation in relation to effort, with this information the blue LED was set as a reference, indicating that the participant was in a range between 1400 and 1800 rpm.

Figure 6 shows the vibration and PPM signals, the vibrations values are remained low during the basal state, after the connection of the load, it is observed that the intensity of the vibration increases until arriving at a point in which there is a change in the slope, this interval delimited by two arrows, was denominated zone of overexertion, because here it was observed that the users were not able to continue the activity with normality, and resorted to postural movements with greater effort, to resume performance for a short time to reach the limit of their physical capacity, during this interval was observed an abrupt increase in heart rate to reach its maximum value, held for a few seconds after completing the pedaling, which showed an abnormal physiological behavior. Thus, the activity was ended and the recovery stage was started.

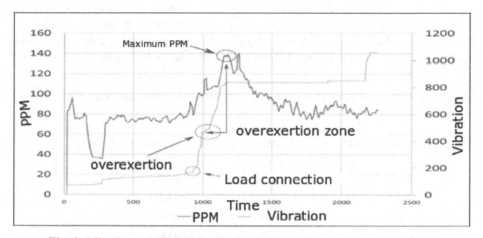

Fig. 6. Vibration and PPW during the first routine of the experimental protocol.

From this analysis, a control could be established to prevent the participant from continuing the activity by detecting these conditions, disabling the power supply to the electromagnet of the generator and consequently the generation of energy.

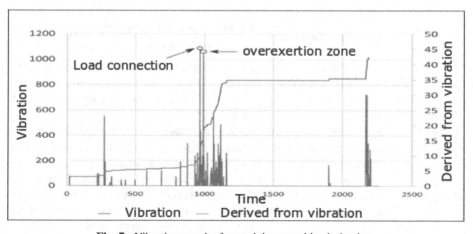

Fig. 7. Vibration graph of a participant and its derivative.

Figure 7 shows the vibration and its derivative from the vibration signal, the value of the vibration derivative when the load is connected is of the same order of magnitude when there is overexertion, suggesting that the derivative value when the load is connected can serve as a threshold for determining overexertion. From this analysis, a second routine of the experiment was established, consisting of the same protocol, with the exception that the moment the system detects that the user is starting overexertion, the generation of electrical energy was disabled, preventing users from undergoing sudden changes in their heart rate.

Once the overexertion zone of the user was identified, the percentage difference in heart rate was calculated. Equation 9 calculates the percentage difference in heart rate, taking into account the maximum PPM value and mean during the basal state at the moment of overexertion detected by the vibration derivative. Table 1 shows the percentage difference, maximum PPP and rule of clinical for heart rate.

Table 1. Information on PPM. Users with (*) correspond to users who participated in the second routine of the experimental protocol.

User	Percentage difference (%)	Maximum PPM	Maximum PPM (%) clinical rule
1	53,67	197	70,55
2	62,00	197	88,83
3	74,07	195	90,76
4	81,25	194	90,86
5	82,77	194	86,08
6*	6,39	197	78,68
7*	8,33	187	82,88
8*	4,11	188	84,04

$$Percentage\ difference = \frac{PPM - mean(PPM\ basal)}{PPM\ basal} \times 100 \qquad (9)$$

The percentage of maximum heart rate of the users during the first routine of the experiment had increased values that between 53.67% reached a value of 82.77% of the maximum heart rate presented, during the second routine of the experimental protocol it was found that the increase was less than 10%.

The external body temperature of the participants was a parameter that did not help to determine the relationship with the performance of the activity; the regulating response of the temperature of each participant behaved differently without a type parameter of the individual, however it was used to monitor that the participants maintained conditions that did not imply health risks, maintaining an external body temperature with a minimum value of 29 °C and a maximum of 34 °C, submitting to an ambient temperature of 25 °C.

The data obtained from the electrical parameters and the energy obtained in the form it is observed that although the voltage levels have a variation, they are in the optimal range for feeding electrical devices with an input level of 110 V RMS. The information obtained from the generation parameters is shown in Table 2 which shows the duration of activity with a load of the subjects, also shows the average voltage, current, power obtained in W and the energy obtained in Wh.

Table 2. Electrical measurements of the electrical energy generated by a conventional bicycle.

User	Time (s)	Average V RMS (volts)	Average I RMS (A)	Average power (W)	Energy (Wh)	Energy (cal)
1	53	117,69	0,64 A	75,32	1,1	946,5
2	78	119,14	0,64 A	76,25	1,65	1419,7
3	36	119,15	0,63 A	75,064	0,756	650,5
4	43	115,73	0,62 A	71,81	0,857	737,4
5	39	106,1	0,58 A	62,28	0,674	579,9
6*	40	125,28	0,72 A	90,95	1,01	869,0
7*	30	115,1	0,65 A	74,81	0,623	536,0
8*	30	103,01	0,59 A	60,77	0,506	435,4

The energy generated by the users of the first routine was a total of 5,037 Wh, with an average of 1,0074 Wh per user and with an average consumption of 866 calories (Cal) per person, the production of the participants of the second routine was 2,139 Wh, with an average of 0,713 Wh per person, equivalent to an average consumption of 613 Cal.

The user 2 presented a calorie consumption superior to 70% of the average diet, at the end of his routine, he presented decompensation and dizziness, for which he had to be attended, hydrated and put in rest until recovering his normal physiological parameters, with which it is evident that the inadequate use of the system can put the life in risk.

4   Conclusions

It was concluded that it is possible to estimate a non-physiological parameter for the safe use of a bicycle in the generation of electrical energy, by means of the derivation of vibration, identifying the instant in which the individual over-stresses, the intensity of movement of the individual has a close relationship with his physical capacity to maintain a continuous exercise and the heart rate.

Measuring physiological parameters is interesting, but can be uncomfortable for individuals, and involve risks that are not suitable for domestic environments, using the vibration sensor, implemented low-cost and simple to use, non-invasive and reusable.

Considering the short period that the users lasted, the energy obtained and the situation occurred with user 2, it is concluded that the generation of energy with this type of system is not justified and that life can be put at risk, the percentage difference of PPM presented a greater increase with ranges between 53.68% and 82.77%, and a disproportionate increase in heart rate in the subjects of the first routine, removing the load, it was possible to avoid these conditions for the subjects of the second routine who had a percentage difference of PPM less than 10%, demonstrating safe operating conditions. By identifying overexertion and avoiding it, the integrity of the participants can be safeguarded.

The generation of electrical energy from physical exercise is limited by the daily caloric consumption that a person can use, as the promised diet is 2000 Cal, a normal person could only use approximately 27% of his caloric consumption, this is equivalent to an approximate of 540 cal or 0.627 Wh, the results reflected values close to 1000 cal, taking into account the physiological characteristics of individuals, the system is not efficient for generating energy, however, the system may be appropriate for performing controlled exercise routines, by means of a dimmer or similar system that regulates the load of the system, which will be reflected in the effort required for pedalling.

References

1. Kong, X., Liu, X., Ma, L., Lee, K.Y.: Hierarchical distributed model predictive control of standalone Wind/Solar/Battery power system. IEEE Trans. Syst. Man Cybern. Syst. **49**, 1570–1581 (2019)
2. Von Drais, K., Mccall, T.: Diseño de un Sistema de generación de energía eléctrica a partir de bicicletas estáticas, p. 10 (2014)
3. Márquez, J.J., García, V., Ardila, R.: Ejercicio y prevención de obesidad y diabetes mellitus gestacional. Rev. Chil. Obstet. Ginecol. **77**(5), 401–406 (2012)
4. Suarez, G., Marquez, J., Marquez, J.: Beneficial effects of exercise in patients with heart failure, vol. 32, pp. 58–65 (2013)
5. Prabhu, R.S., Vasudev, N., Nandu, V., Lokesh, K.J., Anudev, J.: Design and implementation of a power conversion system on a bicycle with utilisation by sensors. In: Proceedings International Conference I-SMAC (IoT in Social, Mobile, Analytics and Cloud), I-SMAC 2018, pp. 117–121 (2019)
6. Carrión, D., Ortiz, L.: Generación distribuida a partir de bicicletas estáticas y sistemas híbridos. Ingenius **10**, 44–48 (2017)
7. Osma, G., Durán, J., Gil, A., Solano, J., Ordóñez, G.: Design and implementation of a power generation system using an stationary bicycle, pp. 15–17 (2015)
8. Mudaliar, S.M., Soman, A.R.: Electrical power generation harnessing human energy and its analysis. In: International Conference on Energy Systems and Applications, ICESA 2015, pp. 333–337 (2016)
9. Corno, M., Berretta, D., Spagnol, P., Savaresi, S.M.: Design, control, and validation of a charge-sustaining parallel hybrid bicycle. IEEE Trans. Control Syst. Technol. **24**(3), 817–829 (2016)
10. Webster, J.G.: The Measurement Instrumentation and Sensors Handbook, p. 2588. IEEE Press, Boca Raton (1999). no. 6
11. AdvancerTechnologies: MyoWare Muscle Sensor AT-04-001 Datasheet (2015). https://cdn.sparkfun.com/datasheets/Sensors/Biometric/MyowareUserManualAT-04-001.pdf. Accessed 23 July 2019
12. Webster, J.: Medical Instrumentation: Application and Design Student Edition, 4th edn. Wiley, Hoboken (2010). 2015
13. Rangayyan, R.M.: Biomedical Signal Analysis, 2nd edn. Wiley, New York (2015)
14. Subramanian, B.: ECG signal classification and parameter estimation using multiwavelet transform. Biomed. Res. **28**(7), 3187–3193 (2017)

15. Argüello Prada, E.J., Serna Maldonado, R.D.: A novel and low-complexity peak detection algorithm for heart rate estimation from low-amplitude photoplethysmographic (PPG) signals. J. Med. Eng. Technol. **42**(8), 569–577 (2018)
16. Parák, J., Havlík, J.: ECG signal processing and heart rate frequency detection methods. In: Proceedings of Technical Computing Prague, January 2011
17. Chapman, S.: Máquinas eléctricas, vol. 53, no. 9 (2013)
18. Alexander Charles, K., Sadiku Matthew, N.O.: Fundamentos de circuitos elétricos 5ed. Mcgraw-Hill/Interamericana Editores, S.A. de C.V (2013)
19. Freedman, R.A., Zemansky, S.: Física universitaria (Volume 1), 12th edn. (2009)
20. Instituto Colombiano de Normas Técnicas: Norma Técnica Colombiana NTC-IEC 60601-1-1 equipos electromédicos (2013)
21. Castro-Llanos, D.A., Carvajal-Escobar, Y., Medio, H.: Análisis de tendencia en la precipitación pluvial anual y mensual en el departamento del Valle del Cauca Analysis of the Trend in Annual and Monthly Rainfall in the Department of Valle del Cauca (2009)
22. Llamosa, L., Meza, L., Parra Lara, H.: Fundamentos para el diseño de la prueba de Seguridad electríca para equipo biomedico con base en la norma ntc-iso-iec-60601-1. Sci. Tech. **1**(30), 321–326 (2006)
23. Instituto Colombiano de Normas Técnicas: Norma Técnica Colombiana NTC-4120 Efectos de la corriente sobre los seres humanos y los animales domésticos (1997)
24. Ministerio de Minas Y Energia: Reglamento Técnico De Instalaciones Eléctricas (RETIE) (2013). https://www.asei-ingenieria.com/documents/retie.pdf. Accessed 18 July 2019
25. Pontzer, H., et al.: Constrained total energy expenditure and metabolic adaptation to physical activity in adult humans. Curr. Biol. **26**(3), 410–417 (2016)
26. Hammond, K.A., Diamond, J.: Maximal sustained energy budgets in humans and animals. Nature **386**, 6 (1997)
27. American Heart Association: Know Your Target Heart Rates for Exercise, Losing Weight and Health (2015). https://www.heart.org/en/healthy-living/fitness/fitness-basics/target-heart-rates. Accessed 12 Sept 2019
28. Aristizábal Rivera, J.C., Jaramillo Londoño, H.N., Rico Sierra, M.: Pautas generales para la prescripción de la actividad física en pacientes con enfermedades cardiovasculares. Iatreia **16**(3), 240–253 (2003)
29. García-Laguna, D.G., García-Salamanca, G.P., Tapiero-Paipa, Y.T., Ramos, D.M.: Determinants of lifestyles and their implications in Young University Students' Health determinantes Dos Estilos. Hacia la Promoción la Salud **17**(2), 169–185 (2012)

Platform for Adaptation of Myoelectric Prostheses in People with Upper Limb Amputation

Edgar Francisco Arcos Hurtado$^{(\boxtimes)}$ (iD), Andrés Felipe Ortegón Sanchez (iD),
Juberth Rentería (iD), Javier Ferney Castillo Garcia (iD),
and Maria del Mar Millán Castro (iD)

Universidad Santiago de Cali, Cali 760036, Colombia
edgar.arcos00@usc.edu.co

Abstract. This paper describes a platform for adaptation of myoelectric prostheses in people with upper limb amputation. The design of the platform is based on the anthropometry and biomechanics of human upper limb, servomotors are used to drive each degree of freedom, except in the articulation of the elbow, in which a gear motor is used. The myoelectric signal acquisition system includes Myoware myoelectric signal sensors from the company Advancer Technologies, an embedded system based on Arduino and a graphic interface to visualize myoelectric signals in real time. The implementation platform allows to replicate flexion/extension movements for the elbow, wrist, and each finger of the hand, pronation/supination of the wrist, and adduction/abduction of the thumb. The data acquisition system allows to visualize in real time, muscular activity concerning for 4 muscles, and was tested in people with upper limb amputation registering significant values for different movement intentions. The platform presented provides a feedback that could improve the adaptation of a superior limb amputee to a myoelectric prosthesis. The characterization of myoelectric signals generated by the residual limb of a person with upper limb amputation, allows to generate control signals according to a movement intention that would be replicated in the platform.

Keywords: Myoelectric prostheses · Upper limb amputation · Medical robotics

1 Introduction

An upper limb amputation is a surgical procedure through which part, or all, of the limb is removed, some of the causes may be accidents, infections, burns, diseases, etc. Any amputation is an experience that changes a person's life, it produces both physical and psychological negative effects that not only affect the person who suffers the amputation, but also those around him; communication, recreational activities are affected due to the limitation of movement resulting from the amputation, a problem that worsens the greater the degree of the same (see Fig. 1). Having an accurate number of the population with disability due to amputation is difficult, since there are no fully updated records worldwide, there are studies at the local level, for example, at the United States, based

© Springer Nature Switzerland AG 2020
M. Botto-Tobar et al. (Eds.): ICAT 2019, CCIS 1195, pp. 192–204, 2020.
https://doi.org/10.1007/978-3-030-42531-9_16

on information from National Center for Health Statistics, existence of 350,000 persons with amputations, 30% have upper limb loss, most common is partial hand amputation with loss of 1 or more fingers, and 50,000 new amputations every year. In Colombia, according to the registry for the location and characterization of people with disabilities, there are more than 530,000 people with disabilities due to amputations or alterations in hands, arms or legs. The study presented in [1] projects more than 3 million of amputations for 2050 around the world.

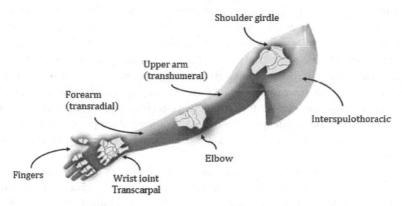

Fig. 1. Levels of upper limb amputation

Upper limb prostheses are medical devices used to improve quality of life in people with upper limb amputation. These can be divided into two types: passive and active prostheses [2]. Passive prostheses have a mostly aesthetic function, although they also have a certain degree of functionality allowing the user to hold objects. Active prostheses can perform rotation and grasp movements of objects through an activation function either by a force of the same body, or by an external force. Usually, prostheses that are activated by a force exerted by the same body, do so through a cable that adjusts through a harness to the body of the user, its operation is based on the extension of the cable through the harness to the opening or closing of the final element of the prosthesis, which emulates hand functions. On the other hand, the prostheses that are activated by an external force generally use electric motors, these can be controlled by buttons [3], or by signals captured through sensors that mainly measure muscle activity [4], reflecting a movement intention, these prostheses, known as myoelectric prostheses make use of electromyography signals (EMG), i.e., the electrical signals produced by a muscle during the process of contraction and relaxation, these signals are conducted to a signal processing system, and then use them as control signals for the actuator elements who execute the movement of the prosthesis. Finally, prostheses that combine different techniques to capture data that reflect the movement intention of the user, and thus provide more precise control of the prosthesis are known as hybrid prostheses [5]. A more detailed analysis of the classification of upper limb prostheses is presented in [2] and [6].

Myoelectric prostheses are one of the greatest technological advances used to improve the quality of life of people with upper limb amputation, although there is still a need to improve control techniques that imply better adaptation, mainly to higher degrees of amputation (e.g., transhumeral). In the traditional control strategy, manufacturers of myoelectric prostheses, use two electrodes positioned on two antagonistic muscles of the residual limb (e.g., flexor and extensor in the forearm or biceps and triceps in the upper arm) to produce control signals that activate one degree of freedom at time; to activate another degree of freedom is required a switch function that the user must generate, normally through a co-contraction, this strategy of control is very robust, but slowly and unnatural [7] it is limited by the patient's ability to remember and perform the trigger motions, potentially leading to the abandonment of the device [8]. In an attempt to reduce the mental load of the patient and provide a more intuitive control of upper limb prosthetic devices, Different studies based mainly on machine learning have been carried out to improve the adaptation of myoelectric prostheses to the user [9–11] pattern recognition methods have been extensively investigated over the last few decades. The input to the classifier in this case would be the electromyographic signals and the output would be a class corresponding to the intended grasp [12]. Myoelectric training systems to improve the adaptation of the prostheses to the amputated are presented in [13], some of them are game-based like in [14, 15], and others, using real and virtual environments like in [16, 17].

The platform for adaptation of myoelectric prostheses in people with upper limb amputation presented in this article, aim to improve the adaptation of myoelectric upper limb prostheses, its allows to implement different control strategies, this can be used for people with different levels of upper limb amputation, and allows to replicate flexion/extension movements for the elbow, wrist, and each finger of the hand, pronation/supination of the wrist, and adduction/abduction of the thumb. Additionally, it has a four-channel myoelectric signal acquisition system with a simultaneous real-time visualization interface.

2   Material and Method

The design methodology was based on the creation of a physical platform that allows to replicate movements of the upper limb, constituted by articulations powered by electric motors, and a system of acquisition of myoelectric signals that allow generating control signals to activate the platform according to an intention of movement indicated.

Stablished design requirements for the platform for adaptation of myoelectric prostheses in people with upper limb amputation presented in this article were:

- The platform must allow to replicate flexion/extension movements for the elbow, wrist, and each finger of the hand, pronation/supination of the wrist, and adduction/abduction of the thumb.
- The Joint complexes of the platform must be analogous to anthropometry and biomechanics of the upper limb.
- The platform must have a four-channel myoelectric signal acquisition system with a simultaneous real-time visualization interface.

2.1 Mechanical Design

Table 1 presents data on the anthropometric dimensions of the Colombian population, resulting from the evaluation of n population, both male and female, between the ages of 20 and 59 [18]. These data are considered taking into account the local context, the size of the population evaluated, the age range and the different dimensions observed, being useful in the design, in terms of similarity of measures between an upper limb and an upper limb prosthesis. Finally, the average of the resulting means of both populations per each dimension is calculated, establishing the lengths that parameterize the design.

Table 1. Anthropometric measures of upper limb in Colombian population

Segment	Data for women (mm)	Data for men (mm)	Average (mm)
Metacarpal width	74	84	79
Hand length	166	183	174,5
Palm length	93	102	97,5
Perimeter of the carpus	146	164	155
Arm perimeter	280	296	288
Perimeter of the forearm	235	268	251,5
Acromial height	1272	1379	1325,5
Radial height	981	1064	1022,5
Styloid height	752	813	782,5

Hand Design. To determine the diameter of the fingers, the metacarpal width was taken as the reference, four contiguous circumferences were made, with symmetry restriction of 2,00 mm in the spaces between the metacarpus, and outer space of the metacarpus two and five, comprised on a symmetry restriction of 79,00 mm, resulting in four circumferences with a diameter of 17,25 mm; for metacarpus one (thumb) the diameter value is set equal. With respect to the length of the fingers, the length of the hand and the length of the palm of the hand are taken as the reference, to obtain the measure of the middle finger and use it as a guide in proportion for the other fingers. Then, to determine the lengths of the phalanx, several percentages of finger are considered, 36% for proximal phalanx, 33% for middle phalanx, and 31% for distal phalanx, these percentages applied for index finger, middle finger, ring finger, and Little finger; for the thumb, 55% for proximal phalanx, and 45% for distal phalanx. The Table 2 shows the resulting lengths.

The design includes cuts of 45° in each phalanx, allowing flexion/extension movements; in addition, in each finger three holes of four mm in diameter are made, which are the path of the material that acts as an flexor/tensor tendon (see Fig. 2).

The design of the back and palm of the hand had as reference the length and width of the palm of the hand. In the upper part of the palm a 45° chamfer was made, which together with the cut of the fingers determined in this area, provides an angle of 90°

Table 2. Lengths of fingers and phalanx

	Length (mm)	Proximal phalanx (mm)	Middle phalanx (mm)	Distal phalanx (mm)
Middle finger	77	27,72	25,41	23,87
Ring finger	72	25,92	23,76	22,32
Index finger	69	24,84	22,77	21,39
Little finger	62	22,32	20,46	19,22
Thumb finger	63	34,65	n/a	28,35

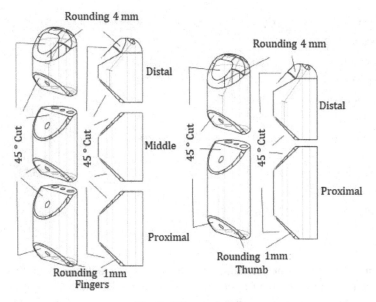

Fig. 2. Fingers design

for better mobility of the fingers, additionally, symmetrical holes to the position of the index finger to little finger are included, these holes lead the elements that promote the flexion and extension of the fingers by subjecting them to micro servomotors that are located in the palm of the hand. The thumb is attached to a base that can perform a rotation of 90°, it is placed in such a way that it can perform a flexion up to 80° from the proximal phalanx. The design of the base of the thumb includes locations to two micro servomotors, one of them rotates the base for the gesture of the thumb, and the other one performs flexion and extension of the finger.

For the wrist design, the perimeter of the wrist was taken as the reference, a guide circumference of diameter 49,338 mm is determined, and a half cylinder with a height of 40 mm and a rounding of 49 mm is constructed at the bottom of the curved area. In addition, a space is adapted for the placement of the bushing of the servomotor what executes the wrist flexion/extension.

Finally, to hide the components of the hand and the base of the thumb, covers with fixing holes are designed; for micro servomotors of the fingers supports are designed to assemble them in the hand, and a coupler to tie the material of the flexor tendon and execute the movement to pull.

Forearm Design. To determine the dimensions of the forearm, the measurements of the radial height, the styloid height, and the perimeter of the forearm presented in Table 1 were used as reference, resulting: length for the design of the forearm 240 mm and radius for the forearm design 40,0275 mm. The forearm design is divided into three sections: proximal section, middle section, and distal section. The proximal section responsible for performing joint movement with the arm, joining with the humeral section, and prono-supination, joining with the medial section, is modeled with a diameter of 80,055 mm and a length of 70 mm. The proximal section performs articular movement through straight bevel gears, the driving gear from the arm, and that driven in the forearm. In the proximal part of the forearm is located a servomotor that performs the pronosupination movement.

The design of the middle section consists of a hollow cylinder, at the bottom it has holes for the bushing of the servo motor what executes pronosupination, and space to wire the micro servomotors. The diameter corresponds to the same of the proximal section and the height is 110 mm. This section has space in order to adapt the wiring or components such as batteries to power the system; The opening is covered by a lid.

The design of the distal section is based on a half cylinder (transverse cut) with 49 mm rounding at the bottom, and symmetrical cuts to adapt the shape surrounding the servo motor that acts as a wrist flexion/extension.

Arm Design. For the design of the arm, the length and diameter of the arm are taken as reference (see Table 1), from which a radius of 45,8366 mm and a length of 151,5 mm is obtained. The arm section is divided into three sections, the first along with the proximal part of the forearm, forming the elbow flexion/ extension joint complex. In the second section, mounting holes are established for the DC motor support and power drivers. The third section performs the function of securing the prosthesis to a support, which provides stability, and allows the platform to perform the movements according to the constructed joint complexes. The acquisition and movement control card is located in this area of the platform.

2.2 Data Acquisition System

The acquisition of myoelectric signals is carried out by using the Myoware sensor of the ADVANCER TECHNOLOGIES company, in conjunction with surface electrodes of the company COVIDIEN. The Myoware sensor has a single reading channel with variable gain, it only allows sensing a muscle, through three electrodes, the reference electrode must be placed on a bony or nonadjacent muscular part of the body near the targeted muscle, and the sensor must be placed so one of the connected electrodes is in the middle of the muscle body. The other electrode should line up in the direction of the muscle length, the Myoware sensor obtains the signal corresponding to the activity of a muscle when it contracts and relaxes, and then filters and amplifies it, providing an analog signal that can be read by an analog/digital converter, a microcontroller, or a development card such as Arduino, Raspberry Pi, etc.

The acquisition system consists of 4 Myoware sensors, an Arduino Uno development card, and a graphical interface developed in Python. The output signal of each Myoware sensor is connected to an analog input of the Arduino Uno development card, in which the analog/digital conversion is performed using a 10-bit converter. The signal from the 4 myoelectric sensors is read by the Arduino Uno simultaneously at a sampling frequency of 300 Hz, and sent via serial communication to a computer to visualize it in real time using a graphical interface developed in Python with the Matplotlib library.

2.3 Actuation System

So that the platform replicate flexion/extension movements for the elbow, wrist, and each finger of the hand, pronation/supination of the wrist, and adduction/abduction of the thumb, electric motors were implemented as actuators of the platform. For the movement of flexion and extension of the fingers, as well as for the rotation of the thumb, Tower Pro MG90S micro servomotors were installed, which provides a torque of 2,2 Kgr.cm with a power supply of 6 V. To perform flexion/extension, and pronosupination of the wrist, two Hitec HS-645MG servomotors were installed, which provide a torque of 19 Kgr.cm with a 6 V supply. Finally, to perform the elbow flexion and extension, a DC gear motor with a ratio of 100:1 was used that provides a torque of 34 kg.cm, at 12 V, with a current consumption of 150 mA without load, this motor is coupled to a pair of bevel gears that allow to make a change of axis of rotation and increase the torque in a 3:1 ratio. Additionally, this gear motor has an integrated quadrature encoder that provides a resolution of 64 counts per revolution of the motor shaft, which corresponds to 6,533 counts per revolution of the gearbox's output shaft. Each of the installed motors is activated through a driver based on the integrated monolithic circuit L298. It is a high voltage, high current dual full-bridge driver designed to accept standard TTL logic levels and drive inductive loads such as relays, solenoids, DC and stepping motors.

3 Results and Discussions

3.1 Mechanical Design and Actuation System

The construction of the platform was carried out in the Creative Lab laboratory of the Universidad Santiago de Cali - Colombia, mainly through the 3D printing process. The developed platform allows to replicate flexion/extension movements for the elbow, wrist, and each finger of the hand, pronation/supination of the wrist, and adduction/abduction of the thumb. Below are specifications:

- The interaction of the interphalangeal movements of the index, middle, ring, and little fingers develops angles of 90° for flexion. The interaction of the interphalangeal movements of the thumb develops angles of 80° for flexion (see Fig. 3).
- Opposition movement of the thumb, and flexion movement of fingers, allow to grab objects of different geometries (see Fig. 3).

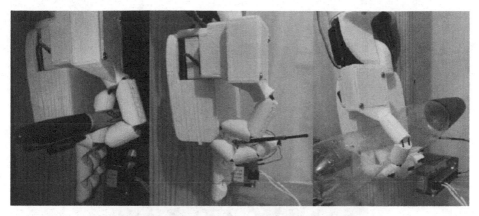

Fig. 3. Grasping objects of different geometries

- Wrist joint develops 90° for active flexion and 80° for active extension (see Fig. 4).
- Wrist develops 80° for pronation, and 85° for supination (see Fig. 5).
- Flexion/extension of the elbow has a range of motion of 0° (complete extension) to 120° (flexion) (see Fig. 6).

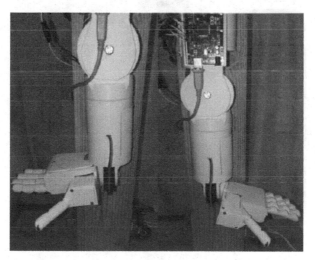

Fig. 4. Flexion/extension of wrist

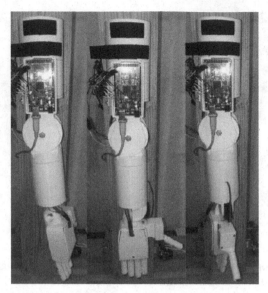

Fig. 5. Pronation/supination

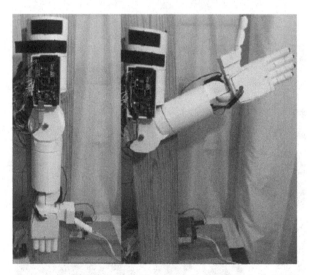

Fig. 6. Flexion/extension of elbow

3.2 Data Acquisition System

The myoelectric signal acquisition system developed allows obtaining simultaneous information from 4 sensors with a sampling frequency of 300 Hz, and with real-time visualization through a graphical interface developed in Python. Two types of trials were performed, one indicating a user when activating the biceps and triceps muscles without performing movement in the elbow joint, and another indicating a user perform the elbow flexion and extension movement.

Figures 7 and 8 present myoelectric signals generated by the biceps and triceps muscles of two different people, Fig. 7 corresponds to the myoelectric signals of a person who performs gym practices daily, and Fig. 8 corresponds to the myoelectric signals of a person with an elbow joint disarticulation. In both trials the data acquisition system records the biceps and triceps muscle activity, when people were told when to activate each muscle, without performing movement. From Fig. 7, is clearly see that the person who frequently visits the gym, controls the activity of each muscle very well, being reflected in the levels of activity that are presented in the graph, specifically, the signal generated by the biceps muscle It has a greater amplitude than the triceps when it is activated. On the other hand, from Fig. 8, it is possible to say that the signal acquisition system registers for the person with elbow disarticulation, relevant amplitudes in the signal of the biceps and triceps muscles, unlike Fig. 7, for The person with elbow disarticulation shows a higher level of activity when the triceps is activated.

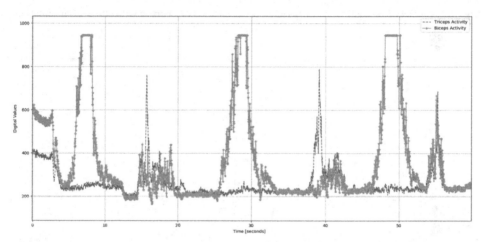

Fig. 7. Myoelectric signals from biceps and triceps muscles of a person who practice exercise daily at gym

Figure 9 presents the record of the biceps and triceps muscle activity, in this trial two sensors were located in each muscle, and the user was instructed to perform the movement of flexion and extension of the elbow joint, the system of Acquisition of myoelectric signals developed, records values according to the muscular activity carried out in each of the sensor locations, being more significant, those that are directly involved in the execution of the movement.

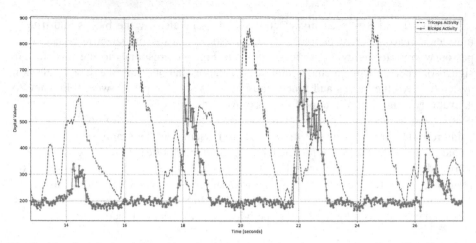

Fig. 8. Myoelectric signals from biceps and triceps muscles of a person with elbow disarticulation

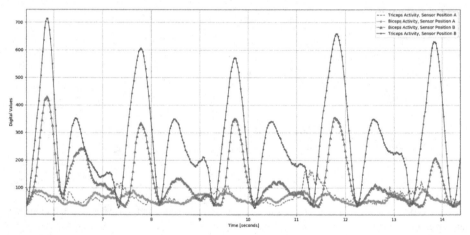

Fig. 9. Myoelectric signals registered by four sensors located at different zones of biceps and triceps when a user executed flexion/extension movement of elbow

4   Conclusions

The platform presented enhances the development and experimentation of control methods of myoelectric prostheses, this can be used for people with different levels of amputation, because it allows to replicate flexion/extension movements for the elbow, wrist, and each finger of the hand, pronation/supination of the wrist, and adduction/abduction of the thumb.

The data acquisition system allows to save myoelectric signals generated by the residual limb of a person for different gestures or movement intentions, through a simultaneous reading of 4 channels with a frequency of 300 Hz, with this, it is possible to generate datasets for later use in the development of control strategies based on machine learning.

The platform presented in this article provides a preliminary step for the implementation of a prosthesis in a patient with upper limb amputation, its main contribution is to enhance the development and experimentation of control strategies that allow a better adaptation of the user, for this reason, adjustments in mechanical design and actuation system like presented in [19], will be necessary to ensure proper functionality of the prosthesis to be built for a specific user.

The acquisition of myoelectric signals was performed using Myoware sensors of the Advancer Technologies Company, and no results were compared with another sensor, so it is recommended to analyze different sensors like in [20] to ensure greater user comfort.

Acknowledgments. The authors are thankful for the support provided by DGI of Universidad Santiago de Cali, Colombia, project No. 819-621119-421.

Disclosure Statement. No potential conflict of interest was reported by the authors.

References

1. Maduri, P., Akhondi, H.: Upper limb amputation. In: StatPearls [Internet]. StatPearls Publishing (2019)
2. Ribeiro, J., et al.: Analysis of man-machine interfaces in upper-limb prosthesis: a review. Robotics **8**(1), 16 (2019)
3. Dar, F.M., Asgher, U., Malik, D., Adil, E., Shahzad, H., Ali, A.: Automation of prosthetic upper limbs for transhumeral amputees using switch-controlled motors. arXiv preprint arXiv: 1401.5181 (2014)
4. Geethanjali, P.: Myoelectric control of prosthetic hands: state-of-the-art review. Med. Dev. (Auckland, NZ) **9**, 247 (2016)
5. Grimm, F., Walter, A., Spüler, M., Naros, G., Rosenstiel, W., Gharabaghi, A.: Hybrid neuro-prosthesis for the upper limb: combining brain-controlled neuromuscular stimulation with a multi-joint arm exoskeleton. Front. Neurosci. **10**, 367 (2016)
6. Nader, H.G.: Otto Bock Prosthetic Compendium-Upper Limb Prostheses, 2nd edn. Schiele & Schon, Berlin (2002)
7. Hahne, J.M., Markovic, M., Farina, D.: User adaptation in myoelectric man-machine interfaces. Sci. Rep. **7**(1), 4437 (2017)
8. Biddiss, E.A., Chau, T.T.: Upper limb prosthesis use and abandonment: a survey of the last 25 years. Prosthet. Orthot. Int. **31**(3), 236–257 (2007)
9. Hahne, J.M., Graimann, B., Muller, K.R.: Spatial filtering for robust myoelectric control. IEEE Trans. Biomed. Eng. **59**(5), 1436–1443 (2012)
10. Young, A.J., Smith, L.H., Rouse, E.J., Hargrove, L.J.: Classification of simultaneous movements using surface EMG pattern recognition. IEEE Trans. Biomed. Eng. **60**(5), 1250–1258 (2012)
11. Ameri, A., Kamavuako, E.N., Scheme, E.J., Englehart, K.B., Parker, P.A.: Support vector regression for improved real-time, simultaneous myoelectric control. IEEE Trans. Neural Syst. Rehabil. Eng. **22**(6), 1198–1209 (2014)
12. Kyranou, I., Vijayakumar, S., Erden, M.S.: Causes of performance degradation in non-invasive electromyographic pattern recognition in upper limbs prostheses. Front. Neurorobotics **12**, 58 (2018)

13. Dawson, M.R., Carey, J.P., Fahimi, F.: Myoelectric training systems. Expert Rev. Med. Devices **8**(5), 581–589 (2011)
14. Prahm, C., Vujaklija, I., Kayali, F., Purgathofer, P., Aszmann, O.C.: Game-based rehabilitation for myoelectric prosthesis control. JMIR Serious Games **5**(1), e3 (2017)
15. Radhakrishnan, M., Smailagic, A., French, B., Siewiorek, D. P., Balan, R.K.: Design and assessment of myoelectric games for prosthesis training of upper limb amputees. In: 2019 IEEE International Conference on Pervasive Computing and Communications Workshops (PerCom Workshops), pp. 151–157. IEEE, March 2019
16. Austin, J., Shehata, A.W., Dawson, M.R., Carey, J., Hebert, J.S.: Improving performance of pattern recognition-based myoelectric control using a desktop robotic arm training tool. In: 2018 IEEE Life Sciences Conference (LSC), pp. 231–234. IEEE, October 2018
17. Dombrowski, M., Smith, Peter A., Buyssens, R.: Utilizing digital game environments for training prosthetic use. In: Lackey, S., Shumaker, R. (eds.) VAMR 2016. LNCS, vol. 9740, pp. 481–489. Springer, Cham (2016). https://doi.org/10.1007/978-3-319-39907-2_46
18. Ávila Chaurand, R., Prado León, L.R., González Muñoz, E.L.: Dimensiones antropométricas de población latinoamericana. Universidad de Guadalajara, CUAAD (2007)
19. Bennett, D.A., Mitchell, J.E., Truex, D., Goldfarb, M.: Design of a myoelectric transhumeral prosthesis. IEEE/ASME Trans. Mechatron. **21**(4), 1868–1879 (2016)
20. Calado, A.L.A.: Comparison between low-cost and high-end sEMG sensors for the control of a transradial myoelectric prosthesis (Doctoral dissertation) (2017)

Determination of Electrical Bioimpedance Characteristics for the Study of People with Type II Diabetes

Luis Carlos Rodríguez Timaná(iD) and Javier Ferney Castillo García(⊠) (iD)

Grupo de Investigación en Electrónica Industrial y Ambiental – GIEIAM,
Universidad Santiago de Cali, Cali, Colombia
{luis.rodriguez11,javier.castillo00}@usc.edu.co

Abstract. Diabetes is a disease that causes the death of one person every seven seconds worldwide and is also costly, in 2014 was invested 600 billion dollars to be treated worldwide, that is why there is a need to develop technological projects to analyze patterns determined in people who suffer from this disease, in order to detect the pathology in a non-invasive way and reduce costs. That is why an electrical bioimpedance analyzer was developed for the analysis of diabetes. For this purpose, the integrated AD5933 was used as an acquisition device for bioimpedance signals and a beaglebone black development platform to process such data. Electrical bioimpedance data were taken from healthy people and people with the pathology. The data were processed using mathematical methods that allowed parameters to be found to differentiate between the signals of people who have diabetes and people who do not. These methods and the performance measures of the device were evaluated through the Confusion Matrix which determined that the best ratio to decree people with and without diabetes was the quotient between the magnitude of bioimpedance at frequencies of 10 kHz with the magnitude of bioimpedance at frequencies of 100 kHz.

Keywords: Diabetes · Bioimpedance · Confusion Matrix

1 Introduction

Diabetes is a disease that without proper treatment can cause death. The World Health Organization estimated that in the world about 347 million people had diabetes in 2013 and it was also estimated that in 2012, 1.5 million people died from this disease, it is estimated that by 2030, diabetes will be the seventh leading cause of death [1]. Rodríguez and Plata explain that diabetes mellitus type II because of the complications it can have, because of its chronic nature and because of the means it requires for its treatment, is considered a highly expensive disease [2]. Evidence from recent years shows that early diagnosis and good control of diabetes reduce the progression of chronic complications of the disease, such as retinopathy, nephropathy, neuropathy and death, while improving the quality of life of these people [3].

The search for methods that are fast, accurate, easily accessible, and inexpensive to analyze the likelihood that a person has diabetes is a latent need. "In Colombia, between

© Springer Nature Switzerland AG 2020
M. Botto-Tobar et al. (Eds.): ICAT 2019, CCIS 1195, pp. 205–218, 2020.
https://doi.org/10.1007/978-3-030-42531-9_17

7 and 8% of adults may have diabetes, which means that we would be talking about 7 to 8 out of 100 people over 30 years of age who have it. These statistics correspond to type II diabetes which, in more than a third of those who have it, tend to develop chronic complications of the kidneys (renal insufficiency) due to the lack of control of their blood glucose levels, explains Pablo Aschner Montoya, endocrinologist, clinical epidemiologist and Scientific subdirector of the Colombian Diabetes Association" [4].

As well as the above statistics, there are many more, both for Colombia and for the rest of the world. That is why if there is a fast, accurate and non-invasive method to determine whether a person has diabetes, the global statistics would change, since the disease could be controlled and treated in time, and the follow-up to it would be much simpler and even less expensive. There are different methods to measure blood sugar levels, currently the most used method is invasive and is glucometry. This method uses a device called a glucometer which subjects a drop of the patient's blood to an enzyme called glucose oxidase and then applies a small voltage to this compound causing an electrical current to be generated which is measured by the device that calculates and delivers the glucose value of the drop of blood. This method can become very expensive if used for a long time because the glucose enzyme oxidase comes in strips which have a single use as well as the needles used to obtain blood.

1.1 Related Works

Within the implementation of different solutions to this problem, there are other non-invasive methods such as photoplethysmography. In 2012, Paul, Manuel and Alex used photoplethysmography as a technique to apply infrared light to the skin and be able to detect sugar levels depending on the rate of absorption of infrared radiation from the blood because the higher the absorption is the higher the sugar level, but the method has a problem and is that it requires a sensor to detect the heart rate, which is expensive [5].

On the other hand, in 2014, Kamat, Bagul and Patil made an electronic device that allows to relate glucose levels with the impedance response of the human body. For this purpose, they used the electric bioimpedance method and conventional glucometry to find a relationship with the reading of these two devices, obtaining positive results, but requiring invasive tests for their study [6].

Subsequently, Anas in 2016 proposed a non-invasive glucose measurement method using a single frequency of 50 kHz and its measurement consists of 4 electrodes on the finger and the calculation of impedance with mathematical equations that consider incremental arterial impedance, tissue impedance and a total. Finally, a predictive result of blood glucose is arrived at by performing a quadratic regression analysis [7]. However, your predictive model values show too much measurement error.

In 2018 Satish carried out the development and implementation of non-invasive blood glucose monitoring methods using bioimpedance spectroscopy to verify that changes in glucose produce effective variations in parameters obtained from a spectroscopic sample, conducting experiments by injecting glucose into blood samples in controlled environments [8]. The problem with this research is that invasive testing of patients is required.

A study carried out in 2019, like that of Kamat and others, is carried out by Sulla, Talavera, Supo and Montoya, who use an AFE4300 development card which requires a configuration of 4 electrodes, making the equipment non-invasive in the same way. The study is based on the change in time of the bioimpedance values obtained after ingesting glucose, finding a difference between this signal and the concentration of glucose in the blood [9]. However, the study requires blood to be drawn from people and, in addition, the electrodes were affected by skin temperature which caused discomfort in the measured signals.

Knowing then that this disease causes the death of people all over the world, that it is expensive, in some cases difficult to access for treatment and that there are different researches and developments that try to study diabetes in a non-invasive way, but they are expensive and of high complexity, this article presents the development of a team which is an alternative method to study type II diabetes in a non-invasive, painless way and at a low cost. It is important to note that the pursuit of these developments directly benefits those who suffer from this pathology and require a painful, uncomfortable and invasive follow-up. The team proposed in this research allows to eliminate these discomforts and promotes the study of a topic that promises to be beneficial not only in the study of diabetes but other pathologies, such as electrical bioimpedance.

The equipment is based on the study of the electrical bioimpedance of the human body. A pair of electrodes, an AD5933 bioimpedance analysis chip and a beaglebone black development platform are used to do the study and determine if a person allegedly suffers from this pathology. This equipment does not require a calibration with the person's sugar levels.

Before addressing the issue in depth and knowing the solution to the research problem, some important concepts must be known. Then, the required theories will be known.

1.2 Diabetes

Guisan, wrote in his encyclopedia that diabetes is a disease that causes an alteration and a serious disorder of the organic metabolism. These metabolic alterations of diabetes are due to an insufficient absolute or relative availability of the hormone called insulin, which is produced by the pancreas [10]. Insulin is responsible for regulating the amount of glucose in the blood. Within diabetes, there are several fundamental groups or types of diabetes, the most common being type 1 diabetes mellitus and type 2 diabetes mellitus. The website of the Consejería de Salud explains that type 1 diabetes mellitus can affect people of any age, but more is given in children and young people, usually diagnosed before the age of 30 or 40 years, affects more men in the first half of life and women in the second [11].

People with this disease, their pancreas, are unable to produce enough insulin, so they need insulin injections to control blood glucose levels so they can live. Basically, your pancreas does not produce enough insulin. On the other hand, type 2 diabetes mellitus affects 90–95% of people who have diabetes. It is the most common diabetes in adults and the elderly, although there have been cases in which this type of diabetes is diagnosed in children and young people, but the most common age of onset is after the age of 30 or 40. The most serious thing about this disease is that it is diagnosed after many years of suffering from it, this by personal carelessness, by not showing symptoms or even by carrying out a good medical control [12].

Type 2 diabetes mellitus is characterized by the fact that, although your pancreas produces insulin, it sometimes does not produce it in the right amounts (sometimes less sometimes more) and the body is not able to administer this insulin adequately. Heredity is a basic factor in the transmission of diabetes, age, sex and dietary transgressions have a very limited etiopathogenic value. The hereditary factor is of great importance. Obesity is one of the most notorious predisposing factors. Although not all obese people suffer from or become diabetic, statistics clearly show that excess body weight contributes to the development of diabetes. Another factor closely related to diabetes is nutrition and is clearly influenced by social position.

1.3 Electric Bioimpedance

An alternating current electrical circuit is defined by four variables: current, voltage, impedance and alternance. The impedance is the opposition of a body to the electric current, its unit of measurement is the ohm. When the alternating electric current circulates through the medium, the impedance will depend on the facility of that medium to carry that current and is proportional to the resistivity of the medium. If the circuit also consists of capacitors, the impedance will depend on the number of capacitors that the current has to pass through, as well as the ease of loading and unloading them. The impedance component (Z) due to the bad conductivity of the medium is called resistance (R) and the component due to the action produced by the capacitors is called capacitive reactance (Xc), which is also known as reactance. In Eq. 1 the relationship of these parameters is observed [13].

$$Z = R^2 + X_c^2 \tag{1}$$

An alternating current circuit is defined by two waves that have different amplitudes, but the same frequency, the intensity wave and the voltage wave. If the peaks of these waves coincide, the intensity is said to be in phase with the voltage. If there are capacitors in the circuit, charging and discharging them generates a delay of the voltage wave with respect to the current wave, causing the current to be out of phase. This phase is represented in the form of an angle and this is called the phase angle. This represented mathematically is observed in Eq. 2.

$$\tan \theta = \frac{X_c}{R} \tag{2}$$

Figure 1 shows the representation of the phase angle.

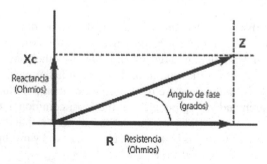

Fig. 1. Impedance angle triangle. Source Own.

Electric Bioimpedance represents the opposition of a biological medium to the passage of alternating current and has the resistance and reactance components mentioned in the previous paragraph. The resistance (R) is conditioned by the resistivity of the different tissues to the electrical conduction. Fat and bone tissues have high resistivity, while intracellular and extracellular fluids easily conduct electric current. The reactance (Xc) in the biological medium is produced by the insulating effect of the cell membranes, which behave like capacitors charging and discharging the passage of the current. In other words, while resistance (R) determines the state of hydration of the body, reactance (Xc) ends the nutritional state of the body.

Following the relationship of the human tissue with an electrical circuit, the Cole-Cole circuit appears. This circuit allows us to understand why, at different frequencies, different impedance responses are obtained. Figure 2 shows the electrical circuit that simulates human tissue. For low frequencies, the charge and discharge process are slow enough for the two capacitors to charge, the total capacity would be C1 + C2. For high frequencies, the C1 capacitor cannot be charged and discharged at the rate of variation of the applied voltage, it is as if it were not, thus being the equivalent capacity C2.

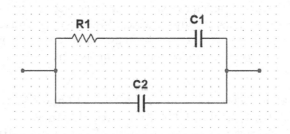

Fig. 2. Cole-Cole circuit. Source: Own.

Figure 3 is the representation of the electrical impedance response at different frequencies to a person. The dotted curve is the representation closest to the impedance curve. This representation is given by a potential curve. The mathematical model of the potential function is presented in Eq. 3.

$$Y = aX^b \tag{3}$$

2 Materials and Methods

2.1 Materials

The elements used in the implementation process of the electric bioimpedance equipment are described below.

Integrated AD5933. The AD5933 integrated circuit is a high-precision impedance analyzer that combines a frequency generator with a 12-bit 1 MSPS analog-to-digital converter (ADC). It can generate frequencies up to 100 kHz and with an impedance measurement range from 100 Ω to 10 MΩ. The received signal is sampled by the ADC and

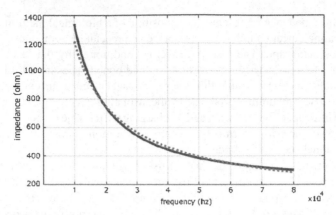

Fig. 3. Impedance curve of a person. Source Own.

processed by an integrated digital signal processor that performs the Fourier transform. The integrated takes 6 shots in the same sweep, averaging the harmonics and delivering the best curve. Me-diante communication I2C, the integrated returns the real (R) and imaginary (I) value of the signal already processed [14]. This device was used to generate the signal at the desired frequencies and obtain the bioimpedance signal of each person. This integrated one needs a calibration stage, this is explained in the methodology section.

BeagleBone Black. It is a free hardware card that has a Cortex-A8 1 GHz ARM CPU, 3D graphics accelerator, a pair of 32-bit SS RISC PRU, 512 MB RAM and 2 GB internal storage, plus a microSD slot. It has a USB connection, Ethernet, micro-HDMI output and two 46-pin connectors. This device was used to process the impedance data delivered by the AD5933 [15].

Other Devices. General purpose electrodes were used to interface the integrated AD5933 with the human body. These are ideal, since they have a good adherence to the skin, they have a low probability of generating infections or similar problems, they are economic and, in addition, they present a low impedance which allows to obtain the bioimpedance signals with little noise, the flexibility of these electrodes allows to adjust in a good way to make a good capture of signal.

2.2 Methods

The following mathematical methods were used to characterize the bioimpedance signals obtained from people.

Calibration of the Bioimpedance Analyzer. The bioimpedance analyzer has as fundamental element the integrated AD5933, this device requires a calibration stage before being able to take bioimpedance. For this purpose, a high precision resistance must be placed on the Vref and Vout pins of the integrated device in order to have a reference of the magnitude of the impedance to be measured. This same resistance must be placed in the output of the integrated one, being this withdrawn now of making the bioimpedance taking. Different resistance values were used for this, concluding that the best representation of the received signal was obtained with a resistance of 510 Ω with a tolerance of 1%. Frequency values of 10 kHz and 100 kHz are chosen according to the literature to cross the intra and extra cellular tissue [16].

Wilcoxon Method. The field of free or non-parametric distribution design statistics has had such a large development, that one has for almost any research design, valid alternative statistical tests that can be used to produce results about a hypothesis. One of those statistical tests used and reliability is that of the Wilcoxon method [17].

Mathematically, if you have a simple random sample of size $n1$ from one population and another of size $n2$ from another population and there are n observations in total, where $n = n1 + n2$, you can calculate the range of the n observations. This is done by adding the W ranges of the group with less sum of ranges. If the two populations have the same continuous distribution, then W has mean, which is shown in Eqs. 8 and 9.

$$\mu_W = \frac{n_1(n+1)}{2} \tag{8}$$

and standard deviation:

$$\sigma_W = \sqrt{\frac{n_1 n_2(n+1)}{12}} \tag{9}$$

Where n_1 will be the sample size of the group with the lowest sum of range.

The Wilcoxon range sum test rejects the null hypothesis that populations have the same distribution when the sum of W ranges is far from their mean, this method allows to indicate a rejection of the null hypothesis in relation to the 5% significance level.

Confusion Matrix. The Confusion Matrix is an important tool when evaluating a classification algorithm. This matrix allows us to understand how this algorithm is being classified based on a count of the successes and errors of each of the classes. With this matrix it is possible to check if the algorithm is classifying in an adequate way or not the classes [18]. To determine this process, the following performance measures should be considered:

- Accuracy is the proportion of the total number of predictions that were correct.

$$A_C = \frac{a+d}{a+b+c+d} \tag{10}$$

- The True Positive Ratio is the proportion of positive cases that were correctly identified.

$$TPrate = \frac{d}{c+d} \tag{11}$$

- The False Positive Ratio is the proportion of negative cases that have been incorrectly classified as positive.

$$FPrate = \frac{b}{a+b} \tag{12}$$

- The True Negative Ratio is the proportion of negative cases that have been correctly classified.

$$TNrate = \frac{a}{a+b} \tag{13}$$

- The False Negative Ratio is the proportion of positive cases that were incorrectly classified as negative.

$$FNrate = \frac{c}{c+d} \tag{14}$$

- Accuracy is the proportion of positive predicted cases that were correct.

$$P = \frac{d}{b+d} \tag{15}$$

- Sensitivity. That is, sensitivity characterizes the ability of the test to detect disease in sick subjects. *1-Se = FNrate.*
- Specificity. Specificity indicates the capacity of our estimator to give healthy cases as negative cases. *1-Sp = FPrate.*

Protocols. At the time of data collection, different inclusion and exclusion criteria were considered in order to avoid factors that alter blood glucose, such as constant alcohol consumption or women in the gestation period or menstrual cycle. Bearing this in mind, the ages of the people who would participate in the project were also limited in order to avoid errors in the analysis of the results. Twenty-two people were evaluated, of which 12 per medical diagnosis do not have diabetes and 12 per medical diagnosis if they have type II diabetes. The average age range of people who do not have the pathology is 45.5 years and 58.25 years for those who do. The body mass composition index is an important fact. For women between 36 and 45 years old, the index should be 25% and 27%, which is why the women in our case study have an index between 25.71%, 25.04% and 25.21%. For men between 36 and 50 years old, the index should be 21% and 23%, so it is fulfilled in our case study since values of 22.39% and 21.52% were obtained. It is also worth mentioning that all these people are mulattos. The tests were performed at the San Juan de Dios hospital in the city of Cali, Colombia, and were approved by the ethics committee of that institution, through the CEIHSJ001-019 act.

After identifying the inclusion/exclusion criteria, the following recommendations should be met:

- You must not present in your body any metallic object.
- It should not take more than 5 h without consuming any food.

- You should not have consumed foods with a high percentage of sugars (choco-lates).
- You should not have any electronic device with you.
- You must not have been physically active in the 2 h prior to the test.
- You must not have had any symptoms of excessive fluid loss.
- Not to have ingested drinks with high alcohol content.

Test Procedure

- The patient should be seated with the palms of the hands facing up and placed on their legs.
- The forearm area of the left hand is cleaned to remove the dead cells present in the skin in order to improve the contact interface and ensure good adherence for the placement of electrodes, the placement of electrodes is on the front face of the forearm due to the low amount of fatty tissue, this area is not exposed to the sun very often and additionally has no capillary tissue.
- Having calibrated the bioimpedance analyser, the data is taken, and the signal is applied to the body for 10 s, which are distributed as follows. The first 5 s the electric current is applied at a frequency of 10 kHz and the final 5 s are applied at 100 kHz.

Figure 4 presents the general scheme of the equipment built. The computer is optional since the bioimpedance equipment is the one that performs the processing to the obtained impedance data, but also has the possibility of these data being sent by I2C communication so that another equipment can process or analyze them in a different way.

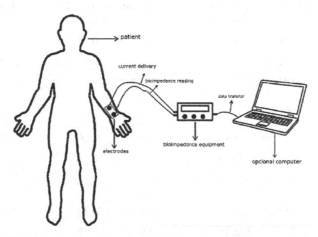

Fig. 4. General scheme of the electric bioimpedance equipment. Source Own.

3 Results

Now of processing the obtained data and by means of characteristics extraction, different relations were determined between the impedance obtained in the frequency at 10 kHz (A) and the impedance obtained in the frequency at 100 kHz (B). After analyzing the confusion matrix for the mathematical relation of A-B, A/B and the Angle of these two magnitudes $\tan^{-1}(A/B)$, it was determined that the best relation to determine whether people have type II diabetes is the relation of the A/B quotient. Table 1 shows different parameters obtained from people with diabetes and healthy people. The Wilcoxon statistic was used for nonparametric samples and it was found that there is a significant difference between the means of the control populations and the patients with type ii diabetes.

According to what was obtained in Table 1, where the A/B ratio presented statistical significance, an analysis of the data related to the bioimpedance values at 10 kHz and 100 kHz was carried out. This analysis consisted in finding the threshold that maximized the success rate greater than 81% (kappa greater than 0.62).

Figure 5 shows the A/B data of the impedance results for each of the users.

Table 2 presents the values of thresholds and the relation of a confusion matrix for characteristic A/B, this table was found that for the threshold of 3.5 the highest success rate corresponding to 83 was obtained. 33% and a kappa value of 0.67 which shows that this value is adequate to implement a discriminator that separates the control populations

Table 1. Relationship of different characteristics of healthy people and people with diabetes.

Characteristics	Patient		Control		Statistical analysis
	Medium	Standard deviation	Medium	Standard deviation	Wilcoxon (P)
Age (years)	58.25	14.68	45.50	20.12	0.2256
Weight (Kg)	72.09	8.11	70.81	18.54	0.3852
IMC	28.30	3.79	70.81	18.54	0.5025
Phase (grades)					
Phase 10 KΩ	−67.32	4.27	−66.25	3.69	0.4262
Phase 100 KΩ	−33.20	6.85	−30.90	6.80	0.4708
Phase 10 KΩ/100 KΩ	2.09	0.35	2.21	0.36	0.5024
Impedance (Ω)					
A 10 KΩ	1911.42	443.69	1701.17	256.47	0.3602
B 100 KΩ	521.00	132.26	534.00	86.17	0.6066
A-B (Ω)	1390.42	364.94	1167.17	226.93	0.2571
A/B (Ω)	**3.89**	**0.37**	**3.23**	**0.54**	**0.0394**
$\tan^{-1}$ (A/B)	74.75	73.40	72.57	71.43	0.2851

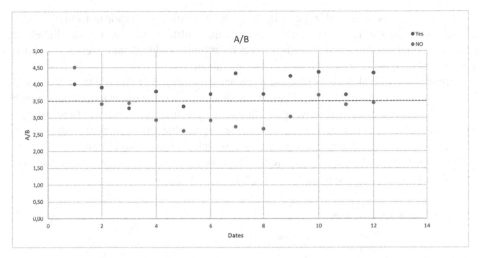

Fig. 5. Relationship between quotient A and B. Source: Own.

and those that present the pathology, in addition the relation of real positives (people that present the pathology) have been correctly predicted (sensitivity) with 83.33% and the negative predictions (people that do not present the pathology - control) with 83.33%.

Table 2. Confusion Matrix for relationship between Bioimpedance at 10 kHz and Bioimpedance at 100 kHz at different thresholds.

Characteristic	Umbral	Specificity	Sensitivity	Accuracy	Kappa
a/b	3.2	66.67%	100%	75%	0.5
a/b	3.3	64.71%	85.71%	70.83%	0.41
a/b	3.4	71.43%	80%	75%	0.5
a/b	**3.5**	**83.33%**	**83.33%**	**83.33%**	**0.67**
a/b	3.6	80.33%	79.65%	70.33%	0.42
a/b	3.7	87.5%	68.75%	75%	0.5

The physiological explanation of these results is given by the physical characteristic of healthy and diabetic people. Type II diabetics have a higher number of glucose cells in their blood compared to healthy people. These cells are composed of a cell membrane which, when viewed electrically, functions as a condenser. As the signal applied by the equipment is synodal, if the frequency is low, the signal will only pass through the intracellular and extracellular liquid, thus obtaining a resistive response (real), but if the frequency is high, the signal will pass through the cell membrane and an impedance response of reactance and resistance will be obtained (imaginary more real).

That is why people with type II diabetes have a different response to people who do not have it, since the same signal applied to the healthy must travel in the diabetic a greater amount of intracellular fluids, extracellular fluids and will get different reactance values by crossing a greater amount of cell membranes.

Figure 6A and B show how glucose is absorbed by a cell. For glucose to be processed in the cells to be converted into energy, the insulin cells sent by the pancreas must reach the insulin receptors so that they open the glucose channel and can enter these sugars. The different minerals such as magnesium are responsible for regenerating the insulin receptors so that they can again have an effective relationship with insulin. People who suffer from diabetes have difficulties in the absorption of these minerals, causing glucose cannot be processed and thus generate high levels of sugars.

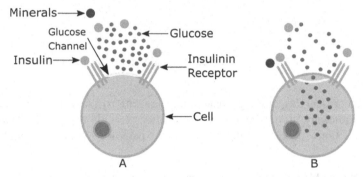

Fig. 6. Glucose absorption process. Source: Own.

Figure 7 illustrates the difference when the electrical signal applied to the body at high frequencies (100 kHz in this case) passes through the cells with and without insulin. Although at high frequencies the signal will always pass through the cells, a difference in bioimpedance will be obtained when the signal finds glucose within them. If insulin cannot allow glucose to enter the cells, this sugar remains outside the cell and bioimpedance at low frequencies (10 kHz in this case) determined this event.

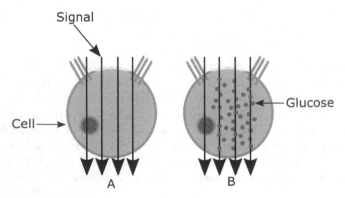

Fig. 7. Signal attacking the cells. Source Own.

4 Conclusions and Discussions

It was determined in this research, that it is possible by extracting characteristics from mathematical relationships of different impedances, to compare people who have type II diabetes with people who do not have it.

Unlike the conventional invasive method, this equipment uses a technique that prevents the person to be studied from being pricked to obtain a drop of blood, thus preventing pain and possible infections. This is an alternative method that, without being expensive in contrast to other developments, can help to study this pathology and contribute to its study. It is important to know in studies like this one, the physiological part of the human body since this investigation was carried out with the purpose of finding different characteristics that would allow differentiating people with type II diabetes using a non-invasive method.

There are some devices that currently serve for measuring blood glucose and not for determining diabetes as proposed in this document, with this study has shown that it is possible to design a low-cost equipment that only uses two study frequencies which allows the system to be less expensive because it will not use specialized hardware and will also be less complex in its software.

As future work and with the results obtained can be projected the use of this equipment to monitor treatments or evidence the evolution of this pathology. The study is projected to carry out a non-invasive continuous glucose measuring equipment using electric bioimpedance.

References

1. de la Salud, O.M.: Diabetes. Organización Mundial de la Salud (2016)
2. Rodríguez, G., Plata, L.: La calidad de vida percibida en pacientes diabéticos tipo 2, revista javeriana (2015)
3. Dittmar, M., Reber, H., Kahaly, G.J.: Bioimpedance phase angle indicates catabolism in Type 2 diabetes. Diabet. Med. 32(9), 1177–1185 (2015)
4. Ortega, M.: Diabetes, un dulce enemigo de la vida moderna (2012)
5. Paul, B., Manuel, M.P., Alex, Z.C.: Design and development of non invasive glucose measurement system. In: 2012 1st International Symposium on Physics and Technology of Sensors, pp. 43–46 (2012)
6. Kamat, D.K., Bagul, D., Patil, P.M.: Blood glucose measurement using bioimpedance technique. Adv. Electron. 2014, 1–5 (2014)
7. Korenevskiy, N.A., et al.: Designing multipurpose diagnostic units on the basis of AFE interfaces. Biomed. Eng. (NY) 50(4), 1–4 (2016)
8. Satish, K.S., Anand, S.: Impedance spectroscopy of aqueous solution samples of different glucose concentrations for the exploration of non-invasive-continuous-blood-glucose-monitoring. Mapan - J. Metrol. Soc. India 33(2), 185–190 (2018)
9. Sulla, T.R., Talavera, S.J., Supo, C.E., Montoya, A.A.: Non-invasive glucose monitor based on electric bioimpedance using AFE4300. In: Proceedings of the 2019 IEEE 26th International Conference on Electronics, Electrical Engineering and Computing, INTERCON 2019 (2019)
10. Guisán, S.: Gran enciclopedia de la ciencia y de la técnica, 4th ed. vol. 12, pp. 740–742. Océano (1998)
11. de Salud, C.: Portal de la Consejería de Salud (2012)

12. de Salud, M., Social, P.: Analisis de la Situacion de Salud (ASIS) Colombia 2015. Inst. Nac. Salud. 175 (2015)
13. Lopez Lopez, C., et al.: Medicina del Deporte. Med. del Deport. **3**(1), 170–178 (2011)
14. Analog Devices: AD5933: 1 MSPS, 12-Bit Impedance Converter, Network Analyzer. Datasheet, p. 40 (2013)
15. Coley, G.: Beaglbone Black System Reference Manual. San Francisco, California (2013)
16. Yang, Y., Zhang, W., Sun, Q.: Design and preliminary test of a palm bio-impedance spectroscopy measurement system for biometric authentication. In: 2014 International Symposium on Computer, Consumer and Control, no. February, pp. 824–827 (2014)
17. Larocque, D.: The wilcoxon signed-rank test for cluster correlated data. In: Duchesne, P., RÉMillard, B. (eds.) Statistical Modeling and Analysis for Complex Data Problems. Springer, Boston (2005). https://doi.org/10.1007/0-387-24555-3_15
18. Sánchez Muñoz, J.: Análisis de Calidad Cartográfica mediante el estudio de la Matriz de Confusión. Pensam. Matemático **6**(2), 9–26 (2016)

Technical Feasibility for the Mobile Measurement of Noise Pollution by Remotely Piloted Aircraft System

Luis Carlos Rodríguez Timaná(iD), Diego Fernando Saavedra Lozano(iD), María Fernanda Díaz Velásquez(iD), and Javier Ferney Castillo García(✉)(iD)

Grupo de Investigación en Electrónica Industrial y Ambiental – GIEIAM, Universidad Santiago de Cali, Cali, Colombia
javier.castillo00@usc.edu.co

Abstract. Excessive noise causes gradual hearing loss and interferes with sleep, reading and concentration. It can even cause physiological disturbances in the cardiovascular system. Noise quantification is usually performed using multiple static measurements with sound level meters. This article implements the technical feasibility analysis to perform mobile noise measurements using a Remotely Piloted Aircraft System-Drone. Initially the acoustic power emitted by a Drone Matrice 100 was estimated, for which a parallelepiped is defined taking as indications the ISO3744 standard and by means of an audio capture system. For the measurement a semi-anechoic chamber was established in a football field and the measurements were made in the early hours of the morning. The acoustic power of this type of drone was 84.6 dB, which determined that the signal-to-noise ratio had a very high value. An intervention in the design of the drone propellants is suggested to reduce the noise of the drones, so that previously the technical viability for applications of measurement of acoustic pollution is discarded.

Keywords: Acoustic pollution · Drone · Noise

1 Introduction

Noise has a major impact on people's health, especially in cities. According to the European Environment Agency, the medium-term health risk caused by noise is much higher than that of passive smoking and air pollution by ozone and particulate matter, issues that receive much greater attention from public administrations and the media. Like air pollution, it comes largely from road traffic (80% of noise exposure in urban environments). Therefore, measures to control them would significantly reduce these risk factors, while at the same time improving the quality of life and health of citizens. The World Health Organization-WHO recommendation as the final target for night-time limit values is 40 dBA with intermediate targets (until final establishment) of 55 dBA. These values were selected because of the health effects that start at 30 dBA, increase significantly from 40 dBA and can start to produce effects in the cardiovascular system from 55 dBA [1].

M. Botto-Tobar et al. (Eds.): ICAT 2019, CCIS 1195, pp. 219–230, 2020.
https://doi.org/10.1007/978-3-030-42531-9_18

A device called a sound level meter is normally used to measure the amount of noise. The sound level meter is an instrument that allows the sound pressure level to be measured objectively. The results are expressed in dB. To determine the hearing damage, we work using a weighting scale "A" that lets pass only the frequencies at which the human ear is more sensitive, responding to the sound in a similar way that it does.

To have an electronic equipment that allows to measure in real time and of instantaneous way the noise in a zone would serve to predict if it is required to make the complete measurement with the sonometers or not. Therefore, the need arose to make an electronic equipment that allows predicting where it is necessary to make a complete measurement with a sound level meter to determine noise levels. However, following the ISO 3744 standard, which is responsible for determining sound power levels and sound energy levels of noise sources using sound pressure, it was established that the sound power of the drone was very high and because of this could not characterize the ambient noise. The tests were conducted at the Universidad Santiago de Cali - Colombia and it was determined that 98% of the noise of the drone is between 0 and 220 Hz.

1.1 Related Works

Within this research, there are few developments that have been made for this problem because trying to determine noise pollution with an equipment that generates high levels of noise such as a drone is a big challenge, even so, Klapel in 2014, made a methodology with which would have some results but not 100% successful. The problem within the methodology implemented by Klapel was that it used a mobile phone as a signal acquisition device, which did not allow it to obtain a good interpretation of the signal to be measured [1].

1.2 Sound

Sound is a change of air pressure, which moves like a circular wave from the source, like the waves that form when we throw a stone into the water. These pressure changes enter the ear canal, are transmitted from the air to the eardrum, which in turn moves the ossicles of the middle ear. The ossicles function as a mechanical amplifier and pass the movements to the snail, where they move the lymphatic fluid it contains. As it moves, it stimulates the hair cells, which in turn react by generating nerve impulses that are sent to the brain [2].

1.3 Contamination

Pollution is the presence or incorporation into the environment of toxic substances or elements that are harmful to humans or ecosystems (living beings). The most important types of pollution are those that affect basic natural resources: air, soil and water. Some of the most serious environmental alterations related to pollution phenomena are radioactive leaks, smog, the greenhouse effect, acid rain, destruction of the ozone layer, eutrophication of water or oil slicks. There are different types of pollution that depend on certain factors and that affect each environment differently [3]. There are different types of pollution such as atmospheric pollution, water pollution, soil and subsoil pollution, radioactive pollution, thermal pollution, visual pollution, light pollution, electromagnetic pollution and acoustic pollution [4]. The latter is the subject of this investigation.

1.4 Noise Pollution

Noise pollution is defined as the presence in the environment of noises or vibrations, whatever the acoustic emitter that originates them, that imply nuisance, risk or damage for people, for the development of their activities or for goods of any nature, or that cause significant effects on the environment. Noise is defined as the generally unpleasant, inarticulate auditory sensation that bothers the ear. Technically, noise is spoken of when its intensity is high, even to the detriment of human health [5].

The Table 1 shows typical sound pressure values (dBSPL) and possible health problems.

Table 1. Sound values and their effects on the organism. Source: [6].

Sound pressure (dB)	Environments or activities	Sensation/Effects in the ear
140–160	Explosion, firecracker at 1 m	Immediate permanent ear damage, ruptured eardrum
130	Aircraft taking off at 10 m, firearm fired	Pain threshold
120	Airplane engine running, pneumatic hammer pylon (1 m)	Permanent damage to the ear from short-term exposure
110	Rock concert, motorcycle to free escape to 1 m	
100	Circular saw at 1 m, discotheque, ambulance siren at 10 m	Unbearable sensation and need to leave the environment
90	Main street at 10 m, mechanic workshop	Disturbing sensation, permanent damage to the ear from long-term exposure
80	Lively bar, noisy street at 10 m	
70	Normal car at 10 m, vacuum cleaner at 1 m, conversation aloud	Uncomfortable background noise for conversation
60	Animated conversation, television at normal volume at 1 m	Pleasant background noise for social life
50	Office, normal conversation, 1 m away	
40	Library, whispered conversation	Necessary background level to rest
30	Silent fridge, bedroom	
20	Very quiet room, soft rumor of the leaves of a tree	
10	Quiet breathing	
0	Hearing threshold	Silence

Decibel (dB). When we speak of noise in technical terms, we speak of sound pressure. Sound pressure is usually measured in decibels (dB). The decibel is a relative and logarithmic value, which expresses the ratio of the measured value to a reference value. Logarithmic means that we do not measure on a linear scale, but exponential [5].

The reference value is the limit of perceptibility of the human ear, a sound pressure of 20 uPa. Therefore, 0 dB means a sound pressure that is at the edge of perceptibility. Given the logarithmic property of the dB scale, we must calculate in powers. An increase of 6 dB is equivalent to a doubling of the sound pressure. 60 dB means doubling 10 times and therefore a pressure 1,024 times higher than 0 dB, and 66 dB is already 2,048 times more. However, the subjective perception of the human ear is different, and we perceive an increase in sound pressure of approximately 10 dB (slightly more than three times the volume) as being double the volume. For example, an increase in sound pressure of 60 dB would mean a perceived volume 64 times higher, i.e. the sound pressure increases 1024 times, but we perceive it as an increase of 64x. It is important to know this difference because the real sound pressure is the one to which the ear is exposed and which causes possible direct damage, while the subjective volume is the one that bothers and causes discomfort and stress [5].

dB$_A$ Value. Volume perception depends not only on the sound pressure, but also on the type of sound. A high-pitched sound, for example, is perceived to be higher than a deaf one, even if they have the same sound pressure. In order to take this characteristic of the ear into account, a weighting factor is usually applied to the different frequencies through a filter when sound measurements are made. The most common is the so-called "A" filter, which represents in a simplified way the different sensitivity of the ear for different frequencies. Values measured with this filter take the unit dB(A) or dBA, as opposed to dB or dBSPL (SPL = Sound Pressure Level). Figure 1 shows that low frequencies (low sounds) count 5–20 dB less (or 1.5–4 times less) because they are perceived as lower by the human ear. As a result, the values measured in dBA and dBSPL may vary fundamentally due to the application of the filter. For example, if we imagine the noise of a bus and a motorcycle that arrive at our house with the same sound pressure and we measure the sound pressure in dBSPL, they would cause the same impact, while applying filter A, the sound of the bus would be evaluated as lower because it is of lower frequency and less annoying [5].

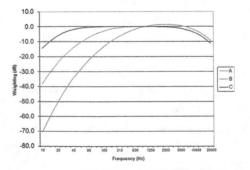

Fig. 1. Weighting curves. Source: [5].

2 Materials and Methods

2.1 Materials

Raspberry Pi 3 Model B

This platform was chosen because of its powerful performance and processing capacity. Here are some of its features [7]:

- Quad Core 1.2 GHz Broadcom BCM2837 64bit CPU
- 1 GB RAM
- BCM43438 wireless LAN and Bluetooth Low Energy (BLE) on board
- 100 Base Ethernet
- 40-pin extended GPIO
- 4 USB 2 ports
- 4 Pole stereo output and composite video port
- Full size HDMI
- CSI camera port for connecting a Raspberry Pi camera
- DSI display port for connecting a Raspberry Pi touchscreen display
- Micro SD port for loading your operating system and storing data
- Upgraded switched Micro USB power source up to 2.5A

Matrice 100 Drone

A DJI Matrice 100 flight platform was used, which provides a stable, flexible and powerful flight. Up to 500 g can be loaded for a flight of approximately 20 min. This Drone was chosen to perform this research precisely to use its load capacity and install the audio card and microphone to make the recordings [8].

Behringer ECM 8000 Microphone

Behringer ecm8000 is an ultra-linear measuring condenser microphone, used for room equalization applications with high-resolution studio recordings and live applications exceptionally flat frequency response and ultra-high sound resolution, true omnidirectional pattern, works with a phantom power from 15 to 48. 3-pin XLR connector gold plated for greater signal integrity. This microphone has a good sound from all angles and a flat frequency response of 15 Hz to 20 kHz, and omnidirectional polar pattern give you a clear and accurate reading of the unique sound characteristics of a room. Like standard condenser microphones used for recording or performance, the ecm8000 has phantom power from 15 V to 48 V [9].

Behringer U-phoria Um2 Audio Card

It is an audio interface capable of connecting the ECM 8000 microphone to the raspberry pi. It was chosen for its low cost and high performance [10].

- Low Latency Low Latency Supports: Core Audio/ASIO
- USB Audio 2x In 2x Out

- Sampling Rate Maximum Sampling Rate: 48 kHz
- Mic Preamps 1x XENYX preamp
- Phantom Power +48 V
- Inputs: 1x XLR/TRS combo jack mic/line input,
- 1x 1/4" (6.3 mm) instrument input
- Outputs: 2x RCA (L, R), 1x 1/4" (6.3 mm) headphone output
- Zero-Latency Direct Monitoring Yes
- Power USB bus power
- Kensington Lock Support Yes

Others

An XLR cable was needed for the microphone, a micro USB cable for the raspberry, 2 m of metal tube for adjustment in the drone and microphone and a Lipo battery of 11.4 V for the power supply of the raspberry and the audio card, plus a 5 V voltage regulator.

2.2 Methods

The following mathematical methods were used to determine the power of the drone and to perform the acoustic measurements.

ISO 3744 Standard. For the determination of the acoustic power of a noise source, there are several procedures depending on the desired degree of precision and the acoustic environment. In this research, grade 2 was implemented, which refers to the use of ISO 3744. To carry out the measurements, it is necessary to first define a reference surface that must include the source, excluding those protruding elements that are not effective acoustic energy radiators. The different positions of the microphones are distributed on the measuring surface, a surface that surrounds both the source and the reference surface [11]. In Fig. 2 se you can see the two alternatives that you have to make the measurements.

In this study the surface of the parallelepiped was selected, due to its easy distribution of measurement elements.

According to the regulations, the positions of the microphones in the distribution of the parallelepiped must be determined. The following equations were used.

$$S = 4(ab + bc + ca) \tag{1}$$

where:

$a = 0.5l_1 + d$
$b = 0.5l_2 + d$
$c = l_3 + d$

l_1, l_2 y l_3 are the sides of the device to measure, in this case, the drone.

In this case, $l_1, = 0.5\,\text{m}\ l_2 = 1.1\,\text{m}$ y $l_3 = 0.22\,\text{m}.\ Lad = 1\,\text{m}$. Applying the formulas, one obtains a parallelepiped area of 21.44 m^2.

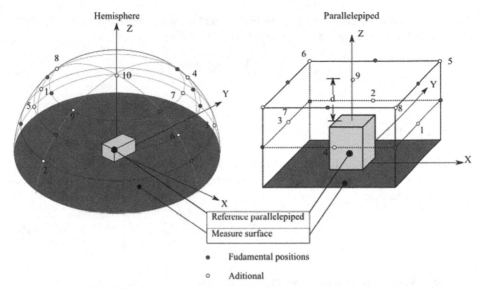

Fig. 2. Surfaces for acoustic measurements. Source: Own.

When making sound recordings, the following equations should be applied.

Regarding the observation period during which the pressure level of our source is determined, the standard specifies that for frequency bands centered at or below 160 Hz, the observation period should be at least 30 s; and for frequency bands centered at or above 200 Hz, the observation period should be at least 10 s. Once these parameters have been defined, the only thing left to do is to measure the pressure level at each of the points, and proceed to determine the power level according to the equations:

$$\overline{L'_{PA}} = 10.\log\left[\frac{1}{N}\sum_{i=1}^{N} 10^{0.1.L'_{PA}}\right] \tag{2}$$

where:
L'_{PA} is the sound pressure level averaged over the surface of the measurement in dB, with the source test running.
L'_{PA} is the sound pressure level measured at the i-th position of the microphone in dB.

$$\overline{L''_{PA}} = 10.\log\left[\frac{1}{N}\sum_{i=1}^{N} 10^{0.1.L''_{PAi}}\right] \tag{3}$$

where:
L''_{PA} is the sound pressure level of the background noise averaged over the measurement surface, in dB.
L''_{PAi} is the sound pressure level of the background noise measured at the i-th position of the microphone, in dB.
N is the number of microphone positions.

Once the pressure levels have been measured, all that remains is to calculate and introduce the necessary corrections to counteract the effects of background noise and the acoustic environment. The correction for background noise is carried out by determining the factor k_1, which is given by the following expression:

$$k_{1A} = -10.\log\left[1 - 10^{-0.1\Delta L_A}\right] \tag{4}$$

Where:

$$\Delta L_A = \overline{L'_{PA}} + \overline{L''_{PA}}$$

The next step is to calculate the reverberation time. Once the room reverberation time has been calculated, the equivalent absorption area of the chamber is calculated from Sabine's formula:

$$A = 0.16\left(\frac{V}{T}\right) \tag{5}$$

where:
V: is the volume of the test chamber in cubic meters.
T: is the reverberation time of the chamber, in seconds, for weighting A or frequency bands.

The correction coefficient for acoustic environment must now be calculated using the expression:

$$k_{2A} = -10.\log\left[1 + \frac{S}{A}\right] dB \tag{6}$$

where:
S is the area of the measurement surface.

Once the two correction coefficients have been calculated, the surface sound pressure level is calculated, which is no more than the level measured with the source in operation.

$$\overline{L_{PFA}} = \overline{L'_{PA}} + -k_{1A} - k_{2A} \tag{7}$$

$$L_{WA} = \overline{L_{PFA}} + 10.\log\left(\frac{S}{S_o}\right) dB \tag{8}$$

where:
S_0 is the reference surface that has a value of 1 m^2.

With Eq. 8, you can finally find the acoustic power of the element that is being studied, in this case the drone.

Fast Fourier Transform. Fast Fourier Transform (FFT) is an efficient algorithm for calculating the Discrete Fourier Transform (DFT) and its inverse. The FFT is useful for digital signal processing and general digital filtering to solve equations in partial derivatives or rapid multiplication algorithms of large integers. The FFT algorithm imposes some limitations on the signal and the resulting spectrum since the signal sampled and to be transformed must consist of several samples equal to a power of two. Most FFT analyzers allow the transformation of 512, 1024, 2048 or 4096 samples. The frequency range covered by the FFT analysis depends on the number of samples collected and the sampling rate. In Eqs. 3 and 4, the mathematical relationship is observed [12].

$$X(K) = \sum_{j=1}^{N} x(j) w_N 1^{(j-1)(k-1)} \tag{9}$$

$$x(j) = \frac{1}{N} \sum_{k=1}^{N} x(k) w_N 1^{-(j-1)(k-1)} \tag{10}$$

$$w_N = \exp\left(\frac{-2\pi i}{N}\right) \tag{11}$$

With the calculation of the FFT, the decibels of the acoustic power generated by the drone were determined. These values are observed in later sections.

Protocol

The drone was equipped with the audio card, microphone, Raspberry and battery to start the flights and the process of recording the audio signal. The Raspberry was established the algorithm that would allow it to record audio signals at 48 kHz and 24 bits, this code was made in Python. There were 5 flights in an open field (soccer) with a schedule for tests from 5am to 6am, at which time did not interfere any additional noise source to that of the same drone. The drone made recordings with its microphone incorporated and in the same way, in the open field was made the assembly of the 9 microphones that would conform the parallelepiped that would allow to analyze the acoustic power of the drone (the same microphones and Behringer audio cards that were implemented in the drone), thus would have the recordings made by the same drone and the recordings by the 9 microphones with the guidelines of ISO 3744.

At the end of the 5 flights and with the audio signals stored (recorded from the drone and from the parallelepiped), we proceeded to calculate the acoustic power of the drone. This would allow in the first instance to know if the acoustic signature of this element would allow to determine parameters to obtain the ambient noise.

Calibration

For the measurement of different physical variables, it is very important that these measuring elements comply with norms and standards. Within these requirements, the equipment must be properly calibrated [13]. That is why, following ISO 3744, 2 equipment's were used that would be of reference to the measuring equipment properly implemented. For this purpose, a class 1 Quest sound level meter and its pistonphone of the same brand were used. With these elements, the calibration process of the developed equipment was carried out and served as a standard to corroborate the measurements it made. Figure 3 shows the calibration process applied by the system and how it responded appropriately when applying a signal to 1 kHz.

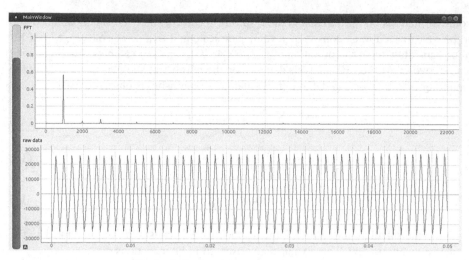

Fig. 3. FFT signal to 1 kHz. Source: Own.

3   Results

Using the Fast Fourier Transform in Matlab, the audios obtained in the flights were processed and the decibels were calculated in each one of the 9 microphones located spatially in the parallelepiped. Taking these decibel values and applying the equations required

Table 2. Acoustic power emitted by the drone Matrice 100.

Microphones (dB)	70,45	72,90	74,16	68,97	70,12	72,12	68,89	69,12	70,45
e1	11,1e6	19,5e6	26,1e6	7,9e6	10,3e6	16,3e6	7,7e6	8,2e6	11,1e6
$\sum$ e1	10,7e7	/	/	/	/	/	/	/	10,7e7
e2	13,4e6	/	/	/	/	/	/	/	13,4e6
L'pa (dB)	71,26	/	/	/	/	/	/	/	71,26
value (dB)	37,63	38,12	37,52	37,62	37,63	38,63	37,01	37,42	37,63
e1	5,8e3	6,5e3	5,6e3	5,8e3	5,8e3	7,3e3	5,0e3	5,5e3	5,8e3
$\sum$e1	47,3e3	/	/	/	/	/	/	/	47,3e3
e2	5,9e3	/	/	/	/	/	/	/	5,9e3
L''pa (dB)	37,72	/	/	/	/	/	/	/	37,72
Δ_La (dB)	33,54	/	/	/	/	/	/	/	33,54
K1A	0,00	/	/	/	/	/	/	/	0,00
K2	0,00	/	/	/	/	/	/	/	0,00
Avr._PFA	**71,26**								
Lwa (dB)	**84,57**								

by ISO 3744 shown in the previous section, the acoustic power emitted by the drone was determined. Table 2 shows the calculations made to determine this acoustic power. It should be noted that as the tests were performed in an open field, the reverberation time was estimated as 0, so k_{1A} y k_2 are 0.

As evidenced in the table above, the acoustic power of the drone is too high (84.57 dB) to be able to perform digital processing and determine ambient noise. These values, which were taken with the own acquisition system, were verified by the sound level meter. It should be noted that every rule imposed by ISO was strictly complied with, from protocol to equipment to be used.

In Fig. 4, there is an original photograph of the flight made in the soccer field. This shot was enhanced while verifying the load capacity of the drone with the audio capture equipment.

Fig. 4. Audio capture system performing test flight. Source: Own.

4   Conclusions and Discussions

Although it was not an adequate tool to determine noise pollution in a non-conventional way, it is of great importance to have these studies for future research, as one of the important processes that must be done in any research is a state of the art and know that it has been done to solve different problems. A research finding shows a future problem when the use of drones is widespread, for transport of packages and others, due to the high noise that they generate.

In order to measure acoustic pollution, equipment is required that does not precisely generate any source of noise. What this research was looking for was to be able to determine the acoustic signature of the drone in order to be able to use digital processing to find the ambient noise without the drone signal affecting it. The main idea of making these noise measurements with a drone, was to be able with lower costs, make a faster measurement and allow in less time to estimate if any area required a complete measurement with professional sound level meters, in addition to being able to reach areas difficult to access in which there are more operator risks with sound level meters.

References

1. Klapel, J.: Acoustic measurements with a quadcopter: embedded system implementations for recording audio from above. Ph.D. thesis. Norwegian University of Science and Technology (2014)
2. Hitage and the A ts Environment Division Department of Environment, Parks, Noise Measurement Procedures Manual, 2nd July 2008
3. Bermudez, M.: Contaminación y Turísmo Sostenible (2010)
4. Elsom, D.: La contaminación atmosférica. Ediciones Cátedra SA (1990)
5. Martínez Llorente, J., Peters, J.: Contaminación acústica y ruido. Ecol. en Acción, vol. 6 (2015)
6. Berglund, B., Lindvall, T., Schwela, D.H., World Health Organization, Occupational and Environmental Health Team: Guidelines for community noise. World Health Organization, p. This document is the outcome of the WHO-expert task force meeting held in London, United Kingdom, in April 1999. It bases on the document entitled "Community noise" that was prepared for the World Health Organization and published in 1995 by the Stockholm University and Karolinska Institute (1999)
7. Raspberry. raspberrypi.org
8. DJI, Manual de Usuario: Drone Matrice 100 (2004). https://dl.djicdn.com/downloads/m100/M100_User_Manual_EN.pdf
9. Behringer: Measurement Condenser Microphone ECM8000 Technical Specifications (2013). https://media63.music-group.com/media/sys_master/h47/hde/8849927929886.pdf
10. Behringer: Quick Start Guide: U-PHORIA (2017). https://www.bhphotovideo.com/lit_files/374154.pdf
11. ISO: ISO 3744 (2010)
12. McLoughlin, I.V.: Basic audio processing. In: Speech and Audio Processing: A MATLAB®-based Approach, pp. 9–53. Cambridge University Press (2016). https://doi.org/10.1017/CBO9781316084205.004
13. López García, R.G.: Caracterización y optimización de un sistema de sonido profesional (2013)

Organic Constructions and Airplane Type Hostels in Isolated Places Supplied with Solar Energy

Daniel Icaza[1,2](✉) ⓘ, Carlos Flores-Vázquez[1,2] ⓘ, Juan-Carlos Cobos-Torres[1] ⓘ, and Santiago Pulla Galindo[1,2] ⓘ

[1] GIRVyP Grupo de Radiación Visible y Prototipado, Cuenca, Ecuador
juan.cobos@ucacue.edu.ec
[2] Universidad Católica de Cuenca Ecuador, Cuenca, Ecuador
{dicazaa,cfloresv,gpullag}@ucacue.edu.ec

Abstract. For this research work, it was considered a renewable energy source that harness the energy of solar radiation to transform itself into electrical energy and supply the organic constructions and airplane type hostels located between the mountains in places of high tourist potential. In the present work of investigation also presents the constructive case of the hostel type airplane, its characteristics, design, simulations and relevant data of the construction, the feasibility of implementing these autonomous constructions was analyzed to give greater value to the Ecuadorian areas with high potential tourist. The research process consisted in the collection of data on solar radiation, temperature, through meteorological stations located in various sectors of the Cuenca-Ecuador Canton.

The simulations were carried out in MATLAB/Simulink based on a mathematical model established for this case.

In the end, we present the results of this successful experience from the technical point of view.

Keywords: Isolated constructions · Renewable energy · Modeling · Solar panel · Sustainable architecture · Rural development

1 Introduction

The flight of the birds, the shapes of the plants, the color of the flowers, the sprouting of the waters, among other prodigies of nature, were the inspiration for the multiple and revolutionary inventions that have been made so far and that over the years human beings continue to develop for the benefit of the countries and their continents [13].

Organic architecture is a philosophy of architecture that promotes harmony between the human habitat and the natural world. Through design, it seeks to understand and integrate the territory, through real territorial development plans, to small complementary works in public or private spaces [9]. Larger buildings, such as buildings, furniture, housing and the surroundings, are propitious spaces for them to become part of a unified and correlated composition [6]. Among the most prominent architects in this type of

© Springer Nature Switzerland AG 2020
M. Botto-Tobar et al. (Eds.): ICAT 2019, CCIS 1195, pp. 231–243, 2020.
https://doi.org/10.1007/978-3-030-42531-9_19

projects are the architects Gustav Stickley, Antoni Gaudí, Frank Lloyd Wright, Imre Makovecz, Javier Senosiain and Antón Alberts.

Specifically, in what has to do with the organic architecture we can highlight the case of Javier Senosiain that with his works published in his book [6], inspire the desire to live more in contact with nature, in the same way his extraordinary presentations with full audiences express the developments in this area that are a wonder and a true taste to live in architectural environments developed by him as those highlighted in Figs. 1 and 2.

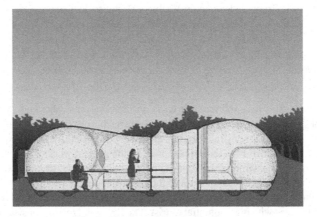

Fig. 1. Design of the cacahuate set.

Fig. 2. Construction of the cacahuate set.

One of the most outstanding interventions was at the Catholic University of Cuenca Ecuador on October 3 of 2018, with the project of the organic Amiba house shown in Figs. 3 and 4. According to Fig. 3 born from the idea of creating a space adapted to man according to their environmental needs, physical and psychological, taking into account their origin in nature.

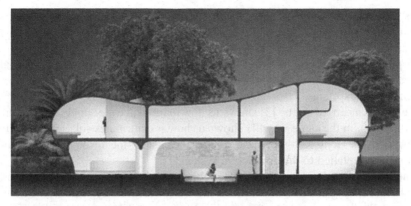

Fig. 3. Design of the organic Amiba house.

Fig. 4. Construction of the organic Amiba house.

Other important developments that are related to nature were presented in Nagasaki Japan by [9], an interesting development of a plant to create shade in parks and recreational sites. One of the few experiences that beyond fulfilling a purpose strictly to have a natural contact, also allows to be provided with internet and renewable energy [10].

In this article we address more than these architectures related to the environment and have organic characteristics, are supplied by renewable energy, such is the case of solar, wind, hydraulic or other that fits the architectural environment and take advantage of the benefits that can arrange the place where the sites are made [5].

While there is no breakthrough regarding the influence of renewable energies on organic constructions worldwide, it is precisely this article that aims to publicize a study and development of a hotel type airplane powered by solar energy in Ecuador, where this country is in the middle of the world the solar radiation is quite intense and takes advantage of measurements made in the vicinity where this construction was implemented and that the final finishes are being made [4].

Several studies carried out where solar energy fulfills an interesting development factor should be discarded and can be better exploited in isolated rural areas or far from the electricity distribution networks.

[2] presented the future of smart grids in Ecuador with a very important analysis aimed at electrification in remote areas of low and medium voltage and a general review of electric power systems.

The research carried out by [3] shows us how to influence the supply of solar energy in South Africa, in the same way [4] shows us how it contributes solar energy within a hybrid system for Hong Kong, in these sources it can show the development that allows the countries in relation to the productive system [1].

Other studies were carried out by [4] highlighting the production of solar energy to supply homes in England and the implementation of electrical systems from renewable energies totally disconnected from the public electricity grid. In our case with the purpose of analyzing its feasibility, we take as a reference successful studies in the vicinity where the first hotel was built, which is the Quingeo-Ecuador Sector, presented by [6] where measurements of important parameters such as solar radiation, wind speed and temperature through a weather station. Similar study was conducted in Chordeleg-Ecuador by [14] to supply solar energy to a Tourist Center, the mathematical model is obtained and the respective measurements and comparisons are made.

This document describes the simulation in matlab in different conditions of solar radiation for the validation of the construction of the airplane type hotel with organic constructive characteristics. The system will be supplied by solar energy and must operate regularly taking into account that its purpose is to guarantee the lighting service, recreation rooms and special loads [11]. The energy will be stored in batteries.

2   Location of Research

The project referring to organic architecture where especially a plane-type hotel has been made in the Rural Parish El Valle, a place that is two minutes from the main road Cuenca - Sigsig. The place is characterized by having a beautiful view of the river and surrounding and green mountain ranges. See Fig. 5.

Fig. 5. Location of the hotel type airplane.

Fig. 6. First phase of construction of the hotel type airplane.

Fig. 7. Second phase of construction of the hotel type airplane.

As shown in Figs. 6 and 7, the construction process of the hotel type airplane is identified, the same one that in the upper part will be equipped with solar panels to capture the sun's rays and transform it into electrical energy in direct current, then it goes to a charge controller to be stored in 12 V batteries and with an inverter to obtain alternating current that basically will serve to supply the electrical system that basically consists of lighting and outlets [7]. We must specify that strictly for the kitchen equipment will be supplied by liquefied petroleum gas (LPG) to be subsidized by the Ecuadorian state for cooking.

It should be noted that it is intended to make a network of hotels in nearby places with the same characteristics, studies and market analysis are favorable as their implementation, their implementation costs are not too high but very attractive for recurring tourists from these areas [14]. The hotels will be equipped with communication systems and all basic services for the benefit of the clients [13].

Then, in Fig. 8 we can identify the general scheme where the contribution of photovoltaic energy to the hotel type airplane is studied, which is the purpose of the investigation, which is subject to simulations in Matlab to see its behavior according to the different operating conditions. It is clear that in our case study we contemplate it without connection to the public distribution network.

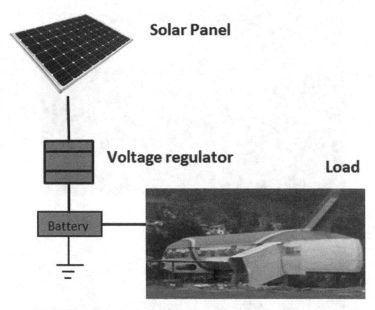

Fig. 8. General scheme of electrical transformation.

3 Mathematical Modeling

In the mathematical model that is indicated below, the most representative parameters that will influence the final objective, which is the production of electrical energy for the airplane-type hotel by capturing solar radiation on the surface of solar panels, are included. This process involves finding the best option for the design of the system provided by solar panels at the top of the hotel, which leads to even better developments based on much more developed mathematical models [7].

3.1 Photovoltaic System

The solar panel that will be used in the application is determined according to the manufacturer's data. The necessary mathematical model has been written in MATLAB. Figure 9 shows the equivalent circuit of the photovoltaic panel [6].

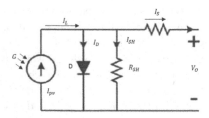

Fig. 9. Mathematical model of the photovoltaic module.

The normalized working temperature (T_O) has been obtained using:

$$T_O = 273 + 25 \tag{1}$$

Equation (2) has been used to determine the working temperature (T_K) of the panel. The operating characteristics of the panel at different temperatures [14] have been obtained as indicated below:

$$T_K = 273 + T_C \tag{2}$$

The thermal energy absorbed by the Photovoltaic system is;

$$P_{pv} = \eta_p * A * G_1 \tag{3}$$

Where;

η_p = Solar collector efficiency.
A = Solar collector area (m^2)
G_1 = Solar irradiation (W/m^2).
η_{pv} = Photovoltaic system performance.

The behavior of the I vs V curve of the photovoltaic cell is described by Eqs. (4), (5) and (6).

$$V_t = mN_s k \frac{(T_1 + 273)}{qe} \tag{4}$$

$$I = I_L(G_1, T_1) - N_p I_0 \left[e^{\left(\frac{V + IR_s}{V_t} - 1\right)} \right] - \frac{V + IR_s}{R_p} \tag{5}$$

$$I_0 = \frac{I_{sc} - \frac{V_{oc}}{R_p}}{e^{\left(\frac{V_{oc}}{V_t}\right)} - 1} \tag{6}$$

Where:

N_s: Number of solar cells in series.
N_p: Number of cells in parallel.
K: Boltzman constant.
Qe: Charge of the electron.
M: Diode ideality factor.
T1:   Working temperature of the solar panel in °C.
R_s: Series resistor.
R_p: Parallel resistance.
I_L (G1, T1): Short-circuit current Isc (G1, T1).
I_0:   Inverse saturation current of the diode.
V_{oc}:   Open circuit voltage.

The electric PV power output in DC taking into account the efficiency of conversion to electric energy is;

$$P_{PV} = \eta_1 I_{PV}.V_{PV} \tag{7}$$

η_1 = Efficiency of conversion to DC.

3.2 Controller

Generally, the controller power output is given by;

$$P_C = V_{bat}(I_{PV}) \tag{8}$$

Where; V_{bat} is multiplication of the nominal voltage DC in the battery for I_{PV} represent the output current of PV.

3.3 Battery Charging and Discharging Model

During the charging period, the voltage-current relationship can be described (Castro C. et al. 2018);

$$V = V_1 + \frac{I\left(\frac{0.189}{(1.142 - soc) + R_i}\right)}{AH} + (soc - 0.9)\ln\left(300\frac{I}{AH} + 1.0\right) \tag{9}$$

$$V_1(V) = 2.094[1.0 - 0.001(T - 25\,°\mathrm{C})] \tag{10}$$

During the discharging process and using Eq. (11), the current-voltage can be;

$$V = V_1 + \frac{I}{AH}\left(\frac{0.189}{soc} + R_i\right) \tag{11}$$

$R_i(\Omega)$: Internal resistance of the cell.
T : Ambient temperature.
AH : Ampere hour rating of the battery

$$P = VI_{OUT} \tag{12}$$

Where I_{OUT} represent the total output current of the rectifier in DC.

4 Blocks Diagram

Figure 9 shows the mathematical model developed in Matlab/Simulink, the simulation is developed according to the characteristic parameters of the photovoltaic system as the area of the panels, number of panels, usual radiation.

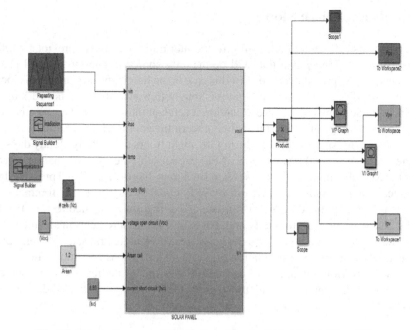

Fig. 10. Block diagram of the airplane type hotel in Matlab/Simulink

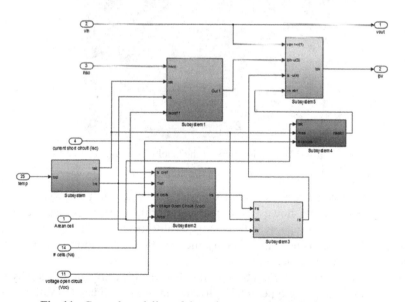

Fig. 11. General modeling of the solar system in Matlab/Simulink

5   Results and Discussions

To solve the Eqs. (1) to (11) according to the literature determined previously related to the solar generation system that will be the only source of energy that will provide enough energy to supply the load that in this case is the hotel type airplane that is located in an energetically isolated area and that it is sought that according to a network of rural hotels in strategic points of Cuenca-Ecuador, it is taken into account that there is a bank of batteries for storage and later through a modern investor to obtain alternating current and provide energy simultaneously during the night hours or on fairly cloudy days. The fundamental purpose is the validation of this model with the use of dynamic software such as the Matlab/Simulink that, in several situations, has been used and presented with great success as the studies carried out by [14] and the coding of the aforementioned equations previously. In addition, to validate and adjust the simulated results, the most coherent data were brought to reality and, based on the measurements made, the internal parts of the airplane-type hotel were designed as shown in its first stage in Fig. 12; The data was used to validate the simulation program under various conditions. In this same section, the corresponding analyzes and the discussions of the results are presented in curves characterized compared with those predicted, consolidating the validations of the solar system.

Fig. 12.   Interior view of the hotel type airplane.

It should be noted that it is sought that during the day to take advantage of the maximum natural lighting, however it is necessary for the client to close those windows for privacy. The 15 solar panels will be strategically located on the sides of the main opening and the equipment that makes up the electrical generation system in a safe, ventilated, clean and dry space.

Figure 13 shows the solar radiation profile that was measured in the vicinity where the location of this airplane type hotel is located in the Localidad del Valle. It should be noted that the measurements with the weather station were not made on the site since security could not be installed in this secluded site. The station was located in the Quingeo Parish and its measurements correspond to several months of the year 2018 at different times of the day.

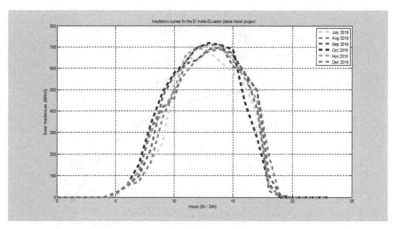

Fig. 13. Solar irradiances (W/m^2) Profile July 2018–Dec 2018.

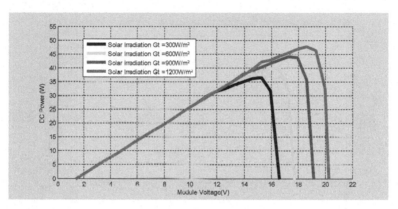

Fig. 14. Voltage-Power curve for different values of solar irradiation.

5.1 PV Simulation

Figure 14 shows the relationship between solar radiation and the production of electrical energy in the photovoltaic system of the hotel type airplane in the area of tourist intervention, it represents and analyzes the electrical voltage in comparison with the power generated. In the same way, in Fig. 15 the result of the matlab simulation is obtained, where the voltage is represented as a function of the DC electric current.

5.2 Validation of the Simulation Model

Next, Fig. 16 is constructed to compare the results of the model used with the experimental results of the photovoltaic system of the airplane type hotel.

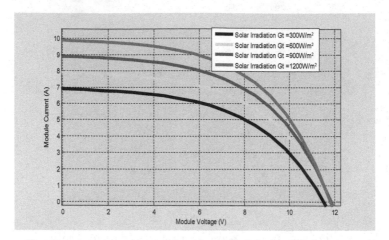

Fig. 15. Voltage-Current curve for different values of solar irradiation.

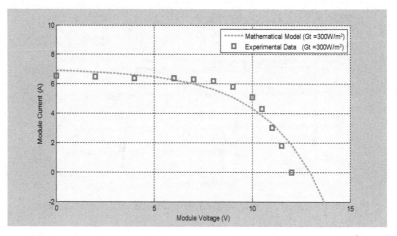

Fig. 16. PV output data compared to model prediction at 300 W/m².

6 Conclusions

The photovoltaic system that is discussed in this article is implemented at the moment and presents a great benefit to the place and stands out in the distance the medium construction of the hotel type airplane that is a reference to replicate in other nearby places where there is a high level of tourism.

The production of electrical energy is sufficient for the lighting system and electrical outlets in the rooms, it becomes an opportunity to supply energy autonomously since the public electricity grid is impossible to reach these remote areas of the population centers and rather, tourists are interested in finding places where peace and tranquility reign.

In relation to the production of solar energy shown in Fig. 16, the results are quite interesting since the prediction model proposed has a behavior pattern quite similar to that of the measurements.

This project avoids the indiscriminate use of noisy generators and fuels that attack the environment as the flora and fauna of the place, this generation system uses clean and renewable energy and above all it is cheap.

Acknowledgments. We thank the Catholic University of Cuenca-Ecuador and the San Agustin University of Arequipa-Peru.

References

1. González, A.E., et al.: Photovoltaic energy to face an earthquake. Int. J. Phys. Sci. Eng. (IJPSE) **1**(3), 19–30 (2017)
2. Arauz, W.M., et al.: The future of micro-grids in Ecuador. Int. J. Phys. Sci. Eng. (IJPSE) **1**(3), 1–8 (2017)
3. Mulaudzi, S.K., et al.: Investigation of the solar energy production and contribution in South Africa: research note. Afr. J. Sci. Technol. Innov. Dev. **4**(4), 233–254 (2012)
4. Ma, T., et al.: Technical feasibility study on a standalone hybrid solar-wind system with pumped hydro storage for a remote island in Hong Kong. Renewable Energy **69**, 7–15 (2014)
5. Duan, X., Redfern, M.A.: The value of PV electricity generation for domestic properties in the West of England. In: 2014 49th International Universities Power Engineering Conference (UPEC), pp. 1–5. IEEE (2014)
6. Portoviejo, J., et al.: Modeling and simulation of a hybrid system solar panel and wind turbine in the Quingeo Heritage Center in Ecuador. World Academy of Science, Engineering and Technology International Journal of Energy and Environmental Engineering, vol. 12, no. 6, Paris- Francia (2018). https://doi.org/10.1999/1307-6892/10009217
7. Icaza, D., et al.: Monitoring of illegal activities in the border area between Ecuador and Colombia using telecommunications networks and microcameras supplied by solar energy installed in native birds. In: 2018 IEEE International Conference on Automation/XXIII Congress of the Chilean Association of Automatic Control (ICA-ACCA), pp. 1–6. IEEE (2018)
8. Javier, S.: Arquitectura Organica, Memoria de la exposición en el museo nacional de arquitectura. AM Editores S.A., pp. 1–176 (2017). Impreso en Chile. ISBN 978-607-437-414-8
9. Avila, M., et al.: Intelligent multifunctional solar urban furniture: a multidisciplinary methodological vision of technology. In: 2018 International Conference on Smart Grid (icSmartGrid), pp. 184–194. IEEE (2018)
10. Rashid, M., et al.: simulation based energy and cost optimization for home users in a community smart grid. Int. J. Renewable Energy Res. (IJRER) **8**(3), 1281–1287 (2018)
11. Kola, S.: A review on optimal allocation and sizing techniques for DG in distribution systems. Int. J. Renewable Energy Res. (IJRER) **8**(3), 1236–1256 (2018)
12. Cedeno, M., et al.: Regulatory framework for renewable energy sources in Ecuador case study province of Manabi. Int. J. Soc. Sci. Humanit. **1**(2), 29–42 (2017)
13. Boyle, G.: Renewable Energy, pp. 456. Oxford University Press, May 2004. ISBN-10: 0199261784. ISBN-13: 9780199261789, 456
14. Castro, C. et al.: Renewable energy system eolic-photovoltaic for the Touristic Center La Tranca-Chordeleg in Ecuador. In: World Academy of Science, Engineering and Technology International Journal of Energy and Environmental Engineering, vol. 12, no. 6 (2018)

Automation of a Lathe to Increase Productivity in the Manufacture of Stems of a Metalworking Company

José Varela-Aldás(✉) ⓘ, Pablo Chávez-Ruiz ⓘ, and Jorge Buele ⓘ

SISAu Research Group, Universidad Tecnológica Indoamérica, 180103 Ambato, Ecuador
{josevarela,jorgebuele}@uti.edu.ec, pablochavez824@gmail.com

Abstract. This project performs the optimization of the process for the manufacture of stems for the gas passage valves produced by the company INDUMETAL M&M, the problem is generated in the process of the elaboration of stems due to the lack of machinery for perform the machining of sufficient stems, the process had a working productivity of 59 units processed/hour of production of stems, which were not sufficient to meet the production requirement, so it was proposed to implement an automated system that solve the problem of production deficiency in the area of stems. The proposal was to reinvigorate the semi-automatic lathe Hardinge AHC (TH-05) existing in the area in very bad conditions, which occupied physical space and could fulfill the required work. For the implementation, a Programmable Logic Controller (SIEMENS S7 1200 PLC) and a Human Machine Interface (HMI DELTA) are used, increasing productivity to 89 units processed/hour of stems, fulfilling the objective set.

Keywords: Automation · Productivity · Manufacturing · PLC · HMI

1 Introduction

According to the exponential growth of society in recent decades, global energy demand is projected to increase gradually [1–4]. The US Department of Energy in 2013 has made a projection that global energy consumption will increase by 56% from 524 billion BTU in 2010 to 820 billion BTU in 2020[1]. Despite efforts to take better advantage of renewable energy production [5] (greens), this amount may not meet the significant increase in demand; i.e. that 76% of the energy will come from carbon-based sources (gas, oil and coal) in 2040[2]. Natural gas being the most prepared to increase its rate to a higher one (1.7% per year) compared to liquid fuel and coal [6]. Almost 80% of the global demand for natural gas is met by conventional sources, although there are conventional sources that have stood out in recent years such as: el tight gas, shale gas and coal bedmethane[3] [7].

---

[1] https://www.eia.gov/outlooks/aeo/pdf/0383(2013).pdf.

[2] https://corporate.exxonmobil.com/Energy-and-environment/Energy-resources/Outlook-for-Energy.

[3] https://www.eia.gov/outlooks/aeo/pdf/0383(2012).pdf.

M. Botto-Tobar et al. (Eds.): ICAT 2019, CCIS 1195, pp. 244–254, 2020.
https://doi.org/10.1007/978-3-030-42531-9_20

Liquefied petroleum gas (LPG) is generated from natural gas or petroleum, which is composed of the combination of propane and butane (heavy gases) [8, 9]. This economical and versatile fuel that is used as fuel in different activities at a commercial, industrial level, as an input for obtaining other products (petrochemical) and essentially in the domestic sphere [10]. It is used in food cooking, air conditioning (in air conditioning or heating systems, water heating by heating and in drying clothes); This means that care must be taken in handling and control. [11–13]. Control devices called pass valves, efficiently start, regulate or stop the passage of gases through the pipe connecting the supply (or gas cylinder) to the gas appliance (cooker, heater, etc.) used in a living place. They are usually male or ball wrenches, which have a conical male or a sphere with a hole through which the fluid passes when it is aligned with the driving shaft [14]. These valves must be completely safe when working with fuel and must ensure a durable installation that is proof of material wear. They are also known as cutting devices or key cutting and are found in all types of domestic installations, where their operation, mechanics and materials are strictly regulated [15]. That is why its components must be prepared in compliance with national and international regulations; inside its structure you have: shank, washers, die-cut knob and other accessories (shichlor, gasket, ½ inch nut and bolt).

Over the years, the empirical design of these products in an artisanal and personalized way, has been replaced by a mass production, focusing the design to increase profits. In this way, greater functionalities can be offered, minimizing production costs, since it uses a high proportion of machinery and energy in relation to workers. In addition, process automation generates lower labor costs and a faster rate of production, capital and energy increases, while total expenditure per unit of product decreases. Mass production systems allow increasing efficiency and productivity in product development, which leads to reduced working hours, generating standardized products that can reach a greater number of consumers [16, 17].

2   Related Works

The change in operating conditions and the business environment provides greater competitive advantages and improved performance [18, 19]. However, few organizations choose to update their systems, either due to lack of planning or shortage of economic resources. Using obsolete systems runs the risk of losing technical support, slowing down processes and generating bottlenecks in the performance and functionality of the systems. That is why, the use of technology for process improvement is applied in various fields of science. As seen in [20] a new process for the elaboration of large-scale industrial chemicals is implemented; despite the environmental, geographical, political and economic challenges associated with energy and manufacturing demands. In addition, incorporating personalized production imposes new requirements on companies that wish to remain competitive in the market. They have to redesign their production systems to be flexible enough to produce a wide variety of products in changing conditions according to market fluctuation. Parallel to [21], the design of a production system with automatic optimization is shown, according to a hierarchical system model. Each level can be considered as an automatic optimization system in itself, which controls the interacting subsystems. The automation of engineering processes requires the development of relevant mathematical support and computer software. The functional tests validate this proposal that demonstrates the importance of the organization and modernization of the processes in the organizations, in the search of their improvement.

The implementation of automated systems allows the best product design and delivery of better services, as described briefly in [22]. This manuscript presents the procedure to determine the geometry of the machining of oblique round-tipped winches without a tip, with the use of vector/matrix transformations. Such an approach allows integration into modern packages of mathematical software as opposed to the traditional analytical description. This advantage is very promising to develop an automated control of the preproduction process, reduces production times and in the long term represents an increase in production. For its part [23] shows the design of a machine that can print customized printed circuit boards (PCBs) by automating the control of a brushless DC motor (BLDC). The design is implemented to demonstrate precisely how to control multiple BLDC motors simultaneously using G-Codes that are encoded in LabVIEW software. The user can monitor the system status and fault conditions and correct them in a timely manner. In addition to the design, another important aspect is the adequate preventive maintenance of the machinery, which increases the reliability of proper long-term operation, as described in [24]. In this document, an imperfect preventive maintenance strategy for the turret system of a CNC lathe is proposed, with the objective of minimizing the total maintenance time and cost in general. Finally, the optimal results of preventive maintenance are discussed under different cost parameters.

This project presents the automation of a damaged lathe to improve the productivity of the production process of stems for gas valves a metalworking company. The document is divided into six sections, including the introduction in Sect. 1, related works in Sect. 2 and the analysis of the initial situation in Sect. 3. Section 4 presents the development of the proposal and Sect. 5 describes the results obtained. Finally, the conclusions are presented in Sect. 6.

3   Initial Situation

As case study, there is a company that operates in the metallurgical field, with an approximate production of 7000 valves per week, which regulates the passage of gas for industrial use (Fig. 1 shows the valve manufactured by INDUMETAL M M). The need for products locally and nationally, have motivated the development of a greater variety of products, which differ in color (blue, silver, tropical or black) and in the design on the front, without modifying their functionality or components used for its elaboration. Thus, in the last year 248,000 copies were made, which reiterates the positioning of the product and the gradual growth of demand.

As a result of the continuous work of the machinery and the incorrect handling of the operators when performing the different procedures, one of the lathes is out of operation (Hardinge AHC, TH-05). All this produces a decrease in the production of stems, an essential part in the elaboration of the valves of passage, which is evidenced in Table 1.

To contrast the machinery owned by the company, its location and other details that make up the production area, the general plan of distribution of the plant is presented, as shown in Fig. 2, marking the position of the damaged lathe in a circle red color.

Fig. 1. Gas valve manufactured by the company INDUMETAL M&M.

Table 1. Stems weekly production: quantity per machine.

Machine	Weekly production	Total production
Hardinge AHC lathe TH01	1500	5650
Hardinge AHC lathe TH02	1350	
Hardinge AHC lathe TH03	1350	
Hardinge AHC lathe TH04	1450	
Hardinge AHC lathe TH05	0	

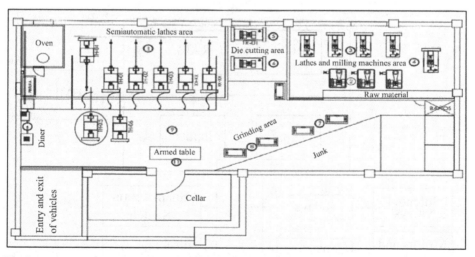

Fig. 2. Diagram of the plant distribution of the metalworking company INDUMETAL M&M, with the location of the TH-05 semi-automatic lathe. (Color figure online)

Productivity relates the efficiency with which capital, inputs and human talent are used to produce economic value; High productivity represents generating higher income without altering the resources available. In this proposal, productivity is calculated based on the number of units produced (stems), as described in (*1*). Where there is a weekly production of 5650 stems, prepared by 2 employees who work 8 h a day and for 6 days a week. Based on the aforementioned, having machinery out of operation has caused a decrease in the amount of production that should be greater than 7000 rods, which means the presence of a bottleneck, which delays the other processes of the company. The productivity prior to this proposal is 59 units per hour as detailed in (*2*) and (*3*).

$$Productivity \ = \ Units\ processed/Hours\ used \tag{1}$$

$$Productivity \ = \ 5650\ units\ /\ (2\ employees \cdot 48\ hours) \tag{2}$$

$$Productivity \ \approx \ 59\ units\ /\ hour \tag{3}$$

4 Proposal Development

4.1 System Components

The semi-automatic lathe is damaged because all the control components have failed and have been discarded, so it is proposed to implement a system with all the components presented in Fig. 3. The system is controlled from a PLC that is connected to an HMI

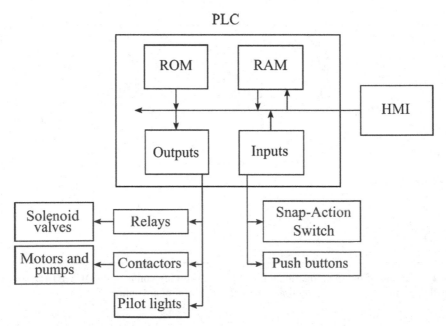

Fig. 3. Scheme of the proposed system to automate the damaged TH-05 lathe, with all the required components

module that allows interaction with the operator, the system inputs are keypads and limit switches, and the outputs are the relays and contactors that control the actuators (solenoid valves, motors and pumps). In addition, pilot lights are activated to indicate operating states.

The lathe has six working tools (each with its respective motor), limit switches, hydraulic drive pumps and lubrication solenoid valves. These components are reused in the repowering of the lathe.

4.2 Electrical Diagram

The electrical diagram of the automatic system is carried out where the main controller is a Siemens S7 1200 PLC and two input and output expansion modules (SM1223 and SM1222) are used. The electrical system contains the connections necessary to install the elements required for lathe automation, Fig. 4 presents a segment of the entire electrical diagram.

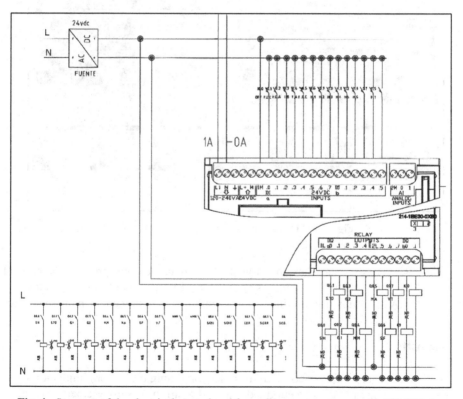

Fig. 4. Segment of the electrical control and force diagram to automate the TH-05 lathe

The PLC contains the programming to automate the machining of stems for gas valves, the process includes sequential drilling with different drill diameters, the cutting of the stem at the predetermined length (splitter) and the collector continues entering the rod to repeat the cycle. In addition, the movements of the reels, the activation of the solenoid valves and lubricating pumps that allow controlling the cutter, the feeder, the taladrina, the hydraulic pump for the pistons and the threader are programmed. The ladder program has been implemented using the TIA PORTAL V14 software.

4.3 HMI

The control interface is implemented in a DELTA HMI using DOP-SOFT software and is physically connected to the PLC via Ethernet communication. Figure 5 shows the screens of the control interface observing the main menu that contains the options of manual and automatic control, and the six menus of each individual tool of the lathe.

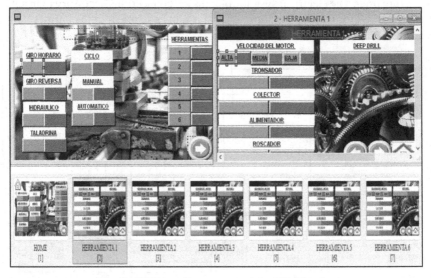

Fig. 5. HMI interface to control the TH-05 lathe.

The CICLO option activates an automated rod manufacturing process, the manual option allows you to control the process one tool at a time as desired by the operator, and the AUTOMATICO function produces stems until it ends with the rod in the manifold.

5   Results

All the components of the proposal are installed, obtaining the system implemented as shown in Fig. 6, the photos present the dashboard of all the control elements, the HMI in operation and the TH-05 lathe in progress. The implementation costs generate a final value of $1,500, which includes the acquisition of control components (PLC, extension modules, HMI, relays, cables and others).

With the TH-05 lathe in operation, a change in the productivity of the stem manufacturing area is obtained, the added lathe produces 1450 stems weekly and the total production per week is 7100 stems, supervised by 2 employees working 8 h a day and for 5 days a week, reducing a work day from the previous condition. Based on the afore-mentioned, the productivity formula (*1*) is applied, obtaining a productivity 89 units per hour as described in (*4*) and (*5*) and evidences an improvement in the efficiency of this production area.

$$Productivity = 7100 \; units \,/ (2 \; employees \cdot 40 \; hours) \qquad (4)$$

$$Productivity \approx 89 \; units \,/\, hour \qquad (5)$$

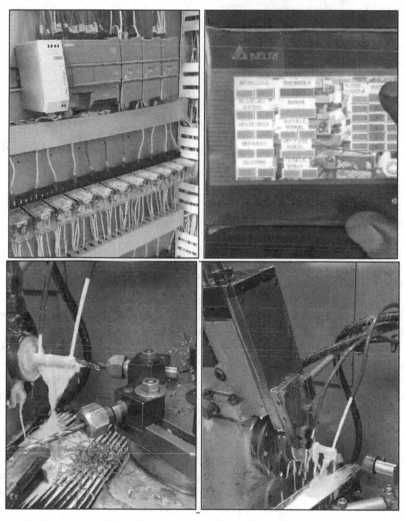

Fig. 6. Photos of the automated system, the control panel, HMI and the TH-05 lathe are in operation.

The results of this proposal are evidenced in the work of 5 lathes in the manufacture of stems. Figure 7 shows the weekly production of stems of each lathe, including the automated lathe (TH-05), and the cumulative production of all the machines for each week that allows to exceed the production requirements (7000 stems weekly).

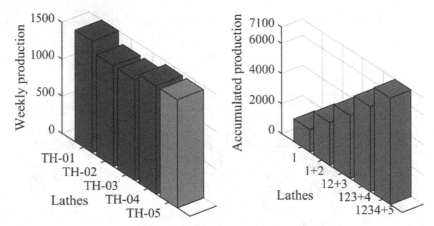

Fig. 7. Weekly production of each lathe and cumulative weekly production of each lathe

6   Discussions and Conclusions

This proposal proposes that the repair of a production machine (Automation of a lathe) improves the productivity in the manufacture of stems, although there are more complex industrial automation works, this work presents a quick and economical solution to the problem of limited production of Business. The related works summarized in this document present advanced automation solutions for similar systems, but this proposal uses a low-cost device that allows the machine elements to be controlled efficiently.

This work describes the implementation of an automatic system to repair a semi-automatic lathe of the Hardinge AHC brand that was damaged. The proposed system consists of a Siemens brand PLC, two input and output extension modules, an HMI display and lathe sensors and actuators are reused. The need for repair arises with the limited production of the area of gas valve valves in the metalworking company INDUMETAL M&M, with a previous productivity of 59 units per hour of work of both employees and a weekly production of 5650 units, which did not satisfy the 7000 units required by the company in the rest of the valve production process.

The results show the automatic system implemented, noting an increase in productivity with 89 units per hour of work of both employees, which is reflected in a production of 7100 units per week. In addition, the proposal implemented has reduced a working day, which result in less wear on the machines and a decrease in the workload for workers. It is recommended to analyze all implementation costs in the development of similar projects.

References

1. Kannan, N., Vakeesan, D.: Solar energy for future world: - A review (2016). https://doi.org/10.1016/j.rser.2016.05.022
2. Sholl, D.S., Lively, R.P.: Seven chemical separations to change the world (2016). https://doi.org/10.1038/532435a
3. Obama, B.: The irreversible momentum of clean energy. Science (2017). https://doi.org/10.1126/science.aam6284
4. Gielen, D., Boshell, F., Saygin, D.: Climate and energy challenges for materials science (2016). https://doi.org/10.1038/nmat4545
5. Mathiesen, B.V., et al.: Smart energy systems for coherent 100% renewable energy and transport solutions (2015). https://doi.org/10.1016/j.apenergy.2015.01.075
6. Chong, Z.R., Yang, S.H.B., Babu, P., Linga, P., Li, X.: Sen: review of natural gas hydrates as an energy resource: Prospects and challenges. Appl. Energy (2016). https://doi.org/10.1016/j.apenergy.2014.12.061
7. Faramawy, S., Zaki, T., Sakr, A.A.E.: Natural gas origin, composition, and processing: a review (2016). https://doi.org/10.1016/j.jngse.2016.06.030
8. Gros, J., et al.: Petroleum dynamics in the sea and influence of subsea dispersant injection during deepwater horizon. Proc. Natl. Acad. Sci. U. S. A. (2017). https://doi.org/10.1073/pnas.1612518114
9. Shen, G., Hays, M.D., Smith, K.R., Williams, C., Faircloth, J.W., Jetter, J.J.: Evaluating the performance of household liquefied petroleum gas cookstoves. Environ. Sci. Technol. (2018). https://doi.org/10.1021/acs.est.7b05155
10. Elmer, T., Worall, M., Wu, S., Riffat, S.B.: Fuel cell technology for domestic built environment applications: state of-the-art review (2015). https://doi.org/10.1016/j.rser.2014.10.080
11. Nie, P., Sousa-Poza, A., Xuc, J.: Fuel for life: domestic cooking fuels and women's health in rural China. Int. J. Environ. Res. Public Health (2016). https://doi.org/10.3390/ijerph13080810
12. Lubwama, M., Yiga, V.A.: Development of groundnut shells and bagasse briquettes as sustainable fuel sources for domestic cooking applications in Uganda. Renew. Energy (2017). https://doi.org/10.1016/j.renene.2017.04.041
13. Martínez-Gómez, J., Ibarra, D., Villacis, S., Cuji, P., Cruz, P.R.: Analysis of LPG, electric and induction cookers during cooking typical Ecuadorian dishes into the national efficient cooking program. Food Policy (2016). https://doi.org/10.1016/j.foodpol.2015.12.010
14. Cui, B., Lin, Z., Zhu, Z., Wang, H., Ma, G.: Influence of opening and closing process of ball valve on external performance and internal flow characteristics. Exp. Therm. Fluid Sci. (2017). https://doi.org/10.1016/j.expthermflusci.2016.08.022
15. Lee, K., Heo, S., Kwon, S., Lee, J.: Study on transient analysis of hot gas valve with pintle. J. Korean Soc. Propuls. Eng. (2018). https://doi.org/10.6108/kspe.2018.22.2.152
16. Arao, Y., Mizuno, Y., Araki, K., Kubouchi, M.: Mass production of high-aspect-ratio few-layer-graphene by high-speed laminar flow. Carbon (2016). https://doi.org/10.1016/j.carbon.2016.02.046
17. Saá, F., Varela-Aldás, J., Latorre, F., Ruales, B.: Automation of the feeding system for washing vehicles using low cost devices. In: Advances in Intelligent Systems and Computing, pp. 131–141 (2020). https://doi.org/10.1007/978-3-030-32033-1_13
18. Sun, B., Jämsä-Jounela, S.L., Todorov, Y., Olivier, L.E., Craig, I.K.: Perspective for equipment automation in process industries. IFAC-PapersOnLine. (2017). https://doi.org/10.1016/j.ifacol.2017.12.012

19. Franklin, T.-O., Tubon-Nunez, E.E., Carrillo, S., Buele, J., Franklin, S.-L.: Quality management system based on the ISO 9001:2015: study case of a coachwork company. In: 2019 14th Iberian Conference on Information Systems and Technologies (CISTI), pp. 1–6. IEEE, Coimbra (2019). https://doi.org/10.23919/CISTI.2019.8760816
20. Clomburg, J.M., Crumbley, A.M., Gonzalez, R.: Industrial biomanufacturing: the future of chemical production (2017). https://doi.org/10.1126/science.aag0804
21. Schlick, C.M., Faber, M., Kuz, S., Bützler, J.: A symbolic approach to self-optimisation in production system analysis and control. In: Advances in Production Technology, pp. 147–160 (2014). https://doi.org/10.1007/978-3-319-12304-2_11
22. Filippov, A. V., Tarasov, S.Y., Podgornyh, O.A., Shamarin, N.N., Filippova, E.O.: Mathematical support for automated geometry analysis of lathe machining of oblique peakless round-nose tools. J. Phys. Conf. Ser. (2017). https://doi.org/10.1088/1742-6596/803/1/012041
23. Shaer, B., Frigon, T., Ferguson, A., Bethel, D.: Application of embedded systems with a universal plotter (2015). https://doi.org/10.1109/secon.2015.7132958
24. Chen, F., et al.: Research on imperfect preventive maintenance strategy for turret system of the CNC lathe. In: Proceedings of 2016 11th International Conference on Reliability, Maintainability and Safety: Integrating Big Data, Improving Reliability and Serving Personalization, ICRMS 2016 (2017). https://doi.org/10.1109/ICRMS.2016.8050075

Optimal-Robust Controller Applied to an Inverted Pendulum-Cart System: A Graphic Performance Analysis

Marco Herrera[1](✉), Xavier Aguas[1](✉), Oscar Gonzales[2](✉), and Oscar Camacho[1](✉)

[1] Escuela Politécnica Nacional, Ladrón de Guevara E11.253, Quito, Ecuador
{marco.herrera,xavier.aguas,oscar.camacho}@epn.edu.ec
[2] Universidad de las Américas,
Calle Queri S/N y Av. De los Granados, Quito, Ecuador
oscar.gonzales@udla.edu.ec

Abstract. In this work a performance graphic analysis approach based on radar charts for an optimal-robust controller with different switching functions is presented. For purpose of taking an overall performance criteria of control algorithm, this graphic analysis is used. The stabilization of the Car-Pendulum System is performed through the optimal-robust controller based on the Variable Structure Control (VSC) and the Linear Quadratic Regulator (LQR) as sliding surface. Different chattering reduction methods are tuned by using Particle Swarm Optimization (PSO) methodology. The performance based on radar graphs are performed using ISE, IAE, $\%M_p$ and TV indexes through initial conditions, disturbances and uncertain parameter tests by simulations.

Keywords: Inverted pendulum-cart system · LQR · PSO · Radar chart · VSC

1 Introduction

Many processes are highly non-linear, this represent a challenge for control engineers. In order to design a control system the linearized model as better option is used, due the controllers based on non-linear models are greater mathematical complexity [1]. One of the most useful test bench is the inverted cart – pendulum system. This is an unstable non-linear system of fast dynamics, where the control system should keep the pendulum balanced at its operation point [2]. In [3], the inverted cart – pendulum control is performed by a Linear Quadratic Gaussian regulator (LQG). The mathematical model is taken from Lagrange algorithm. Then, the model is linearized through Taylor series at the operation point. This approach is affected by oscillations in the control response and the angular position when white noise is added to the plant and measurements through of simulations. Other algorithms have shown more complex designs as in [4], where a

© Springer Nature Switzerland AG 2020
M. Botto-Tobar et al. (Eds.): ICAT 2019, CCIS 1195, pp. 255–269, 2020.
https://doi.org/10.1007/978-3-030-42531-9_21

hybrid scheme between a fuzzy controller and a Linear Matrix Inequalities (LMI) approach is presented. The pendulum movement from position is performed by fuzzy control and the equilibrium is performed by LMI control. However, an approach of robustness at equilibrium point is not adopted.

Hybrid controllers are good alternatives to improve the control performance in the inverted cart – pendulum system, especially when the pendulum reaches instability due to an external force applied at the operation point. Then, [5] proposed three control schemes – comparison to stabilize the inverted pendulum. For swing phase, an energy – based controller is proposed to raise the pendulum from its position. At the equilibrium point, the performance of 3 controllers were analyzed: Linear Quadratic Regulator (LRQ), Sliding Mode Controller (SMC) and Sliding Mode Controller with Integral term (ISMC). The ISMC presented better performance compared to the other two regulators because the control action was smoothed due to the integral term. On the other hand, a risk of a saturated control action is presented by cause of the integral term. Robust algorithms such as non-linear schemes [6] or μ - synthesis [7] present more mathematical complexity than the controllers previously described.

The Variable Structure Controller (VSC) is a versatile regulator scheme that has generated several works on robotics and process control. [8] shows the objectives achieved by the VSC, especially in cases where exist a fast-dynamic plant and it needs to be robust at the point of operation [9,10].

Several robust control algorithms, such as SMC or VSC, use a discontinuous function to accelerate the tracking of the reference in the transient state. The discontinuous function makes the process susceptible to chattering, which is the generation of a very high frequency control signal which several real systems cannot assimilate. Therefore, several techniques manage to chattering reduce through mathematical expressions in order to adapt the control law to real processes, without neglecting the objective of achieving a short settling time [5]; one of this objectives is to compare several methods to smooth chattering and use them in a fast dynamic process, such as the inverted cart - pendulum. Normally, goals accomplishment of several controllers is evaluated by performance indexes, such as: IAE, ISE, TV, among others [11]. However, many results in these cases are biased because a global view of performance is not observed in terms of comparison, also one or two performance criteria are considered and are not enough conclusive. Works such as, [8], shows results of tracking performance of for two-input and two-output networked control systems, test results are projected in a 3D-graphic of tracking errors, but other features such us process performance, were not considered. In [12], a optimal-robust controller is designed in order to control a Furuta's Pendulum, where the robustness performance is analyzed by ISE, however, the control effort is not considered and there is no overall perspective of controller performance.

In this work, a graphic method to evaluate the results of the application of optimal-robust controller based on VSC and LQR as sliding surfaces with different reduction chattering methods (Dead-zone, ramp, hyperbolic tangent switching functions) on Cart-pendulum system. This approach uses several indexes of performance quantification that are placed in a radar chart. This method is used in order to evaluate the performance [13]. Finally, a more global criterion is determined on which reduction chattering methods generates better global control results. Therefore, the aim in this work is to implement an optimal-robust controller in an inverted pendulum car to test the robustness of the controller against external disturbances and parametric uncertainties under the influence of different sliding surfaces.

This paper is organized as follows: in Sect. 2 the Cart-Pendulum System Modelling is developed. The Optimal-Robust Controller based on VSC and the LQR as Sliding surface is designed in Sect. 3. Simulation results of the proposed controller are presented in Sect. 4. Finally, the conclusions are presented in Sect. 5.

2   The Cart-Pendulum System Modelling

The cart-pendulum system is shown in Fig. 1, it is consists of a cart of mass M, with constant of friction b, and its horizontal movement is denoted by displacement x. On the upper side, there is a rigid bar which rotates freely on its point of support with a negligible moment of inertia. Mass m is assumed to be concentrated at a point located at distance l from the cart. An external force F is applied on the cart in order to move the cart-pendulum system, while the variable N is the normal force.

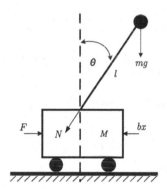

Fig. 1. Cart - pendulum system

In Table 1, the parameters of the cart-pendulum system are presented:

The differential equations describe the dynamics behavior of the cart-pendulum system using Newton's Laws on the cart and the moving mass m. The cart-pendulum model is defined as follow:

$$M\ddot{x} + b\dot{x} = F - N\sin\theta \tag{1}$$

$$m\frac{d^2(x + l\sin\theta)}{dt^2} = N\sin\theta \tag{2}$$

Table 1. Parameters of cart-inverted pendulum system.

Parameter	Description	Unit
M	Mass of the cart	1.2 [kg]
m	Mass of the pendulum	0.32 [kg]
b	Friction of the cart	0.1 [N/m/seg]
l	Length to pendulum center of mass	0.36 [m]
F	Force applied to the cart	$[N]$
g	Gravity	9.8 [m/s^2]
θ	Pendulum angle from vertical	$[rad]$

$$m\frac{d^2(l\cos\theta)}{dt^2} = N\cos\theta - mg \tag{3}$$

In order to obtain a linear model of cart-inverted pendulum system, Eqs. (1)–(3) are linearized at the equilibrium point: $\theta = 0$, $cos(\theta) = 0$ and $\theta\dot\theta^2 = 0$ [14]. Thus, the linearized equations are given by:

$$\ddot{x} = \frac{-mg\theta - b\dot{x} + F}{M} \tag{4}$$

$$\ddot{\theta} = \frac{(m+M)g\theta + b\dot{x} - F}{Ml} \tag{5}$$

By taking into consideration the state-space variables $x(t)$ and the input $u(t)$ of the cart- pendulum system as follows:

$$x(t) = \begin{bmatrix} x_1 & x_2 & x_3 & x_4 \end{bmatrix}^T = \begin{bmatrix} x & \dot{x} & \theta & \dot{\theta} \end{bmatrix}^T$$

$$u(t) = F$$

where from Eqs. (4) and (5):

$$\dot{x}_1 = x_2$$

$$\dot{x}_2 = \frac{-mgx_3 - bx_2 + u}{M}$$

$$\dot{x}_3 = x_4 \tag{6}$$

$$\dot{x}_4 = \frac{(m+M)gx_3 + bx_2 - u}{Ml}$$

Finally, by considering which the state variables are measurable, the linear state-space representation of cart-pendulum system is:

$$\dot{x}(t) = Ax(t) + Bu(t)$$

$$y(t) = x(t)$$

(7)

where:

$$A = \begin{bmatrix} 0 & 1 & 0 & 0 \\ 0 & \dfrac{-b}{M} & \dfrac{-mg}{M} & 0 \\ 0 & 0 & 0 & 1 \\ 0 & \dfrac{b}{lM} & \dfrac{(M+m)g}{lM} & 1 \end{bmatrix}, \quad B = \begin{bmatrix} 1 \\ \dfrac{1}{M} \\ 0 \\ \dfrac{-1}{lM} \end{bmatrix}$$

(8)

3   Controller Design

3.1   Linear Quadratic Regulator

The linear quadratic regulator (LQR) is an optimal state feedback controller, which is designed in order to minimize a quadratic index [15]. The performance index is written as follows:

$$J = \int_0^\infty \left[x^T(t)Qx(t) + u^T(t)Ru(t) \right] dt$$

(9)

Where: $Q \geq 0$ is a positive semi-definite matrix which contains the weights for penalizing the states, and $R > 0$ is a positive definite matrix with weights which penalize the input. Thus, the Riccati algebraic equation to optimize is given by:

$$PA + A^T P - PBR^{-1}B^T P + Q = 0$$

(10)

The vector P is the solution of (10) and the optimal feedback gains are computed by [16]:

$$K = R^{-1}B^T P$$

(11)

Finally, the control law of the LQR is given by:

$$u = -Kx(t)$$

(12)

Where K is the feedback optimal matrix of states. To tune this controller, it is necessary to select the weights for each matrix Q and R according to the relationship between the response time behaviour and control effort [17]. The selection of the weights q_i and ρ for Q and R are done through of the inverse of the square of the maximum value for the corresponding $x_i(t)$ or $u(t)$ [18]. The matrices Q and R are the following:

$$Q = \begin{bmatrix} q_1 & 0 & 0 & 0 \\ 0 & q_2 & 0 & 0 \\ 0 & 0 & q_3 & 0 \\ 0 & 0 & 0 & q_4 \end{bmatrix} \quad R = \begin{bmatrix} \rho \end{bmatrix}$$

(13)

3.2 Variable Structure Control (VSC) with a LQR as Sliding Surface

The VSC is a robust control which is insensitive to the estimation errors of the system parameters, even if these values vary [19]. The main feature of VSC is its sliding mode operation based on a sliding surface. The system remains insensitive to parameters and disturbances variations and its trajectories are kept on the sliding surfaces. However, the VSC control law is characterized by abruptly change, this problem is called chattering effect. In order to design this controller, it is assumed which $A \epsilon \Re^{n \times n}$ and $B \epsilon \Re^{n \times m}$ is a pair controllable. In addition, it necessary to define the tracking error as $e(t) = x_r - x(t)$, $x_r = 0$, this error should tend to zero. The sliding surface is defined as:

$$\sigma(t) = Se(t), \quad S \epsilon \Re^{1 \times n} \tag{14}$$

Where S is the feedback optimal gains vector calculated in the design of Linear Quadratic Regulator. In order to satisfy the reaching condition, the VSC needs to select a control structure through the switching conditions [20]:

$$\begin{aligned} if \quad \sigma(t) &< 0 \quad then \quad \dot{\sigma}(t) = K_d \\ if \quad \sigma(t) &= 0 \quad then \quad \dot{\sigma}(t) = 0 \\ if \quad \sigma(t) &> 0 \quad then \quad \dot{\sigma}(t) = -K_d \end{aligned} \tag{15}$$

Therefore, $\dot{\sigma}(t)$ can be written as:

$$\dot{\sigma}(t) = -K_d sign(\sigma(t)) \tag{16}$$

where $K_d > 0$ and $sign(\sigma(t))$ is the sign function. By differentiation (14) and replacing (8), thus:

$$\dot{\sigma}(t) = -S(Ax(t) + Bu(t)) = -K_d sign(\sigma(t)) \tag{17}$$

Therefore, in order to satisfy the stability and the performance specifications in closed-loop system. The control law which guarantees $\dot{\sigma}(x) = 0$ is given by:

$$u(t) = -(SB)^{-1}[SAx(t) - K_d sign(\sigma(t))] \tag{18}$$

For the purpose of reducing a chattering effect, the sign function can be replaced with a switching function. These functions are presented in Fig. 2.

3.3 Tuning by Particle Swarm Optimization

Particle Swarm Optimization (PSO) is a powerful alternative to solve high-complexity optimization problems [21]. This method is inspired by the collaborative behavior of biological systems which are grouped by swarms in nature. Thus, the PSO algorithm seeks optimal values for VSC parameters. In order to tune the reaching part of the control law, the PSO performs the minimization of a fitness function. In this case the Integral Square Error (ISE) performance index is considered as fitness function. A candidate solution vector in the search space

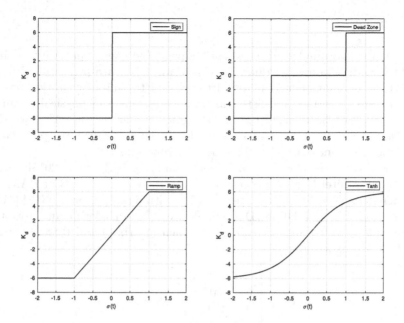

Fig. 2. Switching functions to reduce chattering effect.

is a vector containing all required information [22] to construct the reaching part of VSC controller. This vector is:

$$y = [\delta \ K_d] \qquad (19)$$

Where δ is the limit of switching conditions and K_d is a constant tuning. The procedure of PSO is to iterate the following equations:

$$v_{ij}^{k+1} = wv_{ij}^{k} + c_1 r_1 \left(pbest_{ij}^{k} - y_{ij}^{k} \right) + c_2 r_2 \left(gbest_{ij}^{k} - y_{ij}^{k} \right) \qquad (20)$$

$$y_{ij}^{k+1} = y_{ij}^{k} + v_{ij}^{k+1} \qquad (21)$$

Where: i is the particle number, j is the parameter number of discontinuous part of VSC controller, k is the iteration number, y is the parameter vector of discontinuous part of controller, v is the speed of particle, *pbest* is an individual best solution, *gbest* is the global best solution, r_1 and r_2 are random numbers between 0 and 1, c_1 and c_2 are positive constant learning rates and w is the constriction factor [23].

The objective function f is defined as the Integral Square Error (ISE) index:

$$f = \int e_1(t)^2 dt \qquad (22)$$

Where: $e_1(t) = x_{r1}(t) - x_1(t)$ and Eq. (22) will be used as the objective function to seek a set of parameters such that the feedback control system has minimum performance index.

4   Results

In this section the simulation results of the proposed controller with four differ-ent switching functions to reduce the chattering effect are presented. The per-formance of the controller is analyzed through of the initial condition test and the robustness is verified by disturbances and uncertain in physical parameter tests. The Radar Charts based on ISE, Integral Absolute Error (IAE), overshoot ($\%M_p$) and Total Variation (TV) are used in order to analyze the performance of the proposed controller with the switching functions.

The proposed controller was implemented in Matlab/Simulink 2018b and run on a computer Intel Core i7 processor @ 2.4 GHz with 16.00 GB of RAM. The simulation in each test has a duration of 15 [s] with a sample time of 0.01 [s]. The solver method used is ODE45 (Dorman-Prince). By considering an error of $\epsilon = 0.8$ [m] and $\theta = 1/18$ [rad], the weights for each matrix Q and R were obtained through of [18] as follows:

$$Q = \begin{bmatrix} 0.8 & 0 & 0 & 0 \\ 0 & 0 & 0 & 0 \\ 0 & 0 & 1/18 & 0 \\ 0 & 0 & 0 & 0 \end{bmatrix} \quad R = \begin{bmatrix} 1 \end{bmatrix} \tag{23}$$

By resolving the Eqs. (9) and (11), the feedback gains K are given by:

$$K = \begin{bmatrix} 1.00 & 2.20 & 36.28 & 6.32 \end{bmatrix} \tag{24}$$

Finally, the parameters of Optimal-Robust controller δ and K_d were gotten by Particle Swarm Optimization method. The PSO tuning parameters of Cart-pendulum system are: 30 iterations, 20 particles with a rank of [0 10], $c_1 = 1.7$, $c_2 = 1.3$ and $w = 0.95$. According to the results: $\delta = 0.01$ and $K_d = 6$.

4.1   Initial Condition Test

In this test from the initial condition $x_o = \begin{bmatrix} 0 & 0 & 0.1 & 0 \end{bmatrix}$ [rad] the Cart-pendulum system is released with the purpose that it can stabilize on the equilibrium. The performance of the system is evaluated using the ISE, IAE, $\%M_p$ and TV indexes. The TV index is computed as follows:

$$TV = \sum_{i=0}^{n-1} |u_{i-1} - u_i| \tag{25}$$

The evolution of the pendulum angle θ for initial condition test is illustrated in Fig. 3, where the proposed controller for all switching functions is able to stabilize the Cart-pendulum system.

The evolution of control actions for the initial condition test are shown in Fig. 4, where only the Sign function presents the chattering effect.

In Table 2, shows the ISE, IAE, TV and $\%M_p$ performance indexes for each switching function in order to reduce the chattering effect.

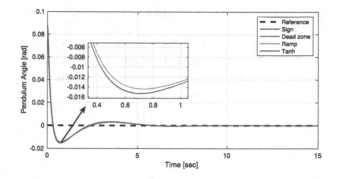

Fig. 3. Evolution of pendulum angle in the initial condition test.

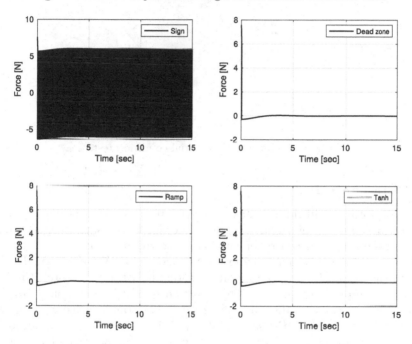

Fig. 4. Evolution of control actions for the initial condition test.

Figure 5 shows a radar chart which represents the performance of the proposed controller with four different functions in order to reduce the chattering effect. Where the Dead-zone switching function presents the better global performance and the Sign function has the biggest TV, IAE, $\%M_p$ indexes.

Table 2. ISE and TV comparison - initial condition test.

Index	Sign	Dead zone	Ramp	Tanh
ISE	0.001128	0.001109	0.001129	0.001126
IAE	0.0417	0.0402	0.0416	0.0416
TV	12.01	6.35e−08	7.86e−09	7.85e−09
%Mp	17.87	16.56	17.83	17.81

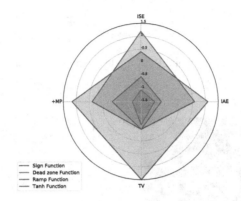

Fig. 5. Radar chart for Initial condition test.

4.2   Disturbance Test

In this test, from equilibrium point ($x_o = \begin{bmatrix} 0\ 0\ 0\ 0 \end{bmatrix}$ [rad]), the car-pendulum system is displaced different angular values θ in order to measure the performance indexes of the proposed controller for each switching function.

The measured performance indexes: ISE, IAE and TV were normalized for graphing the radar charts. To calculate a normalized value (z-score), the Excel Standardized Function was used. This function is based on standard deviation and arithmetic mean of a distribution. A z-score or standard score is a manner of standardizing scores on the same scale by dividing a score's deviation by the standard deviation in a data set [24]. This value can be positive or negative. A negative value means a value less than the mean. On the other hand, a positive value indicates a value higher than the mean. Equation (26) represents how to calculate the standard score o z-score.

$$z_i = \frac{d_i - \bar{d}}{\rho} \tag{26}$$

where: z_i is the z-score, d_i is the value of the element, $\bar{d}$ is the arithmetic mean and ρ is the standard deviation.

Figures 6(a) and (b) show the ISE and IAE radar performance chart respectively for each switching function, where the Sign switching function presents the better global performance. Figure 7 shows the TV radar performance chart, where Sign switching function has the biggest TV.

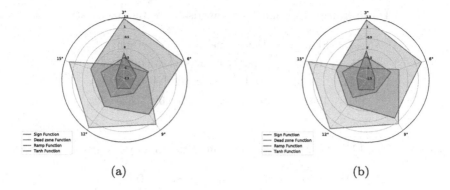

(a)   (b)

Fig. 6. (a) ISE and (b) IAE Radar charts for perturbation test.

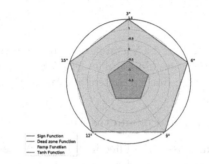

Fig. 7. TV Radar chart for perturbation test.

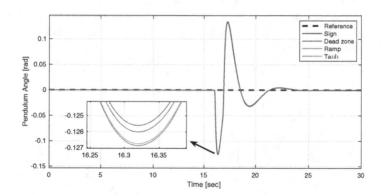

Fig. 8. Evolution of the pendulum angle with a disturbance of 9°.

Figure 8 illustrates the evolution of pendulum angle when a disturbance of 9° appears at 16 [s] with a duration of 0.1 [s].

Table 3. ISE, IAE and TV comparison - disturbance test.

Index	Sign	Dead zone	Ramp	Tanh
ISE	0.001108	0.001129	0.001126	0.001112
IAE	0.0407	0.0416	0.0420	0.0409
TV	12.01	6.35e−08	7.86e−09	7.85e−09

Table 4. ISE, IAE and TV comparison - uncertain in physical parameter test.

Index	Sign	Dead zone	Ramp	Tanh
ISE	0.00953	0.0990	0.00927	0.00923
IAE	0.0360	0.0375	0.0368	0.0362
TV	12.01	9.275e−07	2.28e−08	2.34e−08

Table 3 presents ISE, IAE and TV comparison in the disturbance test when a disturbance appears on the pendulum angle. The VSC controller with sign zone function has the performance but its control actions are high.

4.3   Uncertain in Physical Parameter Test

In this test, the pendulum mass is modified in different percentages −20%, −10%, +10%, +20% in order to measure the robustness of the controller with each switching function. Figures 9(a) and (b) show the ISE and IAE radar performance chart respectively for each switching function; in ISE radar chart, the Tanh switching function presents the better performance whereas in IAE radar chart the Sign and Tanh switching functions present the better performance. Figure 10 shows the TV radar performance chart, where Sign switching function has the biggest TV index.

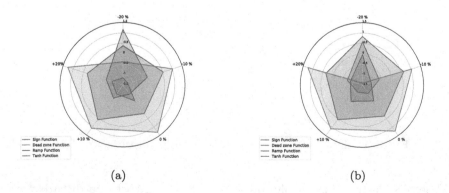

(a)   (b)

Fig. 9. (a) ISE and (b) IAE Radar charts for uncertain test.

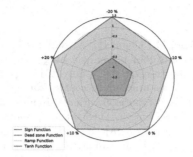

Fig. 10. TV Radar chart - uncertain test.

Figure 11 illustrates the evolution of pendulum angle when the pendulum mass increases a 20%. Otherwise, Table 4 presents ISE, IAE and TV comparison in the test when the pendulum mass increases a 20%. The VSC controller with dead zone function is not recommended if a physical parameter changes in the model.

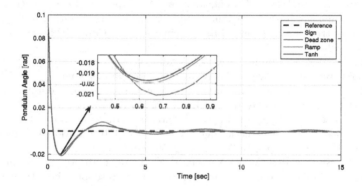

Fig. 11. Evolution of the pendulum angle in the uncertain in physical parameter test.

5 Conclusions

In this work an optimal-robust controller with different switching functions in order to reduced a chattering effect was designed for to stabilize the Car-pendulum system. A performance analysis of proposed controller has been made through radar chart using ISE, IAE, $\%M_p$ and TV indexes for initial condition, disturbance and uncertain parameter tests by simulations. The parameters of switch functions are tuned by the Particle Swarm Optimization methodology. Performance analysis based on radial charts is a good alternative in order to determine the overall performance of the proposed controller.

Acknowledgements. Authors thank to PIS-17-04 Project of the Escuela Politécnica Nacional, for its sponsorship for the realization of this work.

References

1. Feng, Y., Zhao, H., Zhao, M., Chen, H.: A feedback linearization control scheme based on direct torque control for permanent magnet synchronous motor. In: 2018 37th Chinese Control Conference (CCC), July 2018, pp. 87–92 (2018)
2. Chatterjee, S., Das, S.K.: Sampled-data control for optimal gain margin of cart inverted pendulum system: comparison with continuous-time control. In: 2018 15th International Conference on Control, Automation, Robotics and Vision (ICARCV), November 2018, pp. 1153–1157 (2018)
3. Mahapatra, C., Chauhan, S., Hemakumar, B.: Servo control and stabilization of linear inverted pendulum on a cart using LQG. In: 2018 International Conference on Power Energy, Environment and Intelligent Control (PEEIC). IEEE, 2018, pp. 783–788 (2018)
4. Agustinah, T., Jazidie, A., Nuh, M.: Hybrid fuzzy control for swinging up and stabilizing of the pendulum-cart system. In: 2011 IEEE International Conference on Computer Science and Automation Engineering, vol. 4, pp. 109–113. IEEE (2011)
5. Patel, N., Borkar, A.: Hybrid control design for swing up and stabilization of cart pendulum system. In: 2017 International Conference on Intelligent Computing, Instrumentation and Control Technologies (ICICICT), pp. 1051–1057. IEEE (2017)
6. Soria-López, A., Martínez-García, J.C., et al.: Experimental evaluation of regulated non-linear under-actuated mechanical systems via saturation-functions-based bounded control: the cart-pendulum system case. IET Control Theory Appl. 7(12), 1642–1650 (2013)
7. Kumari, R., Dey, J., Pandey, S.K., Chakraborty, A., Mondal, R.: μ-synthesis controller for robust stabilization of cart inverted pendulum system. In: 2017 4th IEEE Uttar Pradesh Section International Conference on Electrical, Computer and Electronics (UPCON), pp. 300–304. IEEE (2017)
8. Wang, J., Yao, L., Wang, S., Li, L.: A variable structure control law for hypersonic vehicles based on genetic algorithm. In: 2014 International Conference on Mechatronics and Control (ICMC), pp. 2259–2262. IEEE (2014)
9. Farivar, F., Shoorehdeli, M.A., Nekoui, M.A., Teshnehlab, M.: Synchronization of underactuated unknown heavy symmetric chaotic gyroscopes via optimal Gaussian radial basis adaptive variable structure control. IEEE Trans. Control Syst. Technol. 21(6), 2374–2379 (2013)
10. Rahmani, B., Markazi, A.H.: Variable selective control method for networked control systems. IEEE Trans. Control Syst. Technol. 21(3), 975–982 (2012)
11. Marzaki, M.H., Tajjudin, M., Rahiman, M.H.F., Adnan, R.: Performance of FOPI with error filter based on controllers performance criterion (ISE, IAE and ITAE). In: 2015 10th Asian Control Conference (ASCC), pp. 1–6. IEEE (2015)
12. Paredes, I., Sarzosa, M., Herrera, M., Leica, P., Camacho, O.: Optimal-robust controller for furuta pendulum based on linear model. In: 2017 IEEE Second Ecuador Technical Chapters Meeting (ETCM), October 2017, pp. 1–6 (2017)
13. Peng, W., Li, Y., Fang, Y., Wu, Y., Li, Q.: Radar chart for estimation performance evaluation. IEEE Access 7, 113 880–113 888 (2019)
14. Ghosh, A., Krishnan, T., Subudhi, B.: Robust proportional-integral-derivative compensation of an inverted cart-pendulum system: an experimental study. IET Control Theory Appl. 6(8), 1145–1152 (2012)
15. Costanza, V., Rivadeneira, P.S., Munera, J.A.G.: Numerical treatment of the bounded-control LQR problem by updating the final phase value. IEEE Lat. Am. Trans. 14(6), 2687–2692 (2016)

16. Zhang, Y., Gao, F., Zeng, T.: A sliding mode controller design for vertical take-off and landing based on model decoupling. In: Proceedings of the 33rd Chinese Control Conference, July 2014, pp. 115–119 (2014)
17. Herrera, M., Leica, P., Chávez, D., Camacho, O.: A blended sliding mode control with linear quadratic integral control based on reduced order model for a VTOL system. In: Proceedings of the 14th International Conference on Informatics in Control, Automation and Robotics - Volume 1: ICINCO, INSTICC, pp. 606–612. SciTePress (2017)
18. Murray, R.: Optimization based-control (California Institute of Technology) (2009)
19. Ignaciuk, P., Morawski, M.: Quasi-soft variable structure control of discrete-time systems with input saturation. IEEE Trans. Control Syst. Technol. **27**(3), 1244–1249 (2018)
20. Al-Hadithi, B.M., Jiménez, A., Delgado, J., Barragán, A., Andújar, J.: Diseño de un controlador borroso basado en estructura variable con modos deslizantes sin chattering. In: Simposio CEA de Control Inteligente, vol. 1, p. 4 (2014)
21. Xue, H., Bai, Y., Hu, H., Xu, T., Liang, H.: A novel hybrid model based on TVIW-PSO-GSA algorithm and support vector machine for classification problems. IEEE Access **7**, 27 789–27 801 (2019)
22. Biswas, P., Maiti, R., Kolay, A., Sharma, K.D., Sarkar, G.: PSO based PID controller design for twin rotor MIMO system. In: Proceedings of the 2014 International Conference on Control, pp. 56–60. Instrumentation, Energy and Communication (CIEC) (2014)
23. Noureddine, B., Djamel, B., Boudjema, F.: Tuning fuzzy fractional order PID sliding-mode controller using PSO algorithm for nonlinear systems. In: 3rd International Conference on Systems and Control, October 2013, pp. 797–803 (2013)
24. Brown, A.M.: A step-by-step guide to non-linear regression analysis of experimental data using a Microsoft Excel spreadsheet. Comput. Methods Programs Biomed. **65**(3), 191–200 (2001)

Smart Battery Charge: A Fiware Open Source Platform and Microcontroller Based IOT Application

Geovanny Raura[1(✉)], Efraín R. Fonseca C.[1(✉)], and Sang Guun Yoo[1,2(✉)]

[1] Departamento de Ciencias de la Computación,
Universidad de las Fuerzas Armadas ESPE, Sangolquí, Ecuador
{jgraura,erfonseca,yysang}@espe.edu.ec
[2] Departamento de Informática y Ciencias de la Computación,
Escuela Politécnica Nacional, Quito, Ecuador
sang.yoo@epn.edu.ec

Abstract. *Context:* Extension of battery lifetime on mobile devices is an aspect which is continuously studied by both manufacturers and applications developers. *Problem:* Most studies are focused on extending Li-Ion batteries lifetime (commonly used in mobile devices), on the premise that charge cycles in this kind of batteries do not reach 100% of their capacity. *Aim:* We have proposed an autonomous system to control the maximum charge level of a mobile device's battery. The system also gathers/analyzes data regarding the battery charge cycles in real-time by using the open source FIWARE platform and the ESP8266 micro-controller. *Methodology:* We have performed a simulation of the battery charge cycle as a proof of concept. *Results:* The preliminary tests were performed on the prototype which allowed us (1) to maintain a relatively constant level of charge by automatically switching on and off the smart plug, (2) to send the charge and uncharge levels of the device in real-time through the an Android application, and (3) to display all information on a time series chart by using the grafana tool.

Keywords: FIWARE · Internet of Things · IoT · Smart battery · Energy consumption

1 Introduction

The primary factor in extending the batteries' operational life of mobile devices is its appropriate use. E.g., even though charging at 100% of the load of a smartphone's battery is a common practice, it is not recommended. Li-ion batteries (commonly used in smartphones) progressively lose the performance of their energy cells during current charge cycles. This behavior has been widely studied in different works [5, 8, 19].

Most of people have the common practice of charging their smartphones during resting hours, which means that the devices are connected to the power

© Springer Nature Switzerland AG 2020
M. Botto-Tobar et al. (Eds.): ICAT 2019, CCIS 1195, pp. 270–281, 2020.
https://doi.org/10.1007/978-3-030-42531-9_22

grid for prolonged period of time [9,16]. The unique charge control in batteries is generally delivered by the manufacturer of the smartphone which interrupts the charging process when the battery is fully charged. This procedure allows the battery to always be at 100% of charge, but does not consider the degradation of the battery life due to excessive charging time.

The current information technologies propose emerging paradigms such as the Internet of Things (IoT), through which the batteries charge management could be considerably improved. The battery charge process could be done autonomously using IoT, maintaining communication between sensors and actuators, and without user intervention. Furthermore, large data volumes could be collected, whose analysis could allow us to understand the habits of smartphone users regarding charging and energy consumption.

With this antecedent, we propose a solution based on the IoT FIWARE platform [12] that could improve the process of charging batteries of mobile devices. Our solution informs a microcontroller configured as a smart plug that the preset battery charge or discharge level has been reached. Next, the connected device is automatically activated or deactivated at the power supply level. Additionally, the proposal collects data regarding the charge or discharge process obtained through a mobile application's APIs. During the charging and discharging battery process, the user intervention is not necessary, which we believe will make the solution viable to increase the battery durability when the device is connected to the power supply for long periods.

The rest of the content of this work is structured as follows. The related works regarding the research subject are presented in Sect. 2. The architecture is detailed in Sect. 3, which served as the basis for the conceptual model proposed. Section 4 presents the technological platform. Finally, in Sect. 5, the conclusions and future work are detailed.

2   Background and Related Works

There are several proposals focused on the optimization of mobile devices' battery life. We found 250 mobile applications (apps) in the Google Play Store through the search string "battery charge". The most relevant features in the applications range from issuing alerts to the user when the battery is charged, monitoring and predicting battery consumption, informing the user about applications that consume energy improperly, to freeing up memory when processes are closed in the background.

As we said before, Li-ion batteries are affected by a high average charge for extended period of time [17]. However, applications identified in Google Play do not offer features that allow managing an effective interruption of the battery charge when it reaches a certain charge level in order to improve its lifetime. Some particular proposals regarding battery charge management based on software and (or) hardware are described below.

Aranagi [2] proposes an application to control the battery's charge level. This app works managing some kernel's configuration files. However, the author advises users that this app only works if the phone has access to root mode, which is usually restricted for security reasons. The user could lose the phone warranty when access to this feature. These restrictions have possibly made software-based solutions not to have commercial developments.

Additionally, we have found some interesting studies to highlight that combine software and hardware.

Choi et al. [4] propose a controlled charge mechanism based on the *contactless* technology, using a *Class-E* converter. This proposal controls the transition between direct voltage and current through a charge algorithm, directly measured from the charge circuit. However, this proposal does not include the recording of measurement data.

Kudo et al. [14] base their work on the LPC1768 micro-controller to stop the charge when there is a transition between direct current to voltage. This proposal is aimed on reducing the charge time with the possibility of being used in places such as free charge sites in public places.

Bai et al. [3] propose a design for charging batteries using a wireless network and an intelligent charger operated by a micro-controller. More specifically, this design can adjust the voltage and current signal according to the environment's temperature. The battery charge status is displayed on a smartphone via a wireless network. The design does not specify communication protocols for IoT applications in the cloud.

Maussion et al. [15] present a proposal to diagnose the battery's state of charge and its condition. The proposal is based on a micro-controller (similar to [3]) and a mobile application (app) for smartphones. Charge control is performed via Bluetooth, and the app is used to configure and receive current parameters from the charger.

Prostl et al. [17] present a solution aimed at mitigating capacity fading. The proposal has a probabilistic predictor which determines the appropriate charge per cycle in a smartphone. Although the proposal mentions the use of a micro-controller, the tests only show the efficiency of the algorithm with a software solution.

The solutions reviewed in this work are not useful without an adequate understanding of users' consumption habits in real usage scenarios. In this sense, we have found studies such as those of Ferreira et al. [9] and Oliver [16], who demonstrate that the common practice of users is to leave mobile phones connected overnight. This practice causes that the charge level of mobile phones reaches higher values for several hours, which significantly affects the battery's life.

Clemm et al. [6] analyze data from a base containing the state of health of Li-ion batteries. Users registered this status for several years through the CoconutBattery application [18]. The main contribution of this study is a predictive algorithm to determine the battery status based on data stored. The authors indicate that the collection of this information is essential since the actual conditions of battery use differ from the conditions set up in the laboratory. The authors indicate as limitations the lack of data of other factors such as ambient temperature, aspects that could be corrected if there were real-time measurements.

As a corollary it is necessary to indicate that we have not been able to identify a solution that incorporates a mechanism that is not intrusive and violates the securities that mobile devices bring from the factory, allows monitoring and recording data in real-time battery consumption using low-cost technologies, and shows communication protocols commonly used in the Internet of Things' applications.

3 Base Architecture of the Proposed Solution

For the development of the proposed solution, we have relied on the FIWARE platform. FIWARE is a open source platform developed by the European Commision's FI-PPP (Future Internet Public-Private Partnership) Programme which provides a set of components to accelerate the development of smart solutions for multiple fields of application [12]. The basic feature of FIWARE is to capture data generated within a *context*. A context is any source of data capable of transmitting or receiving information which can help the fulfillment of an objective and decision making. Here are some examples of those source of data i.e. final users, mobile applications, sensor networks, information systems (such as Customer Relationship Management - CRM) and social networks [12].

FIWARE's architecture provides an open source API called *Context Broker*, which is responsible for orchestrating requests in a component-based development ecosystem. The Context Broker interacts with the context data generated from various sources such as robots, IoT interfaces and third party's systems. Additionally, it also offers a series of components that fulfill specialized functions such as (1) processing, analysis and visualization of context data, (2) management and publication of information, as well as (3) tools for deployment and configuration of the platform. Figure 1, presents a conceptual diagram that shows in a general way the components of the FIWARE platform.

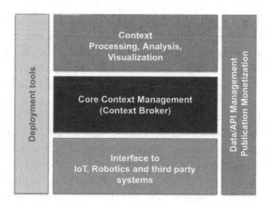

Fig. 1. Conceptual diagram of FIWARE platform (Taken from [13])

The main and only mandatory component of the FIWARE platform is the *Context Broker*, which is also known as Orion Context Borker (OCB). OCB allows the publication of information (taken from *context providers*) for *context consumers*, who are interested in processing such information. Both context providers and consumers deliver and consume data using a subscription mechanism. For example, a smartphone can act as a context consumer receiving the data sent by a temperature sensor subscribed to the OCB.

FIWARE is designed to manage the exchange and communication of data from different context providers and consumers through middleware-type components based on REST services. In the specific case of our solution, we have used a set of middleware components for sending and consuming information between a smartphone and smartplug using the Message Queuing Telemetry Transport (MQTT) protocol [1].

Communication between the different components of the OCB high-level architecture is done through the RESTful NGSI v2 API, which is based on the OMA NGSI specification [11]. The context information in OMA NGSI is represented by using data structures called ContextElements, which have an unique EntityId and EntityType that allows the identification of the entity to which the context data refers. A sequence of one or more attributes of data elements (triplets), and optional metadata linked to attributes (also triplets) are represented by JSON type objects. Figure 2 shows a graphic representation of the OMA NGSI model.

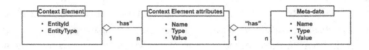

Fig. 2. Graphic representation of OMA NGSI model (Taken from [11])

As indicated before, the interaction between OCB and context providers/consumers is carried out by means of middleware-type components, which act as a bridge between OCB and IOT devices. These components are known as *FIWARE IOT Agents* and they use a facade type pattern and OMA NGSI model to transform the context data that comes from the different IOT devices into their own transport mechanisms and data definition protocols.

In scenarios which is required the usage of lightweight (low bandwidth and low power consumption) transport protocols such as MQTT [1], *FIWARE IOT Agents* require the implementation of a central communication point called *IOT Broker*. *IOT Broker* is the responsible for sending/receiving messages among different devices and systems that have subscribed to a specific topic of the protocol. The devices and systems do not have to know each other and they just have to communicate with the IOT Broker through the topic to which they are subscribed (based on the concept of *publish/subscribe messaging protocol*). This architecture allows the development of highly scalable solutions without dependencies between data providers and consumers [10]. Figure 3 shows the architecture taken as the basis for communication between the context generator (a smartphone) which sends data through RESTful services, and a context consumer (a smartplug) which receives the data using the MQTT protocol.

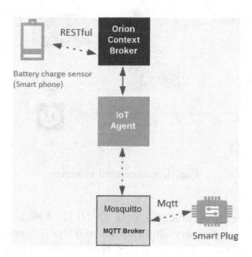

Fig. 3. Base architecture of the proposed solution

4 Proposed Solution

In this section, we present the proposed solution for the management of battery charge of a mobile device using the FIWARE platform and a microcontroller (smart plug). This section is organized as follows. First, the proposed conceptual model is shown. Then, the process of installation of different components used for the implementation of the system is explained. Finally, the results of experimental tests are detailed.

4.1 Conceptual Model of the Proposed Solution

Figure 4 presents the conceptual diagram that shows the components of the proposed energy management platform for mobile devices. The system consists of a specific application which uses the FIWARE architecture and MQTT protocol.

The platform is made up of the components described in Sect. 3: Orion Context Broker, IOT Agent and Mosquitto MQTT Broker. These components use the NoSQL MangoDB engine as their data repository. For storage and visualization of time series data (dashboards accesed through web browsers), we have used QuantumLeap (implemented with CrateDB, a NoSQL database) and Grafana.

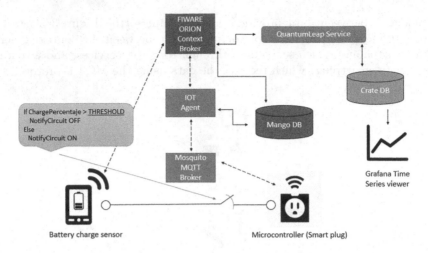

Fig. 4. Conceptual model

The mobile device communicates with the IOT Agent using the RESTFul services and it sends the battery charge level to a microcontroller that acts as a smart plug that is capable of interrupting the electricity flow at a certain level of charge, which is previously defined by the user. Figure 5 shows the process model used by the proposed solution.

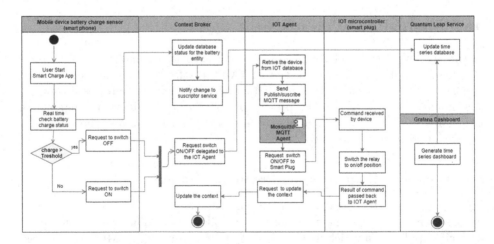

Fig. 5. Process model of the proposed solution

As you can see, the process begins when the user starts the charging service using an application installed on his/her mobile device. Once started the service, the device verifies the level of battery charge and sends the data to the Context Broker for real time data update. The Context broker notifies to the subscribers of the service about the changes using the QuantumLeap Service which keeps the updated data i.e. time series database. This data is consumed by the Grafana tool for the generation of a dashboard of time series.

In the event that the battery reaches an optimal limit of charge (THRESH-OLD), the smart plug receives a notification through the Mosquito MQTT Broker for closing the power supply to the mobile device. This notification is sent by the Orion Context Broker to the IOT Agent who forwards to the Mosquitto MQTT Broker. The results of this process are communicated to the Context Broker through the IOT Agent.

4.2 Details of the Proposed Solution

The following activities were carried out for testing the conceptual model::

- Installation and configuration of FIWARE platform
- Development of an Android application
- Programming of a Smart Plug.
- Real-time battery charge and discharge tests

In the following subsections, we have explained some relevant aspects of each activity.

Installation and Configuration of FIWARE Platform. First of all, FIWARE platform was installed on a laptop computer with Windows 10 using Docker containers. Table 1 shows the services and ports used in the *docker-compose.yml* docker configuration file.

Table 1. Fiware plaform services

No	Service	Image	Ports
1	Orion	fiware//orion: $\{ORION_VERSION:-2.0.0\}	1026:1026
2	Mongo	mongo:3.2.19	27017:27017
3	Iot-agent	fiware/iotagent-ul	4061:4061 - 7896:7896
4	Quantumleap	QL_IMAGE:-smartsdk/quantumleap	8668:8668
5	Crate	crate: $\{CRATE_VERSION:-3.1.2\}	4200:4200 - 4300:4300
6	Grafana	grafana/grafana	3000:3000
7	Redis	redis	6379:6379
8	Mosquitto	eclipse-mosquitto	1883:1883 - 9001:9001

Development of an Android Application. Based on [7], an mobile application for Android was developed using Java and Retrofit2 library. This application communicates with the other components of the system using Wifi netwowork and REST services. In order to obtain the energy consumption data, two components were developed: a service generator (BatteryService) and a service consumer (BatteryReceiver).

Figure 6 shows the user interface of the application developed with the purpose of testing the proposed solution. The interface has a single button that allows the user to start the battery charge monitoring service. The interface also has a control bar at the top that allows the user to set the maximum charge level of the battery (*treshold*), which is recommended to be less than 100%.

Fig. 6. Battery charge service application's interface

The application was installed on a Huawei P9 Lite smartphone (it incorporates Android 7.0) with 3.0 GB of RAM, 16 GB of storage and a battery usage time of approximately 2.5 years.

Programming of a Smart Plug. For experimental purposes, a commercial smart plug based on the ESP8266 microcontroller was used, which was re-programmed using the Arduino IDE. The communication between the smart plug and the Mosquitto Context Broker was carried out using Wifi network and Mqtt with the Wifi.h and PubSubClient.h libraries. Figure 7 shows the smart plug re-programming process using a USB TTL (serial) converter.

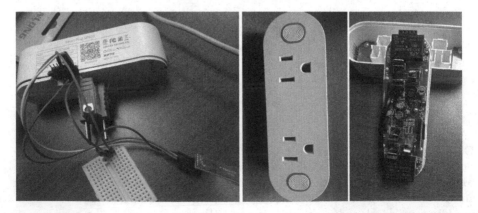

Fig. 7. Re-programming (flashing) of a commercial smart plug

Real-Time Battery Charge and Discharge Tests. An energy monitoring test was performed during a complete charging cycle. In this process, the charging and discharging behavior of mobile device's battery could be visualized by using a time series dashboard built with the Grafana tool. Figure 8 shows the values of a charge cycle measured during 12 h.

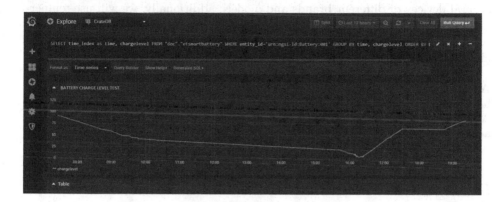

Fig. 8. Grafana time series, battery monitor

The cycle started at a default *Threshold* value of 90%. At this value, the smart plug closed the circuit (energy flow) and the percentage of consumption was measured simulating the habitual use of a user in his/her mobile device. As shown in the figure, during the first three hours the percentage of charge decreases below 50% due to the simulated use of Facebook and YouTube applications. Then, there is a gradual discharge during approximately six hours, when WhatsApp (messaging application), Gmail and Chrome were used. Subsequently, an irregular discharge behavior is observed for a period of approximately 30 min, when the battery level is dropped abruptly from 25% to 3%, which is the configured minimum level (this could be due to several factors including the aging of the battery; although this behavior is not the object of the present study). When the minimum level was reached, the mobile device was reconnected to the energy flow by the smart plug. Then, we changed the recharge level with a Threshold of 65%, and we kept it for approximately one hour. Finally, we raised the level of Threshold to reach 80% of charge.

5 Conclusions and Future Works

This work describes a proposal to autonomously manage the battery charge of a mobile device connected to a smart plug using an Open Source platform called FIWARE. Commands for turning the smart plug on and off are sent using the MQTT protocol and REST service calls provided by the FIWARE services and APIs. The proposed solution allows the user to select the battery charge level using a mobile application created for this purpose.

Preliminary tests of the developed prototype allowed (1) to maintain a relatively constant level of charge by automatically switching on and off the smart plug, (2) to send the charge and uncharge levels of the device in real-time through the developed Android application, and (3) to display all the aforementioned information on a time series chart by using the grafana tool. As future work, we will validate the proposed solution by installing the developed application on several devices of different brands and models; additionally, we will use temperature sensors to correlate the temperature data with the energy level of batteries to understand how it can affect to the battery life in different equipments, especially in mobile devices.

Acknowledgments. This research was funded in part by the line "Grupos de Trabajo" of the Corporación Ecuatoriana para el Desarrollo de la Investigación y la Academia (CEDIA) for the Work Group: "The Internet of Things and Smart Cities", and in part by the line "Estancias de Investigación" of the Universidad de las Fuerzas Armadas ESPE of Ecuador.

References

1. Banks, A., Briggs, E., Borgendale, K., Gupta, R.: MQTT version 5.0 (2019). https://docs.oasis-open.org/mqtt/mqtt/v5.0/mqtt-v5.0.html. Accessed 01 May 2019
2. Arangi, S.: Battery charge limit (2017). https://github.com/sriharshaarangi/BatteryChargeLimit. Accessed 21 Aug 2019
3. Bai, Y., Huang, H.: Automatic charging voltage and current adjustment through the wireless message transmission of a smart charger. In: 2017 IEEE 6th Global Conference on Consumer Electronics (GCCE), pp. 1–2, October 2017
4. Choi, B.H., Nguyen, D.T., Yoo, S.J., Kim, J.H., Rim, C.T.: A novel source-side monitored capacitive power transfer system for contactless mobile charger using class-e converter. In: 2014 IEEE 79th Vehicular Technology Conference (VTC Spring), pp. 1–5, May 2014
5. Choi, S., Lim, H.: Factors that affect cycle-life and possible degradation mechanisms of a li-ion cell based on LiCoO2. J. Power Sour. **111**, 130–136 (2002)
6. Clemm, C., Sinai, C., Ferkinghoff, C., Dethlefs, N., Nissen, N.F., Lang, K.: Durability and cycle frequency of smartphone and tablet lithium-ion batteries in the field. In: 2016 Electronics Goes Green 2016+ (EGG), pp. 1–7, September 2016
7. Developers, A.: Monitor the battery level and charging state (2019). https://developer.android.com/training/monitoring-device-state/battery-monitoring. Accessed 23 Sept 2019
8. Ecker, M., et al.: Development of a lifetime prediction model for lithium-ion batteries based on extended accelerated aging test data. J. Power Sour. **215**, 248–257 (2012). http://www.sciencedirect.com/science/article/pii/S0378775312008671
9. Ferreira, D., Dey, A.K., Kostakos, V.: Understanding human-smartphone concerns: a study of battery life. In: Lyons, K., Hightower, J., Huang, E.M. (eds.) Pervasive 2011. LNCS, vol. 6696, pp. 19–33. Springer, Heidelberg (2011). https://doi.org/10.1007/978-3-642-21726-5_2
10. Fiware.org: FIWARE IoT over MQTT (2011). https://fiware-tutorials.readthedocs.io/en/latest/iot-over-mqtt/index.html. Accessed 01 Mar 2019

11. Fiware.org: FIWARE-NGSI v2 specification (2011). https://fiware.github.io/specifications/ngsiv2/stable/. Accessed 01 Mar 2019
12. Fiware.org: FIWARE context broker (2019). https://www.fiware.org/. Accessed 21 Aug 2019
13. Fiware.org: What is FIWARE (2019). https://www.fiware.org/developers/. Accessed 06 May 2019
14. Kudo, Y., Tagai, Y., Taniguchi, K., Ehara, M., Ito, M.: A study of the efficiency of free charging space using a quick charger with charge limiting function. In: 2017 IEEE 6th Global Conference on Consumer Electronics (GCCE), pp. 1–4 (Oct 2017)
15. Maussion, P., Dung, P.Q., Chi, L.T., Dagues, B.: Diagnostic of batteries based on microcontroller and smartphone. In: 2017 International Conference on System Science and Engineering (ICSSE), pp. 728–732, July 2017
16. Oliver, E., Keshav, S.: An empirical approach to smartphone energy level prediction, pp. 345 354, September 2011
17. Pröbstl, A., Kindt, P., Regnath, E., Chakraborty, S.: Smart2: smart charging for smart phones. In: 2015 IEEE 21st International Conference on Embedded and Real-Time Computing Systems and Applications, pp. 41–50, August 2015
18. Sinai, C.: coconutBattery computer software (2016). http://www.coconutflavour.com/coconutbattery/. Accessed 23 Sept 2019
19. Takei, K., et al.: Cycle life estimation of lithium secondary battery by extrapolation method and accelerated aging test. J. Power Sour. **97–98**, 697–701 (2001). http://www.sciencedirect.com/science/article/pii/S0378775301006462. Proceedings of the 10th International Meeting on Lithium Batteries

Hardware and Software Filter Design for ECG Signal Acquisition and Processing

Paul D. Rosero-Montalvo[1,2]([⊠]), Edgar Maya-Olalla[1],
Marcelo Zambrano Vizuete[1], Pamela Godoy-Trujillo[1], Ana Checa-Ramirez[3],
Julio Andrade-Collahuazo[3], and Christian Montalvo-Loza[3]

[1] Universidad Técnica del Norte, Ibarra, Ecuador
pdrosero@utn.edu.ec
[2] Universidad de Salamanca, Salamanca, Spain
[3] Instituto Tecnológico Superior 17 de Julio, Ibarra, Ecuador

Abstract. Heart data acquisition is actually common these days to prevent its atypical functioning. However, it presents some issues like noise or the overlapping of spectra of the rest of the human body signals. Consequently, the electrocardiogram (ECG) is the most common way of heart monitoring. However, ECG electronic systems have not a portability criterion. To do so, the present system shows filter hardware and software design to improve ECG data acquisition through signal processing. For the one hand, it presents the sensor design, signal coupling, and band-pass filter Sallen-key structure. For another hand, the system implements a function transfer with Triangular and Gaussian filter stages. As a remarkable result, the output signal is a significant noise reduction.

Keywords: ECG processing · Filer design · Signal denoising

1 Introduction

At present, the acquisition of bioelectric signals from the human body has taken an increasingly interest. This is due to the psychological, muscular and organic information with which diagnoses can be made and a subsequent reactivation stage [1]. In this sense, the heart is one of the most important organs because of its vital functioning in living beings. For its analysis, the use of an electrocardiogram (ECG) is necessary. It is a diagnostic procedure that obtains a graphic record of the electrical activity of the heart as a function of time [2], where its frequency range to be studied is between 0.5 and 300 Hz and its greater information it is available in the range of 0.5 and 150 Hz [3].

With the technological advancements, it is sought that these ECG devices can include the parameters of portability, size, weight, low energy consumption, among others [4]. In this way, you can monitor a person's vital signs in their daily activities [5]. However, this signal is contaminated by noise and the overlapping spectra of the rest of the human body bio-signals. In addition, being of

© Springer Nature Switzerland AG 2020
M. Botto-Tobar et al. (Eds.): ICAT 2019, CCIS 1195, pp. 282–293, 2020.
https://doi.org/10.1007/978-3-030-42531-9_23

very small amplitude, when it is amplified the harmonic noise is generated. This is due to the non-linear voltage-current characteristics of the electronic components caused by the distortion of the signal waveform. As a result, this directly affects the signal/noise measurement (SNR) [1,6]. Numerous ECG sensors are already available in the market. However, they fail to comply with the portability parameters set [7]. In addition, they are not designed under free platforms, consequently, it limits their rapid development and their medical applications [5].

With the above mentioned, the Discrete Fourier Transform (DFT) is a tool widely used in the processing of non-stationary signals that provides time and frequency information. In this way, the superposed noise of the acquired signal can be detected. Consequently, once the DFT is used, a device is necessary that discriminates the signal that passes through it [2]. To do this, it is necessary to use active filters, both in hardware and software. On the one hand, the hardware is necessary for a correct coupling between the sensors and a processing system, in such a way that by means of a high input impedance in relation to a low output impedance, it allows to acquire the largest amount of signal components and eliminate the non-linearity noise [5]. On the other hand, the use of filters in software, are linear time-invariant systems (LTI) that show the frequency spectrum of the input signal $X(w)$, according to the frequency response $H(w)$ (better known as transfer function), to get an output signal with spectrum $Y(w) = H(w) * X(w)$. In this way, $H(w)$ acts as a weighting function or spectral conformation function for the different frequency components of the input signal. These LTI systems can be: Finite Impulse Response (FIR) which are non-recursive systems, and Infinite Impulse Response (IIR), where their main feature is the feedback on the output signal [6,8]. To achieve these LTI systems, there are some electronic devices that allow the process of digital signal processing (DSP) [1,9].

The present system shows a new scheme of acquisition, coupling and filtering of the electrical signal of the heart for later analysis. For this, a non-invasive electronic circuit is designed by sensors in order to properly acquire the signal, then a high impedance coupling stage is designed and finally, a Sallen-Key active electronic band pass filter is made in the hardware part. On the other hand, in software, an implementation of different FIR filters, Triangular Smoothing Filter and a Gaussian Filter is presented. As a result, the noise components produced by the different factors are eliminated.

The rest of the document is structured as follows. Section 2 shows the acquisition stage together with the signal coupling. The design of the filtering in hardware and software is shown in Sect. 3. The implementation and tests are presented in Sect. 4. Finally, the conclusions and future work are presented in Sect. 5.

2   Data Acquisition Electronic System Design

The ECG signal consists of five waves where the horizontal axis of a wave represents the time and the vertical of a wave that includes the height and depth represent the voltage. The normal ECG wave consists of a series of positive and negative waveforms, such as the P wave, the QRS complex, and the T wave. Where the P wave represents the first upward deflection and atrial depolarization. The QRS complex is composed of three waves Q, R and S represent ventricular depolarization and the T wave represents the repolarization of the ventricles.

There are different sensors to acquire the heart signal. Generally, it is done by using conventional disposable silver chloride electrodes. These electrodes provide excellent signal quality for demanding ECG measurements. However, you need skin preparation, such as shaving and cleaning the electrode spots with alcohol before putting them on. The electrodes that work without gel are considered dry. They are used in physical exercise applications for a long period of time, unfortunately, they are greatly affected by movements of the person [10].

A non-invasive approach is through the use of infrared sensors. These sensors detect the pulsations due to the increase in the absorption of light when the artery expands (oxygen saturation in the blood). Oxygenated hemoglobin absorbs infrared light and lets in more red light. Deoxygenated hemoglobin absorbs red light and lets in more infrared light. To do this, you need two emitting LEDs, red (630–660 nm) and infrared (800–940 nm) to have a contrast between oxyhemoglobin and hemoglobin. However, preprocessing stages (filtering and coupling) must be implemented. For this reason, the use of infrared sensors is chosen due to their versatility in the implementation (fingers of the hand or earlobe) [11].

In Fig. 1 the connection of the gentlemen with respect to the location of the limb of the person (index finger) is shown.

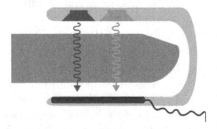

Fig. 1. ECG sensor coupling

One of the biggest drawbacks in DSP systems is to make sure that the information acquired by the sensor is correct (loss of electronic materials). Because of this, it is important to properly calibrate them in hardware or software before developing any analysis. In addition, having a low-value signal (ECG), when using sensors with an external voltage source with non-linear elements, essential heart rate components (decrease in signal) are lost for further analysis. For this reason, an impedance coupling allows counting the same signal from the input to the output. With respect to the hardware, different electronic elements can be used to perform the coupling. Among the most common, are the amplifiers operations, due to their high input impedance and high amplification factor [4]. In Fig. 2 the operational amplifier configuration is presented as impedance matching.

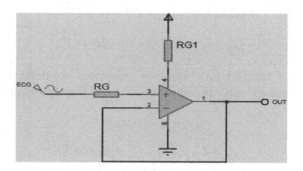

Fig. 2. operational amplifier as coupling

3   Data Filtering

A filter is a system that amplifies or attenuates in amplitude certain electrical signals that are in a certain frequency range. In addition, the phase of the input signal to the filter [12] can be modified. In this section, the design of filters in hardware and software is presented.

3.1   Hardware

According to the literature, the largest number of components of the ECG is found in the 60 Hz [5]. In addition, the non-linear noise from the external source and components is up to 20 Hz [6]. For this reason, a bandpass filter is proposed. However, Sallen-Key settings become complicated by increasing the order of the filter. For this reason, a low pass filter is designed up to 65 Hz and a high pass filter up to 55 Hz of the sixth order (three-second order filters). A Butterworth approximation is chosen since a flat response is obtained in the passing band. This is reflected in a constant output voltage up to the cutoff frequencies. Due to its flat response, it is often used in anti-aliasing filters and data conversion applications. In general, where it is necessary to achieve good measurement accuracy in the passband. Consequently, the Sallen-Key configuration is used, since it is a circuit producing a low pass or high pass filter of two poles using resistors R_i, capacitors C_i in relation to the coefficients a_i and b_i according to the order of the filter and an amplifier without gain. To obtain a higher-order filter, several stages can be cascaded. A filtering stage is performed and then the amplification stage. This is due to a better analysis of each stage. Its transfer function of a second-order filter passes low is as follows:

$$F(s) = 1/[1 + (a_i * s) + (b_i * s^2)] \tag{1}$$

where, $a_i = w_c * C_1 * (R_1 + R_2)$ y $b_i = w_c^2 * R_1 * R_2 * C_1 * C_2$

At the same way, transfer function high-pass filter is:

$$F(s) = 1/(1 + a_i * s^{-1} + b_i * s^{-2}) \tag{2}$$

where, $a_i = 1/(w_c * R_1 * C)$ y $b_i = 1/(w_c^2 * R_1 * R_2 * C^2)$

Regarding their transfer functions, the equations are defined to determine the resistance values R_i and capacitors C_i. For low pass filters, it is as follow:

$$C_2 \geq C_1 * [4b_i/a_i^2] \tag{3}$$

$$R_{1,2} = \frac{a_i * C_2 \pm [a_i^2 * C_2^2 - 4a_i C_1 C_2]^{1/2}}{(4\pi * f_c * C_1 C_2)} \tag{4}$$

High-pass filter equations are:

$$C_1 = C_2 \tag{5}$$

$$R_1 = \frac{1}{\pi * f_c * C * a_i} \tag{6}$$

$$R_2 = \frac{a_i}{4\pi * f_c * C * b_i} \tag{7}$$

Subsequently, an amplification stage is performed to reach adequate levels of acquisition of a DSP (between 3.3 and 5 V). For this, an inverting amplifier is made that allows the return of the initial state of the signal after the filtering stage. The equation for amplification is defined between the ratio of two resistance at the negative terminal of the operational amplifier.

$$A = -(R_f/R_i n) \tag{8}$$

Finally, the entire electronic filter design is showed at Fig. 3.

Resistors and capacitors obtained for each stage are in Table 1 .

3.2   Software

An FIR filter stage is implemented for its stability, ease of signal comprehension, implementation, among others. In this way, you can ensure ECG readings are as appropriate as possible. The Triangular Smoothing Filter is one whose objective is to eliminate small details in the acquired components of the signal and fill in small missing spaces. In addition, this filter helps us eliminate noise. Its process

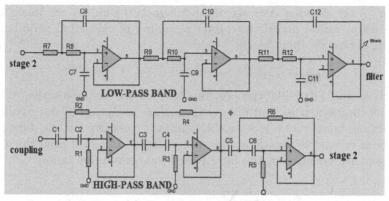

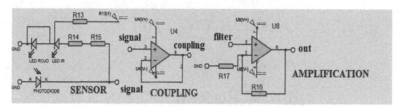

(a) filter band-pass stage

(b) Coupling stage

Fig. 3. Electronic design propose

Table 1. List of passive electronics elements

Resistors	Value
R1, R2, R4, R6	6.8 kΩ
R3, R16	10 kΩ
R5, R12	27 kΩ
R7	18 kΩ
R8	12 kΩ
R9, R15	33 kΩ
R10	56 kΩ
R11	8.2 kΩ
R13	330 Ω
R14	680 Ω
R17	1 kΩ
Capacitors	Value
C1, C2, C3, C4, C5, C6, C7, C9, C11	47 μF
C8, C10, C12	100 nF

is similar to the Moving Average filter, where two samples are taken before and two samples after and divided for the number of calculated periods or the smoothing period (in this case 9).

$$S_j = (x_{i-2} + 2x_{i-1} + 3x_j + 2x_{j+1} + x_{j+2})/9 \tag{9}$$

The Gaussian Filter like the previous one has the same objective to soften signals and eliminate noise, but different masks are used, the difference compared to the previous one is that it is separable; that is, it can carry out one-dimensional convolutions instead of two-dimensional ones. To do this, you need the average μ, the standard deviation σ, the filter G and the convolution $and[i]$.

$$\mu = \frac{1}{N} \sum_{i=0}^{N-1} x_i \tag{10}$$

$$\sigma = \left[\frac{1}{N-1} \sum_{i=0}^{N-1} (x_i - \mu)^2 \right]^{1/2} \tag{11}$$

$$G = e^{-x^2/2\sigma^2} \tag{12}$$

$$y[i] = \sum_{j=0}^{N-1} h[j]x[i-j] \tag{13}$$

4   Implementation and Tests

The different hardware measurements are made with a professional-use KEYSIGHT oscilloscope with an update rate of 50,000 wfms/s. In this way, the entire process of filtering noise components can be validated. With regard to software, the Arduino DUE DSP is available. This is due to its development on free platforms. When using FIR filters for its implementation, it is necessary to have sampled $x[n]$, where n is equal to 1000. The whole system implementation process is shown in Fig. 4, starting with the stage of the sensor until finalization with the visualization by serial communication of the filtered data (Arduino serial plot). All the system is represented in stages how is showed in Fig. 3.

4.1   Hardware Tests

Being an infrared sensor, very susceptible to the movement of the person, the cardiac signal cannot be acquired properly. For this reason, you can only acquire the peaks of the R wave that represents the considered pulse of a person. In Fig. 5, the acquisition of the sensor is shown on the one hand and the hardware coupling stage on the other. As can be seen, the non-linear errors of the electronic components have been eliminated and there is a square signal.

Subsequently, the tests of the high pass filter operation are performed in order to eliminate the distortions of the signal. Consequently, the low pass filter can be implemented to eliminate harmonic signals. This process can be seen in Figs. 6 and 7.

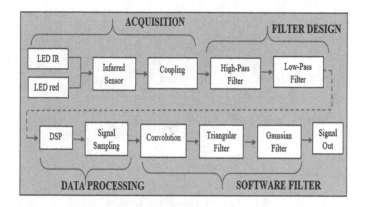

Fig. 4. Electronic design bloc diagram

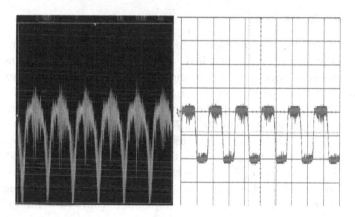

Fig. 5. Adquisición y acoplamiento de Hardware

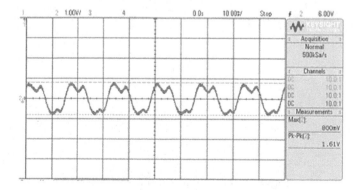

Fig. 6. High-pass filter design

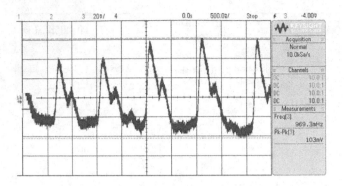

Fig. 7. Low-pass filter Design

4.2 Software Tests

With the hardware designed properly, we proceed to perform the software stage. The development of these filters is in C language compiled within the arduino DUE using the equations present in the previous sections. For visualization, use the tooling of the Arduino environment itself to make graphs. In order to get the right set of samples $x[n]$, the sampling frequency is very relevant. The number of heartbeats is between 60 to 75 per second. In some cases, it can be 40 beats minute (0.67 Hz). Taking Nyquist's theorem into account, the sampling frequency should be twice the signal. For this reason, taking between 200 and 300 samples per beat is adequate. To ensure the acquisition of all signal components. 250 samples are established per heartbeat. This is defined in the time between the times of peak R. In Figs. 8 and 9 the implementation of the filters is shown.

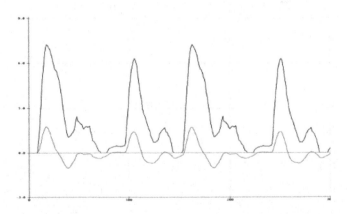

Fig. 8. Convolution and software filter

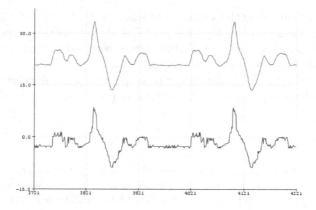

Fig. 9. Triangular filter

With the union of the hardware and software filters, the reconstructed and filtered ECG signal can be seen. In Fig. 10 it is shown the row output of the circuit.

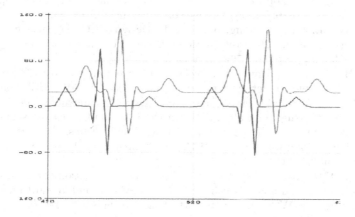

Fig. 10. Signal output after Gaussian filter

5   Conclusions and Future Works

The ECG signal provides information on the functioning of the heart, its analysis leads to the prevention of many diseases or critical situations. For this reason, the use of portable systems, allow having cardiac monitoring of the daily activities of the human being. To do this, the use of hardware and software filters are complemented to eliminate the different sources of noise when acquiring this signal. Due to this, the use of filter structures in hardware must be used in order greater than 3 and its amplification in a separate system to avoid the insertion of non-linearity errors of components. With respect to the software, there are a variety of filters that allow the signal to be smoothed out that together with the convolution within a transfer function an ECG signal can be adequately represented. In this case, the selection of these filters was subsequently implemented several times that did not fulfil the assigned task.

As future work, with ECG signal acquired appropriately, an exhaustive analysis is sought to detect anomalies early way and improve the system to be portable.

References

1. Toan, N.V.H., Duc, T.Q.: Design an open DSP-based system to acquire and process the bioelectric signal in realtime. In: 2016 International Conference on Biomedical Engineering (BME-HUST), pp. 90–94. IEEE, October 2016. http://ieeexplore.ieee.org/document/7782108/
2. Shiu, B.-Y., Wang, S.-W., Chu, Y.-S., Tsai, T.-H.: Low-power low-noise ECG acquisition system with DSP for heart disease identification. In: 2013 IEEE Biomedical Circuits and Systems Conference (BioCAS), pp. 21–24. IEEE, October 2013. http://ieeexplore.ieee.org/document/6679630/
3. Balasubramaniam, D., Nedumaran, D.: Implementation of ECG signal processing and analysis techniques in digital signal processor based system. In: 2009 IEEE International Workshop on Medical Measurements and Applications, pp. 60–63. IEEE, May 2009. http://ieeexplore.ieee.org/document/5167955/
4. Gao, Z., Wu, J., Zhou, J., Jiang, W., Feng, L.: Design of ECG signal acquisition and processing system. In: 2012 International Conference on Biomedical Engineering and Biotechnology, pp. 762–764, May 2012
5. Jani, A.B., Bagree, R., Roy, A.K.: Design of a low-power, low-cost ECG and EMG sensor for wearable biometric and medical application. In: 2017 IEEE Sensors, pp. 1–3. IEEE, October 2017. http://ieeexplore.ieee.org/document/8234427/
6. Eminaga, Y., Coskun, A., Kale, I.: IIR wavelet filter banks for ECG signal denoising. In: 2018 Signal Processing: Algorithms, Architectures, Arrangements, and Applications (SPA), pp. 130–133. IEEE, September 2018. https://ieeexplore.ieee.org/document/8563418/
7. El Hassan, E.M., Karim, M.: An FPGA-based implementation of a pre-processing stage for ECG signal analysis using DWT. In: 2014 Second World Conference on Complex Systems (WCCS), pp. 649–654. IEEE, November 2014. http://ieeexplore.ieee.org/document/7060929/
8. Eminaga, Y., Coskun, A., Kale, I.: Hybrid IIR/FIR wavelet filter banks for ECG signal denoising. In: 2018 IEEE Biomedical Circuits and Systems Conference (BioCAS), pp. 1–4. IEEE, October 2018. https://ieeexplore.ieee.org/document/8584717/
9. Wong, K.-I.: Real-time heart rate variability detection on sensor node. In: 2009 IEEE Sensors Applications Symposium, pp. 184–187. IEEE, February 2009. http://ieeexplore.ieee.org/document/4801803/
10. Cassim Munshi, M., Soetiono, E.: Wireless ecg plaster for body sensor network. In: 2008 5th International Summer School and Symposium on Medical Devices and Biosensors, pp. 310–313, June 2008

11. Chi, Y.M., Cauwenberghs, G.: Wireless non-contact EEG/ECG electrodes for body sensor networks. In: 2010 International Conference on Body Sensor Networks, pp. 297–301. IEEE, June 2010. http://ieeexplore.ieee.org/document/5504769/
12. Shemi, P.M., Shareena, E.M.: Analysis of ECG signal denoising using discrete wavelet transform. In: 2016 IEEE International Conference on Engineering and Technology (ICETECH), pp. 713–718. IEEE, March 2016. http://ieeexplore.ieee.org/document/7569341/

Implementation of DeviceNet Communication Driver Prototypes and Electronic Data Sheets (EDS) for Analog and Discrete Industrial Sensors

María Gamboa[✉], Silvana Gamboa[✉], María Trujillo[✉], and Ana Rodas[✉]

Escuela Politécnica Nacional, Quito 17-01-2759, Ecuador
{maria.gamboa,silvana.gamboa,maria.trujillo01,ana.rodas}@epn.eu.ec

Abstract. The development of DeviceNet communication drivers and their electronic data sheets (EDS) for configuring them in automation software applications are proposed. In this regard, Common Industrial Protocol (CIP) Standard established by ODVA is reviewed, and a commercial DeviceNet network is analyzed in order to define hardware and software requirements for implementing the proposed drivers. Then, prototypes for discrete as well as analog sensors are implemented; their EDS files are developed too. After, the implemented drivers are integrated in a commercial DeviceNet network for validating their performance by monitoring their operation through RSNetWorx for DeviceNet. The developed prototypes and their EDS files shown a proper operation according to proposed aims. Therefore, by this work, the basis for the development of DeviceNet communication drivers for sensors were established.

Keywords: Industrial network · DeviceNet · CIP · Ethernet/IP · Communication driver

1 Introduction

Nowadays, the industry growth is marked by the integration of new communication and information technologies (ICT) for the purpose of achieving an industry more competitive within a globalized market. The integration of such technology is limited in Pymes, small and mid-sized Ecuadorian industries, because it entails a high initial investment costs that cannot be made by those industries. As a result, the Pymes will not be able to benefit by the advantage that using ICT in their process and maybe they will not be enough competitive to operate in current market. Therefore, the development of low-cost industrial automation devices and software could contribute to reduce the gap between Pymes and the great industry, when the aim is to position themselves in the market.

On this issue, this work presents the development of low-cost DeviceNet communication drivers and their electronic data sheets (EDS). The proposed drivers

Supported by Escuela Politécnica Nacional, Quito, Ecuador.

© Springer Nature Switzerland AG 2020
M. Botto-Tobar et al. (Eds.): ICAT 2019, CCIS 1195, pp. 294–304, 2020.
https://doi.org/10.1007/978-3-030-42531-9_24

are intended to enable communication of sensors that currently are installed in any process and their process values are acquired through direct hard wiring. But, with these drivers the output signal from sensors will be connected to the input of the driver and their process value will be sent through a DeviceNet communication network. This proposal aims to reduce the cost of migration from sensors without communication capabilities to sensors that do have these.

DeviceNet drivers were selected justified by the fact that it is based on the CIP (Common Industrial Protocol) standard in that is based Ethernet/IP too. Therefore, DeviceNet is compatible with Ethernet/IP, which is becoming one of the most widespread protocols in the worldwide industry together with ProfiNet. Thus, DeviceNet as a field network will enable the integration of field level with the higher industry automation levels by the interaction with Ethernet/IP networks. This would allow the access to whole plant information avoiding that some process areas could stay isolated. As result, acquired data could be used for implementing automation and control techniques in order to improve the process.

With this background the first stage of the project for developing the proposed drivers began, and in this stage the main objectives were (1) to study the theoretical basis and the regulations related to the DeviceNet networks, as well as the characteristics of the communication in this industrial network, (2) determine the formats of the data frames that should be implemented in the communication drivers, as well as the format of the EDS for configuring DeviceNet devices in industrial automation software, (3) establish the hardware and software requirements for implementing DeviceNet communication drivers for industrial sensors, (4) implement the hardware and the software program necessary to ensure proper operation of developed drivers and their EDS files. As a result of this stage the requirements for implementing DeviceNet drivers are defined, and the prototypes of them are implemented.

This paper is organized as follow, Sect. 2 presents some basic concepts of the CIP protocol and the DeviceNet industrial communication. Section 3 presents the establishment of requirements for implementing the DeviceNet communication drivers. Section 4 shows the implementation and validation of the proposed prototypes. Finally, in Sect. 5 conclusions are drawn.

2   Background: CIP and DeviceNet Network

CIP was proposed according to OSI Reference Model as a media-independent platform protocol, and for this reason it is implemented in a variety of networking technologies. CIP uses an object-oriented data model that allows an abstract representation of the devices connected to the network. They are represented by Instances from a Class that share common attributes as is shown in Fig. 1. Whereas a publisher/subscriber mode is implemented as a communication model which provides versatility to adjust it at the different exchange information requirements.

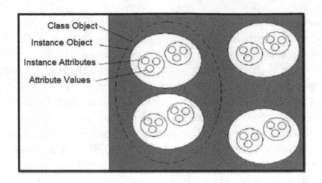

Fig. 1. Object model CIP node [1].

CIP versatility proposes four variations, one of these variations is DeviceNet that is a CIP adaptation to a subset of the CAN protocol frames in order to communicate simple devices such as intelligent electronic devices (IEDs), sensors and actuators. This adaptation is accomplished by shortening CIP explicit messages to 8 bytes or less and defining a master/slave communications mode to minimize the connection establishment overhead. Although DeviceNet is the simplest form of CIP, the interoperability with other networks such as Ethernet/IP or ControlNet are feasible [1]. This feature allows a full integration between the different automation levels in the industry.

Because CIP uses publisher/subscriber mode for communicating, to establish the connection between the nodes that exchange information previously the beginning of data transmission must be done. This connection is represented through a numerical identifier defined as "Connection-ID" or CID. Since DeviceNet incorporates CAN protocol in the data link and physical layers, a specific format is used and rules the 11-bit identifier defined in the CAN protocol is specified for DeviceNet.

Identifier or Connection-ID is made up of a *MAC-ID* and a *Message-ID* fields, also the MAC-ID (Media Access Control) is a 6 bits field which contains the source or destination address from 00 until 63. The Message-ID is the field to identify the message with a variable extension because it depends on message groups belongs to since DeviceNet divides the Connection-ID range into 4 message groups which are detailed in Fig. 2.

Connection ID = CAN Identifier (bits 10:0)											Used for
10	9	8	7	6	5	4	3	2	1	0	
0	Message ID				Source MAC ID						Message Group 1
1	0	MAC ID						Message ID			Message Group 2
1	1	Message ID			Source MAC ID						Message Group 3
1	1	1	1	1	Message ID						Message Group 4
1	1	1	1	1	1	1	x	x	x	x	Invalid CAN Identifiers

Fig. 2. Distribution of the 4 message groups defined by DeviceNet [1].

In this work, the two first groups are the most important due to Message group 1 enables to exchange data to set as high priority data, then such messages are used for slaves to send information such as process variables states to master. Meanwhile, Message group 2 is oriented to establish the connection "Predefined Master / Slave Connection Set", it is one of the methods that allows communication between a master device and a slave device in a simplified way, for this reason it will be used.

Additionally, CIP guideline establishes the methods for device configuration how certain parameters and characteristics that have been preestablished by the device manufacturer because they require to be changed. The modifications are according to the network's requirements that was configured to device operation. Between the proposed methods is the Electronic Data Sheet (EDS) who represents a simple programming method (EDS for configuring DeviceNet devices in industrial automation software) for the user compared with other methods. An EDS is a text file written in ASCII code that contains the most important information of the device such as I/O support connections, device identification, values assigned by the vendor, type of data it supports, among others. An EDS file is structured by sections, in where "File" and "Device" sections are mandatory for all EDS, because this information identifies the device.

3   Requirements for Driver Implementation

In order to implement the proposed drivers, the requirements are defined. For this propose ODVA guidelines will contemplate with the results from analysis of data exchange between DeviceNet network commercial devices. In addition, other consideration to developed drivers is conditioning the output signal sensor to a standard range of values since 0 to 10V. Also, it does not require additional devices such as external sources for the driver installation, but the connection terminals to the network need to be included. Then, each driver boards include the obligatory circuits for accomplishing the requirements.

3.1   Analysis of Communication in DeviceNet Networks

With the aim of establish the requirements for the DeviceNet driver's implementation some specific characteristics of Master / Slave communication in a DeviceNet network must be determined. Then, the way how the connection is established, and a regular communication is accomplished are analyzed by the operation of commercial devices in a DeviceNet network. For the experiment, the master is a PLC CompactLogix with a 1769-SDN DeviceNet scanner module, and a photoelectric sensor is used as a slave. The communication between them is analyzed through the USB-CAN Tool V2.02 software installed on a PC connected to the DeviceNet network.

During network analysis the information exchange between master and slave is accomplished in two stages through messages from group 1 and group 2. At the beginning of communication, values on the range of 400-5ff are identified in

Message-ID field, therefore it is concluded that messages used for this communication belong to the Group of Messages 2 which are defined as the Predefined Master/Slave Connection Set. For the purpose of finding for slave devices and their specification, then such messages aim a "Pre-Establishment of the Communication" which are depicted in Fig. 3. After communication is established, a sequential frame exchange is observed because each slave sends periodically messages from Group 1 with process values and master acknowledge to a message from Group 2. This second stage can be considered as the regular "Data Exchange" that is represented in Fig. 4, and the gathered data from network analysis and its corresponding description are detailed in Table 1 in that DLC is Data Length Code.

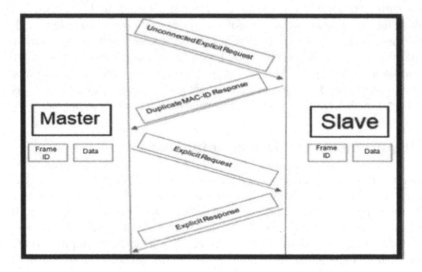

Fig. 3. Master/slave communication establishment.

4 Implementation and Validation of DeviceNet Communication Drivers

4.1 Prototype Implementation

After establishing the requirements, two prototypes of communication drivers are developed, one for discrete sensors and the other for analog sensors, as is shown in Fig. 5. In addition, their respective EDS files were implemented.

For driver implementation, the AT90CAN32 micro controller generates and processes CAN data frames in order to reduce processing time and communication delay. In addition, the CAN L9616 transceiver is applied because it enables to micro controller to work with the differential voltage defined for the CAN Bus. Hardware related with signal conditioning and others ancillary circuits such as voltage source have been implemented in the driver circuit boards.

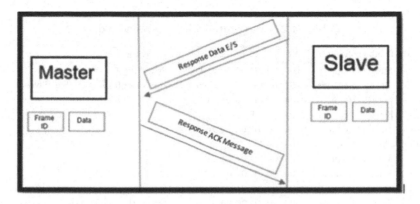

Fig. 4. Master/slave data exchange.

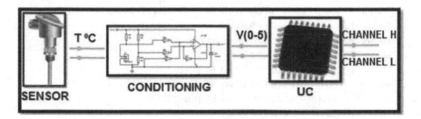

Fig. 5. Hardware components for proposed drivers.

The electronic data sheet (EDS) is a plain text file that is written in ASCII code. The "File" and "Device" sections are mandatory fields according with CIP guidelines. The "File" section contains the name of the device, date of creation of the EDS, web address to access the online EDS of the device, among others. The "Device" section contains the identifying information assigned by the device manufacturer. Additionally, in this section there are [IO_Info] and [Variant_IO_Info] parameters. The first parameter indicates the data type supported by the device and the number of bytes used (see Fig. 6) and the second parameter is implemented to permit the modification of the byte number in [IO_Info] parameter as it is shown in Fig. 7.

4.2 Validation Tests

For validating the developed prototypes, some different kind of sensor were used. A PT-100 temperature sensor and a differential pressure level sensor were connected to driver prototype for analog sensors. Meanwhile, a light sensor, a presence sensor and smoke sensors were integrated with the driver for discrete sensors.

With a view to evaluate the performance of implemented prototypes and their interoperability with commercial devices, the prototypes were integrated into an

Table 1. Network data with slave connected.

FrameID	Sender	Type	DLC	Data	Function
0x044E	Master	Request	0x06	00 4B 03 01 01 00	Searching for slaves
0x044F	Slave	Response	0x07	00 01 00 2B F5 0 A 50	Response from available slaves
0x044E	Master	Request	0x06	00 4B 03 01 01 00	
0x044B	Slave	Response	0x04	00 CB 00	
0x044C	Master	Request	0x06	00 4B 03 01 10 00	
0x044B	Slave	Response	0x03	00 CB 00	
0x044C	Master	Request	0x05	00 0E 01 01 01	
0x044B	Slave	Response	0x04	00 8E 01 00	
0x044C	Master	Request	0x05	00 0E 01 01 02	Request from master for information
0x044B	Slave	Response	0x04	00 8E 06 00	set by the manufacturer of slave
0x044C	Master	Request	0x05	00 0E 01 01 03	device and their respective response
0x044B	Slave	Response	0x04	00 8E 2C 00	(identification number, device type,
0x044C	Master	Request	0x05	00 0E 01 01 04	product code, revision, status,
0x044B	Slave	Response	0x04	00 8E 01 06	serial number)
0x044C	Master	Request	0x06	00 10 05 01 0 C 03	
0x044B	Slave	Response	0x02	00 90	
0x044C	Master	Request	0x06	00 10 2B 01 01 10 00	
0x044B	Slave	Response	0x04	00 90 10 00	
0x044C	Master	Request	0x07	00 10 05 04 11 01 00	
0x044B	Slave	Response	0x04	00 90 08 00	
0x044C	Master	Request	0x05	00 0E 05 02 07	Request for polled input data
0x044B	Slave	Response	0x04	00 94 16 FF	Response from slave
0x044C	Master	Request	0x05	00 0E 05 04 07	Request for COS input data
0x044B	Slave	Response	0x04	00 8E 01 00	Response from slave
0x044C	Master	Request	0x05	00 0E 05 02 08	Request for polled output data
0x044B	Slave	Response	0x04	00 94 16 FF	Response from slave
0x044C	Master	Request	0x05	00 0E 05 04 08	Request for COS output data
0x044B	Slave	Response	0x04	00 8E 00 00	Response from slave
0x044C	Master	Request	0x07	00 10 05 04 09 FA 00	Request for expected packet rate
0x044B	Slave	Response	0x04	00 90 00 01	Response from slave
0x0349	Slave	Data	0x03	00 00 01	Slave COS or Polled message
0x044A	Master	Ack	0x00		Master acknowledgment

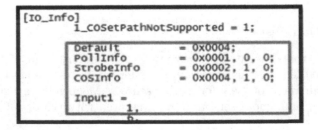

Fig. 6. IO_Info parameter in photoelectric sensor.

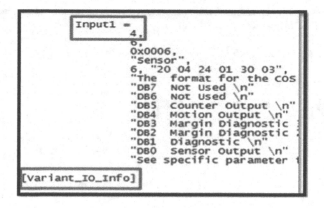

Fig. 7. IO_Info and variant_IO_Info parameters.

industrial DeviceNet network together with commercial devices such as a PanelView 300, a photoelectric sensor and a PowerFLex700-VFD. The implemented network was configured in the RSNetWorx software, in which prototypes were recognized in a similar way as a commercial device. In Fig. 8 the implemented architecture is depicted, in which developed prototypes (nodes 08, 09 and 10) are identified, also the I/O parameters configuration in the DeviceNet scanner for them are shown in Fig. 9.

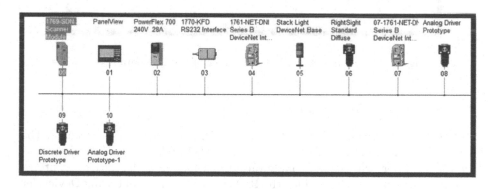

Fig. 8. The recognition of the elements that make up the network.

The USB-CAN Tool V2.02 software was used to verify the communication during connection establishment as well as after it is accomplished and a Master/Slave data exchange is maintained.

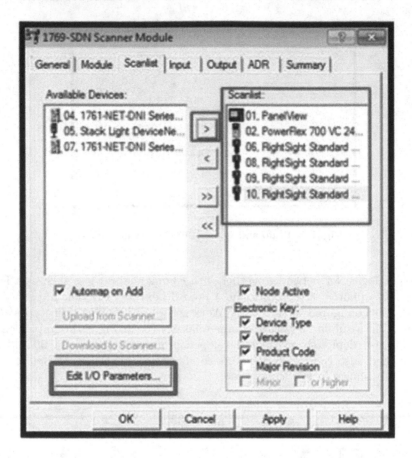

Fig. 9. The configuration in the scanner of the I/O parameters.

4.3   Results and Discussion

Through the experiments carried out, the implemented EDS files as well as the developed communication drivers were evaluated. In relation to EDS files, these shown a good performance as configuration method since the developed prototypes were correctly recognized for the RSNetworx application during DeviceNet network configuration. In regards to the developed drivers, their functioning were according with the expected operation because connection establishment and then the master/slave communication were accomplished correctly. In general, we observed that the transmission of data from the slave to the master is carried out periodically and the master responds with an acknowledgment message which indicates that the sent data by the slave has been recognized. Such condition is shown below in Fig. 10.   According with the results the developed DeviceNet drivers presented an adequate working during their interaction with configuration applications as well as a proper operation within a DeviceNet network in which prototypes exchange information with commercial devices.

Frame ID	Type	Format	DLC	Data
0x034A	Data	Standard	0x01	x| 00
0x0452	Data	Standard	0x00	x|
0x0348	Data	Standard	0x01	x| 12
0x0442	Data	Standard	0x00	x|
0x0349	Data	Standard	0x03	x| 00 00 01
0x044A	Data	Standard	0x00	x|

Fig. 10. Master/slave frames during data exchange.

Therefore, the implementation of a external communication drivers for sensors without communication capabilities were successfully accomplished through an adequate implementation of the data frame, communication rules and EDS files for DeviceNet. In this way, the proposal for implementing low-cost communication drivers is feasible.

5 Conclusions

Development of communication drivers and their EDS files that enable to communicate analog and discrete sensors to a commercial DeviceNet network was presented. For validating the developed prototypes, some sensors were connected to them, such is the case of a PT100 and a differential pressure sensor that were chosen for the analog drivers; while sensors of light, presence and smoke for the discrete drivers. Subsequently, the sensors with the drivers were integrated in a DeviceNet network together with commercial devices to verify their performance and their interoperability. Also, the implemented EDS files were verified by using them as configuration method in a commercial engineering software. Testing results allow to verify the feasibility of implementation of this communication driver, since prototypes can establish and maintain communication with a DeviceNet master and EDS files show to be a proper method for configuring them.

The proposed prototypes permit that Ecuadorian Pymes take advantage of the benefits of industrial communication and ICT technologies in their process and achieve an enough competitive to operate in a globalized market without the necessity for expensive commercial devices.

With regard to future works, they can be directed towards two objectives. The first is the development of drivers for sending commands to actuators through a DeviceNet network to enable control in addition to monitoring. Also, the necessary modifications in the developed drivers could be implemented to integrate into DeviceNet network more complex devices besides sensors.

References

1. Schiffer, V.: Common Industrial Protocol (CIPTM) and the Family of CIP Networks. ODVA (2016)
2. Rinaldi, J.: DeviceNet Protocol Overview. Real Time Automation Inc. (2018)
3. Rinaldi, J.: CIP - The Common Industrial Protocol. Real Time Automation Inc. (2019)
4. Schiffer, V.: The Common Industrial Protocol (CIP) and the Family of CIP Networks. Real Time Automation (2018)
5. Rinaldi, J.: An Overview of EtherNet/IP^{TM}. Real Time Automation Inc. (2017)
6. Schiffer, V.: CIP on CAN Technology. ODVA Inc. (2016)
7. Jaramillo, A.: Diseño y construcción de una red de sensores CAN controlados y supervisados a nivel de planta mediante el protocolo Ethernet industrial (2016)
8. Valladares, C., Nacimba, J. C.: Diseño e implementación de un módulo didáctico para una red DeviceNet (2010)
9. Bartelt, T.: Industrial Automated Systems: Instrumentation and Motion Control. DELMAR(2011)
10. Zurawski, R.: Industrial Communication Technology Handbook. ISA Group (2015)
11. Lawrenz, W. (ed.): CAN System Engineering. Springer, London (2013). https://doi.org/10.1007/978-1-4471-5613-0
12. Natale, M., Zeng, H., Giusto, P., Ghosal, A.: Understanding and Using the Controller Area Network Communication Protocol, vol. 1. Springer, Heidelberg (2012). https://doi.org/10.1007/978-1-4614-0314-2
13. Rinaldi, J., Wendorf, J.: ETHERNET/IP The Everyman's Guide to The Industry's Leading Automation Protocol. Real Time Automation Inc. (2018)

Michell-Banki a Promise Turbine
for Pico-Hydro in Water Irrigation Channel

Lenin Ibañez[1], Luis Escobar[1], Andrés Hidalgo[1] (iD), Carlos Gordón[1](✉) (iD),
and Myriam Cumbajín[2] (iD)

[1] Facultad de Ingeniería Civil y Mecánica, Facultad de Ingeniería en Sistemas, Electrónica e
Industrial, Universidad Técnica de Ambato, UTA, 180150 Ambato, Ecuador
{le.ibanez,leescobar,andresshidalgo,cd.gordon}@uta.edu.ec
[2] Facultad de Ingeniería y Tecnologías de la Información y la Comunicación,
Universidad Tecnológica Indoamérica, UTI, 180103 Ambato, Ecuador
myriamcumbajin@uti.edu.ec

Abstract. We report the design, manufacture, and testing of the Michell-Banki
turbine by using the hydraulic data of the Ambato - Huachi - Pelileo water irrigation channel in the Tungurahua province in Ecuador. The turbine has the blade,
impeller, flange and shaft that are purely plastic materials because they will be
subject to the action of water and thus be able to extend the life of the components. For an optimal design it was considered an efficient alternative, which is the
manipulation of the turbine, it should be portable and as light as possible. When
performing the tests, it was determined that there is an error around 14% between
speed and torque calculations, while the greater efficiency of the turbine is at the
exit of each oval of the channel. The main contribution of the present work is
to provide the required promise component in a Pico-Hydro that is expected to
be implemented in the water irrigation channel. Also this work aims to provide
several benefits to the society bordering the irrigation channel, such as generating
energy for self-consumption as a contribution to the lighting of the channel at no
cost to the people.

Keywords: Michell-Banki · Turbine · Pico-hydro · Water · Irrigation · Channel

1 Introduction

The main sources of electricity generation worldwide are biomass, solar and geothermal
with 13.1%, and hydroelectric with 16.6% [1]. Therefore, the reduction of the polluting
effects of renewable generation technologies will have a positive impact on the environment, making practices directed towards the production of electricity sustainable [2].
The Electricity Master Plan 2016–2025 defines that, "Ecuador within its state policies,
encourages the use of renewable energies, due to its environmental characteristics and
mainly because they are linked to the sustainable development of the electricity sector, such as: hydroelectric, wind, biomass and geothermal energy" [3, 4]. In addition,
in Ecuador the generation of electrical energy by 47% depends on the combustion of
fossils, and 51% in water sources, whether these dams or reservoirs [5], which reveals

© Springer Nature Switzerland AG 2020
M. Botto-Tobar et al. (Eds.): ICAT 2019, CCIS 1195, pp. 305–317, 2020.
https://doi.org/10.1007/978-3-030-42531-9_25

that the greater production of electrical energy in this country is renewable based on hydroelectric plants.

In the province of Tungurahua in Ecuador, which is located in the Andean zone, due to its varied and abrupt geography, it is possible to find slopes in its topographic profiles, in which there are 6 Public channels transferred to the Provincial GAD (Autonomous Decentralized Government). There are also 264 ditches and community channels built with the effort of the peasant families. Therefore, it is common to find waterfalls, which are used in the different hydroelectric plants that the country has. And currently, the reservoirs generated from the main rivers generate electricity for the province and the country [6].

Considering the hydraulic characteristics of the Ambato-Huachi-Pelileo irrigation channel, it is determined that the Michell-Banki type turbine is the most suitable, since it is a mechanism used mainly for low hydroelectric uses [7]. The main advantages that can be found in these turbines is its easy design and simple construction, which attracts attention to produce it on a large scale for the cost benefit it generates [8]. Turbines with capacities of 1 KW to 750 KW can be designed, with a maximum efficiency of 82%.

The main objective of this work is to develop the design, manufacture and testing of the Michell-Banki turbine whose main function is to take advantage of the Ambato-Huachi-Pelileo water irrigation channel in the Tungurahua province in Ecuador for the implementation of a Pico-Hydro power plant capable of generating energy for various uses such as providing luminosity inside the channel for maintenance tasks, luminosity typical of the channel at night reducing the danger to passersby through the channel areas and providing electricity for remote sectors that do not own it or to reduce the cost of those who have energy supply. Finally, the results obtained reveal a minimum torque range of 1 Nm and a maximum of 30 Nm and revolutions ranging from 70 rpm to 110 rpm.

2   Methodology

The methodology carried out in this work includes the procedure of analysis of the theoretical foundation, selection of alternative solutions, design, manufacture and testing of the Michell-Banki turbine.

2.1   Theoretical Foundation

Pico-Hydro
It generates a range of energy from 1 kW to 10 kW, they are usually installed in distant places where the power grid does not reach and in some cases provides electricity to small industries.

Energy From Water
It must be taken into account that to generate energy from water it is necessary to have two factors, the flow and the jump or height difference, it should be noted that the useful

energy delivered by the system is being lost, either by friction, noise, heat or due to different circumstances that cause loss of energy [9].

Plant Factor
It is directly proportional to the ratio of the energy we obtain through power, multiplied by the time of the use power, and inversely proportional to the available energy obtained from the installed power for a period considered.

Flow Measurement
Due to the lack of information regarding hydrology studies, it is necessary to carry out data collection by using methods that help us determine the flow of rivers throughout the year, the most used methods are the following:

- Salt solution method.
- Container method.
- Speed area method.
- Control section method and graduated rule.
- Landfill method and thin wall.

It should be noted that it is necessary to consider the characteristics of the different methods in order to apply them in the most appropriate way.

Flow Regulation
Different flow control or regulation systems can be used which uses tubes, nozzles or holes of different characteristics, which allows us to regulate the flow rate.

Hydraulic Machines
It is considered as a mechanism that can generate mechanical energy, either this motor by means of turbines or generator by means of pumps. To achieve the effect of transforming the current into mechanical energy, it is necessary to use a revolution mechanism, which rotates on its own axis, this mechanism consists of one or several wheels, which contains several blades that are distributed around the impeller, in such a way that it allows to take advantage of the energy of the water current [9].

Hydraulic Turbines
To perform the transformation of fluids to mechanical energy, there are different machines that can perform this process or its action in vice-versa and are classified as follows:

a. Gravimetric machines; where the variation of the geodetic energy of the fluid is used.
b. Displacement or hydrostatic machines; they generally use the energy changes of the pressures generated from the fluid.
c. Turbomachinery or rotodynamic machines; harness the kinetic energy generated by the fluid.

Already reviewed the classification of turbomachines these are basically made up of three parts: diffuser, impeller and distributor.

Constitutive Elements

Diffuser: it is the drain pipe where the water flows to the river or channel. It also allows to generate an aspiration effect, which recovers part of the energy of the kinetic energy.

Impeller: It could say that it is the heart of the machine, since it contains the blades that will help generate mechanical energy.

Distributor: The main function of directing the flow of water from the machine inlet to the impeller and depending on the size of the injector allows regulating the water inlet [9].

Types of Hydraulic Turbines

These turbines are classified depending on the variation of the pressure that affects the impeller, they are classified as follows.

(a) Action or drive turbines.

The water pressure is atmospheric when leaving the distributor and reaches the impeller with the same pressure, here all the potential energy generated in the jump is transmitted directly to the impeller in kinetic energy. Turbina Pelton de uno o más inyectores.

- Turgo Turbine.
- Michell-Banki turbine.

(b) Reaction or overpressure turbines.

The pressure of the water that leaves the distributor tends to decrease as the water advances through the blades of the impeller, so the pressure output tends to be zero or in some cases negative, here the jump power energy is divided into two parts, kinetic energy and pressure energy [9].

- Rotary pump operated as a turbine.
- Francis turbine, whether this: fast, normal or slow.
- Deriaz turbine.
- Kaplan and Propeller turbine.
- Axial turbines, having as variants: bulb, tubular and peripheral generator m^3/s.

Michell-Banki Turbine

The Michell-Banki turbine, also known as cross flow, is an action turbine, radial inlet, transverse flow and partial admission, whose operating ranges from 1 m to 100 m high, with a flow range of 0.2 m^3/s to 7 m^3/s to generate a power less than 1 MW. Basically, it consists of two stages, loading and unloading. The first stage delivers an average of 70% of the total energy transferred to the rotor and the second around the remaining 30% [10].

It consists of the following parts:

1. Transmission part.
2. Injector.
3. Roll over.
4. Guideline palette.
5. Housing.

In Fig. 1, the parts of the Michell-Banki turbine listed above are sketched.

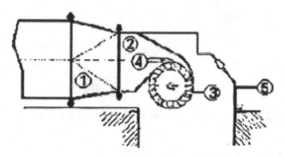

Fig. 1. Michell-Banki turbine parts.

Main Features

The most relevant characteristics of a Michell-Banki type turbine and that have been considered suitable for use in the Ambato-Huachi-Pelileo irrigation channel, are the following [11]:

- Wide range of turning speed.
- Efficiency of 82% for an abundant range of flows.
- Simple construction.
- Lower costs in operation and maintenance.
- Featured turbine for use in rural populations.

Operating Principle

Keep in mind that, if the turbine is divided into two stages, which also gives this machine the name of double-acting turbine, on the other hand, the performance will not vary, for example, if the rotor is divided into equal parts, that is, 1/3, 2/3 or the impeller in its entirety [11]. In Fig. 2, partial transverse flow of the Michell-Banki type turbine is shown.

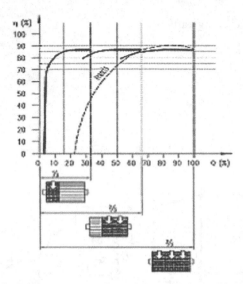

Fig. 2. Partial transverse flow of the Michell-Banki turbine.

2.2 Selection of Alternatives

When selecting the appropriate design for the Michell-Banki turbine, the data obtained in the field about the irrigation channel was considered, which are:

(a) Channel width.
(b) Speed in the channel.
(c) Channel flow.
(d) Accessibility to the channel.

With the information obtained in the field, 3 alternatives were modeled, which are detailed below.

Alternative 1
As can be seen in Fig. 3, alternative 1 consists of a set of runners stacked in series; the speed and flow of the fluid will be controlled with a gate, which will be anchored by concrete columns that are submerged in the channel.

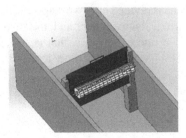

Fig. 3. Alternative 1. Serial wheels with gate.

Advantages:

(a) Vary the speed and flow rate of the impeller.
(b) Simple construction.
(c) Ideal coupling between structure and turbine.

Disadvantages:

(a) High cost due to the impression of the impeller assembly.
(b) Fluid overflow due to excessive rainfall.
(c) Gate obstruction due to debris dragged along the channel.

Alternative 2

In Fig. 4, a fluid speed regulation section and a protection grid can be seen that will help keep the components free of any debris that could obstruct the turbine.

Fig. 4. Alternative 2. Speed regulation section and protection grid.

Advantages:

(a) Protection of the components.
(b) Medium low cost.

Disadvantages:

(a) Complexity in construction.
(b) Obstruction of the fluid due to the speed regulation section.
(c) Difficulty when assembling the structure in the channel

Alternative 3.

As shown in Fig. 5, alternative 3 is a simple and easy-to-assemble construction that has a protective grid, which prevents obstruction in the impeller of debris dragged along the channel.

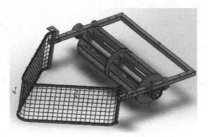

Fig. 5. Alternative 3. Protection grid.

Advantages:

(a) Protection grid.
(b) Low construction cost.
(c) Facility when assembling the structure in the channel.
(d) Simple construction.

Disadvantages:

(a) Work with channel speeds.

Considering the advantages and disadvantages with the characteristics of the Ambato-Huachi-Pelileo irrigation channel, the design and manufacture of Alternative 3 was selected.

2.3 Turbine Design

For the turbine design, it was based on the data obtained in the channel and the basic principles of the theory of cross flow turbines, for the subsequent design of the hydraulic and mechanical part.

Design Parameters

(a) Measurement of the channel geometry.
     The initial data collected in the field were measured by using a rigid measuring tape from which the following information was obtained:
     Channel Width: 1.63 m
     Total channel depth: 1.7 m

(b) Speed measurement.
     In order to obtain a more real data of the channel speed, the measurement was carried out using a pinwheel; the readings were made at three different points along the width of the channel and at two different heights. The minimum distance to obtain speed data is 20% from the surface of the water [12]. The measurement results are depicted in Table 1.

Table 1. Measure taken from 20% of the water line down.

Measurements	Distances (m)		
	0.4	0.8	1.2
First	0,93 m/s	1,58 m/s	1,44 m/s
Second	0,91 m/s	1,63 m/s	1,36 m/s
Third	0,94 m/s	1,52 m/s	1,31 m/s
Average by measurement	0,93 m/s	1,58 m/s	1,37 m/s
Total average		1,29 m/s	

The simplest method to determine the average speed is to place the windlass at a depth of 60% of the depth from the surface of the water, since at this depth it is like the average speed [13]. The measurement results are presented in Table 2.

Table 2. Measure taken from 60% of the water line down.

Measurements	Distances (m)		
	0.4	0.8	1.2
First	1,63 m/s	1,68 m/s	1,2 m/s
Second	1,65 m/s	1,66 m/s	1,22 m/s
Third	1,67 m/s	1,64 m/s	1,26 m/s
Average by measurement	1,65 m/s	1,66 m/s	1,227 m/s
Total average		1,512 m/s	

Specific Energy (H)

In open channels it is necessary to specify the energy of the flow in the corresponding area of interest, this is measured with the relationship of the template of the channel, which is a combination of the potential energy that relates the depth of the fluid, plus the kinetic energy due to the fluid flow [14].

$$H = y + (V \wedge 2)/2g$$

Where:

$y =$ Depth (m)
$v =$ Speed of the fluid (m/s)
$g =$ Gravity (m/s2)

Diameter Selection

In the Eighth Ibero-American Congress of Mechanical Engineering [10], it is recommended that for low power hydro-energy uses, the diameters used have a range of 200 mm to 500 mm. In the same way, it can be selected with the flow and height value as shown in Table 3.

Table 3. Rotor diameter selection.

$Q/\sqrt{H}$	Rotor diameter (mm)
0.02236–0.04743	200
0.04743–0.07906	300
0.07906–0.11068	400
0.11068–0.15812	500

Number of Rotor Blades (Z)

Depending on the diameter, the number of blades is considered. Table 4 shows the number of optimum blades according to the diameter of the rotor. A limited number of blades can produce pulsations at the time of power generation.

Table 4. Number of blades according to rotor diameter.

Diameter of rotor	Number of blades
200	22
300	24
400	26
500	28

At the end of the design the technical sheet of the Michell-Banki Turbine is shown Fig. 6.

2.4 Turbine Manufacturing

The manufacture of the turbine was carried out in the workshops of the Technical University of Ambato. Figure 7 depicts the manufacturing process where it is presented: (a) Welding process, (b) 3D printing, (c) Finished mesh, and (d) Michell-Banki turbine, respectively.

FICHA DE:	MÁQUINA	EQUIPO	X	SISTEMA	
		INGENIERÍA MECÁNICA			

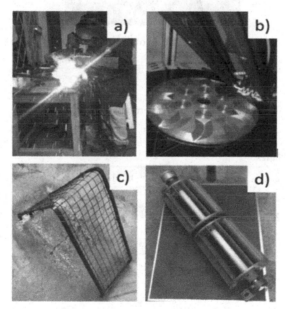

CARACTERÍSTICAS GENERALES	
DIMENSIONES	916,5x726,9x237 mm
PESO	33,35 kg
REVOLUCIONES	110 rpm
TORQUE	26 Nm
POTENCIA	22,88 W
DIÁMETRO DEL EJE	0.019 m
CAUDAL	0.0936 m³/s

Fig. 6. Michell-Banki Turbine Data Sheet.

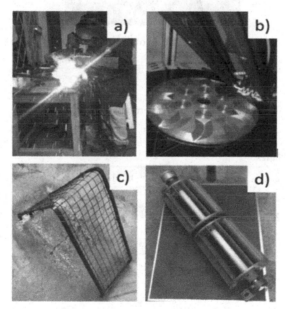

Fig. 7. Manufacturing, (a) Welding process, (b) 3D printing, (c) Finished mesh, and (d) Michell-Banki turbine.

3   Measurements and Results

The results were obtained after starting the turbine as shown in Fig. 8. The torque was also analyzed, and the results indicated in Table 5 were obtained, which were achieved by performing the calculations and experimentally by submerging the turbine to different depths.

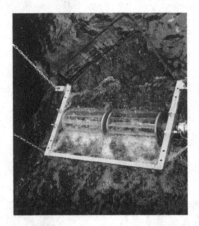

Fig. 8. Start-up of the turbine.

Table 5. Torque and speed results at different flows.

Outcome	Number blades	Blades water	Flow m^3/s	Torque Nm	Speed rpm
Calculated	12	2	0,0117	1.32	72,08
Calculated	12	5	0,0936	26.30	109,81
Measured	12	2	0,0117	1.100	72,08
Measured	12	5	0,0936	30.10	110,00

4   Conclusions

It is determined that with the hydraulic data of the Ambato-Huachi-Pelileo water irrigation channel, the sizing of the Michell-Banki type turbine was carried out, from which the required parameters were obtained. In addition, the results of the turbine calculated in relation to mechanical energy with a minimum torque of 1 Nm and a maximum of 30 Nm and revolutions ranging from 70 rpm to 110 rpm. Finally, it was observed that the revolutions taken in the field of the Michell-Banki turbine have an error of 19% with the calculated data, also when comparing the calculated torque with the simulation, it can be concluded that there is an error of 5%. So, these results show us successfully that the prototype is suitable for installation in the Ambato-Huachi-Pelileo water irrigation channel.

Acknowledgements. The authors thank the invaluable contribution of the Technological University Indoamerica in Ambato - Ecuador with the project "Estudio de Energía Eléctrica de Baja Potencia en los Canales de Riego como Fuentes Hídricas", project code: 151.100.2018. Also, the authors thank the Technical University of Ambato - Ecuador and the "Dirección de Investigación y Desarrollo (DIDE)", for their support in carrying out this research, in the execution of the project "Obtención de electricidad a través de canales de riego como fuentes energéticas" code of the project: PFICM15.

References

1. Bonilla, S., Cordero, J.: La dimensión jurídica de la energía eléctrica y las energías renovables en México. Revista Digital de Derecho Administrativo **22**, 299–333 (2019)
2. Chica, R., Yilmar, A.: Generación de Energía Eléctrica a través de la Tecnología de Microturbina en la finca La Pomba, zona rural de Fusagasugá-Cundinamarca (2019)
3. CELEC. Plan maestro de electricidad 2016–2025 (2019). https://www.celec.gob.ec/hidroagoyan/index.php/plan-maestro-de-electricidad-2016–2025. Accessed 30 Aug 2019
4. Rodríguez, V., Gómez, G., Chou, R.: Ecuador De Cara A La Sustentabilidad En El Siglo XXI: Ley De Eficiencia Energética. Identidad Bolivariana **3**(1), 1–8 (2019)
5. Wang, S., Shifeng, W.: Implications of improving energy efficiency for water resources. Energy **140**, 922–928 (2017)
6. Ponce, M., Castro, M., Samaniego, R., Espinoza, J., Ruiz, E.: Electricity sector in Ecuador: an overview of the 2007–2017 decade. Energy Policy **113**, 513–522 (2018)
7. Galarza, M., Chávez, A.: Un Estudio De La Turbina De Flujo Cruzado (Efecto Del Ángulo De Ataque, Ángulo De Entrada Del Álabe Y Relación De Diámetros En La Eficiencia Hidráulica). Sciéndo **15**(2) (2014)
8. Woldemariam, E., Hirpa, G.: Numerical simulation-based effect characterization and design optimization of a micro cross-flow turbine. Strojniski Vestnik/J. Mech. Eng. **65**(6), 386–397 (2019)
9. Coz, F., et al.: Manual de mini y microcentrales hidráulicas; una guía para el desarrollo de proyectos. no. P06 C6 (1995)
10. Elalaoui, R.: Investigation and analysis of static and dynamic behaviour of a new natural composite material of a wind turbine blade using the finite element method. Int. J. Renew. Energy Res. (IJRER) **9**(1), 363–373 (2019)
11. ITDG. Ficha Técnica Turbina Michell-Banki. https://solucionespracticas.org.pe/ficha-tecnica-n2-turbina-michell-banki. Accessed 30 Aug 2019
12. Llerena, C., Caracterización de la curva de consumo diario de la red de agua potable del sector Huachi Loreto II del cantón Ambato (Bachelor's thesis, Universidad Técnica de Ambato. Facultad de Ingeniería Civil y Mecánica. Carrera de Ingeniería Civil). http://repo.uta.edu.ec/. Accessed 30 Aug 2019
13. Kennedy, A., Fragoza, F., Peña, E., Moreno E.: Manual de aforos (1991)
14. Mott, R.: Mecánica de fluidos y máquinas Hidráulicas, 6th edn. Pearson Educación de México, México DF (2006)

Multiband Broadband Modulator Implementation on Field-Programmable Gate Array

Cristhian Castro[1], Carlos Gordón[2]([✉]) [iD], Patricio Encalada[3] [iD], and Myriam Cumbajín[4] [iD]

[1] Universidad Politécnica de Valencia, 46022 Valencia, Spain
cricaspe@alumni.upv.es
[2] Facultad de Ingeniería en Sistemas, Electrónica e Industrial, Universidad Técnica de Ambato, UTA, 180150 Ambato, Ecuador
cd.gordon@uta.edu.ec
[3] Facultad de Ingeniería Mecánica, Escuela Superior Politécnica de Chimborazo ESPOCH, 060106 Riobamba, Ecuador
patricio.encalada@espoch.edu.ec
[4] Facultad de Ingeniería y Tecnologías de la Información y la Comunicación, Universidad Tecnológica Indoamérica, UTI, 180103 Ambato, Ecuador
myriamcumbajin@uti.edu.ec

Abstract. The proper management of resources available in FPGA's is one of the main issues that designers must consider when implementing a high bandwidth communications system. For this reason, we report the hardware-efficient implementation, for mapping stages and pulse shaping, of broadband multi-level QAM signals, in Field-Programmable Gate Array (FPGA) devices. The process for designing the system is based on the large capacity of analog-digital (ADC) converters that exist today, in this case the ADC has a sampling rate of 5 GSPS, which allows the transmission of signals with bandwidths of about 2.5 GHz. The model implements in the same polyphase FIR structure multiplier-less the mapping schemes Q-PSK, 16-QAM, 64-QAM y 256-QAM together with the RRC filter. As a result, this implementation shows that the proposed architecture eliminates the use of dedicated multipliers which would be around 3150 if conventional methods were used. The Error Vector Module is used as a figure of merit in the selection of the RRC filter and the digital quantization levels. We achieved the target frequency for hardware operation at 312.5 MHz con un factor de interpolation de 16 and an EVM < 2%. Also, Hardware Description Language (HDL) models are validates in test benches with reference to the finite precision models of Simulink.

Keywords: RRC · FPGA · Polyphase structures · Digital modulation · Multiplier less FIR · HDL

© Springer Nature Switzerland AG 2020
M. Botto-Tobar et al. (Eds.): ICAT 2019, CCIS 1195, pp. 318–330, 2020.
https://doi.org/10.1007/978-3-030-42531-9_26

1   Introduction

Fiber-optic communications systems enable the transmission of signals with a high bandwidth. For this reason, electronics manufacturers have made great efforts in developing DAC's and FPGA's that take advantage of these favorable characteristics.

The increase in the characteristics of the DACs bring the digital sections of the communications system closer to the radiation front. Nowadays, it is possible to generate certain RF frequencies digitally, leaving only the filtering and amplification for analog electronics.

This project presents the HDL design of the stages of a high bandwidth digital transmitter based on FPGA, for a 5 GSPS A/D converter, with 16-channel digital interface and 12-bit resolution. The FPGA device on which the transmitter is implemented is the development board VC707 of xilinx, which, hosts an FPGA of the Virtex 7 family with 2800 dedicated DSP blocks (DSP48).

The objective is to design a multiband, multi-modulation transmitter in FPGA to send signals with bandwidths around 2.5 GHz. So, polyphase division algorithms are used so that the hardware works at 312.5 MHz, the performance of the system is evaluated through the Error Vector Magnitude (EVM) [1], and the hardware is verified by HDL test bench, that compare the finite precision model of Simulink with the hardware encoded in HDL.

2   Broadband System Model

The D/A converter device has a digital interface of 16 channels, that are sampled at 5 GSPS, with a resolution of 12 bits. To achieve the maximum performance of the converter the 16 channels must operate at 312.5 MHz in simultaneous. By the Nyquist theorem the bandwidth is limited to half the sampling frequency. Thus, the upper limit of the bandwidth will be at 2.5 GHz, in this space you may be introduced 7 channels, each of 312.5 MHz, sufficiently separated to avoid inter-symbolic interference (ISI). Based on these characteristics, the system shown in the Fig. 1 is proposed.

Each branch of system forms a communication channel with a bandwidth of 1/16 of the sampling frequency. Each channel is moved to one of the 7 intermediate frequency carriers, generated by the Digital Up Converter (DUC). The blocks that make up each communication channel can be classified into two groups, according to your sampling rate, from the up sampler. The data source and the baseband modulator are in the lower area of the sampling rate $\left(\frac{1}{16} f_{sDAC} \right)$, while, the rest of blocks must work at the sampling frequency of the DAC (5 GSPS). Thus, techniques should be used to transfer these blocks to the lower area of the sampling frequency.

2.1   Pulse Shaping Filter

Due to the dual property of the Fourier transform, it can be established that, if the spectrum of a rectangular pulse is a sinc, thus, a signal in the time domain in the form of sinc, will have a spectrum like a rectangular pulse. That is, changing the rectangular shape of the pulse to a sinc in the time domain, we would have in the frequency domain

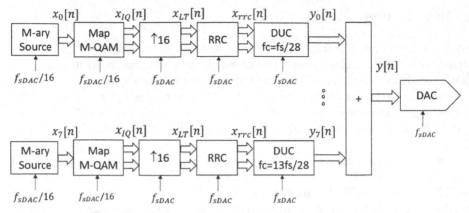

Fig. 1. Block diagram of broadband digital transmission system

a spectrum of rectangular shape of limited band, thence, that this type of filters is called pulse shapers or Nyquist filters [2].

Within the family of Nyquist filters, the most used in communication systems for its favorable characteristics before Jitter, zero crossings each T_{sym} and rapid decay in the cutting frequency, is the Raised Cosine Root filter (RRC) [3].

One of the design parameters of the RRC filter is the excess bandwidth factor, also known as *roll-off* and represented by β, whose range is $0 \leq \beta \leq 1$. The pulse bandwidth is defined by $(1 + \beta)/2T_{sym}$, for values of $\beta = 0$ the bandwidth normalized to f_s Will be $BW_{rrc} = 1/2$, while for, $\beta = 1$ have a bandwidth of 1 that is the bandwidth of the filter will be equal to the pulse period, (see Fig. 2), the spectral and temporal response of a RRC filter for different values of β is observed.

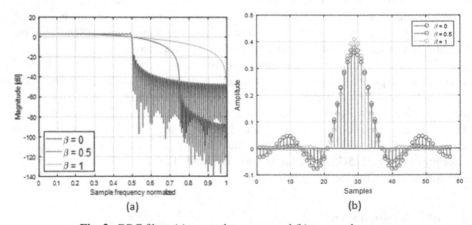

Fig. 2. RRC filter, (a) spectral response and (b) temporal response

In practice, the calculation of the RRC filter will depend on the interpolation factor (L), and the *span*. The *span* indicates the number of coefficients to which the ideal filter response will be limited, the ideality of their response and the cost of implementation depends on the appropriate choice of this value [4].

The number of RRC filter coefficients is defined as $N_c = span * L + 1$, as high as the span will be the cost of implementation and more resemble an ideal filter, as the span decreases the secondary lobes increase their amplitude, (see Fig. 3), which could cause interference with adjacent samples, due to the inherent replications of the interpolation process, in addition to, the system is more vulnerable to Jitter's effects [2].

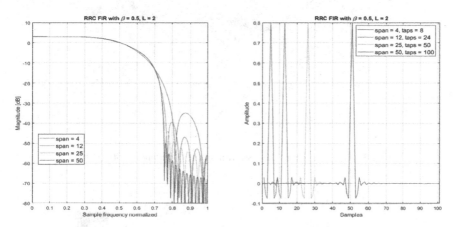

Fig. 3. Responses of an RRC filter for different span values

An appropriate value to start with the design of the RRC filter is to take $\beta = 0.3$, which is a usual value in communications systems [5], and a criterion for calculating the span is presented in [6], in which the relationship is established $span = -44\beta + 33$, for values of β in $0.2 < \beta < 0.75$.

Implementing the proposed system in the Fig. 1 in Simulink with initial values for the RRC filter of $\beta = 0.3$, $L = 16$ y $span = 20$, several iterations of simulation of a transmitter 256-QAM are carried out, for 7 carriers through an AWGN channel with $EbNo = 1 \times 10^3$ dB. In each interaction the value of β is adjusted until a least-cost design treaty that maintains the $EVM < 2\%$ is achieved and an enough margin of freedom for the quantification process.

In the simulation process is established that $\beta = 0.14$ is an appropriate value with which a theoretical bandwidth of 0.0356 is obtained, who transferred to IF would be 0.0712, this means that the multi-carrier system would occupy 0.4987 of the DAC sampling rates. Figure 4 shows the distribution in the spectrum of the 7 channels of the simulated model, which shows that the busy bandwidth is 0.4543 that is 2.272 GHz.

The performance of the channel is evaluated by the constellation diagram, which is observed in Fig. 5, from which the EVM is obtained, for the simulated model is $EVM_{rms} = 0.5\%$ with a maximum peak of 1.1%.

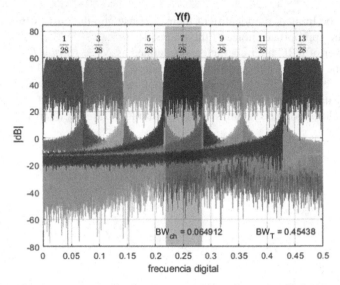

Fig. 4. Distribution in the spectrum of the 7 channels 256-QAM

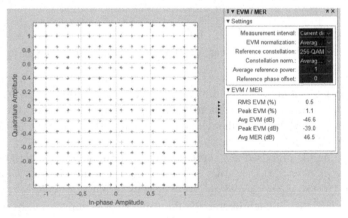

Fig. 5. Constellation diagram for 256-QAM transmitter, of 7 carriers without quantification

2.2 Quantization

The representation of numbers and arithmetic operations in digital systems are carried out by binary coding, using a certain finite number of bits. The number of bits with which a number is represented is inversely proportional to the quantization error, which is obtained through the error probability density function. For finite precision models with rounding function, the variance of the error is calculated using: $\sigma_Q^2 = Q^2/12$, where Q represents the resolution $Q = 2^{-b}$ and b the number of bits of the fractional part of the number you want to represent [7].

The effects that quantization causes on filter performance are the main source of errors in the transmission of limited band binary information. The quantization of the filter coefficients affects the frequency response, when cutting resolution in algebraic operations rounding noise occurs [8].

Knowing that the A/D converter has a resolution of 12 bits, It would not be practical to use a lot of bits in the stages before this one, as, in the converter it will be necessary to cut the word length to 12 bits, although you can maintain a good resolution in algebraic operations taking advantage of the hardware features in the FPGA.

Quantification points are established for the system as shown in Fig. 6.

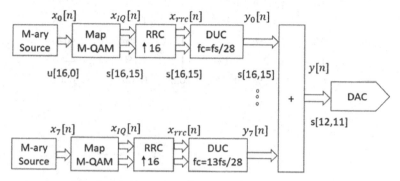

Fig. 6. Multi-carrier transmitter quantization points

The numeric format of each quantization point is represented as follows:

s[N, b]: Signed integer, where N is the number of bits of the word and b the fractional part, is mathematically represented as:

$$X = \left(-x_{N-1}2^{N-1} + \sum_{i=0}^{N-2} x_i 2^i\right) Q \tag{1}$$

where Q is the resolution and X has a range of $\left[-2^{N-1}Q, (2^{N-1} - 1)Q\right]$.

u[N]: Unsigned integer, where N is the number of bits of the word, is mathematically represented as:

$$X = \sum_{i=0}^{N-1} x_i 2^i \tag{2}$$

and it has a range of $\left[0, (2^N - 1)\right]$.

On the other hand, arithmetic operations for DSP are performed on dedicated blocks DSP48, which has multipliers of 18×25 bits with accumulators of 48 bits. The architecture implemented by the DSP48 is optimal for performing symmetrical filters, where, filter coefficients are in the filter channel 18 bits and are encoded in format s[N, b], N = 18 and b = 17.

Applying the finite precision model for the multi-carrier transmitter and maintaining the parameters of previous simulations, you get the following results for various *span* values, shown in Table 1 and the Fig. 7, in which it is observed that, the most appropriate value, to maintain the performance of the system with the lowest cost is *span* = 0.14.

Table 1. Comparison of the EVM in the stages of the multi-carrier model for: $L = 16$, $\beta = 0,14$ y 256-QAM.

Span	Full precision	DAC	M-QAM	FIR	Up-converter	DSP's
10	4.9%	4.9%	4.9%	4.9%	4.9%	2254
12	2.7%	2.8%	2.8%	2.8%	2.8%	2702
14	1.2%	1.4%	1.4%	1.4%	1.3%	3150
16	1.0%	1.2%	1.2%	1.2%	1.1%	3598
18	0.9%	1.0%	1.1%	1.1%	1.0%	4046
20	1.1%	1.2%	1.2%	1.2%	1.1%	4494
27	0.5%	0.7%	0.7%	0.8%	0.6%	6062

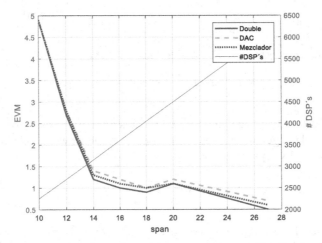

Fig. 7. Comparison between EVM vs span, and cost of implementation

3 Mapping and Polyphase High-Speed FIR Structure

Once the RRC filter has been designed, hardware deployment technique should be established, the challenges in implementing this filter are: keep the filter size, minimum clock frequency 312.5 MHz and don't exceed the hardware resources. To achieve these objectives, the polyphase division technique is used [9].

3.1 Polyphase Structure for Interpolation Filter

The selected filter has a total of 225 coefficients, which must interpolate by 16 to reach the DAC sampling rate. Using the polyphase division technique, it is possible to divide a filter of N coefficients into L sub-filters that work at $1/L$ times the sampling rate [10].

Noble's identities exchange between transfer functions and interpolation/decimation blocks, this translates the FIR blocks to the low sampling rate zone and to the upper area of the sample rate the interpolators and delays, which in practice are implicit in the operation of the DAC, (see Fig. 8), so, only the implementation of the 16 FIR sub-blocks is necessary, with the distribution presented in Fig. 9 [11].

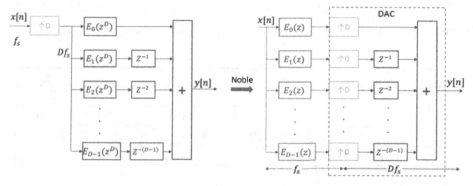

Fig. 8. Converting the sampling rate using Noble identities

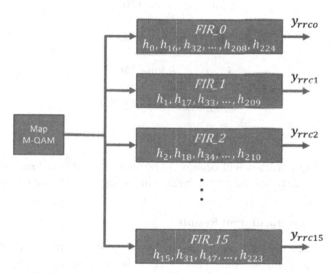

Fig. 9. Distribution of coefficients in the polyphase filter

3.2 LUT for Multi-modulation Schemes

The simulation model feeds from a block that randomly generates unsigned M-size integers in Gray code. Each point of the constellation on the I-Q axes has an amplitude given by: $\pm\frac{d}{2}, \pm\frac{3d}{2}, \pm\frac{5d}{2}, \ldots, \pm\frac{\sqrt{M}-1}{2}$ where M is the size of the constellation, d the distance between points and the number of bits to form the constellation is: $k = log_2(M)$ [12].

Knowing the value of the real and imaginary part of the dots that make up the constellations: Q-PSK, 16-QAM, 64-QAM y 256-QAM, us can set a memory distribution, where, all the points for these modulations are stored, and will be addressed with the bits of the input data [13], this distribution is presented in Table 2.

Table 2. Comparison of the EVM in the stages of the multi-carrier model for: $L = 16, \beta = 0, 14$ y 256-QAM.

b_7	b_6	b_5	b_4	b_3	b_2	b_1	b_0
							Q-PSK
				16-QAM (Re)		16-QAM (Im)	
		64-QAM (Re)			64-QAM (Im)		
256-QAM (Re)				256-QAM (Im)			

To store the four constellations, you will need a vector of:

$$k_{16QAM} = \log_2(16)$$

$$k_{64QAM} = \log_2(64)$$

$$k_{265QAM} = \log_2(256)$$

$$k_{QPSK} = \log_2(4)$$

$$N_{LUT} = 2^{k_{16QAM}/2} + 2^{k_{64QAM}/2} + 2^{k_{256QAM}/2} + 2^{k_{QPSK}/2} = 32\,posiciones$$

Each of the I-Q branches will occupy 32 positions, and this in turn will consist of numbers in format s[16, 15], therefore the size of the memory should be 1024 bits.

3.3 Hardware Implementation Results

The architecture selected for the implementation of the RRC filter, is the FIR structure of the Direct Form-1, which is shown in Fig. 10. This structure is modified to embed the baseband mapping in the filtering process.

Taking advantage of the input data and the filter coefficient are known exactly in each branch of the FIR, it is possible to store in LUT's the pre-processed values between the mapping vector and the corresponding coefficient, respecting natural growth through the binary multiplication process [14]. Then, instead of storing only the mapping vectors are stored the pre-calculated products, so, memory size increases to 2176 bits, but the use of multipliers is avoided, which leads to increased processing speed, since, the critical path consists only of one adder block in the FIR structure [15].

The traditional structure of the FIR is included with a delay vector, whose function is to avoid unnecessary sample output when start processing, this effect is caused by

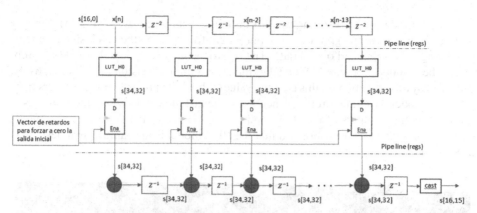

Fig. 10. FIR RRC filter with embedded mapping based on LUT's

the zero initialization of the registers, what causes memory assumes that there is a zero-value data at the input, which is incorrect, to correct this a delay vector is introduced that enables memory output only when there is a valid input.

Verification. Hardware model verification is performed with the help of the finite precision model developed in Simulink, from which input stimulus and output values are obtained, that will be purchased with the HDL model outputs, through a test bench developed in HDL, which is shown in Fig. 11.

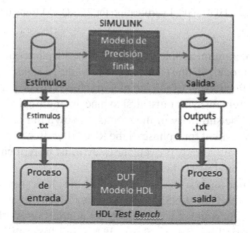

Fig. 11. Flowchart for HDL model verification

The Test Bench is responsible for reading the text files with the input stimulus, generate the clock to 312.5 MHz and generate the signals needed to enable the Device Under Test (DUT), During the output process, the Test Bench receives the DUT data and compares it with the text file containing the finite precision model outputs (Simulink), quantifying errors in the HDL model in this way.

Figure 12 shows the resulting waveforms of the test process for 256-QAM. Starting with the first row of this graph is the input signal, followed by the clock signal, signals indicating valid input and output data. The two rows marked with (s_M) and (s_F) represent the outputs of branch I of the HDL model and finite precision model respectively, followed by an error counter, this is, if the value of the finite precision model differs from the HDL model the counter register increases. The last three rows show: the comparison for the Q branch outputs of the HDL model, (sin_M) and of the finite precision model (sim_F). In both cases it is observed that the HDL model is the same as that developed in Simulink.

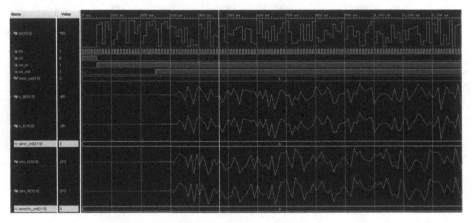

Fig. 12. HDL model verification for 256-QAM transmitter

To measure the maximum sample rate, the Xilinx Vivado compiler is used, which, more than the HDL model, it must also contain a file of constraints, specifying the clock parameters and the port on which the measurement will be performed. For Vivado to perform this measurement, you must first synthesis and implement the HDL model on the FPGA device. The summary of the results is shown in Fig. 13, where, hardware resource occupancy is verified for a phase of the RRC filter. Because for the multi-carrier transmitter model only this already proven hardware must be replicated, can specify that the rest of the model would work the same.

Vivado performs time analysis based on reaching the clock specified in the constraint file, in this case 3.0 ns, and get WNS (Worst Negative Slack) what is it, the value of the worst timing of all model routes for maximum delay analysis. With this value you get the minimum clock period by $T_{min} = T_{clk} - WNS$ and from this the maximum clock frequency [16], Fig. 14, shows the RTL diagram for measuring the maximum operating frequency f_{max} and the Vivado timing report.

$$T_{min} = T_{clk} - WNS = 3\,ns - 0.912\,ns = 2.088\,ns$$

$$f_{max} \frac{1}{T_{min}} = 478.93\,MHz$$

Utilization	Post-Synthesis	Post-Implementation	
		Graph	Table
Resource	Utilization	Available	Utilization...
LUT	1293	303600	0.43
LUTRAM	1	130800	0.01
FF	2015	607200	0.33
IO	46	700	6.57
BUFG	1	32	3.13

Fig. 13. Hardware utilization report for a phase of the RRC filter

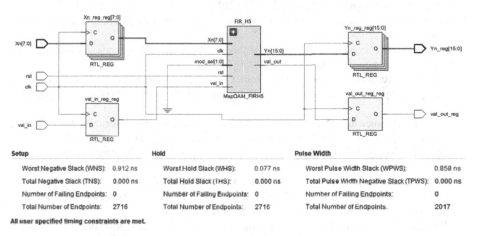

Setup		Hold		Pulse Width	
Worst Negative Slack (WNS):	0.912 ns	Worst Hold Slack (WHS):	0.077 ns	Worst Pulse Width Slack (WPWS):	0.858 ns
Total Negative Slack (TNS):	0.000 ns	Total Hold Slack (THS):	0.000 ns	Total Pulse Width Negative Slack (TPWS):	0.000 ns
Number of Failing Endpoints:	0	Number of Failing Endpoints:	0	Number of Failing Endpoints:	0
Total Number of Endpoints:	2716	Total Number of Endpoints:	2716	Total Number of Endpoints.	2017

All user specified timing constraints are met.

Fig. 14. RTL diagram of the RRC filter for f_{max} measuring

4   Conclusions

With the model of the communications system proposed in Fig. 6, has been able to generate a 2.27 GHz signal of bandwidth distributed over 7 IF channels. Simulation iterations have estimated that the RRC filter values should be: $\beta = 0.14, span = 14$ y $L = 16$ to maintain the $EVM < 2\%$, in the specified range with the lowest hardware resource occupation.

In the architecture selected for the implementation of the RRC filter, the multipliers have been exchanged for LUT's, in which pre-calculated values of all possible products of input data are stored with the respective coefficient to the FIR branch, with this technique has eliminated the use of multipliers, reducing hardware area and increasing processing speed. With this technique it has been achieved that the hardware works at 478.93 MHz well above the 312.5 MHz that was targeted.

Acknowledgments. The authors thank the Technical University of Ambato and the "Dirección de Investigación y Desarrollo" (DIDE) for their support in carrying out this research, in the execution of the project "Plataforma Móvil Omnidireccional KUKA dotada de Inteligencia Artificial utilizando estrategias de Machine Learning para Navegación Segura en Espacios no Controlados", project code: PFISEI27.

References

1. Rishad, A., Shahriar, R., Razibul, I., Nabil, S.: On the error vector magnitude as a performance metric and comparative analysis. In: International Conference on Emerging Technologies, pp. 27–31 (2006)
2. Gentile, K.: The care and feeding of digital, pulse-shaping filters. RF Mixed Signal **25**, 50–61 (2002)
3. Mehra, R., Devi, S.: FPGA implementation of high speed pulse shaping filter for SDR applications. In: Meghanathan, N., Boumerdassi, S., Chaki, N., Nagamalai, D. (eds.) ASUC/NeCoM/VLSI/WeST/WiMoN -2010. CCIS, vol. 90, pp. 214–222. Springer, Heidelberg (2010). https://doi.org/10.1007/978-3-642-14493-6_23
4. Matworks: "rcosdesign," Matworks Documentation. https://www.mathworks.com/help/signal/ref/rcosdesign.html. Accessed 21 Oct 2019
5. Anderson, J.B.: Digital Transmission Engineering. IEEE Press Editorial Board, Piscataway (2005)
6. Zoltowski, M.: Equations for the raised cosine and square-root raised cosine shapes. Communication Systems Division (2013)
7. Dehner, G., Rudolf, R., Schafer, M., Strobl, C.: Analysis of the quantization error in digital multipliers with small wordlength. In: Processing Conference (EUSIPCO), pp. 848–1852 (2016)
8. Chan, D., Rabiner, L.: Analysis of quantization errors in the direct form for finite impulse response digital filters. IEEE Trans. Audio Electroacust. **4**(AU-21), 354–366 (2016)
9. Denis, D., Cordeiro, R., Oliveira, R., Viera, J., Silva, J., Silva, T.: Fully Parallel architecture for designing frequency-agile and real-time reconfigurable FPGA-based RF digital transmitters. IEEE Trans. Microw. Theory Tech. **3**(66), 1489–1499 (2008)
10. Milic, L.: Multirate Filtering for Digital Signal Processing Matlab Applications. IGI Global, New York (2009). Information Science Reference
11. Zhen-dog, Z., Bin, W., Yu-mei, Z.: Multipath pipelined polyphase structures for FIR interpolation and decimation in MIMO OFDM systems. ISRN Signal Process. **2011** (2011). 4 pages
12. Nguyen, B., Shwedyk, E.: A First Course in Digital Communications. Cambridge University Press, Cambridge (2009)
13. Klymyshyn, D., Haluzan, D.: FPGA implementation of multiplierless M-QAM modulator. Electron. Lett. **38**(10), 461–462 (2002)
14. Dehner, G., Rabenstein, R., Schafer M., Strobl, C.: Analysis of the quantization error in digital multipliers with small wordlength. In: European Signal Processing Conference (EUSIPCO), pp. 1848–1852 (2016)
15. Marin-Roig, J., Angarita, F., Valls, J., Almenar, V.: Diseno de Moduladores Basados en Tablas para Software Radio (2014)
16. Vivado Design Suite User Guide: Using Constraints, Xilinx (2017)

Centralized Trajectory Tracking Controller for a Multi-robot System

Christian Beltrán⬤, Andrés Cabrera(✉)⬤, Gabriel Delgado⬤,
and Daniel Iturralde⬤

Universidad del Azuay, Cuenca, Ecuador
cebt@es.uazuay.edu.ec,
{apcabrera,gabrieldelgado,diturralde}@uazuay.edu.ec
http://www.uazuay.edu.ec

Abstract. This work shows the development and implementation of a centralized trajectory tracking system for multi-robot systems, which is based on a kinematic trajectory controller for unicycle robots and subsequently transforming it to differential kinematics, a wireless network is also created for the communication of the master with the slave robots, additionally a method of prevention and avoidance of collisions between the robots is implemented.

Keywords: Trajectory tracking · Velocity obstacle · Centralized system · Multi-robot system · Differential kinematics · Mobile robot

1 Introduction

Multi-robot systems (MRS) are composed of a set of the same or different robots associated in an orderly manner to work together; in this way they can reach a goal or perform a task which would be impossible for a single robot [7]. The collective goal can be achieved through the cooperation of the different robots in a large task or by breaking down this task into simple sub tasks which will be addressed by the robots individually. This is very useful in the industry since the cost-benefit ratio is usually lower by applying MRS compared to a complex robot that has the ability to carry out the entire task [5].

The paper is organized as follows: it starts with a brief review of related works in Sect. 1.1. In Sect. 1.2, the problem to be addressed is defined. Section 2 defines the mathematical models of the mobile robots that are going to be part of the system. Also, the centralized controller is proposed in Sect. 2.3 to follow trajectories and apply geometrical methods to avoid collisions. In Sect. 2.5, the laboratory set up is briefly described and the algorithms implemented in the centralized controller are shown. Section 3 show the simulations and experiments performed. Finally, Sect. 4 analyzes data gathered in the simulation and laboratory experiments.

© Springer Nature Switzerland AG 2020
M. Botto-Tobar et al. (Eds.): ICAT 2019, CCIS 1195, pp. 331–345, 2020.
https://doi.org/10.1007/978-3-030-42531-9_27

1.1 Related Work

Given the importance of MRS, several research projects have used these systems as a solution to various problems, such as exploration and mapping, collective manipulation, surveillance, etc.

One of the main uses of MRS is in the field of exploration is presented in [3]. A probabilistic method is presented to optimize the area of exploration covered by each robot and prevent robots from covering areas already discovered by other robots, thus minimizing the time needed to cover the entire land to be explored.

In [10], Soltero et al. use mobile robots for closed trajectory tracking. When the robot passes through an area, it eliminates its uncertainty, this uncertainty increases over time if it is not eliminated, so robots tend to prioritize reaching areas that have high uncertainty.

Collective manipulation by MRS is also possible, as in [11] and [4], where a decentralized algorithm controls the robots to perform the manipulation of an object, which cannot be moved by a single robot. The robots do not have communication between them, but they use force feedback to synchronize the forces in such a way that the object moves as desired.

The research in [1] presents a behavior-based control architecture to control the robots to act as part of a herd. Since the processing for this type of control is carried out in a decentralized manner, the robot requires information from adjacent robots or the immediate environment.

In the case of mapping using MRS, authors in [8] use multiple position graphs obtained by different robots to generate maps of an area by overlaying equal points of interest on maps obtained by different robot.

1.2 Problem Definition

Consider a group of n robots, each one labeled as R_i where $i \in \{1, 2, 3, ..., n\}$. Each one is described geometrically as a circle with radius r_{Ri}, which represents the distance from the center of the robot to its physical edge. Also, each robot has velocity constraints given by $v_{min} < v_{Ri} < v_{max}$ where $v_{min} > 0$. Each robot has a parametric trajectory $T_i(t) \in \mathbb{R}^2$ associated with it. The position of each robot in a time τ is given by $P_{Ri}(\tau)$. Robots lack of sensors to detect the environment, so they don't have information about their positions. All the robots have a simplex channel of communication with a server that has all the information about position and direction of all robots in real time, and it sends control inputs to follow the trajectories minimizing error. In case of collision between robots, a controller in the server is needed to adjust robots' trajectories to avoid collisions and follow the trajectories minimizing errors.

2 Methods

2.1 Unicycle Robot Model

The unicycle robot, as shown in Fig. 1, is an ideal representation of a mobile robot, which describes it as a point located in the center of the robot's wheel axis.

This point has non-holonomic restrictions, so to describe its movement a linear velocity and an angular velocity is required. Due to its simplicity, it is one of the most used models when designing position controllers, trajectory tracking, etc. [9,13].

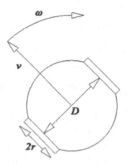

Fig. 1. Unicycle model representation.

The equations that describe the movement of a control point in a 2D plane, referenced to the origin, are:

$$\dot{x}_c = v \cdot \cos(\varphi) - a \cdot \omega \cdot \sin(\varphi)$$
$$\dot{y}_c = v \cdot \sin(\varphi) - a \cdot \omega \cdot \cos(\varphi) \tag{1}$$
$$\dot{\varphi} = \omega$$

where

- φ is the angle between the positive x axis and robots heading
- a is the distance between the middle of the wheels axis to the control point
- $\dot{x}_c$ is the x-direction velocity
- $\dot{y}_c$ is the y-direction velocity
- ω is the angular velocity
- v is the linear velocity

2.2 Differential Robot

The differential robot model, shown in Fig. 2, is the most widely used of all mobile robots, and consists of 2 independent active wheels and one or more passive wheels to improve stability.

Unlike the unicycle model, the differential model requires additional information such as the distance between wheels, the wheel radius, etc. The equations that describe the movement of the differential robot in a 2D plane [6] are:

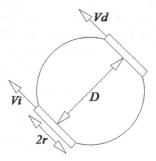

Fig. 2. Differential drive model representation.

$$\dot{x} = \frac{r}{2} \cdot (v_d + v_i) \cdot \cos(\varphi)$$
$$\dot{y} = \frac{r}{2} \cdot (v_d + v_i) \cdot \sin(\varphi) \tag{2}$$
$$\dot{\varphi} = \frac{r}{D} \cdot (v_d - v_i)$$

where

- $\dot{x}$ is the x-direction velocity of the center of the robot
- $\dot{y}$ is the y-direction velocity of the center of the robot
- φ is the angular velocity
- v_d is the angular velocity of the right wheel
- v_i is the angular velocity of the left wheel
- r is the wheel radius
- D is the distance between wheels

Relation Unicycle-Differential. As mentioned earlier, the unicycle model is the most applied model when designing controllers, since its level of abstraction represents the robot in the simplest way possible. On the other hand, when applying control systems in a real environment, their implementation is complex given that it is an ideal model. In practice, robots usually have different actuators to control their movement, as is the case with differential robots, so a way to convert the speeds of the unicycle model to the differential model is required [6]. This is achieved using Eqs. 1 and 2, and solving for v_d and v_i.

$$v_d = \frac{2v + \omega D}{2r}$$
$$v_i = \frac{2v - \omega D}{2r} \tag{3}$$

2.3   Trajectory Tracking Controller

A trajectory $\boldsymbol{T}(t) \in \mathbb{R}^2$ with $\boldsymbol{T}(t) = (x_d, y_d)$ is a set of points that represent the desired position of a moving point at a given time. With a given trajectory it is possible to obtain the velocities needed at each point of the trajectory by taking the derivative of the trajectory with respect to time $\dot{\boldsymbol{T}}(t) = (\dot{x}_d, \dot{y}_d)$. Once these are obtained, they are processed to obtain the inputs required for a unicycle type robot (v and ω) using the inverse Jacobian of the system given by the first two relations in Eq. 2.

$$\begin{bmatrix} v \\ \omega \end{bmatrix} = \begin{bmatrix} \cos\varphi & -a \cdot \sin(\varphi) \\ \sin\varphi & -a \cdot \cos(\varphi) \end{bmatrix}^{-1} \begin{bmatrix} \dot{x}_d \\ \dot{y}_d \end{bmatrix} \tag{4}$$

If the error in the trajectory is accounted, an extra term in 4 can be added to create a proportional controller:

$$\begin{bmatrix} v \\ \omega \end{bmatrix} = \begin{bmatrix} \cos\varphi & -a \cdot \sin(\varphi) \\ \sin\varphi & -a \cdot \cos(\varphi) \end{bmatrix}^{-1} \left(\begin{bmatrix} \dot{x}_d \\ \dot{y}_d \end{bmatrix} + \begin{bmatrix} k_p & 0 \\ 0 & k_p \end{bmatrix} \begin{bmatrix} x_d - x \\ y_d - y \end{bmatrix} \right) \tag{5}$$

where

- k_p is a proportional gain constant
- x_d and y_d are the coordinates given by the trajectory
- x and y are the robot's current position coordinates

2.4   Velocity Obstacle

A Velocity Obstacle (VO) is defined as the set of all possible speeds that an object A with radius r_a can take which would produce a collision with an object B with radius r_b at a future instant of time. Geometrically, VO can be understood, as shown in Fig. 3, starting from the Minkowski sum between objects A and B, denoted as $A \oplus B$, such that:

$$A \oplus B = \{a + b \mid a \in A, \; b \in B\} \tag{6}$$

Defining $\lambda(p, v)$ as the line that starts in p and has a direction v such that:

$$\lambda(p, v) = \{p + t \cdot v \mid t \geq 0\} \tag{7}$$

If there is a line that originates at the central point of object A and a direction given by the relative velocity between objects A and B, denoted (v_A-v_B), inside $A \oplus B$, then v_A is in VO of object B and is defined by:

$$VO_B^A(v_B) = \{v_A \mid \lambda(p_A, v_A - v_B) \cap A \oplus B \neq \emptyset\} \tag{8}$$

This means that if $v_A \in VO_B^A(v_B)$, or if λ (p_A, v_A - v_B) is tangential to $A \oplus B$ (a "collision cone") then objects A and B will collide in the future if they keep the same trajectory [12].

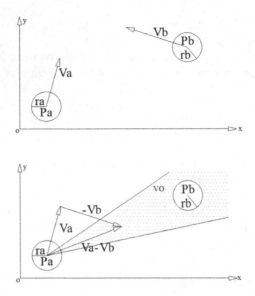

Fig. 3. Geometric representation of Velocity Obstacle.

2.5   System Setup

The system consist of a centralized controller programmed in a server computer which contains the parametric trajectories of the robots and the controller algorithm. The feedback system consists in a motion capture system comprised of several cameras developed by Arbito et al. in [2], which uses computer vision to capture the movement of multiple robots in a workspace space and gives information about position and orientation. The system was calibrated to have a measure of 0.25 cm per pixel. The server communicates with the robots using a wireless connection via the user datagram protocol (UDP). The robots were configured as UDP receivers and were given a unique Internet Protocol (IP) address on the network, so that the server can communicate with them.

The controller sends unicycle commands to the robots, each one contains a simple program to convert the inputs to right and left wheel velocities, and subsequently to electric signals (Pulse Width Modulation) to control the motors.

Once the trajectory tracking is applied to a differential robot with the control point a, a criterion for collision avoidance must be applied. For this, VO method was applied, which requires verifying whether the relative velocity between the two objects is in the collision cone. The evasion criterion is shown in Fig. 4, such that if $limit_{lower} < \angle(v_a - v_b) < limit_{upper}$ relative speed is in the collision cone.

To verify the condition $limit_{lower} < \angle(v_a - v_b) < limit_{upper}$, Algorithm 1 must be applied.

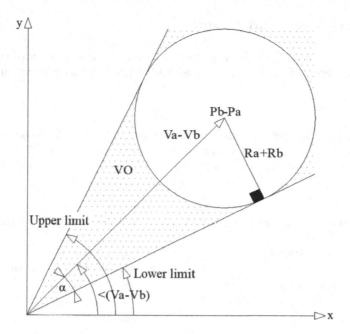

Fig. 4. Velocity obstacle and collision cone avoidance.

Algorithm 1. Velocity Obstacle

1: **procedure** VELOCITY OBSTACLE
2:     $distance \leftarrow \sqrt{(x_a - x_b)^2 + (y_a - y_b)^2}$
3:     $r \leftarrow r_a + r_b$
4:     $v_r \leftarrow v_a - v_b$
5:     $v_\varphi \leftarrow \arctan(v_y/v_x)$
6:     $\alpha \leftarrow \arcsin(r/distance)$
7:     $lim_{upper} \leftarrow v_\varphi + \alpha$
8:     $lim_{lower} \leftarrow v_\varphi - \alpha$
9:     **if** $lim_{lower} < v_\varphi < lim_{upper}$ **then**
10:         $v_r \leftarrow lim_{upper} + v_b$

The server procedure is shown in Algorithm 2.

Algorithm 2.

1: **procedure** MULTI ROBOT CONTROLLER
2:     **for** all $T_i \in T$ **do**   ▷ T is Trajectory List
3:         **for** all $R_i \in R$ **do**   ▷ R is Robot List
4:             Obtain position x, y, ϕ
5:             Compare position T_i
6:             Calculate new velocities
7:             **for** all $(R_k \in R) \neq R_j$ **do**
8:                 Apply Velocity Obstacle
9:             Update Velocities
10:            Send Data

---

3   Experiments and Results

Different experiments have been proposed to verify the operation of the system in different areas, which were simulated and applied in the real system.

3.1   Simulations

Non-colliding Trajectories. First, a set of paths was designed which contains non-colliding trajectories to test the system capabilities. The trajectories for three robots are shown in Fig. 5. In Table 1, the error between the desired trajectory and the path described in the simulation test is shown.

Table 1. Statistical table of errors obtained in the simulation of non-colliding test.

	Trajectory		Percentile 10–100	
	Mean error	Mean squared error	Mean error	Mean squared error
Blue robot	0.864	1.89	0.319	0.397
Green robot	1.195	2.89	0.360	0.419
Red robot	0.889	2.01	0.309	0.577

Colliding Trajectories. Data obtained by simulating colliding trajectories for three robots is shown in Fig. 6. Data in Fig. 7 shows the relative distances between robots throughout the test, showing no graph close to level zero. This information is summarized in Table 2.

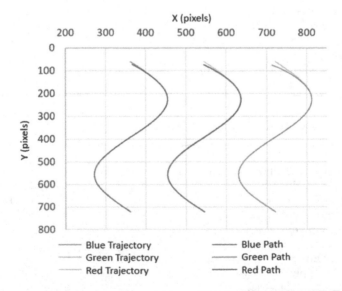

Fig. 5. Non-colliding trajectories in simulation test.

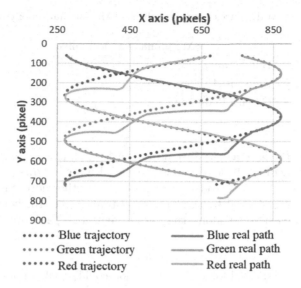

Fig. 6. Colliding trajectories simulation test.

3.2 Laboratory Tests

After simulation experiments, the same tests were carried out in the laboratory system and the same analysis was carried out on the data obtained in order to contrast it with the simulations.

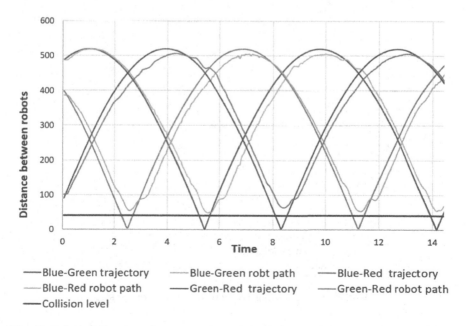

Fig. 7. Relative distances between robots for colliding trajectories simulation test.

Table 2. Minimum distances between robots in the simulation of colliding test.

	Minimum distances (pixels)
Blue - Green	56.83
Blue - Red	54.77
Green - Red	56.98

Non-colliding Trajectories. Just as in the first simulation experiment, the trajectory tracking of multiple robots was tested. Figure 8 shows the ideal trajectories, as well as the paths traveled by the robots. Furthermore, Fig. 9 shows the trail of each robot captured by the camera system. Figure 10 shows the instantaneous error of each robot along the entire path, and Table 3 summarizes the errors.

Table 3. Statistical table of errors of non-colliding laboratory test.

	Trajectory		Percentile 10–100	
	Mean error	Mean squared error	Mean error	Mean squared error
Blue robot	13.684	1.84	14.214	0.908
Green robot	15.787	1.78	16.309	0.838
Red robot	14.814	1.22	14.820	0.992

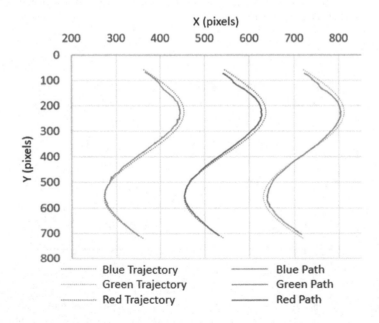

Fig. 8. Non-colliding trajectories laboratory test.

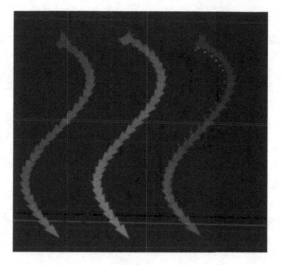

Fig. 9. Robot trails for non-colliding trajectories laboratory test.

Colliding Trajectories. Data obtained by colliding trajectories for three robots is shown in Fig. 11. Data in Fig. 12 shows the relative distances between robots throughout the test. Information is summarized in Table 4. Figure 13 shows the trail of each robot captured by the camera system.

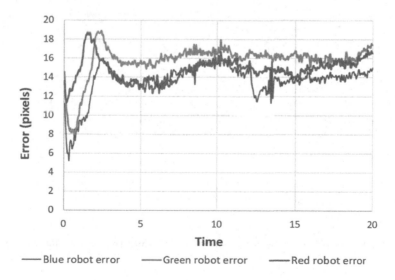

Fig. 10. Error with respect to time in non-colliding laboratory test.

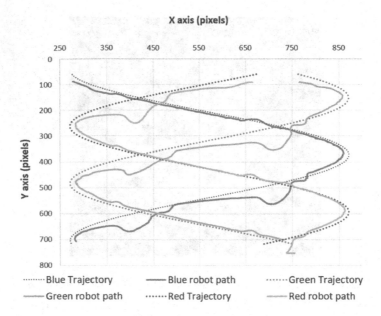

Fig. 11. Colliding trajectories laboratory test.

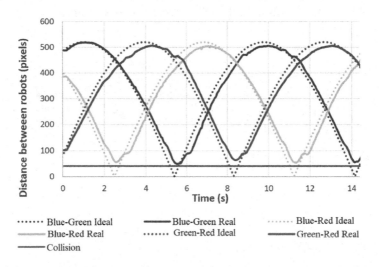

Fig. 12. Relative distances between robots for colliding trajectories laboratory test.

Table 4. Minimum distances between robots in colliding laboratory test.

	Minimum distances (pixels)
Robots Blue - Green	48.64
Robots Blue - Red	53.28
Robots Green - Red	57.13

Fig. 13. Robot trails in colliding trajectories laboratory test.

4   Conclusions and Future Work

Very early tests show an initial error in individual trajectories that decreases significantly as the controller acts to minimize error. However, there are certain points where the error increases due to pronounced changes of direction, which can be interpreted as a discontinuities or high derivative values in the trajectories, and this causes the required speeds to be outside the robot motors limitations. The data obtained in the laboratory tests average an error of 14.44 pixels, which is significantly higher with respect to the simulation.

In both the simulation and the laboratory experiment, whose results are shown in the box plot of Fig. 14, it is observed that most of the data is not scattered, which translates to a small box. This represents an almost null quadratic error, except for the beginning of the trajectory in which the initial positioning of the robot has to be taken into account. Likewise, the whiskers are short, which means that most of the data that is outside the box do not move away from its limits. In this case, the main difference between the simulation and the actual experiment lies in the average error and as in the previous test, it presents a constant error along the entire trajectory.

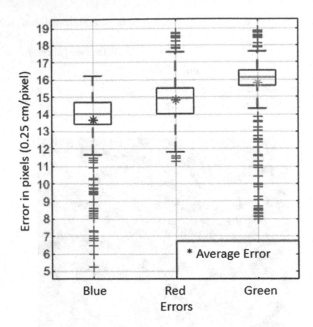

Fig. 14. Box plot for laboratory experiment results.

Acknowledgments. This research was funded by Project UDA 2019-0083, UDA 2019-0084 and UDA 2019-0230.

References

1. Antonelli, G., Arrichiello, F., Chiaverini, S.: Flocking for multi-robot systems via the null-space-based behavioral control. Swarm Intell. **4**(1), 37 (2010)
2. Arbito Chica, P.F.: Implementación de un Sistema de Posicionamiento Óptico para un Robot Móvil dentro de un Entorno de Trabajo. B.S. thesis, Universidad del Azuay (2019)
3. Burgard, W., Moors, M., Fox, D., Simmons, R., Thrun, S.: Collaborative multi-robot exploration. In: ICRA, pp. 476–481 (2000)
4. Faal, S.G., Kalat, S.T., Onal, C.D.: Decentralized obstacle avoidance in collective object manipulation. In: 2017 NASA/ESA Conference on Adaptive Hardware and Systems (AHS), pp. 133–138. IEEE (2017)
5. Gautam, A., Mohan, S.: A review of research in multi-robot systems. In: 2012 IEEE 7th International Conference on Industrial and Information Systems (ICIIS), pp. 1–5. IEEE (2012)
6. Guzmán, L.E.S., Villa, M.A.M., Vásquez, E.L.R.: Seguimiento de trayectorias con un robot móvil de configuración diferencial. Ingenierías USBMed **5**(1), 26–34 (2014)
7. Khamis, A., Hussein, A., Elmogy, A.: Multi-robot task allocation: a review of the state-of-the-art. In: Koubâa, A., Martínez-de Dios, J.R. (eds.) Cooperative Robots and Sensor Networks 2015. SCI, vol. 604, pp. 31–51. Springer, Cham (2015). https://doi.org/10.1007/978-3-319-18299-5_2

8. Kim, B., et al.: Multiple relative pose graphs for robust cooperative mapping. In: 2010 IEEE International Conference on Robotics and Automation, pp. 3185–3192. IEEE (2010)
9. Płaskonka, J.: The path following control of a unicycle based on the chained form of a kinematic model derived with respect to the serret-frenet frame. In: 2012 17th International Conference on Methods & Models in Automation & Robotics (MMAR), pp. 617–620a. IEEE (2012)
10. Soltero, D.E., Smith, S.L., Rus, D.: Collision avoidance for persistent monitoring in multi-robot systems with intersecting trajectories. In: 2011 IEEE/RSJ International Conference on Intelligent Robots and Systems, pp. 3645–3652. IEEE (2011)
11. Wang, Z., Schwager, M.: Kinematic multi-robot manipulation with no communication using force feedback. In: 2016 IEEE International Conference on Robotics and Automation (ICRA), pp. 427–432. IEEE (2016)
12. Wilkie, D., Van Den Berg, J., Manocha, D.: Generalized velocity obstacles. In: 2009 IEEE/RSJ International Conference on Intelligent Robots and Systems, pp. 5573–5578. IEEE (2009)
13. Xie, D., Wang, S., Wang, Y.: Trajectory tracking control of differential drive mobile robot based on improved kinematics controller algorithm. In: 2018 Chinese Automation Congress (CAC), pp. 2675–2680. IEEE (2018)

Hardening of Metal Matrix Composites
with Ceramic Nanoparticles

Victor M. Cardenas$^{(\boxtimes)}$ and Carlos A. Villarreal B.

Technical University of the North, Av 17 de Julio 5-21, Ibarra, Ecuador
{vmcardenas,cavillarreal}@utn.edu.ec

Abstract. The importance that in the last decades have acquired the composite materials of metallic matrix with reinforcements of nano ceramic particles, not only for their extraordinary mechanical properties, finding applications in different branches of industrial technology such as automotive, naval, aerospace and others. This work aims to show how the hardening of this type of materials depends on: the type of reinforcement, the size and its characteristics, the interaction of the dislocations with the defects, the process of obtaining these materials and the grain size of the matrix for the materials obtained by fusion or the particle size for those obtained by sintered compacting.

Keywords: Metals hardening · Nanoparticles · Nano compounds

Nomenclature

MMC   Metal matrix compounds
PMC   Polymeric matrix compounds
CMC   Ceramic matrix compounds
CNT   Carbon nanotubes
MMNCs   Nanocomposite metal matrix materials
CTE   Coefficient of Thermal Expansion

1 Introduction

Composite materials are engineering or natural materials that contain two or more different materials with different mechanical properties. In general, the properties of composite materials are superior to those of monolithic components. There are different classifications for composite materials, but the most common is based on the nature of the matrix: metal matrix compounds (MMC), polymeric matrix compounds (PMC) and ceramic matrix compounds (CMC) [1]. Nano particles can improve the base material in terms of wear resistance, damping properties and mechanical strength. Different types of metals, predominantly Al, Mg and Cu, have been used for the production of compounds reinforced by nano-emic particles such as carbides, nitrides, oxides and carbon nanotubes.

© Springer Nature Switzerland AG 2020
M. Botto-Tobar et al. (Eds.): ICAT 2019, CCIS 1195, pp. 346–358, 2020.
https://doi.org/10.1007/978-3-030-42531-9_28

Metal matrix compounds (MMC) have gained considerable interest in the last three decades. The driving force has been the fact that the addition of ceramic reinforcement in the metal matrix can improve specific strength, stiffness, wear, fatigue and creep properties compared to conventional engineering materials [2, 3].

MMCs are widely used in several industrial areas, such as aerospace, automotive and electronics [4]. It has been observed that the properties of MMCs are greatly influenced by the nature of the reinforcement and its distribution in the metal matrix. The properties of the compounds are also influenced by the chemical nature of the components, the morphology of the particles, their distribution and interface reactions [5]. Particle size, however, is an important factor.

The processing methods used to manufacture MMC can be grouped according to the metal matrix temperature during processing MMCs, in general, are mainly manufactured using powder metallurgy (P/M) and agitation molding techniques [1]. To reduce the cost and improve the properties, the solid-state technique, that is, the powder metallurgy route, is of great importance. The extended the advantage of using the P/M technique is that it makes use of lower temperature compared to other processing methods and there is less interaction between the matrix and the reinforcement. The P/M technique gives more homogeneous distribution of particles in the metal matrix with or without interaction between the matrix and the reinforcement phase. Much work has been done using aluminium as a matrix material but there are very few reports that it uses iron as a metal matrix; that is directly related to the strength of the compounds [6]. There have been significant advances in processing techniques to control the microstructure and mechanical properties resulting from MMC [7].

The processing methods used to manufacture MMC can be grouped according to the metal matrix temperature during processing. MMCs, in general, are mainly manufactured using powder metallurgy (P/M) and agitation molding techniques [1]. To reduce the cost and improve the properties, the solid-state technique, that is, the powder metallurgy route, is of great importance. The extended the advantage of using the P/M technique is that it makes use of lower temperature compared to other processing methods and there is less interaction between the matrix and the reinforcement. The P/M technique gives more homogeneous distribution of particles in the metal matrix with or without interaction between the matrix and the reinforcement phase. Much work has been done using aluminium as a matrix material but there are very few reports that it uses iron as a metal matrix [8].

Metal matrix compounds (MMC) are an important class of engineering materials that are increasingly replacing a series of conventional materials in the automotive, aerospace, marine and sports industry due to their light weight and superior mechanical properties. In MMCs, non-metallic materials are embedded in metals or alloys as reinforcements to obtain a novel material with attractive engineering properties, such as improved tensile strength, ductility, toughness and tribological behaviour. These parameters include material parameters (size, shape, volume fraction and type of reinforcements), mechanical parameters (normal loading and sliding speed), and physical parameters (temperature and environment). In general, it was shown that the wear resistance and the friction coefficient of the MMCs are improved by increasing the volume fraction of the reinforcements. As normal loading and sliding speed increase, the wear rate of the compounds increases and the coefficient of friction of the compounds decreases. The rate of wear and the coefficient of friction decreases with the increase in temperature to a critical temperature, and then both the rate of wear and the coefficient of friction increase increasing temperature The nano compounds showed the best friction and wear performance compared to the micro compounds [9].

Because of its low melting point and the facilities it presents for processing, aluminum is the most used and studied among metallic matrices [10].

In the literature, different kinds of matrix metals have been coupled with several types of nanometric phases. Ceramic compounds (SiC, Al2O3, etc.), intermetallic materials and carbon allotropes were used to reinforce Al, Mg, Cu and other metals and alloys. Importance is attached to carbon nanotubes (CNT), which are characterized by very high strength, stiffness and electrical conductivity. These properties confer greater mechanical strength and in turn improve the electrical and thermal properties of the base material. In addition, MMnCs proved capable of improving other interesting engineering properties, such as damping capacity, wear resistance and creep behaviour [11].

MMNCs display superior tribological properties, such as surface hardness and wear resistance. Ultrasonic treatment has been advantageous to enhance the surface properties by uniform dispersion of nano particles and avoid the formation of porosity. Improvement in the surface hardness by 75% has been achieved with a reinforcement of 5 wt% of SiC in Mg alloy (AZ91D) by ultrasonic-assisted casting. Using a similar casting process, Li observed a 20% hardness improvement in Al 356 alloy with the addition of 2 vol.% SiC nanoparticles.

However, very few studies have been conducted on the tribological properties of MMNCs produced by ultrasonic assisted casting. In one of the studies on Al alloy, produced the nano B4C-Al composite by ultrasonic-assisted stir casting and conducted the dry sliding friction and wear test against EN31 hardened steel; the addition of 8 wt% B4C decreased the wear rate by ~100% compared with pure Al. The coefficient of friction has also decreased with the addition of B4C in Al, as exemplified for Al-8 wt% B4C composites. This lowering of the wear rate and the coefficient of friction was observed due to formation of a mechanically mixed layer during sliding, and such a layer acted as a solid lubricant film and protected the surfaces. B4C-AA6061 composites were fabricated by ultrasonic-assisted casting and, where the friction and wear were measured; AA6061 reinforced with 1.5 vol.% of nano B4C particle had lower weight loss (136% lesser than the unreinforced AA6061 alloy) possibly due to the improved hardness by the uniform distribution of nano particles that served as load-bearing elements in the matrix [12].

2 The Material and Method

There are three important factors that can determine MMC performance: they are (1) the composition and microstructure of MMC; (2) the size, volume fraction and distribution of particles in metal matrices; and (3) the interface properties between metal matrices and reinforcements.

The main problem to face in the production of MMCs is the low wettability of the ceramic nano particles that do not allow the use of conventional methods of smelting.

Small dust aggregates are prone to grouping and not dispersing homogeneously in the matrix for hardening of the material [11].

The techniques most used in the processing of nanoparticulate compounds, of metal matrix are: (i) in a liquid state, with the infiltration and dispersion of nano particles, (ii) in solid state by compacting-sintering, and (iii) in solid-liquid state [13].

Also, a critical factor in the hardening in this type of materials, is the processing of the same. Several advanced synthesis techniques such as agitation and ultrasonic mixing can be applied for the homogeneous distribution of particles in the foundry. In powder processing, manufacturing methods such as extrusion and lamination are essential in processing and postprocessing to improve the physical properties of the compounds redistributing reinforcement arrangements [14].

Among the hardening mechanisms with nano ceramic particles are the effect of load transfer from the matrix to the nano particles, the grain size of the matrix (Hall-Petch effect), the Orowan effect of interaction of nano particles with the particles. dislocations and defects and differences in the coefficient of thermal expansion and Yang modulus between the matrix and the particles [11].

The quantity, size, shape and distribution of the hard particles embedded in the matrix have some effects on the hardening of these materials. In addition, the interfacial union between the reinforcements and the matrices are another important factor that affects the mechanical and tribology properties of MMCs. In general, it is an admissible opinion that the hardness of the particles as reinforcements in the matrix increase the resistance and resistance to wear. of MMCs, however, the ductility of the compounds decreases. On the other hand, soft particles generally act as a solid lubricant and therefore reduce friction. MMNC coefficient [10].

Metal matrix composite materials reinforced with ceramic particles, have great potential in stiffness and strength, compared to conventional structural alloys. But the increase in mechanical resistance leads to a significant decrease in ductility [8].

Of practical interest are aluminum matrix composites reinforced with boron-containing nanopowders. Composites reinforced with B4C and graphite-like BN nanoparticles were prepared. Powder grinding to a nanoscale value was carried out in a high-energy ultrasonic mill. Samples reinforced with boron-containing nanopowders were subjected to mechanical tests. The test results showed that the most durable are composites reinforced with B4C and BN nanoparticles [7].

In the study of MMCs reinforced with synthetic nanodiamonds, aluminum and its alloys, as well as copper, were used as matrix materials. At present, the strong and wear-resistant copper-based metal matrix composite hardened by nanodiamonds has been well studied. The initial nanocopper and nanodiamond have a spherical shape; after compaction, the nanodiamond, evenly distributed over the volume of the composite, provides its high strength and wear-resistant properties [13].

The use of such metal composites is very diverse. In particular, the medical matrix composite reinforced with nanodiamonds is promising for the manufacture of a loaded electric contactor operating at high dynamic loads, as well as units requiring high wear resistance.

Improving the characteristics of wear resistance (friction coefficient, wear rate, local heating value) depend on the hardness and compressive strength of the composites.

It was experimentally established that when compositing samples from Al + SiC, Al + BN, and Al + B4C composites with increasing dynamic pressure to a certain value, the strength characteristics of the samples increase. A further increase in pressure leads to their destruction [14].

The mechanical properties (tensile and compressive strength, microhardness, wear resistance) of MMCs reinforced with SiC and BN nanopowders are high, which makes it possible to recommend these MMCs for mechanical engineering as structural and bearing materials, for the electric power industry as contact power groups operating under high shock conditions loads and friction. Aluminum matrix composites reinforced with boron-containing nanoparticles are promising for use in nuclear energy as neutron-protective materials [15].

3 Results and Discussion

In Table 1, some important material properties of ceramics. reinforcements commonly used in Al MMC/MMNC are summarized [13, 16]. The thermo physical properties listed here are based on measurements at room temperature. The CTE values for these materials were approximately linear over the experimental temperature range [17]. Because ceramic oxide is generally very susceptible to plastic deformation at high temperatures, they are not considered structural materials in high temperature applications [18].

Table 1. Particle size

Type of compound	Size range reinforcing particle (μm)	Range of the volumetric fraction of the reinforcement (%)
MMC	<500	<60
MMNC	<0.1	<10

Table 2 shows the typical ranges of reinforcement. sizes, volume fractions of reinforcements and metal matrix grain sizes that are often observed in Al MMC/MMNC. In the current work, we categorize Al MMNC as samples with embedded particle size of less than 100 nm. Depending on the processing methods, different factors must be taken into account to produce high quality compounds. For example, with PM processing, matrix compositions and types of reinforcements can be controlled relatively independently; However, in casting, they are intimately linked through the reactivity between reinforcements and matrix in them state [10].

In Fig. 1, it is clear that the behaviour of creep resistance and compressive strength of metal matrix materials reinforced with micro particles depend on the type of particle, although in both cases a growth of these properties is observed with the increase of the volumetric fraction, until reaching a maximum, and then decrease. In the same graph but literal c the elongation before the breakdown decreases differently for each type of reinforcement, worsening the ductility of the materials.

Figure 1 shows how the creep resistance of a pure aluminum matrix compound with alumina micro particles, silicon carbide of different sizes varies. The size of the

Table 2. Particle properties

Reinforcement	Elasticity modulus E (GPa)	Critical stress current factor K_{IC} (MPa.m$^{-1/2}$)	Ultimate tensile strength (MPa)	Coefficient of thermal expansion CTE α (10^{-6} K^{-1})	Density ρ (g/m^3)	Poisson module μ
SiC	450	40	310	4.3	3.21	0.17
Al$_2$O$_3$	390	4.0	260–300	8.1	3.96	0.25
B$_4$C	308	2.5	261	5.0	3.25	0.25

Source: [13]

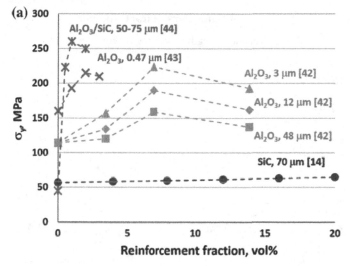

Fig. 1. Creep resistance vs. volumetric fractionation [17]

silicon carbide particles is 70 microns and it is observed that creep resistance practically remains constant because the dislocations contour the particles. In the green lines when we reduce the size of the micro particle, the creep resistance increases, until reaching a maximum, when the volumetric fraction is 7%. The maximum value of the creep resistance is achieved with a mixture of alumina particles and silicon carbide (Fig. 2).

As in the case of microparticles, the growth of mechanical resistance depends on the size of the particles, the smaller the size, the faster the growth of mechanical properties.

Elongation in compounds with micro particles decreases rapidly, while in compounds with nano particles their decrease is moderate and they retain a degree of ductility [19].

The variation of tensile strength with the size of micro particles and the percentage of reinforcements is similar to the creep resistance behavior, with the difference that the compound with silicon carbide undergoes an increase in the range of 15 to 20% volumetric fraction.

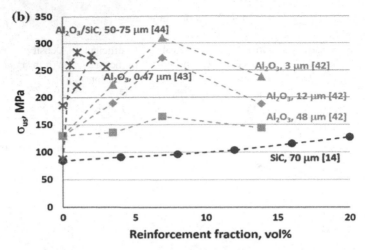

Fig. 2. Tensile strength vs volumetric fraction [17]

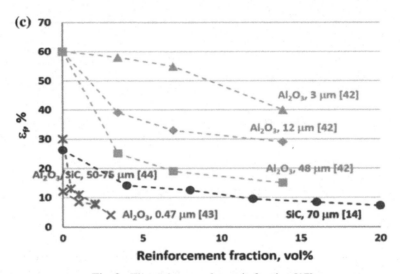

Fig. 3. Elongation vs volumetric fraction [17]

From Fig. 3 it can be seen that the ductility of the compound decreases with the increase in particle size and the percentage of reinforcement. It should be noted that when the particle size is large and its elastic modulus is high, the ductility decreases very little (Table 3).

The nanoparticulate compounds have a behaviour similar to microparticles, that is to say that the mechanical resistance increases with the increase in the percentage of volumetric fraction. It is possible to notice unlike the microparticles, the nanoparticles have a monotonous growth of the mechanical properties up to 10% of volumetric fraction.

Table 3. Properties of nanoparticulate compounds

Reinforcement	Manufacturing process	Volumetric fraction V_f (%)	Particle size Sp (nm).	Stress to fluency σ_y (MPa)	Ultimate tensile strength σ_{us} (MPa)	Elongation ε(%)
SiC	Milling and agitation (MA)	0–7	50	164–269	302–448	22.5–5.5
Al$_2$O$_3$	Powder metallurgy and extrusion (MP)	0–7	50	75–185 (1.3)	150–250 (1.2)	27–8
B$_4$C	High temperature compression (HPT)	0–15 wt,	10–60	324–420	371–485	16.3–12.1
Al$_2$O$_3$ y B$_4$C	Milling and agitation (MA)	0–4	50	129–241	161–279	

Source: [17]

Percentages greater than 20% volumetric fraction are not used since the nano particles are prone to coalescence and their effect would be significantly reduced [20].

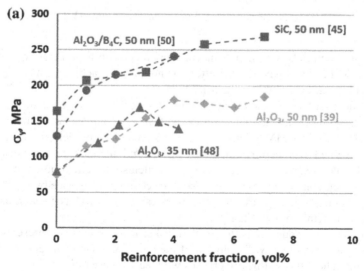

Fig. 4. Creep resistance vs. volumetric fraction [17]

The MMNCs have the nanoparticles dispersed as a mechanism of hardening of the material, for this reason when the at a certain percentage of volumetric fraction decreases the particle size leads to a decrease in the distance between the particles, which increases the tension required for dislocation movements, thus increasing the resistance of the compounds. In addition, smaller particles will indirectly increase grain growth resistance during processing (i.e. grain refinement mechanism).

Because the nanoparticles tend to group together the percentages of the volumetric fraction do not exceed 10%.

Figures 4 and 5 show us that with the decrease in nanoparticle size and the increase in the percentage of reinforcement, creep resistance and tensile strength increase, but in most cases that variation is monotonous (Fig. 6).

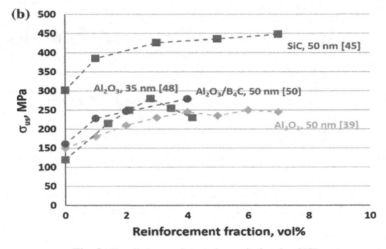

Fig. 5. Tensile strength vs volumetric fraction [17]

Composite materials with metal matrix reinforced with nano ceramic particles, in the last decade, have received special attention not only for achieving high mechanical strength but for achieving greater ductility [13].

The nanoparticulate reinforcements, by increasing their volume fraction, reduce the ductility of the compound, but to a lesser extent than what happens with micro particles.

The grain size of the MMNC processed by fusion and the particle size of those same materials processed by sintered compacting play a fundamental role in the resistance of this type of materials. In both cases the nano particles can refine the grain or prevent its growth, which contributes to an increase in mechanical resistance by the Hall-Petch mechanism. Figure 4 clearly shows that the creep resistance of MMNC materials depends on the size of the grain or particle [7].

The hardness of a material is the mechanical property that best represents the phenomenon of the hardening by dissolution of the micro and nano particles; This is how the graph shows how the hardness increases with the increase of the volumetric fraction until it reaches a maximum limit and then decreases due to the coalescence of micro particles, which facilitate the movement of dislocations [12].

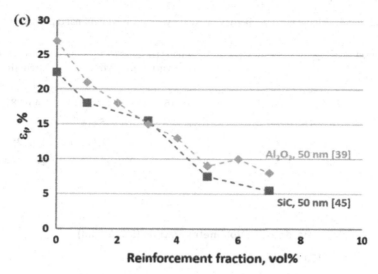

Fig. 6. Elongation vs volumetric fraction [17]

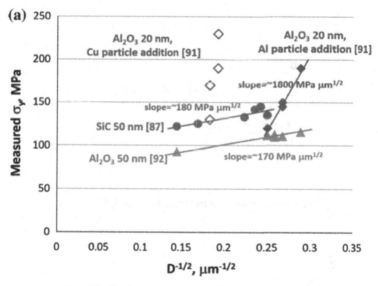

Fig. 7. Creep resistance vs grain size [21]

Grain limits act as obstacles to the movement of dislocations and contribute efficiently to hardening of the material, as shown in Fig. 7 (Table 4, Figs. 8 and 9).

The hardness of nano-particulate materials also grows with the increase in the volumetric fraction, but they do not always have a maximum but rather have a monotonous increase. From the graphs it can be concluded that the hardening of a material depends strongly on the type of nanoparticle, especially its properties (Fig. 10).

Table 4. Mechanical properties of Al alloys reinforced with nano particles

Reinforcement	Alloys	Volumetric fraction V_f (%)	Grain size Gs (μm)	Stress to fluency σ_y (MPa)	Ultimate tensile strength σ_{ut} (MPa)
SiC	356AA	0–4.5	48–16	122–145 (3.5)	145–283 (3.5)
Al_2O_3	2024AA	0–2	25	85–155 (1)	153–210 (1)
ZrO_2	LM13AA	0–15		120–183 (12)	170–258
TiB_2	358AA	0–5		237–277 (1.5)	242–364 (1.5)

Source: [17]

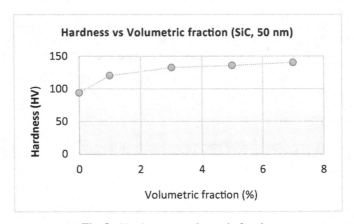

Fig. 8. Hardness vs. volumetric fraction

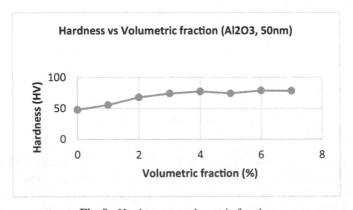

Fig. 9. Hardness vs. volumetric fraction

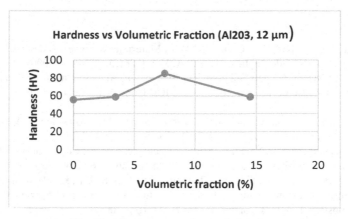

Fig. 10. Hardness vs. volumetric fraction

The previous results are corroborated with the numerical methods, which use a classic plasticity model, which demonstrates that in the absence of material failure, knowing the average particle size, the elastoplastic behaviour of the compound can be predicted.

The numerical results also justify the experimental results on: (i) the effects of morphology and volumetric fractionation in the process of hardening due to deformation of the compound, (i) the pronounced influence of the reinforcement grouping on mechanical resistance, (iii) ductile failure due to the growth of the vacuum of the matrix, (iv) the insensitivity of the resistance to change of the microstructure of the matrix, and (v) the dependence of the ductility of the microstructure, morphology and distribution of the reinforcement [13].

4 Conclusions

The hardening by dissolution of ceramic particles of the materials of metallic matrix is due to the process of obtaining the material, the transfer of load of the matrix to the ceramic particles, the Orowan effect and the Hall-Petch phenomenon.

The characteristics of the nano particles and their volumetric fraction largely determine the hardening process of this type of materials, due to the interaction of the dislocations with the nano particles.

Although the hardness is not the only property that indicates the level of hardening of this type of materials, creep and tensile strength help us to establish this phenomenon to a large extent.

Acknowledgment. We would like to thank the Technical University of the North for sponsoring the development of this research.

References

1. Da Costa, C.E., López, F.V., Castelló, J.M.T.: Materiales compuestos de matriz metalica. I parte. Tipos, propiedades, aplicaciones. Rev. Metal. **36**(3), 179–192 (2000)
2. Mohsin, M., Mohd, A., Arif Siddiqui, M., Suhaib, M., Arif, S.: Effect of alumina on green properties of Al-Fe-Cr powder composites. IOP Conf. Ser. Mater. Sci. Eng. **225**, 012171 (2017)
3. Öksüz, K.E., Çevik, M., Bozdağ, A.E., Özer, A., Şimşir, M.: Production of (V-B) reinforced Fe matrix composites. Int. J. Mater. Metall. Eng. **8**(8), 800–804 (2014)
4. Zakeri, M., Zanganeh, T., Najafi, A.: High-frequency induction heated sintering of ball milled Fe-WC nanocomposites. Int. J. Miner. Metall. Mater. **20**(7), 693–699 (2013)
5. Reddy, B.S.B., Rajasekhar, K., Venu, M., Dilip, J.J.S., Das, S., Das, K.: Mechanical activation-assisted solid-state combustion synthesis of in situ aluminum matrix hybrid (Al_3Ni/Al_2O_3) nanocomposites. J. Alloys Compd. **465**(1–2), 97–105 (2008)
6. Vani, V.V., Chak, S.K.: The effect of process parameters in aluminum metal matrix composites with powder metallurgy. Manuf. Rev. **5**, 7 (2018)
7. Kang, Y.C., Chan, S.L.I.: Tensile properties of nanometric Al_2O_3 particulate-reinforced aluminum matrix composites. Mater. Chem. Phys. **85**(2–3), 438–443 (2004)
8. Kim, H.H., Babu, J.S.S., Kang, C.G.: Fabrication of A356 aluminum alloy matrix composite with CNTs/Al_2O_3 hybrid reinforcements. Mater. Sci. Eng. A **573**, 92–99 (2013)
9. Menezes, P.L., Ingole, S.P.. Nosonovsky, M., Kailas, S.V., Lovell, M.R.: Preface, vol. 9781461419457 (2013)
10. Hashim, J., Looney, L., Hashmi, M.S.J.: Metal matrix composites: production by the stir casting method. J. Mater. Process. Technol. **92–93**, 1–7 (1999)
11. Niu, Y., et al.: Effect of in situ nano-particles on the microstructure and mechanical properties of ferritic steel. Steel Res. Int. **87**(11), 1389–1394 (2016)
12. Attar, S., Nagaral, M., Reddappa, H.N., Auradi, V.: A review on particulate reinforced aluminum metal matrix composites. J. Emerg. Technol. Innov. Res. **2**(2), 225–229 (2015)
13. Su, H., Gao, W., Feng, Z., Lu, Z.: Processing, microstructure and tensile properties of nano-sized Al_2O_3 particle reinforced aluminum matrix composites. Mater. Des. **36**, 590–596 (2012)
14. Yamasaki, T., Zheng, Y.J., Ogino, Y., Terasawa, M., Mitamura, T., Fukami, T.: Formation of metal-TiN/TiC nanocomposite powders by mechanical alloying and their consolidation. Mater. Sci. Eng., A **350**(1–2), 168–172 (2003)
15. Tang, F., Hagiwara, M., Schoenung, J.M.: Microstructure and tensile properties of bulk nanostructured Al-5083/SiCp composites prepared by cryomilling. Mater. Sci. Eng., A **407**(1–2), 306–314 (2005)
16. Xu, N., Zong, B.Y.: Stress in particulate reinforcements and overall stress response on aluminum alloy matrix composites during straining by analytical and numerical modeling. Comput. Mater. Sci. **43**(4), 1094–1100 (2008)
17. Kim, C.S., Cho, K., Manjili, M.H., Nezafati, M.: Mechanical performance of particulate-reinforced Al metal-matrix composites (MMCs) and Al metal-matrix nano-composites (MMNCs). J. Mater. Sci. **52**(23), 13319–13349 (2017)
18. U. City: Waku_JMS_1998.pdf, vol. 3, pp. 1217–1225 (1973)
19. Mirzaei, M., Najafi, M., Niasari, H.: Experimental and numerical analysis of dynamic rupture of steel pipes under internal high-speed moving pressures. Int. J. Impact Eng **85**, 27–36 (2015)
20. Zhang, Z., Chen, D.L.: Consideration of Orowan strengthening effect in particulate-reinforced metal matrix nanocomposites: a model for predicting their yield strength. Scr. Mater. **54**(7), 1321–1326 (2006)
21. Mazahery, A., Abdizadeh, H., Baharvandi, H.R.: Development of high-performance A356/nano-Al_2O_3 composites. Mater. Sci. Eng., A **518**(1–2), 61–64 (2009)

Development of a Prototype Solution for Hearing Problems in Noise in People with Disabilities, Using an Acoustic Beamforming System with a FPGA Card

Fabián Sáenz[1,2](✉) ⓘ, Paúl Bernal[1], Carlos Romero[1,2],
and Marcelo Zambrano Vizuete[3]

[1] Universidad de las Fuerzas Armadas ESPE, Latacunga, Ecuador
{fgsaenz,cpbernal,cgromero}@espe.edu.ec
[2] Universidad Nacional de La Plata, La Plata, Argentina
[3] Instituto Superior Tecnológico Rumiñahui, Sangolqui, Ecuador
Marcelo.zambrano@ister.edu.ec

Abstract. The study of voice signals is an important issue, since a part of society has hearing impairments. This implementation aims to help people with hearing problems, through enhanced voice; using a microphone array with hemispherical methodology broadband beamforming, which can distinguish signals arriving from different directions. A semi-spherical microphone array adapts better to human anatomy because it captures finer sound field.

Keywords: Beamforming · Finite precision · Adaptative algorithm

1 Introduction

The voice is the main form of communication of the human being. The voice process begins with the thought of a message represented abstractly in the brain of the announcer and through the complex process of voice production, finally the information becomes an acoustic signal.

The voice is characterized for being the combination of several frequencies with their corresponding harmonics. However, compared to the full range of human hearing, which goes from 20 Hz to 20 kHz, the voice covers a relatively small range of frequencies between 100 Hz to 6 kHz.

The voice is a non-stationary signal, but it can be assumed through intervals (small sample blocks) as locally stationary. Intervals between 20 and 30 ms are the most suitable for nearly all applications.

The processing of voice signals, for numerous applications, is related to the analysis of their significant characteristics, for example we can mention the pitch (fundamental tone or frequency of the vocal cord's vibration) and its harmonics (peak spectrum of an audible sound). The male voice has a pitch between 100 and 200 Hz and the female voice is typically between 150 and 300 Hz.

© Springer Nature Switzerland AG 2020
M. Botto-Tobar et al. (Eds.): ICAT 2019, CCIS 1195, pp. 359–375, 2020.
https://doi.org/10.1007/978-3-030-42531-9_29

1.1 Initial Mathematical Analysis

An array of sensors is a set of isotropic elements distributed in each geometry, in order to obtain information of the wave fields in the mean in which they propagate. Sensor arrays allow each sensor to have greater directivity and sensitivity. The most commonly used sensor arrays are the Uniform Linear Array (ULA) and the Uniform Circular Array (UCA).

If you have a flat wave that reaches the point $\vec{r}$ at a time t you get Eq. 1. A flat wave is characterized because it has the same amplitude and phase.

$$s(\mathbf{r}, t) = Ae^{j(\boldsymbol{\beta}.\mathbf{r}-\omega t)} con\left\{\beta = \|\boldsymbol{\beta}\| = \frac{2\pi}{\lambda} = \frac{2\pi}{\vartheta/f}\right. \tag{1}$$

Where A is the wave amplitude, $\boldsymbol{\beta}$ the wave vector (propagation), β wave factor (number of waves), λ is the wavelength, ϑ wave propagation speed, f is the frequency.

The flat wave signal in Eq. 2 is considered to arrive at a ULA array, as shown in Fig. 1, at the position (r_x, r_y, r_z) and up to the origin (0, 0, 0) you have:

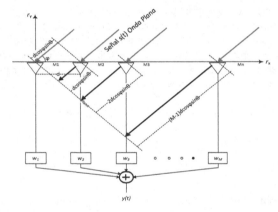

Fig. 1. Uniform Lineal Array ULA. *Source*: (Yang, Cho and Choo 2012)

$$s(\mathbf{r}, t) = s(\mathbf{0}, t)e^{j\beta(r_x \cos\varphi \sin\theta + r_y \cos\varphi \sin\theta + r_z \cos\varphi)} \tag{2}$$

Where φ y θ represent the azimuth angle and the elevation angle respectively.

1.2 Signals Processing

Digital processing of voice signals is an interdisciplinary topic that involves phonetics, physiology, acoustics, among other disciplines, in addition to the theory of digital signal processing. This last one has had a great advance thanks to the development of the digital signal processor's technology, being found innumerable applications in the modern life whether it is in the voice coding, recognition or synthesis. For the development of this implementations, it is used the adaptive algorithms of the Householder family, the unconstrained algorithms NLMS (Normalized Least Mean Squares) and the CG (Conjugate Gradient).

Spatial Filtering or Beamforming is a technique that uses an array of sensors; where the main signal is estimated using linear combinations of the different outputs of each of the array sensors, so that unwanted disturbances coming from different directions are attenuated by the phenomenon of spatial directivity or arrangement selectivity (Fig. 2).

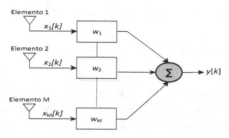

Fig. 2. Narrowband beamforming. Source: (Madisetti 2010)

The study of voice signals is an important issue, since a large part of society has some form of hearing impairment. Hearing disability is considered as those quantitative alterations in a correct perception of hearing. The present implementation seeks to help people with hearing problems, by enhancing the voice; using a semi-spherical arrangement of microphones with the beamforming broadband methodology, that can distinguish signals coming from different directions. It uses a semi-spherical arrangement of microphones that adapts better to human anatomy, and which will allow to better capture the sound field, as studied in the thesis project Acoustic Signal Optimization in a Semi-spherical Microphone Array Using the Beamforming Broadband Methodology.

LCMV adaptive algorithms are divided into three families: Linearly Constrained, such is the case of CLMS (Constrained Least Mean Square), among others. In addition, the GSC structure algorithms (Generalized Sidelobe Canceler) that allows any unconstrained algorithm to be used as constrained. And finally, we have those with Householder structure that through the matrix Q and its Householder's reflectors, they accomplish as the GSC but computationally more efficient.

2 Adaptive Algorithms

LCMV (Linearly Constrained Minimum Variance) adaptive algorithms aim to restrict beamformer in amplitude and output phase to signals coming from one or more directions of no interest. The filter weights are selected in such a way that it minimizes the variance or power of the error subject to a set of linear constraints, as shown in Eq. 3. In Fig. 3 it is shown an adaptive broadband beamforming structure with M sensors y N weights (number of filter coefficients).

$$\min_{\mathbf{w}} \xi[k] \ subject\ to\ a \quad \mathbf{C}^H \mathbf{w} = \mathbf{f} \tag{3}$$

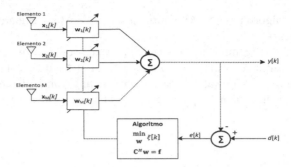

Fig. 3. Adaptive broadband beamforming structure. Source: (Apolinario and de Campos 2014)

Where signal error $e[k]$ is related with the target function $\xi[k] = E\{|e[k]|^2\} = E\{e[k]e^*[k]\}$, **C** is the dimension restriction matrix **MN x p**, being **p** the number of restrictions and **f** the dimension gainance vector **p x 1**.

By imposing linear restrictions, the need for a signal can be often dismissed $d[k] = 0$ LCMV adaptive algorithms are divided into three families: *Linearly Constrained*, with GSC (*Generalized Sidelobe Canceler*) structure, that allows that any *unconstrained* algorithmZZZ be used as constrained and finally there are those of *Householder* structure.

The *Householder* structure is the one with the best performance compared to the other two structures with *unconstrained* NLMS (*Normalized Least Mean Squares*) adaptive algorithms and CG (*Conjugate Gradient*) for the development of this implementation.

The matrix **Q** is an orthogonal rotational matrix that is used as the transformation that will generate a vector of modified coefficient $\overline{w}[k]$ that relates to $w[k]$.

The matrix **Q** should be chosen in such a way that $\mathbf{QQ}^H = \mathbf{I}$.

$$\overline{w}[k] = \mathbf{Q}w[k] \tag{4}$$

$$\overline{\mathbf{C}}\left\{\overline{\mathbf{C}}^H\overline{\mathbf{C}}\right\}^{-1}\overline{\mathbf{C}}^H = \begin{bmatrix} \mathbf{I}_{p\times p} & \mathbf{0} \\ \mathbf{0} & \mathbf{0} \end{bmatrix} \tag{5}$$

Then $\overline{\mathbf{C}} = \mathbf{QC}$ satisfies $\mathbf{f} = \overline{\mathbf{C}}^H\overline{w}[k+1]$ and the projection matrix transformation is given by:

$$\overline{\mathbf{P}} = \mathbf{QPQ}^H = \mathbf{I} - \overline{\mathbf{C}}\left\{\overline{\mathbf{C}}^H\overline{\mathbf{C}}\right\}^{-1}\overline{\mathbf{C}}^H = \begin{bmatrix} \mathbf{0}_{p\times p} & \mathbf{0} \\ \mathbf{0} & \mathbf{I} \end{bmatrix} \tag{6}$$

If $\overline{w}[0]$ is initialized according to

$$\overline{w}[0] = \overline{\mathbf{C}}\left\{\overline{\mathbf{C}}^H\overline{\mathbf{C}}\right\}^{-1}\mathbf{f} = \mathbf{QF} \tag{7}$$

The first p elements of $\overline{w}[0]$ don't need to be updated. The solution $\overline{w}[k]$ is based on the transformation **Q** to the output signal and therefore the output error is not modified by the transformation.

The HNCLMS algorithm has a slow speed of convergence and its computational cost is low $(2p + 3)N - (p^2 + p - 1)$, so the algorithm becomes desirable for the implementation on devices with limited hardware capabilities.

The HCCG algorithm has a fast convergence and its computational cost $(3N^2 + (10 - 4p)N + p^2 - 8p + 2)$ is higher compared to the HNCLMS algorithm one, so it is desirable when its implementation on a hardware has abundant resources.

2.1 Calculations in Finite Precision

In a digital implementation of an adaptive filtering algorithm, the input data and internal calculations of the algorithm are performed with finite precision, and the cost of digital implementation of an algorithm is influenced by the number of bits (precision) available to perform numerical calculations associated with the algorithm.

The simulation will be done with the Matlab® tool that emulates the operation of finite precision; working with the number of bits with which the hardware works, in this case of 16 bits. The simulation will be performed for 8, 12 and 16 bits.

The theory of adaptive filtering considers that all variables involved in calculations and input signals can be represented in finite precision, thus facilitating mathematical analysis, but the practical implementation in digital signal processors is limited by the number of bits that can be used in internal mathematical calculations and the accuracy with which the values used are stored.

In a digital implementation of an adaptive filter there are essentially two sources of quantization errors to be considered:

- Analogue Conversion – digital
- Finite length of word arithmetic

Analogue Conversion/Digital
The analogue-digital conversion (A/D) can be visualized by an ideal continuous-discrete converter (C/D), followed by a quantizer. The quantization operation will be represented by:

$$\bar{x}[k] = Q\{x[k]\} \tag{8}$$

Where the operator $Q\{.\}$ performs a non-linear rounding operation of the value of $x[k]$ for the nearest quantization level. The spacing of quantization levels defines the step of quantization, uniform or not uniform. For example, a 3-bit uniform quantization is seen in Fig. 4. It is noted that the 3 bits correspond to $2^3 = 8$ levels of quantization. In addition, it is shown on the figure that $x(k) > \frac{7\Delta}{2}$ or $x(k) = \frac{-9\Delta}{2}$, is going to have a saturation. In digital signal processing, we have an output to the A/D converter, value belonging to one of the possible quantization levels, represented according to a numbering system.

The quantization introduces an error (quantization error) defined by:

$$e[k] = x[k] - \bar{x}[k] \tag{9}$$

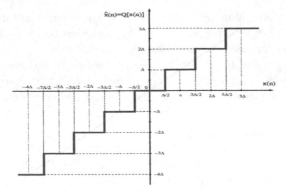

Fig. 4. 3 bits quantification examples

So that, in the case of an example of uniform quantization, there is no saturation (overflow) $-\Delta/2 \leq e(k) \leq \Delta/2$.

The average error is zero, and its variance is given by:

$$\sigma_e^2 = \frac{\Delta^2}{12} = \frac{4X_m^2 2^{-2\#}}{12} = \frac{X_m^2 2^{-2(\#-1)}}{12} \tag{10}$$

Where # is the bits numbers.

2.2 Programming

The Matlab® simulation tool works internally with a high numerical accuracy of 32 or 64 bits. In this project the implementation hardware a FPGA NI myRIO works with 16 bits, so to carry out finite precision analysis it is used the qround function, which emulates the nearest integer.

The ground function will allow to quantify the decimal part of each variable by rounding b bits, as can be seen below.

function Vq = qround(V,b)

  Vq = 2^(-b)*round(V*2^b);

end

3   Results Analysis

By varying the number of bits between 8, 12 and 16 for the HNCLMS algorithm, the MSE starts to suffer variations, so as the number of bits increases the HNCLMS algorithm presents a better performance, decreasing its MSE, as can be seen in Fig. 5.

Figure 6 shows the behavior of the HCCG algorithm by varying the size of bits from 8, 12 and 16. In the HCCG algorithm, its performance varies with the increasing of bit size, as its MSE starts to decrease, the number of bits increases.

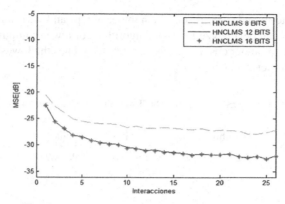

Fig. 5. HNCLMS algorithm for different bits sizes

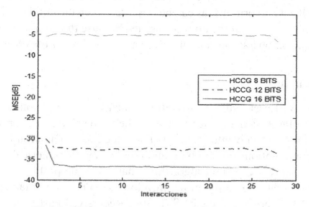

Fig. 6. HNCLMS algorithm for different bits sizes

3.1 Comparison of Results

As mentioned, the cost of digital implementation is influenced by the number of bits available to perform numerical calculations associated with the algorithm. For the algorithms to be implemented, the computational complexity of the algorithms is given by the number of multiplications detailed in Table 1.

Table 1. Computational cost of LCMV algorithms

Algorithm	
NLMS	$(2p + 3)N - (p^2 + p - 1)$
CG	$3N^2 + (10 - 4p)N + p^2 - 8p + 2$

Where N is determined to represent the number of taps and p the number of restrictions. In Table 2, it can be analyzed that the algorithms of lower computational cost are NLMS and the one of higher cost is CG. The structure that has the lowest computational cost is the Householder.

Table 2. MSE in dB for HNCLMS and HCCG algorithms

Algorithm	8 bits	12 bits	16 bits
HNCLMS	−26.0071	−29.6076	−29.6826
HCCG	−5.1213	−32.3649	−36.4347

Table 2 presents a summary of the MSE for the different bit numbers used for the HNCLMS and HCCG algorithms, as can be observed when the number of bits increases the MSE is smaller for each of the algorithms, and because the number of bits is smaller there is an increase in operations and therefore a propagation of the error.

3.2 Lattice Structure

The RLS (Recursive Least Squares) algorithm which, compared to other adaptive algorithms, presents a faster convergence rate and a better response in the presence of disturbance, but with the disadvantage that its hardware implementation is quite difficult due to its high computational complexity and problems with numerical stability.

Theoretically there are several algorithms that solve the problem of least squares recursively. In particular, the Lattice structure allows to reduce computational complexity (in the order of N). Therefore, the LRLS (Lattice Recursive Least Squares) structure is considered a quick implementation for the RLS algorithm problem.

The LRLS algorithm is a cascade structure based on forward and backward linear prediction filters that allows to describe the properties of the input signal, based on the development of least squares to reduce the quadratic error of the mentioned filters, it also updates the reflection coefficients as a function of time.

The performance of LRLS algorithms when implemented with infinite precision arithmetic is identical to those of any RLS algorithm, but with finite precision arithmetic, each algorithm has a different response.

3.3 Recursive Least-Squares Prediction

Forward and backward RLS predictions are essential to derive the order-updating equations inherent in LRLS algorithms. For both cases the results are obtained by following the derivation procedure of the conventional RLS algorithm, since the only distinguishing feature of the prediction problems is the definition of the reference signal $d[k]$. In the case of forward prediction, you have that $d[k] = x[k]$, while the input signal vector has the sample $x[k-1]$ as the most recent data. For backward prediction $d[k] = x[k-i-1]$, where the index i defines the sample of the past to be predicted and the input vector signal $x[k]$ has as the most recent data.

The goal of forward prediction is to predict a future sample given an input sequence, using the current information of the available sequence. For example, you can try to predict the value $x[k]$ using samples passed as $x[k-1]x[k-2]$ through a FIR prediction filter with $i+1$ coefficient as shown in the following equation:

$$y_f[k, i+1] = \mathbf{w}_f^T[k, i+1]\mathbf{x}[k-1, i+1] \tag{11}$$

Where $y_f[k, i+1]$ is the output prediction signal

$$\mathbf{w}_f[k, i+1] = \{\mathbf{w}_{fo}[k]\mathbf{w}_{f1}[k]\ldots\mathbf{w}_{fi}[k]\}^T \tag{12}$$

This is the vector of forward FIR prediction coefficients

$$\mathbf{x}[k-1, i+1] = \{x[k-1]x[k-2]\ldots x[k-i-1]\}^T \tag{13}$$

$\mathbf{x}[k-1, i+1]$ is the available input signal vector. The second variable included in the vector of Eq. (11) shows the dimension of the vector and is required in the order-updating equations of the LRLS algorithm.

The subsequent instant error of the forward prediction is given by:

$$\boldsymbol{\varepsilon}_f[k, i+1] = x[k] - \mathbf{w}_f^T[k, i+1]\mathbf{x}[k-1, i+1] \tag{14}$$

For the RLS formulation of the forward prediction problem, the next prediction weighted error vector is defined as:

$$\boldsymbol{\varepsilon}_f[k, i+1] = \hat{\mathbf{x}}[k] - \mathbf{X}^T[k-1, i+1]\mathbf{w}_f[k, i+1] \tag{15}$$

Where:

$$\hat{\mathbf{x}}[k] = \left\{x[k]\lambda^{1/2}x[k-1]\lambda x[k-2]\ldots\lambda^{k/2}x[0]\right\}^T \tag{16}$$

$$\boldsymbol{\varepsilon}_f[k, i+1] = \left\{\varepsilon_f[k, i+1]\lambda^{1/2}\varepsilon_f[k-1, i+1]\lambda\varepsilon_f[k-2, i+1]\ldots\lambda^{k/2}\varepsilon_f[0, i+1]\right\}^T \tag{17}$$

$$[k-1, i+1]$$
$$= \begin{bmatrix} x[k-1] & \lambda^{1/2}x[k-2] & \cdots & \lambda^{[k-2]/2}x[1] & \lambda^{[k-1]/2}x[0] & 0 & 0 \\ x[k-2] & \lambda^{1/2}x[k-3] & \cdots & -\lambda^{[k-2]/2}x[0] & 0 & 0 & 0 \\ \vdots & \vdots & \vdots & \vdots & \vdots & \vdots & \vdots \\ x[k-i-1] & \lambda^{1/2}[k-i-2] & \cdots & 0 & 0 & 0 & 0 \end{bmatrix} \tag{18}$$

The error vector $\boldsymbol{\varepsilon}_f[k, i+1]$ can be defined as:

$$\boldsymbol{\varepsilon}_f[k, i+1] = \mathbf{x}^T[k, i+2]\left\{\begin{matrix} 1 \\ -\mathbf{w}_f[k, i+1] \end{matrix}\right\} \tag{19}$$

The objective function to be minimized in the forward prediction problem is given by:

$$\xi_f^d[k, i+1] = \mathbf{e}_f^T[k, i+1]\boldsymbol{\varepsilon}_f[k, i+1] \tag{20}$$

$$\xi_f^d[k, i + 1] = \sum_{i=0}^{k} \lambda^{k-1} \mathbf{e}_f^2[l, i + 1] \tag{21}$$

$$\xi_f^d[k, i + 1] = \sum_{l=0}^{k} \lambda^{k-1} \left\{ x[l] - \mathbf{x}^T[l - 1, i + 1]\mathbf{w}_f[k, i + 1] \right\}^2 \tag{22}$$

The optimal solution for the coefficient vector is:

$$\mathbf{w}_f[k, i + 1] = \mathbf{R}_{Df}^{-1}[k - 1, i + 1]\mathbf{p}_{Df}[k, i + 1] \tag{23}$$

Where $\mathbf{R}_{Df}[k - 1, i + 1]$ is equal to deterministic correlation matrix $\mathbf{R}_D[k - 1]$ of order $i + 1$ y $\mathbf{p}_{Df}[k, i + 1]$ is the deterministic vector of cross-correlation between $x[l]$ and $\mathbf{x}[l - 1, i + 1]$.

The minimum value of $\xi_f^d[k]$ is given by:

$$\xi_{fmin}^d[k, i + 1] = \sigma_f^2[k] - \mathbf{w}_f^T[k, i + 1]\mathbf{p}_{Df}[k, i + 1] \tag{24}$$

Combining Eqs. 23 and 24 you obtain:

$$\mathbf{R}_D[k, i + 2] \begin{bmatrix} 1 \\ -\mathbf{w}_f[k, i + 1] \end{bmatrix} = \begin{bmatrix} \xi_{fmin}^d[k, i + 1] \\ 0 \end{bmatrix} \tag{25}$$

Where $\mathbf{R}_D[k, i + 2]$ is equal to $\mathbf{R}_D[k]$ of dimension $i + 2$. The previous equation refers to the deterministic order correlation matrix $i + 2$.

The purpose of the return prediction is to generate an estimate of a past sample of a given input sequence, using the current available sequence information

$$y_b[k, i + 1] = \mathbf{w}_b^T[k, i + 1]\mathbf{x}[k, i + 1] \tag{26}$$

Where $y_b[k, i + 1]$ is return prediction output signal, and

$$\mathbf{w}_b^T[k, i + 1] = \{w_{b0}[k]w_{b1}[k] \ldots w_{bi}[k]\}^T \tag{27}$$

It is the return FIR prediction coefficient vector. The return instant prediction error is given by:

$$\varepsilon_b[k, i + 1] = x[k - i - 1] - \mathbf{w}_b^T[k, i + 1]\mathbf{x}[k, i + 1] \tag{28}$$

The weighted backward error vector is represented by:

$$\varepsilon_b[k, i + 1] = \hat{\mathbf{x}}[k] - \mathbf{X}^T[k - 1, i + 1]\mathbf{w}_b[k, i + 1] \tag{29}$$

Where:

$$\hat{\mathbf{x}}[k - i - 1] = \left\{ x[k - i - 1]\lambda^{1/2}x[k - i - 2] \ldots \lambda^{[k-i-1]/2}x[0]0 \ldots 0 \right\}^T \tag{30}$$

$$\varepsilon_b[k, i + 1] = \left\{ \varepsilon_b[k, i + 1]\lambda^{1/2}\varepsilon_b[k - 1, i + 1] \ldots \lambda^{k/2}\varepsilon_b[0, i + 1] \right\}^T \tag{31}$$

$$\mathbf{x}[k, i+1] = \begin{bmatrix} x[k] & \lambda^{1/2}x[k-1] & \cdots & \lambda^{(k-1/2)}x[1] & \lambda^{(k)/2}x[0] \\ x[k-1] & \lambda^{1/2}x[k-2] & \cdots & -\lambda^{[k-2]/2}x[0] & 0 \\ \vdots & \vdots & \vdots & \vdots & \vdots \\ x[k-i] & \lambda^{1/2}[k-i-1] & \cdots & 0 & 0 \end{bmatrix} \tag{32}$$

The error vector $\varepsilon_b[k, i+1]$ can be defined as:

$$\varepsilon_b[k, i+1] = \mathbf{X}^T[k, i+2]\left\{ \begin{matrix} -\mathbf{w}_b\lfloor k, i+1\rfloor\} \\ 1 \end{matrix} \right\} \tag{33}$$

The objective function to be minimized in the return prediction problem is shown as:

$$\xi_b^d[k, i+1] = \sum_{l=0}^{k} \lambda^{k-1}\left\{ x[l-i-1] - \mathbf{x}^T[l, i+1]\mathbf{w}_b[k, i+1] \right\}^2 \tag{34}$$

The optimal solution for the coefficient vector is:

$$\mathbf{w}_b[k, i+1] = \mathbf{R}_{Df}^{-1}[k, i+1]\mathbf{p}_{Df}[k, i+1] \tag{35}$$

Where $\mathbf{R}_{Db}[k, i+1]$ is equal to deterministic correlation matrix $\mathbf{R}_D[k]$ of order $i+1$ and $\mathbf{p}_{Db}[k, i+1]$ is the deterministic vector of cross-correlation between $x[l-i-1]$ and $\mathbf{x}[l, i+1]$.

The minimum value for $\xi_b^d[k]$ is given by:

$$\xi_{bmin}^d[k, i+1] = \sigma_b^2[k] - \mathbf{w}_b^T[k, i+1]\mathbf{p}_{Db}[k, i+1] \tag{36}$$

Combining Eqs. 35 y 36, you get:

$$\mathbf{R}_D[k, i+2]\begin{bmatrix} -\mathbf{w}_b\lfloor k, i+1\rfloor \\ 1 \end{bmatrix} = \begin{bmatrix} o \\ \xi_{bmin}^d[k, i+1] \end{bmatrix} \tag{37}$$

Where $\mathbf{R}_D[k, i+2]$ is equal to $\mathbf{R}_D[k]$ of dimensions $i+2$. The above equation refers to the deterministic order correlation matrix $i+1$.

4   Algorithm Implementation

A microphone serves as an acoustic sensor to record audio signals and monitor sounds levels. MEMS ADMP504 microphones were used for this project. The ADMP504 consists of a MEMS microphone element, an impedance converter and an output amplifier. The sensitivity specification makes it an excellent choice for both near field and far field applications. The ADMP504 has very high signal/noise ratio and extended broadband frequency response, resulting in a natural sound with ba high intelligibility (Figs. 7 and 8).

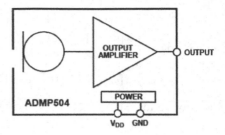

Fig. 7. Microphone MEMS ADMP504   **Fig. 8.** Functional microphone MEMS ADMP504 block diagram

4.1 Data Acquisition

The response of the microphones used in this project was evaluated. The array of sensors must have an isotropic behavior.

For the analysis we performed a ULA arrangement that complies with the Nyquist theorem, where the sampling frequency is greater than or equal to twice the maximum component of signal frequency and thus avoid aliasing (overlap) frequently. The overlap occurs when the separation between the microphones is not correct, causing the microphones to be unable to differentiate the incoming signals from different directions.

Based on the Nyquist criterion, 4 microphones were used equidistant between them by 0.1 m. in front of a source that casts AWGN signals that by its mathematical characteristics its spectrum covers all frequencies spaced to 1 m. relative to the microphone array and 90 to a microphone to which we will nominate M4, as shown in Fig. 9.

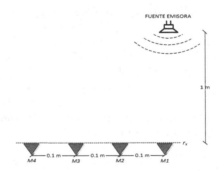

Fig. 9. Microphone ULA arrangement

4.2 NI myRIO 1900 Card Technical Specifications

It has aCortex™-A9 dual core processor of real-time performance and customized I/O, taking advantage of the default FPGA configuration, which they can customize according to the projects, by means of their components internal data, access to transparent software and resource library. Programable with Labview, C or adaptable.

4.3 Construction of the MEMS Microphone Interface Circuit

The amplifier circuit for microphones is constructed as seen in Fig. 10, where the microphone output signal will be connected directly to the analog MXP inputs of the NI myRIO card.

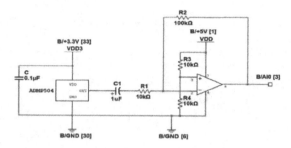

Fig. 10. MEMS microphone circuit with Analog Input (AI)

4.4 Interface with NI Labview

Data acquisition will be done from the FPGA card. A FPGA.vi file is generated where analog inputs are created for the 4 microphones that are connected (Fig. 11).

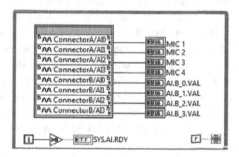

Fig. 11. Analogous entries for data acquisition in the FPGA

The data acquisition must be executed at 8000 Hz, which is no more than the voice encoding process, using the Timed Loop icon that executes each loop iteration in the period specified in this case.

Data acquired at a constant rate ($125\,\mu s$) will be displayed using the Waveform Chart icon, which is a numerical indicator that maintains a data history.

$$\text{history length} = 8000\,\text{samples/s} \times 40\,\text{s} = 320,000\,\text{samples} \tag{38}$$

4.5 Frequency Microphone Response Interface

Frequency microphone responses are presented in Fig. 12, where the behavior of microphones is seen to be different. In order to compensate for the differences between the microphones used in their manufacture, the system identification structure is applied and the M1 is used as a reference.

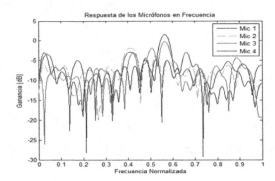

Fig. 12. Frequency microphone response for a ULA array

Because the signals were not acquired in an anechoic cabin (a room designed to absorb all reflections produced by acoustic or electromagnetic waves on any of the surfaces forming it (floor, ceiling and side walls), in turn, the camera is isolated from the outside of any external noise source or sound influence) is executed the RLS algorithm to obtain the same reference signal that is acquired by taking the white noise signal as a signal desired and the input signal of the M1 microphone, this acquired signal is the reference signal for M2, M3 and M4 in the system identification structure.

By offsetting the delay of the signals, which occur due to the hardware, processing and propagation of the signal, it is seen in Fig. 13 that the response of the microphones in frequency has changed and the behavior between them is similar. The identification structure of the system generates the coefficients with which a transfer function is estimated to perform the equalization of the channel and thus compensate for the linear distortion caused by the channel.

NI myRIO is an embedded hardware specifically designed to develop advanced engineering systems more quickly. NI myRIO has a fully programmable dual-core ARM Cortex-A9 processor that runs a real-time OS, as well as a FPGA. The system identification structure generates the coefficients with which a transfer function will be estimated to perform the equalization of the channel and thus compensate for the linear distortion caused by the channel.

The MSE is further illustrated in Fig. 14 where the two algorithms are represented with all interactions, it can be observed how the algorithms converge reaching the HNCLMS algorithm an average MSE of -28.8352 dB, while the HCCG algorithm reaches an MSE lower than -33.8471 dB. Figure 14 shows the beampattern of the HNCLMS and HCCG algorithms, according to this figure the angle obtained matches the input signal of $90°$. The two algorithms have a high resolution.

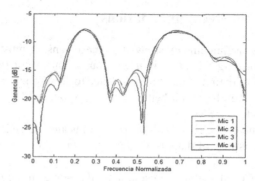

Fig. 13. Frequency microphone compensated response for a ULA arrangement

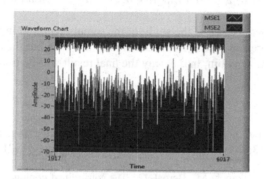

Fig. 14. Comparison of Householder algorithms to MSE

The HCCG algorithm has a high performance and this can be corroborated when comparing the beampattern, as can be seen in Fig. 15, in which the gain of the HCCG algorithm is acceptable.

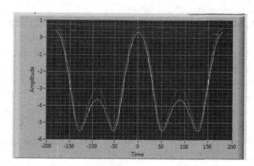

Fig. 15. Comparison of Householder algorithms to the beampattern for a semi-spherical array

5 Conclusions and Recommendations

The theory of sensors arrangements shows that these sensors must have an isotropic behavior, when performing the analysis it was found that in practical cases does not comply; this is typical of their manufacture, attributed to the physical-chemical properties of the materials used, therefore their behavior was approximated by the equalization of the same, taking as reference Mic 1.

The execution time of the HCCG algorithm is 8 ms and the HCNLMS algorithm is 6 ms; due to the acquisition of data, processing of signals, algorithms executed in the Matlab Math Scrip.

The NLMS and CG algorithms present a similar value in their MSE and a good execution when performing graph analysis. However, it should be considered that the HCNLMS algorithm has a shorter run time because its algorithm has a smaller number of operations.

It is recommended to extend the study of the signals acquired in a suitable environment, since in the present research AWGN signals are used but these signals were not acquired in an anechoic cabin, in this way the final result will be improved.

References

1. Agilent EEsof EDA Software: Herramienta Advanced Design System. Recuperado el 7 de Agosto de 2013 (2000). http://www.home.agilent.com/en/pc-1297113/advanced-design-system
2. Apolinário, J., de Campos, M., Bernal, C.: The constrained conjugate gradient algorithm. IEEE Signal Process. Lett. **7**(12) (2000)
3. Papoulis, A., Pillai, U.: Probability, Random Variables and Stochastic Processes. International Edition. McGraw-Hill, New York (2002)
4. Apolinário, J.: Processamento Digital de Sinais. Bookman Editora, São Paulo (2003)
5. Apolinário, J.A.: QDR-RLS Adaptive Filtering. Springer, Boston (2009). https://doi.org/10.1007/978-0-387-09734-3
6. Apolinario, J., de Campos, M.: Instituto Militar de Engenharia. Recuperado el 21 de 12 de 2014 (2011). http://aquarius.ime.eb.br/~apolin
7. Benesty, J., Chen, J., Huang, Y.: Microphone Array Signal Processing. Springer, Heidelberg (2008). https://doi.org/10.1007/978-3-540-78612-2
8. Bernal Oñate, C.: Principios y Aplicaciones de CDMA "Code Division multiple access" con implementación de algoritmos para la detección de multiusuarios. Tesis, Quito (2000)
9. Bernal, P., Sáenz, F., Romero, C.: Análisis de Señales Acústicas. Departamento de Eléctrica y Electrónica, Universidad de las Fuerzas Armadas ESPE (2014)
10. Caisapanta, A.: Optimización de las señales acústicas en un arreglo semiesférico de micrófonos utilizando la metodología de beamforming de banda ancha. ESPE, Quito (2015)
11. Chandran, S.: Adaptive Antenna Arrays Trends and Applications. Springer, Heidelberg (2004). https://doi.org/10.1007/978-3-662-05592-2
12. de Campos, M., Werner, S., Apolinário, J.: Constrained adaptation algorithms employing householder transformation. IEEE Trans. Signal Process. **50**(9), 9 (2002)
13. Diniz, P.: Adaptive Filtering: Algorithms and Practical Implementation, 4th edn. Springer, Rio de Janeiro (2013). https://doi.org/10.1007/978-1-4614-4106-9
14. Golub, G., Van Loan, C.: Matrix Computations, 4th edn. The Johns Hopkins University Press, Baltimore (2013)

15. Gundersen, K., Hakon Husoy, J.: Preconditioner structures for the CLMS adaptive filtering algorithm. In: IEEE (2006)
16. Huang, Z., Balanis, C.: Adaptive beamforming using spherical array. In: IEEE (2005)
17. Liu, W., Weiss, S.: Wideband Beamforming: Concepts and Techniques. Wiley, Chichester (2010)
18. Madisetti, V.: The Digital Signal Processing Handbook, 2nd edn. Taylor and Francis Group, LLC, Boca Raton (2010)
19. Medina, C.A., Rodríguez, C.V., Apolinário, J.A., León, R.D.: Implementación de un arreglo superdirectivo de micrófonos con múltiples líneas de retardo. Quito (2000)
20. Monzingo, R., Haupt, R., Miller, T.: Introduction to Adaptive Arrays, 2nd edn. SciTech Publishing Inc, Raleigh (2011)
21. Rabiner, L., Schafer, R.W.: Theory and Application of Digital Speech Processing. Prentice Hall, Englewood Cliffs (2009)
22. Sansaloni, T., Valls, J.: Simulador de Sistemas Digitales de Preisión Finita (2000)
23. Valle, S. d.: Manual Práctico de Acústica, Terceira edn. Música & Tecnología, Rio de Janeiro (2009)
24. Van Veen, B., Buckley, K.: Beamforming Techniques for Spatial Filtering. CRCnetBASE (2000)
25. Werner, S., Apolinário, J., de Campos, M.L.R.: On the Equivalence of the Constrained RLS and the GSC-RLS Beamformers. Helsinki University of Technology, Instituto Militar de Engenharia, and Universidade Federal do Rio de Janeiro (s.f.)

e-Learning

Assignment of Groups for the Execution of a Collaborative Work Using Emerging Algorithms

Dunia Inés Jara-Roa[1](✉), María-Soledad Ramírez-Montoya[2](✉), Marcos Cabezas G.[3](✉), and Luis Barba-Guamán[1](✉)

[1] Universidad Técnica Particular de Loja, San Cayetano Alto, Loja, Ecuador
{dijara,lrbarba}@utpl.edu.ec
[2] Tecnologico de Monterrey, Avda. Garza Sada 2501 Sur. Col Tec. Monterrey, Monterrey, Mexico
solramirez@tec.mx
[3] Universidad de Salamanca, Paseo de Canalejas 169, 37008 Salamanca, Spain
mcabezasgo@usal.es

Abstract. In educational institutions collaborative work is used as a strategy to enhance active learning. One of the organizational tasks that is in charge of the teacher is the assignment of groups. Hence the purpose of this article, which is to show how emerging algorithms with their self-organization characteristics, can be used in group formation to carry out a collaborative task. Showing that performance and small groups do not necessarily go hand in hand. The methodology used is a case study and the sample corresponds to 62 students of the subject of Artificial Intelligence of Distance Modality of the Universidad Técnica Particular de Loja, in the academic period April-August/2018, to whom a dichotomous 16-item survey was applied based on the three phases of the Zimmerman self-regulated learning cycle. Among the remarkable results, we can mention that the synergy of individual regulation known as socially shared regulation influenced the execution of the collaborative task. Likewise, the cohesion of a group is not a determining variable to achieve meaningful learning since the less cohesion the greater regulation of socially shared learning. The contribution of the present study is given in the field of Computer Supported Cooperative Learning (CSCL) to alleviate one of the administrative tasks of teachers "Group Assignment", which can be replicated in classroom learning environments or in any of the variations of e-learning.

Keywords: Emerging algorithms · Self-regulation · Group assignment

1 Introduction

Society is a set of living beings that relate to each other in order to achieve an objective; to keep it in balance, it is essential that standards of organization and behavior are established. Societies within the animal kingdom show to us like human beings how working together leads to better results than individual work. One of them is the ant

© Springer Nature Switzerland AG 2020
M. Botto-Tobar et al. (Eds.): ICAT 2019, CCIS 1195, pp. 379–390, 2020.
https://doi.org/10.1007/978-3-030-42531-9_30

society. In these societies the communication is carried out by means of a chemical called pheromone that is a chemical signal deposited in the soil that informs the physiological state, reproductive, social, age, sex and even the possible relationship with the issuer [1].

Optimization based on ant colonies constitutes a metaheuristic, with the understanding that metaheuristics allows us to find the best solution, in the shortest time, to optimization problems [2]. The metaheuristics of ant colonies are inspired by the behavior of ants to find the shortest paths between food sources and anthill [3]. Ants move between food sources and the anthill following the pheromone trail, if there is no trace, they move randomly; the choice that ants make between the different paths to follow, constitutes a probabilistic decision biased by the amount of pheromone, The stronger the trail, the greater the probability of choosing it [4].

Among other features of the nonlinear model present in ants, according to [5] are:

- The idea of fork;
- The basic interaction scheme;
- Synchronization of activities;
- The size of the colonies.

The characteristics indicated are fundamental for the emergent behavior of the ants; therefore, they constitute a fundamental part of the theory of emerging systems. The term emergency, in its basic definition, is applicable to those properties of a complex system that arise from a certain level of complexity [6]. The emerging models of the ant colony are: food search, division of labor, recruitment (nest migration), organization of the environment (nest building, etc.), aggregation (graveyard, breeding classification), and transportation of objects.

Given the nature of the article, the aggregation model (graveyard, offspring classification) is described, "Aggregation processes have a relevant role in the emergence of cooperation processes and assignment of tasks in the colonies. The phenomenon of aggregation is of particular interest, because it is a prerequisite for the development of other forms of cooperation in an insect society. [...] but really how do these patterns arise? For example, ants initiate the formation of such patterns by modulating the emission of an attraction signal" [7]. As indicated [8] in the aggregation phenomenon, two dynamics arise: (a) animals are grouped, despite the heterogeneity of the environment, and (b) the group of animals regulates their activities, through social inter-attractions. The metaheuristics of the ant colony aggregation model uses a stochastic scheme, nondeterministic, it plans a process of grouping elements, in which elements that are different from those of their neighbors are or should be isolated by what has been applied to the assignment of work groups for the execution of a collaborative task, where students who have heterogeneous characteristics are removed to form a community of students with similar characteristics considering self-regulation as a differentiating element, those results showed the efficiency of the formation of homogeneous groups for the accomplishment of collaborative tasks.

The sociocultural school, within the theoretical perspectives of the constructivist pedagogical model, argues that when learning one of the most important elements is the socialization of experiences and knowledge. Therefore, one of the best ways to learn is to do it together with others [9], one of the main elements to achieve the effectiveness of computer-assisted collaborative learning - CSCL- is collaboration, but this is not spontaneous, it occurs through motivation and fundamentally the sense of belonging to the group. [10] indicate that collaboration is a process in which the learning context, personality, experience, prior knowledge and learning skills of individual students are interrelated. However, learning is a personal and dynamic process, when the human being needs to learn something new, it is necessary to define the objectives to be achieved and it is through the motivation and monitoring of the cognitive processes that regulates their learning, this process is called learning self-regulation. It is understood that self-regulation is "the control that the subject performs on her thoughts, actions, emotions and motivation through personal strategies to achieve the objectives she has established" [11]. Likewise, [12] mentions that self-regulation is a "process formed by self-generated thoughts, emotions and actions that are planned and cyclically adapted to achieve personal goals." Self-regulation or regulation of learning allows the student to be the protagonist of her own learning, for this, commitment, reflexive knowledge, responsibility, and above all motivation are required. It is a process that requires coordination and regulation of activities [13]. Socially shared regulation can contribute to the learning achievements of groups if activated at the right time and place [14].

The moment that each of the people is part of a group for the construction of knowledge is fundamental the capacity of regulation of the group known as socially shared regulation, that goes beyond the individual regulations, that is the regulation of learning exercised by the group; in other words, it is the synergy of individual regulations, where the group members act as a collective entity [15]. The regulation of socially shared learning refers to the processes through which the members of the group regulate their activity collectively [16]. This type of regulation reciprocally depends on interdependent or collectively shared regulations of processes, beliefs and knowledge available at the service of a shared or co-constructed result [17]. The regulation of socially shared learning supports to carry out, maintain and regulate productive collaboration processes leading to significant learning.

However, each of the members of the group must be aware of their cognitive, social, motivational and emotional aspects, identifying the way in which they learn alone, with others or from others. In the process of social regulation it is assumed that metacognitive processes must be systematically observed or measured in such a way that when the group of students perceive a discrepancy between where they are (individually or collectively) and where they pretend to be, an opportunity arises to strategically change thinking, feelings or actions [...] it is argued that success in achieving CSCL depends on (a) self-regulation skills and strategies; (b) temporary assistance established among themselves to facilitate self-regulation competence within the group (co-regulation); and (c) collective learning regulation such as metacommunicative awareness, regulation of shared motivation, and successful coordination of strategies (shared regulation) [18].

Each member of the group has the responsibility to regulate her learning; likewise, each member of the group supports the other members of the group to regulate her own learning and the group regulates the learning processes in a continuous and productive way towards the achievement of the group objectives; for this to happen, it is important to know the individual and group strategies and goals. To this [16], they add that the shared social regulation of learning has three basic principles: (1) increased student awareness of her own learning process and the one from others, (2) support in the learning process by performing her own tasks and/or the tasks from others, thus helping to share and interact, and (3) causing the acquisition and activation of regulatory processes.

For the realization of the virtual collaborative task, one of the organizational tasks that the teacher has, is the formation of groups. [19] indicate that a virtual group is a defined set of students (3 to 5 members) who work in an interdependent, coordinated and committed manner in a shared virtual environment to achieve a common goal. To this [20] they add that the groups must be heterogeneous and that "performance and small groups go hand by hand" (p. 9). For [21]; as well as for [22] there are three typical ways of organizing groups; like this: puzzle, star and chain; in the puzzle, the tasks are divided, it is established who does what and when? they decide which activities or aspects are divided, and appoint a person in charge to join the contributions and develop a unique product among the different contributions. In the star organization, each of the participants resolves the issue of collaborative work to later jointly develop a unique product. In the chain organization, one of the members of the group makes a partial, initial or final contribution of the task solution and puts it to the group's consideration, then together they ratify, rectify, aggregate, negotiate the task solution.

While [23] they mention that generally the learning groups are ad-hoc and that they are initially ineffective since they lack mutual trust in not knowing their competencies, these groups [24] are called low-familiarity groups or zero-history groups, in which dialogue, agreements, negotiation disagreements, and therefore the construction of knowledge is slower, in contrast to the groups of high level of familiarity where group norms, exploratory criteria, communication and social construction of knowledge occurs in less time. The group development models can be progressive, cyclic and non-sequential linear, the definition and stages can be observed in [25].

Groups usually have their own rules, [26] indicates that there are rules that are important to consider: "Expect that those who participate in the group have a good mood [...]; the group coordinator must be aware of what the group technique marks [...]; clearly define what the purpose is to carry out a specific technique [...]; they need to be actively involved [...]; once the technique is decided it must be respected [...]; the techniques must be studied and its risks assessed in advance [...]" (p. 5).

From the observation, there are several criteria for the organization of groups, but there is a lack of research in which reference is made to the results of learning processes with the assignment, conformation or distribution of groups, hence the hypothesis of the present research is: the use of emerging algorithms for the assignment of groups in the execution of a collaborative task, allows us to consider self-regulation as a differentiating element to produce better learning.

2 Materials and Methods

The research design is a case study in which the class of Artificial Intelligence was chosen included in the eighth cycle of the micro curriculum of the Computer Science Program of Distance Modality of the Universidad Técnica Particular Loja, in the academic period April-August/2018. The participants were 82 students from class A (50) and B (32) to whom a 16-item dichotomous survey was developed in Suverymonkey. The survey was constructed based on the three phases of the self-regulated learning cycle of [12] that is: previous phase, completion phase and reflection phase (Table 1).

Table 1. Survey summary considering Zimmerman's self-regulated learning cycle

Phases	Nro. items	Indicator
Previous phase	Two ítems	(Planning and time allocation)
Realization phase	Ten ítems	(Information search, regulation of actions towards goals, strategies to address the task, defense of their points of view, cognitive altruism, mental images, argumentation, focus of attention)
Reflection phase	Four ítems	(Periodic self-evaluation, final self-evaluation, strategy evaluation, satisfaction/dissatisfaction reactions)

The survey was taken by 27 students from class A and 25 students from class B, in order to apply the ant colony aggregation mode, the responses to the survey are tabulated with the following values 1 = Yes, 0 = No. So Table 2:

Table 2. Sample tabulation of responses to survey items

Stu-id	Time	Search	Processes	Goals	Regulation	Learning	Attention	Reflection	Defend	...
1	1	1	1	1	1	1	1	1	0	
2	1	1	0	0	0	1	1	1	1	
3	1	1	0	1	1	1	1	0	1	
4	0	1	0	0	1	1	1	0	1	
5	1	1	1	1	1	1	1	1	1	
6	1	1	1	0	1	0	0	1	1	
7	1	1	1	0	1	0	1	1	1	
8	1	1	1	1	1	1	1	1	0	
9	1	1	0	0	1	0	1	1	1	
10	1	0	1	1	0	1	0	1	1	
...										

For the present article, the results presented correspond to class A, in which the following options were obtained when using metaheuristics Tables 3, 4 and 5:
Option 1: Group
Report; open class.csv (Ecs1); 27 individuals
K1 = 0.0; K2 = 0.3; Threshold1 = 0.0; Threshold2 = 0.3

Table 3. Result of the first grouping

Community	Individuals	Total individuals
Community 1	26; 23; 24; 5; 13	5
Community 2	3; 16; 19; 14; 12; 1; 8	7
Community 3	21; 4; 15; 9; 7; 25; 22	7
Community 4	6; 2; 18; 11; 20; 17; 10; 27	8

Option 2: Group
Report; open class.csv (Ecs1); 27 individuals
K1 = 0.0; K2 = 0.5; Threshold1 = 0.0; Threshold2 = 0.2

Table 4. Result of the second grouping

Community	Individuals	Total individuals
Community 1	24; 23; 22; 12; 17	5
Community 2	1; 11; 5; 16	4
Community 3	27; 18; 26; 9; 2; 10; 7; 6	8
Community 4	15; 21; 4; 14	4
Community 5	20; 3; 13; 19; 8; 25	6

Opción 3: Group
Report; open class.csv (Ecs1); 27 individuals
K1 = 0.0; K2 = 0.6; Threshold1 = 0.0; Threshold2 = 0.2

Table 5. Result of the third grouping

Community	Individuals	Total individuals
Community 1	25; 24; 23; 22; 20; 17	6
Community 2	15	1
Community 3	19; 13; 3; 5; 8; 11	6
Community 4	16; 1	2
Community 5	4; 14; 6; 7; 21	5

The values of the grouping metric are called cohesion and separation [8, 27]. When applying grouping metric definitions, you can select the best form of team grouping, bearing in mind that the cohesion is the lowest and separation is the highest; therefore, of the three options, option 1 was chosen, since the cohesion level is 0 and the separation level is 3.

3   Results

The levels of cohesion and separation of each of the communities of option 1 are presented below (Fig. 1):

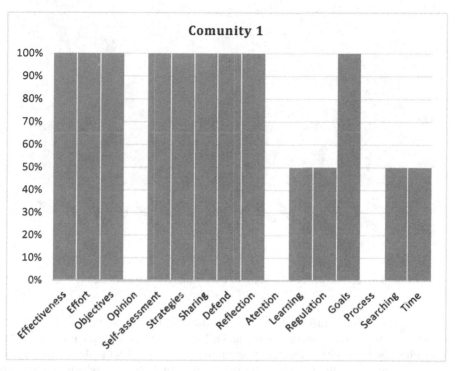

Fig. 1. Answers to the items of the community questionnaire 1.

As shown in community one, we have 100% cohesion in the response of 9 items, 50% cohesion in four items; likewise, there is a separation in three items, one oriented to the previous phase (management of mental processes towards the achievement of goals), and two in the phase of realization (argumentation of opinions and attention to relevant things).

In the community 2, there are 9 items answered with 100%, there two items with the answers with 80%, three items with answers with 65% and two items with answers of 50%, both oriented to the reflection phase (attention to relevant things and reflection on dense or difficult topics) (Fig. 2).

From what can be observed in community 3, there are six items that have 100% cohesion, four items with a cohesion over 70%, two items with 50% one oriented to the reflection phase (periodic verification of the scope of the proposed objectives) and the other oriented to the reflection phase (analysis and reflection of dense or difficult texts), three items with 25%, two of them correspond to the previous phase (time organization and management of mental processes to achieve goals), while the other item corresponds

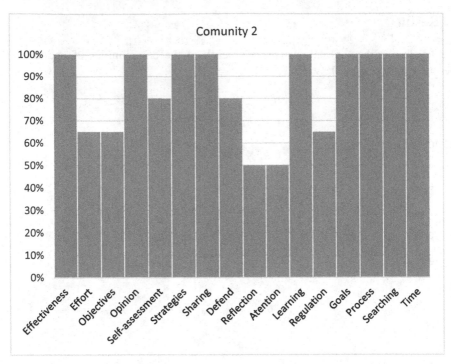

Fig. 2. Answers to the items of the community questionnaire 2.

to the realization phase (information search); likewise, there is an item that marks the level of separation within the community and is located in the realization phase (effort to defend what you know or ask for an explanation of what you do not understand) (Fig. 3).

In this community, the level of cohesion is given by 9 items to which all members respond in affirmative and a separation provided by 7 items, one oriented to the planning phase (time organization), five to the realization phase (periodic verification of the scope of the proposed objectives, argumentation of opinions, availability to share knowledge, analysis and reflection of dense or difficult texts and one to the reflection phase (periodic verification of the scope of the proposed objectives) (Fig. 4).

Once the groups were formed, students were informed about the group to which they belonged; as well as the role they must play within the group. For the execution of the collaborative task that had a period of six months, a star-type organization was made since everyone had to complete the entire activity individually to elaborate subsequently the final product jointly from the individual elaborations.

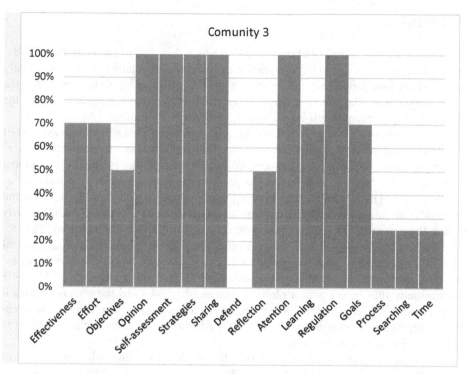

Fig. 3. Answers to the items of the community questionnaire 3.

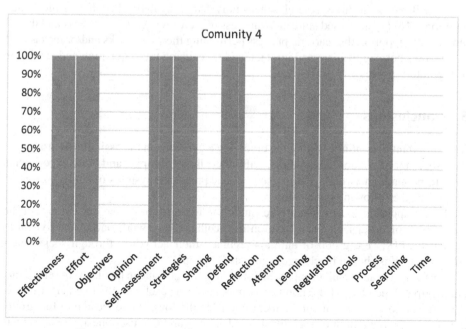

Fig. 4. Answers to the items of the community questionnaire 4.

4   Discussion

Once the academic period of class finished in which they had to carry out the collaborative task, we observed how the synergy of individual regulation known as socially shared regulation influenced the execution of the collaborative task, confirming the study hypothesis: The use of emerging algorithms for group assignment, where the differentiating element is self-regulation allows for better learning.

The community 1 composed of five people, concluded the task with an average of 38.94/40 which means that cohesion in the realization phase was a fundamental element to complete the collaborative task successfully, considering that it began with a global cohesion of the 56.25%, this forced the group to regulate its activity collectively as indicated in [16] mainly in the process of arguing opinions; as well as, in paying attention to the relevant things, since the metacognitive processes must be measured continuously having the opportunity to change thoughts, actions fulfilling what it mentions [18].

Community 2 composed of seven people, completed the task with an average of 33.74/40, a community that began with a global cohesion of 84.68%. Likewise, Community 3 composed of seven people, concluded the task with an average of 35.72/40, a community that began with a global cohesion of 65.94%. In these communities it is observed that in a group of low familiarity the dialogue, the agreements, disagreements, negotiation is slower, therefore, they need more time for the social construction of knowledge, according to [24].

Community 4 composed of eight people completed the task with an average of 37.14/40, started with a global cohesion of 56.25%. in this community it is observed that there were strategies of self-regulation, coregulation and collective regulation according to [18]. Likewise, the three principles of socially shared regulation become visible, which mentions [16] (1) increased student awareness of their own learning process and that of others, (2) support in the learning process performing their own tasks and/or the tasks of others, thus helping to share and interact, and (3) causing the acquisition and activation of regulatory processes.

5   Conclusions

It is important to continue testing the emerging algorithms in the assignment groups for the execution of collaborative works, with many larger samples and these experiments need to be made in virtual, semi presential, and presential systems of study, so we can generalize the following conclusions:

When applying the metaheuristic model of aggregation of the ant colony, in the assignment of groups for the execution of a collaborative work one of the dynamics indicated in [8] "the group of animals regulates their activities, through social inter-attractions", this should be changed animals for people.

Performance and small groups will not necessarily go hand in hand, it is observed that the group independent of the number of members can reach an effective performance. With regard to cohesion, it can be mentioned that the lower the cohesion of the group, the greater the regulation of socially shared learning, and that the cohesion of a group is not a determining variable to achieve meaningful learning.

Regarding Zimmerman's self-regulated learning cycle, it can be mentioned that the indicators of the previous phase and the reflection phase are of personal responsibility and they can be modified in the execution or completion of the collaborative task; meanwhile, the indicators of the realization phase can be changed in the execution of the collaborative task through socially shared regulation.

From the observation, the assignment of groups must not necessarily be composed of three to five people to work in a committed way in a shared virtual environment to achieve a common objective as mentioned [19]. The assignment of groups must not necessarily be composed of three to five people to work in a compromised way in a shared virtual environment to achieve a common goal. The number of people in a group is irrelevant, since the performance of a group does not necessarily depend on the number of members as indicated by several authors.

References

1. Sancho, F.: Algoritmos de hormigas y el problema del viajante (2018). http://www.cs.us.es/~fsancho/?e=71
2. Márquez, M.: Las metaheurísticas : tendencias actuales y su aplicabilidad en la ergonomía, Ing. Ind. Actual. y Nuevas Tendencias, vol. IV, no. 12, pp. 108–120 (2014)
3. Alonso, S., Cordon, O., Fernández de Viana, I., Herrera, F.: La Metaheurística de Optimización Basada en Colonias de Hormigas: Modelos y Nuevos Enfoques, vol. 2014, p. 51 (2003)
4. Goss, S., Aron, S., Deneubourg, J., Pasteels, J.: Self-organized shortcuts in the Argentine ant. Naturwissenschaften **76**(12), 579–581 (1989). https://doi.org/10.1007/BF00462870
5. Depickère, S., Fresneau, D., Deneubourg, J.: A basis for spatial and social patterns in ant species: dynamics and mechanisms of aggregation. J. Insect Behav. **17**(1), 81–97 (2004). https://doi.org/10.1023/B:JOIR.0000025134.06111.be
6. Johnson, S.: Sistemas emergentes. O qué tienen en común hormigas, neuronas, ciudades y software, EURE., vol. 24, no. 101, pp. 142–145 (2008). https://doi.org/10.4067/s0250-71612008000100008
7. Aguilar, J.: Introducción a los Sistemas Emergentes, Primera Ed. Mérida Venezuela: Universidad de Los Andes (2014)
8. De Wolf, T., Holvoet, T.: Using UML 2 activity diagrams to design information flows and feedback-loops in self-organising emergent systems. In: Proceedings of the 2nd International Workshop on Engineering Emergence in Decentralised Autonomic Systems, pp. 52–61 (2007)
9. Erkens, M., Bodemer, D.: Improving collaborative learning: guiding knowledge exchange through the provision of information about learning partners and learning contents. Comput. Educ. **128**, 452–472 (2019). https://doi.org/10.1016/j.compedu.2018.10.009
10. Koivuniemi, M., Järvenoja, H., Järvelä, S.: Teacher education students' strategic activities in challenging collaborative learning situations. Learn. Cult. Soc. Interact. **19**(May), 109–123 (2018). https://doi.org/10.1016/j.lcsi.2018.05.002
11. Panadero, E., Alonso-Tapia, J.: ¿Cómo autorregulan nuestros alumnos? modelo de Zimmerman sobre estrategias de aprendizaje. An. Psicol., vol. 30, no. 2, pp. 450–462 (2014). https://doi.org/10.6018/analesps.30.2.167221
12. Zimmerman, J.: Attaining self-regulation: A social cognitive perspective. In: Self-regulation, pp. 13–40. Academic Press, San Diego, California (2000)
13. Grau, V., Whitebread, D.: Self and social regulation of learning during collaborative activities in the classroom: the interplay of individual and group cognition. Learn. Instr. **22**(6), 401–412 (2012). https://doi.org/10.1016/j.learninstruc.2012.03.003

14. Järvelä, S., Järvenoja, H., Malmberg, J., Isohätälä, J., Sobocinski, M.: ¿Cómo los tipos de interacción y las fases del aprendizaje autorregulado establecen un escenario para el compromiso colaborativo?, Aprendiz. e Instr., vol. 43, pp. 39–51 (2016). https://doi.org/10.1016/j.learninstruc.2016.01.005

15. Castellanos, J., Onrubia, J.: Regulación compartida en entornos de aprendizaje colaborativo mediado por ordenador: diferencias en grupos de alto y bajo rendimiento, RIED. Rev. Iberoam. Educ. a Distancia, vol. 19, no. 1, pp. 233–251 (2016). https://doi.org/10.5944/ried.19.1.14036

16. Järvelä, S., Kirschner, P., Panadero, E., Malmberg, J.: Enhancing socially shared regulation in collaborative learning groups: designing for CSCL regulation tools. Educ. Technol. Res. Dev. (2014). https://doi.org/10.1007/s11423-014-9358-1

17. Hadwin, A., Järvelä, S., Miller, M.: Self-regulated, co-regulated, and socially shared regulation of learning. In: Zimmerman, B.J., Schunk, D.H., (eds.) Handbook of Self-regulation of Learning and Performance. Educational Psychology Handbook Series, pp. 65–85. Routledge/Taylor & Francis Group, New York, NY, USA (2011). https://doi.org/10.4324/9780203839010.ch5

18. Järvelä, S., Hadwin, A.F.: New frontiers: regulating learning in CSCL. Educ. Psychol. 48(1), 25–39 (2013). https://doi.org/10.1080/00461520.2012.748006

19. Dalsgaard, C., Paulsen, M.: Transparency in Cooperative Online Education (2009). http://www.irrodl.org/index.php/irrodl/article/view/671/1267.   https://doi.org/10.19173/irrodl.v10i3.671

20. Johnson, D.W., Johnson, R.I.: Los elementos básicos del aprendizaje cooperativo. In: Aprender juntos y solos. Aprendizaje cooperativo, competitivo e individualista, Primera ed., Buenos Aires: Grupo Editorial Aique S.A., pp. 107–135 (1999)

21. Engel, A., Onrubia, J.: Patrones de organización grupal y fases de construcción del conocimiento en entornos virtuales de aprendizaje colaborativo, Infanc. y Aprendiz., vol. 33, no. 4, pp. 515–528 (2010)

22. Mayordomo, R., Onrubia, J.: Work coordination and collaborative knowledge construction in a small group collaborative virtual task. Internet High. Educ. 25(2015), 96–104 (2015). https://doi.org/10.1016/j.iheduc.2015.02.003

23. Lewicki, R., Bunker, B.: Trust in relationships: a model of trust development and decline. In: Kramer, R., Tyler, T. (eds.) Trust in Organizations, pp. 114–139. Sage, Thousand Oaks (1996)

24. Janssen, J., Erkens, G., Kirschner, P., Kanselaar, G.: Influence of group member familiarity on online collaborative learning. Comput. Human Behav. 25(1), 161–170 (2009). https://doi.org/10.3115/1599600.1599657

25. Fransen, J., Weinberger, A., Kirschner, P.A.: Team effectiveness and team development in CSCL. Educ. Psychol. 48(1), 9–24 (2013). https://doi.org/10.1080/00461520.2012.747947

26. Ortega, O.: Dinámica de grupos. Técnicas de organización de eventos. Bogotá, Colombia: ECOE Ediciones (2016)

27. Waddell, S., Khagram, S.: Multi-stakeholder global networks: emerging systems for the global common good. In: Glasbergen, P., Biermann, F., Mol, A.P.J. (eds.) Partnerships, Governance and Sustainable Development: Reflections on Theory and Practice, pp. 216–287. Edward Elgar Publishing, Cheltenham Glos (2007)

Design of a Mobile Application for Access to the Remote Laboratory

Pedro Salinas-Sagbay$^{(\boxtimes)}$ ⓘ, Celia Paola Sarango-Lapo$^{(\boxtimes)}$ ⓘ,
and Rodrigo Barba$^{(\boxtimes)}$ ⓘ

Universidad Técnica Particular de Loja, Loja, Ecuador
{pjsalinasl, cpsarango, lrbarba}@utpl.edu.ec
https://www.utpl.edu.ec

Abstract. Information and Communications Technology (ICT) have play an important role in education which has given way to new lines of work and research such as Mobile Learning (M-Learning). Nowadays, more and more applications are designed and developed for the M-Learning. Experimentation with remote laboratories (RL) has become a technological achievement that improves student's autonomous and experimental learning activities. This paper shows the aspects considered for the design of a mobile application using Ionic framework that allow the access to a remote physics laboratory aimed to the students enrolled of a distance programs to carry out experimental practices. The methodology was applied in phases: analysis, design, development, implementation and evaluation. As a result, an optimized and cross-platform mobile application was obtained, with a graphical user interface (GUI) with a responsive design capable of adapting to any mobile device such as iOS and Android based on resolution ranges. The functional testing of the application accomplishes the requirements for which it was required.

Keywords: Remote laboratory · M-Learning · IONIC · Mobile applications

1 Introduction

The rapid development of Information and Communication Technologies (ICT) has significantly contributed to distance education. The educational model of distance education with ICT support presents opportunities to improve the interaction between the actors of the process of teaching and learning [2]. Teachers should integrate the use of ICTs into their teaching practices as integrated and innovative elements [3]. Hence the use of mobile technological devices in educational practices constitutes an innovative alternative. In recent years, technological devices such as smartphones, tablets, are accessible because of their availability, benefits and costs [4]. Smartphones are no longer conceived only as communication tools, but as instruments of people's social, working and academic life [14]. Because of this, mobile learning or M-learning is presented as a new option for education, allowing the development of skills and the construction of knowledge [5, 15]. One of the applications that can be adapted and recreated as learning scenarios by means of mobile devices are the Remote Laboratories (RL), thus avoiding forcing students to sit in front of a fixed computer but rather

© Springer Nature Switzerland AG 2020
M. Botto-Tobar et al. (Eds.): ICAT 2019, CCIS 1195, pp. 391–402, 2020.
https://doi.org/10.1007/978-3-030-42531-9_31

providing a more flexible and ubiquitous learning environment [5], which allows the experience of learning [6].

Several researchers have defined an RL. It is technology composed by a set of real physical devices, located in certain institutions, equipped with a set of instruments, sensors, motors, video cameras, etc., so that they can be manipulated remotely through the Internet, allowing experimentation on real devices without the need to be physically in a laboratory [9]. A RL is software and hardware tool that allows students to remotely access real equipment located in the university through the Internet [16]. The basic design of an RL is as follows: on the one hand, the plant, whose sensors and actuators allow interaction with it, is connected to the host PC through an acquisition card (DAC) [17].

The RL adaptation for mobile devices began with the use of web technologies that are compatible with older mobile devices, which were then adapted to be compatible with the new platforms [18]. The diffusion of new advanced mobile platforms such as the iPhone or Android among students has generated a new challenge and increases the opportunities to exploit these devices in their education; due to the characteristics and features that a mobile phone offers, a student will be able to use or validate experiments and compare results with other students outside the physical lab [16]. There are several frameworks for mobile devices that allow the adaptation of RL to mobile devices, one of them is IONIC which comprises the development of open source based on HTML5, CSS, JavaScript and other technologies to write web applications, and build an experience close to the native mobile application [19].

Also, there are several researches that have been oriented to RL design. Some researchers have been concerned about providing RL for experimentation in physics [7, 10] where it is necessary to make use of new technologies such as mobile applications that offer the student a better user experience, and an alternative to the use of the computer. On the other hand, there are studies focused on the experimentation of electronics [11, 13]. Some studies provide experiences of working with RL through mobile devices [8, 12]. Of these studies describe the implementation of a low-cost, web-based RL with a GUI that can be used from students' mobile devices (smart-phones or tablets) and compiled by a computer, allowing teachers and students to parameterize and observe the behavior of Raspberry Pi controllers/systems connected by sensors to laboratory devices [8]. The result was the implementation of a low-cost web-based RL with a GUI that can be used from students' mobile devices. In addition, another research describe the development of an RL project built at low-cost and effective hardware and software components, including Raspberry Pi single board computers and Arduino prototyping platforms based on 8-bit microcontrollers [12]. An RL system was obtained that allows remote control of three thermal plants, magnetic levitation and a hydraulic tank system by means of a low-cost microcontroller. As a result of these studies reveals the need for an RL that presents a graphical user interface optimized for mobile devices, because the implementation of RL is a mature technology and being adapted via web in mobile devices, it is not reflected that many studies suggest the construction of a mobile application for the use of an RL, which is why its implementation plays an important role in the use of new technologies, in addition to improving the user experience.

The mobile application developed for the RL system emerges as an institutional necessity, undertaking a new service. The use of new technologies such as mobile devices is essential today, providing a better feedback to the student. Given the above, the purpose of this research is to present the methodology that is conducted for the design and implementation of a hybrid mobile application based on the framework IONIC directed for students, and optimized for Android and iOS.

2 Methodology

The RL system was developed using four phases. Table 1 presents the components of methodology and then details each of the phases [10].

Table 1. Phases of methodology.

Phases	Description
Analysis	Collection of requirements and identification of users
Design	Design of prototypes and architecture of the system
Implementation (development)	Definition of both technical and pedagogical tools
Tests (evaluation)	Field tests

2.1 Analysis

This base defines the functional and non-functional requirements that the RL must meet. Once the problem has been defined and the solution proposed, it is important to identify the objectives to be achieved when developing this work.

Functional Requirements
The goal is to develop a multiplatform mobile application (Android, iOS) that allows interaction with the RL through the Internet, making use of web services [10], in addition to having the following user interfaces:

- List of practices with information regarding each practice.
- Reservation of schedules that will allow the user to separate his schedule for practice.
- Manipulation of the model according to the activities described by the teacher for the realization of academic practices in a real environment.
- Development of analysis questions and questionnaire questions.

Non-Functional Requirements Availability

- The system must be available 24 h a day, 7 days a week, according to the proposed architecture, and must provide mechanisms or components that assure the continuity of the system without failure.

Security

- Identification and Authentication: Authentication must be done at the server and client level.
- Roles: Access to information can also be controlled through the function or role of the user that requires such access according to the identified users, which can be grouped into: Student role.

Usability

- The system must have properly structured user manuals.
- The system must have commented source code, and make use of good development practices.
- The system must have well-structured graphical interfaces.
- The mobile application must have a responsive design in order to ensure adequate visualization in multiple computers, tablets and smart phones.

Efficiency

- The system must be able to process 100 transactions per second.

2.2   Design

This phase presents the proposed architecture for the mobile application of RL, which contains the integration of the components of the RL that are: main server, model server, network with Internet output and models (Fig. 1).

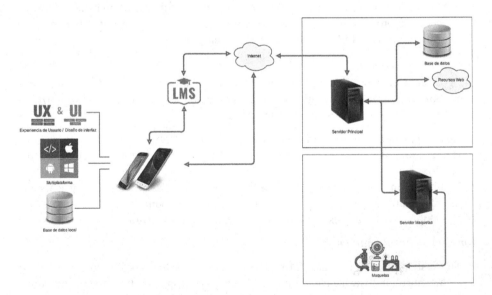

Fig. 1. Proposal architecture.

In general, the physical architecture of the solution requires the use of a mobile device. The student, through the mobile device, accesses the LMS through the internet. The user then selects the course and goes to tasks where you will find the corresponding activity that will redirect the student to the mobile application through a communication module under LTI standard in Canvas LMS, authentication through Moodle is integrated as an external application. Canvas LMS supports additional integrations using LTI to offer a more integrated experience and allow a greater personalization of the product. LTI allows instructors to modify course settings so that additional third-party software can be linked to the class [20]. Once selected, the standard activity LTI proceeds to redirect the mobile application, which will access through the plugin Smartlinks offered by Ionic/Cordova. This plugin facilitates the response to the links through custom URL schemes and Universal/App Links in iOS and Android [20]. The student data collection is through the OAuth2 protocol that allows third-party applications to be authenticated to perform actions as a user, without obtaining the password of the same [21]. By accessing application, the student will be able to manage the reservation of practice and execution of it. The components of the RL are the following: Main server, this is responsible for managing services that provide access to users and storage of information and a Model server, responsible for controlling the electronic models and components.

2.3 Development

For the construction of the mobile application, the use of the SCRUM software development methodology has been convenient. This is based on flexibility, adaptability and productivity in a volatile environment, allowing developers to choose the techniques, methods and software development practices specific to the process of implementation and inclusion of frequent management activities [22]. SCRUM defines the utility and efficiency in adapting the mobile method for the development of mobile applications, in addition to being really effective in delivering mobile applications in a timely manner [23].

For development purposes a three-role team was considered. (1) The Product Owner is the most important role, since it is the one which determines the priority of the characteristics to be implemented. The product owner represents the voice of customers and end users. (2) The Scrum Master helps the team adopt SCRUM processes, making sure that the controls and reviews are carried out correctly and regularly, the quality of user histories is up to date, among others. (3) The Scrum Team is made up of developers, testers and others [26].

SCRUM defines a framework for project management; software development is done through iterations called sprints. A sprint is the smallest block of SCRUM that has a small team that works on the assigned task, it has the duration of one to three weeks. Each task for a sprint is decided by a sprint backlog. The sprint backlog is a documentation of all the requirements for the current sprint. The product backlog is a list of requirements that are determined by the product owner and are called user histories that are divided into Sprint Backlogs followed by a Sprint Planning that includes methods for conducting a Sprint [24]. Each Sprint results in an executable increment that is shown to the customer. Another important feature is the meetings throughout the project, including the fifteen-minute daily meeting of the development team for coordination and integration [1].

The project had User Acceptance Testing (UAT) at the end of each Sprint, in order to verify if the application is suitable for use. These tests are generally functional and are based on the requirements defined by the customer and must be done before production.

1. Sprint 1: In this sprint the analysis of requirements, design of the graphic interface prototype and integration with Canvas LMS and Moodle LMS was carried out. The latter consisted of the integration of the LMS using interoperability standards with the objective of integrating an external learning course or activity more fully with the institutional LMS and, in addition to establishing data communication between both systems without compromising functionality or access security [27]. The link between the RL system and the LMS is based on the creation of a new activity configured as an external application, this is done by the teacher in charge of the course.

2. Sprint 2: This sprint was divided into four user stories that comprise the programming of the authentication and practical services. The authentication service allows access to the user through the use of APIs provided by the LMS, as an alternative access to the application against integration through the LTI protocol. The Practical service allows the exchange and manipulation of data with the main server of the RL that corresponds to data related to the experimental practices assigned to the student. Once the service programming was finished, the Login screens that provide a form for user authentication and the Home component that shows the practices and a brief detail of them were implemented.

3. This sprint was divided into four user stories. The sprint had the task of developing the reservation service, which is necessary for the execution of the practice; as well as the development of the Instructions, Questionnaire and Reserve components which show all the information related to the practice, questionnaire forms and the manipulation of reservations for the execution of the project.

4. Sprint 4: This sprint focuses on the development of the Practical component, which allows the execution of the practices of the different models, based on functions that distinguish the type of practice, rendered as follows. This component makes use of the services described previously and the connection through sockets with the Main Server and Maquette Server [10] to establish a continuous full-duplex connection, between the mobile application and servers. Thus also the development of analysis question forms corresponding to each practice.

At the end of the construction of the application based on the SCRUM methodology, the corresponding tests were performed, which were divided into three types of acceptance tests, these are: (1) Development tests of the application, focused on connection tests, such as: loading speed, download speeds, latency, loss percentage, packet corruption, etc. It also includes performance tests to determine the application behavior, and memory tests that determine the use of application resources. These tests were performed using Chrome DevTools, which is a set of web creation and debugging tools built into Google Chrome. The use of simulators also fulfilled a key aspect in the tests, because this allowed to define the specifications so that the application works correctly on multiple devices. (2) Connection tests to servers; these were carried out under two scenarios: connection to the main server of the RL and model server. (3) Authentication tests were defined under two scenarios: integration of the RL through the LTI standard with Canvas LMS, and integration with Moodle LMS. The design of user acceptance test cases sought to include the main execution scenarios of the application, determining that the requirements have been correctly understood and that the tests to be performed on the functionality were sufficient.

The application development tests were carried out under software testing techniques called Test Driven Development (TDD), used in agile software development methodologies, among these SCRUM. TDD is a technique that changes the order established in terms of first developing (programming) and then testing, so that tests are first defined (test cases) and from these the functionality is developed, repeating the cycle.

2.4 Evaluation

The evaluation methods used were based on graphical user interface, network and black box tests.

1. Graphic Interface Testing: GUI testing is the process of testing the system's Graphical User Interface of the Application Under Test.
2. Network Testing: The primary goal of network testing is to find faults in the network in order to correct them, but a secondary goal is to know the limitations of a given kind of network.
3. Black box testing: Black box tests are tests that are carried out in the graphic interface of the software. A black box test examines some fundamental aspects of a system with little concern for the internal logical structure of the software. Black box tests, also called behavioral tests. Focus on the functional requirements of the software; that is, black box test techniques allow derivative sets of input conditions that will completely review all functional requirements for a software [25].

Evaluation Results
Graphic Interface Testing Results
Figure 2 shows the adaptability in three different mobile devices, the first one a tablet with 768 × 1024 px, the second one is a smart phone with a 317 × 667 px and the last a smart phone with a 320 × 568 px. In all devices the design responds and adapts to the dimensions of the screen without affecting the graphic interface.

Network Testing Results
For the network tests performed, the Chrome DevTools by Google Chrome were used, making use of the network panel, which ensures that the resources are downloaded or loaded as expected and other tasks such as inspecting the properties of an individual resource, their HTTP headers, content, size, and so on.

The purpose of these tests was to measure the performance of the mobile application when the practices are executed in two types of networks, a wireless network and a 3G mobile network. Figure 3 show the network activity in the Network Log, in a wireless network with a speed of 6.0 Mbps. The Network Log shows the image of the practice in execution without interruptions and a charge time lower than 1000 ms. Figure 3 show the network activity in the Network Log, in a wireless network with a

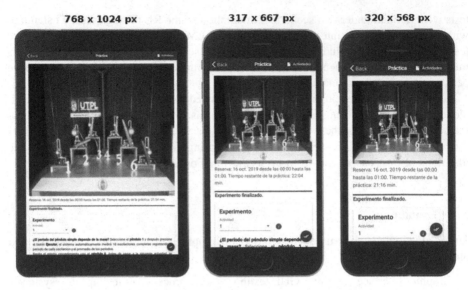

Fig. 2. Responsive design on mobile phones and tablet.

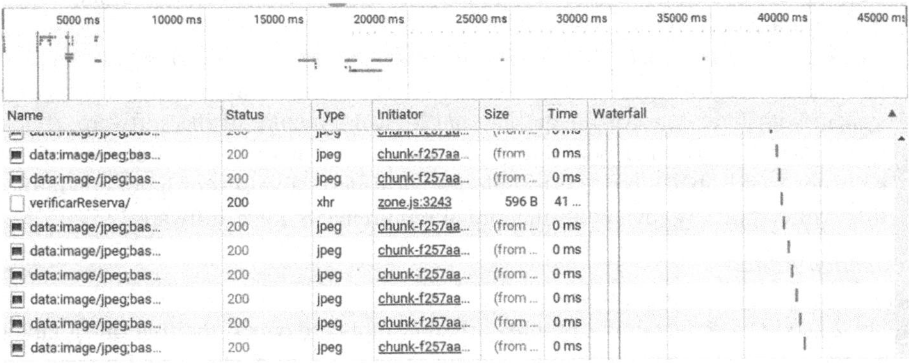

Fig. 3. Speed tests in wireless network.

speed of 6.0 Mbps. The Network Log shows the image of the practice in execution without interruptions and a charge time of the image lower than 1000 ms.

Figure 4 show the network activity in the Network Log, in a 3G network with an approximate speed of 2.7 Mbps. In this test the image load took a little more than 1000 ms.

Black Box Testing Results
The tests carried out were focused on the execution of the seven experimental practices that the RL has. Each practice has forms validations that don't allow the user to enter values not allowed by the system and thus avoid errors in the main server and model server. The mobile application was designed with the purpose of executing the

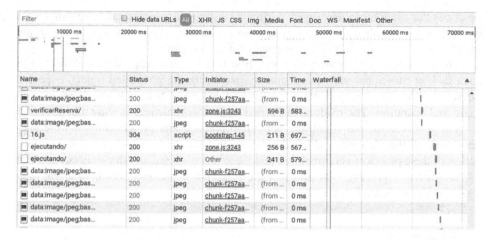

Name	Status	Type	Initiator	Size	Time	Waterfall
data:image/jpeg;bas...	200	jpeg	chunk-f257aa...	(from ...	0 ms	
verificarReserva/	200	xhr	zone.js:3243	596 B	583...	
data:image/jpeg;bas...	200	jpeg	chunk-f257aa...	(from ...	0 ms	
16.js	304	script	bootstrap:145	211 B	697...	
ejecutando/	200	xhr	zone.js:3243	256 B	567...	
ejecutando/	200	xhr	Other	241 B	579...	
data:image/jpeg;bas...	200	jpeg	chunk-f257aa...	(from ...	0 ms	
data:image/jpeg;bas...	200	jpeg	chunk-f257aa...	(from ...	0 ms	
data:image/jpeg;bas...	200	jpeg	chunk-f257aa...	(from ...	0 ms	
data:image/jpeg;bas...	200	jpeg	chunk-f257aa...	(from ...	0 ms	
data:image/jpeg;bas...	200	jpeg	chunk-f257aa...	(from ...	0 ms	

Fig. 4. Speed tests in 3G network.

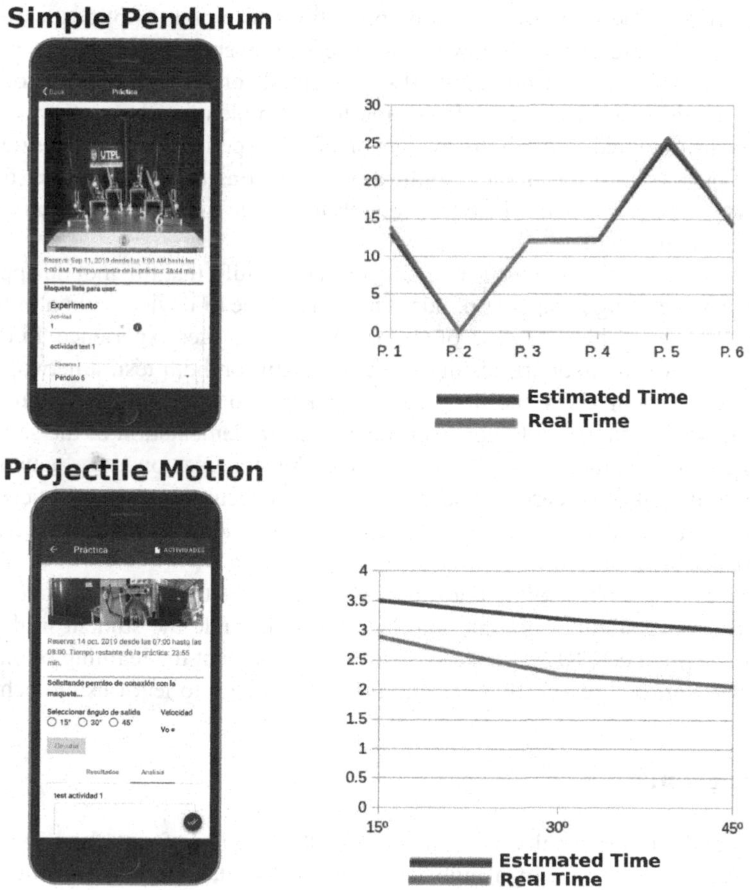

Fig. 5. Black box testing on simple pendulum and projectile motion, real time vs estimated time.

practices that the RL has. However, during the testing stage errors can arise that do not depend on the mobile application, either due to functionality or network or due to the maintenance of the models or some change in the system.

The black box tests were performed, based on the task tests, which allow to test each task or functional unit independently, analyzing the controlled inputs, expected outputs and outputs obtained; the objective of this type of tests is to discover errors in logic and operation. The evaluation carried out in two practices is shown below.

The tests carried out in simple pendulum practice and project motion were successful in all the elements, which determines that the operation of the mobile application in these practices is correct and that the Errors obtained and that may occur are at the server level. The Fig. 5 shows that the execution of the practices is in a real time less than the estimated time.

3 Discussion

According to [5, 8], an RL system must have a responsive GUI, emphasizing the user experience (UX). The migration of web applications to mobile applications is a necessary change, the use of mobile devices is increasing every year and brings a number of advantages. The study of related works is essential for the development of an RL, since they provide the necessary information for its implementation.

The results obtained through the evaluation of the experimental practices determine the correct operation of the mobile application, as well as the performance, functionality, network and graphic interface tests establish that the mobile applications adapt to this type of technology.

The results of graphical interface level, you can identify that the mobile application have a responsive design, capable of adapting to any type of device without interfering graphical interface in the execution of the practices or the user experience. In the other hand the results of the network testing were successful on both test, a network with a stable connection will allow the image of the practice to load without failures and in real time. However, you should consider the correct implementation of the server side, since this would be crucial for the execution of the practices over the network. The black box tests that were carried out resulted in the execution of the practices in less time than estimated, determining that the execution of the practice are optimal in the mobile application.

The developed mobile application provides the student with an intuitive learning environment and a friendly graphic interface that will guide the student in the development of the practices. RL's are a tool that can complement the learning of physics in a way never seen before and that can motivate the student to learn using technology.

4 Conclusions

According to the found results, we can conclude that the use of a methodology for the design and implementation of a mobile application is vital, since it provides a well-defined structure in the development process and serves as an indicator for future implementations. Although some tests were carried out in more than one round, more tests may be necessary to determine errors and obtain alternatives to the elements that represent discomfort or risks to the interaction with the RL.

The app's design will allow the students to have flexibility by eliminating the need for learning to occur at a specific time and place. Students have the advantage of accessing content wherever and whenever they want. The app designed as a hybrid application allowed a rapid and low-cost development.

References

1. Becerra, P., Sanjuan, M.: Revisión de estado del arte del ciclo de vida de desarrollo de software seguro con la metodología SCRUM — Investigación y Desarrollo en TIC (2018). http://revistas.unisimon.edu.co/index.php/identic/article/view/2474
2. Dormido, S., Sanchez, J., Morilla, F.: Laboratorios virtuales remotos para la práctica a distancia de la automática (2016)
3. Gonzalez, J.C.: ICT and the transformation of educational practice in the context of knowledge societies. RUSC. Rev. Univ. Soc. Conocimiento **5**(2), 1–8 (2008). https://doi.org/10.7238/rusc.v5i2.330
4. Papagiannakis, G., Singh, G., Magnenat-Thalmann, N.: A survey of mobile and wireless technologies for augmented reality systems. CAVW **19**(1), 3–22 (2008)
5. Wang, N., Chen, X., Song, G., Lan, Q., Parsaei, H.R.: Design of a new mobile-optimized remote laboratory application architecture for M-learning. IEEE Trans. Ind. Electron. **64**(3), 2382–2391 (2017). https://doi.org/10.1109/tie.2016.2620102
6. Matarrita, C.A., Concari, S.B.: Hacia un estado del arte de los laboratorios remotos en la ensenanza de la fisica. Rev. Ensenanza Fisica **27**(2), 133–139 (2015). https://revistas.unc.edu.ar/index.php/revistaEF/article/view/12596/12872
7. Arguedas Matarrita, C.A.: Diseño y desarrollo de un Laboratorio Remoto para la enseñanza de la física en la UNED de Costa Rica. Escucla de Ciencias Exactas y Naturales, Universidad Estatal a Distancia, Costa Rica. Universidad Estatal a Distancia de Costa Rica (UNED) (2011)
8. Bermudez-Ortega, J., Besada-Portas, E., López-Orozco, J.A., Bonache-Seco, J.A., De la Cruz, J.M.: Remote web-based control laboratory for mobile devices based on EJsS, Raspberry Pi and Node. js. IFAC-PapersOnLine **48**(29), 158–163 (2015). https://doi.org/10.1016/j.ifacol.2015.11.230
9. Concari, S.: Tecnologías emergentes¿ cuáles usamos. Latin Am. J. Phys. Educ. **8**(3), 494–503 (2014)
10. Contreras-Mendieta, J.A., Sarango-Lapo, C.P., Jara-Roa, D.I., Agila-Palacios, M.V.: Implementación de un Laboratorio Remoto (LR), como recurso de apoyo en un sistema de Educación a Distancia (2019)
11. Grout, I.: Remote laboratories to support electrical and information engineering (EIE) laboratory access for students with disabilities. In: Proceedings of the 25th International Conference on European Association for Education in Electrical and Information Engineering, EAEEIE 2014, pp. 21–24 (2014). https://doi.org/10.1109/EAEEIE.2014.6879377
12. Kalúz, M., Čirka, Ľ., Valo, R., Fikar, M.: ArPi lab: a low-cost remote laboratory for control education. In: IFAC Proceedings Volumes (IFAC-PapersOnline), vol. 19. IFAC (2014). https://doi.org/10.3182/20140824-6-ZA-1003.00963

13. Marchisio, S., Lerro, F., Von Pamel, O.: Empleo de un laboratorio remoto para promover aprendizajes significativos en la enseñanza de los dispositivos electrónicos (2011)
14. Vázquez-Cano, E., García, L.S.: El smartphone en la educación superior. Un estudio comparativo del uso educativo, social y ubicuo en universidades españolas e hispanoamericanas. Signo Pensamiento **34**(67), 132–149 (2015). https://doi.org/10.11144/Javeriana. syp34-67.sese
15. Ponce, L.B., Antonio, J., Méndez, J., José, F., Peñalvo, G.: Dispositivos móviles y apps: Características y uso actual en educación médica. Rev. Asoc. Técnicos Inf. **231**, 86–91 (2015). https://doi.org/10.1016/j.jsat.2015.06.018
16. Orduña, P., García-Zubia, J., Irurzun, J., López-de-Ipiña, D., Rodriguez-Gil, L.: Enabling mobile access to Remote Laboratories. In: 2011 IEEE Global Engineering Education Conference, EDUCON 2011, pp. 312–318 (2011). https://doi.org/10.1109/EDUCON.2011. 5773154
17. Chacon, J., Vargas, H., Farias, G., Sanchez, J., Dormido, S.: EJS, JIL server, and LabVIEW: an architecture for rapid development of remote labs. IEEE Trans. Learn. Technol. **8**(4), 393–401 (2015)
18. De Lima, J.P.C., Rochadel, W., Silva, A.M., Simão, J.P.S., Da Silva, J.B., Alves, J.B.M.: Application of remote experiments in basic education through mobile devices. In: IEEE Global Engineering Education Conference, EDUCON, pp. 1093–1096, April 2014. https:// doi.org/10.1109/EDUCON.2014.6826245
19. Yang, Y., Zhang, Y., Xia, P., Li, B., Ren, Z.: Mobile terminal development plan of cross-platform mobile application service platform based on ionic and Cordova. In: Proceedings - 2017 International Conference on Industrial Informatics - Computing Technology, Intelligent Technology, Industrial Information Integration, ICIICII 2017, 2017-Decem, pp. 100–103 (2018). https://doi.org/10.1109/ICIICII.2017.28
20. Fecil'ak, P., Fecil'aková, K., Jakab, F.: Networking academy-the way we live, we learn and play, pp. 95–99, October 2013, https://doi.org/10.1109/ICETA.2013.6674411
21. Ionic-team: Ionic plugin deeplinks (2019). https://github.com/ionic-team/ionic-plugin-deeplinks
22. Flora, H.K.: Adopting an agile approach for the development of mobile applications, pp. 1–26 (2012)
23. Mahmud, D.M., Abdullah, N.A.S.: Reviews on agile methods in mobile application development process, pp. 161–165 (2015)
24. Srivastava, A., Bhardwaj, S., Saraswat, S.: SCRUM model for agile methodology. In: Proceeding - IEEE International Conference on Computing, Communication and Automation, ICCCA 2017, pp. 864–869 (2017). https://doi.org/10.1109/CCAA.2017.8229928
25. Pressman, R.S.: Ingeniería del software: un enfoque práctico (Séptima ed) (2010)
26. Mundra, A., Misra, S., Dhawale, C.A.: Practical scrum-scrum team: way to produce successful and quality software. In: Proceedings of the 2013 13th International Conference on Computational Science and Its Applications, ICCSA 2013, pp. 119–123 (2013). https:// doi.org/10.1109/ICCSA.2013.25
27. Soto, C., Menéndez, V., Aguilar, R.: Interoperabilidad entre el LMS Moodle y las aplicaciones educativas de propósito específico utilizando servicios del IMS-LTI. Apertura **7** (2), 56–66 (2015)

Research and ICT Mediated Learning Styles

Nancy Dalida Martínez Barragán[1]([⊠]), Andrea Aparicio Gallo[1]([⊠]),
and Jennifer Catalina Murcia Rodríguez[2]([⊠])

[1] Universidad ECCI, Bogotá, D.C, Colombia
{nmartinezb,aapariciog}@ecci.edu.co
[2] Corporación Universitaria Minuto de Dios, Bogotá, D.C, Colombia
jennifer.murcia@uniminuto.edu

Abstract. Taking into account technology goes ahead quickly and the teaching-learning processes for each person are different and the way to carry out this process should be at vanguard, Information and communications technology (ICT) play a role very important because they allow to create virtual objects for learning through software platforms, where they make knowledge is captured in a way more interactive, also making investigative process more dynamic and efficient.

By an autonomous learning, a building critical thinking and well-structured forming purposeful, creative and innovative professionals who contribute suitable solutions to their environment.

Besides all above, the professor also takes technological knowledge and developing new strategies and group dynamics, not only inside the classroom, but outside too, thus building a strong string between knowledge and working in site.

Regarding above, it is made a study with a focus group to watch how ITC contributes to develop knowledge and investigative processes, concluding the students use these artefacts as a complementary tool to make their knowledge stronger.

Keywords: Knowledge · Teaching · ITC · Investigation

1 Introduction

The challenges of current education propose learning environments that overcome traditional methodologies and break the physical and geographical spaces to propose students new ways of learning, resources on virtual platforms and access to web resources that make learning an experience with multiple options for autonomous work and also for student-professor and student-student interaction, proposing from the teaching person's novel planning and didactic forms that carry off the student to multidisciplinary environments; in such a way that autonomous learning is encouraged using and applying friendly technologies where the professor or virtual tutor becomes a mediator and companion of the student for the development of skills and the study of content allowing with the use of ICT to intervene the formation of reflexive, ethical, critical and competent people in an increasingly diverse and changing environment [1].

Taking into account that learning through ICTs as proposed by Grasha and Riechmann (1,974) the users of virtual platforms and websites learn individually or in

© Springer Nature Switzerland AG 2020
M. Botto-Tobar et al. (Eds.): ICAT 2019, CCIS 1195, pp. 403–414, 2020.
https://doi.org/10.1007/978-3-030-42531-9_32

groups in three dimensions: autonomous/dependent, collaborative/competitive and participatory/non-participatory [2]; it is necessary a professor prepares for new ways of proposing content, tools and learning resources and also to become a virtual environment into a classroom, a research space, throughout with technological advances to modify significantly the paradigms of teaching-learning.

ICT-mediated learning implies a careful process of selection and organization of resources and contents, considering that the virtual environment can be accessed by people with different learning rhythms and styles, it is necessary to use different content managers and content platforms in a way that allows synchronous and asynchronous connection and provides all resources for deepening, exploring and applying knowledge; turning the ICT-mediated learning environment into a research space where the student can access to contents, but also build explanations, reasoned approaches to knowledge advancement and novelties that can modify and make products, processes, designs and in general speaking, academic productions that prove they have researched and applied knowledge.

1.1 Reference Framework

When talking about learning, it is necessary to know that all human beings have different ways of learning, which makes us have different ways of communication. The foregoing is so complex that several thinkers, psychologists, pedagogues and even at these times, coaching leaders have been concerned with understanding the way in which human beings learn.

There are several authors who have been working and generating theories about what is estimated as learning style: Witkin (1954), "cognitive styles", authors such as Holzman and Clein (1954); Eriksen (1954); Golstein and Scheerer (1951), Dunn or Dunn, and Price, for whom learning styles reflect "the way in which basic stimuli affect the ability to a person to absorb and retain information"; for Hunt (1979: 27), these "describe the conditions under which a student is in the best situation to learn, or what structure the student needs to learn better"; Claxton, and Ralston (1978) learning style, "is a consistent way to respond and use stimuli in a learning context" [3].

Taking Ingrid Mosquera's article entitled "Learning styles: sensory classification and Kolb's proposal", he presents two differentiated learning styles: sensory and Kolb's. The sensory learning style is based on the human brain being divided into two hemispheres, the right hemisphere and the left hemisphere. The left hemisphere of the brain is focused on observation, analysis, experience and language. While the right hemisphere has the capacity to synthesize information, to understand images, it is where imagination and creativity develop [4]. According to this, the way in which each one learns, is based on which hemisphere we develop the most, hence the sensory language as the name implies has to do with the experienced sensations becoming the sense of preference that leads the baton at the time of learning; this is why the sensory learning style is classified as: visual, auditory and kinetic. If the sense of preference is sight, it means that they will learn much more through images, maps, drawings, photos, among others; in the same way if the auditory is preferential, the learning will take place through the actions of speaking and listening, it should be noted that the knowledge will be appropriate through talks, recordings, films, round tables and other actions that generate they need an auditory exchange; in kinetic learning, the development of concepts will be carried out with the sense of touch, of experience, in doing, therefore activities such as comparing and interpreting everyday situations, laboratory practices, field trips, and other tasks that involve contact, sense of relationship and belonging [3].

In addition to the learning styles shown by Kolb is the proposal by Fariñas, G. (1995), who presents 4 basic dimensions for learning through a holistic conception of it: "(1) The approach of objectives, tasks and the temporary organization of its execution through steps or stages. (2) The search for information and its understanding. (3) Communication about your performance. (4) The solution or problem statement." [1].

Once you have understood some of the learning styles that have been studied and developed, you can talk about research and its relation to learning in students at different stages of it; Therefore, according to the dictionary of the Royal Academy of the Spanish Language, the research is that it aims at expanding scientific knowledge, without pursuing, in principle, any practical application [5]. Hence, the research is based mainly on the observation of the environment and the identification of any problem in any aspect, whether social, technical, technological, environmental, educational, among many others. As Tamayo (2003) quotes in his text: "the process of scientific research" to Arias Galicia "[...] research can be defined as a series of methods to solve problems whose solutions need to be obtained through a series of operations logical, based on objective data." [6].

Given the above, research becomes a systemic process that leads to achieve concrete results to "To see the reality that others have not seen" [6]. So that the investigation has the rigor that it deserves, it is leveraged in the scientific method, which gives it a rigorous character in terms of the observance of reality and the theoretical construction that allows it to generate objective conclusions; through the following steps: The approach to the problem, stage in which the observation and discovery of the situation or situations that are inconsistent in relation to knowledge are made, allows the problem question to be formulated. A theoretical model that allows the selection of variables and the generation of hypotheses. Test of the hypothesis, at this stage a series of procedures are generated for the design and performance of tests that will lead to data collection, classification, evaluation and analysis. Finally - The Conclusions that give rise to the verification and/or denial of the hypotheses raised for the solution of the problem found [7]. With this, it could be said that research is implicit in each of the learning styles of individuals due to whatever form of appropriation of knowledge the same process is always carried out: observation, through the senses; identification of a problem, the way in which the observed thing is related to the environment; hypothesis generation, questions that student is asked about the subject being treated; Test of the hypothesis, when student tries to solve those questions through consultations and class activities and finally the conclusions, they are established when student to appropriate the knowledge. This demonstrates the relationship between learning and research.

It should be borne in mind that when talking about a learning environment, in addition to the tools that exist today to carry out the teaching-learning process, terms such as: M-Learning, E-Learning and Learning. According to the author's research Aguirre [8], where he quotes that: "The technological resources that currently allow teaching proposals supported by virtuality are based on two fundamental concepts, M-Learning and

E-Learning. The first one joins the proposals of the information society to support the learning proposal throughout life and especially its continuity in adulthood; the concept of e-Learning is a teaching-learning modality that consists in the design, implementation and evolution of a course or training plan developed through computer networks".

Based on the foregoing and according to the studies carried out in the research, it can be concluded that the described technologies have been and are directly or indirectly involved in the teaching-learning processes. In the article of [9], they highlight "The impact of technologies on education" and recognize the importance of having them as main tools in the classes, to allow student to interact, to experience, to associate and to recognize the knowledge that is abstract to them when it is only explained to them from the theoretical; with this, the information is brought within their reach, allowing them to reflect, observe and understand to put it into practice in their personal and working environment.

As a complement to the above, at this moment the Information and communications technologies are indispensable for the good development not only of the different learning processes but also in the implementation of the research in the classroom and strictly speaking; in such a way that it is evident that there are few investigations in Colombia about this subject, some of them are based on the EVAS (Virtual Learning Environments) those are a type of virtual education based mainly on the permanent internet connection and online software. In this perspective of virtual training, Spanish authors stand out who are at the forefront such as: (Fernández 2015), Professor of Didactics and School Organization at the University of Castilla la Mancha and Julio Cabero Almenara of the University of Seville (2008). Additionally, there is the research conducted by (Vera 2014) of the University of Malaga entitled. "Virtual reality and educational possibilities", where it raises the theme of Virtual Reality in the classroom as a research challenge; it revolved around the question. "What can Virtual Reality technology bring to current training environments?"; concluding that Virtual Reality is a technology applicable to the context of education, mainly for its ability to visualize the processes under study, regardless of the discipline to be treated. That way, students can appropriate artificial scenarios that show them processes under study that would otherwise be unaffordable for them.

However, it is important to highlight that these technological developments have been managed in students for entertainment purposes and to generate communication networks between their contacts and friends, but when incorporating these technologies and others such as chat, video conferences, educational games with virtual reality, social networks or guided tours with augmented reality, they do not recognize them as academic resources, and although they have the ability to navigate and consulting digital media, they do not recognize them in class and they have difficulties in interactions, this identified in one of the experiences commented in the book of Cortes and Murcia [10], where a workshop held to students of engineering programs, the theme developed was focused on scalar magnitudes, this to know the physical dimensions of objects and spaces, using virtual reality as a technological resource, where the results were a better remembrance of the different magnitudes, greater interest in the class, more participation of the groups and more assimilation of concepts. It was also found that they show difficulty in handling the technology with the device (VR goggles) and the software, they were accompanied and advised by the professor, to achieve the objective of the classes.

Other research found, it is Alicante University's research, in Spain, they designed a remote laboratory with virtual technology for the robotics area, this in order to mitigate access problems such as unavailable schedules, limited times, laboratory equipment not available [11].

2   ICT, Virtual Environments and Research

2.1   New Information and Communication Technologies as a Teaching Tool

ICT-mediated learning environments are today a constant before educational practices, these environments involve leaving the paradigm of traditional education to take on the challenge of interacting with students through the web [2]; Information and Communication Technologies allow both students and professors, not only the use of platforms, software to manage content and the combination of educational media preload on virtual platforms, but the combination of these ones with social networks options to be used on an open and informal communication for supporting formal educational strategies such as courses and contents of a syllabus and propose new ways to access and building knowledge.

Current professionals require a communicative skills that allows them to interact with people in a synchronous and asynchronous way, establishing feedback and an effective communication, making the use of ICTs promote autonomous learning, comprehension skills, construction, disseminate knowledge in a wide and diverse context which is constantly changing. For the professor they constitute an alternative mechanism in their educational action, through which they can boost the learning styles mentioned above, generating both individual and group educational proposals; developing cognitive styles mentioned by Grasha and Riechmann (1974) propose educational experiences in three dimensions: autonomous/dependent, collaborative/competitive and participatory/non-participatory [9].

ICTs have advanced by leaps and bounds, where in addition to platforms, content controllers, the web and social networks; new empathy technologies have appeared that seek to propose the game as a learning tool; they apply softwares and tools that make use of augmented reality, virtual reality, tangible programming, 360 environments, to explore content, discover and share knowledge, through the game, interaction and exploration of realities intentionally proposed by the professor to achieve learning objectives. Becoming another challenge for higher education, where new educational experiences open paths that were visualized since the incorporation of new computers in Universities and as Adell (1977) had already predicted, digitalization is the main support of knowledge and the fact itself to know [2, 12].

In addition, several authors agree that the use of technology makes learning a holistic process Jonassen, Campbell and Davidson (1994), and also integrating and acquiring knowledge is a constructive process according to Viejo, Cabezas and Martínez (2013) which is achieved through ICT, also in a collaborative way, therefore it means technology is also considered a cognitive tool, because its use falls on the student's learning who generates autonomously knowledge [13].

That generation of autonomous knowledge in the student, developing step by step, a methodology that allows him/her to advance in the research area, because he/she begins to contextualize and conceptualize his/her environment in a more concrete way, with his/her own criteria, which leads to build a critical and well structured thinking, which results in a proactive, innovative, creative professional who shows appropriate solutions in accordance with social, economic, political and business environments. Likewise, ICTs have forced professor to change the way to teach knowledge, nowadays more than standing in front of a whiteboard and conducting a master class it is about being a guide in the route of appropriation of student's knowledge, using new strategies and new group dynamics inside and outside of the classroom.

2.2 Research as a Process in Virtual Learning Environments

In the context of higher education, one of the most controversial aspects is scientific research, and in virtual environments this process requires to be prepared and also scheduling those strategies that motivate significant moments for student to relate the study of content and the building of knowledge, with the practices of learning to investigate and professor with the methodology to research and proposing to the student approaches with science (Hernández 2005).

Higher education Institutions are making progresses in recognizing and appropriating strategies and methods so that students, through the use of ICTs have access to content designed in such a way that they propose cognitive imbalances, problematic and casuistic situations that lead them to delve into the subjects, to the search of reliable sources of information and contents and therefore to the investigative development to excuse of the disciplinary contents.

However, the practice of teaching is still conditioned by the low motivation to develop demanding projects, based on real needs and also conditioned by the gaps between schools and higher education (Aponte 2005 and Vasco 2006) that do not allow a true research in a Colombian University [14]. This before the reality that teaching staff were not either formed for scientific research. Researching in ICT-mediated environments implies access to digitalized content as part of teaching and research and as a strategy to generate academic-scientific trajectory [14].

The interaction between student and professor in the virtual environment implies, as mention before, the use of ICT to communicating, interacting, learning and teaching, all this is extended to the vision of supporting a culture of research, which exceeds the access to information and contents to propose transformations in the classroom, the educational context. (See Fig. 1)

ICTs are tools that make science possible through animations, simulations, videos, three-dimensional models that connect student with nature, technological environments and all of this constitutes supporting elements for scientific education [15]. These technological tools allow the professor to prepare the instructional design of the virtual environment and propose diverse web resources that give student an opportunity to access a multitude of concepts, themes, visions, experiences, experiments and digitized contents that motivate critical and analytical thinking. In addition to proposing activities that promote meaningful learning from the design of forums of analysis and purposeful forums, tasks such as blog, communication wall, designs such as timelines, infographics,

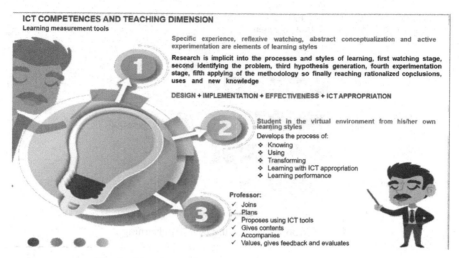

Fig. 1. Learning and research styles. Source: self made

voice notes, recordings, animations, projects, applications; all of them in an entertaining way allow to transmit what you have learned, expand content, showing research and conclusions or scientific approaches; all of this in the context of an open classroom university, transformer and enhancer of research skills.

3   Methodology

The current study is analytical-descriptive; for its development, the first stage was the documentary review of the theories incident on ICT-mediated learning and learning styles; then it is defined to apply the qualitative method and the combination of techniques: direct watching from the teaching role, in a group of higher education students and the online survey to subsequently analyze the data and describing the results contrasting them with the theories of base for the investigation.

4   Results and Discussion

For the study, the behaviors of a group of 39 higher education students were analyzed, in relation to the use and technological preferences in learning, learning styles and investigative behaviors in the mentioned process; finding the following results (Figs. 2, 3, 4, 5, 6, 7, 8, 9):

Watching the 39 students of the selected sample, the results of the strengthening of education with the use of ICT and the incursion of virtual reality, show that students using virtual classrooms focus on sending activities such as homework and forum with a result of 79.5%, showing less interest in classroom's e-mail and its syllabus and general speaking students prefer more the individual activities (61.5%) than collaborative and autonomous development of content (94.9%); which is an educational paradigm and of

Do you know the resources of a virtual classroom and have used them to strengthen your education? Mention the most frequent.

40 answers

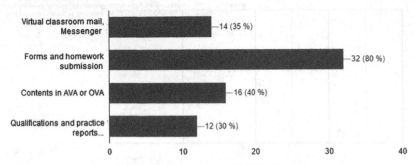

Fig. 2. Knowledge and use of ICT in learning.

In a virtual classroom, what are the activities of your choice?

40 answers

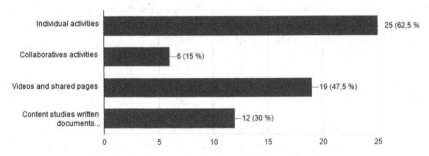

Fig. 3. Preferences in the use of ICT in education.

His activity in a virtual classroom is:

40 answers

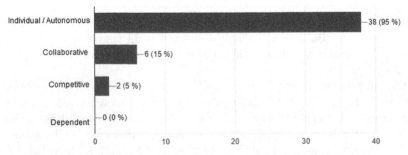

Fig. 4. Learning styles according to Grasha and Riechmann (1,974).

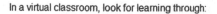
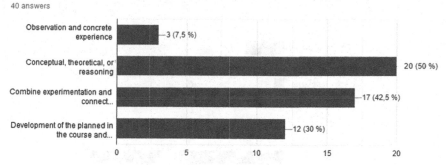

In a virtual classroom, look for learning through:
40 answers

Fig. 5. Learning styles Mosquera (2,017) Kolb analysis (1,970).

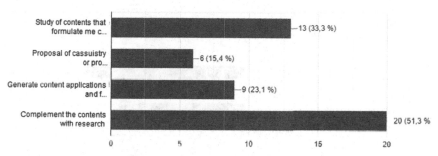

In a virtual classroom, you can research on a topic of interest or content:
39 answers

Fig. 6. Research in TIC-mediated learning.

the same design of the activities and the learning environment in the virtual classroom; it must be planned from the teaching role.

It is also observed that the students surveyed are drawn to the learning process through the implementation of virtual reality (52.6%), taking into account that the majority of respondents have had contact with this technology through video games (80%) and their experience in the use of it has been satisfactory (60%). In addition to this, some subjects were chosen in which learning can be made through virtual reality, watching most of them would find it easier to learn subjects based on technical drawing. using this technology (50%), due to the visualization of objects and structures dimensioning and projecting their forms.

From the above, it can be concluded that the support of ICTs through virtual class-rooms allows student to adopt their own learning style in which he/she can visualize and appropriate in an independent way the knowledge, generating a habit of permanent consultation associated with a research process of the topics proposed in the subject by professor; likewise, the implementation of virtual reality tools in some subjects, increases the student's cognitive processes by creating skills and abilities by virtual interacting with the elements of study. In fact, it has been possible to show that students who use virtual classrooms or virtual reality for their learning, not only improve their grades but also their capacity for analysis, critical thinking showing innovative proposals in the classroom.

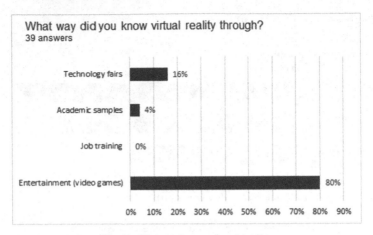

Fig. 7. Ways to know virtual reality.

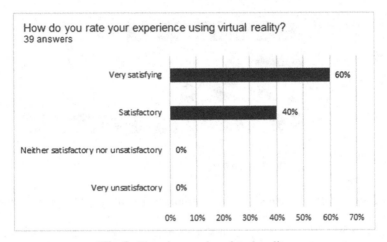

Fig. 8. Experience using virtual reality.

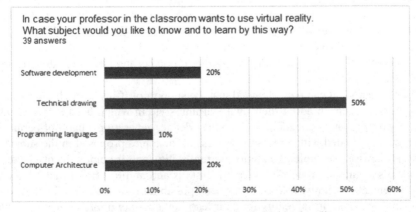

Fig. 9. Thematic for learning through virtual reality.

5 Conclusions

Student's learning process is in itself a dynamic, permanent and sequential process; the student is building, generating and expanding knowledge as the same time he/she receives the motivation and mediation from professor; with the use of technologies this mediation and accompaniment in the learning process becomes more striking and implies the use of a large number of methodological strategies that help student to access knowledge through the web, media and communication tools, the new software and diversity of pages and resources for knowledge creation; in such a way that according to their own learning style, the use of ICTs and the intentional proposition of teaching strategies and teaching by teaching staff achieve a significant learning, which according to Ausubel [14] make use or retake the concepts and learning that student already brings and expands with new learning that he/she later manages to appropriate and apply.

The learning process with the use of ICT and augmented reality becomes more autonomous, reflective and with a high research component, since in the mediated learning by the range of technologies to which we now have access, professor is a companion and engine of the process and student is an investigator whose action is depth, so that the learning action is carried out by itself, this is how he/she builds and proposes elaborations, creations, adaptations and understandings of concepts, processes, prototypes, procedures where the cognitive, the procedural and the knowledge application are put into action.

On the other hand, in relation to the diagnosis made to students of different academic programs of higher education, it could be evidenced that they definitely only handle the technology for entertainment and leisure spaces, and when making use in these fields, they consider it assertive since it allows them to interact and because it is a dynamic way to play alone or online with a group of students, and they are constantly updating the latest trends in these resources, from software to hardware; on the other hand, they stated that if in institutions they implement technology such as virtual reality for learning, the area that had more interest or more acceptance was technical drawing, due to interacting with spaces and objects, it allows them to have a better approach in aspects of dimensions, perspectives of design and setting of the places, for later students to be able to project them with their own proposals.

It is necessary that both educational institutions and students, receive advice on how to make use of technologies different to conventional ones, so that there is more appropriation of knowledge and more collective participation by the study groups, thus in this way classes and subjects, be more enriching and with more learning.

References

1. Martínez, N.: Pedagogía: Currículo y uso de TIC para cursos virtuales. Revista ED Experiencia Docente. Universidad ECCI. Bogotá Colombia. IOP Web (2016). http://experienciadocente. ecci.edu.co/index.php/experienciadoc/article/view/43/30
2. Martínez, N.: Influencia de la red social Twitter en la interacción, comunicación y nivel académico de los docentes de un curso de actualización. Editorial Académica Española (2014). ISBN: 978-3-639-67097-4

3. Cabrera, A., Juan, S., Fariñas, L.G.: El estudio de los estilos de aprendizaje desde una perspectiva vigostkiana: una aproximación conceptual. Revista Iberoamericana de Educación. UNIR (2019). (ISSN: 1681-5653). IOP Web: http://www2.udec.cl/~hbrinkma/estilos_de_aprendizaje_perspectiva_vigotskiana.pdf
4. I. Mosquera G., Estilos de aprendizaje: clasificación sensorial y propuesta de Kolb UNIR (2017). IOP Web: https://www.unir.net/educacion/revista/noticias/estilos-de-aprendizaje-clasificacion-sensorial-y-propuesta-de-kolb/549201749973/. Accedido el 28 de julio de 2019
5. Investigaciónl Definición de investigación - Diccionario de la lengua española - Edición del Tricentenario (2017). IOP Web: https://dle.rae.es/?id=M3YxV5t. Accedido el 30 de julio de 2019
6. Tamayo y Tamayo, M.: and Instituto Colombiano para el Fomento de la Educación Superior., *La investigación*. Icfes. (1999)
7. Bunge, M.: La Ciencia, Su Método Y Su Filosofía. Laetoli (2013)
8. Aguirre, C.: Desarrollo de competencias de investigación en estudiantes de educación superior con la mediación de herramientas de m-learning & e-learning. Revista de Inclusión y desarrollo – Uniminuto, pp. 68–83 (2017)
9. Yang, X., Cheng, P.-Y., Yang, X.: The impact of three types of virtual reality scene on learning. International Conference of Educational Innovation through Technology (EITT) (2017). ISBN: 978-1-5386-0629-2
10. Cortés, J., Murcia, C.: REALIDAD VIRTUAL EN LOS PROCESOS DE ENSEÑANZA EN LA EDUCACIÓN SUPERIOR. Bogotá: Corporación Universitaria Minuto de Dios-UNIMINUTO (2019)
11. Candelas, F., Fernando Torres, P.G.: LABORATORIO VIRTUAL REMOTO PARA ROBÓTICA Y EVALUACIÓN DE SU IMPACTO EN LA DOCENCIA. Alicante (2004). https://rua.ua.es/dspace/bitstream/10045/4609/1/CandelasA-Laboratorio_Virtual_remoto_para_robotica_y_evaluacion-RiaiI1-2.pdf
12. Martínez, N.: Evaluación del aprendizaje en ambientes mediados por TIC: Influencia de las rúbricas en el rendimiento académico en educación superior. Tesis doctoral Universidad internacional de la RIOJA. España (2018)
13. Steve, F.: Bolonia y las TIC: de la docencia 1.0 al aprendizaje 2.0. Universidad Politécnica de Madrid (2009). IOP Web: http://polired.upm.es/index.php/lacuestionuniversitaria/article/view/3337/3402. Accedido el 30 de julio de 2019
14. Aparicio, O.: Las TIC como herramienta cognitiva. Revista interamericana de Investigación, educación y pedagogía. Universidad Santo Tomás, vol. 11, no. 1, pp. 67–80 (2018). IOP Web: http://www.redalyc.org/articulo.oa?id=561059324005. Accedido el 30 de julio de 2019
15. Rojas, M., Méndez, R.: Cómo enseñar a investigar. Un reto para la pedagogía universitaria. *Educ.* Universidad de la Sabana Universidad Industrial de Santander. Escuela de trabajo social. Bucaramanga. Colombia, vol. 16, no. 1. (2013). https://dialnet.unirioja.es/servlet/articulo?codigo=5468365. Accedido el 30 de julio de 2019
16. Lemke, J.: Investigar para el futuro de la educación científica. Nuevas forma de aprender, nuevas formas de vivir. Enseñanza de las ciencias: revista de investigación y experiencias didácticas, vol. 24 no. 1, pp. 5–12. (2006). https://www.raco.cat/index.php/Ensenanza/article/view/73528 Accedido el 30 de julio de 2019
17. Ausubel, D.: Adquisición y retención del conocimiento. Una perspectiva cognitiva. Editorial Paidós. Barcelona. España (2002)
18. Kolb. Fundamentos teórico-metodológicos de la educación distancia: Estilos de aprendizaje. Universidad autónoma del Estado Hidalgo. Sistema de universidad Virtual (1970)
19. Del Carmen Avendaño, V., Rangel Ibarra, R., Chao González, M.M.: Paakat : revista de technología y sociedad, vol. 1, no. 1. Universidad de Guadalajara (2011)

Learning Analytics as a Tool to Support Teaching

Ma. Carmen Cabrera-Loayza[✉], Elizabeth Cadme, René Elizalde,
and Nelson Piedra

Research Group Knowledge-Based System,
Universidad Técnica Particular de Loja, San Cayetano, 1101608 Loja, Ecuador
{mccabrerax,iecadme,rrelizalde,nopiedra}@utpl.edu.ec
https://investigacion.utpl.edu.ec/grupos/kbs

Abstract. Nowadays open online courses have become a powerful alternative in the teaching-learning process worldwide. Also, the use of Virtual Learning Environments for delivery of these courses has generated information sources contain large data sets about student interactions (content, resources and learning activities) creating research opportunities about students' behavior in online courses. However, these type of courses faces an important challenge: high dropout rates during the course. This is a problem has become generalized in the different initiatives of online courses. This work, it is describing a dynamical visualization tool based on Learning Analytics using interaction events discovered in tracking logs. This tool can be used as a support to identify students at risk of dropping the course and to help teachers or instructors to take the necessary and appropriate actions.

Keywords: Open courses online · Learning Analytics · Drop out · Log files · Tracking logs

1 Introduction

In the field of education, the use of virtual learning environments has become widespread, especially in higher education where learning technologies tend to be adaptive. New and appropriate evaluation and feedback methods are needed for these environments. The traditional methods used to monitor and evaluate learning behavior are not effective or appropriate for virtual learning environments. However, web technologies have allowed a new way to collect data on learning behavior based on capturing student interactions through log files that provide a rich source of data [1]. The follow-up records provide the basic structures that contain the learning actions and the interactions of the students. The follow-up records included the basic structures that contain the learning actions and student interactions. This information is valuable and can be used to analyze

UTPL, Research Group Knowledge-Based System and the Open Campus initiative.

M. Botto-Tobar et al. (Eds.): ICAT 2019, CCIS 1195, pp. 415 425, 2020.
https://doi.org/10.1007/978-3-030-42531-9_33

students' academic progress, predict future behaviors as well as to alert teachers, tutors and students during the development of a course [13].

Datasets allow do descriptive or predictive analysis, which has led to the development of two lines of research on educational data: Learning Analytics (LA) and Educational Data Mining (EDM) [2]. According to [3], the analytics of learning is the measurement, collection, analysis, and reporting of data of students and their contexts, in order to understand and optimize learning and the contexts in which it occurs. A variety of jobs that analyze student behavior when developing online activities. The data contained in the archives has become the raw material that has given rise to different investigations from different approaches, so we have [9] where tasks of collaborative learning are analyzed and discover patterns to give some guides on student behavior. On the other hand, [10] describes the analysis of the relationship between a student's behavior and their performance in a given course. In [11] the relationship between learning objectives and student interactions is studied. Also, we have found tools developments like [12] that describe a tool for predicting learning performance-based in checkpoint assignments (theory tests, home assignments, project assignments and final test). In [4, 6, 7] they refer to EDM as a discipline that focuses on the development of methods of exploring specific types of data that come from the educational context. Finally, the general objective is to understand how students learn and identify those aspects that can improve learning and other educational aspects.

Use of Learning Analytics in institutions of higher education, in the study of [13], indicates that despite having a development time, they require teachers, tutors, administrators, among others, should familiarize themselves with the methods of application of this field.

Based on these approaches and the analytical cycle proposed by [3], in this work is proposed a different approach, with the purpose of carrying out the analysis of the interactivity of students and tutors of open courses online offered by OpenCampus initiative.

The analytical cycle proposed in [3] includes 4 generic phases: (1) Establishment of objectives and metrics; (2) Data collection; (3) information analysis; and, (4) Action according to the results required in the previous analysis. The goal is the development of a tool that facilitates teachers to know the progress of their course. Some documents such as reports and requests from teachers and students will be used as input to determine key indicators during the course development. The information collection and analysis phase is described below in this section. The most important aspects of the actions that were carried out based on the analysis developed are highlighted in the discussion and conclusions section.

2   Methodology

For the development of this work the following process has been determined (see Fig. 1): Identification of the sources of information, Data Preprocessing, Identification of variables, Analysis, and visualization of results.

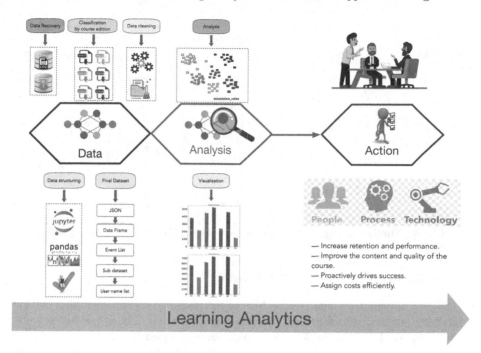

Fig. 1. Methodology process.

2.1 Identification of Sources of Information

Data sources used are the log files generated in April - June 2019 academic offer of the courses developed in the OpenCampus initiative. The number of enrolled in 44 courses offered, reaching a total of 15800 participants is shown below (see Fig. 2).

Besides, it is relevant to mention that Open Campus is implemented under the OpenEdx platform, which classifies student interactions 22 types of defined events. This classification helps determine which are the events that register more activity on the part of the students. Table 1 describes 5 of the main events generated in the courses offered.

Table 1. Types of interaction event - OpenEdx Platform

Event type	Description
Navigation	The number of navigation interactions on the platform
Video	The number of video interactions watched by students
Problem	The number of interactions to problems solved by students
Assessments	The number of interactions to peer evaluations do by students
Forum	The number of interactions in the discussion forums made by the students
Certificates	Identify if the student has received a certificate at the end of the course

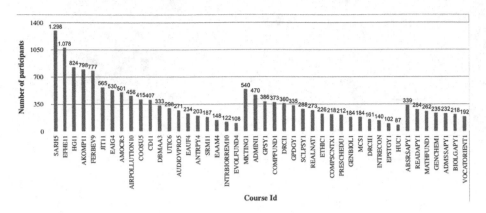

Fig. 2. Number of registrants per course - Open Campus offer April 2019.

2.2 Data Preprocessing and Cleaning

The source information is in the log files of the platform server; such information must have entered into a strong pre-processing process. The steps taken were: (a) Reading each line of the log files; (b) Transformation to Json format of each line of the file; (c) Review and transformation of the data types of each column to types that allow obtaining statistics more efficiently, example: transformation to datetime format. Another point is that, in this step new columns of data were created in the dataset.

Finally, in this phase do the processes of cleaning, transformation and integration of data are carried out. In the cleaning process, irrelevant data is removed, missing data is determined and outliers are eliminated. For the data cleaning process, the five types of events identified in the previous phase are considered. In the transformation process the data discretization is performed, where certain continuous values become discrete. Finally, in the integration process, the extraction of user-profiles is performed to later associate the interactions with the student's data. At this stage, approximately 2,800,000 million interaction records are initially involved, as well as information from 9,500 user profiles.

2.3 Identification of Variables

The main objective of this phase is to identify patterns of student interaction throughout the offer and for each course. For this, the following questions and the associated criteria or variables for their analysis are established Table 2:

As mentioned in the previous section, the sources of information for the analysis of the variables are the student interaction log files. This type of file allows you to know at any given time what the student has done? How has he done it? How much time has he spent? And what content and activities have you worked on? The degree of detail and the amount of stored data allows greater accuracy in the analysis of the identified variables.

Table 2. Variable identification.

Questions	Analysis variables
What are the **most active courses**?	Number of interactions per course
What are the students' **peak connection** times on the platform?	Connection time
How is the evolution (timeline) of student **interactions per week**?	Number of interactions per offer and per course
How many **average interactions** does a student make from entering until leaving the platform?	Number of interactions per user
What evaluation **activities are the most carried out**?	Number of interactions per event - type of problem

For the first and second variables, the Log files of the entire course offer are considered. While for the remaining variables the Log files of the four courses with the greatest interaction are analyzed: MATHFUND1, SARH5, EFHE11, and AKOMP11.

2.4   Analysis and Visualization of Results

For the analysis, descriptive learning analytical techniques [7,8] have been applied to the variables defined in the previous section. There are three main ways in which ordinal data distributions and intervals can be described. First, the measure of the central tendency, where it is located on the measurement scale. Second, the dispersion, the degree of propagation. And thirdly, the form. For nominal data distributions, only the central tendency measure is applied. Measures can be used to describe each of these characteristics of distribution and can be displayed graphically.

Next, the analysis and visualization of each of the variables is presented.

Number of Interactions per Course. For this variable, the number of interactions that students have made for each of the five interaction events is analyzed in order to see the trend in the development of content and activities. The analysis of this variable gives the teacher an idea about the students' interest in the course. In addition, with the information collected from this variable, you can answer questions such as: what resources do students interact most? Is the course planning followed or are the tasks done at the last moment? What types of resources capture more student attention? among others.

After the analysis, it has been obtained that the greatest maximum of interactions is 125289 interactions, the minimum value is 8662 interactions, and a global average of interactions is 42991 interactions for this offer (see Fig. 3).

With the analysis, it has also been discovered that not necessarily the number of interactions is directly proportional to the number of participants in the

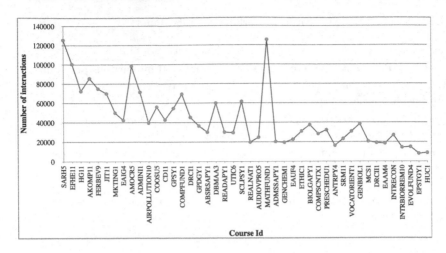

Fig. 3. The most active courses - Open Campus offer April 2019

course. However, the MATHFUND1 course has 39% of participants with respect to the course with the maximum number of participants in the offer. However, the MATHFUND1 course has 10% more interactions than that course.

Connection Time. The general objective of this variable is to analyze the descriptive question When did the user take a specific action? Specifically, we want to predict the peak hours that course participants register more activity within the platform, this will help establish an interactive timeline and predict actions such as the number of effective hours of dedication and if this influences the percentage of participants who pass the course (Fig. 4).

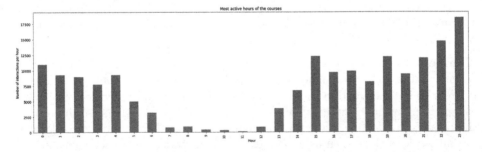

Fig. 4. Comparison of students' peak connection times on the platform - Open Campus offer April 2019

The analysis is performed considering the actual time and connection time per student and the number of interactions 24 h a day. It is determined that the users mostly connect between 7:00 p.m. and 11:00 p.m. (see Fig. 3). Analyzing this range it is concluded that a large number of participants in the course do not have enough time during the day to carry out the planned activities, it can be by study, work or family obligations. However, interest in continuing and participating in the courses is maintained.

Number of Interactions per Offer and per Course. The analysis of this variable shows how the interaction of students is weekly. It is observed that the greatest activity is concentrated between the first week until the fifth week, decreasing as the course ends.

This variable is very important since it can help us predict when students leave the course and take measures to avoid it. Considering that there is an average of 5% of students who unwind before starting the course, 60% who drop them during the course and 35% who finish the course and pass it (see Fig. 5).

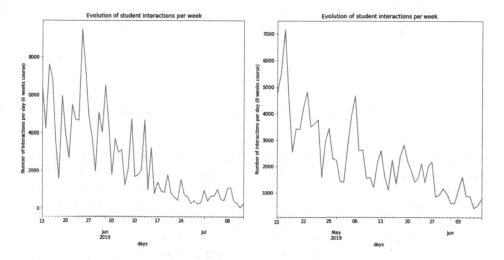

Fig. 5. Student interactions per week (6 weeks course and 8 weeks course)

Number of Interactions per User. This variable helps determine the interaction behavior by each user in the different activities and content uploaded in the course. You can determine what are the user preferences and how are the learning paths that you create per week until the end of the course. One of the learning paths that has been determined is that 60% of students, only observing audiovisual resources, can solve problem-type activities and pass the course. However, in 30% of other students also review the document-type resources and perform peer reviews. Finally, 10% of the students comply in detail with all the proposed activities and contents.

Analyzing the results, the maximum number of interactions per student is 7073 interaction and an average of 272 interactions. The average obtained is relatively low considering the courses are planned in a range of 6 to 8 weeks (see Fig. 6).

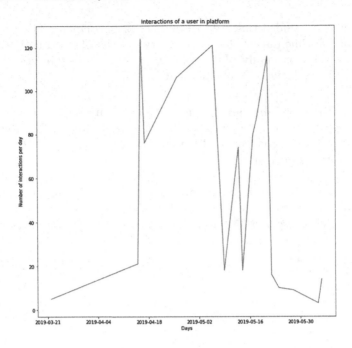

Fig. 6. Number of interactions per user - Open Campus offer April 2019

Number of Interactions per Event - Type of Problem. In the OpenCampus platform courses, teachers in their planning enter some types of activities to be carried out by the participants; one of the activities is the test resolution of the type of problem check component. The graph shows the number of interactions the component has in relation to the selected courses.

A high number of teachers propose the resolution of tests at the end of each week of study, in addition a final test is proposed that includes the topics studied in all the weeks of the course, said component is showed in the final weeks (see Fig. 7). More interaction is visualized in this space of time (the courses have a duration of six to eight weeks).

To get a better insight into the importance of the variables, it is important to analyze and measure the impact of input variables on the level of success at the end of the courses. In this case, the number of interactions per users is a key variable to identify which are the most predominant events and which the students focus on to meet the proposed objectives in the course. Also, based on the results obtained, several student behaviors can be interpreted in the course, as well as learning paths that can be used to predict the success or failure of future participants based on their behavior within the platform. For example, with the variable of the number of interactions per event, it is possible to determine if both the learning activities and the learning resources are of complete interest for the students and is a predominant variable in the success or failure of the courses.

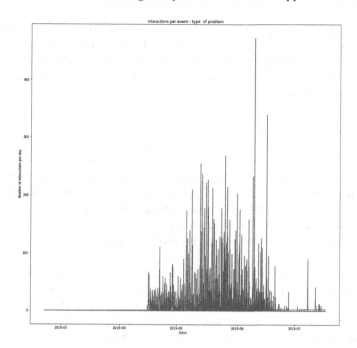

Fig. 7. Number of interactions per event - type of problem. - Open Campus offer April 2019

3   Discussion

After analyzing the information from the results visualizations, the team of researchers built a review protocol to be applied to each of the OpenCampus platform courses. The protocol was socialized and refined with the teaching team, detailed below:

Course name; course edition; teaching team; start and end date, dedication and weekly effort of teachers, expressed in hours, type of educational resources uploaded to the course (documents, weblinks, audiovisuals); number of evaluations to be developed by students in the course, number of co-assessment activities generated in the course, percentage of advance estimated in the previous configuration of the course, use is made of a scale: Minimum (10%–30%), Acceptable (31%–60%), Complete (61%–100%); interactions of the teaching team in the development of the course; student academic results (number of active, inactive and approved students), and a section that includes general observations or recommendations from the OpenCampus team.

The described protocol was executed in 44 courses of the first academic offer of the platform of the year 2019; after the implementation of the protocol, the consolidated report was brought to the attention of academic departments of the institution with the objective that the performance and improvement of the courses can be evaluated in a next edition.

With the information obtained from interactions of students, teachers and protocols applied to the courses; It remains as future work, to complete the cycle of analysis of learning of educational data, the implementation of techniques in the scope of three approaches such as Educational data mining, academic analytics, and learning analytics.

4   Conclusions

In today's world, in which the trend is oriented towards adaptive learning, the use of learning analytics especially in higher education has become essential. Some platforms provide teachers with information about their students' performance through built-in tools. Even so, it is not enough and other data are relevant and that allows us to have other criteria on how to guide teaching-learning strategies in online courses. This has led us to the analysis of interactivity through the log files.

In general terms, with the use of learning analytics, it is possible to know the behavior of our students to (a) prevent possible failures, (b) understand the different events that occur in the virtual learning environment, (c) check the suitability and analyze the use of educational content and resources, (d) Promote offline and online tutoring, and (e) audit online courses for continuous improvement.

Descriptive analysis of student interaction records, through log files, can be used to provide valuable information to course instructors about the use of the virtual learning environment, the use of resources, the learning behavior and task performance. Based on the analysis carried out, the trend on the decrease in the number of interactions continues as the course progresses, this is mainly due to the early dropout of students. Of the 100% of students enrolled at the end of the course, they remain active between 30% and 10%. Besides, it is identified that students take more advantage of weekends to carry out the planned activities in the courses, as well as schedules outside the working day.

Finally, it is important to highlight that this project is a work in progress that aims to trace student behavior routes in support of the teaching team in making decisions and actions to reduce the degree of early abandonment in the courses.

Acknowledgement. This research was supported by the Knowledge-Based System Research Group of the Universidad Técnica Particular de Loja and teacher's teams that design and published your courses in Open Campus initiative (http://opencampus.utpl. edu.ec).

References

1. Bogarín, A., Cerezo, R., Romero, C.: A survey on educational process mining. Wiley Interdisc. Rev.: Data Mining Knowl. Disc. **8**(1), e1230 (2018)
2. Lang, C., Siemens, G., Wise, A., Gasevic, D. (eds.): Handbook of Learning Analytics. SOLAR, Society for Learning Analytics and Research (2017)

3. Amo, D., Santiago, R.: Learning Analytics - La narración del aprendizaje a través de los datos. UOC (2017)
4. Siemens, G., Baker, R.S.: Learning analytics and educational data mining: towards communication and collaboration. In: Proceedings of the 2nd International Conference on Learning Analytics and Knowledge, pp. 252–254. ACM, April 2012
5. Romero, C., Ventura, S.: Data mining in education. Wiley Interdisc. Rev.: Data Mining Knowl. Disc. **3**(1), 12–27 (2013)
6. Romero, C., Ventura, S., Pechenizkiy, M., Baker, R.S.: Handbook of Educational Data Mining. CRC Press, Boca Raton (2010)
7. Pazmiño-Maji, R.A., García-Peñalvo, F.J., Conde-González, M.A.: Approximation of statistical implicative analysis to learning analytics: a systematic review. In: Proceedings of the Fourth International Conference on Technological Ecosystems for Enhancing Multiculturality, pp. 355–376. ACM, November 2016
8. Wong, B.T.M.: Learning analytics in higher education: an analysis of case studies. Asian Assoc. Open Univ. J. **12**(1), 21–40 (2017)
9. Rodríguez-Triana, M.J., Prieto, L.P., Martínez-Monés, A., Asensio-Pérez, J.I., Dimitriadis, Y.: Monitoring collaborative learning activities: exploring the differential value of collaborative flow patterns for learning analytics. In: 2018 IEEE 18th International Conference on Advanced Learning Technologies (ICALT), pp. 155–159. IEEE, July 2018
10. Goldstein, S.C., Zhang, H., Sakr, M., An, H., Dashti, C.: Understanding how work habits influence student performance. In: Proceedings of the 2019 ACM Conference on Innovation and Technology in Computer Science Education, pp. 154–160. ACM, July 2019
11. Costa, L., Souza, M., Salvador, L., Amorim, R.: Monitoring students performance in e-learning based on learning analytics and learning educational objectives. In: 2019 IEEE 19th International Conference on Advanced Learning Technologies (ICALT), vol. 2161, pp. 102–103. IEEE, July 2019
12. Bystrova, T., Larionova, V., Sinitsyn, E., Tolmachev, A.: Learning Analytics in Massive Open Online Courses as a Tool for Predicting Learner Performance (2018)
13. Avella, J.T., Kebritchi, M., Nunn, S.G., Kanai, T.: Learning analytics methods, benefits, and challenges in higher education: a systematic literature review. Online Learn. **20**(2), 13–29 (2016)

Automation of the Generation of Accessible Digital Educational Material for Students with Visual Disabilities

Boris Cabrera Medina[1](✉) and Miguel Zuñiga-Prieto[2](✉)

[1] Facultad de Ingeniería, Universidad de Cuenca, Av. 12 de Abril, 010107 Cuenca, Ecuador
boro101094@gmail.com
[2] Departamento de Ciencias de la Computación, Av. 12 de Abril, 010107 Cuenca, Ecuador
miguel.zunigap@ucuenca.edu.ec

Abstract. Online learning has grown in the last years, where educational institutions are offering courses or study programs in different knowledge areas. Online learning allows students to participate actively in cooperative learning activities, interacting without the preconceived notions of disability that other participants could have, which affects the relationship. However, these advantages have often not become a reality for most people with disabilities, especially in the educational context. For instance, courses' web pages are not accessible for people with visual disabilities, which makes the experience of taking a course frustrating and tedious.

This article proposes a Model-Driven Development approach for supporting the design and generation of accessible educational material, for example, accessible Learning Objects (LO). This approach provides a software infrastructure that includes: (i) A Domain-Specific Language and its corresponding graphic editor that supports accessible LO's design. Helping teachers during the instructional design and allowing them to describe accessibility requirements for students with visual disabilities. (ii) A LO's generation engine that takes as input design artifacts and generates the source code that implements accessible LO. Abstracting teachers from technological aspects (e.g., programming language instructions) necessary to construct LO with accessibility features. The applicability of this approach is illustrated by using the DSL and the generation engine to design and automatically implement an accessible LO according to the accessibility profile specified during design. Finally, the generated LO was published in the Learning Management System Moodle.

1 Introduction

Since the mid-1990s, the number of colleges and universities that offer courses and degree programs through distance education has been growing dramatically [1].

The asynchronous (e.g., email) and synchronous (e.g., chat) communication characteristics of online learning favor the growth mentioned above. It, by easing communication among students and allowing them to participate in cooperative learning activities. Additionally, Internet communication tools facilitate students to interact with each other without the preconceived notions of disability affecting the relationship [2].

© Springer Nature Switzerland AG 2020
M. Botto-Tobar et al. (Eds.): ICAT 2019, CCIS 1195, pp. 426–439, 2020.
https://doi.org/10.1007/978-3-030-42531-9_34

The perspective promised with the digital age has often not become a reality for most people with disabilities, especially in the educational context. Studies reveal that leading organizations in online education have a high percentage of inaccessible pages. For instance, [3] shows that 33% of them did not know if their websites followed accessibility guidelines, 28% followed the guidelines moderately, and 18% followed the guidelines to a lesser extent. Web pages use inadequate color or small font size, preventing students with visual disabilities from understanding pages' content or interacting with it. Visual disability is a disorder that is not corrected either with regular glasses or contact lenses or medications or surgery [4]). Approximately 1.3 billion people worldwide live with visual disabilities [10], whereas, in Ecuador, about 11.79% of its population suffers these disabilities [11]. Therefore, it is essential to redesign traditional pedagogical approaches by integrating information and communication technologies in courses to offer distance education programs using the Internet [5].

Learning Objects (LO), digital resources used in virtual education environments, mediate the teaching-learning process. LO design and construction is based on didactic, pedagogical, and technological aspects [17]. Teachers are not experts in technology, which makes it difficult for them to construct accessible LO (barrier-free learning content). The difficulty level increases with the heterogeneity of technological resources involved in the construction of LO. For instance, different: authoring tools (e.g., eXeLearning, Ardora), used by teachers to authoring web-based e-learning content; programming languages, used to incorporate dynamic accessible characteristics (e.g., java scripts); educational standards, used to publish interactive content (e.g., SCORM, IMS). The importance of accessibility in digital resources is widely recognized today from a technological point of view. The Web Accessibility Initiative (WAI) of the World Wide Web Consortium (W3C), has played an important role, developing standards and supporting material that helps in promoting the importance of accessibility and developing a framework for accessible web resources [6]. The Web Content Accessibility Guidelines (WCAG) are part of a series of web accessibility guidelines published by the WAI.

This paper proposes a technological solution (hereafter referred to as solution) to support teachers during the construction of accessible LO for students with visual disabilities. This proposal is based on a Model-Driven Development (MDD) approach to overcome the heterogeneity in technological tools that teachers require to construct accessible LO. This solution prevents teachers from (i) needing to know how to use technology (e.g., a programming language instructions that implements accessibility), because the solution embeds technological knowledge; and (ii) building a new LO in case there are new accessibility or technological requirements because teachers reuse the course design. MDD is a software engineering approach that focuses on the creation and exploitation of domain models as major artifacts of the development process, where model-to-text (M2T) transformation algorithms use the information described in models (e.g., instructional design) to generate different versions of source code (e.g., web pages).

This proposal, a software infrastructure, extends a previous work [18] allowing teachers, in addition to supporting different activities of the LO construction process, to take into account aspects of accessibility through (i) A Domain-Specific Language (DSL) and its corresponding graphic editor that supports LO design; facilitating not only the instructional design of courses but the specification of accessibility requirements of students with visual disabilities. (ii) A LO generation engine that takes as input the information described during the design and automatically creates the accessible LO web pages, preventing developers from knowing technological aspects of how to implement accessibility features. The applicability of this proposal has been proven through designing a LO using the graphic editor, then using the LO generation engine to automatically obtain an accessible LO as a SCORM package (Sharable Content Object Reference Model) according to the accessibility profiles specified during the design. The LO was published in the Learning Management System (LMS) Moodle.

2   Related Work

In [7] the authors claim to meet the accessibility needs of MOOC users, with an approach based on the creation of user-profiles and the use of questionnaires to define specific accessibility preferences (e.g., text size, color contrast, line spacing): From that point on, the presentation of adaptive content is automatically applied to the content. However, this proposal requires different content databases with different presentations according to the content type (e.g., video, images, text).

The work presented in [8] proposes an approach to the development of LO that focuses on the specification of a LO architecture where developers identify customizable elements, customizable learning objects (e.g., animations, images). The authors propose a DSL for creating models of customizable LO that will be stored on a repository to be consumed by teachers through authoring tools, enabling teachers to change specific LO components. Then students access a new LO version. In [9], the authors propose learning patterns implemented as templates for accessible and adaptable LO, allowing teachers to use them to design accessible LO that derive from existing patterns.

The works cited above propose approaches to address the need to provide accessible content to people with different disability profiles. However, these works require that developers of LO design and implement different LO, as many as disability profiles for which they need to provide accessible content. It implies additional teachers' effort during the LO designing or creation time. Additionally, teachers require to have prior knowledge about designing or implementing LO for different disabilities. Therefore, teachers require solutions that abstract them from knowing both visualization/interaction alternatives as well as technical aspects that they need to take into account for the design and implementation of accessible learning objects.

3   Design of the Technological Solution

To design the technological solution for supporting teachers during the construction of accessible LO for students with visual disabilities, we made decisions regarding the following aspects: (i) The visual disabilities of users for whom the generated LO will be accessible. (ii) The methodology for the construction of accessible LO that the solution will allow applying. (iii) The authoring tool with which the generated LO will be compatible.

3.1 Visual Disabilities of Users for Whom the Generated LO Will Be Accessible

The solution proposes in this work will provide a DSL for assisting teachers in designing assessable LO as well as a generation engine that automatically implement accessible objects according to the design. Both of these solution components require to work with Web pages' elements (e.g., text, images) whose configuration (property values) will vary during the design and generation of LO accessible for students with visual disabilities. Therefore, visual disabilities are the requirements that guide the solution development.

WCAG describes what people with low vision need for electronic content in a technology-neutral language, providing guidelines and accessibility requirements to implement into web pages in order to improve the experience of people with visual disabilities when interacting with Web content [4]. WCAG introduces five visual disability categories that impact the Web (not including total blindness) whose requirements determine the configuration alternatives for web pages' elements.

Visual Acuity (Clarity): Is the clarity or sharpness of vision. Requirements for people with blurry vision are:

- Perceiving: people need to recognize individual letters based on their characteristics (e.g., text size, font, style, capitalization, size of all elements).
- Spacing for Reading: space between lines and space between words impacts readability (leading, letter spacing, word spacing, justification, margins and borders, elements spacing).
- Identifying Elements: distinguishing elements such as headings and lists (element-level customization, proportional text increase).

Light Sensitivity: For some people, the typical brightness of a computer screen with a light background is not readable and painful. They need to change the background to a darker color. Requirements for people with light sensitivity are:

- Brightness and Color: brightness relates to luminance and luminosity (brightness overall, text contrast, not relying on color).

Contrast Sensitivity: Is the ability to detect differences in brightness; for instance, colors that look very different (such as red, blue, green) can have similar brightness, not providing sufficient contrast. Requirements for people with light sensitivity are:

- Brightness and Color.

Field of Vision: The area where a person's eye can collect visual information when looking forward is known as the field of vision or visual field. Some people have a smaller field of vision, which is called field loss. There are three types of visual field loss: Central field loss, where vision is reduced or absent in the middle of people's vision; peripheral field loss, where people only see in the central part of their visual field, sometimes called "tunnel vision"; and other field loss, where people have dispersed hidden vision patches. Requirements related to the field of vision are:

- Tracking: following along the lines of text, including getting from the end of one line to the beginning of the next line of text (rewrap for one direction scrolling, reflow to a single column, flexible text areas, line length, justification, hyphenation).
- Point of Regard and Proximity: the point of regard is the area that the user is viewing, whereas proximity is using space to group related content (maintain point of regard, the proximity of related information, scrollbars).

Color Vision: Also called "color blindness." It is when people cannot see specific colors well or at all. It is usually due to deficiencies in the cone receptors of eyes, which are responsible for color perception. Requirements related to color blindness are:

- Brightness and Color.

3.2 Methodology for the Construction of Accessible LO that the Solution Will Allow Applying

Teachers should build LO following approaches that guide the process and take into account pedagogical aspects of educational material. In this work, in order to provide a solution that takes into account those aspects, and not only abstract teachers from knowing visualization/interaction alternatives and technological issues, the proposed solution supports the process suggested in the methodology *Design, Creation and Building of Learning Objects* (DICREVOA – from Spanish Diseño, Creación y Evaluación de Objetos de Aprendizaje). DICREVOA [14] is a methodology based on learning theories and the design of educational materials so that teachers can create an OA optimally for their students. This methodology proposes five phases (i.e., Analysis, Design, Implementation, Evaluation, and Publication). The DSL provided for the solution supports the execution of the two first phases of the DICREVOA methodology, adapting these phases in order to allow the specification of accessibility requirements. On the other hand, the generation engine automates the third phase, implementing accessibility features in the generated LO.

3.3 Authoring Tool with Which the Generated LO Will Be Compatible

The e-Learning XHTML (eXe) editor is an Author program for content development. This tool is especially suitable for education professionals (teachers and instructional designers) dedicated to the development and publication of teaching and learning materials through the web. Being an authoring tool avoids the user who wants to create web-based content having to have previous knowledge of the programming languages necessary to develop content on the Internet (e.g., html, XML, javascript, ajax) [12]. Additionally, it is quite useful for teachers since they will not depend on designers or programmers to be able to make their content and present it to their students, that is why we choose the eXelearning editor as a starting point for the creation of learning objects.

In this work, we analyzed the set of artifacts that eXelearning produce to implement LO implementation, and we made our generation engine produce the same set of artifacts but including accessibility functionalities into them, generating accessible LO.

The e*Xelearning editor packages the LO* for deployment as SCORM packages, which is a ZIP file that contains certain content defined by the SCORM standard. The file is known as Package Interchange File (PIF) and contains all the artifacts needed to deliver the content package through the SCORM or LMS runtime environment. SCORM packages include the following artifacts:

- A manifest XML file (imsmanifest.xml),
- Schema and definition files (i.e., .xsd and .dtd files) referenced within the manifest,
- Resource files (e.g., .js, .html, .css files) used by the content package and its learning activities. References to external files or absolute URLs are not allowed [13].

4 Overview of Technological Approximation

This section presents the software infrastructure that has been designed and implemented for the generation of accessible OA. The software infrastructure provides:

- DSLs to facilitate the documentation of the decisions made during the analysis and design of accessible LO; these include (i) A metamodel that defines the abstract syntax, concepts, and relationships between DSL concepts. (ii) A graphic editor that defines the specific syntax of the DSLs.
- A generation engine, which implements M2T transformations that generate SCORM packages. Artifacts are generated according to the type of disability that the teacher defines when designing the OA.

For the development of the software infrastructure, Obeo Designer was used. It is an integrated development environment based on Eclipse that integrates modeling tools for creating metamodels as well as graphic editor builders [15]. The metamodel used and graphical editor proposed in this work was created by analyzing the LO creation process suggested in DICREVOA as well as the interaction mechanisms (known as iDevices) supported by eXelearning. The resulting metamodel (http://bit.ly/2YLimfm) allows the documenting of the analysis and design of accessible LO. Regarding the construction of the generation engine, Acceleo was used. It provides facilities to create MT2 transformations that automatically produce source code [16] from models. In this work, models that describe LO' analysis/design decisions are created with graphic editors.

Next, excerpts from the graphic editor, which show the interfaces provided to (i) Specify the disability to which the LO will adapt; (ii) Define the LO structure; (iii) Describe the LO content; (iv) Generate accessible LO.

4.1 Specify the Disability to Which the LO Will Adapt

During the analysis phase, the teacher will have a palette on the right side that contains all the information (e.g., Impairment) to be specified in this phase in order to analyze LO requirements (see Fig. 1).

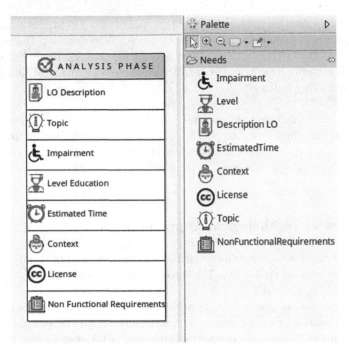

Fig. 1. Analysis phase information

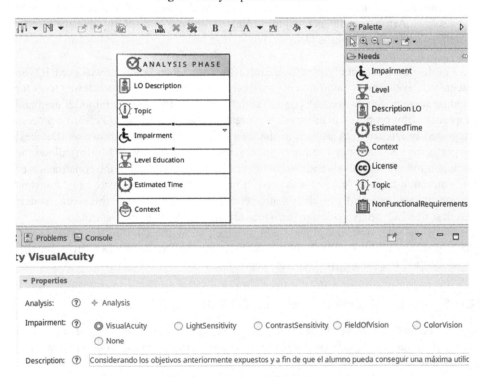

Fig. 2. Impairment information

Regarding impairment information, during analysis, teachers have to specify the type of impairment for which the LO implementation will be compatible with (see Fig. 2).

4.2 Define the LO Structure

During the instructional design phase, teachers are allowed to structure the LO, as shown in Fig. 3.

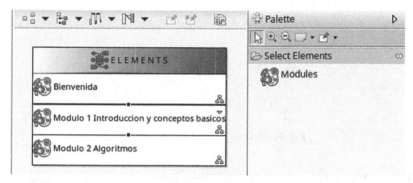

Fig. 3. Structuring of modules or themes for the OA

Teachers will be able to add the modules or themes to the LO. For instance, Fig. 3 shows that there are three modules already added, having the possibility of adding new modules. Additionally, when a module is selected, teachers define the module structure by defining the content elements that will be part of the module and their corresponding types (e.g., Content/Information, Activities, Self-appraisal), see Fig. 4.

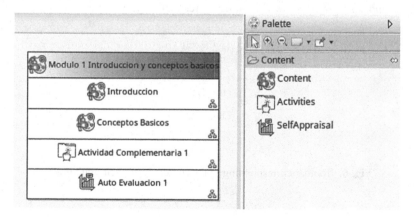

Fig. 4. Module content structure

Each content element can be composed by one o more pages, as shown in Fig. 5.

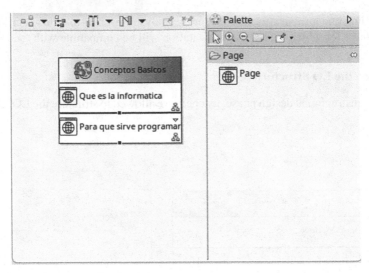

Fig. 5. Module content structure pages

When teachers select a page, they describe the page content by including iDevices elements.

4.3 Describe the LO Content

For *describing* the LO content, teachers describe the elements to be included in the pages corresponding to the module structure. These elements are iDevices which support the interaction with students by either showing information or receiving students' feedback. Figures 6, 7 and 8 show the corresponding toolbox according to the elements content-type: Self-appraisal, *Information, or Activity,* respectively.

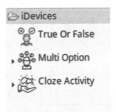

Fig. 6. Toolbar corresponding to the content type "Self-appraisal"

Fig. 7. Toolbar corresponding to the content type "Information"

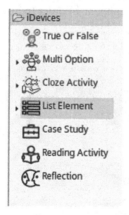

Fig. 8. Toolbar corresponding to the content type "Activity"

4.4   Generate Accessible LO

Generation engine will generate SCORM packages whose web pages (artifacts) implement accessibility menus that allow students to change the web page´s elements configurations (e.g., background color). These accessibility menus *(see* Figs. 9, 11 and 12*)* change according to the impairment specified during analysis, allowing students to adapt the way they interact with the LO content. It is important to emphasize that the teacher will not have to worry about copying any file, nor packing the created content, the generation engine provided in this work *generate* a .zip file ready to be deployed in an LSM.

Fig. 9. Accessibility menu for color vision, light sensitivity, and contrast sensitivity impairments

When any of the options presented in the accessibility menu of Fig. 9 is selected, the window presented in Fig. 10 will appear in order to allow students to change the color configuration.

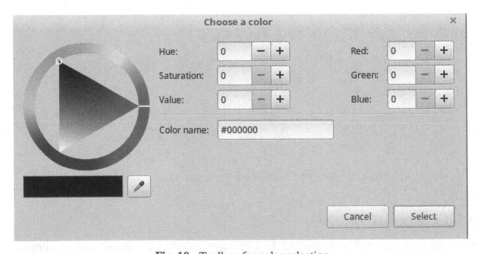

Fig. 10. Toolbox for color selection

The color configuration window shown in Fig. 10 allows students to have the flexibility to choose any color within the entire spectrum of colors for their OA, so students can adapt their LO with the combination of colors that best suits their needs.

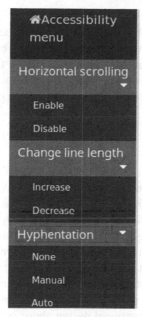

Fig. 11. Accessibility menu field of vision impairment

Fig. 12. Accessibility menu for visual acuity impairment

A particular feature of the accessibility menu in Fig. 12 is that students can choose the section to which they want to make the changes (see the bottom part of Fig. 12), all the titles of each section of the page are added with a checkbox so that students will know to which section he will make the changes. These functionalities are added only within the visual acuity disability since the W3C recommends that the student can work with different configurations for different sections of the page.

5   Conclusions

This work proposes a solution for the creation of accessible LO that allows teachers to focus their attention on the instructional design of the LO, abstracting them of technical aspects related to providing LO with accessibility characteristics. The proposed solution is based on the model-driven software development approach and provides: (i) a domain-specific language and its graphics editor, which allows teachers to describe and document the design of LO, including accessibility requirements for students with visual disabilities. (ii) A LO generation engine that takes as input the design documentation and generates different versions of source code that implements the LO designed according to the specified accessibility features. Separating the design from the implementation allows teachers to reuse the instructional design; therefore, if the LO is required to meet other accessibility requirements, teachers specify the new accessibility requirements and generate the new version of the LO. As future work, new disability criteria (e.g., auditory, motor, cognitive) will be integrated, which implies identifying and implementing accessibility characteristics in LO.

Acknowledgment. This research is supported by the DIUC_XIV_2016_038 project.

References

1. Kinash, S., Crichton, S., Kim-Rupnow, W.S.: A review of 2000-2003 literature at the intersection of online learning and disability. Am. J. Distance Educ. **18**(1), 5–19 (2004)
2. Clark, J., Bellamy, A.: Internet utilization by persons with disabilities. In: Presentation at the Annual Conference of CSUN (California State University, Northridge): Technology and Persons with Disabilities-Where Assistive Technology Meets the Information Age, Los Angeles (1999)
3. Tabs, E.D., Waits, T., Lewis, L.: Distance Education at Degree-Granting Postsecondary Institutions: 2000-2001. US Department of Education, Washington, DC (2003)
4. Allan, J., Kirkpatrick, A., Henry, S.L.: Accessibility requirements for people with low vision (2016). https://www.w3.org/TR/low-vision-needs/#visual-impairments
5. Arrigo, M.: E-learning accessibility for blind students. In: Recent Research Developments in Learning Technologies (2005)
6. Kelly, B., Phipps, L., Swift, E.: Developing a holistic approach for e-learning accessibility. Can. J. Learn. Technol./La revue canadienne de l'apprentissage et de la technologie **30**(3) (2004)
7. Sánchez Gordón, S., Luján-Mora, S.: Adaptive content presentation extension for open edX. Enhancing MOOCs accessibility for users with disabilities (2015)

8. Maria de Fátima, C., de Castro Filho, J.A., Andrade, R.M.: Model-driven development in the production of customizable learning objects. In: 2010 10th IEEE International Conference on Advanced Learning Technologies, pp. 701–702. IEEE, July 2010
9. Green, S., Jones, R., Pearson, E., Gkatzidou, S.: Accessibility and adaptability of learning objects: responding to metadata, learning patterns and profiles of needs and preferences. ALT J. **14**(1), 117–129 (2006)
10. Bourne, R.R., et al.: Magnitude, temporal trends, and projections of the global prevalence of blindness and distance and near vision impairment: a systematic review and meta-analysis. Lancet Glob. Health **5**(9), e888–e897 (2017)
11. Consejo Nacional para la Igualdad de Discapacidades. Estadísticas de discapacidad (2019). shorturl.at/kwyEF
12. Cubero, S.: Elaboración de contenidos con eXelearning (2008). http://www.iesgabrielciscar.org/eXe
13. JCA solutions. SCORM content packages (2017). http://www.scormsoft.com/scorm/cam/contentPackages
14. Maldonado, J.J., Bermeo, J.L., Mejía, M.: Diseño, Creación y Evaluación de Objetos de Aprendizaje (2017)
15. Foundation Eclipse. Sirius overview (2019). https://www.eclipse.org/sirius/overview.html
16. Foundation Eclipse. Acceleo overview (2019). https://www.eclipse.org/acceleo/overview.html
17. Pianucci, I., Chiarani, M., Tapia, M.: Elaboración de materiales educativos digitales. In: 1er Congr. Int. Punta Este
18. Bermeo, J., Zuñiga, M., Cabrera, B.: Proposal of an assistant for the automation of the design and creation process of learning objects. In: CLEI 2018. SLIS (2018)

e-Government and e-Participation

Optimization of Assembly Processes Based on Lean Manufacturing Tools. Case Studies: Television and Printed Circuit Boards (PCB) Assemblers

Silvana Cuesta[1] , Lorena Siguenza-Guzman[2] , and Juan Llivisaca[3](✉)

[1] Faculty of Chemical Sciences, Universidad de Cuenca, Cuenca, Ecuador
silvana.cuestac14@ucuenca.edu.ec
[2] Department of Computer Sciences, Faculty of Engineering,
Universidad de Cuenca, Cuenca, Ecuador
lorena.siguenza@ucuenca.edu.ec
[3] Department of Applied Chemistry and Systems of Production, Faculty of Chemical Sciences,
Universidad de Cuenca, Cuenca, Ecuador
juan.llivisaca@ucuenca.edu.ec

Abstract. In the current global context, where competition is growing, it is necessary to change the ways how companies operate, eliminating waste through the implementation of optimization tools such as the ones included in the Lean Manufacturing (LM) philosophy. LM is defined as a systematic process of waste elimination, which achieves a sustained rate of improvement over time. This research describes an optimization proposal with LM tools, performing an analysis of the processes' state of two companies focused on the assembly of televisions and Printed Circuit Boards (PCB) for televisions, respectively. Through Value Stream Mapping (VSM), it was possible to identify problems in the production processes within the two case studies. Regarding televisions, the use of various tools such as 5S and Workloads led to the elimination of one workstation, projecting an increase of almost 5% of the units produced in the assembly capacity of the plant. In the case of PCBs, the distances traveled by operators was reduced with the use of plant distribution strategies and the creation of a supermarket to supply post-assembly activities. These actions allowed the company to reduce 35% in traveled distances and increase 3.69% in the number of produced units. Validation of the optimization proposal was done through computer simulations using a process modeling software.

Keywords: Assembly companies · Lean Manufacturing · Process simulation

1 Introduction

Companies in the industrial sector must face uncertainty and demanding trends by making products that are increasingly competitive in terms of cost and quality while circumventing the challenges that sustainability and efficiency bring [1]. Industrial managers

© Springer Nature Switzerland AG 2020
M. Botto-Tobar et al. (Eds.): ICAT 2019, CCIS 1195, pp. 443–454, 2020.
https://doi.org/10.1007/978-3-030-42531-9_35

seek to change the way how processes are operated in order to optimize them and eliminate waste [2, 3].

Lean Manufacturing (LM) is seen as a methodological process that allows the identification and elimination of waste, considering waste as everything that does not add value to the process [4]. This concept is a versatile alternative to adapt to different scenarios within the industrial sector [5]. LM is not only the use of tools but also a complete change for operating businesses [7]. LM has been used differently to instill improvement. There is an attempt to correlate LM with the reduction of environmental waste, therefore, creating a balance between environmental and economic parts [1]. With the application of LM, less of each resource is used, properly distributing the available space [8]. In addition, different objectives can be optimized while considering costs and efficiency [9].

Several different applications of LM tools can be found in the literature, highlighting that the implementation of its principles has a favorable impact on the industry [6–9]. For instance, one of the main LM tools is Value Stream Mapping (VSM). It is a graphical representation of production and information elements, which are the basis for process's current situation analysis [10]. This analysis is the identification of the process flow that allows visualizing where the value and the waste are located. For example, [11] carry out an analysis of the current situation of industrial plants using the VSM tool. In this work, it is observed that by taking corrective measures, there is an increase in productivity, an increase in bottleneck capacity and improvements in production homogeneity. The 5S tools are other LM techniques aimed at creating a culture of order and cleanliness to create tidy workplaces in order to achieve the reduction of search times and to improve working conditions. These tools are considered a basic method for optimization and they have proven to be a technique that instills positive changes [12, 13].

Unlike previous researches, this study provides an idea of the possible results of optimizing processes before their real implementation in the enterprise. Moreover, by using an optimization proposal using specialized software, this work allows managers to facilitate the interpretation of the effects produced by problem-solving.

2   Materials and Methods

The main objective of this study is to present a proposal for process optimization based on LM tools. To this end, two case studies were analyzed, corresponding to two assembly companies, one focused on televisions and another on Printed Circuit Boards (PCB) for televisions. A proposed methodology was applied since the objective is the theoretical, descriptive, and computational verification of the success of LM tools utilizing the programmed system "FlexSim". For the sake of complying with the confidentiality agreement signed with the analyzed enterprises, code names were given to each of the companies as well as their corresponding assembly models. Moreover, the optimization methodology comprised four stages: Stage 1, collection and analysis of data for the mapping of the current situation; Stage 2, identification of problems and selection of tools; Stage 3, optimization proposal; and Stage 4, simulation of the optimization proposal.

2.1 Stage 1: Data Collection and Analysis for the Mapping of the Current Situation

For the analysis of the current situation of the two case studies, data were taken into consideration from [14] that reports that the television model generating more sales in 2017 was TV3, as well as its PCBs since they were the main raw material for the assembly of these televisions.

Concerning the case of televisions, the labor force was nine operators. The time available for the work was 771800 s per month. That was one shift of 12 h, five days a week, for four weeks a month, subtracting non-productive time (half-hour of lunch, preparation time at the beginning of the shift). On average, the monthly demand for TV3 was 14068 TVs per month. The takt time, i.e. the rhythm of production to reach the clients' demand, was calculated by dividing the hours of work available by the demand of the product chosen for the case study. In this case, the takt time was 54.86 s.

With all the collected data, it was possible to map the current situation of the TV case. Figure 1 contains how to carry out the process with suppliers and customers. It also highlighted the problems encountered, which corresponded to waits between processes and initial inventory excess. The processing time, i.e., the time needed to produce a TV3 was 340 s.

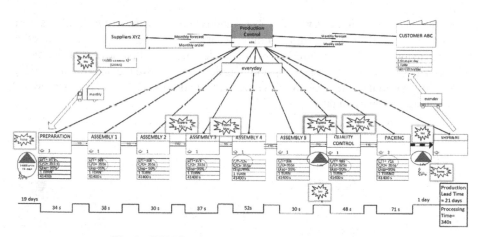

Fig. 1. VSM for the case of assembly of televisions.

Regarding the PCB assembler, there was a workforce of three operators, the available time was 772580 s per month, with a monthly demand of 13000 PCBs for the TV3 model and a takt time of 59.42 s. Figure 2 shows that the sequence of the assembly process is not a straight-line flow. Also, it is pointed out that the problems are waits between processes and transports and inventories. In addition, the processing time is 294 s.

2.2 Stage 2: Identification of Problems and Tool's Selection

The analysis of the current situation of the production processes of the two case studies using the VSM tool led to the identification of the waste or wastes that existed along the

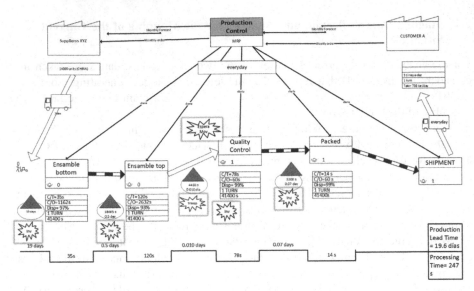

Fig. 2. VSM case assembler of printed circuit boards.

production lines. Additionally, with the observations of the process *in situ*, problems were identified and prioritized according to their occurrence in order to propose corrective measures to mitigate them. Figure 3 shows the cycle time and takt time of the television's case activities. It is observed that the packaging activity is above the takt timeline, being the activity that marks the rhythm of the process. In addition, the assembly activities 2 and 5 are also below the takt time.

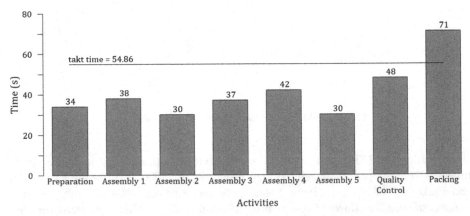

Fig. 3. Cycle time vs. Takt time for the case of televisions.

Based on the current context of televisions, the LM tools selected to mitigate the main problems were: 5S and Load Leveling. These tools were selected since the problems with the highest occurrence rate were disorder, unnecessary movements in search of tools or materials, and the cycle time of the assembly activities (it is above the takt time found in stage 1). Regarding PCBs, the LM tools selected were: 5S, Biphase plant distribution proposed in flexible manufacturing environment by the analytic hierarchy process (Plant Distribution) and Supermarkets.

2.3 Stage 3: Optimization Proposal

Based on LM tools, it was proposed to implement 5S in the two case studies to create a culture of order and cleanliness because it does not require investment. It requires the involvement and commitment of the staff. In the case of televisions, the workloads were analyzed, and it was determined that they were not balanced. Therefore, it was proposed to divide the activities to continue below the takt time. This provided the operator with time to perform internal activities. The authors in [15] mention that when there is a balanced assembly line, each worker is assigned as much work as possible. In the case of PCBs, a plant distribution was carried out for the automatic assembly area, trying to improve problems associated with distances traveled [16]. It was determined that currently for the transportation of raw material from the warehouse to the beginning of the line, the operator must walk a distance of 22.81 m, while, for the transportation of finished products from the packing area to the finished products dispatch area took 32.81 m.

Continuing with PCBs, in order to mitigate the wait among processes, the creation of a supermarket system was proposed, since, according to [17], the demand can be satisfied employing a "buffer". In this buffer, the material that was consumed should be filled or replaced, acting as a shock absorber, in a manner that the material seems to flow continuously, and the waiting times reduced. The maximum and minimum buffer capacity is calculated based on the monthly production and considering its deviation. The security inventory is determined by three zones: Zone 3 (green) is the initial part of the buffer, the inventory can be consumed to fulfill orders, that is, to satisfy the demand (Inventory > 2/3 of TIL[1]). Zone 2 (yellow): the variability and uncertainty consume part or all of this segment (1/3 of TIL < inventory < 2/3 of TIL). Zone 1: important is that this buffer segment is not entirely consumed (Inventory < 1/3 of TIL).

$$TIL = 1303.405 + 2(1024) * 1 = 3351.4 \tag{1}$$

For each buffer zone, an amount of inventory is allocated, which is calculated for daily production based on monthly production data. This results: in Zone 1, a maximum inventory of 112 units; in Zone 2, it must be less than 112 and greater than 56; and, in Zone 3, a minimum inventory of 56 units in order to reduce the waiting times between processes.

2.4 Stage 4: Simulation of the Current and Future Situation of the Cases of Televisions and PCBs

The current situation for televisions and PCBs were validated by simulation, it allowed representing a production system through objects and observing how the process was

---

[1] TIL = Target Inventory Level, i.e. average daily demand (last month) + (2 standard deviation * basic historical replacement time).

performed with each element that integrated the flow, as similar as possible to the reality of how the plant distribution was carried out.

To simulate the future situation of the television case, first, discrete events were considered. The probabilistic distribution was carried out with the times taken from the work of [14], obtaining the statistical distribution of times, shown in Table 1. It was possible to portray the reality with the support of the "Stat Fit" tool of the "ProModel" software, which yields times with a normal and logarithmic distribution, from a base of 10 takes of time of each activity of the process. All this through a curve fit analysis and data analysis for the simulation. Moreover, 30 replicas were performed to verify the stability of the system. According to the optimization proposal that was carried out previously, the changes could be observed in Fig. 4, where there were free corridors of boxes or materials.

For the simulation of the PCBs, in the same way, the statistical distribution was made with the times observed by [14], obtaining, as a result, a normal distribution for the quality control and packing activities, as shown in Table 2. In addition, since the two main assembly activities were automatic, the times of these depended only on the programming of each machine. In the same way, 30 replicas were made to annul the variability of the system as they were stochastic processes and thus ensured its stability.

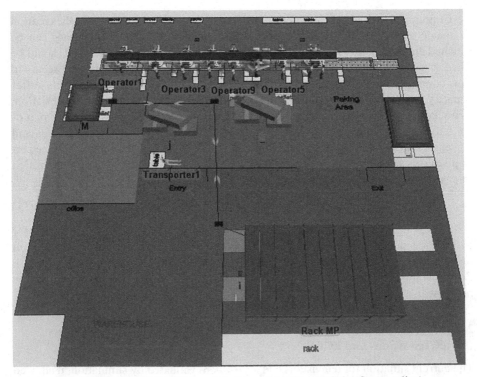

Fig. 4. Simulation of the future situation of televisions. (Color figure online)

Table 1. Probability Distribution of times in the case of televisions.

Activities	Distribution	Cycle time (s)
Preparation	Lognormal, LN (γ, μ, σ)	LN (22.2; 1.06; 0.507)
Assembly 1	Lognormal, LN (γ, μ, σ)	LN (43.5; 0.909; 1.39)
Assembly 2	Normal, N (μ, σ)	N (36.4; 4.79)
Assembly 3	Lognormal, LN (γ, μ, σ)	LN (27.1; 1.96; 0.292)
Assembly 4	Lognormal, LN (γ, μ, σ)	LN (16.1; 2.05; 0.727)
Quality	Lognormal, LN (γ, μ, σ)	LN (27.7; 1.69; 0.64)
Packed	Normal, N (μ, σ)	N (47.2; 2.76)

Note: Note: Lognormal (γ, μ, σ); Normal (μ, σ); μ = Mean; σ = Standard deviation; γ − Localization.

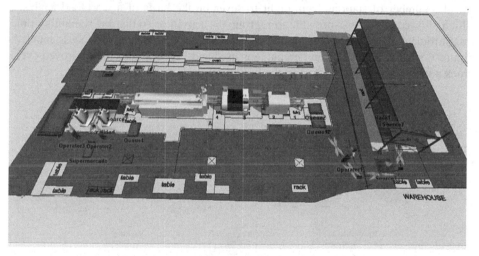

Fig. 5. Simulation of the future situation of PCBs. (Color figure online)

Figure 5 shows the new distribution of the process plant, the direction of the line flow

Table 2. Probability Distribution of times in the case of PCBs.

Activities	Distribution	Cycle time (s)
Assembly bottom		36
Assembly top		120
Quality control	Normal, N (μ, σ)	N (51.8; 1.29)
Packed	Normal, N (μ, σ)	N (22.6; 25.6)

Note: Normal (μ, σ); μ = Mean; σ = Standard deviation.

is changed, the quality control and packaging stations are placed at the end of the line, thus achieving a straight-line flow for the assembly process.

3 Results

In regard to the case of televisions, a reduction of 5% was achieved in search times with the application of 5S. This value was based on the analysis in Stage 2 in the works of [18] and by simulating the reduction in time that was obtained with the provision of label dispensers and sleeves for finished products. It meant that time available will increase, which also increases production capacity. By making these changes and improvements, it was possible to produce 682 units.

With the application of the process optimization proposal, the percentage of the bottleneck activity load was reduced, with the packaging activity continuing to set the pace of production. In addition, the number of operators was reduced from nine to eight and the number of stations from eight to seven on the basis of a workload analysis, which showed that it was possible to regroup the activities; so that the remaining time was sufficient to be able to perform the same internal activities that the process entailed. Figure 6 shows the utilization percentages used and Fig. 7 shows the improved cycle times and takt time (represented by the horizontal line) of the TV activities.

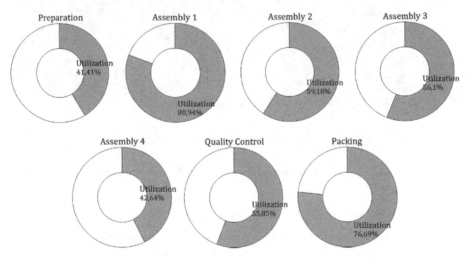

Fig. 6. Percentage of use of the activities in case of televisions.

In the case of PCBs, when applying the optimization proposal to the process and making the corresponding improvements with the simulation of the future situation, 674 units could be assembled. This result was achieved with the creation of a supermarket, which supplied the quality control activity with a maximum inventory of 112 units and a minimum of 56, which was supplied on a time basis. The integration of the quality control and packing activities were also carried out at the end of the assembly line; thus, there was a favorable increase in the number of units produced and a decrease in waiting

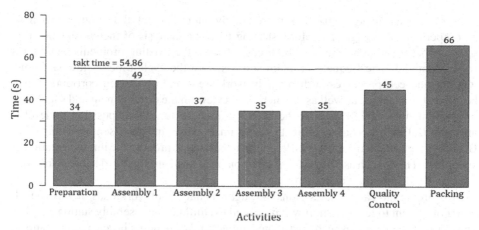

Fig. 7. Improved cycle time vs. takt time for the case of televisions.

times, which was reflected in the percentage of use of the activities. Figure 8 shows a high percentage of the use of quality control and finished product packaging activities at the beginning of the shift. By implementing a supermarket system before quality control, these activities begin their work simultaneously with the assembly activity. Finally, it was possible to reduce the distances covered by the operators for the supply of raw material from the warehouse to the beginning of the 14.68 m. For the dispatch of finished product, from the packing station there was a reduction of 19.98 m.

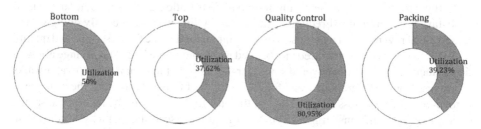

Fig. 8. Future simulation of the usage percentage of PCBs assembly activities

4   Discussion

Nowadays, competitiveness in the market is the main challenge companies face due to the changing and challenging demands of clients. In addition, since technology advances every day, it arises the necessity to implement tools of Lean Manufacturing to stand out or to stay afloat. Improving processes is based on the refusal to accept waste by increasing the flexibility of the process.

The main objective of this research is the process optimization through the application of LM tools to increase the productivity of companies because of the continuous changes in the market. It forces organizations to work daily to look for tools that allow them to have a competitive advantage. Therefore, starting from the analysis of the current situation of the process through VSM, for both case studies, the existing problems and wastes were identified. The frequent problem sources were the cycle times below takt time, waiting between processes, a disorder in work areas and obstructed corridors. Then, based on the analysis, as well as the literature review on the development and successful implementations of LM tools in the manufacturing sector, it was possible to develop an optimization proposal to mitigate or eliminate waste in two assembly companies. Based on the collected data, it was determined the need to propose the implementation of specific LM tools such as 5S, Plant Distribution (industrial installation design), Workload Leveling and supermarket system.

Regarding the case of televisions, through an analysis of workloads, it was considered convenient to level them. It was proposed to eliminate an assembly station and thus an operator; the activities were distributed among eight operators in seven workstations, increasing the productive capacity by 4.92%. On average, 650 units were initially produced, while with the new workload allocation, a total of 682 units per day were going to be assembled, with a 12.5% reduction in labor costs, which meant producing more units with fewer personnel resources. By proposing the implementation of the 5S tool, it was expected additional improvements by creating a culture of order and cleanliness within the working areas and by reducing the occupational accidents rate through space liberation in the corridor. In addition, it was intended to reduce unnecessary movements by suggesting that the shelves should be placed in front of the operators at an adequate height; thus, the operator could have easy access to the components for the TV assembly, expecting a reduction of up to 5% in time for searching materials.

In the case of PCBs, by applying the plant distribution and through an analysis of the distances covered, the direction of the assembly line was changed. By doing so, the warehouse of raw material was close to the beginning of the line for its supply, and quality control activities were also placed and packed at the end of the line. This change allows a 35% reduction in distances covered since, for the supply of materials, the operator walks 8.13 m less from the warehouse, and for the dispatch of finished products, the distance to be covered is 12.97 m less from the end of the line. Likewise, with the incorporation of a supermarket system, consisting of a buffer or minimum-security, quality control station was supplied with a maximum inventory of 112 and a minimum of 56 units. With this change, an increase of 3.69% was achieved in the production capacity referring to the number of units produced since it was possible to produce 674 units per day, eliminating the waiting time between the assembly processes.

5 Conclusions

At the end of this research, it was possible to verify that the optimization proposal based on LM tools provided favorable results for the assembly companies. Initially, with the VSM design and on-site observations, existing problems were identified throughout the process. Based on this information, LM tools were selected, such as inventory levels, 5S, which resulted in a reduction of search times by 5%, an increase in production capacity by 4.92% and a 12.5% reduction in labor costs. With an industrial installation design and the supermarket system, a 35% reduction was achieved in the distances covered by operators and a 3.69% increase in production capacity with its application. By the simulation and the elimination of data variability, it was possible to corroborate the viability of the implementation of the selected LM tools, providing a stable system and an environment similar to reality. This contributed to simulate the optimization proposal and its possible consequences, as well as to make decisions without the need to modify the plant. This research is a useful starting point for future research as a basis to parameterize a model that pinpoints the problems of each organization.

Acknowledgments. This study is part of the research project "Modelo de Gestión para la Optimización de Procesos y Costos en la Industria de Ensamblaje," supported by the Research Department of the University of Cuenca (DIUC). The authors gratefully acknowledge the contributions and feedback provided by the IMAGINE Project team; similarly, to the management and operational staff of the enterprises, for their willingness to being analyzed as case studies.

References

1. Nujoom, R., Mohammed, A., Wang, Q.: Drafting a cost-effective approach towards a sustainable manufacturing system design. Comput. Ind. Eng. **133**, 317–330 (2019). https://doi.org/10.1016/j.cie.2019.05.007
2. Barcia, K., De Loor, C.: Metodología para Mejorar un Proceso de Ensamble Aplicando el Mapeo de la Cadena de Valor (VSM). Revista Tecnológica - ESPOL **20**, 31–38 (2007)
3. Achieng, O.H., Githii, W., Ombati, O.T.: Lean supply chain and performance enablers at Homa Lime company. AJIBM **08**, 1157–1171 (2018). https://doi.org/10.4236/ajibm.2018.85080
4. Socconini, L.: Lean Manufacturing. Paso a Paso. Marge Books (2019)
5. Sarria Yépez, M.P., Fonseca Villamarín, G.A., Bocanegra-Herrera, C.C.: Modelo metodológico de implementación de lean manufacturing. Revista EAN 51–71 (2017). https://doi.org/10.21158/01208160.n83.2017.1825
6. Matt, D.T., Rauch, E.: Implementation of lean production in small sized enterprises. Procedia CIRP **12**, 420–425 (2013). https://doi.org/10.1016/j.procir.2013.09.072
7. Rajadell Carreras, M.R., Sánchez García, J.L.S.: Lean Manufacturing. La evidencia de una necesidad. Ediciones Díaz de Santos (2010)
8. Arrieta, J.G., Domínguez, J.D.M., Echeverri, A.S., Gutiérrez, S.S.: Aplicación lean manufacturing en la industria colombiana. Revisión de literatura en tesis y proyectos de grado. Presented at the Ninth LACCEI Latin American and Caribbean Conference (LACCEI 2011), Engineering for a Smart Planet, Innovation, Information Technology and Computational Tools for Sustainable Development, Medellin, Colombia (2011)
9. Sanz Horcas, J., Gisbert Soler, V.: Lean manufacturing en PYMES. 3c Empresa: investigación y pensamiento crítico, pp. 101–107 (2017). http://dx.doi.org/10.17993/3cemp.2017.especial.101-107/
10. Stamm, M., Neitzert, T.: Value stream mapping (VSM) in a manufacture-to-order small and medium enterprise. Presented at the 3rd World Conference on Production and Operations Management, Tokyo, Japan (2012)
11. Fortuny-Santos, J., Arbós, L.C., Castellsaques, O.C., Nadal, J.O.: Metodología de implantación de la gestión lean en plantas industriales. Universia Bus. Rev. 28–41 (2008)

12. Randhawa, J.S., Ahuja, I.S.: An investigation into manufacturing performance achievements accrued by Indian manufacturing organization through strategic 5S practices. Int. J. Prod. Perform. Manag. **67**, 754–787 (2018). https://doi.org/10.1108/IJPPM-06-2017-0149
13. Diez, J., Abreu, J.L.: Impacto de la capacitación interna en la productividad y estandarización de procesos productivos: un estudio de caso. Revista Daena (Int. J. Good Consci.) **4**, 97–144 (2009)
14. Guerrero, P.: Tiempos estándar y modelización de procesos de ensamblaje: televisores y tarjetas electrónicas usando programación no lineal y BPMN (2018). http://dspace.ucuenca.edu.ec/handle/123456789/31279
15. Meyers, F.E., Stephens, M.P.: Diseño de instalaciones de manufactura y manejo de materiales. Pearson Educación, México (2006)
16. Salazar, A.F., Vargas, L.C., Añasco, C.E., Orejuela, J.P.: Biphase plant distribution proposed in flexible manufacturing environment by the analytic hierarchy process. Revista EIA 161–175 (2010)
17. Hernández Matías, J.M., Vizán Idoipe, A.: Lean manufacturing: Conceptos, técnicas e implantación. Fundación EOI, Madrid (2013)
18. Lobo, F.G.P., Sánchez, N.T.C., Colmenares, C.E.I., Maldonado, M.G.U.: Manufactura esbelta en la PYME. Pequeños cambios grandes resultados. XI Congreso de Ingeniería de Organización, pp. 1281–1289 (2007)

Prediction of Standard Times in Assembly Lines Using Least Squares in Multivariable Linear Models

Jhon Ramirez[1] , Rodrigo Guaman[2] , Eliezer Colina Morles[3] ,
and Lorena Siguenza-Guzman[3] ([⊠])

[1] Faculty of Chemical Sciences, Universidad de Cuenca, Cuenca, Ecuador
jhon.ramirez1707@ucuenca.ec
[2] Department of Applied Chemistry and Systems of Production, Faculty of Chemical Sciences,
Universidad de Cuenca, Cuenca, Ecuador
rodrigo.guaman@ucuenca.edu.ec
[3] Department of Computer Sciences, Faculty of Engineering, Universidad de Cuenca,
Cuenca, Ecuador
{eliezer.colina,lorena.siguenza}@ucuenca.edu.ec

Abstract. Currently, the highly competitive environment of the assembly industries has been an engine for them to seek differentiating factors for improving their
efficiency. One of these factors is the study of times and methods (referred to the
analysis and the critical and systematic examination of how a task is presently
performed, facilitating to find more effective methods), which allows alleviat-
ing internal and external aspects that affect productivity and provides the basis
for management decision-making. The present work has two primary objectives;
firstly, the calculation of standard times within the enterprise operative area and,
additionally, the development of a mathematical model for time prediction. For the
fulfillment of these purposes, a referential conceptual framework was established
about the study of time and the multiple linear regression model. This framework
allowed elaborating a procedure for the development of the mathematical prediction model, together with its validation. The study concludes with a discussion on
the importance of having models to estimate standard times in business decision
making, and the establishment of relevant conclusions.

Keywords: Assembly · Linear regression · Process times · Work cells · Standard
times

1 Introduction

Ecuadorian assembly companies face increasingly complex challenges generated by
both external and internal factors. For instance, in the motorcycle assembly sector, there
has been loss of market places as a result of government policies, which together with
the dynamism of the Ecuadorian economy, the low purchasing power of citizens and the
high unemployment rate, have generated a decrease in sales and therefore in motorcycle
production [1]. Similarly, the automotive industry has been impacted by policies that

© Springer Nature Switzerland AG 2020
M. Botto-Tobar et al. (Eds.): ICAT 2019, CCIS 1195, pp. 455–466, 2020.
https://doi.org/10.1007/978-3-030-42531-9_36

affect its ability to compete fairly with imported vehicles, which enter the country with 0% tariffs [2]. In addition to the external factors mentioned, the assembly industries also present challenges caused by internal factors, such as limited resources and low productivity, which cause inefficient business performance, reflected in economic losses and market share. The most representative aspects of low productivity are the reprocesses, poor management of resources and methods, and downtimes [3]. Moreover, the decrease in productivity is greatly influenced by an excessive demand for operators' effort [4]. These factors can be summarized in terms of incorrect work-study.

Method engineering represents a systematic conception for the development of strategies that increase productivity in assembly industries, significantly optimizing their resources and providing tools to raise levels of competitiveness. Over the years, method engineering has developed improvement techniques focused on the study of work, in order to solve problems related to the inadequate administration of times and movements. The main objective of the study of work is to detect, reduce, or eliminate downtime by creating standards for the execution of tasks [5].

This work contemplates two intimately related fundamental aspects that, according to [6], are: the study of methods and the study of times. Through the former, the movements that an operator performs when executing a task are analyzed in order to find improvements to reduce or minimize the operating time [3, 7]. The measurements of the latter are taken as inputs to determine optimal times; that is, the time required for a trained worker to perform a specific activity [8]. In addition, with the establishment of standard times, it is possible to carry out other strategic processes such as production planning and cost calculation and productivity. Therefore, it is essential to focus on the study of times to raise the level of competitiveness. In turn, due to the changes that occur in the industrial assembly sector, it is necessary to develop tools that allow anticipating the internal behavior of the processes, with the aid of mathematical tools such as regression models.

2   Theoretical Background

The industrial and technological advancement led to the development of new tools to facilitate the work of the time analyst, allowing the conception of techniques for the determination of standard times [6]. This calculation can be obtained utilizing the following alternatives: estimates made by analysts, historical records, predetermined time systems, and chronometer time study [5]. The estimates made by analysts are based on the expertise of a person trained to determine the standard time most adjusted to the reality of the activity [9]. The determination of standard times T_E, by means of historical records, is based on time data of tasks performed in the past. For this, three values of time are taken into account: optimal time or optimistic time T_o, modal time or most probable time T_m, and most bulky time or pessimistic time T_a. For the calculation of the standard time, a weighted average of the mentioned values is used, according to the formula given by (1) [10].

$$T_E = \frac{T_o + 4T_m + T_a}{6} \tag{1}$$

One of the most advanced techniques for the study of times is the so-called Pre-determined Time Systems, which is based on the use of databases with information on movements and their respective durations for the establishment of standard times [5]. Finally, the time study with a chronometer is the primary technique for measuring works. It is a direct method since the calculation of the standard time is based on the observation and timing of the various activities in a certain number of cycles [5]. The basic elements to carry out in this time study are a chronometer, time study form, and observation board [11]. The study of times with a chronometer can be divided into four steps, preparation, execution, evaluation and determination of supplements [12]. However, the International Labor Organization summarizes these steps in three: the selection of work to study, recording by direct observation of the process, and calculation of the standard time [11].

Standard times are indispensable inputs for correct decision-making [13], and therefore, they are significant factors to consider. With this argument, it is necessary to determine prediction models that allow obtaining standard times without the need to re-conduct field studies. A classical statistical technique to represent a process relies on linear regression models, which allow quantifying the link between one or more dependent variables based on values adopted by independent variables or regressors [14, 15].

To estimate the behavior of the dependent variable y, based on the values of the independent variables $x_1, x_2, x_3, \ldots, x_p$, it is necessary to construct a mathematical model as described in (2), based on a set of observations y_i, $i = 1, 2, \ldots n$, made on the production process. The estimated value of the dependent variable will be called y_e and can be represented by the linear, algebraic mathematical model, given by (3).

$$y - f(x_1, x_2, x_3, \ldots, x_p) \tag{2}$$

$$y_e = \beta_0 + \beta_1 x_1 + \beta_2 x_2 + \beta_3 x_3 + \ldots + \beta_p x_p \tag{3}$$

By defining the vector of coefficients $\vec{\beta} = (\beta_0 \beta_1, \beta_2, \ldots .\beta_p)^T$, and the inclusion of the independent variables in the vector $\vec{x} = (1, x_1, x_2, \ldots x_p)^T$, Eq. (3) can be rewritten in vector form, as showed in (4).

$$y_e = \vec{\beta}^T \vec{x} \tag{4}$$

The coefficients of the β vector are calculated using the least-squares method, by defining an objective function that reflects the quadratic differences between the measurements and the estimated value, as defined in Eq. (5).

Each observation y_i corresponds to a vector $\vec{x}_i$, and the concatenation of the vectors $\vec{x}_i$, $i = 1, 2, \ldots, n$ allows defining the matrix (pxn) of values $X = [\vec{x}_1 \vec{x}_2 \ldots .\vec{x}_n]$. In turn, the observation y_i $i = 1, 2, \ldots, n$ defines the vector of observations $\vec{y} = (y_1, y_2, \ldots, y_n)^T$. The coefficients β_i, $i = 0, 1, \ldots, p$ are calculated appropriately utilizing an optimization procedure. The solution to the problem of minimizing the objective function (5) is presented in (6).

$$J = \frac{1}{2} \sum_{i=1}^{n} (y_i - y_{ei})^2 \tag{5}$$

$$\vec{\beta} = \left(X^T X\right)^{-1} (X^T \vec{y}) \tag{6}$$

The correlation between the dependent variable and the independent variables can be determined using the coefficient of determination R^2, defined by the equation in (7).

$$R^2 = \frac{SS_R}{SS_T} \tag{7}$$

In (7), SS_R represents the sum of squares of the regression given by (8), while SS_T is the sum of total squares given by (9).

$$SS_R = \beta^T X^T y - \frac{\left(\sum_{i=1}^n y_i\right)^2}{n} \tag{8}$$

$$SS_T = y^T y - \frac{\left(\sum_{i=1}^n y_i\right)^2}{n} \tag{9}$$

The value of the coefficient of determination belongs to the interval [0, 1], and its interpretation is as follows, the closer to 1 the value of R^2 is, the better the estimate given by (4); otherwise, the estimate will be inaccurate. Therefore, it is necessary to find R^2 values closest to 1 [16]. The linear correlation coefficient allows identifying the influence that an independent variable exerts on the dependent variable. This coefficient, defined through (10), is a good measure of the goodness of the regression line fit, and its values belong to the interval [−1, 1].

$$r^2 = \frac{S_{xy}^2}{S_x^2 S_y^2} \tag{10}$$

Where,

$S_{xy}^2 = $ Covariance of xy
$S_x^2 = $ Standard deviation of x
$S_y^2 = $ Standard deviation of y

If the value of r^2 is equal to 1, then there will be an exact linear relationship between the independent variable and the dependent variable.

3   Materials and Methods

The present study contemplates the analysis of a motorcycle assembly plant; therefore, in the first instance, it is based on the processes carried out in [17]. Then, being the primary objective constructing linear mathematical models, which serve as instruments to predict standard times, variables related to the work environment, and the operator information of the motorcycle assembly plant were used. This plant produces seven different motorcycle models and consists of six assembly cells. In each cell, two operators work by performing simultaneous tasks both in the front and the rear of the motorcycle, in order to complete the product. The population consists of each motorcycle model and all operators within the assembly area, that is, 12 workers. The coding, M1, M2, M3, M4, M5, M6, and M7, was used for motorcycle models, respecting the confidentiality agreement established with the company.

3.1 Methodology

The research represents a case study of a longitudinal-non-experimental type since the analyst was in charge of handling the predetermined variables through n observations. It is also of a mixed nature due to the need for a documentary review of the various theories, strategies, and models about time standardization and multiple linear regression. The work required a field investigation for the collection of information directly from the source.

For the development of the time study, the methodology applied by the International Labour Organization (ILO) was used as a baseline. This is structured in three phases [11], selection of the job or position to study, registration of the process by direct observation, and calculation of standard time.

Phase 1. Selection of the Job or Position to Study. During the development of this phase, a detailed study was carried out on the process of assembling the products. Likewise, through direct observation, a diagram of the precedence of the activities of the process could be defined.

Phase 2: Registration of the Process by Direct Observation Using Appropriate Techniques. Once the job to be studied was selected, it was divided into several operations and these into activities with a clear beginning and end. To determine the operating cycle time, an initial sample was taken to define the number of cycles to be timed by using the Westinghouse table. This table provides the number of observations necessary depending on the duration of the process cycle [13, 18], which for this particular case resulted in three observations; however, five observations were made for a better interpretation of the actual data.

Once the number of observations was known, the time was recorded using three primary instruments: chronometer, observation board, and time study form [11]. For illustrative purposes, Table 1 shows a record of times observed on the rear part of motorcycles, in Cell 1.

Table 1. Times observed on the rear part, of Cell 1

	Observations					Average observed time
	1 (min)	2 (min)	3 (min)	4 (min)	5 (min)	T_{Op} (min)
M1	70.31	70.04	69.97	70.62	70.14	70.21
M2	78.39	77.47	75.62	77.89	78.56	77.59
M3	54.18	52.47	52.42	52.88	52.29	52.85
M4	49.00	49.19	49.19	49.60	47.14	48.82
M5	59.91	57.00	59.95	56.80	58.52	58.44
M6	57.48	57.53	57.73	56.65	57.72	57.42
M7	66.66	64.08	63.99	64.97	64.84	64.91

Finally, it was necessary to calculate the normal time T_N, which represents the qualification of the operator's work rhythm when performing a task. This is defined as the "time it takes for a qualified operator to perform a certain task or activity at a standard speed, without any delays due to personal or external situations" [19]. Normal time is calculated using (11).

$$T_N = T_{Op} \, x \, C \tag{11}$$

Where,

T_N = Normal time
T_{Op} = Average time observed
C = Performance qualification

The assignment of the work rate of the operators was carried out utilizing the Westinghouse method. The method, developed by Westinghouse Electric Corporation, takes into consideration four elements for assessing the pace of work: skill, effort, qualification, and consistency [9]. This method provided the data in Table 2 for the "Performance Qualification" of each operator. Table 3 presents an example of the calculation of normal time, based on the data in Table 1 relative to Cell 1.

Table 2. Westinghouse qualification system.

Operator	Ability	Effort	Conditions	Consistency	Qualification
Operator 1	0.03	0.02	0	0.03	1.08
Operator 2	0.06	0.08	0	0.03	1.17
Operator 3	0.03	0.02	0	0.01	1.06
Operator 4	0.06	0.02	0	0.01	1.09
Operator 5	0.06	0.06	0	0.03	1.15
Operator 6	0.03	0.02	0	0.01	1.06
Operator 7	0.03	0.06	0	0.01	1.1
Operator 8	0.06	0.06	0	0.03	1.15
Operator 9	0.06	0.06	0	0.01	1.13
Operator 10	0.03	0.06	0	0.01	1.1
Operator 11	0.03	0.02	0	0.01	1.06
Operator 12	0.06	0.02	0	0.03	1.11

Phase 3. Standard Time Calculation. With the knowledge of the normal time, the standard time T_E is calculated using the formula given by (12).

$$T_E = T_N(1 + S) \tag{12}$$

Where,

S = Supplements.

The value of the supplements is established by direct observation in the workplace, analyzing various aspects such as standing work, improper posture, use of force, light intensity, visual tension, mental tension, and mental tedium.

Table 3. The normal time of the rear - Cell 1.

	Average time observed (min)	Qualification	Normal time (min)
M1	70.21	1.17	82.15
M2	77.59	1.17	90.78
M3	52.85	1.17	61.83
M4	48.82	1.17	57.12
M5	58.44	1.17	68.37
M6	57.42	1.17	67.18
M7	64.91	1.17	75.94

For the development of the prediction model using the structure of multiple linear regression, it is necessary to select those variables that have more influence on the determination of the standard time. For this purpose, each value of the correlation coefficients was analyzed with respect to the standard time, defined by (10) [20]. As a result of this analysis, five independent variables $x_i, i = 1, 2, 3, 4, 5$, corresponding to age, weight, height, noise and illumination were selected.

Table 4 includes the correlation coefficient values of independent variables with respect to the standard time, based on the rear of the M7 model. Note that illumination and noise are the most correlated variables with the prediction of the standard time, followed by age and weight, while height affects less than 10% on the prediction. However, by introducing this variable in the linear model, an important adjustment in the prediction values was achieved.

Table 4. Selection of variables.

Variables	Coefficient of correlation r^2
Age	0.137216543
Weight	0.123469244
High	0.081088858
Noise	0.261844676
Illumination	0.397216472

Tables 5 and 6 show the selected variables and their measured values, which are expressed in the following units: [age] → years; [weight] → kilograms; [height] → centimeters; [noise] → decibels; [lighting] → luxes.

Thus, by matching the dependent variable y_e defined in (4) with the estimated standard time T_{Ee}, the mathematical model given by (13) is obtained, valid for both the front and the rear part of each motorcycle model.

$$T_{Eel} = \beta_0 + \sum_{i=1}^{5} \beta_i x_i \quad l = 1, 2, \ldots, 7 \tag{13}$$

Table 5. Independent variables front-part from the motorcycle.

Variables	Cell 1	Cell 2	Cell 3	Cell 4	Cell 5	Cell 6
Age	38	33	21	19	22	27
Weight	61	63	54	66	66	63
High	160	165	164	176	165	165
Noise	90	94	88	86	93	91
Illumination	194	187	214	178	189	194

Table 6. Independent variables back-part from the motorcycle.

Variables	Cell 1	Cell 2	Cell 3	Cell 4	Cell 5	Cell 6
Age	38	28	30	24	23	23
Weight	54	66	54	56	68	62
High	160	175	160	171	163	168
Noise	90	94	88	86	93	91
Illumination	194	187	214	178	189	194

By defining the vector $\vec{\beta} = (\beta_0, \beta_1, \ldots, \beta_5)^T$, and the vector $x = (1, x_1, \ldots, x_5)^T$, (13) can be represented in the vector form given by (14).

$$T_{Ee} = \vec{\beta}^T \vec{x} \tag{14}$$

The values of the model parameters are obtained by minimizing the objective function given by (15).

$$J_l = \frac{1}{2}(T_{El} - T_{Eel})^2 \quad l = 1, 2, \ldots, 7 \tag{15}$$

4 Results

Tables 7 and 8 include the standard times obtained from (12) for the motorcycle models considered.

Table 7. Standard time T_E for the front (min).

Model	Cell 1	Cell 2	Cell 3	Cell 4	Cell 5	Cell 6
M1	85.19	84.38	89.96	85.62	88.14	83.80
M2	89.18	89.88	86.80	89.74	91.35	87.15
M3	75.11	75.29	77.79	75.43	76.34	72.06
M4	62.07	58.93	64.14	60.87	58.79	58.49
M5	72.85	73.07	76.56	74.05	74.53	71.16
M6	66.47	63.23	69.27	67.53	68.00	63.68
M7	84.07	83.92	87.41	85.28	87.47	82.40

Table 8. Standard time T_E for the rear (min).

Model	Cell 1	Cell 2	Cell 3	Cell 4	Cell 5	Cell 6
M1	95.49	92.68	88.12	93.89	89.94	90.57
M2	107.12	105.65	99.17	107.47	100.31	102.62
M3	72.54	74.70	66.44	69.95	67.83	68.10
M4	67.41	66.91	62.59	65.72	63.42	64.86
M5	80.68	80.02	72.64	78.62	77.38	76.72
M6	79.27	77.66	73.18	78.54	75.00	75.30
M7	83.26	78.88	76.38	82.45	78.53	78.86

The minimization of the objective function was carried out by programming a spreadsheet, which allowed performing the matrix operations defined by (15). Tables 9 and 10 contains the linear models for the prediction of standard times for each motorcycle.

The use of (7) to calculate the coefficients of determination allowed to perform an analysis to corroborate the validity of the constructed regression models, resulting in 1 of both the front and rear part of each motorcycle model.

Table 9. Time prediction model for the front-part of the motorcycle.

Model	Equations
M1	$T_{Ee} = 815.92 - 1.16x_1 - 2.29x_2 - 1.87x_3 - 0.23x_4 - 1.17x_5$
M2	$T_{Ee} = 660.91 - 0.78x_1 - 1.65x_2 - 1.45x_3 - 0.03x_4 - 1.07x_5$
M3	$T_{Ee} = 921.05 - 1.17x_1 - 2.98x_2 - 1.98x_3 - 0.10x_4 - 1.51x_5$
M4	$T_{Ee} = 592.12 - 0.59x_1 - 1.85x_2 - 1.15x_3 - 0.58x_4 - 0.81x_5$
M5	$T_{Ee} = 721.91 - 0.96x_1 - 2.31x_2 - 1.51x_3 - 0.09x_4 - 1.14x_5$
M6	$T_{Ee} = 957.91 - 1.28x_1 - 2.46x_2 - 2.24x_3 - 0.77x_4 - 1.36x_5$
M7	$T_{Ee} = 885.64 - 1.23x_1 - 2.50x_2 - 2.01x_3 - 0.19x_4 - 1.36x_5$

Table 10. Time prediction model for the rear-part of the motorcycle.

Model	Equations
M1	$T_{Ee} = 88.19 - 0.23x_1 - 1.18x_2 - 0.10x_3 + 1.95x_4 - 0.41x_5$
M2	$T_{Ee} = 66.29 - 0.56x_1 - 1.99x_2 - 0.03x_3 + 3.25x_4 - 0.61x_5$
M3	$T_{Ee} = -16.77 + 0.07x_1 - 0.85x_2 + 0.17x_3 + 1.95x_4 - 0.37x_5$
M4	$T_{Ee} = 0.65 - 0.56x_1 - 1.68x_2 - 0.08x_3 + 3.05x_4 - 0.43x_5$
M5	$T_{Ee} = 54.04 - 0.23x_1 - 1.08x_2 - 0.12x_3 + 2.19x_4 - 0.43x_5$
M6	$T_{Ee} = 77.58 - 0.07x_1 - 0.75x_2 - 0.03x_3 + 1.24x_4 - 0.32x_5$
M7	$T_{Ee} = 120.62 - 0.23x_1 - 0.94x_2 - 0.20x_3 + 1.32x_4 - 0.34x_5$

5   Discussion

It is well known that the study of times represents an essential discipline for decision-making due to its contribution to the operational control of industries. This serves as a reflection of the situation they are living in and may raise awareness of improvement situations. In the present work, it was possible to determine various activities within the production process that do not add value such as transport and storage, the latter due to the nature of the production planning managed within the plant.

Referring to the standard time, it should be noted that it has a significant variation concerning the observed time, which ranges between values close to 30%. The present fluctuation is due to the manual nature of the work, which is executed in assembly cells made up of two operators. This value represents fatigue for them, among others considered for the determination of supplements, within the study of time with a chronometer.

It is worth mentioning that, according to the study [21], the chronometer time study has the participation of 89.5% concerning the other methods mentioned above. While it is true that there are more advanced techniques such as the Predetermined Time System, based on databases for the calculation of standard time, most time analysts, opt for taking time with a stopwatch. Although it represents a longer time, its main advantage is the reflection of the reality of the plant.

A recent study suggests the existence of a relationship between productivity, working conditions, and the environment, proposing a set of appropriate conditions for the good performance of a worker [22]. Likewise, it is known that ergonomics and productivity are interwoven in the prevention of ergonomic risks [23]. Thus, these arguments were considered in the selection of quantitative and qualitative variables for the construction of the time prediction model, which also constitutes a factor closely related to productivity. As a result of this approach, the variables illumination, noise, age, weight, and height served as the basis for the construction of linear prediction models suitable for estimating standard times associated with the assembly of seven motorcycle models. While it is true that regression models have been widely used in manufacturing processes, there is no background on its uses for predicting assembly line times.

Multiple linear regression analysis is essential to define the relationship between the dependent and independent variables in order to issue estimates and predictions within an adequate confidence interval. The present case shows a perfect relationship ($R^2 = 1$) between the selected independent variables (illumination, noise, age, weight, and height) and the dependent variable (standard time).

6   Conclusions

The standard time setting is a technique that, together with the work measurement, allows determining optimal times to operate processes, minimizing the amount of work, eliminating unnecessary movements, and replacing methods. Standard times thus facilitate the detection and reduction of downtime, to generate higher added value.

This article proposes a multiple linear prediction model structure for time prediction, whose main objective is to provide inputs for decision-making that allows for increased productivity. The study let to select important variables to model the behavior of the standard time and to validate the models constructed using the coefficient of determination, which concerning the accuracy of the adjustment. The model construction approach applies to other business scenarios with predictive purposes, such as sales forecast, staff turnover rate, among other possibilities.

The present study serves as the basis for future analysis on the prediction of times, in which it is possible to include other ergonomic variables, such as energy wear, mental load, and workload, to build better models.

Acknowledgments. This study is part of the research project "Modelo de Gestión para la Optimización de Procesos y Costos en la Industria de Ensamblaje," supported by the Research Department of the University of Cuenca (DIUC). The authors gratefully acknowledge the contributions and feedback provided by the IMAGINE Project team; similarly, to the management and operational staff of the motorcycle assembly, for their willingness to being analyzed as a case study.

References

1. Guevara, J.E.C., del Carmen Yacelga Rosero, C.: Análisis de los efectos de la aplicación de las salvaguardias en las importaciones y exportaciones en el intercambio comercial por carretera Ecuador-Colombia. SATHIRI 42–60 (2016)
2. Pico, L.M.P., Coello, R.R.C.: Análisis de la restricción a las importaciones del sector automotriz en el Ecuador periodo 2010–2015 y su impacto en la economía. INNOVA Res. J. **2**, 128–142 (2017)
3. Cardona Márquez, M.J.: Mejoramiento del tiempo de operación en procesos de ensamble bimanual basado en técnicas de optimización computacional (2016)
4. Moreno, L.A.M., Maestre, M.M., Flórez, L.A.F., Palomino, L.M.P., Villamizar, J.M.V.: Avances en el análisis del estrés laboral a partir de la captura de Neuroseñales en el cliente interno dentro de una organización textil en la ciudad de Pamplona. FACE Rev. Fac. Cienc. Económicas Empres. **17**, 81–90 (2017). https://doi.org/10.24054/01204211.v2.n2.2017.2648
5. Baca, G., et al.: Introducción a la Ingeniería Industrial. Grupo Editorial Patria, México (2014)
6. Rico, L., Maldonado, A., Escobedo, M.T., De la Riva, J.: Técnicas utilizadas para el estudio de tiempos: un análisis comparativo. Rev. CULCyT **11**, 9–18 (2005)
7. Rojas Ruiz, D.: Propuesta de estandarización de métodos y tiempos en el proceso productivo de la Empresa Industrias SUR EU (2016)
8. Maynard, H.B.: Maynard's Industrial Engineering Handbook. McGraw-Hill Education, New York (2001)
9. Freivalds, A., Niebel, B.: Niebel's Methods, Standards, & Work Design, 13th edn. McGraw-Hill Higher Education, New York (2013)
10. Caso Neira, A.: Técnicas de medición del trabajo. FC Editorial, Spain (2006)
11. Kanawaty, G.: Introduccion al Estudio Del Trabajo. OIT (1996)
12. Meyers, F.E.: Motion and Time Study: Improving Work Methods and Management. Prentice Hall, Upper Saddle River (1992)
13. Meyers, F.E., Stewart, J.R.: Motion and Time Study for Lean Manufacturing. Prentice Hall, Upper Saddle River (2002)
14. Castillo Morales, A.: Estadística aplicada. Editorial Trillas (2013)
15. Spiegel, M.R., Schiller, J.J., Alu Srinivasan, R.: Schaum's Outline of Probability and Statistics: 897 Solved Problems + 20 Videos, 4th edn. McGraw Hill Professional, New York (2013)
16. Freund, R.J., Wilson, W.J., Mohr, D.: Statistical Methods. Academic Press, Cambridge (2010)
17. Benavídez Vera, E.X., Segarra Farfán, E.M., Colina-Morles, E., Siguenza-Guzman, L., Arcentales-Carrion, R.: Levantamiento de procesos como base para la aplicación de sistemas de costeo basado en actividades en empresas de ensamblaje. Rev. Econ. Política. **30**, 40–71 (2019). https://doi.org/10.25097/rep.n30.2019.03
18. García, R.: Estudio del trabajo: ingeniería de métodos. McGraw-Hill, México (2000)
19. García, V., García, N., Patiño, V., Rondón, L.: Reubicación del almacén de equipos reparados y disminución de traslados de la empresa HIDROBOMBAS C.A para la mejora en su proceso aplicando las herramientas de Ingeniería de Métodos (2009)
20. Pértega Díaz, S., Pita Fernández, S.: Técnicas de regresión: Regresión Lineal Múltiple. Cad Aten Primaria. **7**, 173–176 (2000)
21. Ovalle, A.M., Cárdenas, D.M.: ¿Qué ha pasado con la aplicación del estudio de tiempos y movimientos en las últimas dos décadas?: Revisión de la literatura. Ing. Investig. Desarro. **I2D**(16), 12–31 (2016)
22. Nicolaci, M.: Condiciones y medio ambiente de trabajo (CyMAT). Hologramática. **8**, 3–48 (2008)
23. CROEM: Prevención de Riesgos Ergonómicos (2013)

Towards the Information Security Governance for Institutions of Higher Education: Harmonization of Standards

Hugo Heredia[1,2]([⊠]) [iD] and Vicente Merchán[3,4]([⊠]) [iD]

[1] Instituto Tecnológico Superior Cordillera, Quito, Ecuador
hugo.heredia@cordillera.edu.ec, hugoheredia79@gmail.com
[2] Maestría en Sistemas de Información, Universidad Técnica de Ambato, Ambato, Ecuador
[3] Universidad de las Fuerzas Armadas ESPE, Sangolquí, Ecuador
vrmerchan@espe.edu.ec
[4] Universidad de Otavalo, Otavalo, Ecuador
vmerchan@uotavalo.edu.ec

Abstract. Institutions of Higher Education have been continually threatened by the lack of direction and control from the perspective of information security in the context of information technology governance. The ISO/IEC 27014:2013 standard represents an opportunity to govern information security; however, it suffers from a clear alignment that allows it to articulate its activities with the IT governance and provide visibility to the organizational government. This exploratory and document-level study has carried out a harmonization process between the ISO/IEC 27014:2013 and ISO/IEC 38500:2015 standards with the purpose of identifying overlapping problems and strongly related elements that contribute to a consistent model of information security governance at three levels: principles (responsibility, performance, strategy, risk analysis, compliance and human behavior), objectives and indicators. As a result, the components of the information security governance model have been defined as strongly related to information technology governance. This work contributes to the knowledge and collaboration of decision-makers in the strategic steering and information security control committees of Ecuador's higher education institutions. Future work will focus in the relation of substantives components of law of higher education, the factorial analysis of components of the model with the participation of actors from the institutions, in order to consolidate it towards what the institutions cannot do without.

Keywords: Information security · Information security government · Information technology government

1 Introduction

A good implementation of information security government must offer a strategic alignment, risk management, and resource management, for this, it is essential to identify the critical factors that allow achieving the strategic success of information security in the long term in organization [1].

© Springer Nature Switzerland AG 2020
M. Botto-Tobar et al. (Eds.): ICAT 2019, CCIS 1195, pp. 467–481, 2020.
https://doi.org/10.1007/978-3-030-42531-9_37

Similarly, [2] in the proposed information security governance framework show the relevance of adopting and employing a mature approach to the ability to manage and control information security with the use of a common business-focused language that allows organizations to establish appropriate security standards according to the nature of each business and leverage resources to achieve a level of information security, generating confidence and business advantage.

On the other hand, [3] states that the benefits of an information security government enhance trust in customer relationships, protect the reputation of the organization, hand over responsibility for safeguarding information from critical business activities; meanwhile, Luqman Ayodele [4] concludes that inadequate governance over information security affects organizations in the management and processing of information by inconsistency in the configuration of their information systems.

Da Veiga and Eloff [5] that in order to implement an information security governance framework, behavior and a level of culture must be generated at all levels of the organization, that is, from the top executives to the operational levels, with a view to reducing the impact generated by the loss or theft of information in the organization.

It is important that the organization effectively governs information security, its components, policies, and metrics holistically by developing behaviors among the actors that go hand in hand with an information security governance model.

Clark and Sitko [6] ensure that the implementation of an information security framework will allow the organization to significantly improve its corporate governance processes; just as CGI Group [7] that security and governance cannot be separated nor can they be achieved by deploying technical solutions alone.

Carcary et al. [2] argue that governance processes are intended to enhance the ability of any organization to direct, supervise, and control actions, processes, and procedures to safeguard information assets, as well as to provide confidentiality, integrity, availability, and accessibility of data found in information systems.

That is why Bowen, Hash and Wilson [8] establish a conceptualization of what information security governance is guaranteeing its implementation proactively while at the same time managing it. An information security government has a set of requirements, challenges, activities, and structures that allows it to identify key roles and responsibilities that influence the implementation of information security policies and procedures.

Finally, De Oliveira Alves, Rust da Costa Carmo and Ribeiro [9] conclude that while corporate governance concepts are well known, information security governance remains a major challenge for organizations.

These definitions help us to thinking that many institutions of higher education have yet to establish real information security governance. There are many reasons behind this; our goal is not to list them but rather, to propose a model to facilitate the implementation of a governance process adapted to the realities of each institution. But, first, let's harmonization look at governance and management activities to better understand what we are talking about and why it is important together worked in information technologies and information security.

In particular, the ISO/IEC 38500:2015 standard for the Governance of IT, not only covers all the good governance principles, e.g. responsibility, accountability and outcomes strategy alignment but also includes (implicitly) the governance of information security. The same applies for the ISO/IEC 27014: 2013 standard which is not limited to those areas of organizational governance that are specifically related to information security activities. Information security governance include subjects such as defining the governance structure; strategic alignment, value creation, accountability, security adequacy, investment decision process, and compliance with standards.

We believe that both standards: have overlapped issues, need some coordination and compatibility to be coherent and moreover, there should be some hierarchy between them. All these possible design issues produce practitioner's misunderstandings and standardization drawbacks in the current version of both standards.

The present work has been structured. In Sect. 2, the theoretical background. In Sect. 3, the research methodology is presented. In Sect. 4, the results obtained are analyzed. In Sect. 5, the discussions and conclusions of the study are presented.

2 Background

2.1 ISO/IEC 38500:2015

ISO/IEC 38500:2015 is the international standard that speaks about elements of governance of Information Technology (IT) in organizations, it sets standards for processes, procedures and decision making in terms of reference to information systems and technologies, on the other hand, describes that a model is a set of components that are related to describing the functioning of an object, system or concept [10].

The ISO/IEC 38500:2015 governance model is based on three main axes, the first evaluating the current and future use of IT, the second preparing for the implementation of policies and strategies to ensure that the use of IT meets business objectives, and the third establishing the monitoring of compliance with policies and performance in relation to established strategies, i.e., it shows a governance model that Evaluates, Directs and Monitors [10].

Figure 1 shows the model for IT governance proposed by ISO/IEC 38500:2015 in which three main elements can be seen to evaluate, direct and monitor strategies, policies, plans and purposes in the achievement of the organization's strategic objectives [10, 11].

Merchán and Rodríguez [12] that within the ISO/IEC 38500:2015 standard, guiding principles are also defined, which are applied to any organization. The principles of responsibility, strategy, procurement, performance, compliance establish the conduct by which directors, executives and will be guided in the best decision making. On the other hand [10] establishes a model composed of three main activities: management (Direct), evaluation (Evaluate) and follow-up (Monitor).

2.2 ISO/IEC 27014:2013

ISO/IEC 27014:2013 [13] is a guide to information security governance, providing concepts and principles by which organizations can assess, manage, monitor and communicate information security- related activities, as well as develop a holistic view in the organization's board of directors on security governance issues.

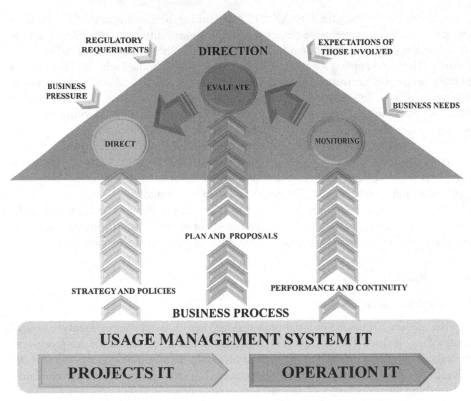

REGULATORY
REQUERIMENTS

DIRECTION

EXPECTATIONS OF
THOSE INVOLVED

BUSINESS
PRESSURE

EVALUATE

BUSINESS NEEDS

DIRECT

MONITORING

PLAN AND PROPOSALS

STRATEGY AND POLICIES

PERFORMANCE AND CONTINUITY

BUSINESS PROCESS

USAGE MANAGEMENT SYSTEM IT

PROJECTS IT

OPERATION IT

Fig. 1. Model for IT governance [10]

However, ISO/IEC 27014:2013 establishes certain results that must be evaluated when implementing information security governance, among which are the visibility of the directory on the state of security, an agile approach to decision making and information risks, as well as efficient and effective investments in terms of information security complying with external requirements (legal, regulatory or contractual).

ISO/IEC 27014:2013 presents six principles: establish information security throughout the organization, adopt a risk-based approach, establish the direction of investment decisions, ensure compliance with internal and external requirements, foster a positive security environment and performance of opinion in relation to business results, through which corporate governance can design and implement its information security governance framework, listing the responsibilities they must take into account [13].

Unlike ISO/IEC 38500:2015, which presents a model of evaluate-direct-monitoring and lets the governance committee creates its particular governance framework; ISO/IEC 27014:2013 shows a proportionate framework for the management of information security defined in five areas with a flow of communication, among them, focused on monitoring, evaluation, communication, direction and, finally, assurance; that is, evaluate - direct - monitor - communicate - secure (see Fig. 2).

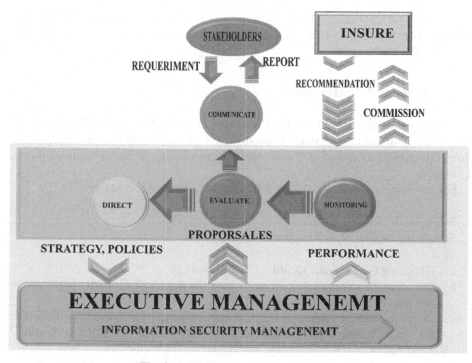

Fig. 2. Information security model [13]

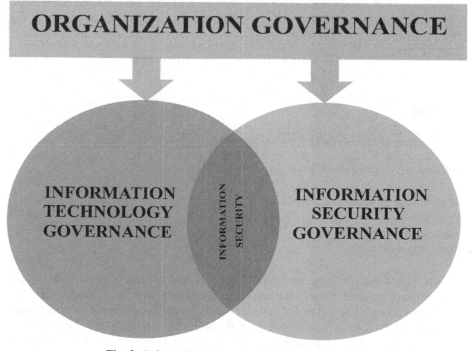

Fig. 3. Information security and IT government [13]

Figure 3 presents something very important that consists of some relationship between IT governance and information security governance, which is ultimately the reason for this study.

3   Methods and Materials

For the purpose of this research, ISO/IEC 38500:2015 [10] and ISO/IEC 27014:2013 [13] standards were taken into account. Then, difficulties were identified, and a comparison of objectives, policies, models and processes was made; using the harmonization process of [14–16].

For the mapping of standards, the following steps were executed [16]:

1. Selection of elements to compare from both standards.
2. Standards mapping design, in the following terms:

   a. Obtaining the elements identified in the first step;
   b. Definition of a comparison scale, to show the degree of similarity between the two standards; and
   c. Definition of the comparison template through which it was determined whether the scale values represent the ratio of ISO/IEC 27014:2013 in ISO/IEC 38500:2015.

3. Execution of the mapping of standards through a process of valuation of the main elements and components of the standards. Where the rows are made up of the elements of ISO/IEC 38500:2015 and in the columns are the elements of ISO/IEC 27014:2013.

4   Results

4.1   Selection of Elements to Be Compared

The following elements were considered for the comparative analysis:

- Government Objectives
- Principles of governance
- Models of government
- Governance activities

Each one of the objective elements, principles and models allowed to know the scopes, areas of applicability of each one of the norms, for example, as much the principles of the government of security of the information as of technologies of the information are oriented to guarantee the attainment of the objectives raised by the organizational government; as for the model of governance the two norms establish a model of two levels with processes of government by segregation of functions.

The governance activities of each of the standards studied are determined by evaluation, management, and monitoring, as common elements; however, communication is explicit in ISO/IEC 38500:2015 while in ISO/IEC 27014:2013 communication and assurance towards the fulfillment of organizational objectives is an essential part of the model.

4.2 Standards Mapping Design

Once the elements in each of the standards have been identified, the level of relationship that exists between them was determined using a similarity scale, using the Holmes matrix as a tool for comparison, analysis and prioritization of each of the criteria, as presented in Table 1 to establish the importance of the elements of both standards [17].

Table 1. Holmes weighting scale

Scale	Verbal scale
0.5	Value of the main diagonal of the matrix considering the comparison with itself
1	Whether the criterion is more important than the other criteria
0	Whether the criterion is less important than the other criteria

With the parameters or criteria established and defined, Holmes' matrix allowed the decision making based on the criteria and value judgments according to the scale determined based on the quantification with respect to each element determined in Table 2.

Table 2. Definition of criteria

Criteria	Definition
Effectiveness	Refers to information generated that is relevant and pertinent to the business, allowing to achieve strategic goals and improvements to business processes
Efficiency	Efficiency is about delivering or providing quality information to services faster by allowing IT departments to look for ways to achieve it, with strategies that contribute to this goal
Confidentiality	It relates to the characteristic of protection, privacy and access to information and to the policies and actions necessary to guarantee it

(continued)

Table 2. (*continued*)

Criteria	Definition
Integrity	Refers to the integrity of the data that are processed to generate information, these must be accurate, valid and consistent with mechanisms that prevent unauthorized removal, modification and disposal [18]
Availability	It refers to the information that must be available at the time it is required by any business unit, as well as the IT services that the business requirements need
Reliability	[19] work it as the provision of appropriate information that IT services provide to be considered in decision-making
Strategic alignment	They are the strategies of IT governance as well as information security support the business strategy
Meeting the needs of stakeholders	It is understood as the information needs that each one of the interested parties seeks to obtain for decision making, evaluating the benefit and associated risks
Cover the organization in a comprehensive manner	All the processes and functions necessary for the governance and administration of the entire organization, including IT services, are contemplated
Organizational structures	Defines its responsibilities to IT governance and information security in order to ensure the stated objectives
Risk management	It is considered as the adequate management of the risks associated with the use and generation of information by IT and each business unit of the organization
Measuring performance	It is the value generated by IT and information security governance strategies in the execution and control of projects, performances focused on cost-benefit
Resource management	It is defined as the adequate management that each of the available resources of the organization must have in order to guarantee the fulfillment of the organizational strategies

The comparison was made considering a superior triangular matrix that is completed with the opposites to the scale as corresponds to the analysis obtaining at the end of a type L matrix. Subsequently, the sum was made for each of the criteria or parameters to quantitatively determine the importance of the criterion or parameter in order from highest to lowest.

Once the results were obtained, the Pareto rule was applied to make visible the choice of criteria or parameters under which the analysis of the two government standards was carried out (see Table 3).

Table 3. Application of the Pareto rule

Parameters	Importance	Accumulated importance	% Sum	% Sum accumulated
Confidentiality	11,5	11,50	12%	12%
Integrity	10,5	22,00	11%	22%
Availability	10,5	32,50	11%	33%
Strategic alignment	10,5	43,00	11%	44%
Value delivery	9,5	52,50	10%	54%
Effectiveness	7,5	60,00	8%	61%
Meeting the needs of stakcholders	7,5	67,50	8%	69%
Reliability	6,5	74,00	7%	76%
Efficiency	5,5	79,50	6%	81%
Cover the organization in a comprehensive manner	4,5	84,00	5%	86%
Measuring performance	4,5	88,50	5%	90%
Risk management	3,5	92,00	4%	94%
Resource management	3,5	95,50	4%	97%
Organizational structures	2,5	98,00	3%	100%

Figure 4 shows the result of applying the Pareto rule, the focal criteria are: confidentiality, integrity, availability and strategic alignment. This means that the four criteria or parameters are of major importance for assessing the relationship between the standards studied.

According to the above figure, the four focal criteria constitute the minimum desirable elements in an information security governance model. Holmes' matrix helped determine the categorical and numerical values for each of the criteria (see Table 4), from which a relational valuation matrix was defined, as shown in Table 5.

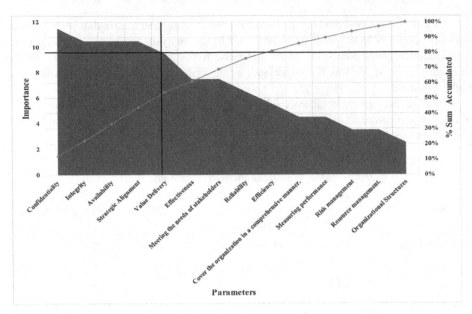

Fig. 4. Pareto diagram

Table 4. Matrix of Holmes selected criteria

Criteria	Confidentiality	Integrity	Availability	Strategic alignment	SUM	Weighting factor
Confidentiality	0,5	1	1	1	4	0,44
Integrity	0	0,5	1	0	2	0,19
Availability	0	0	0,5	1	2	0,19
Strategic alignment	0	1	0	1	2	0,19

Table 5. Relational valuation scale

CRITERIA	1-NR	2 -PR	3-MR	4 – FR
Confidentiality	Does not facilitate the confidentiality of information	Facilitates a little the confidentiality of the information	Mildly facilitates the confidentiality of information	Completely facilitates the confidentiality of information
Integrity	Does not take into account any element of information integrity	It takes into account some elements that guarantee the integrity of the information	It takes into account most of the elements that guarantee the integrity of the information	Takes into account all the elements that guarantee the integrity of the information
Availability	Does not comply with information availability policies	Complies with some information availability policies	Complies with most information availability policies	Complies with all information availability policies
Strategic Alignment	Does not facilitate strategic alignment	Facilitates in a few aspects the strategic alignment	Facilitates in several aspects the strategic alignment	Completely facilitates strategic alignment

4.3 Execution of the Comparison

Confidentiality Criteria

The strongly related element between the two standards represents a two-tier system: management body and corporate governance. In the same way the principles, mitigate the risk of directors not complying with their obligations, strategy, performance, human behavior, responsibility, compliance, procurement, IT governance, balance the risks and promote the opportunities derived from the use of IT, establish and sustain a suitable environment and monitor, as to the activities of greatest relative importance are: evaluate, manage, add value to the board of directors and stakeholders, monitor, provide alignment between information security strategies and objectives with business strategies and objectives to ensure that information and risks are being adequately addressed, through assertive communication.

Integrity Criteria

The mapping under integrity determined that in a two-tier system that brings together the bodies of management and corporate governance should be focused on performance, accountability, strategy trying to mitigate the risk of directors who failed to meet their obligations, on procurement and especially on human behavior to seek compliance in IT governance, balancing the risks and encouraging opportunities arising from the use of IT to establish and sustain a fit environment, ensuring compliance with obligations relating to the acceptable use of IT with a monitoring of activities.

Availability Criteria

It is established that to guarantee the availability of information, the model must have a two-tier system that combines management and corporate governance bodies focused on performance, responsibility, strategy trying to mitigate the risk of directors who did not comply with their obligations, on acquisition and above all on human behavior to seek compliance in IT governance, balancing the risks and promoting the opportunities derived from the use of IT to establish and sustain a suitable environment ensuring compliance with obligations related to the acceptable use of IT with a monitoring of activities.

Strategic Alignment Criteria

The best results in terms of ISO 38500:2015 is obtained by having a two-tier system that brings together management and corporate governance bodies focused on performance, responsibility and strategy; seeking to mitigate the risk of directors who did not comply with their obligations, in procurement and especially in human behavior to seek compliance in IT governance, balancing risks and promoting opportunities arising from the use of IT, to establish and sustain a suitable environment ensuring compliance with obligations relating to the acceptable use of IT with a monitoring of activities.

To perform a strategic alignment as seen from ISO/IEC 27014:2013 must be assessed, managed and monitored; it will add value to the board of directors and stakeholders by ensuring that risk-based information is being properly treated and thus ensuring information integrity to provide alignment between information security strategies and objectives with business strategies and objectives by means of efficient communication that are marked as being of greatest relative importance.

To achieve an integration mapping between ISO/IEC 38500:2015 and ISO/IEC 27014:2013 and have agreement with the results for each of its elements, a consolidated matrix was established in which both standards present evidence of a strong and moderate relationship between model, objectives, activities and principles of the two standards, which allows confirming that the information security governance is not totally misaligned from the IT governance, as shown in Table 6.

Table 6. ISO/IEC 27014:2013 related to ISO/IEC 38500:2015

ISO/IEC 38500:2015	Model: Two-level system (Executive management and corporate governance)	Aims: Provide alignment between information security objectives and strategies and business objectives and strategies	Aims: Adding value to the board of directors and stakeholders	Aims: Ensure that information risks are being adequately addressed	Act: Evaluate	Act: Direct	Act: Monitor	Act: Communicate	Act: Insure	Act: Establish Information Security Across the Organization	Prin: Adopt a risk-based approach	Prin: Set the direction of investment decisions	Prin: Ensure compliance with internal and external requirements	Prin: Fostering a positive security environment	Prin: Performance of opinion in relation to business results
Model Two-tier system (management body and corporate governance)	FR		MR	MR	FR	FR	FR	FR	FR	FR	PR	MR	MR	PR	FR
Objectives Balance risks and promote opportunities arising from the use of IT.	FR									MR	PR	MR	MR	PR	FR
Mitigate the risk of directors failing to meet their obligations	PR	MR			FR	FR	FR	MR	MR	MR	FR	MR			PR
Ensure compliance with obligations relating to acceptable use of IT.	FR	MR	FR							MR					
Ensure that the use of IT contributes positively to the organization's performance		FR	MR					MR	MR	FR	MR	FR	MR	MR	FR
Activities Evaluate	FR	PR	PR		FR	PR			PR		PR		PR		FR
Direct	FR	MR	MR		MR	FR			MR	FR		MR	MR		
Monitor	MR	MR	FR	FR	MR	MR	FR	PR		PR	FR	MR		PR	
Principles Liability		FR	MR		FR	FR	FR			MR	MR	MR	MR	MR	MR
Strategy		MR	FR	MR	FR	FR	FR	MR			MR	MR	MR	MR	
Acquisition		MR	MR	FR	FR	FR				PR	MR		MR	MR	
Performance	PR	MR		FR	FR	FR	FR			MR	PR	MR	FR	MR	MR
Conformity		FR	FR	MR	FR	FR	FR	MR	MR	MR	MR	PR	PR	MR	MR
Human Behavior		FR	FR	FR	FR	FR			MR	MR	PR	MR	MR	PR	MR
ISO/IEC 38501:2015															
Establishing and sustaining an enabling environment	MR		FR	MR	FR	FR	PR	FR	FR		MR	MR			FR
Governing IT	FR	FR	PR	FR	MR	MR	MR	FR	FR	MR	FR	PR	PR	PR	PR
Continuous Review		MR	MR	MR	FR	FR	FR								

Model

ISO/IEC 27014:2013 shows a strong relationship with ISO/IEC 38500:2015 from the sectional point of view: management and governance. In addition, they share a strong relationship with activities and elements.

It can also be observed that the ISO/IEC 27014:2013 standard is strongly related to the balancing of risks and the promotion of opportunities derived from IT in the fulfillment of obligations for the acceptable use of IT and government properties corresponding to the ISO/IEC 38500:2015 standard.

On the other hand, the establishment of information security policies will make it possible to correctly measure performance in relation to business results.

Principles

At the time of mapping, we found that ISO/IEC 27014:2013 has a strong relationship with five of the six principles of ISO/IEC 38500:2015: responsibility, strategy, performance, compliance, and human behavior; which enable information security to be established throughout the organization by adopting a risk-based approach to measuring performance in relation to business results.

Finally, the principles of responsibility, strategy, performance, human behavior, compliance, performance, and risk analysis are strongly related in the two standards. Each one of them with its descriptions and conceptualizations that allow describing the activities related to the security, integrity, and reliability of the information.

Activities

The activities of evaluating, directing, monitoring, communicating and assuring the ISO/IEC 27014:2013 standard are strongly related to the IT governance model (management and corporate governance), in addition three of them (evaluating, directing, monitoring) are strongly related to the objective of the ISO/IEC 38500:2015 standard to mitigate the risk of directors not complying with their obligations.

On the other hand, there is a moderately strong relationship with the six principles of the ISO/IEC 38500:2015 governance model, directly with responsibility, strategy, human behavior, compliance, and performance.

Objectives

The objective to add value to the board of directors and stakeholders, to provide alignment between the information security objectives, strategies and business of ISO/IEC 27014:2013, is strongly related to the objective of ensuring compliance with the obligations relating to the acceptable use of IT, to ensure that the use of IT contributes positively to the performance of the ISO/IEC 38500:2015 standard organization.

In addition, a moderate relationship is established by providing alignment between information and security objectives, mitigating the risks that directors have by failing to comply with their obligations and ensuring compliance with obligations relating to the acceptable use of IT at the level of integrity, reliability, and availability of information within the organization.

5 Discussions and Conclusions

A model of information security governance for higher education institutions would be strongly based on both standards in an integrated manner. The ISO/IEC 38500:2015 standard is mainly present at the first level of the model in terms of principles (responsibility, performance, strategy, and human behavior), with two substantial elements (risk analysis and compliance) of the ISO 27014:2013 standard that include the actions of directing, evaluating, monitoring, communicating, and ensuring.

In this study, a harmonization process has been carried out using a mapping for the comparison of both standards, identifying the related elements, following the guidelines of [16] and [3], and with the help of Pareto's rule it has been possible to summarize in Table 6 the correspondence that exists between the two standards in order to define MoGSIIES levels.

The governance of information security is a specific part of IT governance, although it can be seen separately the two affect the strategic processes of organizations.

Another important aspect that has been carried out is the understanding of the importance of government information security on IT governance and being aware that the responsibility for making decisions rests with a strategic steering committee of the institution.

This study has contributed to the knowledge and collaboration of decision-makers in the strategic steering committee for information security in institutions, overcoming the visibility barrier that an organizational government suffers. Future work will focus on strengthening the model through substantives components and factorial analysis of components with the participation of actors from Ecuador's higher education institutions.

References

1. Gashgari, G., Walters, R., Wills, G.: A proposed best-practice framework for information security governance. In: Proceedings of the 2nd International Conference on Internet of Things, Big Data and Security, (IoTBDS), pp. 295–301 (2017). https://doi.org/10.5220/0006303102950301
2. Carcary, M., Renaud, K., McLaughlin, S., O'Brien, C.: A framework for information security governance and management. IT Prof. **18**(2), 22–30 (2016). https://doi.org/10.1109/MITP.2016.27
3. Tenorio Chacón, O.: Government information security, myth or reality. In: ISACA (ed.) IX Congress ISACA Costa Rica, pp. 1–21 (2016). http://m.isaca.org/chapters12/costa-rica/events/Documents/PresentacionescongresoIsaca2016/13.GovernmentInformationSecurity.pdf
4. Luqman Ayodele, P.: Information Security Governance: an action plan for a non-profit organization based in the Nordics (Thesis, Laurea University of Applied Sciences) (2018). https://www.theseus.fi/bitstream/handle/10024/147149/Information_Security.pdf?sequence=1
5. Da Veiga, A., Eloff, J.H.P.: An information security governance framework. Inf. Syst. Manag. **24**(4), 361–372 (2007). https://doi.org/10.1080/10580530701586136
6. Clark, T.L., Sitko, T.D.: Information security governance: standardizing the practice of information Security. Res. Bull. **2008**(17), 1–11 (2008)
7. CGI Group: IT Security Governance—A holistic approach. CGI Group INC, pp. 1–8 (2016)
8. Bowen, P., Hash, J., Wilson, M.: Information Security Handbook: A Guide for Managers. NIST Special Publication 800-100, (October), 137 (2006). https://doi.org/10.6028/NIST.SP.800-100
9. De Oliveira Alves, G.A., Rust da Costa Carmo, L.F., Ribeiro Dustra de Almeida, A.C.: Enterprice security governance a practical guide to implement and control Information Security Governance (ISG). In: IEEE/IFIP Business Driven IT Management, pp. 71–80 (2006). https://doi.org/10.1109/BDIM.2006.1649213
10. INEN-ISO/IEC: Information Technology-IT Governance for the Organization (ISO/IEC 38500:2015, IDT), pp. 1–5. INEN, Quito (2019)
11. Quintanilla, M.Y.: Reference model of information technology governance for university institutions. Interfaces **9**(9), 87–116 (2016)

12. Merchán, V., Rodríguez, R.N.: Analysis of information technology government models and their relationship with the Ibero-American Model of Excellence. In: R. of U. with C. in I. (RedUNCI) (ed.) XXI Congreso Argentino de Ciencias de la Computación, vol. 1, p. 10 (2015). http://sedici.unlp.edu.ar/handle/10915/50028

13. NTE INEN-ISO/IECN: Information Technologies-Security Techniques-Information Security Government (ISO/IEC 27014:2013, IDT), pp. 1–5. INEN, Quito (2016)

14. Baldassarre, M.T., Caivano, D., Pino, F.J., Piattini, M., Visaggio, G.: Harmonization of ISO/IEC 9001: 2000 and CMMI-DEV: from a theoretical comparison to a real case application. Softw. Qual. J **20**(2), 309–335 (2012)

15. Pardo, C., Pino, F.J., Garcia, F., Baldassarre, M.T., Piattini, M.: From chaos to the systematic harmonization of multiple reference models: a harmonization framework applied in two case studies. J. Syst. Softw. **86**, 125–143 (2013)

16. Serrano, A., Gomez, B., Juiz, C.: Why the governance of projects, programs and portfolios (PPP) cannot be separated from the governance of IT standard. In: 2017 National Information Technology Conference, NITC 2017, September 2017, pp. 106–111 (2018). https://doi.org/10.1109/NITC.2017.8285661

17. Albán, P., Saavedra, R.: Proposal for a Strategic Control Plan and System, Applying the Balanced Scorecard Methodology, in the company Kilikos Flowers Cia. Ltda, dedicated to the production and commercialization of roses, located in the Canton Pedro Moncayo. National Polytechnic School (2009)

18. Gelbstein, E.: Data integrity: the most neglected aspect of information security. ISACA J. **6**(1), 6 (2011)

19. Fernández, A., Llorenz, F.: IT governance for universities. In: Conferencia de Rectores de las Universidades Españolas (ed.) Igarss 2014 (CRUE) (2014). https://doi.org/10.1007/s13398-014-0173-7.2

Author Index

Printed in the United States
By Bookmasters